D1599203

John Cardinal Krol and the Cultural Revolution

John Cardinal Krol and the Cultural Revolution

by E. Michael Jones

Fidelity Press
206 Marquette Ave.
South Bend, IN 46617

Fidelity Press

206 Marquette Avenue

South Bend, IN 46617

Printed and bound in the United States of America by
Thomson-Shore

ISBN 0-929891-02-3: $35

Library of Congress Catalogue Number: 95-060525

*Cover by Michael Murphy, pictures courtesy of the Temple
University Urban Archives*

How this book came to be written

In the fall of 1989, right around the time that the Berlin Wall fell, I was sitting in my parent's home in Philadelphia reading a recent biography of Joseph Cardinal Bernardin trying to contain feelings of annoyance that were too large and insistent to ignore. The book was not only based on little more than newspaper articles, articles which I had read; it was based on a selective and dishonest redaction of those articles. The whole story of the Bernardin-Greeley conspiracy had appeared in articles that were easily accessible, and here was the author trimming them to make an ideological point. The Catholic Church deserved better scholarship, I remember thinking at the time.

Another thought that crossed my mind was that once again John Cardinal Krol showed up as a minor character in another book that I was reading. My own situation bears some elucidation in this regard. For the past eight years I had been the editor of *Fidelity*, a Catholic counterrevolutionary magazine. I was also involved in a series of biographical sketches which would appear in that magazine and eventually as a book under the title *Degenerate Moderns*. I had also reached the point where I was beginning to see the shortcomings of the ideological divisions that had arisen in the Church since the rebellion over *Humanae Vitae* orchestrated by Father Charles Curran in 1968. *Fidelity* was decidedly anti-Modernist, but it also had no time for cults and phoney apparitions, which were finding increasing favor among "conservative" Catholics. In the fall of 1989, *Fidelity* had just weathered an attack from just these "conservative" friends over an article we had done exposing one of these organizations.

It was a time of crisis for me. I was sick of the warmed-over and essentially dishonest platitudes of the liberals that were appearing in things like the Bernardin biography. But I was also under increasing attack from the right, whose support of things equally dubious was equally repugnant to me. The Church, as I was to say later, had broken down into two main groups following the Council—heretics on the Left and lunatics on the Right. Instead of the Catholic synthesis of faith and reason, the Catholic Church in the United States was dominated by liberal heretics, who had established the university as their base of operation and believed in reason without faith, and the lunatics, who had established the numerous Marian pieties as their base of operations and believed in faith without reason.

It was over that Thanksgiving weekend in Philadelphia in 1989 that I decided to see if I could do a biography of Cardinal Krol. I wanted access to primary documents; I wanted to dig down beneath the current ideological configuration in the Church and come up with a description of how things had happened. I was also interested in understanding the city where I grew up. The decay that characterizes that city has become so pervasive that at some point it simply ceased to need an explanation. In this, Philadelphia was not unlike other cities in this country. "Inner city" has become a euphemism, if not a synonym for decay, violence and race. Why this was so needed some explanation I thought.

The first hurdle in a project of this magnitude is getting the cooperation of the subject. After a number of preliminary meetings, on June 29, 1990, Cardinal Krol sent a letter to the Rev. Joseph Pepe, chancellor of the archdiocese of Philadelphia, granting me access to his papers. "Michael Jones," the cardinal wrote, "has my permission to study the archives for material to be used in writing a biography. No other such or similar permission has to date been given."

With this hurdle cleared, the next one stared me in the face, namely, what to do with over 200 cubic feet of documents, whose contents were still *terra incognita* to the keepers of the archives themselves. It is difficult to convey at this point in time just how overwhelmed I felt at the magnitude of the task before me. There was no preliminary book to work from as a guide, and the project seemed to be doomed from the start by the sheer magnitude of documentation. But with the help of my research assistant, Sister Mary of Victory O'Brien, IHM, the contents of the boxes found their way one by one to a computerized index, which will be a major source of information for future scholars.

Gradually a coherent pattern began to emerge, along with the sense, that the biography would have to break down into two volumes, the first dealing with the Cardinal's early life and the upheavals of the '60s, the time of our cultural revolution. At this point, I would just like to state unequivocally that Cardinal Krol is the hero of this book and a hero in a cultural struggle for the soul of this country, a struggle still in progress. This is not to say that he hasn't made mistakes. But it is to say that the country in general and the city of Philadelphia in particular are immeasurably poorer because they did not heed his warnings.

No book of this size and scope can be written without the collaboration of a number of different people. At this point, I would like to thank Cardinal Krol for his cooperation, especially in making available to me the Krol Archives of the Archdiocese of Philadelphia. I would also like to thank Msgr. Thomas Herron, who endorsed the project at a crucial time, and Msgr. Daniel Murray, former rector of St. Charles Borromeo Seminary, whose hospitality allowed me to spend the time I needed at St. Charles doing research. I'd also like to thank Michael J. Mazza for proofreading this manuscript. Last but not least I would like to thank my research assistant, Sister Mary of Victory O'Brien, IHM, who did a masterful job of codifying the over 200 boxes of material that make up the Krol Archives. This book would not have been possible without her assistance. She has also done a major service for scholars, who now have an important source of information about one of the Catholic Church's most turbulent periods.

E. Michael Jones

South Bend, Indiana

February 1995

Contents

Prologue:

Leo Pfeffer Declares Victory

It must have been difficult for Leo Pfeffer to suppress a smile of satisfaction as he stepped to the podium to deliver his talk to the Society for the Scientific Study of Religion at the end of October in 1976. The title of the talk gives some indication that Pfeffer had come to Philadelphia to gloat. It was called "Issues that Divide: The Triumph of Secular Humanism" and it provided a catalogue of the revolutionary changes that had transformed American culture during the 15 years prior to Pfeffer's talk. During the period in question, America had quite simply revised its culture. If America were a computer, one could say that the default settings had been changed. At the beginning of the seventh decade of the twentieth century, the culture of the country was based on a pan-Protestant reading of Christianity whose assumptions favored, in imperfect form albeit, a rough approximation of the moral law. By the end of the decade, the default settings had been changed in favor of a culture that was individualistic, rationalistic, and hedonistic, especially in matters sexual. It was not just that people's behavior had changed; those changes had been inscribed in the culture, in the constitution, or at least how it was interpreted, in the rules that governed people's lives, and Leo Pfeffer was one of the main agents of that change.

But who was Leo Pfeffer, and why was he so disposed to view the events of the past 15 years with such satisfaction? At the time of his talk in Philadelphia, Pfeffer was professor of constitutional law and chairman of the Department of Political Science at Long Island University in Brooklyn, New York. The credentials seemed hardly distinguished. In a profession where prestige exists in inverse proportion to the amount of time an academic spends in the classroom, Professor Pfeffer had what seemed to be a distinctly unglamorous joint appointment in an undistinguished state school.

A look at the awards he had garnered in the years before the talk, however, gives a better indication of his accomplishments and the changes he himself was instrumental in bringing about. Born in Hungary on Christmas Day in 1910, Pfeffer arrived in the United States at the age of two, was naturalized a citizen in 1917, and married in 1937. At the time of his speech in Philadelphia in 1976, Pfeffer had received awards from Americans [formerly Protestants and Other Americans] United for the Separation of Church and State, the Minnesota Jewish Community Council, the New York Unitarian Universalist Church, the Brooklyn Civil Liberties Union, the Horace Mann League, the Unitarian-Universalist Association, the American Jewish Congress, and the Committee for Public Education and Religious Liberty.

At the time of his talk he was Special Counsel to the American Jewish Congress, as well as counsel for the Religious Coalition for Abortion Rights, and a member of the advisory committee on the National Project for Film and the Humanities. In the years following his talk he would receive an award from the American Jewish Congress in 1980 and the Humanist of the Year Award in 1988. Pfeffer's bio reads like a road map of the revolutionary changes that had swept through American society over the previous 20 years. If Pfeffer had come to talk about the "triumph of secular humanism," he was well-qualified. He had been intimately involved in virtually all of the battles that had brought about that triumph. Beginning with the *Schempp v. Abington* decision in the early '60s and ending with the *Lemon v. Kurtzman* decision in 1970, Pfeffer was the architect of the legal strategy which removed the last vestiges of Protestant culture from the public schools and denied government funding to Catholic schools. If his listeners wanted a description of how the triumph came about, it was clear that Pfeffer could give a first hand account.

The fact that he was in Philadelphia for the talk was significant, too, for a number of reasons. First of all, the nation's bicentennial celebration had just taken place in that city. It had been a lackluster affair, in many ways the perfect mirror of a country still staggering under the changes that Pfeffer had wrought, but also a country still under the shadow of the Watergate scandal and not too sure that it was in the mood to celebrate anything at all. One of the terms that Pfeffer used synonymously with secular humanism was deism. Deism was the word that allowed Pfeffer to situate his revolutionary changes in the context of the country's founding. The founding fathers, according to a view Pfeffer propounded throughout his later career, were secular humanists who deliberately excluded mention of God from the Constitution.

It was an attempt to read a political philosophy back into history that excluded a lot of material. Washington's farewell address comes most immediately to mind. "Of all the dispositions and habits, which lead to political prosperity," opined the father of our country, "Religion and morality are indispensable supports. . . . Reason and experience both forbid us to expect that national morality can prevail in exclusion of religious principle."

If Pfeffer was going to situate the beginnings of his revolution in the Philadelphia of two hundred years earlier, it was clear that his was going to be a selective reading of history. But there were other reasons why his appearance in Philadelphia to announce the "triumph of secular humanism" was significant. With the candor of a victor who had nothing more to fear from his opponents, Pfeffer was never vague about who it was he had been fighting all these years.

In recent years, the term cultural revolution has become a shibboleth dividing the political tribes in the United States. The conservatives define it vaguely, oftentimes so vaguely that it comes across as an effect without a cause. The liberals, for their part, since they were the victors in the struggle, claim, for tactical purposes perhaps, that the term itself is a figment of the conservatives' perfervid and overheated imagination. Conservatives, the liberal victors seem to be saying, just failed to get their point of view across in an effective manner in any of the institutions which really count in this country, and now, like sore losers, they are claiming to be the victim of some shadowy conspiracy which they can't even describe in any cogent fashion.

Pfeffer, however, takes a different tack. Not only does he claim victory in a struggle which his fellow humanists are embarrassed to admit existed in the first place; he also names names. Pfeffer tells us all who exactly the enemy was in the, from his perspective at least, successfully concluded cultural wars in the United States. Not for Pfeffer the shadowy opponent behind the scenes. Not for Pfeffer vague accusations against groups defined vaguely as "the Establishment." Not for Pfeffer the straw man heroics of fellow revolutionary and Supreme Court Justice William O. Douglas, who in his 1970 polemic *Points of Rebellion* announced:

> We must realize that today's Establishment is the new George III. Whether it will continue to adhere to his tactics, we do not know. If it does, the redress, honored in tradition, is also revolution.

No, Pfeffer was at once more specific and more frank than Douglas and his liberal epigoni. For Pfeffer, the enemy was, quite simply, the Catholic Church. In a memoir which appeared a year before his talk in Philadelphia (published with mordant irony in the liberal Catholic magazine *Commonweal*), Pfeffer went to some length to explain his animus against the Catholic Church. "I did not like it," Pfeffer wrote,

> because it was monolithic and authoritarian and big and frighteningly powerful. I was repelled by the idea that any human being could claim infallibility in any area, much less in the universe of faith and morals, and repelled even more by the arrogance of condemning to eternal damnation those who did not believe it.

The Church which Pfeffer grew up hating (if that is not too strong a word) was the Church he got to know as a Jewish immigrant in New York City. During the time Pfeffer was growing up and getting started in the legal profession, the Catholic Church was, in his opinion, "one if not the single most powerful political force in the nation." It was a time, when, to use his own words,

> Pius XI and Pius XII reigned over the Catholic world and Cardinal Spellman ruled in the United States. It was the pre-John XXIII-Vatican II era, and it was during this period that my feelings towards the Catholic Church were formed.

In the *Commonweal* memoir, Pfeffer refers to his daughter's threat when she didn't get her way to "marry a Catholic army officer from Alabama," because that particular configuration of Catholicism, the military, and the South embodied all that Pfeffer did not like about America. At another point Pfeffer talked about the impression Catholic schools made on him as a young man:

> I often saw children lined up in separate classes as they marched in. All the children were white; each group was monosexual; all the boys wore dark blue trousers and white shirts, all the girls dark blue jumpers and white blouses; all the teachers were white and wore the same nuns' habits.

Once Pfeffer gets started, the reasons for his animus against the Catholic Church start to pour forth in an increasingly frank as well as an increasingly hostile litany of offenses against the liberal *Weltanschauung*. Pfeffer did not like the fact that the Church opposed the Equal Rights Amendment; he is annoyed that "among the children outside the parochial school on the way to my office there are only a sprinkling of black faces"; he does not like the fact that the Vatican still defends papal infallibility and *Humanae Vitae*, the 1968 encyclical banning the use of contraceptives; he even opposes the practice of having first confession before first communion. ("I know it's none of my business," he adds as if realizing that his animus is getting out of control even by his own standards, "but you asked didn't you?") Pfeffer dislikes the Church because of its size and because of its unity and because of its internal coherence and because of its universality. He dislikes it, in other words, because of its claim to be "Catholic." Pfeffer dislikes the Catholic Church because it is big and because it is "monolithic," because with "monolithity," he tells us, "goes authoritarianism."

Pfeffer has nothing against religion per se; he only opposes "monolithic," "authoritarian" religions, i.e., religions with enough clout to have a say in how the culture gets organized. But even that is misstating the case somewhat. As James Hitchcock has noted, neither Pfeffer nor the liberal media objected in 1973 when the Supreme Court established as the law of the land a policy on abortion virtually identical with the position of the United Methodist Church; nor did the fact that Justice Blackmun, the author of the opinion, was himself a Methodist cause them much concern (Hitchcock, p. 197). The reason is most probably because the media by and large agreed wholeheartedly with the decision. When it comes to the separation of church and state, some religions are more equal than others, and some are clearly more threatening than others as well, and in Pfeffer's view Catholicism stood alone in this regard.

One major difference between the Catholic Church and all other churches and synagogues, according to Pfeffer, was its unity; another was its authority. No other denomination was as threatening to the view of the world Pfeffer held because no other denomination made the same magnitude of belief claims on its adherents. "The difference," according to Pfeffer,

> is that the hassidim of one rabbi need not accept . . . the infallibility of other rabbis, and the overwhelming majority of Jews, who are not hassidim and in fact not Orthodox, deny the infallibility of any rabbi, and this without fear of excommunication or loss of salvation. Therein lay the basic difference between the Catholic Church and Orthodox Judaism or fundamentalist Protestantism; in the latter instances, orthodoxy was just one of many voices reflecting the faith; in the former there were no alternatives.

If the Catholic Church had been willing to declare fornication and abortion the eighth and ninth sacraments respectively, it seems doubtful that the liberals would have been upset by her authoritarianism. The fact remains, however, that she wasn't and therein lies the real reason for the animus of the liberals and the *causus belli* in our *Kulturkampf*. During the entire post-World War II period in the United States, the Catholic Church opposed the main article of faith of secular humanism, namely, sexual liberation. Beginning with the creation of the Legion of Decency in 1933 and culminating in the opposition to *Roe v. Wade* 40 years later, the Catholic Church consistently picked up the banner of sexual morality which the mainstream Protestant denominations had let fall. The one great thaw in the liberal animus toward the Church came in the early '60s during the Second Vatican Council when it looked as if the Church might reach a *modus vivendi* with modernity by legitimatizing the use of contraceptives. That dream was laid to rest in 1968 when Pope Paul VI slammed the door shut on the *conditio sine qua non* of cooperation with the liberal regime. When *Humanae Vitae* hit the streets, the liberals broke off relations and turned instead to a combination of open hostility and fomenting rebellion within the ranks. The lull in the fighting in the liberals' ongoing *Kulturkampf* with the Catholic Church ended abruptly in 1968. Thereafter, the hostilities were out in the open again.

Pfeffer's animus toward the Church never really changed, but it did abate somewhat, primarily because the Church's influence in society had diminished, and because the confusion in its own ranks increased—in no small measure because of Pfeffer's activities. "What do I think about the Church today?" Pfeffer asked rhetorically in the mid '70s,

> In short, I still do not like it, but I do not like it less than I did not like during that period, and the reason is that, while it is still what it was before, it is considerably less so, if you can make out what I mean.

We can without too much difficulty make out what Pfeffer means. The only good Church was a confused Church. The more it approached the divided and tentative condition of Judaism and the Protestant denominations, the more Pfeffer liked it. If the Church was less powerful in 1976 than it had been under Pope Pius XII and Cardinal Spellman, Leo Pfeffer was in no small way responsible for that diminution of power and influence.

So what was this "triumph of secular humanism"? It was simply one side declaring victory in a cultural revolution which had begun in the early '60s. But even the term cultural revolution has the air of *fait accompli* to it. If the revolution had not been successful, it is doubtful that anyone would have called it a revolution. Only successful revolutions earn the name. So, to take a step back even further, what Pfeffer was describing was the successful (from his point of view) completion of a struggle for the control of the instruments of culture, for the determination of the society's default settings when it came to certain issues dear to the secular humanist heart. From the perspective of a struggle that has not yet been concluded, perhaps the best description of what happened in this country then would be the German word *Kulturkampf*. What we witnessed during those years was a struggle for the control of the instruments of culture which was remarkably similar to the struggle in Germany 90 years before. What we witnessed in the '60s in the United States was America's *Kulturkampf*.

The similarities between what happened in Germany in the 1870s and in the United States in the 1960s are more than merely semantic. Both the German and the American *Kulturkampf* involved a conflict between the Enlightenment and the Catholic Church. Leo Pfeffer is quite candid not only about his animosity toward the Catholic Church, but also about seeing himself as a latter day Deist, i.e., a secular humanist who traces his heritage back to the tradition of the *philosophes* and the French Revolution. In both Germany in the 1870s and in the United States in the 1960s, the struggle for control of the culture began with the question of whose values controlled the elementary schools. In both instances, the Catholics found themselves facing the opposition of both liberals and conservatives. In Germany, the heirs of the failed revolutions of 1848 united with Prussian Junkers under what was a nominally protestant, but actually liberal, agenda legitimatized as "free and independent science" (*die freien Wissenschaften*). The unification of Germany in 1870 brought the German Catholic populations of the Rhineland and Bavaria into union with Protestant Prussia under Prussia's cultural and political hegemony. *Kulturkampf* was the Prussians' attempt to unify the culture in their own favor, according to their rules. The new culture was to take its tone from the philosophies of Kant and Hegel, which were by turns German, Protestant, and "scientific." When the Catholics, whose culture was simply not as powerful, demurred at accepting the unity of religion, language, and education, which both the liberals and Prussian conservatives felt was necessary for the political unity of the newly-founded German nation, they were perceived as an alien element in the new empire which had to be either assimilated or exterminated.

Interestingly enough, Germany found itself in a similar situation after the reunification of 1989. The predominantly Catholic *Bundesrepublik* founded after World War II, suddenly with the fall of the Berlin Wall and the Communist regime in the east found itself absorbed into a country that was predominantly secular and socialist and at least nominally Protestant. (The Soviets sequestered the traditionally protestant sections of Germany when they created the now defunct German Democratic Republic.)

In a speech in Bremen in January 1993, Eduard Reuter, CEO of Daimler-Benz, reopened the issue of *Kulturkampf* once again by wondering if there was a place for Catholics in the newly unified Germany.

> Unter diesen Umständen scheint es mir an der Zeit, hart und unerbitterlich die Frage zu Ende zu denken, ob eine neue deutsche Republik überhaupt mit den tradtionellen "Reichsfeinde," den rheinischen, den bajuwarischen oder gar polnischen Bevölkerungsteilen, sinnvoll und vernünftig ins Werk gesetzt werden kann? Oder haben die katholischen Länder zu Zeiten der alten Bundesrepublik etwa nicht immer wieder die Spaltung betrieben, insbesondere versucht, den unabhängigen Status dieser stolzen protestantischen Hansestadt zu unterminieren?(*Offerten Zeitung*, Nr. 4/ April 1993, p. 14).

"Under conditions such as these," opined Reuter referring to the new confessional configuration in Germany after the reunification of 1989,

> it appears to me that the time has come to think this question rigorously to its logical conclusion. The question, of course, is whether a new German republic is at all possible if it includes the traditional enemies of the Reich, namely, the [traditionally Catholic] populations of the Rhineland, and Bavaria and even the Poles. Or isn't it really the case that the Catholic states ever since the founding of the Federal Republic have always been a divisive element, one that has especially attempted to undermine the independent status of this proud Hanseatic city?

Since one of the main issues dividing Germany is the issue of abortion, it seemed that history was repeating itself. Just as the American *Kulturkampf* of the 1960s was a continuation of what was launched in Prussia in the 1870s, so, too, the neo-post-1989 *Kulturkampf* in Germany seemed to possess uncanny similarities with what had happened in America 20-some years earlier. In both instances, Protestantism was used as a stalking horse for what was essentially a secular humanist agenda.

Just as the Prussian Junkers aligned themselves with the liberal, humanist heirs of the Enlightenment in Germany in the 1870s, so too in the United States in the '60s, there was a similar alliance between the old line anti-Catholicism of groups like Protestants and Others United for the Separation of Church and State with liberal, humanist, and, oftentimes, liberal Jewish organizations and the various left-wing acolytes of sexual liberation. In some instances, as with the Episcopalian Church in Pennsylvania and the American Friends Service Committee headquartered in Philadelphia, the line between the old and the new anti-Catholicism begin to blur. When the mainline denominations became advocates of contraception, the etiolated nativism of the 1840s was given a new infusion of vitality through the advocacy of sexual liberation.

One of the best thumbnail sketches of the liberal/conservative alliance which Catholics faced in the American *Kulturkampf* of the 1960s was the alliance between Hugo Black and William O. Douglas on the Supreme Court. Black made a name for himself in Alabama defending a member of the Ku Klux Klan who murdered a Catholic priest. Supreme Court Justice Black's son once wrote a memoir in which he claimed that "the Ku Klux Klan and Daddy, so far as I could tell, only had one thing in common. He suspected the Catholic Church. He used to read all of Paul Blanshard's books exposing power abuse in the Catholic Church." Fellow jurist William O. Douglas was a practitioner of sexual liberation as well as an absolutist when it came to the right to purvey smut. Black along with Douglas provided the rationale on the Warren and early Burger courts for engineering the change in American culture from one consonant with a pan-Protestant reading of Christianity to the secular humanist culture we have today. If the two groups—conservative Protestants and liberal humanists—seemed at odds with each other, each was able to overlook their differences in opposing Catholicism. As James Hitchcock has noted,

> Anti-Catholicism, as exemplified in Justice Douglas's 1973 *Lemon* opinion, brings together strange bedfellows indeed—conserva-

tive Protestants and liberal humanists who are ordinarily anathema to one another.

In each instance, the animus against the Catholic Church on the part of the mainline Protestant denominations arose in large measure because the Catholics were now defending standards that the Protestants themselves had erected and then abandoned. There was a certain lull in the hostilities coinciding with the convoking of the Vatican council in the early '60s, but it was more a lull of anticipation than anything else. The liberals wanted to see if the Catholic Church was going to abandon the teachings which were most repugnant to modern sensibilities. When it became obvious that they were not, the hostilities renewed with increased vigor.

The reaction following Vatican II brings us to another similarity between Germany and the United States. Both the German *Kulturkampf* of the 1870s and the American one of the 1960s were spawned by an ecumenical council. The reactions were, however, initially quite different. The German liberals were quite simply outraged by Pius IX's *Syllabus of Errors* and the doctrine of infallibility and turned that outrage on their German Catholic compatriots. If someone could believe such things, his patriotism was in question. His status as a German was in doubt. He was quite simply under the suspicion of subverting the regime. The effect of Vatican I on German Catholics was, however, quite the opposite. After languishing as cultural second-class citizens, German Catholics were suddenly reinfused with a new sense of identity and purpose that was bound to make itself felt in the newly unified country, a country whose unification was to take place under the unspoken aegis of German philosophy, German science, and Prussian Protestantism.

The *Kulturkampf* which took place in the United States during the 1960s followed on the heels of a council as well, in this case Vatican II. But its trajectory was different. Unlike the *Syllabus of Errors*, Vatican II sought to be as irenic as possible in its approach to modernity. So irenic was the council, in fact, that a large segment of the Catholic population felt that its mission was to convert the Church to the categories of modernity. When it became obvious that the Church was not going to modernize to the satisfaction of the liberals, the American *Kulturkampf* began in earnest. *Humanae Vitae* was the opening shot, *Roe v. Wade* the liberals' major counteroffensive. The irenic approach of Vatican II to the modern world gave the liberals within the Catholic Church their major opening, and it also provided the secular humanists with a major foothold in weakening the Church's opposition to its agenda.

Which brings us to one of the major differences between the *Kulturkampf* in 1870 and the one in 1960. In Prussia, Bismarck tried to divide the Church, but in vain. In America, the secular humanists were much more successful in finding a fifth column within the Church to do their bidding. Bismarck's attack on the Catholic Church in Ermland was a frontal assault. He expelled the Jesuits and other religious from Germany. (Gerard Manley Hopkins' poem, "The Wreck of the Deutschland" is about one such group of nuns seeking refuge in England.) When he attempted to force the bishop of Ermland, a Catholic enclave in eastern Prussia (now Poland), to accept an Old Catholic as a religion teacher in the Braunsberg Gymnasium, the Catholics held firm. As a result of Catholic unity in face of frontal assault, the *Kulturkampf* of 1870 was a much more violent fever which, as a result, passed much more quickly.

In America, the assault was much subtler. The carrot of government funding, publishing contracts, foundation money, and *pro bono* legal services was proffered more readily than the stick of government regulation. As a result, the cultural revolutionaries in America in the 1960s found a fifth column within the Church willing to aid and abet their plans. By subsidizing an obviously schismatic group like the Old Catholics, Bismarck guaranteed Catholic solidarity. There was no Prussian Charles Curran, no Prussian Theodore Hesburgh. The story of the cultural revolution in America in the 1960s is the story of the Catholic Church at war on two fronts. There was the enemy outside the gates, people like Pfeffer, and there were the collaborators within, who were often taking the money of the cultural revolutionaries to undermine the Church's position. Pfeffer, it should be remembered, published the memoir of his campaign against the church in a Catholic magazine. He also included in the same article a group of Catholics he found congenial to his cause. "I voted for John Kennedy in 1960," Pfeffer tells the *Commonweal* readership, and then goes on to give a list of liberal Catholics he could also conceive of voting for in the future. They would include "Robert Drinan, Justice William Brennan, Eugene McCarthy, Senator Phillip and/or Jane Hart, Dorothy Day, Theodore Hesburgh, and almost any member of the editorial board of *Commonweal*, although," he adds with a wry touch, "I would not necessarily want my daughter to marry them."

When Bismarck declared war on the Catholic Church in Germany 1870, "the German Catholics," according to the *Catholic Encyclopedia*, "so long eliminated from the political and economic and educational life of their nation, rallied to the defense of the faith against liberalism." When Leo Pfeffer declared victory over the Catholic Church in the United States in 1976, he could publish his memoir in a Catholic magazine. Vatican II was an occasion for liberal apostasy. Perhaps because it was a much more blatantly sexual revolution that the German one, the American Catholic liberals went over to the other side in the revolution body and soul—for the most part, body first.

Which brings us to the various theaters of combat in the cultural war. Pfeffer delineates three major areas of contestation. First, as in the *Kulturkampf* in Germany beginning in 1870, there was the battle over the schools. As counsel for the the American Jewish Congress, Pfeffer was the architect of a two pronged campaign which sought first of all to root out the last vestiges of Protestant culture from the public schools and secondly to deny funding to non-public schools, the great majority of which were Catholic. Pfeffer was the successful litigant in the *Schempp* and *Engel* cases in the early '60s which prohibited prayer from the public schools, and he was the equally successful litigant in *Lemon v. Kurtzman* which denied public funding to parochial schools in 1970.

The second area of contestation he mentions is obscenity in general and film in particular. As one of the signs of Cardinal Spellman's inordinate influence over American culture, Pfeffer mentions the fact that the Roberto Rosellini film *The Miracle* was declared blasphemous in the state of New York in the early '50s. In 1952, the New York State blasphemy law was struck down by the Supreme Court in the case of *Joseph Burstyn, Inc. v. Wilson*. Twenty-one years later, to give just one indication of the revolutionary changes in *mores* that had taken place, two of the top grossing films of 1973 were *Deep Throat* and *The Devil in Miss Jones*. By the 1980s, the United States was saddled with a pornography industry whose gross receipts ranged anywhere from $8 to $10 billion a year. Because of the decisions of the Supreme Court, this industry was essentially beyond the reach of the law.

In 1957, in the *Roth* case, the Supreme Court got into the pornography business by applying the First Amendment's guarantees of freedom of speech to anti-obscenity laws. In 1964, in the *Jacobellis* case, the Court opined that it couldn't define obscenity and gave us in *lieu* of definition the famous dictum, "I know it when I see it." Thereafter, viewing pornography became a regular feature of working on the Supreme Court with randy law clerks viewing pornographic films and crying out at particularly outrageous moments, "I know it when I see it." (cf. *The Brethren*.) "The Supreme Court decisions," according to Pfeffer, "did not cause the sexual revolution of the 1960s and '70s; it is closer to the truth to say that they reflected it. They did, however, accord it constitutional sanction and thereby contributed to its acceptability."

The final area of cultural revolution delineated by Pfeffer had to do with whose idea of the family would dominate in the culture. The major issue in the '60s was contraception, but that was soon replaced by abortion in the '70s. In the early '60s, to give some indication of the magnitude of the change which took place later, it was illegal in many places in the United States to sell contraceptives. By the end of that decade the government was not only not prohibiting the sale of contraceptives; it was distributing them itself. The two instances are not only indications of the situation before and after the revolution; they are causally related as well. The law had to go because the revolutionaries wanted government to get into the contraceptive business. According to Pfeffer,

> the anti-contraception laws had to be removed from the books because their presence made it impossible for the state to encourage contraception, something it now increasingly deems necessary to do. The middle income and the affluent, married and unmarried, use contraceptives; the poor have babies. When the poor, often racial minorities, are on the welfare rolls, taxpaying Americans rebel and expect the state to do something about it.

Why did it take a more activist approach to anti-contraception laws? The answer may lie in the fact that the justices recognized the need to get the laws off the books to enable the States to take affirmative action toward encouraging and assisting birth control, or at the very least not to prevent private groups from doing so; but they also realized that as a matter of political reality the States were not going to repeal the laws, as the twice-unsuccessful effort in Connecticut evidenced.

In addition to describing the areas of contestation in America's *Kulturkampf*, Pfeffer also describes his view of the contending parties. On the one hand, there were the Catholics, who

hope for an America in which, if not all will be Catholics, all will adhere to Catholic values: no divorce, no contraception, no abortion, no obscene books or pictures, no homosexuality, everybody worshipping God in his own way, government solicitous of and helpful to religion, and children and adults equally obedient to their parents and lawful authority (Pfeffer, *God, Caesar*, p. 20).

Arrayed on the other side of the front lines of the cultural war are "liberal Protestants, liberal Jews, and deists [i.e., secular humanists] ," who

seek a different America: one in which individuals enjoy maximum freedom of thought and expression, contraception is used and encouraged to control population and avoid the birth of babies that are unwanted or cannot adequately be cared for, women's right to control their own bodies is recognized and respected, the sexual practices of adults, whether of the same or of different sexes, are of no concern to anyone but themselves, governmental institutions avoid manifestations of religiosity, public schools are free of sectarianism, and citizens are not forced to fight in a war they deem immoral or in any war (Pfeffer, *God, Caesar*, pp. 20-1).

As can be gathered from Pfeffer's description of the two sides in the cultural war, the major issue was sexuality. If there was a residual anti-Catholic feeling in the United States as evidenced in the Blaine Amendments (Mr. Blaine coined the phrase "Rum, Romanism and Rebellion" as a description of the Democratic Party), it was quickly subsumed into (or re-energized by) the secular humanists' determination to liberate American mores from what they perceived to be the shackles of Christian morals. What often presented itself as a theoretical discussion of issues of state—the separation of church and state, let us say, as one example—turned out upon closer inspection to be an attempt to put the legitimatizing aura of law around behavior that had hitherto been deemed immoral.

James Hitchcock cites the case of Paul Blanshard, whose influence on Chief Justice Hugo Black has already been noted, as an illustrative example:

> Although his anti-Catholic attacks were always cast in terms of true Americanism and concern for separation of church and state, Blanshard reveals in his autobiography, *Personal and Controversial*, that he was an "utterly typical example of the sexual revolution of the 1920s" and that he was first stirred to write about the Catholic Church when he chanced upon a book about Catholic sexual morality.

The concern about the separation of church and state evinced by thinkers like Pfeffer and Blanshard shows itself upon closer examination to be a fear that the Catholic schools might prosper, and that specter inspires fear among the secular humanists because of the sexual consequences they see resulting from it. Parochial schools have a significant impact on the culture, and from that impact there is at least the possibility that a society would come into being in which, as Pfeffer said, there would be "no divorce, no contraception, no abortion, no obscene books or pictures, no homosexuality, everybody worshipping God in his own way, government solicitous of and helpful to religion, and children and adults equally obedient to their parents and lawful authority." What the liberals feared in short was a society in which social mores were congruent with the moral law, specifically the moral law regulating sexual behavior. What the liberals sought to bring about in their cultural war was the minimization of the effect the Catholic Church could have over the culture, the exclusion of Catholics from the forum of ideas, the marginalization of the Catholic contribution to the moral tone of society, and the substitution of secular humanism for the social laws and regulations the Protestants had for all practical purposes erected and abandoned.

This is what *Kulturkampf* meant in America in the 1960s, and this was why Leo Pfeffer came to Philadelphia in 1976 on the two-hundreth anniversary of the declaration of independence to claim victory in the cultural wars and proclaim the triumph of secular humanism.

But Pfeffer's appearance in Philadelphia to proclaim the triumph of his worldview was significant for another reason as well. If Pfeffer had his attitudes toward the Church formed under the reign of Cardinal Spellman of New York, it was John Cardinal Krol, the archbishop of Philadelphia, who more often than not, proved to be his actual opponent in the cultural wars. If Pfeffer was at war with the Catholic Church and its teachings and its influence in general during the 1960s and early '70s, he was more often than not at war with John Cardinal Krol of Philadelphia in particular. The most obvious case in point was *Lemon v. Kurtzman*. Krol was the architect of public aid to non-public schools in the state of Pennsylvania, and Pfeffer defeated him in the *Lemon* case before the Supreme Court in 1970.

But the opposition was at once broader and more radical than that one case would indicate. In addition to being the architect behind the bill aiding parochial schools struck down in *Lemon v. Kurtzman*, Krol was head of the episcopal commission for the Legion of Decency when Hollywood decided to challenge the Legion's influence over the culture and overthrow the Production Code in 1965. Krol was also a major opponent on both the state and the national level to government-funded birth control, and in the summer of 1966 fought the state of Pennsylvania to a stand-still by getting that year's budget appropriations bill held up in committee until the state welfare department agreed not to bring up contraception to its clients. Finally, Krol was instrumental in dealing with the liberalism's fifth column within the Church as well. He was the episcopal strategist in Charles Curran's tenure battle at Catholic University, the prelude to the open rebellion of the dissenters which broke out when Pope Paul VI issued *Humanae Vitae*.

Just as Pfeffer could bask in the glow of victory, so Krol could mull over the lessons of defeat in a cultural battle in which the country seemed bent on committing social suicide in the name of liberation from the moral law. In a memoir of his own, delivered also in Philadelphia seven years after Pfeffer's "Triumph of Secular Humanism" speech, Krol acknowledges

Pfeffer as both opponent and victor in the cultural warfare of the past 25 years. He even cites Pfeffer's Philadelphia speech as the basis for his argument. "Leo Pfeffer," Krol stated on the occasion of the Mayor's Prayer Breakfast on April 19, 1983,

> candidly admits that "secular humanism has won out" as the permanent cure for religious divisiveness. He has used the First Amendment to drive all theistic religion into a closet and to establish his own "religion" of secular humanism as the prevailing ethic of American society and American public schools.

If both Krol and Pfeffer agree that secular humanism was the victor in America's cultural wars, Krol is of the opinion that the victory was a pyrrhic one at best. The main loser in the successful campaign the secularists waged has been, not the Church, as Pfeffer might have said, but the social fabric, in the United States in general and in Philadelphia in particular. The main result of what Pfeffer set out to achieve has been spiritual impoverishment—in Krol's words, "the depletion of the religious and moral capital of our nation." As the moral law sanctioned by religion was driven from the public sphere, Philadelphia in particular and the country at large became a more dangerous place. According to Krol, "the progressive decline in morality" has led to a "corresponding increase in crime and corruption."

> Between 1960 and 1970, while the population increased 13 percent, crimes increased 176 percent in the nation and 128 percent in Philadelphia. In 1980, 67 Philadelphia police were detailed to senior and junior high schools. . . . In 1981 in the 260 public school buildings, there were 316 assaults on teachers and 368 on students . . . 12 rapes and 244 cases of weapons possession. . . . The decline in morality and the increase in crime and corruption is all too obvious today.

After naming Pfeffer as its advocate, Krol indicts secular humanism as the cause of the precipitous decline in social well being. "These affirmations," says Krol citing the secular humanist manifestos of 1933 and 1973,

> sweep away all decalogues, rules, and regulations. They deny God's existence and hence the inalienable rights which man derives from God. They deny objective truth and the difference between right and wrong. They accept as the ultimate criterion,

human experience, human need, and human desire. They open the gate not to healthy individualism, but to an uninhibited and frightful egoism and ruthless selfishness. . . . These affirmations are not basically different from the underlying principles of Atheistic Communism and Nazism. . . . The legal situation of the Church-State question is today bogged down in conceptual confusion and contradictions. The Courts seem unable to distinguish between "church" and "religion"; between institutions of religion and the dynamics of religion as such in society.

The two speeches were not unlike the parable of the seven blind Hindus and the elephant, except that in this instance we are talking about the body politic and not pachyderms. That two such men should have such diametrically opposed views of the good of society is in many ways even more remarkable considering the similarities of their background. Born within three months of each other, both Pfeffer and Krol came from Eastern Europe at a time when Eastern Europeans were denied access to the decision-making institutions of American culture. Krol was born in Cleveland, but was taken back to Poland in 1912, the same year that Leo Pfeffer arrived in New York. John Joseph Krol's father once told him that, if it had been economically possible to have raised his family in Poland, he never would never have come to the United States. The older Krol tried to return unsuccessfully two years after his son John was born, but had to return to Cleveland again to seek work. Leo Pfeffer came from Hungary, which is where Krol's father first went to seek work during the early years of this century.

In addition to both being immigrants from Eastern Europe, both Krol and Pfeffer were trained in the law. Pfeffer made a name for himself as a civil lawyer with groups bent on bringing about the secularization of American culture. Krol's rise out of the working class Polish neighborhood in Cleveland, Ohio, to a position where he was sought after by presidents and popes for his advice and expertise took place within the Catholic Church, at first as a priest and finally as a prelate, but—intellectually at least—as a canon lawyer. Both Krol and Pfeffer were trained in the law, and it would be in the courts of law, primarily the Supreme Court, that the final battles of the cultural revolution would be decided. Americans, perhaps because of the absence of traditions in a land carved out of the wilderness, have always accorded the law an unusual amount of respect. In retrospect, when one considers the magnitude of changes that were wrought in such a short period of time, it seems impossible to understand without understanding the influence that law had in this particular culture. The respect for law was so great in fact, that the majority of Americans allowed it to overrule their respect for democracy, as one democratically enacted bill after another was overturned by a Supreme Court which had arrogated to itself the position of unelected legislature. Pfeffer tacitly acknowledges the anti-democratic stance of the courts during the cultural revolution, but since he sympathizes so clearly with the results there is little of the zeal in his defense of the constitutional separation of the branches of government as there is in his defense of the separation of church and state. In explaining why the Supreme Court had to get involved in overturning a statute banning the sale of contraceptive duly enacted by the chosen representatives of the state of Connecticut, Pfeffer proffered the following explanation:

> Why did it take a more activist approach to anti-contraception laws? The answer may lie in the fact that the justices recognized the need to get the laws off the books to enable the States to take affirmative action toward encouraging and assisting birth control, or at the very least not to prevent private groups from doing so; but they also realized that as a matter of political reality the States were not going to repeal the laws, as the twice-unsuccessful effort in Connecticut evidenced (Pfeffer, *God, Caesar*, p. 97).

The strategy of using the courts, in other words, was necessary to circumvent the democratic process. All of the talk about procedure is essentially a subterfuge which is necessary to rationalize results. Since we all know what we want, namely, contraceptives, and, of course, what contraceptives stand for, namely, sexual liberation, and since we all know that the achievement of this end, was, given the social climate of the country in 1960, democratically impossible, we will allow the courts to overrule democracy in the name of social progress:

> In this respect the nine judges on the Supreme Court, being immune to political reprisal since they serve for life, may be performing a significant though quite controversial function; they may be compelling the people to accept what the judges think is good for them, but which they would not accept from elected legislators (Pfeffer, *God, Caesar*, p. 99).

The cultural revolutionaries realized that to get their way they had to circumvent the democratic process, and they realized as well that the only institution which could trump democracy in this culture was the law and the exaggerated respect for it that was peculiar to this country's intellectual history. Krol's rise to a position of prominence as a canon lawyer in the Catholic Church took place at a time when, as Pfeffer put it, "Catholicism took over the mission first launched by Protestantism" (Pfeffer, *Commonweal*, p. 310). In the vacuum created by the effacement of mainstream Protestantism as the guarantor of the social order in this country, Krol and Pfeffer found themselves locked in a battle over whose interpretation of the law would permeate the culture. It was a *Kulturkampf* in just about every sense of the word, and the place of religion as the guarantor of public morality was the main bone of contention.

According to Pfeffer,

> Religious groups, avowedly or not, seek to translate their own particular hierarchy of values into categorical imperatives for the community at large, including that part outside their own respective folds. Since government and law are highly effective means for translating particular values into universal rules of conduct, each competing religious group will seek to prevail upon government to accept its values as the best (Pfeffer, "The Triumph of Secular Humanism," p. 204).

One of the unintended ironies of Pfeffer's account is the fact that in arguing for the separation of church and state what he effected was the establishment of a religion of secular humanism. Given Pfeffer's essentially Nietzschean world view, the body politic is made up of groups which attempt to impose their will on the body politic as a whole. His use of the terminology of the separation of church and state was nothing more than a clever attempt to insure that, in the battle for the public mind and morals, those who were open about their religious affiliations were to be disqualified before they got out of the starting gate. According to Pfeffer's view, someone invariably imposed his views on the majority. This was only wrong when the imposer happened to espouse or represent a religion.

Krol's view of the relation between law and society was, as one might suspect, radically different than Pfeffer's. Because of his training as a canon lawyer, but also because of his familiarity with the Catholic tradition of natural law, Krol began to view the direction the Supreme Court was taking with alarm as early as the early '50s when he was still auxiliary bishop in Cleveland, Ohio. Instead of simplifying the just adjudication of disputes, American legal praxis was becoming progressively more complex and confused because the Supreme Court in particular was, in Krol's view, taking leave of elementary principles of jurisprudence. The law had ceased to be an effective agent in adjudicating disputes because it had taken leave of its foundation in the moral order, an order established by God. The chief villain in this regard, according to Krol, was Oliver Wendell Holmes, who propounded a view of the law that has subsequently become known as legal positivism.

According to Krol, Holmes

> dismissed the idea of Natural Law Principles as a product of mere wishful thinking. He rejected all traditional moral concepts as a set of emotional prejudices. He considered physical force as the essence of all law. He admitted no absolute rights . . . and denied the existence of absolute truth. He maintained that Might is Right.

With the foregoing formulation, the liberal judiciary found itself in a deep metaphysical bind. The liberal judiciary did not believe in truth or in the positive law as based on the moral law, which was in its turn based on the law of God. In short, it did not believe in anything identified with the natural law. The law was, quite simply, what the jurists said it was, and that law was imposed by force on the populace as a whole. At least, this is what they believed theoretically. In praxis, the liberals found themselves hamstrung by their very theory. If the law was not an instantiation or approximation of moral justice, then it was simply the imposition of a set of views on an unwilling recipient. And if this was the case, by what right did they impose the law? In order to preserve liberalism the justices have to back off in enforcing the law, which is precisely what the Warren court did. Oliver Wendell Holmes may have felt no qualms in implementing the rule of might makes right, but his successors, perhaps influenced by how that theory had worked itself out in Nazi Germany and Stalinist Russia, lacked the stomach for its consistent implementation in the United States, even if they could come up with a rationale for consistent implementation.

The result, of course, was social chaos, which is precisely what Krol saw in 1983 as the result of Pfeffer's revolution.

According to Krol,

> Government has the responsibility of articulating a public morality for the common good of society and for the happiness and security of its citizens. If government does not encourage the teaching of virtue and morality, it gives by default free reign to vice.

In formulating his position this way, Krol was entering a debate which had been taking place in this country since before the inception of the Republic. "Is not the law sufficient to protect itself?" Judge Marmaduke Temple exclaims in James Fenimore Cooper's initial volume of the Leatherstocking tales, *The Pioneers*. The answer, then as now, is no. The laws of the land can only function in a broader context which includes the moral law. It is a lesson which this country has had to learn the hard way. It is a lesson which John Cardinal Krol attempted to teach it. It is a lesson which the cultural revolutionaries of the '60s refused to learn, and one they refused to allow to be taught in the cultural institutions which fell under their hegemony.

This book is a description of John Cardinal Krol's contribution to that struggle. It was a struggle which was, in many ways, lost before it began. But it is a struggle which will only cease when there are no more people left to fight it. "If our traditional Judaeo-Christian morality declines," Krol wrote,

> and—God forbid—should go into eclipse, we will witness not only a spiralling crime rate—now in evidence—but also, either increasing social and political chaos or an emergence of government morality by legislation. But morality cannot be secured by laws, and virtue cannot be coerced—not even in a totalitarian police state.

If the liberals were the doctors of the '60s, then the country in general and the city of Philadelphia in particular were their patients. They had come up with a new cure for all of the ills of society, one which solved virtually every social problem by redefining it out of existence. In the name of freedom of the individual to do what he wanted without regard the exigencies of the moral law and the social consequences of disregarding that law, anarchy was loosed on the land. If liberalism was the medicine, then the patient sickened and died. The liberals got virtually everything they wanted in terms of the programs they wanted enacted; they got virtually nothing they expected in terms of outcome.

This book is an attempt to give an account of one man's efforts to stem the tide. Not just any one man, but, as the narrative will bear out, one of the major opponents of the Liberal Regime during the American *Kulturkampf* of the 1960s. When all is said and done, the cultural revolution that took place in this country during the 1960s was pretty much what Leo Pfeffer said it was; it was a contest between the Enlightenment and the Catholic Church. No one is claiming that John Krol was the victor in this struggle; however, in giving a clear picture of what he fought for, I hope to show that, until what he fought for is restored to its rightful place in the republic, there will be no peace.

I
La Dolce Vita

I am convinced that the damage that we have incurred in these
twenty years is due, not to the "true" Council, but to the unleashing within the Church of latent polemical and centrifugal forces;
and outside the church it is due to the confrontation with a
cultural revolution in the West: the success of the upper middle
class, the new "tertiary bourgeoisie," with its liberal-radical ideology of individualistic, rationalistic and hedonistic stamp.

Joseph Cardinal Ratzinger

The Ratzinger Report

Cleveland, Ohio—Rome, February 1961

On February 9, 1961, the Most Reverend John Joseph
Krol, auxiliary bishop of the Archdiocese of Cleveland and titular bishop for the see of Cadi, arrived at Cleveland Airport for a
flight to Rome only to find that his plane had been delayed for
two hours. Krol was on his way to Rome for a meeting of one of
the preparatory commissions established by Pope John XXIII
the year before in preparation for what would come to be known
as the Second Vatican Council. Krol was at the time a rising
young star in a rising young church. In recognition of his administrative abilities, Monsignor Krol had been raised to the
episcopacy in 1953 at the age of 43, and seven years later Bishop
Krol had been placed on one of the Council's preparatory commissions, the Committee on Bishops and Diocesan Government,

the only American to be so named. As fellow Cleveland auxiliary Floyd Begin would say of Krol years later, "Everyone in the diocese felt so much confidence in him that everything landed on his desk. He always had time. He never seemed hurried. He never gave the impression that he had something else to do. Still he was busy all the time. "

Rather than waste the two hour delay by sitting at the airport, Krol called the chancery and finding that a letter he had been expecting had arrived, decided to go back to the office, pick up the letter and take care of some unfinished business. When he got back to the chancery, he found not only the letter he had been expecting but an unexpected call as well—from the apostolic delegate in Washington. When he asked his superior, Archbishop Edward Francis Hoban, ordinary of Cleveland, about the call, he was surprised to hear Hoban tell him to return the call personally. Krol shouldn't have been there to receive it in the first place, and beyond that he had assumed that any message of importance that had been intercepted by Hoban, as this one had, would be conveyed to Krol by Hoban or taken care of by Hoban himself. But an order was an order, even if it was a suggestion, and so not a little bit puzzled (if not annoyed) and with one eye on the clock as the two hour delay for his Rome flight ticked away second by second, he called Washington and was put through to a certain Monsignor Pio Laghi, later Archbishop Pio Laghi, the Vatican's ambassador to the United States during the Reagan administration.

"What's this involve?" Krol wanted to know in a manner that must have struck the diplomatically more acute Laghi as brusque. To Krol's increasing displeasure, Laghi parried the direct question with more indirection. The Apostolic Delegate, Archbishop Egidio Vagnozzi wanted to talk to him personally, but he was not in Washington at this precise moment. Laghi was to find out how much longer Krol would be in Cleveland. A quick glance at the clock showed that the plane was leaving in 30 minutes. With annoyance and puzzlement vying for the place of dominant emotion in the young auxiliary bishop, Krol put down the receiver and decided to do as he was told and wait.

He did not have to wait long. Within a matter of minutes of putting the phone down, it rang again with Archbishop

Vagnozzi on the other end of the line this time telling Bishop Krol that he had just been made ordinary of the Archdiocese of Philadelphia. Krol was, to put it mildly, taken by surprise.

"Have you been out in the sun too long?" he asked Vagnozzi, in his Cleveland manner. After assuring the auxiliary bishop from Cleveland that the appointment was in earnest (and besides the sun was not particularly strong in Washington in February), Vagnozzi told Krol to report to the Congregation for Bishops when he arrived in Rome. For the hurried ride to the airport and for the less hurried flight to Rome, Krol was left to sort out his feelings of ambivalence.

"I wasn't thrilled," was how he put it 25 years later. On the one hand he kept thinking that there were other candidates who were more willing and deserving than he was. Coupled with that there was the feeling that he was quite happy where he was as auxiliary of Cleveland. He had grown up in Cleveland and with the exception of a few years abroad studying in Rome and a period during which he had been taken back to Poland as a child, he had spent his entire life there. He got along well with his ordinary and fellow auxiliaries. Now he was both stunned and annoyed at the direction his life was taking. So stunned or so annoyed, in fact, that in uncharacteristic fashion he delayed going to the congregation to get his appointment. After arriving in Rome, he dutifully called the congregation, but asked for a reprieve of 24 hours.

"Do you mind if I delay this until tomorrow," he asked one of the undersecretaries. "I'm tired."

Perhaps because of his own perplexity in accepting what loomed as a very large and complicated assignment, Krol had difficulty persuading his fellow priests that he had in fact received the assignment. On February 15, 1961 at 12 o'clock noon Rome time, Krol's appointment was announced at that day's session of the Committee on Bishops and Diocesan government by the congregation's presiding officer, Cardinal Mimmi. Krol had known about the appointment for almost a week before it was announced, and during that time had taken part in the general speculation with the rest of his priest peers in Rome. Msgr. William Beckman, spiritual director at the North American College in Rome and also a priest of the Cleveland archdiocese, had discussed the Philadelphia appointment during the week following Krol's return to Rome with Krol and had even shared his list of the most likely candidates with the Cleveland auxiliary, whose name was conspicuous by its absence from the list. When Krol left the meeting of the preparatory commission for lunch on the 15th, Beckman was there to pick him up.

"You were right, monsignor," Krol announced as he got in the car .

"I was?" Beckman replied, "About what?"

Krol was scheduled to have dinner at the North American college that evening, but Beckman wanted him to postpone the engagement because the rector, Archbishop Martin O'Conner, wouldn't be able to attend. Krol, however, insisted on keeping to the original plan because he was going to use the dinner as the place where he would announce his appointment as archbishop of Philadelphia.

"About the announcement for Philadelphia," Krol continued. "They've named someone for Philadelphia."

"Oh," said Beckman, "who is it?"

"It's me," said Krol.

There was a moment of silence.

"Come on now," Beckman said trying again. "Tell me who it is."

When Krol kept repeating that he had been appointed ordinary of Philadelphia, Beckman became increasingly annoyed at what might have been a moderately funny joke the first time, but was now wearing increasingly thin. Finally, Beckman got so annoyed that he refused to press Krol on the matter any further. Then as if to exact his revenge on Krol that evening for the poor joke he had pulled on him in the car that afternoon. Beckman stood up and announced formally at dinner, "His Excellency, Bishop Krol, said that Cardinal Mimmi made the announcement of the appointment of Philadelphia." Beckman was calling Krol's bluff.

Once again Krol was badgered for the name of the new appointee; once again he announced, "It's me, " and once again, no one believed him. It must have made him wonder if his appointment wasn't a case of mistaken identity. The incredulity of his friends was perhaps a function of Krol's own ambivalence in the matter and probably did something to exacerbate it as well. Closer examination of the candidate himself and the type of bishop Rome chose at the time to lead the Church in the United States would show that if Krol's appointment was anything, it was not a case of mistaken identity. Krol was an American bishop in the classic mold.

In his book on the contribution of the American hierarchy to the Second Vatican Council, Msgr. Vincent Yzermans tries to explain why, in effect, the American bishops didn't contribute more to the discussion of important issues at the Council and comes up with his own explanation of the American bishop in the classic mold. As bishops of a growing, developing church, Yzermans tells us

> the American bishops had to become builders, administrators, and financiers. To shirk these duties would mean a real neglect of interests which are essential for the proper functioning of the Church in their country. Secondly, the American bishops' reluctance to speak, if it can be called reluctance, is best explained by the American character itself. An American prefers action to speech. He finds it embarrassing to create tedium by voicing views which another has already expressed. This national temperament had restrained more than one American bishop from addressing the Council assembly (Yzermans, p. 4).

Taken in another light, Yzermans might just as well be explaining why the American bishops contributed so little to the controversies of the Vatican Council. Taken at face value, Yzermans is simply giving expression to the conventional wisdom about American bishops. They were known as brick and mortar guys. Coming from immigrant stock, they had little education and less culture. Their concerns were not unsurprisingly the concerns of the social groups which produced them. They arrived in the United States as part of what were for the most part economically disadvantaged groups (sometimes, as in the case of the Irish, because of their Catholicism, sometimes because of the part of Europe they left) and once they arrived here they became reconfigured as a disadvantaged ethnic enclave in a predominantly Protestant culture whose major concern was getting an economic foothold in a new country and establishing the rudiments of ecclesial life so that the faith could be passed on to successive generations. Because of the fact that the United States was de *facto* a Protestant country, and because the constitution did not (on paper at least) favor the establishment of any one religion or the support of the educational efforts of that religion, the Catholics were faced with the task of creating not only their own system of parishes in dioceses across the country but their own school system as well. When Catholic migration increased significantly in volume throughout the late nineteenth and early twentieth centuries, that creation was seen in a very literal sense as the building of schools and churches across the country for the newly-arrived Catholic immigrants.

By the early 1960s, that movement of expansion was still in full flood, although it was now more the result of the flourishing birthrates among Catholics already in the United States than immigration from the traditionally Catholic parts of Europe. During his tenure as archbishop of Philadelphia, John Joseph Krol lived up to the reputation of the classic American bishop. During the first 15 years alone of his tenure as archbishop of Philadelphia, Krol financed, built and opened 34 new parishes. Before he retired he would in addition build four new Newman Centers, one for each of the major secular universities in the area, as well as a new home for the handicapped and a new home for retired priests. When Krol was installed as archbishop of Philadelphia he arrived to find a diocese millions of dollars in debt to local banks. One bank, perhaps to take advantage of the inexperience of the new man, announced that it was going to increase the interest the diocese was paying by one percent. The announcement prompted Krol to do a bit of research, which led to the archdiocese consolidating its assets in one account and getting out of debt altogether by the end of 1962. Except for one short period to cover expenses, Krol never went back to the banks. Instead he financed the entire building campaign during his 26 year tenure—36 parishes, some with 50-classroom schools, four Newman centers, homes for aged priests and religious—from an internal trust which at times had as much as $42 million in assets. In a country where the bishops had the reputation as being builders, Krol had the reputation of being a financial genius. After his retirement, Krol continued his financial legacy by creating the Papal Endowment, a trust fund whose interest went, oftentimes in personally delivered checks from Krol to Pope John Paul II, to the Holy See and whatever projects the pope deemed worthy.

There are, the cliche goes, only so many hours in the day, and by the time Bishop Krol arrived to take over the archdiocese of Philadelphia, there was some indication that the acumen of the American bishops in erecting buildings had its shadow side as well. The concentration on getting schools built was often at the expense of neglecting what was being taught in them. In 1961, what would become a major problem in grade and high schools ten years later, and what would become a major impetus for the universal catechism some 25 years after that, was virtually nonexistent in an archdiocese like Philadelphia. But perceptive observers were beginning to get disquieting signals from the Catholic institutions of higher learning.

On June 3, 1961, the same Archbishop Egidio Vagnozzi who had announced to Krol over the phone that he was to become the new archbishop of Philadelphia some four months earlier gave the commencement address at Marquette University, a Jesuit-run institution in Milwaukee. Like Yzermans, Vagnozzi praised the American bishops for their virtues; however, the context of the talk, entitled "Thoughts on the Catholic Intellectual," made the praise seem somewhat fainter. In fact, the faint praise offered by Vagnozzi sounds ominously damning at some points. What troubles Vagnozzi most throughout the talk is the defensiveness of Catholic intellectuals in America. These Catholic intellectuals, Vagnozzi tells the graduating class of 1961 in Milwaukee, "seem to feel that the Catholic intellectual effort of today does not measure up satisfactorily with the level of the secular effort."

As a result, the Church seemed to be losing the intellectual war for the minds of its own troops, the very people staffing its own institutions. Catholicism had reached a dangerous point in 1961—nothing in comparison to the disaster which would follow Vatican II—but dangerous in its own way because it led to the disaster and was clearly perceptible to an intelligent observer of the American intellectual scene among Catholics. A sort of fideism was setting in. Catholic academic life was confining itself more and more to the faith and concerning itself less and less with the world, which seemed to function according to principles more ably explicated according to the categories of secular science. In his capacity as the Vatican's observer of the American Catholic scene, Vagnozzi had discerned as early as 1961 a disturbing tendency on the part of the people who staffed the Church's universities "to feel . . . that an excessive attachment to traditional positions appears to prevent the Church from freely facing modern problems with adequate answers and assuring directions."

After taking the measure of American intellectual culture, Vagnozzi was impressed with its overwhelmingly secular character and underwhelmed by the reaction of Catholic intellectuals who were all too willing to accept the categories which secular culture proposed to them at face value. Catholic intellectuals, Vagnozzi felt, were confronted by "the modern, massive opposition of secularism and naturalism" and yet seemed unaware of the massive nature of the contradiction between what they believed and what the culture proposed to them as believable. Vagnozzi detects a disturbing tendency on the part of Catholic intellectuals to take the categories of secular culture for granted and an even more disturbing tendency to allow them "to dominate alone the domain of the mind."

Caught in the middle of the conflict, which at this point of time must have seemed only a moderately-sized cloud on a very clear horizon, were the American bishops, who considered themselves financial enablers and who were chosen with their administrative and financial acumen in mind for tasks that were increasingly viewed as irrelevant when not downright hostile by the very people whose salaries they paid. Vagnozzi, as could be expected in this situation, attempted to be as diplomatic as possible, but it is oftentimes difficult to discern whether he is urging the intellectuals to be more faithful or the bishops to be more observant. In either case, neither group found the task at hand particularly congenial. The intellectuals were chafing under a regime which they often felt lacked intellectual credibility, and the bishops were reluctant to do battle in fields they found alien and beyond their field of expertise. As a result there was oftentimes much pretending going on where the Church was supposed to be doing its thinking and where it was supposed to be educating the upcoming generation in the faith.

"The Holy See," Vagnozzi told the crowd at Marquette, "chooses its bishops with the utmost care, for their intellectual training, superior intelligence and deep understanding as well as for their moral integrity." At this point the Apostolic Delegate begins to slip into a mode that in all honesty has to be described as defensive. "Even if our bishops and priests cannot all be scholars. . . they are equipped to understand and evaluate anything that the intellectuals can say and write about religion . . ." If Vagnozzi meant to reassure the Catholic intellectual elite, he in many ways articulated their fears without allaying them.

The main problem lay not with the bishops, however, but with the constituency which ran Catholic universities. In many ways the bishops had created a whole new set of problems for themselves because of their success as builders and financiers. The Catholic education system had not only been well-established; it was now beginning to flourish. The roots had been sunk and now the tree was bearing fruit. However, an intellectual institution bears intellectual fruit, and it was precisely in this area that the Catholic educational system was beginning to slip away from the bishops who had been its major enablers. While they could provide financial backing, it was not clear that they could provide the same caliber of intellectual direction. And in the absence of this direction from the Church, the Catholic intellectual was beginning to take his cue from the world around him. What Vagnozzi saw among the Catholic intelligentsia in America was an incipient case of Catholic inferiority complex. They had been successful enough—enormously successful—in moving beyond the financial exigencies of their parents or parent's parents to a point where they had the leisure to devote their thoughts to higher things, things of the intellect, only to find that the secular educational establishment held them in veiled contempt. Sensing this, the immediate reaction of the Catholic intellectual was to "build bridges."

"They seem to feel," Vagnozzi said,

> that every effort has to be made in order to build a bridge between modern secular thought and Catholic thought, even to the point of digressing from positions traditionally accepted in the past, in the expectation of being acknowledged and accepted in the intellectual circles of today.

Vagnozzi touched a sensitive spot here. The immigrants who came to this country did not come here to hold this country in contempt. For the most part they aspired to do well; they aspired to be accepted; they aspired to achieve more or less according to the terms propounded to them by the society at large. And the America of the time of the great waves of European immigration for the most part did its part to meet the immigrants' aspirations half way. There was widespread economic exploitation of the newcomer, but the immigrant was free to establish the intermediary structures which made that transition as painless as possible. The Catholic Church, with its vast network of social and educational institutions, throve during this period. Catholics were granted a sort of second class status with regard to the main institutions of the culture, but within that framework did very well for themselves indeed.

Nineteen sixty-one was to prove to be a crucial crossroads in this regard. It was during this year that the first Catholic was elected to the presidency of the United States. In 1928, Al Smith told the pope to unpack his bags when he lost to Herbert Hoover in an election that saw an enormous resurgence of anti-Catholic feeling. In 1961, all of that seemed far in the past, and the Catholic intellectual seemed to be on the threshold of stepping out of the ethnic ghetto and into the mainstream of cultural life in this country for the first time. Perhaps as well as anyone during the period, Michael Novak, a young Catholic of Slovakian heritage from Johnstown, Pennsylvania, seemed to epitomize the Catholic intellectual's aspirations to join the mainstream without sufficient attention being paid to the terms under which the deal was being consummated. His writings throughout the '60s are permeated by an enthusiasm for bridge-building that was giving Archbishop Vagnozzi pause.

"The American secular community," Novak informs us in his 1964 book *A New Generation : American and Catholic*, "regards American Catholics as politically and socially selfish and unenlightened." And Novak seems determined to do everything within his power for the rest of the book to prove the secularists wrong by adopting their categories and attempting to restructure Church culture according to their exigencies. Novak is clearly aware of his existence in two worlds—"there are at present two different 'worlds' for the Catholic in America, the

Catholic world and the secular world" (Novak, *A New Generation*, p. 211). The *Zeitgeist* of the early '60s led Novak to believe that he could have "the best of both worlds," which was precisely the feeling that was causing Archbishop Vagnozzi such consternation. In discussing contemporary art, Vagnozzi wagged his finger at the audience at Marquette:

> We cannot blame our bishops and our priests if they are reluctant to abandon the accepted, traditional forms in order to build churches and fill them with statues and paintings which may be an expression of a genuine feeling and of the talent of an individual artist, but which too often do not respond to the demands of the religious feeling of the Catholic people.

In retrospect, Vagnozzi's caveat on contemporary culture was neither a devastating critique of modern art nor a ringing endorsement of the bishops. But given the spirit of the times, it was more perceptive than what most Catholics had to say on the matter in the Kennedy era, and Vagnozzi, unlike Novak, was perceptive enough to realize that there might not be a complete congruity between the Catholic and the secular worlds.

If Novak recognized any incongruity at the time, the implication was almost invariably that the Church would have to seek help. "The secular campus," Novak tells us making one of the many invidious comparisons which pervade his book, "provides an arena for free, unstructured discussion" unlike the Catholic campus which seems bound to an a priori commitment to defend outmoded traditions and the dead hand of the past. "The secular university," Novak continues, "seems in fact to promote, through the method of liberty, the achievement of a profound personal synthesis in a remarkable number of its graduates" (p. 217). "Catholic pastoral theory," on the other hand, instead of favoring "the strong, the bright, and the critical," "seems clearly to favor the weak, the slow, the undiscerning." Secularists even have better parties: "a cocktail party in a secular environment," Novak informs us, "is open on the world, more pluralistic, more respectful, more favorable to the individual talent."

Given Novak's awe at the time of things secular, his prescriptions for the Catholic intelligentsia are not surprising. They should "build bridges." They should, in other words, lay the

Catholic intellectual life on the procrustean bed of American, liberal, democratic secularism and lop off whatever doesn't fit. The lopping at this stage of the game had mostly to do with philosophical issues; the pleading for doctrinal changes would come later in the decade.

The "Catholic mind," we are told, "does not seem universally convincing" (p. 220). Catholic colleges are "too much dominated by Aquinas." Scholastic arguments "block contemporary insights" and should be replaced instead by "a much more fruitful approach," namely, "the study of the contemporary analysis of language, Dewey, and the existentialists, with only supplementary study of Aristotle and Aquinas" (p. 221).

The heady optimism, the naive bridge-building, the myopic confidence in the secular regime: it all evokes a sense of embarrassment now and wonderment at how someone who professed to be a Catholic and an intellectual could be taken in by fads on the level of "Dewey and the existentialists." Perhaps it was Novak's misfortune to be published so widely while still so young. The more mature Michael Novak gives some indication of having second thoughts about the promise of the early '60s. In an article which appeared in 1992, Novak expresses regret at the loss of "self-confidence, direction and quiet pride" that characterized the Church he railed against 30 years before. If there was a loss, then Novak's efforts at reaching an accommodation with secular culture were a major contributing factor.

With the help of hindsight, he seems to be coming to the same realization himself. "At the very moment during which some of us were urging an "open church," writes Novak in 1992 referring to the title of his own book on the Second Vatican Council published 28 years before,

> and "opening the windows of the church to the world," we neglected to notice that the vehicle in which we were riding was just entering a long tunnel filled with noxious fumes. We opened those windows at an inopportune moment. Thus the "popular" culture in which the young find themselves has at its disposal the most powerful instruments ever—television, cinema, rock music, etc. and is at the same time perhaps the most toxic in history to faith and morals (Novak, *Crisis*, p. 16).

"Let me speak for myself," Novak concludes with the benefit of 30 years' hindsight, " I know that I will have a lot to answer for. . . . I think our generation needs to say we failed."

In 1961, however, when the prospects of collaboration between the Church and the world seemed so promising, it seems remarkable that anyone suspected anything untoward. But that was clearly Vagnozzi's warning at the time; and the benefit of history shows that his warning was just as clearly ignored by the people, like Novak, to whom it was aimed. The American bishops had created an educational system that was moving beyond their intellectual control. Their very acumen in raising money and administration often earned them the contempt of the people whose salaries they paid. In the wake of Vagnozzi's talk the clouds on the horizon grew perceptibly darker. The bishops would within a matter of years become engaged in a major cultural battle over just who controlled these Catholic institutions in the United States. "True intellectuality," Vagnozzi warned,

> must be combined with humility. . . .The true intellectual . . . does not . . . set up his intellect, whose adequate object is truth, in contradiction to the Truth. Rather, he recognizes in awe the limitations of his human intellect when face to face with the infinite wisdom of God.

If this were in fact the case, then it must have become apparent that the Church had a surplus of false intellectuals at the time. But the Apostolic Delegate, perhaps slightly intimidated by the specter he invoked decided to end his speech on a deliberately optimistic note.

> When we consider that a large part of our Catholic people is made up of third and fourth generation children of poor immigrants . . . I think we must be thankful to Almighty God for the results that have been achieved.

If we view Archbishop Vagnozzi's speech at Marquette in Platonic terms, then his description of the typical American bishop could be construed as the shadow on the wall of the cave and John Joseph Krol as the thing casting the shadow. He was quite simply an exaggerated version of the type of bishop Vagnozzi described in his speech. Enormously successful in finance and administration, Krol had made it to the penultimate position of authority in the Church within one generation, not three or four. Yet, like the rest of his episcopal generation, he would arrive on the scene to confront a challenge that was in many ways alien to the gifts which got him where he was. During the '60s Krol and his brothers in the American episcopate would be called upon not so much to build more buildings but to insure that what got taught in the buildings the immigrant Church had established was in fact the Catholic faith.

It must not have seemed a challenge congenial to the man who was born in Cleveland, Ohio on October 26, 1910 the second oldest son and one of seven children born to John Krol, Sr. and Anna Pietruzka. John's father was born into the diocese of Tarnow in what was then the Austro-Hungarian empire on April 30, 1882. John Joseph Krol was born into a family whose main preoccupation was economic survival. His father, who returned to Poland when John was two years old, told him once that the only reason they had come to the United States was because it was impossible for him to raise a family in Europe. John Krol senior left his native village of Siekieczyna in the Tatra mountains of what is now southern Poland and travelled first to seek his fortune in Budapest as a stonecutter. In the course of his stay there he learned enough Hungarian to converse later with one of his son's seminary friends, and he learned in addition that the economic situation there was not propitious for economic prosperity.

From Budapest, Krol Sr. made his way to Baltimore and from Baltimore to Cleveland where he got a job drilling railroad ties for $12 a week. In 1904, John Krol married Anna Pietruzka and the young couple settled in St. Hyacinth's parish in the Kingsbury Run section of Cleveland, an industrial area dominated by the Standard Oil Refinery. When asked if his parents met at some social gathering in Cleveland, Krol's response was "Are you kidding?" The implication was clearly that they had not time for things social so busy were they with the burdens of work. Krol remembers his father as someone who could do virtually anything with his hands. He was by turns a machinist but also a self-taught carpenter, electrician, barber, paperhanger, plumber and cobbler. John Joseph even remembers his father setting a broken bone when one of his sisters broke her leg.

John Joseph's mother, Anna, was born on December 8, 1886 in Poland. She changed her name to Pietruzka, taking the name of her stepfather after her mother remarried on the death of her first husband. Like John Joseph's father, his mother came to the United States because of economic hardship around the turn of the century with the great wave of Polish immigration of the time. Krol's mother came to Cleveland to live with a half-sister there and work at a convent run by the Ursuline nuns. After marrying at the age of 18, she continued to work outside the home for a while as a chambermaid at a hotel in Cleveland. John Joseph remembers having boarders in the home in the period up to and including World War I, but not thereafter, when rising wages and the increasing size of their family made the money unnecessary and the extra people burdensome. The reason for the emigration of both his mother and his father was economic. Poland was under Austrian administration at the time, which for the Catholic population was the most benign alternative to either the Prussians or the Russians.

As soon as the threat of poverty began to abate, John Krol Sr. entertained thoughts about returning to Poland. "If I could feed my family and educate them in Poland," he once told his son John Joseph, "that's where I'd be." In 1912, John Sr. felt that he had accumulated enough capital to try exactly that. He sold his house in Cleveland and moved back to buy a farm in Poland. The trip to Poland was to provide John Joseph with his first memory—and not a particularly pleasant one. He remembers being inoculated and not liking the experience, screaming, as he put it later, "to the high heavens" in protest.

The venture was not a success. John Joseph's brother Stanley was born in Poland in December of 1912, but by 1913 the Krol family was back in Cleveland. There were a number of reasons for the return. Financially things had not worked out; there was a sense that war was imminent, which meant in all probability being drafted into the Austro-Hungarian army; and beyond that John Sr. felt that there were virtually no educational opportunities for his children there. When asked later in life why education was considered so important, Krol just shrugs, confessing that he doesn't know and admitting that these aspirations were unusual for someone from that background and time. John Joseph was the exception among his peers in that he finished high school. Most of the people he knew got jobs at the age of 14 or 15 because the extra money was needed to help out with their families.

"My background," Krol told the *B'nai B'rith* in an address in 1964, "is that of a normal American. I am one of eight children born in Cleveland of Polish immigrants. My parents, like some of yours, had very limited educational and economic resources. They lived in a settlement of Polish immigrants, adjacent to a settlement of Jewish immigrants—many of whom also migrated from Poland. At the age of 9, I began to contribute to the family income, and at the age of 16, after graduating from high school, I went to work. At the age of 18, I was rated a master meat cutter and was the manager of the meat department of a chain store."

John Joseph was no exception to his peers in Cleveland in this regard. At the age of 10 he got a job as a butcher's helper at Kroger's supermarket. His job was clerking, i.e., selling and delivering the meat and cleaning the chopping blocks. Krol remembers learning nothing of value from the latter task, but selling meat in Cleveland in the 1920s was in many ways a linguistic education all by itself. The neighborhoods were still heavily ethnic and command of a number of Slavic and Germanic Languages, not to mention Hungarian, was not only desirable, it was oftentimes necessary. Krol remembers being called in to translate more than once. Ethnic Cleveland in the 1920s was in many ways a rehearsal for Rome in the early '60s, when Krol's administrative and linguistic skills were put to use in running the Second Vatican Council.

What Krol doesn't remember about his apprenticeship at Kroger's was the amount of money he made. It couldn't have been much, and what little there was went to his family to help out with the family finances.

"We were always lacking money," he said later of the time of his childhood. This forced him to be resourceful in other ways. As a child he would frequent the foundries in the area collecting railroad ties which the Krols would then use for heat and cooking in their eisenglass pot bellied stove. One gets the impression that the Krols were serious people. The economic hardships which might have broken a less spiritual family simply hardened this one into a unit of people who felt that life was serious business and that they were put here to perform their duty.

John Joseph graduated from Cleveland's Cathedral Latin High School in 1927 at the age of 16. He graduated from high school early because he started grade school early, at the age of four and a half, at St. Hyacinth's, where he was taught by Polish nuns, the Sisters of St. Joseph of the Third Order of St. Francis. He remembers them more for their discipline and strictness that he does for any academic achievement on his own part. When asked what his grades were like in grade school, he remarks laconically, "I passed." The language of instruction was Polish, although some instruction was done in English as well. Krol remembers translating in grade school as well. When one of the students didn't understand the instructions in English, he would translate them into Polish. When asked if he enjoyed Latin in high school, he replies by saying, "I wouldn't say I liked it." Latin, at Cathedral Latin, was "a subject that you took."

When asked what his main interests in high school were, Krol mentions working. In the summer before his senior year, Krol worked for the Rockefellers at the Standard Oil box factory. For 40 hours a week, Krol would drill holes in wooden boxes which would eventually carry cans of Standard Oil, for which he was paid 25 cents an hour. In characteristic fashion he adds that by the time he left the Rockefeller's employ he was making 35 cents an hour, "which at that time was considered a good wage."

In terms of extracurricular activities during high school, Krol played no sports. He started smoking at the age of 16 because everyone else did, a bad habit that would almost kill him later on in life, after which time he would merely chew cigars without smoking them. He is listed in the yearbook as having been a member of the glee club and on the staff of the yearbook, *The Purple and Gold*, but even there instead of writing for it, he went around to local businesses and solicited ads to help defray the book's cost. John Joseph was the guy who made the yearbook financially viable; he was not the guy who wrote the copy. It was a pattern which would repeat itself throughout Krol's life. If the guy who wrote the copy was dependable, any joint venture with Krol was a success. If not, then it was not. Krol supported the Church to the best of his ability. He was able to enable; he was able to efface himself into the man behind the scenes. He took on the mind of the Church in virtually everything, but when the Church was of two minds, he did not flourish. Krol was a financial enabler who did what he did, not particularly because he liked it but because he felt it was his duty—the word looms large in the evaluation his peers wrote about him upon his graduation from high school:

> The pleasure one feels in the consciousness of having performed his duty is the reward one receives for all his pains. "John" certainly must feel this most delectable sensation. He does his duty, never swerves from it; his conscience tells him that his is right and he leaves the consequences to God.

Upon graduation from high school, John Joseph went to work full time at the meat department at Kroger's and as can be expected in a situation like this he began a steady rise up through the ranks. By the time he was 19 he had become manager of the meat department, owned stock in the company and his own car. During this time the Krol family focused on meeting the economic necessities of life. They seem to have had little time for anything else. Krol remembers sending money to relatives in Poland but he does not remember long discussions about the political situation there. He remembers knowing about the Bolshevik Revolution and Jozef Pilsudski defeating the Communists, but remembers as well that there was not a lot of correspondence between Cleveland and Siekecyzna. Krol's father had a sense that war was coming but probably could not have located Sarajevo on a map when it finally broke out. It was only after Krol arrived in the seminary in the early '30s that it dawned on him what communism was and, as he would put it later, that the communists were "not nice people." This realization came chiefly as a result of listening to the radio broadcasts of Father Charles Coughlin. What he did learn at the seminary was never to identify Russians with Communists. Krol's father didn't talk much about the Communists because he wasn't aware of what they were doing. And he wasn't aware then because most people weren't. Krol spoke Polish at home, but for the most part was completely cut off from what was happening in Poland until he arrived there in the summer of 1939.

The events of the times were refracted as they had always been through the lens of daily routine. Krol's father did not prosper during the '20s because he did not own his own business and as a result the economic pressure which drove consideration of other things from his mind did not relent.

Given this set of circumstances, it would seem that the only way that God could get John Joseph's attention was by sending His directives care of the meat department at Kroger's. Which is pretty much what the Almighty did. If John Joseph had ever entertained the idea of being a priest he had pretty much dismissed it by the time he reached high school. By the time he graduated from high school, he was sure of one thing when it came to career choices, "I did know what I did not want to be, and that was a priest."

By 1929, Krol was the highest paid manager in the store, making $38 a week, which was more than many married men with children were making at the time. One can imagine him continuing his rise in the Kroger organization or starting a business of his own, although it must be admitted that 1929 was not a particularly good year for entrepreneurial ventures. Instead his seriousness came to the attention of the head of the grocery department in the same store, a studious German Lutheran by the name of Herb Riehl who approached Krol one day and asked him if he could discuss religion without getting emotional. Krol opined that he could and found himself confronted with four questions which he couldn't answer. The unanswered questions drove the 19-year-old manager of the meat department to the books and some protracted reflection on the purpose of life, which in turn led to the decision to quit working at Kroger's and to try to go to college.

The ruminations about higher things did not stop there. After achieving a modicum of economic security and—by his peers' standards, at least—prosperity, at the age of 19, Krol was faced not only with the prospect of a long life doing much the same thing, as well as being confronted with the question of what the purpose of that life was supposed to be. Since there were basically two major forces in Krol's life at the time— economic necessity and religious duty—it followed that when the one was taken care of the other would rise to increasing prominence on his intellectual horizon. With the thoroughness of a logic manual, Krol decided that 1) the purpose of being here is to get to heaven and 2) that the shortest way to get to heaven was through the priesthood. Combining thesis one and two, he came up with his conclusion: he would enroll in the seminary.

John Joseph Krol entered St. Mary's College in Orchard Lake, Michigan in the fall of 1931. Krol later said that he chose St. Mary's College and later St. Mary's Seminary because he wanted to learn how to speak and write classical Polish. Krol had grown up with Polish as the language of the home, but had always felt that what he spoke was, if not exactly the local patois, then a language more appropriate to the concerns of farmers rather than scholars or diplomats. His original intention was to return to a parish like the one he left and minister to the blue collar Polish population of Cleveland, perhaps acting as an intermediary between the two cultures as he had done in grade school when he would translate something which his fellow pupils found incomprehensible in English into the language they could understand. In addition to taking all of the subjects that seminarians were expected to take at the time, Krol devoted himself to the study of Latin, Greek, and Hebrew, but even these subjects were taken with the idea of mastery of Polish in mind. "I very deliberately studied every subject I could in Polish," he said later characterizing his days at the seminary. "I took Latin and translated it into Polish and translated Greek into Polish as well."

What he expected was what he got. After his ordination to the priesthood at St. John's Cathedral on February 20, 1937, Father Krol was assigned to Immaculate Conception parish in Cleveland, a blue collar ethnic parish not unlike St. Hyacinth's where he had grown up.

"I expected to be assigned to a Polish parish," Krol said later, "and I was assigned to a Polish parish." Polish was the language of instruction at the parish school. The liturgy was in Latin but the priests at Immaculate Conception were expected to preach in Polish and hear confessions in Polish. "I would say that better than three fourths of what I did was in Polish," Krol recounted later. "It served me in good stead because even today people are amazed that I speak Polish as well as I do. I have preached in Poland without a script. I spoke at the shrine of Our Lady Of Czestochowa and at the seminaries there too."

Krol's business acumen didn't leave him during his time at the seminary any more that his ability for languages did. Bishop Paul Hallinan of Charleston, South Carolina, remembers Krol setting up a commissary and selling cigars—factory rejects—at the seminary. "If he weren't a priest," the former rector of the seminary remarked later, "he would have become a millionaire."

Krol would later say that he would have been content to remain at Immaculate Conception doing what he was doing. But his good qualities, most specifically his ability to get things of a practical nature done, came to the attention of the ordinary, and he was placed on the track for those destined for upward mobility in the Church at that time. In 1938 he was sent to Rome to get an advanced degree in canon law. Canon law is what the people who became bishops studied, primarily because as bishops they were called upon to administer the Church according to the Church's law. American bishops were doubly prone to study canon law because of the role law played in American culture. In the absence of common traditions and in the presence of so many diverse ethnic groups, law was the only agency which integrated such diverse groups into an integrated whole. At the same time that Father Krol was setting off to Rome to study law, the president of the United States was having his own troubles with that country's Supreme Court invalidating his programs for economic recovery. Roosevelt's immediate response to the intransigence of the Supreme Court came to be known as the Court packing scheme, an attempt to raise the number of justices on the highest court of the land. It was an attempt which failed. What Roosevelt did achieve, however, was the appointment of two justices—Hugo Black and William O. Douglas—who would become instrumental in revolutionizing the cultural framework of the republic. Thirty-three years down the road Krol and Douglas would meet in a face-off over aid to nonpublic schools, but as a young seminarian, this sort of thing, needless to say, was not uppermost in the young priest's mind.

Krol arrived in Rome in November of 1938 on the feast of St. Charles Borromeo, the north Italian counterreformation reformer after whom the diocesan seminary in Philadelphia was named.

"We came over on the Volcania," Krol remembered over 50 years after the fact. The half a dozen priests who left for studies in Rome shipped over two to a cabin. Krol remembers spending about 30 hours in Boston harbor because of fog. During the trip, Krol remembers his discussions with fellow priests as "not talking about politics"; rather more "sense and nonsense" is how he put it later.

The contrast between the gravity of the times and the light-heartedness of the priests' conversations is striking. The priests had to get special permits to travel at all, to show that their visit to Italy had some serious purpose and wasn't simply a pleasure trip, and yet from Krol's description at least the conversations of the priest seemed only obliquely related to the gravity of the times. *Mit Brennender Sorge*, Pius XI's condemnation of Nazism had been issued one year before, but when Krol arrived in Italy the connection between the German Nazis and the Italian Fascists was not immediately apparent—not to him at least.

Krol had a room at the Maryknoll house on the Via Sardinia, not far from the famous Hotel Excelsior, epicenter of *La Dolce Vita* on the Via Veneto 20 years later. Because his classes were held at the Gregorian University, Krol would walk to his classes by himself every day. The walk would take him by the Vittoria Emmanuale monument where Mussolini's influence was very much in evidence. When Krol was eventually moved to a room on the Via Aurelia Antiqua at the North American College he would watch the young Fascists lining up in their black shirts for another "spontaneous" demonstration in support of Mussolini and his policies. It was clear, to Father Krol at least, that Mussolini was intent on building an empire. His invasion of Ethiopia had taken place the year before. "There was no secret about the great Italian empire," Krol remembered. "If you talked against it, you got a dose of castor oil." However, the connection between Fascism and Hitler was "not evident" and any connection between the rise of what would come to be known as the axis powers and the situation in Poland was more remote still.

Father Krol was not sent to Rome to watch history unfold. He was sent to master canon law, a subject he would have to study in Latin. And that prospect was intimidating enough all by itself to focus his mind on his studies to the exclusion of almost everything else.

"I had taken a number of courses in Latin at the seminary," Krol said, "but I wasn't sure whether I would be able to catch what was being taught at the Greg. I knew Latin, but I was worried about the amount of courses. Instead of going easy, I went hard. In fact I even took a special course at the Roman Rota so that I would have one year training as a Rota lawyer."

When asked how the gathering storm clouds over Europe affected his studies, Krol gives the impression that they had little effect until the war interrupted them in the spring of 1940 and Krol and his fellow priests were sent back to the United States. Some of this lack of concern may have been a young man's bravado, but much of it had to do with the way priests were trained at the time.

"We didn't have that much time for common talk," is how Krol put it 50 years later. Krol remembers going to a restaurant called Albrecht's on the Via Sicilia which served beer and sauerkraut. He remembers being free to talk, at the restaurant at least, but when asked about the content of the conversations, he draws a blank.

Given the type of training he received, this is not surprising. At the time Father Krol's mind was being formed as a canonist in a language no one spoke outside of the halls of the university where he was studying, education meant an extremely specific type of training for an extremely specific type of purpose. Krol was being groomed to be a bishop when the Church had very definite ideas about what a bishop did and did not do. And he was being educated in a language that no one spoke anymore. Beyond that, there were a whole host of rules governing seminary training which had grown up during the post-reformation, post-Trent period in the church which were extremely strict and extremely explicit and yet by the same token inexplicable to the very people who were expected to hold them.

In an article on the "the historical context in which the Idea of a new Ecumenical Council was Born," the Rev. Giacomo

Martina, S.J. gives some idea of what it was like to study at the Gregorian University 20 years after Father Krol was there, but still before the advent of the changes initiated by the Second Vatican Council. "We left the Gregorian in the '50s," Martina writes, "with a strong feeling of the difference between certain classic, traditional Catholic positions, and the principles commonly accepted by the modern world" (Martina, in Latourelle, p. 51). In addition to this sense of difference, Martina relates a series of rules that the seminarians had to follow which he found inexplicable. Jesuits, for example, were forbidden to talk to non-Jesuits, "following a rule dating from the sixteenth or seventeenth century." Not only did the rule not make sense to Martina, it also did little to encourage collegiality among the members of the universal church gathered in Rome. This also meant that virtually no one in the Church had a broad picture of either the forces affecting the Church as a whole or the proper response of the Church as a whole to those same forces. The post-Reformation seminary training had created experts in the trees who had difficulty seeing the forest because of what were increasingly perceived as senseless traditions whose purpose no one could explain. The Church's future bishops were encouraged to become experts in the law governing the Church, but they were not encouraged to explore the connections between that law and the cultures they inhabited. They were, in effect, confronted with two compartments of life and left to wonder in their spare time—if they had any—how those two compartments—the City of God and the City of Man—were related.

As some indication that the young priests did have spare time and as some indication of the disjunction between the Cities of God and Man at that time, Father Krol decided to take a trip to Poland during the summer vacation of 1939. Nineteen-thirty-nine was about as auspicious for Polish tourism as 1929 was for quitting a well-paying job, but Krol, whose life in Cleveland was saturated with Polish culture and language, was determined to return to the land he had left as a three year old over a quarter of a century before. Father Krol had had virtually no contact with his relatives during the greater part of his life in Cleveland. Perhaps because of that, perhaps because the Krols did not write much anyway, Father Krol decided to arrive in Poland unannounced. Another factor which facilitated his decision was the fact that not only was seminary closed during the summer. His rooms were closed as well.

"You had to spend the time somewhere," he said, "And so I decided to make a *giro*, to take a trip and visit my relatives."

Father Krol left Rome in late July and headed north by train travelling through Switzerland. When he got to Austria he noticed a change in the political climate. While in Vienna he had difficulty getting anyone to tell him where Mass was being said. The *Anschluss* was one year old and the Nazi police state tactics were having their effect on the Catholic population of Austria.

"One woman was willing to talk at first and then she caught herself and clammed up," said Krol slipping into the patois of Cleveland.

In a convent chapel in Vienna, Krol ran into a number of priests who had recently been jailed. When he asked them the reason, Krol was told that the government didn't need a reason anymore. If they didn't like you, that was reason enough. The Vatican was not unaware of the gravity of the situation of Catholics under the Third Reich. When word got around that Krol was planning a trip north, it was suggested to him that he wear a necktie in Germany to avoid difficulties for himself and the Church. Wearing a roman collar was not recommended because of the Reich's increasing hostility to the Church. Priests were often arrested on the suspicion of being spies, perhaps for good reason. When Father Krol finally got to Poland and put on his soutane again, he was informed that foreigners in clerical garb in Poland were suspected automatically of being German spies. Throughout the summer of 1939, the Germans were sending spies dressed up as priests into Catholic Poland as advanced reconnaissance for the invasion which eventually took place on September 1. The United States State Department at the time discouraged travel claiming that the risk factor involved was simply too difficult to gauge in such uncertain times.

Father Krol pressed on nonetheless, arriving in Kattowice at the Polish/Czech border on August 15, 1939. He almost made it no further getting into an altercation with a customs official who refused to believe that a man with an American passport and a Polish name wasn't smuggling contraband to relatives. Father Krol suspected that the man wanted a cut of whatever it was he suspected Krol of smuggling. When Father Krol said he had nothing to declare, the customs official refused to believe him.

"By this time I wasn't in a good mood," Krol related later. "I said to him, 'Are you accusing me of lying?' I insist that you're going to take down those bags and go through all of them and if you find anything I'll apologize. If you don't, then you'll have to apologize, and I will report you to your superiors."

"We got into a hassle over customs, and we got into another hassle over the question of exchanging money and buying a ticket. All the other customs officials were understanding, but this clown was just a little guy playing the big shot. So I insisted that he go through the two bags and give me a clearance or prove that I'm wrong."

By the time the train arrived in Kattowice, Krol's ticket was no longer valid, and he was insisting that he be issued a new one. The customs official, by now had concluded that the American priest with the Polish name was more than he had bargained for. "You talk to this nut," said the customs official to the conductor, who proved more amenable to Father Krol's way of doing business. In all, it seemed a curious way to carry out the Vatican's directive to remain unobtrusive.

From Kattowice Krol took the train to Krakow without incident and from Krakow he headed southeast to Limanouw, which was, as far as taking the train went, the end of the line. Krol picked up his two suitcases and set out for the rest of the way by foot, arriving in Siekeczyna on a humid morning murky with a combination of fog and drizzle. Siekeczyna is not a a large town, and Krol went directly to the family homestead and knocked on the door. When Peter Krol, John Joseph's uncle, came to the door he did not recognize his nephew, whom he had last seen a little more than a quarter of a century before. In a manner in keeping with Krol family traditions, Father Krol was invited in, but the family did not have a formal party for him, lacking either the money or the time. After the evening meal, Father Krol sat on a bench in front of the house, and one by one his relatives and friends of the family would come over to talk.

Father Krol had 22 cousins living in Poland in the summer of 1939. Six years later there were only five left.

"I know a couple of them," he said later, "were blasted skyward. If you were caught sheltering a Jew, feeding them or anything of that sort, you were just shot right then and there. Poland was the only place that I know of where the Nazis had summary executions."

Poland, of course, suffered the brunt of Nazi terror. It was the first country to be invaded and the last to be liberated, if that is the proper word to describe what the Russian occupation involved. At the time, Krol remembers everyone feeling that war was imminent, but it becomes just as clear that no one had much of an idea of just what kind of war it was going to be. Concentration camp was not a part of the general vocabulary at the time, nor was *Blitzkrieg* or holocaust: all these terms have helped shape the consciousness of the latter half of the 20th century.

While walking through the town, Father Krol ran into a few young men roughly his own age who were a little drunk and happy to have the harvest behind them. They looked upon war with Germany as an almost certain thing but saw it roughly on the same level as one final chore that had to be completed after the crops had been gotten in the barn.

"They were going to fight the devil, meaning the Germans," Krol said. When Father Krol wondered what would happen if the Russians became involved in the war too, he was told that in that case "we'll be fighting two devils instead of one."

Not all of the conversation turned on the war though.

"We talked about family and friends. There weren't that many of the Krols that came over to America and the ones that stayed behind in Poland had a common notion that if you were in America you had the chance to make all kinds of money. America was the place to make money and after you made it there you would come back to Poland to live. I told them the streets were not paved with gold and that if you got a job you had to work long hard hours in a factory."

The actual fighting of World War II never really arrived in Sieckeczyna, which is in the uplands of the Tatra Mountains, generally rough terrain possessing no strategic importance and plagued by severe winters which last well into what is Spring in the rest of Europe of similar latitude. But the Nazi's version of ethnic cleansing did arrive there after the country had been conquered. In 1939 there was a synagogue in Limanouw for the orthodox Jews in the area who ran the banks and owned some taverns. Krol claims that there was some anti-Semitism in the area but that it was not a social problem. It quickly became a problem, however, when the Nazis arrived—not just for the Jews but for Krols' relatives as well. When he finally got back to Poland long after the war, and at a time when the Polish communist regime had loosened its restrictions on the Catholic clergy, Krol found the names of three of his relatives who had been summarily executed during the war.

Before too long, the rumors of war became impossible to ignore and the pleasures of family reunion notwithstanding, it became clear to Father Krol that he had better make plans to get out of the country while he still could. Father Krol, of course, still had his return train ticket, but before he seriously entertained using it, he noticed that the Polish government began mobilizing all available man and horsepower for the impending war. Then he found that the borders had been closed and that he was for all practical purposes stranded in a country that scheduled for invasion by the German *Wehrmacht*, which would soon show itself to be the most powerful army Europe had seen since the days of Napoleon.

Feeling suddenly helpless as the events which a few weeks ago seemed nothing more than an annoying background to this study of canon law now threatened to sweep him away with them, Krol turned to the Church and his family for advice. He first consulted the local pastor who claimed that no one could tell for sure what was going to happen and suggested going to Krakow. He then talked with Stan Krol, a relative who was a member of the Sejm, the Polish Parliament at the time. Because of his job, Stan Krol travelled back and forth between Siekeczyna and Warsaw on a regular basis. He also owned a radio and was kept apprised of the developing situation as a result. Between the pastor and his relative in the Sejm, Father Krol came up with a plan of escape. He would circumvent the closed borders by flying over them. With the invasion of Poland and the outbreak of World War II literally hours away, Krol boarded a DC 3 in Krakow and flew back over the Tatra Mountains and the now-closed border to Budapest where he touched down on August 31, 1939. The entire city was talking about war, a war now only hours away. Krol spent the last night of peace in the world for the next six years at the Hotel Bristol in Budapest in a building crowded with refugees whom he remembers as both poor and afraid.

The next day he took the train through the blackout from Budapest to Trieste, then he travelled again by train from Trieste to Venice and then from Venice to Rome in a train with people packed four to a seat talking of war. When he arrived in Rome he was quickly reabsorbed into the Catholic world he had left a few weeks before. It was a world which functioned according to its own schedule, and so while Hitler invaded the East and then then turned on his heel and invaded the West, Father John Krol quietly finished the 1939-40 academic year. At the end of the second semester, he successfully passed his exam for the licenti-ate in Canon law, just in time for he and his fellow priest canon lawyers to be evacuated from Italy in early May on the liner Saturnia. On May 9, when Mussolini declared war, Father Krol was on the high seas, not exactly safe because of the uncertain-ties of submarine warfare in the Atlantic at the time, but soon to be home again with two degrees under his belt, completed on schedule in spite of the war.

In 1942 Father Krol finally received the doctorate in canon law he was supposed to have gotten in Rome from Catholic University in Washington, DC. whereupon he joined the fac-ulty of St. Mary's seminary and began his rise through the ranks of the Archdiocese of Cleveland. Soon after joining the seminary faculty he was appointed Defender of the Bond, then Vice Chancellor of the Archdiocese and then in 1945 Papal Chamberlain with rank of Monsignor. In 1948 he was named President of the Canon Law Society of America. In 1951 he was named Domestic prelate and Chancellor of the Archdiocese of Cleveland.

Just two years later, on July 15, 1953, Amleto Cicognani, Apostolic Delegate to the United States announced that Msgr. Krol had been elevated to the rank of bishop. He was now auxiliary bishop of Cleveland and titular Bishop of Cadi. Krol was consecrated on September 2, 1953, at St. John's Cathedral in Cleveland at the hand of the ordinary, Archbishop Edward Francis Hoban. He chose as his motto "Deus Rex Meus," (God my King) perhaps in partial recognition of his nickname ("Rex") at the seminary which was in turn a play on the translation of his family name from the Polish.

Bishop Krol was now 43 years old, old enough in general to know what is going on and old enough in this particular instance to know that he did not particularly like the direction he saw his country taking in the years following world War II. We have already discussed his increasing unease at the direction that the American judicial system was taking under the aegis of legal positivism. There were other things he saw on the horizon which he did not like as well. Nineteen Fifty-three saw the continued spread of Communism abroad, but something equally pernicious was spreading at home which caused him just as much discomfort. In 1953, an entymologist at the state university in Bloomington, Indiana by the name of Alfred Kinsey issued the second of his two volumes on sexual behavior—this one on the human female—and set off an unprecedented discussion about the nature of sexual mores and morals in this country. The controversy was so great in fact that it prompted a congressional subcommittee chaired by Rep. Carroll Reece of Tennessee to inquire into the effect that foundation funding of projects like Kinsey's sexuality study were having in undermining the institutions of the republic.

Rene Wormser, Reece's legal assistant throughout the hearings, documented in a book published in 1957 not only the dangers posed by foundations to the institutions of the republic, he also documented the influence those foundations and their political allies were bringing to bear on the nation's cultural institutions. The great foundations—Ford, Rockefeller, Carnegie—were for the most part founded as a result of the New Deal as an attempt to prevent the flow of family money into the coffers of the federal government under the tax policies instituted by Roosevelt. Created from the wealth of this country's major capitalists, the foundations soon applied the techniques of the cartel and the trust to the flow of information and the reconfiguration of culture. The foundations would put up money which would serve as "venture capital" in the politics of change. Foundations like those run by the Rockefeller brothers would fund projects like the Kinsey sex surveys which would have been otherwise impossible to support given the constraints of democratically elected government or the simple satisfying of market forces. The foundations would fund research which they found congenial, and this almost invariably involved instigating social change away from a position of congruity with the moral law. They involved more often than not, as the Kinsey studies did, the substitution of "scientific" data for moral principle, and then when the project had received a modicum of public acceptance, the foundations would then turn the funding of the projects over to the government.

This was by and large the mechanism of cultural revolution in this country. The foundations would fund the undermining of some law—generally having to do with sex, the family, morals or religion—the courts would remove any legal roadblocks; the press would proselytize for whatever the social change in question entailed, giving widespread dissemination of the "scientific" surveys which the foundations funded, and eventually the government would set up programs based on what the foundations proposed, funded by government money. The government's involvement in contraception is just one instance of this general rule and one which we will examine in greater detail later.

The Reece Hearings were held through 1954 hard on the heels of the McCarthy hearings, and in the public mind, with the help of liberal pundits across the country, the two became inextricably liked. The Reece Committee in the hands of the nation's newspaper cartoonists became a witch-hunt. This was unfortunate for a number of reasons. In an age in which Moscow was seen as the root of virtually every evil in he world by a conservatism with a severe case of myopia, the Reece Hearings brought out the fact that subversion comes in many varieties, and that the subversion that does the most damage to a country is the one which subverts its most basic institutons, things like the family, in ways which the majority of that country's citizens find congenial.

The Reece Committee cited Rockefeller's funding of the Kinsey sex as especially subversive of the social order. Between

1941 and 1949, the Rockefeller foundations gave Kinsey $414,000 to conduct a study that was not only statistically worthless but which also involved criminal activity. The results of the survey were then purveyed as scientific truth by a press so avid for change in sexual morals that it had little time to dig into the inaccuracies and misrepresentations in the methodology. One professor who found the methodology and results indefensible found it virtually impossible to convey his misgivings to a wider audience. In addition, he found his own access to foundation money severely limited because of his critical stance. The collaboration of foundations, universities, and the media on a project they all deeply desired, namely sexual liberation, made it virtually impossible to get an opposing point of view across to the public, and even more difficult to influence legislation or protect the legislation that these "scientific studies" attacked. "Despite the patent limitations of the study and its persistent bias," Professor Hobbs continued,

> its conclusions regarding sexual behavior were widely believed. They were presented to college classes; medical doctors cited them in lectures; psychiatrists applauded them; a radio program indicated that the findings were serving as a basis for revision of moral codes relating to sex; and an editorial in a college student newspaper admonished the college administration to make provision for sexual outlets for the students in accordance with the "scientific realities" as established by the book (Wormser, p. 102).

Kinsey could claim that child molestation "may have contributed favorably to [the child's] later socio-sexual development." and no one seemed disposed to get upset. Nor did the press take notice of the fact that his data on child sexuality were clearly the result of illegal activity. That this was the case was in large measure due to the prestige of the foundations which funded the survey.

The same Professor Hobbs, cited previously by Wormser, stressed the fact that such pseudoscientific representations could seriously affect public morality.

In the second volume it is stressed, for example, that we object to adult molesters of children primarily because we have become conditioned against such adult molesters of children, and that the children who are molested become emotionally upset, primarily because of the old-fashioned attitudes of their parents about such practices, and the parents (the implication is) are the ones who do the real damage by making a fuss about it if a child is molested, because the molester, and here I quote from Kinsey, "may have contributed favorably to their later socio-sexual development." That is, a molester of children may have actually, Kinsey contends, not only not harmed them, but may have contributed favorably to their later socio-sexual development.

The special responsibility of the Rockefeller Foundation for having financed the Kinsey "best sellers" becomes apparent in a quotation from an article by Albert Deutsch in *Harper's*: "So startling are its revelations, so contrary to what civilized man has been taught for generations, that *they would be unbelievable but for the impressive weight of the scientific agencies backing the survey*" (Wormser, p. 104). Wormser finds it "preposterous to propose that social change should be justified upon empirical inquiry alone" but that is precisely what was happening and would continue to happen for the foreseeable future. A survey would show that a certain percentage of people did not follow the moral law on a particular issue, usually sexual. That survey would then be used as ammunition in attacking the particular law which safeguarded society from the effects of that particular vice. Wormser asked questions in the mid-'50s that so far have yet to be answered:

> Should concepts of value (legal, religious, ethical ideas) be abandoned merely because any number of men find them oppressive and neglect to live up to them? Are we justified in advocating a change in the criminal law because certain types of crimes are practiced widely? Shall we abrogate punishment for speeding, for theft, for adultery, for fraudulent voting, for income-tax evasion, if we find that such illegalities are practiced by a majority? By twenty percent of our people? By eighty percent? What percentage of our population must express itself, either by response to interviews or by action, in favor of an illegality to convince a social scientist that the law proscribing it should be abrogated?

The Constitution of the United States specifies a system of checks and balances in government. By the mid '50s it was clear to people like Reece and Wormser that the foundations circumvented virtually all of the mechanisms which the republic had established to defend itself from subversion. The foundations had enormous wealth on which they paid no taxes, and they had virtually free rein in expending that wealth on projects which would be condoned by neither the free market nor the country's duly elected representatives. As a result, the foundations and the entities they supported attracted a particular class of people. They attracted those who were interested in social change but who could not bring that change about by democratic means. They attracted the Left at a time when the Left had become disillusioned with the program Moscow was supporting and when New Deal liberalism was moving from an economic focus to a cultural one.

> These amazingly like-minded men have contributed substantially to converting into current orthodoxy what were revolutionary ideas during the twenties. They have supported for so long what they euphemistically call the "New Deal" (but what is really a modified form of socialism) that they are no longer capable of recognizing that other concepts of value may be held *bona fide* by thinkers and scholars (Womser, p. 81).

"Very few important cultural projects of any size," Wormser writes, "are consummated in this country without having experienced either the direct or indirect impact of foundation philosophy and influence." The influence of the foundations gets multiplied by the penurious situation of most academics of the time, who in order to get money were willing to do the research that the foundations wanted done and more often than not come up with the results they wanted as well. What this symbiosis of need creates is a class of people whose interests in a particular outcome are tied together, economically to be sure, but professionally as well. These are people who believe in the same sort of thing and make a living by propagating what they believe in.

The result is a system which is in many ways invisible to the eye and embedded in the very institutions of the culture. It can act in ways that make it seem as if the culture itself is acting and as a result becomes difficult to expose. Holding a committee hearing on it, passing a law against it is a bit like what Eliot said of refuting Montaigne's essays: it is like trying to disperse fog with a hand grenade. According to Wormser, this "concentration of power has measurable influence on our cultural life. . . .

No group of men sat down deliberately to plan this thing over-all. It just grew into being, but it is none the less dangerous as a concentration of power" (Wormser, p. 61).

> The emergence of this special class in our society, endowed with immense powers of thought control, is a factor which must be taken into account in judging the merits of contemporary foun-dation operations. The concentration of power, or interlock, which has developed in foundation-supported social-science re-search and social-science education is largely the result of a cap-ture of the integrated organizations by like-minded men. *The plain, simple fact is that the so-called "liberal" movement in the United States has captured most of the major foundations and has done so chiefly through the professional administrator class, which has not hesitated to use these great public trust funds to political ends and with bias* (Wormser, p. 81 [my emphasis]).

If this class has a common ideology it is essentially Nietzsche's project of the transvaluing all values. Henceforth, how the culture acts will be validated by "science," specifically the newly created social sciences. The cultural revolutionary class was by and large a group of moral relativists, especially when it came to sexual morality. Indeed, recent studies have shown that cultural relativism as practiced by people like Mar-garet Mead and Ruth Benedict was in reality nothing more than an attempt to rationalize sexual misconduct. The same sort of thing was noticed by the Reece Committee:

> It seems to this Committee that there is a strong tendency on the part of many of the social scientists whose research is favored by the major foundations toward the concept that there are no abso-lutes, that everything is indeterminate, that no standards of con-duct, morals, ethics and government are to be deemed inviolate, that everything, including basic moral law, is subject to change, and that it is the part of the social scientists to take no principle for granted as a premise in social or juridical reasoning, however fundamental it may heretofore have been deemed to be under our Judeo-Christian moral system (Wormser, p. 105).

Both the Reece Commission and Wormser in his subsequent book point out the mechanisms of cultural revolution in pains-taking detail. But the material they uncovered fell on deaf ears for the most part. This was true for a number of reasons. On the one hand, the liberals were avid for the scientifically-sanctioned sexual liberations which Reece and Co. found subversive. Secondly, Reece was right about the ability of the foundations and their minions in academe and the media to control information. His report was as a result consigned to epistemological limbo. Thirdly, there was the myopia of the conservatives who had become so obsessed with a foreign threat emanating in Moscow that they couldn't perceive a greater threat emanating from the culture at home. In the language of the '50s, subversion and communism had become synonymous. Reece had come up with a definition that was as once too subtle for the anti-communist conservatives and one that the liberals did not want propagated. As a result the warning went unheard. "What does the term 'subversion' mean?" the Reece Committee asked:

> In contemporary usage and practice, it does not refer to outright revolution, but to a promotion of tendencies which lead, in their inevitable consequences, to the destruction of principles through perversion or alienation. Subversion, in modern society, is not a sudden, cataclysmic explosion, but a gradual undermining, a persistent chipping away at foundations upon which beliefs rest. . . . In the modern usage of the term, "subversion," it is no exaggeration to state that in the field of the social sciences many major projects which have been most prominently sponsored by foundations have been subversive (Wormser, pp. 184-6).

"Society," the committee concludes, "does not grant tax exemption for the privilege of undermining itself." The committee was, as history would show, wrong. What the liberals had in effect created was totalitarianism with an American face. Conformity would come not so much from the stick of the police state as from the carrot of consumerism, conveyed by the increasingly powerful media of communication to nooks and crannies unreachable before. What came about as the result of America's experience in winning World War II was a new approach to social control. People like Bernard Berelson had studied the successes of Joseph Goebbels and came up with a new formula; it was in effect the ministry of propaganda without the police state.

Wormser terms the new regime "the Third American Revolution," a revolution

> none the less serious because it is bloodless. This new revolution is a reform movement gone wrong. It has become an attempt to institute the paternal state in which individual liberty is to be

subordinated and forgotten in a misapplication of the theory of the greatest good for the greatest number.

We are too managed by "social science divines" according to the new "scientific method" which can be "applied to the behavior of men as well as to the behavior of electrons."

> And how is this "scientific" management to take place? One gathers from Mr. Chase's book, which seems to represent the official line of the foundation complex, that it is to be through "cultural determinism," via a molding of our minds by propaganda (Wormser, p. 113).

This leads Wormser to wonder just who won the last war— so powerful has the effect of cultural propaganda become.

> Intellectually speaking, this country has a great danger of intellectually trying to imitate the totalitarian approach, in allowing people at centers of financial power—they aren't political powers in this sense—to tell the public what to study and what to work on, and to set up a framework.

In short, what to think.

Perhaps in reaction to the reaction, the Rockefeller Foundation decided to discontinue its financial support of Kinsey's sex project, a decision which so enraged Kinsey that he threatened to reveal the sex histories of anyone who opposed him. Kinsey died before he could make good on his threat, but the nation's morals took a body blow from his research, abetted by a media establishment avid for sexual liberation.

It was a blow from which the nation has yet to recover, and Bishop Krol in Cleveland was beginning to realize that winning two major wars in one century brought with it a series of social ills that the country was ill-equipped to face. In an address to the attorneys of Akron, Ohio given during his tenure as auxiliary bishop of Cleveland, Bishop Krol expressed concern over the rising tide of divorce which followed on the heels of the returning troops. "On the American scene," he told the Akron attorneys, "the divorce ratio climbed from 62 per 1000 in 1890 to 164 per 1000 in 1935. The divorce rate in the United States is the highest in the world. Since the war, the number of divorces has sky-rocketed to astronomical figures."

Krol saw the climb in divorce as a function of legal positivism, which had allowed this country's courts to legitimate what
was morally wrong. He also saw parallels between the situation
in this country and the recent catastrophes in Europe where
entire countries attempted to separate the rule of law from the
moral law with disastrous results. The state cannot make right
what God's law says is wrong. "This notion of total supremacy
of the state," Krol continued,

> is, of course, unadulterated totalitarianism, which took the form
> of Fascism under Mussolini in Italy; Nazism under Hitler in
> Germany, and Communism in Soviet Russia. . . . It seems para-
> doxical that Soviet Russia, which denies the existence of God and
> of the natural law, was much quicker in discovering the greatest
> threat to marriage and the family. In 1929, by way of reaction to
> bourgeois morality, the Soviet Republic promoted free divorces.
> In less that nine years, this government, founded upon a materi-
> alistic philosophy, realized the mistake of easy divorce, and en-
> acted legislation to sustain and preserve marriage and the family
> for the welfare of the nation. This comparison is a sad commen-
> tary upon our national intelligence or morality or both.

The unspoken implication of the comparison is clear. All of
the major regimes in the world had had their flirtation with
modernity with catastrophic results. The United States, in this
regard, would prove to be no exception. The tempting of the
United States would have to do with separating sexual morals
from social sanction and promoting a liberty that would threaten
the social fabric of the country. Liberalism, with its penchant for
sexual liberation, was to the United States what Fascism had
been to Italy, what Nazism was to Germany, and what Communism would be to Russia—a social mistake with untold suffering following from it as its main result. State of the art sexual
liberation in 1953 was the toleration of divorce. Krol would live
to see, and to fight, virtually the entire trajectory of sexual
liberation, battling contraception in the '60s and abortion in the
'70s. But now he was prescient enough to see that the cloud on
the postwar horizon in America was the genie of sexual license
escaping from the bottle.

"Divorce, being tolerated," Krol said quoting what Pope
Leo XIII had said in 1880, "there will be no restraint powerful
enough to keep it within the bounds marked out or
presurmized."

It was a lesson America would have to learn the hard way, and a lesson few seemed willing to entertain in the mid-'50s when the moral law was being pounded into submission by types like Alfred Kinsey in the name of "scientific" objectivity. Later studies would show that Kinsey's "science" was really the cover for personal compulsion, but no one knew this at the time, and the journalists were so avid for what Kinsey proposed that no one seemed willing to challenge what he had to say.

As a result, Krol felt compelled to spell out the consequences to his audience in explicit detail:

> Our system of divorce too frequently places a premium on vice. It rewards the guilty spouse by freeing him from the bond of marriage he ruined, and gives him a fresh opportunity to remarry. The spouse guilty of the crime of adultery, of cruelty, of non-support, of desertion, and of promiscuity is given the license to repeat the damage to other individuals and to society.

As a result, a measure which was initiated in the name of social hygiene quickly becomes worse than the ill it set out to cure: "The remedy is worse than the disease. . . . Divorce, which was introduced as a measure of preserving the family, has been a complete failure."

Beyond that, the atmosphere which condones divorce also condones the behavior which leads to divorce creating a vicious circle of family pathology. With divorce as the escape hatch from every marital problem, there is little incentive to attempt to cure the problems which lead to divorce in the first place.

> The lustful eye of the male and the fickle mind of the female is nursed by the assurance of an easily obtainable divorce. The irresponsible teenager enters marriage as a lark, knowing that he will be married only for as long as he gets along with his spouse; that the divorce courts will free him from a bad bargain and allow him to make a new one. The petty quarrels of the early crucial years of marriage grow into bitter arguments because the stubborn and selfish spouse knows that divorce will resolve all differences, and frequently resorts to divorce as a means of justifying his stubbornness. The irresponsible spouse is willing to risk extra-marital escapades because he knows that a divorce will give him an opportunity to make a new start. Divorce not only fails to curb marriage disasters, it actually promotes them.

Krol's training in the Church's legal system gave him a dual perspective on trends affecting the United States during the aftermath of World War II. First of all, the Church's canon law is rooted in the doctrine of natural law as its matrix. This meant that the Law of God, the moral law, and positive law, while not the same thing, had to be at least congruent. The civil law could not condone what the moral law forbade. In sexual matters, however, that is precisely what was happening with increasing frequency in the United States during the postwar years. Using the social sciences as a cover, the liberal revolutionaries were undermining the social enculturation of the moral law in America's judicial system. The results of this trend, according to Krol, were twofold: first there was an increase in social disruption, particularly among the young as families broke up and the children in them were not socialized. "Juvenile Delinquent" is a term which acquired widespread currency during this period, although few were pointing out its connection with divorce. The increasing availability of divorce was having its effect on the legal system as well. It was breeding disrespect for the rule of law while at the same time breeding an increase in litigation. "Divorce," Krol told the lawyers in Akron,

> not only fosters and abets family pathology it corrupts the judicial system which condones it. [Divorce] leaves a trail of broken homes and hearts, neglected children, juvenile delinquency, and above all it breeds a complete disregard for law and degrades our courts of justice.

Family issues tend to be of one piece. A liberalization in one area tends to create pressure for liberalization in others. So the weakening of the marital bond which resulted from the legal acceptance of divorce increased the demand for contraceptives and tended to drive down the size of families. If the woman was going to be abandoned, she did not want to be left with a lot of children to raise. Similarly, the insecurity stemming from widespread acceptance of divorce increased the pressure on women to get employment outside of the home. The woman who couldn't be sure of her position as wife and mother had to have some economic insurance to fall back on. Widespread acceptance of contraception would lead to pressure to accept abortion as its backup as well as the toleration of homosexuality, because divorce and contraception meant in effect that procreation had really nothing to do with sexual activity, and the State need make no provision for the fact that it did.

As the result of the redefinition of marital relations that began willy nilly with the acceptance of divorce, the family was changed into a voluntary corporation which could pretty much be dissolved at the will of the partners much along the lines of a business venture which had ceased to be profitable for the parties involved. The exigencies of the economic order were imposed on the family, where the fit was contrived at best. Egotism would become the unspoken social philosophy according to which disputes would be adjudicated. Twenty years before the advent of what was dubbed the "Me Decade," Krol warned that "the private good of the litigants receives supreme consideration to the exclusion of Common good." Krol then went on to list a number of specific evil consequences flowing from divorce: the married state becomes precarious, there is a serious disincentive to give birth to and raise children, women's dignity will be lowered, and finally the state itself is threatened with disintegration because of the undermining of the family, the basic cell of the body politic.

During the course of his episcopate, Krol would see his predictions fulfilled one by one. He would go on to fight the trajectory of sexual decay at each of its crucial junctures for the next 30 years. For the moment, in the early '50s, all he could do was make a claim that his culture was finding increasingly incomprehensible: that there was a connection between the nation's respect for the moral law and its well being, that the nation's moral level depends upon its respect for the family; that "the family is the cornerstone of human order and preeminently the principle of social continuity and conservation of human traditions of civilization." Krol concluded his talk by drawing an analogy between the totalitarian ideologies that devastated Europe and the alien sexual ideology which was spreading throughout the American legal system. Both were predicated on a radical disjunction between politics and morals, both erected legal systems in defiance of the moral law; both spelled disasters for their respective countries.

"It took atheistic communism," he concluded, "less than 10 years to realize the damaging effects of free divorce upon the strength of the nation. . . . It is time . . . that we all took some firm measures to safeguard this country from its greatest enemy. We have successfully defended our homes and families from the attack of foreign enemies. Now it is time to defend them from enemies from within which threaten to destroy our national strength."

During the same year that John Joseph Krol was elevated to the episcopate and around the same time that he began to become more distressed with the corrupting effect the post-World War II wave of divorces was having on our legal system and family life, Supreme Court Justice William O. Douglas filed for divorce from Mildred Riddle Douglas his wife of 29 years. The same wave of permissiveness in sexual matters that was causing so much concern to Bishop Krol in postwar American life acted as an enabling device in the life of one of the leading jurists of the land. Douglas, a Roosevelt appointee to the court had a reputation as a womanizer in Washington. "It was not a very well kept secret," his biographer claims, "that the Justice, still in Washington, dallied with other women." Social convention, however, frowned on such activity and Justice Douglas went along with the conventions. In 1950, he was named Father of the Year. In 1952, he wrote "we are a religious people whose institutions presuppose a Supreme Being." Douglas was raised a Presbyterian and according to Douglas's own testimony "Divorce was, in my Presbyterian heritage, a sin, and I looked down on those who had gone that way." One could accuse the justice of hypocrisy, perhaps rightly so, but hypocrisy is at least, as the saying goes, the tribute that vice pays to virtue.

At some point around 1952, Douglas decided that he was no longer willing to pay that tribute. There was an ever-growing divide between his Presbyterian beliefs and his libertine behavior. Faced with the alternative of conforming his behavior to his beliefs or his beliefs to his behavior, Justice Douglas chose the latter course and filed for divorce. It was a decision which would have far-reaching consequences for Douglas's intellectual development and beyond that for the country as a whole. For Douglas was not alone in making this decision. His was just one of an epidemic of divorces which was sweeping the country in the wake of the upheaval caused by war. Divorce had become acceptable to the cultural elite, despite their Protestant upbringing, and praxis was following theory in a predictable fashion. Justice Douglas's legal theory was in many respects the externalization of his sexually-troubled conscience. This would not have been as problematic in a man of lesser influence, but Justice Douglas was in the position to write his troubled conscience into the law of the land. This was the case not simply because Douglas was a Supreme Court justice, but because of the sort of Supreme Court justice he was and the redefinition of the Court's role which took place under his tenure.

Judicial activism is a term that has come into common parlance lately, and it has precisely because of the role Douglas played on what came to be known as the Warren and Burger courts. Douglas was fond of saying he would rather create a precedent than find one, and he spent a good deal of his tenure, especially the latter part, doing just that. "Marriage," Justice Douglas wrote in *Griswold v. Connecticut* in 1965

> is a coming together for better or for worse, hopefully enduring, and intimate to the degree of being sacred. It is an association that promotes a way of life, not causes; a harmony in living, not political faiths, a bilateral loyalty, not commercial or social projects. Yet it is an association for as noble a purpose as any involved in our prior decisions.

These are touching sentiments, especially coming from a man who was in the process of dumping his third wife and picking up a fourth—a young lady 40 years his junior. It's difficult to tell what Douglas had in mind when he wrote the *Griswold* decision, but it was most probably not the constitution of the United States, which had little to say about the right to sell and/or use contraceptives. Perhaps Douglas was remembering a letter from his first wife, the one he divorced twelve years earlier. In 1952, Mildred Riddle Douglas, then Douglas's wife of 28 years wrote to him still reeling from the shock of of the impending divorce he had just inflicted on her.

"The breaking up of a family," she wrote,

> —a fine family—one week—then thirty or fifteen minutes before a judge—it's all over—it never was—or one is supposed to believe it never was—I can't forget 28 years of devotion, loyalty and hard service that quickly and easily. I am physically and emotionally played out. . . . So will you please be patient? You

are a famous and brilliant man. May God help you find it in your heart to forgive yourself, as our children and I do (Simon, p. 287).

With letters like this in the back of his mind, it's not difficult to imagine the parameters of Justice Douglas's troubled conscience. Before long it was a a guilty conscience that would suffuse the legal system of the United States, overturning laws that protected the family in favor of those who favored a more individualistic approach to sexual issues. The noble sentiments which Justice Douglas expressed in regard to the family in *Griswold v. Connecticut* were tainted perhaps by the fact that their purpose was to strike down a Connecticut law banning the sale of contraceptives. In the *Griswold* decision, Douglas had discovered "a right of privacy" "emanating from the penumbras" of the Constitution. The people who were in favor of contraceptives thought of it as brilliant constitutional law; the people who were in favor of constitutional law simply scratched their heads and wondered how these emanations from penumbras had so successfully evaded the legal minds of the past two hundred years.

Douglas was simply in the process of creating what might be called Thelemic Jurisprudence. Instead of the rule of law, Douglas proposed the law of will. "For those who liked the result," said one admirer, "it was scholarship." (Glancy, p. 162). For those who favored sexual liberation, the result of the decision was the ultimate test of its validity. Even those who are sympathetic with the decision have difficulty justifying it on any other grounds. Of Douglas's *Griswold* decision, his biographer says "that Douglas and others on the Court could convert their subjective values into constitutional law" (Simon, p. 349).

> He searched in vain for a right to privacy. Douglas, possessing a more expansive libertarian creed, did not hesitate to look beyond the explicit language of the Constitution to protect what he considered to be the contemporary needs of the nation. To be sure, Douglas collected few accolades in the nation's leading law reviews for his *Griswold* opinion. The criticism was, in part, justified. Douglas did not provide a thorough analysis to support this new constitutional right to privacy. Indeed, his analysis in *Griswold* was not even as persuasive as his earlier writings on the subject had been. But the decision endures because Douglas's conclusion was correct. In declaring a right to privacy, Douglas

had identified the most critical constitutional battleground for human dignity in the modern age (Ibid.).

Those who are more interested in the law than in the social results one can achieve from manipulating it are less enthusiastic about *Griswold*. Judge Robert Bork, who had his own unpleasant experiences at the hands of the cultural revolutionaries in the mid-'80s saw *Griswold* not so much as legal scholarship but rather "an attempt to enlist the Court on one side of one issue in a cultural struggle," namely "on the side of moral relativism in sexual matters."

Douglas was not alone in championing the cause of sexual revolution. Over the years, throughout the '50s and '60s, he implemented on the court what he had taught at Yale Law School. It was a school of legal thought that alternately took its name from the Yale Law School where it was taught or from the name of Douglas and fellow judicial activist Hugo Black themselves. "The Yale thesis," according to Arthur M. Schlesinger, Jr.,

> crudely put, is that any judge chooses his results and reasons backward. The resources of legal artifice, the ambiguity of precedents, the range of applicable doctrine, are all so extensive that in most cases in which there is a reasonable difference of opinion a judge can come out on either side without straining the fabric of legal logic. A naive judge does this unconsciously and conceives himself to be an objective interpreter of the law. A wise judge knows that political choice is inevitable; he makes no false pretense of objectivity and consciously exercises the judicial power with an eye to social results.

Yale Law School presents a number of interesting examples of the interlock between the institutions and personalities which brought about our cultural revolution. William O. Douglas taught at Yale, where he imbibed the philosophy of Thelemic Jurisprudence from its theoretical font. He then went to the Supreme Court where he implemented it as the law of the land. During the '50s a bright young law graduate from Yale by the name of Charles Reich went to Washington to clerk for Justice Hugo Black and fell under the influence of Douglas during long walks with him along the C & O canal. In 1970, Reich synthesized what he had learned at the feet of Black and Douglas into what is probably the prime manifesto of cultural revolution,

The Greening of America, "There is a revolution coming," Reich tells us in the bell-bottom prose style which pervades the book:

> It will not be like revolutions of the past. It will originate with the individual and with the culture, and it will change the political structure only as its final act. It will not require violence to succeed, and it cannot be successfully resisted by violence. The whole emerging pattern, from ideals to campus demonstration to beads and bellbottoms to the Woodstock Festival, makes sense and is part of a consistent philosophy. It is both necessary and inevitable, and in time it will include not only youth but all people in America (Reich, p. 2).

"This is a book about Revolution," Justice Douglas opined in the blurb he wrote endorsing *The Greening of America*, "—not in the Marxist sense, but Revolution against many of the values which Technology has thrust upon us." By 1970 Justice Douglas was claiming to be oppressed by vague faces "which Technology has thrust upon us." In the early '50s the forces which Douglas found intolerable had more to do with being married to the same woman for 29 years and Presbyterian disapproval of divorce. Behind the transformation was an attempt to redefine the parameters of the social order and its connection to the moral law. A major component in making the shift from Consciousness I, America before the cultural revolution, to Consciousness III, the stage of liberation at which the country had arrived in 1970, is redefining the moral element out of what were traditionally seen as areas of moral concern. "Consciousness I," personified by his Jewish immigrant grandfather, Reich tells us

> insisted on seeing the evils of industrialism not for what they were, but as moral problems. If a given number of automobiles are crowded onto a highway, there will be a predictable number of accidents. The moral approach tries to deal with this as a question of individual driver responsibility. It stresses safe driving and criminal penalties. Yet reduction of the accident rate is demonstrably a problem in engineering. Similarly, urban crime is seen as a moral and law enforcement problem, although crime is a product of identifiable environment factors (Reich, p. 40).

Reich's Consciousness III was in many ways just an extrapolation the Yale Thesis to the society as a whole. It was the Miranda law applied to the troubled consciences of the sexually liberated. The more deeply the country plunged into sexual liberation the more it found itself unable to hold anyone to moral standards. Behavior, as a result, was suddenly construed as having its root in technological structures, over which we could only have control after a revolution in consciousness. As Myron Magnet has shown recently, this sort of exculpatory thinking has had a especially devastating effect on the very people who could least afford it. The urban underclass was what it was primarily because of the breakdown of the family and the cultural elite fostered that breakdown by redefining the moral element as irrelevant to successful social behavior. This was a message the urban poor could ill afford to hear. And as the engines of culture dinned it into their ears through television and film but, above all, through the avant garde's appropriation of Negro music, the behavior of just about everyone suffered accordingly and an already tenuous situation went from bad to worse.

After Reich left his clerkship under Justice Black but before he became famous as the savant of the counterculture, he returned to the Yale Law school there to perpetuate the Yale Thesis and Thelemic Jurisprudence among the upcoming legal generation. Bork also taught at Yale's law school but he did not like what he saw there. The notion that judges used the law to argue for foregone conclusions may have been an apt description of how the mind of William O. Douglas worked but it had a corrupting effect on the legal profession as a whole. In the end teaching that all a justice votes for is his own personal interests becomes a self-fulfilling prophecy. "If men are told complacently enough that this is how things are, they will become accustomed to it and accept it. And in the end, this is how things will be" is how Judge Bork put it (Bork, p. 72).

One can argue that this is not how the law should operate, but no one, least of all Judge Bork, would claim that this is not how the law, as read by the Supreme Court, did operate beginning in the '50s and throughout the '60s.

> That is, indeed, how things were during the era of the Warren Court. The judicial philosophy espoused by Black and Douglas came to be a majority philosophy with new appointments, particularly those of Earl Warren as Chief Justice, and Justices Tom

Clark, William J. Brennan, Jr., Arthur Goldberg, Abe Fortas, and Thurgood Marshall.

During the '50s, liberal culture forged the weapons for its successful cultural revolution out of the two elements Krol mentioned as areas of concern as the newly consecrated auxiliary of Cleveland: those elements were legal positivism and sexual liberation. Liberal culture was especially fond of the courts because it found early on that it could not achieve the results it desired through the democratic process. The Supreme Court as a result took on the character of a super-legislature over which there was no possibility of appeal. Like the decisions of the Supreme Pontiff according to the Code of Canon Law, the opinions of the Supreme Court were irreformable. There was neither appeal nor recourse against their decisions, which were taking on more and more the character of decrees.

In coming up with its agenda, the Supreme Court showed itself partial to the theories which found acceptance in academe, and those theories found widespread acceptance there oftentimes because they were financially subsidized by the foundations. By the late '50s, the interlock was virtually complete and by that time the warnings of the Reece commission were long forgotten. We have already mentioned Justice Douglas's connection to academe. But the connection was less one of persons than of ideas. Kinsey's studies began cropping up in legal discussions as did Freud's theories.

The case which Judge Bork described as "the defining event of modern American constitutional law" was intimately tied to the foundations and their attempts at social engineering as well. In 1954, one year after Krol's consecration as bishop and Justice's Douglas's divorce, the Supreme Court handed down *Brown v. Board of Education*, the case which struck down *Plessy v. Ferguson*, which allowed "separate but equal" segregated schools for Negroes, primarily in the South. The Supreme Court based its *Brown* decision in large part on Gunnar Myrdal's study of segregation in the South, *An American Dilemma*. That book in turn was financed by a $250,000 grant from the Carnegie foundation during the '30s. Wormser claims that Carnegie, who had chosen Alger Hiss around the same time to become president of The Carnegie Endowment for International Peace, chose Myrdal "not in spite of his collectivist bias but because of it."

The Left had been trying to exploit the racial situation in the United States for its own ends ever since John Reed and Lenin invited the Jamaican writer Claude McKay to be a delegate to the fourth congress of the Third International in Moscow in 1922. During the '30s the Communists mobilized their forces behind the defendants in the trial of the Scottsboro boys. By the late '40s, according to Harold Cruse, the communists had lost their leverage among the Negro leadership but that is probably because they had lost their leverage among intellectuals in the United States in general. With *Brown v. Board of Education*, a transmutation took place in the Left's racial politics. In the '30s, the Negro in order to succeed both politically and culturally had to become a leftist. In the '50s, the Leftist in order to succeed politically and culturally had to become a Negro.

"Boss," so the story from Mississippi goes about the Negro cotton picker addressing his white overseer, "if you could live like a nigger for one Saturday night, you'd never want to be white again" (Lemann, p. 28). By the mid-'50s, the Left had decided that it wanted to live like niggers. Perhaps the classic expression of this aspiration came in *On the Road*, a novel, published in 1957, but written ten years earlier by Jack Kerouac, a lapsed Catholic of French Canadian extraction from Lowell, Massachusetts who went onto to become one of the founding fathers of the beat generation. While hitchhiking across the country in 1947, Kerouac arrived in Denver and described for posterity the attraction the Negro held for the Bohemian Left:

> At lilac evening I walked with every muscle aching among the lights of 27th and Welton in the Denver colored section, wishing I were a Negro, feeling that the best the white world had offered was not enough ecstasy for me, not enough life, joy, kicks, darkness, music, not enough night.

What liberal culture wanted from the Negro was what Kerouac was to describe in the same book as "Spade kicks," i.e. sex unfettered by marriage vows and the burdens of raising children, jazz, and intoxication. What liberal culture got was social decay and the destruction of virtually all of America's major cities. The attraction of the Negro as the paradigm of sexual liberation was reaching its peak in the late '50s following in the wake of *Brown v. Board of Education* and the civil rights movement it spawned.

In 1958, Norman Mailer was acute enough to analyze the Beatnik phenomenon into its component parts. It was for the most part whites attempting to live like Negroes. Or more accurately, it was white leftists trying to live out their fantasies of sexual liberation by imitating the family pathology they descried in the ghetto. "The only revolution which will be meaningful and natural for the 20th Century," Mailer opined in his seminal essay "The White Negro," will be the sexual revolution" which one senses especially in "the White South terrified of the Birmingham bus strike and the growing power of the Negro. . . ."

To get to specifics, Mailer claimed that "the source of Hip is the Negro." Jazz, he continued, has provided the entry point for "Negro" values (or at least the values Mailer ascribes to Negroes) into mainstream American culture.

In *The Greening of America*, Reich ascribes the same cultural influence to the Negro, his sexuality, and his music:

> Unquestionably, the blacks made a substantial contribution to the writings of the new consciousness. They were left out of the corporate state, and thus they had to have a culture and life-style in opposition to the State. Their music, with its "guts," contrasted with the insipid white music. Their way of life seemed more earthy, more sensual than that of whites. They were the first openly to scorn the Establishment and its values; as Eldridge Cleaver shows in *Soul on Ice* and Malcolm X shows in his autobiography, they were radicalized by the realities of their situation. When their music began to be heard by white teen-agers through the medium of rock'n'roll, and when their view of America became visible through the civil rights movement, it gave new impetus to the subterranean awareness of the beat generation and the Holden Caulfields (Reich, p. 239).

Race has been the Left's most successful weapon in the cultural wars, and it was *Brown v. Board of Education* that gave them their major weapon. *Brown v. Board of Education* had as its direct consequence the Birmingham bus boycott of 1955, and thereafter the institutions of the segregated south from whites' only beaches to segregated golf courses were hauled in front of the courts and excoriated for their baleful psychological effects.

If *Brown* was disruptive to the social order in the South that was nothing compared to its effect on the nation's judicial system. According to Bork, the court felt that it had to violate the Constitution to arrive at what was obviously a moral conclusion, namely, the elimination of segregation in the schools. "The Court," according to Bork,

> judging by its opinion, thought that it had departed from the original understanding in order to do the socially desirable thing. What is more, the Court triumphed over intense political opposition despite that fact. . . . They had issued, so they apparently believed, a ruling based on nothing in the historic Constitution, and that decision had prevailed despite the fact that it had ordered a change in an entrenched social order in much of the nation. . . . The end of state-mandated segregation was the greatest moral triumph constitutional law had ever produced. It is not surprising that academic lawyers were unwilling to give it up; it *had* to be right. Thus, *Brown* has become the high ground of constitutional theory. Theorists of all persuasions seek to capture it, because any theory that seeks acceptance must, as a matter of psychological fact, if not of logical necessity, account for the result in *Brown*.

With *Brown,* the court was thrust into being the conscience of the nation and a superlegislature all at once, and it had come to this position by violating (at least in its own thinking) the Constitution. Its success in triumphing over the significant opposition of a large segment of the country emboldened it to expand its moral fervor to encompass other aspects of the liberal agenda as well. Bork is of the opinion that the same result could have been achieved by following the Constitution, specifically the 14th Amendment, but the fact remains that the court did not think so. And once they achieved such a spectacular success on an issue of such obvious moral import, the apparatus was in place and capable of being expanded further. In fact, since the justices had departed from the original intent of the constitution in achieving what they felt were moral ends there would be and could be no limit put on their interpretations. They henceforth would not interpret the laws: they would write the laws. "Once a court abandons the intention of those who made the law," Bork writes, "the court is necessarily thrust into a legislative posture. It must write the law." The court was encouraged by its success in *Brown* to go "to embark on more adventures in policymaking" (Bork, p. 83).

What resulted from *Brown* was "a new mandarin class," "an unelected, unrepresentative, unaccountable committee of lawyers applying no will but their own." What the court wrought in collaboration with the foundations, academe, and the media was a cultural revolution that effectively took the power of social legislation out of the hand of the country's elected representatives and put it into the hands of an unelected liberal elite. That elite, in the words of Herbert Schlossberg, "has found a vehicle for giving its values the force of law without bothering to take over the political authority of the state" (Bork, p. 138).

Brown v. Board of Education contained a number of ironies. "Separate but equal" is precisely the status to which Catholic education aspired in the United States. There is no indication that that status proved damaging to Catholic children in their separate school systems. In fact, as the public schools became more and more a tool of social engineering, it became more and more obvious that the Catholic system, which would have considered itself fortunate to receive a fraction of the subsidy that went for the support of segregated schools in the South, were proving to be in fact both separate and superior to the public system, a fact which Leo Pfeffer found troubling. At the same time that the court was overturning what it perceived to be burdens on the segregated schools in the South, it was imposing financial burdens on religious schools in the North. Throughout the entire period following the New Deal, the government found ways to support causes it approved. The fact that parochial schools were not one of these institutions leads James Hitchcock to the conclusion that "it seems reasonable to assume that they do not regard the survival of parochial schools as a desirable goal. . . . The facts indicate an immense animosity directed at the parochial schools simply because they are Catholic, and their survival is deemed by many people to be socially undesirable."

Beyond that *Brown* would further impinge on the Catholic Church by enabling a racial politics that would prove to be the undoing of the ethnic neighborhoods in cities in the North in general and in Philadelphia in particular, which meant in effect the sickening of these cities if not their death. By the late '50s, the civil rights movement unleashed by *Brown* was having a revolutionary effect on the mainline Protestant Churches as well. In keeping with the goals of the liberal elite, they began a process of de-emphasizing personal morality in favor of the social gospel as dictated by the civil rights movement. In his book *The Freedom Revolution and the Churches*, Robert W. Spike, who headed the National Council of Churches' civil rights project, captures the fervor for civil rights and the cause of the Negro which swept through the mainline churches: "Not since the abolitionist period have the churches and their people become as conscious of their guilt and their need for action as in recent months" (Spike, p. 34). Spike's first parish was in Greenwich Village in the early '50s, where he frequented places like the White Horse bar and the San Remo, and where he socialized with Jack Kerouac and Allen Ginsburg, and evidently picked up the bad habit of homosexual behavior. "Their sins rise up to haunt them," Spike said of the southern defenders of segregation. Spike's sins eventually came to haunt him as well. In the fall of 1966, he was murdered by a man he picked up in Columbus, Ohio.

Leo Pfeffer lists the civil rights movement as the seminal event for Protestants in this century, equal to the '67 and '73 Arab Israeli wars for the Jews and the Second Vatican Council for the Catholics. If so, the fervor of people like Spike suggests compensation for capitulation in other areas, and sexuality comes most immediately to mind. As a result of its hidden sexual agenda, many liberal social programs during the '60s were like pouring gasoline on the fire, and this was nowhere more evident than in the area of race and poverty which was caused to a large extent by the breakdown of family structure that the liberals were attempting to implement in their own lives.

By the late '50s, virtually everything was in place. The Cultural Revolution was like a plant which needed time to develop a subterranean network of roots before corresponding growth could manifest itself above the ground. That time of subterranean growth was the '50s, during which all of the elements of cultural revolution grew in ever more confident cooperation with each other. The foundations, academe, the media, and the courts all shared a common understanding of law and human nature which converged on several points. The liberal elite believed in moral relativism, sexual liberation, in racial equality, in skepticism on religious matters, and in general they saw the family as an institution which should be prevented from inhibiting an individual's freedom of expression.

In 1958, there was a sense of storm just over the horizon. A deceptive calm had fallen over the Church. Then Pope Pius XII died, and a new era dawned. In attempting to explain why he supported the letter of Vatican II if not the spirit unleashed in its wake in the Church, Joseph Cardinal Ratzinger describes the Council as,

> perhaps, the first council in history to be convoked, not under the pressure of pressing problems or crises, but in a moment of seeming tranquility with respect to ecclesial life. . . . Then came the cultural revolutions and the social convulsions that the Fathers in no way could have foreseen but which have shown how their answers—at the time anticipatory—were those that were needed in the future. . . . The crises erupted later, not only within the Church but in the whole society. Could it not be said . . . that the Church, at all events, would have had to confront those cultural revolutions but that, without the Council, her structure would have been more rigid and the damages could have possibly been even more grave?

It was a rhetorical question the Church was still answering 30 years after the fact. The fact is that the Council unleashed forces in the Church which no one could have anticipated at the time. But as the foregoing analysis has, I think, shown, those forces were gathering on the horizon without regard to what the Church thought of them and would have fallen on the Church whether she had opened her windows or not.

In the fall of 1958, in the conclave immediately following the death of Pius XII, when it became apparent that Angelo Roncalli would be the next pope, Cardinals Ottaviani and Ruffini went to his room and suggested in the strongest terms possible that he call an ecumenical council. In many instances, the Catholic Church would become a battlefield over which liberals fought conservatives for control of the Church in the period following the close of the Second Vatican Council. Like the battle over the constitution that was fought in the judicial system and the Supreme Court of the United States, it was a battle between competing interpretations. However, there is one thing both Catholic liberals and conservatives had in common and that was a common view of the Council. When two opposing groups who otherwise disagree on just about every-thing agree on something, that idea generally becomes firmly embedded in the conventional wisdom on a subject. This is precisely the case about the calling of the Council. Both liberals and conservatives agree that Cardinal Alfredo Ottaviani, pre-fect of the Congregation of the Doctrine of the Faith, or Holy Office at the time, opposed the Council: conservatives applaud the fact; liberals bemoan it; but both accept it as true.

Giving the conservative formulation of the position, Father Gommer de Pauw, founder of the Catholic Traditionalist Move-ment and one of the early opponents of liberalization following the Council, writes

> Since Rome itself has lifted the veil of secrecy from such matters, it can now be said that there would have been no Second Vatican Council and church history would have taken a completely dif-ferent direction, if, upon the death of Pius XII in 1958, the con-clave of cardinals had elected Ottaviani to become Pope Pius XIII, as it ever so nearly did before one Angelo Roncalli finally received the necessary votes that made him Pope John XXIII. And I venture to add that from that day on I, among many, started wondering what percentage in the outcome of papal elec-tions is attributable to the Holy Ghost, and what percentage is the result of politics (de Pauw, p. 5).

Taking the same position but from a diametrically opposed point of view, Xavier Rynne, the pseudonym for Passionist Father Francis X. Murphy, claims that a "self-perpetuating clique in the Curia . . . had thus far successfully resisted all but the most innocuous changes dictated by the exigencies of modern life . . . To these men the announcement of the new Council came as a severe shock." Lest anyone not get his drift, Rynne spells out his morality play of good and evil at the Council in explicit terms. "The leading figure in the group of intransi-gents—or "prophet of doom," to use the pope's phrase—was Cardinal Alfredo Ottaviani." When Pope John XXIII used the phrase "prophets of doom" in the speech announcing the open-ing of the Council, Rynne directs the reader's attention to Car-dinal Ottaviani as the principal suspect: "As the listeners heard these words," Rynne writes, "their attention focussed uncon-sciously on the face of Cardinal Ottaviani."

Paul Johnson makes a much more convincing case that Pope John XXIII was referring to Cardinal Pizzardo with the "prophets of doom" reference. Beyond that, one wonders how Rynne was privy to the consciousness of so many listeners, but beyond that one can hardly deny that his account of the Council has long since settled into the conventional wisdom. The only problem with the account is that it is wrong. Ottaviani not only did not oppose the Council. He was instrumental in getting it called. Just why he should be cast as the villain is obvious, at least from the point of view of the liberals' misrepresentation of the Council. The liberals wanted to portray Vatican II as the Church converting to modernity when in fact the opposite was the case: the Council involved the Church responding to the challenge of modernity. In order to appropriate the Council the liberals had to expropriate the man who called it; hence their need to make Ottaviani the villain, when in fact the calling of the Council was his idea. The thesis that conservatives like Ottaviani opposed the Council leads to quandaries for both the liberals and the conservatives. According to the conservative view, everything was fine. There was no reason to call the Council. It was an act of either supererogation or self-immolation but in either case an effect without a cause. This of course plays nicely into the hands of liberals who can then claim that the conservatives were so myopic they didn't see the obvious need to modernize.

The fact is that the Council was neither a work of supererogation nor an attempt to convert the Church to the ideology of modernity. All of the evidence of the time indicates it was an attempt to help the Church face a threat just over the horizon but one palpable enough to those with eyes to see and ears to hear.

"It must not be forgotten," writes Ottaviani's successor, Joseph Cardinal Ratzinger, "that my predecessor in the Holy Office, Cardinal Ottaviani, also supported the project of an ecumenical council. After Pope John XXIII had announced its convocation, the Roman Curia worked together with the most distinguished representatives of the world episcopate in the preparation of those schemata which were then rejected by the Council fathers as too theoretical, too textbook-like and insufficiently pastoral. Pope John had not reckoned on the possibility of a rejection but was expecting a quick and frictionless balloting on these projects which he had approvingly read."

Father Robert Bonnot, who interviewed Ottaviani in the late '70s just before his death, corroborates Ratzinger's view by stating emphatically "Cardinals Ottaviani and Ruffini had recommended a council to Cardinal Roncalli during the conclave" (Bonnot, p. 54).

> They visited Roncalli's cell on Monday evening (October 26, 1958) with the awareness that he was going to be elected pope. One of their aims was to suggest that it would be a "fine thing" (*bella cosa*) to call an ecumenical council in order to combat the many errors circulating in both Church and world. Evidence that Pope John thought about calling a council long before January is abundant. On October 29, John told Cardinal Feltin of Paris, "I shall summon a council." On October 30, his secretary heard him comment "for the first time in a conversation on the necessity of celebrating an ecumenical council." On November 2, Pope John had several audiences, including one with Ruffini and the idea of a council came up again (p. 54).

Once the role of the undeniably conservative Cardinal Ottaviani in calling the Council becomes clear a number of contentious issues are resolved. First of all, the Council was not the Church's belated conversion to modernity as the liberals would like to portray it. Secondly, it was not an act of self-destructive supererogation as the conservatives would like to portray it. The Church was in serious trouble in 1958, a fact recognized by people like Ottaviani. The dictum "If it ain't' broke, don't fix it" might hold true here but not in the way the conservatives think it should apply. There was something broke, and the Church needed to take time to fix it. The Council was convoked for basically two reasons: internal decay and external threat. The documents of the preparatory commissions called by John XXIII, some of which were written under Cardinal Ottaviani's direction, give ample evidence that the Church had reached a state approaching internal paralysis during the last years of Pope Pius XII and that this was not the best posture for confronting the liberal revolution in morals which was beginning to sweep through the West. Even in Italy, which as late as 1950 had been a predominantly agricultural country, the media, most especially television and film, were ushering society in a direction that deep-thinking prelates like Ottaviani found profoundly disturbing and inimical to social well being and the salvation of souls.

"Television," writes Latourelle in his book on the Council, "acted as a multiplying factor in a process of transformation that was in itself dramatic. . . . The day has gone in which people listened to the Church when it gave instructions in the economic, political, and social fields." The Church of 1958 found itself "on the defensive, immobile in the face of a rapidly changing world," a situation that was in large measure due to the personality of Pope Pius XII, of whom Cardinal Tardini states, he "did not want collaborators but simply executors." "During his papacy," Tardini continues,

> direct personal contact between the Supreme Pontiff and the bishops of the various dioceses was considerably reduced. . . . Thus the Roman curia suffered a certain stagnation, rather like the situation in the body when some irregularity in the circulation of blood sets in. We old people stayed on, standing in the way and preventing fresher and more robust forces than our own from moving forward. . . .

Instead of finding themselves within a Church intimately involved in facing the challenges of modernity, the Church's own officials found a disconcerting immobility at the center of the Church's affairs. However, what the Church lacked in vitality it made up in discipline. One Jesuit describes his perplexity at the myriad senseless rules that dominated Church life at the time. Anyone who challenged the rules was told the parable of the dry stick, referring to the anecdote of the monk who watered a dry stick after being ordered to do so by his superior as part of his duties as the monastery's gardener. The task made no sense, but the monk persisted out of sheer blind obedience and was in the end rewarded when God made the dry stick blossom into a lush plant.

By 1958, the principle of the dry stick had been made to cover a multitude of sins, and the people who were expected to give the Church this sort of blind devotion were becoming increasingly skeptical, especially in light of the liberal ideologies sweeping through the West at the time, ideologies which seemed so reasonable, enlightened and humane by comparison. The already-cited writings of Michael Novak are a good case point.

During the course of his long reign as pope, Pius XII increasingly concentrated the administrative powers of the Church into his own hands. When the position of Secretary of State fell vacant, he filled the position himself. With help of telephone and radio, Pius XII became in many ways the ecclesial equivalent of the totalitarian leaders of his time, micromanaging the Church into a position of paralysis that only increased as his physical powers began to fail him with advancing age. The situation became acute during the '50s, when oftentimes ordinaries of major dioceses would come to Rome only to cool their heels in some antechamber and to go home without seeing the Pope. When asked for his impression of the era, Krol remembers that Archbishop Hoban of Cleveland came to Rome during the '50s and for days found himself unable to meet with the pope. Krol also remembers the punchline of a forgotten joke, "My God, are you here again." It was a reference to the fact that Pius XII during the last years of his papacy was claiming to have apparitions of both Our Lady and Our Lord and Savior Jesus Christ. "It was the first time in nearly two thousand years," Paul Murphy would write, "that any pope—other than Peter, who founded the Church—claimed to have seen Christ" (Murphy, p 275).

Vatican officials were in the process of denying the alleged visions as journalistic fabrication when Pius XII would cause them acute embarrassment by calling the journalists in personally and recounting the alleged apparitions in detail. Celso Cardinal Constantini, chancellor of the Holy Roman Church, characterized the government of the Church in the last days of Pius XII as "Byzantine and weird." Paul Johnson in his biography of Pope John XXIII concurred:

> The tragedy of Pius's decline is that the stifling and unseemly atmosphere of his court began to affect the church as a whole. Decisions were delayed, or taken in secret, often behind the backs of responsible officials. There was a widening chasm between the papal apartments, where all power ultimately resided, and the Curia itself. In many respects, they operated as two separate governments, sometimes in conflict. Though Pius took all the decisions in some spheres, down to the smallest details, in others the Curia was given free rein, and worked on, in its own bureaucratic manner, stifling initiative and strengthening its grip on the routines of the church everywhere. Bishops and cardinals

throughout the world, responsible for vast congregations, faced with problems of great urgency, found that they could not obtain access to the pope when they visited Rome, and were forced to make their own separate deals with Curia officials. There was a feeling, during these years, that the church was almost entirely stagnant, a great machine running down for lack of vital controlling force. Pius had always seen the church as a beleaguered citadel: at the end of his life it became one, in more than a notional sense, but a citadel crumbling from within, manned by a garrison without officers, and with commander increasingly divorced from reality. Pius, wrote Guiselle Dalla Torre, former editor of the official Vatican paper, *L'Osservatore Romano*, "separated himself from direct contact with life, though not, unfortunately, from people who abused his confidence." His own interests became increasingly pietistic and credulous. He was obsessed by the prophecies of the Fatima-miracle children, by the prodigies worked by the Bavarian girl Theresa Neumannn, and by his own mystical visions and dreams, some of which were leaked to the press. Some prelates feared he might suddenly announce a new and controversial dogma: there were rumors, for instance, that he planned to declare the Virgin Mary to be the co-redemptress, and thus plunge the church into mariolatry. In his old age, the great organization he controlled seemed to have lost any semblance of intellectual virility, any sense of pastoral mission, any desire to come to grips with the problems of the real world, and to be settling into a childish, devotional dotage. The church appeared to be dying with him (Johnson, pp. 105-7).

In the fall of 1958 the Church was in a perilous condition and virtually all of the cardinals who arrived in Rome to elect Pius XII's successor felt that something needed to be done. The task at hand was twofold: first of all, restructure the Church from the *de facto* monarchy it had become under Pius XII to an institution where the authority would be more broad-based and, therefore, more effective in dealing with the local situation. This meant a rehabilitation of the role of bishop so that, secondly, it could meet the challenges of secularism head on.

L' Osservatore Romano chose to announce the most momentous Catholic event for the 20th century in its January 26-7, 1959 issue. There were no blazing headlines, just a brief announcement that, in order to meet the errors of the time, and its excessive materialism, the pope intended to hold a synod of the Roman clergy, to call an ecumenical council of the universal church, and to modernize canon law; the Council was also to be "an invitation to the separated communities to search for that unity towards which so many souls aspire." Ottaviani concurred on both the internal and the external goals, and the best demonstration that he felt the Church was facing an external threat can be gleaned from the preparatory documents which got written under his direction.

In a preparatory schema issued on May 7, 1962 entitled "The Esteem of Virginity and Chastity," Ottaviani said quite bluntly that sexual issues were "the most acute and discussed moral problems of our day." They were eternally crucial because "the Church has always shown that she considers conjugal life as the ordinary way of sanctification for the majority of the human race" (*Preparatory Documents*, p. 54). However, that plan was in danger of being thwarted by the combination of sexual permissiveness and the newly-created media of communication which were constantly attempting to inject this same sexual permissiveness into their programming. "Modern life," Ottaviani continued, giving his assessment of the postwar period,

> without doubt, multiplies invitations to evil by such distractions as beauty contests, spectacles, billboards, songs, illustrated magazines, beaches, places of vacation, promiscuity, and certain forms of sport. This is why the Church never ceases to recall to each one the principles of prudence, conscience, and responsibility, the rights and duties of liberty, and the obligation of vigilance and precaution on the part of parents educators and civil authorities. This is also why the church points out as dangerous and condemns as erroneous all theories that are then translated into practice concerning the cult of movie stars, naturalism, the so-called sexual education, pansexualism, and certain injurious aspects of psychoanalysis. . . . it also studied those errors which are directly harmful to marriage, e.g., divorce, or indirectly, Malthusianism, and artificial insemination (*Preparatory Documents*, p. 155).

Eventually the preparatory documents would be rejected by the Council fathers, something that undoubtedly caused Cardinal Ottaviani some consternation. However, the rejection was caused more by the approach of the documents, and the approach the Council wanted to take to modernity rather than their content. Ratzinger describes the rejection of the preparatory documents as "a certain discomforting feeling that the whole enterprise might come to nothing more than mere rubber-stamping of decisions already made. . . . The preparatory commission had undoubtedly worked hard, but their diligence was somewhat distressing." At issue was a new approach to a hostile world. The majority of the assembled bishops had decided the hard line of Pius IX and the Syllabus of Errors simply did not work. Instead of condemnation, they preferred dialogue. Ratzinger speaks of how "the anti-Modernistic neurosis . . . had again and again crippled the Church since the turn of the century" and how with the convoking of the Council the posture of rigid defiance "here seemed to be approaching a cure."

"The real question behind the discussion," Ratzinger wrote,

> could be put this way: Was the intellectual position of "anti-Modernism"—the old policy of exclusiveness, condemnation and defense leading to an almost neurotic denial of all that was new—to be continued? Or would the Church, after it had taken all the necessary precautions to protect the faith turn over a new leaf and move on into a new and positive encounter with its own origins, with its brothers and with the world of today? Since a clear majority of the fathers opted for the second alternative we may even speak of the Council as a new beginning. We may also say that with this decision there was a major advance over Vatican Council I. (Ratzinger, *Theological Highlights of Vatican II*, p. 22)

Whether the Council fathers made the right decision is open to debate. In light of the cultural revolution which followed the Council, the Council documents seem oftentimes naively irenic. "The Church has nothing to fear from the modern world," is how the situation was described in *Lumen Gentium*. Well, in a sense it doesn't, but it a sense it does. And in retrospect the forthrightness of the preparatory documents often times seems a welcome relief from the oftentimes naive optimism of the early '60s. "The moral order," Cardinal Ottaviani wrote in one of the preparatory documents on that topic,

> has the task, not only of leading man to his true end, but of defending him against all doctrines and practices that would enslave him to the minds, modes and passions that are contrary to the dignity of his intellect. . . . In particular the moral order

defends the immutable principles of Christian modesty and chastity. We know the energies spent at the present time by the world of fashion, movies and the press in order to shake the foundations of Christian morality in this regard, as if the Sixth Commandment should be considered outmoded and free rein should be given to all passions, even those against nature. The Council will have something to say concerning this subject. it will clarify and eventually condemn all the attempts to revive paganism and all the trends that in the abuse of psychoanalysis tend to justify even those things which are directly contrary to the moral order (*Preparatory Documents*, p. 52).

In the end, the Council condemned virtually nothing, and did not have a whole lot to say about the Sixth Commandment in particular either. The irony of course is that the Church was accused of being obsessed with such matters at precisely the time when the obsessions were all on the other side. The Church was opening its windows to the world at the same time that the world was opening itself to a bad case of sexual obsession. The process of undermining sexual morals took on a curiously reciprocal relationship involving Italy and America at the time. Film producers like Joseph E. Levine were buying up Italian B-flicks like the Steve Reeves Hercules movies at bargain prices and reissuing them in America. Italian movies produced outside of the Hollywood production code were being increasingly shown in "art film" houses in the United States as a way of weakening the influence of both the Hollywood production code and the Legion of Decency, the Catholic organization which provided the teeth for the code.

The most famous case in this regard was the Roberto Rossellini film *The Miracle* which was repackaged under a more prurient title, *The Ways of Love* and after being hyped by even more prurient advertising, ("Sexier than Hollywood ever dared to be") played to a long run at one of New York's "art" houses until the state film commission declared the film blasphemous. That ruling was eventually overturned and the overturning paved the way for Hollywood's eventual overthrow of the production code some 13 years later. The Catholic Church, primarily under the leadership of Cardinal Spellman of New York, launched an attack on the film in terms that made Catholic intellectuals cringe. The head of the Catholic War Veterans denounced it as part of a communist plot. The film seems innocuous compared to what came afterwards, but then again everything seems innocuous in that light. In retrospect, it seems clear that Hollywood and the cultural elite were working to undermine the code, but, by the same token, the Legion of Decency and Cardinal Spellman and the Catholic VFW seem to have played into their hands by first of all their overheated rhetoric and secondly by being unable to identify the problem in a way that was compelling and realistic. The judges who overturned the blasphemy statute were not impressed with the argumentation of Cardinal Spellman; nor for the most part were Catholic intellectuals like Allen Tate. The Church as a result was dangerously divided, and the hierarchy, in the process, had alienated the very elements it needed to fight the war.

Spellman's reaction to *The Miracle* epitomized for Leo Pfeffer the Church's power in the United States. It must have given him some inkling of a strategy for fighting that power as well. Speaking in 1975, Leo Pfeffer proposes an exercise in cultural imagination to his audience. Think of the ads for abortion clinics in New York's daily newspapers, Pfeffer suggests, and then: "Try to imagine this in the days of Cardinal Spellman, who was able to banish from the city such an innocuous motion picture as *The Miracle. "* If abortion was the *terminus ad quem* of the secular, sexual society, *Joseph Burstyn, Inc. v. Wilson*, was its *terminus a quo*.

At the same time that Italian films were being used to undermine the production code in Hollywood, Hollywood's vision of reality was, as Cardinal Ottaviani noticed, having a deleterious effect on family life in Italy. The only remotely sexy scene which Bosley Crowther could remember from the Italian realist classic *The Bicycle Thief*, was the poster of Rita Hayworth plastered to a wall in Rome. The image of sexual freedom which Hollywood proposed to post-war Italy would reach its apotheosis in Anita Eckberg in Fellini's *La Dolce Vita*. During the press conference Sylvia, the Eckberg character, holds to hype her film, Marcello, the reporter and moral center of the film (or immoral center), discusses her with his Italian girlfriend on the phone. Emma, the girlfriend, wants to know if Sylvia is beautiful.

"Beautiful?" Marcello replies, "Well, yes—if you like the American sort of beauty. A doll. . . yes, a big doll."

Fellini's biographer describes Sylvia as "a blonde, bosomy, and glamorous star." Fellini "had seen the prototype of this woman in a full-page photograph in an American magazine" (Alpert, p. 125). During the press conference, Sylvia announces that she has gotten the part in the upcoming film "because they discovered I have a big talent." She then sticks out her bosom and the reporters laugh.

The trajectories of *La Dolce Vita* and the preparations for the Second Vatican Council parallel each other in an uncanny fashion. In a manner of speaking, Vatican II was the Church's response to *La Dolce Vita*. Looked at in another way, both Federico Fellini and Alfredo Ottaviani were both responding to the same stimulus in their different ways. The film is not without its note of moral condemnation, a note which paralleled much of what Ottaviani railed against in the preparatory documents.

"This evening," Fellini wrote in his diary during May 1958, "I went walking along the Via Veneto, trying to see it clearly, how it has changed from 1950, from the time when I would go there by foot every morning through the Villa Borghese and stop at Rosetti's bookstore, and there meet such as Marcari and Cardarelli the poet." Rome in 1958 was the film capital of the world. Ben Hur was being filmed there at the time. During the period when Pius XII died and the cardinals went into conclave, which is to say, the same time when Ottaviani proposed the idea of a council to Angelo Roncalli, Fellini concluded the final arrangements for *La Dolce Vita*. The world premier of the film took place in Milan on February 5, 1960 four months to the day before John XXIII announced the establishment of the preparatory commissions on June 5, 1960.

The film caused an unprecedented furor in Italy, and the Church took notice, at first praising it for its moral realism and then condemning it for its decadence. Fellini had three years before enlisted the help of his friend, Father Angelo Arpa, in deflecting the censors' blow from his film *Nights of Cabiria*. Arpa had arranged a midnight viewing of the film for Cardinal Siri of Genoa, a prelate even more conservative than Ottaviani. Siri's only comment was 'Poor Cabiria, we must do something for her." It was typical of the reaction of the Church at the time. Both Fellini and Ottaviani had more in common that a superficial juxtaposition of their names would ordinarily indicate. Both *La Dolce Vita* and Ottaviani's preparatory documents show deep reservations about the direction that life was taking in post-war Italy. The prosperity which resulted from technology more often than not lacked any sense of human direction. It was in many ways epitomized by the automobile, which destroyed the Italian landscape, and the television, which destroyed its social life and morals. Fellini was attracted and repulsed by both. His films became increasingly confessional, confessing his infidelities to Giulietta Massina, his wife, nd the woman who had made him a star with the release of *La Strada*. Fellini was fascinated as well by the automobile, particularly the large American variety. Perhaps more than any other artifact the automobile symbolized the pointless freedom of the age. And Fellini both succumbed to it and railed against it, in much the same way that he succumbed to and criticized the sexual freedom of the age.

"Contemporary life," Fellini wrote defending himself against his critics at the time of *La Dolce Vita*'s release, "is filled with contradictions: a frantic, tense, exciting life and, in fact, a terrible emptiness, an immobility. Men, for example, going from one woman to the next, from adventure to adventure. And all this, only to end up revolving around oneself without really budging" (Alpert, p. 150).

It was a passage Cardinal Ottaviani could have written himself. The automobile had become the technological analogue to promiscuity in *La Dolce Vita*. It was an enabling device which made sexual liberation seem plausible. When Marcello and Maddelana, the wealthy nymphomaniac, take Adriana home to her Bauhaus *Wohnmaschine* apartment in the Roman suburbs, they do so in Maddelana's Cadillac convertible. America, as symbolized by the Cadillac, had come to represent freedom from all of the restraints Marcello found burdensome in life, and these had most of all to do with the home. Home, Fellini seems to be saying, oftentimes in spite of himself, no longer makes any sense. And architecturally it doesn't seem much like home anymore either. Adriana lives in a the basement of a poured concrete box with four inches of water on the floor. When Maddelena asks if she has any family, Adriana just laughs and mentions a cousin who is vaguely at work somewhere else. The automobile, the contraceptive, the apartment building all have contributed to the destruction of a culture based on the family and has created in its place a culture of anomic, sexually frenzied individuals who spend a good deal of their time in automobiles travelling from one place to the next. "Adriana's home," we are told in the film's scenario, is "one of these starkly functional housing development buildings, surrounded by raw earth." When the trio arrives in the middle of the night, we are told that "the car stops, but the radio continues to blast away." Fellini, we are told, by his biographer, came under the influence of American writers like William Faulkner and John Steinbeck right around the time that American troops had entered Rome and he imbibed from these writers an impatience with things traditional, which when generalized to the culture at large, would cause Cardinal Ottaviani to feel the Church was in peril. The works of the American writers struck Fellini as "realistic, sensual, adventuresome, palpitating—a sensation of liberty, of landscapes without horizons." Fellini was clever enough to see through the hype as well. Instead of the automobile-is-freedom advertising campaigns that were fusing the new myth with the old in America, Fellini examines the effect of the automobile and what it stood for in America on Italian culture at the time: Marcello, the reporter, with aspirations to be a serious writer sitting outside the Bauhaus *Wohnmaschine* in a Cadillac convertible with two women of dubious virtue and the radio blaring rock and roll.

Marcello's ambivalent attitude toward faith and the family is best expressed in his relationship with his girlfriend, Emma. While attending Sylvia's press conference, Marcello is trying to bridge the two worlds, the American technological and the Italian traditional by talking to his girlfriend Emma, symbol of domesticity and sexual life lived in conformity with the moral code and the canons of traditional family behavior, but the conversation is constantly at cross purposes. Emma wants Marcello to come home, but Marcello is distracted by Sylvia's "big talent." As he tries to link both worlds in a phone conversation, Marcello succeeds in simply seeming distracted:

"I'm waiting for you here," Emma tells Marcello, referring to the apartment, not unlike Adriana's, which functions as a bad simulacrum of the home, "I'll be home all day. What would you like to eat? Something light? Shall I make a nice dish of ravioli? I have everything at home—the pasta, the cheese—all I have to do is buy the salad. Then we can go to the movies or we can stay home—whatever you like. Say you love me!

"Yes," Marcello responds dazzled by the hoopla surrounding Sylvia, the movie goddess, " Ravioli."

Late the same evening "a Negro orchestra is playing softly 'Arrivederci, Roma,'" a schlocky '50s tune based on the resurgence of the film industry in Rome, "Marcello and Sylvia are dancing. Marcello is holding her very close."

"You are everything, Sylvia" Marcello tells her with evidently all thought of ravioli driven from his mind. "Don't you know that you are everything, everything. . . . You are the first woman on the first day of creation. You are the mother, the sister, the lover, the friend, . . an angel, a devil, the earth, the home. . . Yes, that's what you are Sylvia, the home. . . "

Marcello's relationship with the goddess never gets consummated. Dionysian revelry keeps intruding, in ironic fashion, to drive them apart. Shortly after he effuses into Sylvia's ear, Frankie, her husband, appears looking "like a satyr and dressed in a striped sport shirt." When Sylvia and Frankie dance they "are spectacular—sinuous and free, like two young animals." Before Marcello can maneuver Sylvia into a another slow dance, the crowd, who, we are told "wants excitement," starts chanting "We want rock and roll, we want rock and roll." Out of nowhere a rock and roll star complete with tight black pants and a black leather jacket jumps up onto the stage and sings an American rock and roll number. A hideous old lady claps frantically in time. A young homosexual is so overcome with Frankie's animal magnetism that he starts weeping in ecstasy. "Frankie," he cries, "you're wonderful! You're so good. You're so good. Look, I'm crying! You danced like a god."

In the end, Sylvia, in spite of her impressive breasts, is unable to produce any milk. Marcello hoping to maneuver her into bed goes off looking for milk so that Sylvia can feed a stray cat she has found. In the end, dawn arrives to find the two of them standing in the Trevi fountain looking slightly ridiculous as the water suddenly gets turned off.

Religion fares no better than family life in La *Dolce Vita.* Emma's devotion focuses on an obviously fraudulent apparition outside of Rome which quickly degenerates into a media circus. The field on which the children allegedly see the Virgin is, according to the scenario, "transformed into a vast arena where all the technical equipment of modern communication is focused on one point. . . . It looks like the opening of a carnival or the scene of some great national disaster" On the way to the field of the miracle, Emma becomes Fellini's caricature of family life, the mama manque, by constantly shoving food into Marcello's mouth and telling him to chew slowly. When she arrives she offers a prayer to the non-present Madonna: "If he marries me, I'll come here everyday to thank you. I'd come here barefoot to thank you. But I don't even ask for that. All I ask is that he love me and he be all mine, as he used to be."

The scene provides a neat recapitulation of the state of the Church during the last days of Pius XII. Family life in decay as the result of American technology, hedonism and rock and roll, as the Church stands by helplessly and the rank and file are drawn to phoney apparitions in a desperate attempt to fill the vacuum. In the end, the Church could never make up its mind about *La Dolce Vita,* whether to condemn it for its decadence or praise it for the damning portrait of modern materialism it rendered. Fellini's friend, Father Angelo Arpa, professor of theology at the University of Rome, took the latter tack claiming, "never has cinema included in sin such a profound sense of bitterness and weariness, or misfortune and desolation."

Marcello, to put the situation in its simplest formulation, was finding family life implausible as a result of the illusions the American-dominated media were presenting to him.

"Don't you understand," Emma asks, "that you've found the most important thing in life, a woman who really loves you, who would give her life for you as though you were the only man in the world?"

Marcello, looking miserable, evidently does not understand and chooses media-induced fantasy instead of family life Italian-style. He sees domesticity as "the life of a worm? You talk of nothing but the kitchen and the bedroom. Do you understand that a man who accepts a life like that is through?" Marcello starts beating her and screaming "I don't believe in this aggressive, sticky, maternal love of yours. I don't want it! I can't use it! This isn't love. it's bestiality! How can I make you understand that I can't live like that, and don't want to be with you." At an earlier point in the film, Marcello told his friend Steiner, "You know, your home is a real sanctuary. Your children, your wife, your friends—they're all wonderful. Your books, too. . . I'm wasting my time. Will I ever accomplish anything?" But Steiner inexplicably kills himself and Marcello continues his downward trajectory into increasingly sterile decadence. By the end of the film he can't even produce journalism, much less the books he had hoped to write. By the end of the film he has become a PR-man; he now produces the illusions that have undone him. "By 1965," Domino, "the transvestite fairy" (Fellini's heterosexism comes to the fore) announces, "it will be complete depravity. Mama mia, how filthy this world will be!"

Eventually, Fellini, unable to shake the guilt resulting from his own adulterous behavior, would descend into Jung, LSD and the occult and eventually produce films that became a parody of the term Felliniesque. At the world premier of *Juliet of the Spirits*, Fellini sat next to Joseph E. Levine, who had just purchased the American rights to the film. Half-way into the film Fellini realized that Levine had bought the film sight unseen. The Catholic moment by then had both come and gone. Fellini was no longer saying he was producing Christian films and Catholic critics were no longer critiquing according to Catholic principles. The Catholics had become open to a world that was no longer interested in what they thought because for the most part they had lost their identity as Catholics. All of that was to unfold over the next few years, but a number of ironies were already in sight.

In November 1961 seven months after the American premier of *La Dolce Vita* on April 17 of that year, at the 43rd annual meeting of the American bishops' National Catholic Welfare

Conference Archbishop Krol of Philadelphia was named chairman of the NCWC Youth Department and almost as an afterthought appointed chairman of the Bishops' committee for the Legion of Decency. Krol had just signed on to be the episcopal head of the Legion of Decency at what would prove to be the most crucial period in the history of film, the time when Hollywood decided to overturn the production code. "God," Krol would say looking back on his own life, " has a sense of humor."

Making him chairman of the episcopal committee for the Legion of Decency was a good indication of that. What Archbishop Krol was prepared for was one thing. What he got was something else again. He was prepared to administer the Church he had grown up in, building new buildings and enabling people to serve God. What he got was a position on the front lines of a cultural revolution that few could see looming over the horizon at the time. In looking back over his tenure in Philadelphia, Krol saw similarities between himself and Saint John Neumann, the Bohemian bishop who was canonized under his tenure. "One of his outstanding qualities," Krol said of Bishop Neumann, "was his awareness of his own inadequacy and at the same time of the power of God which could work through him." When Neumann came to Philadelphia, the tide of Catholic immigration was just at its beginning, and Neumann in effect created the ethnic parish as the best way to preserve the faith of the Catholics who came to Philadelphia's alien, Anglo-saxon Protestant culture. By the time Krol arrived as his 20th century successor, that system was under attack and would eventually succumb to a number of forces yet to be described. What Krol saw as in common to both himself and his predecessor was a sense of their inadequacy. Neumann, according to Krol, "did not according to human standards, compare favorably with the other bishops who were eloquent orators, and who had perfect command of the English language, which Bishop Neumannn did not.

"According to human standards, [Bishop Neumannn] was somewhat inadequate. But it's the old story that God takes the least and most humble and uses them to produce great works."

The same could be said about Archbishop Krol himself. Krol was a financier sent off to fight a cultural war. Krol had no interest in film; the chairmanship of the Legion of Decency was not a job he sought; nor was it a job which the bishops at that time considered terribly important. Krol got the job primarily because of his avidity in accepting work. The meeting was coming to a close; it was obvious that the more important work had already been done, the bishops were anxious to get back home. Krol was not a film buff: he was the man for the job because he had acquired the reputation for doing what no one else wanted to do. Eventually he would give an award to Joseph E. Levine for a film Krol had himself never seen.

Looking back on the period later in life, Krol talked about the bishops being thrust into more and more fields of life and as a result being more and more at the mercy of their advisors. It was something that was probably unavoidable in an organization as large as the Catholic Church. The problem may have been that bishops were pronouncing on things over which they had no competence. But there was a problem within the problem too. At a time when the bishops were becoming more and more dependent on ever larger staffs of advisors, those advisors, taken from the Church's intelligentsia, were coming more and more under the sway of the ideologies of modernity, and the bishops often found themselves incapable of bringing them back. In fact, as time went on those advisors often became bishops themselves, bishops who because of the historical peculiarities of their training were unable to distinguish between the Catholic faith and the liberal ideology that was undermining that faith.

On the eve of the Council, the Church faced a crisis of hermeneutics. Just whose interpretation was going to be normative, and were the bishops capable of guiding the Church in a manner which its own members, especially its own priests, found plausible? No one knew the answers to these questions at the time; in fact, few knew these were the questions, but before long the bishops would find out just how important a coherent, plausible, intellectual framework was for the Church. This was in effect the main task of the Council: to make the Church plausible to the modern age, to bridge the gap between piety and reason, to situate the gospel in terms the Church's own ministers would find persuasive. In 1961, no one could see the turmoil that would flow from that attempt Had the bishops known they might not have tried, but had they not tried it is doubtful that the Church would have survived the divisions that were lurking beneath her surface any more successfully than she survived the trauma which resulted from facing them openly.

In his apostolic constitution *"Humanae Salutis,"* dated December 25, 1961, Pope John convoked the Second Vatican Council for some time in 1962. "Today," Pope John XXIII said,

> the Church is witnessing a crisis under-way within society. While humanity is on the edge of a new era, tasks of immense gravity and amplitude await the Church, as in the the most tragic periods of its history. It is a question in fact of bringing the modern world into contact with the vivifying and perennial energies of the gospel, a world which exalts itself with its conquests of the technical and scientific fields, but which brings also the consequences of a temporal order which some have wished to reorganize excluding God. This is why modern society is earmarked by a great material progress to which there is not a corresponding advance in the moral field.

By the time he reached retirement, the Council had crystallized in Cardinal Krol's mind as both the most significant event in his own life and the most significant event for the life of the Church in the twentieth century.

"It was divine providence," he said in retrospect, "that inspired Pope John XXIII to convoke the Council." And in that apostolic constitution in which he convoked the Council almost by priority of place he expressed the reasons why he convoked the Council: He expressed the concern about a world which exalts itself and its technological conquests in the scientific fields. Which brings about also the consequences of a temporal order which some wish to reorganize to the exclusion of God. Pope John cited a completely new and disconcerting fact, the existence of militant atheism, which is active on a world level. He spoke about a crisis in society and the spiritual ruin caused by false ideologies. He made it clear that the Church cannot abstract itself from the temporal order. It cannot be insensitive to it; it cannot ignore it. But the Church must vivify and energize that order with the light of Christ, the light of the gospel and it must help men discover within themselves their own nature their own dignity, their own destiny.

The Second Vatican Council did not cause but it was followed by a period of some turbulence and confusion. Some of this was caused by persons who did not read or did not understand the Council documents. Some of it was also caused by the influence of secularization and a consequent religious liberalism. Religious liberals appealing under the principle of freedom favored the democratization of the Church. Some resisted and were actively hostile to the authority of religion. They exalted human judgment to the point where free intellectual inquiry became more important than the truth.

"There was a bit of turbulence," Krol said with characteristic understatement, describing the turmoil that was to descend on the Church and the country as Vatican II provided the backdrop and, in many instances, the pretext for the cultural revolution of the '60s. "Vatican II was a special manifestation of the Holy Spirit that is ever present in the Church." Then lapsing for a moment from the vocabulary he had learned in the seminary and the understatement he cultivates when describing things that denote controversy during his tenure, Krol adds, "It was the event of the century."

II
The Cultural Revolution at home: July 4, 1962

On July 4, 1962, a crowd of 100,000 people, many of them Catholic, gathered at Independence Hall in Philadelphia to hear an Independence Day address from the first Catholic president of the United States. On the podium with John F. Kennedy were David Lawrence, governor of Pennsylvania, who also happened to be a Catholic, and James H. J. Tate, mayor of Philadelphia, who was a Catholic as well. Archbishop John Joseph Krol gave the invocation. Virtually all of the men on the podium were, in addition to being Catholic, newly arrived on the political scene. Kennedy and Lawrence had been elected in 1960; Tate and Krol had both taken their respective offices in 1961. For a Catholic audience most of whom could still remember the Klan marches of 1928 in protest against the presidential campaign of Al Smith, it must have been a remarkable sight. For an audience of Philadelphia Catholics whose history included the anti-Catholic nativist riots of 1844, it must have seemed more remarkable still. It must have seemed as if a new age of acceptance for Catholics had finally dawned. The long night of anti-Catholic bigotry which had characterized this country since well before its beginning in 1776 had finally come to an end. Catholics were finally accepted as full partners in the republic. Catholics had come of age and were now in a position to make their contribution to the common good of the country.

With the benefit of hindsight, we can now see that the euphoria was remarkably short-lived, just as we can see that the conditions for acceptance were less than congenial to Catholic interests. To begin with, there was the fact that President Kennedy's Catholicism was more ethnic than moral, as subsequent biography has shown. Beyond that, the closer Kennedy got to the levers of power the more he proved willing to divest himself of his Catholic identity. The closer President Kennedy got to a policy-making position, the greater became his willingness to promise that his Catholicism would have no influence on his policies. During the 1960 campaign, Kennedy had to promise to a group of Protestant ministers assembled in Houston that his Catholicism would in no way influence his behavior as president. It is difficult to imagine the member of any other denomination in the United States being required to make such humiliating assurances, but Catholicism had always been a special case in this regard.

The hiatus in anti-Catholic feeling in the early '60s had other causes as well. Less than four months away loomed the opening of the Second Vatican Council. We have already discussed what the Council was supposed to accomplish from the Church's point of view. It was to reorganize the Church and make it more effective in dealing with the challenges which modernity posed, specifically the challenges to family life which the culture of liberalism and its increasingly invasive media promulgated. From the outside, however, this was not clear, primarily because the Church was never able to compete with the media's version of what it was supposed to be. As a matter of fact from the outside, it often looked as if the Council had been convoked for the exact opposite purpose; namely, to conform the Church to the superior achievements of the modern age. This was due in large measure to the press the Council got, which was in large measure the result of the efforts of young Catholics who had imbibed the intoxicating atmosphere of the Kennedy age and wanted to use the opportunity of interpreting the Council as a vehicle for upward mobility.

"At the highest position of the Church," wrote Michael Novak as a fairly representative instance of this class,

> down through the majority of the Council of Bishops, the idea of reform had taken hold. The chief point for reform was in the area of liberty. . . . How could the Church of Christ ever have lost liberty? But it had. The wave of enthusiasm and relief that swept the Church and the world were because of the return of liberty,

and at the return of Catholics into the midst of the human race, out of their defensive isolation.

Traditionally hostile American culture was warming in its feelings toward Catholicism for a number of reasons, but foremost was the anticipation that the Church might cease being so aggressively the Church. This was, in fact, ever the condition of acceptance for Catholics in American culture and would continue to be thereafter. If Catholics chose not to impose their views, then they were perfectly acceptable. Imposing their views came to mean exercising the right that other groups took for granted in the republic, but that was just part of the double standard that Catholics had to face and, in many instances, had come to accept. Now, if, as seemed to be the case at the dawn of the Council, the Church itself was willing to endorse the separate peace that so many Catholics had already made, then the basis for cooperation was more or less limitless. Hence the "era of good feeling" which characterized the early '60s. For James Hitchcock, the era of Pope John XXIII and John F. Kennedy was an "unusual and temporary parenthesis in the history of anti-Catholicism" that had pervaded the United States since before its founding. Just how temporary it was would probably prove to be a surprise to many assembled at Independence Hall that day had they been able to look a few years into the future.

However, even in the summer of 1962, there were enough disturbing signs on the horizon to disturb the assembled even then. Less than a month before the July 4 gathering, the Supreme Court had handed down *Engel v. Vitale*, its decision declaring prayer in schools an unconstitutional violation of the separation of Church and state. Writing for the six-man majority, Justice Hugo L. Black claimed that "in this country it is no part of the business of government to compose official prayers for any group of the American people to recite as a part of a religious program carried on by government." Archbishop Krol, as can be imagined, saw the matter differently. Less than a week before his appearance with President Kennedy at Independence Hall he had denounced the decision in the diocesan newspaper as "establishing secularism as a state religion." Krol saw the decision as ignoring "the text of the very amendment it professes to interpret." Since, Krol reasoned, God was the supreme reality in life, acknowledging his existence must be "a supreme factor in education." Otherwise, the health of the body politic would suffer as first religion and then morality were drained out of public discourse to be replaced by self-will, ideologies of selfishness, and the social disorder which would follow naturally from their propagation.

The *Engel* decision unleashed a storm of outrage and sarcasm that provided a discordant preliminary note to the harmony evidenced at Independence Hall on July 4. According to Judge Bork, "the sense of outrage was particularly intense when the Court prohibited prayer in the public schools, and years later even disapproved some moments of silence. The application of the Bill of Rights to the states in this and other matters has done much to alter the moral tone of communities across the country." The change in moral tone did not happen overnight, and was in effect only visible with the gift of many years of hindsight, but the seeds for moral decay were sown by driving religion out of the public sphere, and this was comprehended with dismay throughout the Catholic world. Bishop Bernard J. Topel of Spokane described *Engel* as "a new low" in constitutional law. "How has it come that the Supreme Court makes decisions so contrary to the thinking of 100 years ago?" the bishop asked. Then without pause, Topel answered his own question: "One word gives the answer: secularism." "The time has come for action," Bishop Topel concluded. "No longer can we tolerate such abuse of religion and morality." In August, Francis Cardinal Spellman, then ordinary of New York, called the decision a "two pronged attack on the American way of life" which consisted in "the movement to take God out of the public school and to force the child out of the private school" by denying it its fair share of tax dollars. "This," Spellman concluded, "is the establishment of a new religion of secularism. It should be ruled unconstitutional."

Catholic politicians showed little desire for a fight, however, perhaps because of the accommodations they had to make in order to get elected. President Kennedy, for example, counseled Americans to accept the Supreme Court's school prayer decision and recommended a "very easy remedy for those who disagree with it"—namely, praying at home and in Church.

This disparity between the judiciary and the other two branches of government was in many ways indicative of the path that the Cultural Revolution would take. The Cultural Revolution was never elected to office. It achieved its ends by subverting the democratic process through other institutions, like the Supreme Court and academe, where people were in effect appointed for life and beyond recall. Oftentimes the elected officials were secretly glad to have controversial issues taken off their hands, at least this was the view of Leo Pfeffer, who found the changes congenial. But those who disagreed with the changes were oftentimes left befuddled by the fact that the system seemed to make no provisions for what to do when the Supreme Court was wrong, or when it chose to abuse its power and usurp legislative function from the legislatures. The system of checks and balances proved curiously inadequate when it came to the Supreme Court, which during the Warren Era declared itself unilaterally above the constitution in the very act of ostensibly interpreting it. It was a flaw in the system which no one had noticed up until that point, and the flaw remains uncorrected still. The remedy applied by presidents from Roosevelt up to the present had been packing the court with people of like mind, but that did nothing to remedy the situation in which the country found itself in the early '60s, as millions of concerned Americans watched their institutions fall one by one to the arbitrary will and opaque logic of an unelected tribunal. "The Court," Robert Bork wrote after failing to ascend to its ranks himself because of political pressure from the long since successful Revolution,

> is virtually invulnerable, and *Brown* proved it. The Court can do what it wishes, and there is almost no way to stop it, provided its result has a significant political constituency. (These days the significance of a political constituency is greatly magnified if the constituency includes a large part of the intellectual or knowledge class, which means that the Court has greater freedom to the left than it has to the right.) (Bork, p. 77).

The Supreme Court's attitude toward prayer was not the only thing causing consternation throughout the country. Almost simultaneously with the *Engel* decision, the Court continued the path it had charted for itself in the Roth decision by handing down *Womack*, which made it more difficult for the post office to prevent the dissemination of obscene material though the mails. On June 28, 1962, Rep. Kathryn Granahan (D.

PA) delivered a speech before the United States House of Representatives in which she denounced the *Womack* decision as "an incredible series of judicial rationalizations" which carried with it "frightening implications." According to Justice John M. Harlan who wrote the majority opinion, material is obscene not just when it appeals to "prurient interest" but must instead "go beyond the pale of rudimentary decency." The magazines on trial in *Womack* could not be considered obscene since they catered to homosexuals and hence would not appeal to normal individuals. Rep. Granahan claimed in her speech that a "beast was being turned loose on society unless prompt and informed action is taken to close the loopholes."

It's easy to sympathize with Rep. Granahan's indignation, but difficult to understand the solution she is proposing. The loophole in question is a large one indeed; it is in fact what one might call a fundamental flaw in the American constitutional system. Aside from impeachment, no one knew what to do to curb the excesses of the Court when the Court decided to place itself above the Constitution it was appointed to interpret. "Impeach Earl Warren" was one solution proposed as a slogan which appeared on billboards and automobile bumpers but with no real effect. During the early '70s, the Republicans attempted to impeach William O. Douglas, but neither attempt came to much. By the early '60s, with the glow of *Brown v. Board of Education* still a warm recent memory, the Supreme Court decided that it could do pretty much whatever it wanted to do. At the same time the Court was coming to this realization, the composition of the Court was changing into a decidedly more activist body which saw the implementation of the liberal agenda as something akin to a moral imperative. At the very moment when it seemed that Catholics had reached their place in the sun in American political life, the Black-Douglas faction on the Supreme Court was on its way to becoming a majority on the court.

By 1962, the Black-Douglas faction of the court had become a minority of four in a court of nine. Although the civil rights struggle was by no means over, it looked as if the Court had safely weathered the storm over *Brown v. Board of Education*, which would become the moral justification for further excursions into liberal activism. *Brown*, however, had only come about as a result of the acquiescence of the Frankfurter majority on the the Court. Then in 1962, Justice Charles Whittaker, a crucial part of the Frankfurter majority, announced his intention to retire and the balance in favor of judicial restraint was suddenly an open question.

Wanting a place in history perhaps and attempting to gain favor with the civil rights groups, Robert Kennedy approached Chief Justice Earl Warren with the nomination of William H. Hastie, a black Harvard graduate who was at the time sitting on the U.S. District Court bench. Warren, according to Kennedy, "was violently opposed to having Hastie on the Court." In a move which seemed surprising at the time but not so surprising in light of the Clarence Thomas confirmation hearings, Warren got down to brass tacks: "He's not a liberal and he'd be opposed to all measures that we're interested in." As a result, Judge Hastie was "completely unsatisfactory." Justice William O. Douglas was of much the same opinion. Hastie, he felt, would be "just one more vote for Frankfurter."

The case had uncanny parallels with the nomination of Clarence Thomas to the Supreme Court some 30 years later. In both cases, the liberals, who had the reputation for supporting the cause of the Negro, turned against a black nominee to the Court because that nominee was perceived as a threat to the liberal agenda. Just why this was the case was not difficult to see. With *Brown*, the Left had finally found an effective use of race as the vehicle for their agenda. If racial equality was invoked, the liberals were discovering to their delight, then virtually anything—any intrusive federal program, any violation of the Constitution—would be accepted as a means to that end. With *Brown* the liberals had found an extremely effective way of getting just about anything they wanted in terms of social change. If a prominent black (and a colleague on the Supreme Court was nothing if not that) demurred in the use of race to implement the liberal agenda, it threatened to derail a key part of the liberal strategy of judicial activism. As a result, Hastie's nomination was quietly dropped, and Byron White was nominated and eventually approved to fill the chair of Justice Whittaker.

White was to prove a disappointment to the liberals. But their disappointment did not last long. Shortly after White's appointment, Justice Frankfurter himself fell ill and was forced to retire. Replacing the chief proponent of judicial restraint on the court was Arthur Goldberg, who comfortably fit into the Black-Douglas faction and made it for all practical purposes the new majority, a new majority which felt morally vindicated by *Brown* and ready to take judicial activism in the service of the liberal agenda to new heights. The Catholic reaction to *Engel v. Vitale* was the first warning that the Court was transgressing on things too important to ignore. It was furthermore a warning that no matter who was in the White House and no matter what he professed as his religion, the social order and its moral underpinnings in the law of God were going to be in for rough times. *The Catholic Standard and Times,* the Philadelphia diocesan newspaper, was full of articles denouncing the obscenity and prayer decisions in terms that ranged from the fulminative to the sarcastic. During the summer of 1962, the *Standard and Times* reported on a suit filed in New York which sought to have the national Anthem declared unconstitutional. In early August President Kennedy unveiled a white marble mantle on which a prayer written by John Adams was engraved. "Think the Supreme Court will let it stay?" the *Pittsburgh Catholic* wondered.

When John Joseph Krol arrived at Pennsylvania station at 30th and Market on March 21, 1961, the city's two auxiliary bishops and a number of priests were on hand to meet him. Shortly after Krol's arrival, the Philadelphia archdiocese would split in two, and one of the auxiliaries would go to become the first ordinary of the newly-formed diocese of Allentown. On March 22, 1961, Archbishop Krol was formally installed as the 10th ordinary and sixth metropolitan of the Archdiocese of Philadelphia by Archbishop Vagnozzi at the Cathedral of SS. Peter and Paul. Two weeks later, 20,000 people gathered at Philadelphia's convention hall for the public celebration of his installation. At the time Archbishop Krol took over as ordinary, the Archdiocese of Philadelphia was home to 1,245,000 Catholics, over one third of the total population of the area. In 1961 there were 309 parishes in an archdiocese served by 1,595 priests, 361 brothers and 6,109 sisters in 63 religious orders. Within two months of his arrival in Philadelphia, Archbishop Krol announced the establishment of the first of 34 new parishes which he would found in his first 15 years as archbishop.

During the course of the twentieth century, the Church in Philadelphia gradually took on an Irish flavor that would become synonymous for many with American Catholicism. The seminary, which had come under the control of the Germans by the end of the 19th century, was firmly in Irish hands by the time Krol arrived. Krol, however, perhaps because he was Polish and from Cleveland was more ambivalent toward this fact than his predecessors had been. The issue was enculturation. The Irish had identified firmly with the Church and had come to dominate it because they were so willing to serve it. The Italians in many ways held their distance. They tended to send their children to public schools. The Irish clergy tended to look on them as less generous in supporting the Church when seen in comparison to the Irish. The positive side of the enculturation process was that the faith suffused the life of the neighborhoods and parishes of Philadelphia. The Philadelphia of the neighborhoods was in many ways a world unto itself, with its own social life and its own schools feeding into its own universities, and eventually into a number of professions and businesses dominated by Catholics. This separateness caused the secularist mind, as the testimony of Leo Pfeffer indicated, a good deal of discomfort. It was the liberals' version of the nativist feeling that Catholics weren't really 100 percent American. The upshot of this attitude was a determination on the part of people like Pfeffer, and the advocacy groups he represented, to make the maintaining of the Catholic school system as difficult as possible. In an age when government aid was pouring into any number of private enterprises good, bad and indifferent, the Catholic school system was presented instead with roadblocks to insure that it did not flourish.

But enculturation had its down side as well. Just as the faith suffused the neighborhoods, so also did the neighborhoods suffuse the faith. The negative side of the enculturation of Catholicism that so annoyed Leo Pfeffer was the undeniable fact that the neighborhood was not only transmitting the faith but deforming it as well. This was the problem that the Church had to face on a world-wide basis; it was also the problem the Council would face in the fall of 1962. Philadelphia Catholic culture had become so successful in transmitting the faith that, in many ways, it was in a position to dictate what the faith was to be. This would cause problems in the coming years when the

Church attempted to change the liturgy. For many people, and rightly so, the faith is what they learned while growing up. When the Church attempted to correct what it deemed deformations of the faith that had crept in as a result of that enculturation, as it did during the Second Vatican Council, the people in many instances rebelled. The rebellion was in many ways a tribute to enculturation as well as a caveat against what it could become in the absence of the Church's ongoing direction of it.

From the time of Pope St. Pius X, the Church had been trying to reform the Mass and increase the participation of the faithful in it without diminishing their attendance at it. Krol had been trying to implement these directives in Cleveland, and the announcement of the Council gave new impetus to implementing them in Philadelphia. When he arrived in Philadelphia in 1961, Krol found a lot of people going to mass but found that the participation of those people at mass left a lot to be desired. Part of his task was to get them ready for greater participation in the liturgy because, as he put it, "the church in Philadelphia at that time, not today, but at that time, was following the 'quiet low mass and run' attitude."

"This," Krol continued, "was kind of a refection of the church in Ireland." The enculturation of the Church in Philadelphia had been so successful that the tail was threatening to wag the dog. Krol liked to compare the situation of Catholics of that time with that of the Jews. If there had been no council, if the Church had not attempted to take charge of the interface between faith and culture, the Church ran the danger of splitting up according to political lines. There would be an orthodox segment, a reformed segment, a conservative Catholic Church, etc. The fault lines would be pretty much the same as those along which Judaism cracked and broke.

"Jews," Krol explained, "have moved from the orthodox to the conservative to the reformed to the reconstructionists, four main kind of divisions. Some of our ecumenical friends in the various denominations, they tend to split and separate, whereas the Catholic Church has the capacity of self-renewal. And every time you have change there's a bit of dust, a bit of turbulence, a bit of turmoil. It comes not from the Council itself but it comes from people who have made references to what the spirit of the Council is."

On the other hand, from the point of view of the commonweal, the enculturation of the faith had created an extremely stable social situation in Philadelphia. So stable that its residents often complained of Philadelphia's stodginess. The city was divided into parishes, and from the point of view of Catholics living there, parish boundaries were the definitive geographical coordinates. A Catholic Philadelphian would identify himself as living in St. Malachy's parish in the same way a New Yorker would list his address as Greenwich Village. Each parish in turn had an ethnic flavor. Some in fact were almost exclusively the domain of one ethnic group or another. The result was a social structure which held together with remarkable cohesiveness because of the specificity of the values and culture it shared. Anna Quindlen, an alumna of Southwest Philadelphia who went on to become a columnist for the *New York Times*, described in one of her columns how her father had been subjected to corporal punishment in a fairly short amount of time by a policeman, a nun, and a neighbor. This showed the overlap of reinforcing social structures, and how a parent's burdens in disciplining children were lightened by those supportive social structures. The order established by the ethnic parishes benefited not only parents but the city government as well, which in the first half of the 20th century was relieved of many of the burdens it took on as the omnicompetent state expanded its power during the postwar period. In the early 1990s one priest who had been assigned to a once thriving parish which was now struggling under the burdens that would come to be characterized euphemistically as those of the inner city, put the situation in perspective by recounting the judgment he heard from a priest many years his senior. "In 1952," the older priest had said, "there was no such thing as a poor parish in Philadelphia." At the time the young priest made this remark, the archdiocese under the leadership of Krol's successor was in the process of withdrawing from virtually all of North Philadelphia because it had become financially unfeasible to maintain parishes there.

What happened between 1952 and 1992 was a change of regime in city government. Actually the change preceded the date set by the priest by one year, but its affects did not. In the fall of 1951, Joseph S. Clark was elected mayor of Philadelphia, the first Democrat to head the city in 87 years. Clark was by birth and class a blue-blood Republican from the patrician neighborhood of Chestnut Hill. He and his co-reform Democrat Richardson Dilworth attended Ivy League schools and helped found the Philadelphia branch of Americans for Democratic Action in 1947, a group which would provide much of the cadres that would staff the city's government during their respective tenures as mayor. Both Clark and Dilworth were considered traitors to their class, a term frequently reserved for Franklin D. Roosevelt. The association of terms bespeaks more than coincidence in this instance, for Clark and Dilworth were, in effect, the advent of the New Deal in Philadelphia. Clark and Dilworth forged in Philadelphia the same coalition which Roosevelt had forged nationally some 20 years earlier. In Philadelphia this coalition came down to two major groups, the Negro and the Irish, if we let the Irish act as synechdoche for Catholic ethnics. The Irish Catholics were already in place in stable neighborhoods when Clark-Dilworth brought the New Deal to Philadelphia. The destabilizing element in the coalition would prove to be the Negro, specifically the Negro migration up from the South, which the Democrats on the local as well as the national level found expedient to encourage.

According to Richard A. Kaiser, "Mayor Clark and his reform-minded successor, Richardson Dilworth, . . . began the incorporation of blacks into city government by backing black community leaders (especially clergymen) for elected and appointed offices which heretofore had not been held by blacks" ("The Rise of a Biracial Coalition in Philadelphia" in *Racial Politics in American Cities* ed. Rufus P. Browning, Dale Rogers Marshall, David H. Tabb, 1990, p. 51). Mayor James H. J. Tate continued the coalition by creating a cadre of black supporters "to administer the federally-funded anitpoverty program and placing patronage jobs at their disposal so that they could mobilize others in their neighborhoods." The strategy was not without perils though. The influx of federal money as well as the black migration up from the South which it fostered was putting intolerable strains on the neighborhoods of the white ethnics in Philadelphia who were an increasingly beleaguered part of the increasingly beleaguered New Deal coalition. As the '60s progressed, both black demands, fueled by the civil rights movement, and white complaints, fueled by the anarchy resulting from black migration, increased apace, and the Democratic coalition threatened to collapse under the strain. The Democratic response to the problem was to attempt to placate both sides without resolving the underlying tension. To the blacks, the Democrats promised more money and more of a share in administering the distribution of government largesse. To the whites, the Democrats proposed a man: Frank Rizzo, the policeman who would get tough with urban crime. The two proposals were, in a political sense, contradictory, a fact which became apparent when Rizzo, as Democratic mayor of Philadelphia, endorsed Richard Nixon as president of the United States. But by that time Clark was a United States Senator and a shill for Planned Parenthood and telling everyone in Philadelphia who would listen that Tate and Rizzo had betrayed what he and Dilworth had started. Rizzo would eventually fail in getting the city charter changed so that he could run for a third term, which set the scene for black ascendancy in the city under Mayor Wilson Goode.

Krol arrived on the scene just about 10 years after the Democrats took over the city but at the moment during which the forces which they had set in motion were beginning to shake the city's institutions to their foundations. In their separate ways, both the Negro and the Irish overwhelmed the city with their immigration and created significant backlash in the process. The Irish arrived in great numbers during the mid-19th century, and the anti-Catholic nativist riots were the result. The Irish arrived when Philadelphia was on the upward slope of industrialization, at the same time the country as a whole was following the same trajectory, and the Irish arrived to man the city's industries. The Baldwin Locomotive factory on Broad St. was just one of the factories that drew the Irish to Philadelphia like a magnet.

Black migration up from the South began in much the same way, but at a much later date, beginning in earnest during World War I and repeating itself on a larger scale during and following World War II. At this point the similarities begin to break down. The Irish were by and large socialized as a result of their allegiance to the Catholic Church, which provided a plethora of intermediary structures that allowed them to become stable home-owning residents of the neighborhoods they dominated. The blacks, although in many ways extremely religious, did not have a church with the same unity and cohesiveness the Catholic Church provided. As a result, they all too often succumbed to the antinomian atmosphere of the big cities. The release from the rigors of the segregated South often led to lawlessness and family breakdown, already a problem in the South, but one which was exacerbated by the lack of intermediary social organizations in the urban ghettoes of the North.

If the blacks had arrived in Philadelphia at a different time, if the black migration had taken place more gradually allowing them to take over the structures the whites left behind in more orderly fashion, things might have turned out differently. But none of this was to be. The great migration of blacks from the sharecropping segregation system of the South into the inner cities of the North took place under the banner of the New Deal with its ever-increasing appetite for expanding government. Roosevelt had won the blacks over from the party of Lincoln, and the Democrats cemented the deal in a way that would prove difficult to maintain, by steadily increasing the scope of government and including ever-increasing numbers of blacks on the government payroll as either its beneficiaries, as in the case of welfare, or the distributors of that largesse in the ever-expanding social welfare bureaucracies in the nation's northern cities. Senator Daniel Patrick Moynihan of New York describes the blackmail that took place under the rhetoric of civil rights during the 60s as "for many an altogether intoxicating experience." "Do this," the civil rights movement informed Washington or Philadelphia and any number of cities of the North, "or the cities will burn."

Moynihan felt that the black leadership had

> been greatly encouraged in this course by white rhetoric of the Kerner Commission variety. But most important of all, the existence of a large marginal, if not dependent, black urban lower class has at last given the black middle class an opportunity to establish a secure and rewarding power base in American Society—as the provider of social services to the black lower class. . . . What building contracts and police graft were to the 19th-century urban Irish, the welfare department, Head Start, and Black Studies programs will be to the coming generation of Negroes. They are of course very wise in this respect. These are expanding areas of economic opportunity.

"In 1970," Nicholas Lemann points out in his book on black migration, "government employed 57 percent of black male college graduates and 72 percent of black female college graduates." In the intervening years the percentages have only increased. Upward mobility for blacks meant, for the most part, getting a government job, which more often than not adminstering a program for other blacks of the less fortunate sort. It would be wrong to focus simply on welfare as the magnet which drew the blacks up from the South. Welfare was just the entry level position in an ever expanding series of government jobs that blossomed during the entire postwar period. Beginning with the practical implementation of the mechanical cotton picker in the '40s to the introduction of pesticides and a national minimum wage standard in the late 60s, the Negro agricultural worker was becoming more and more superfluous in the South. At the same time, the increasingly liberal welfare laws of the North provided a magnet which would pour federal money into the coffers of newly-Democratic big cities like Philadelphia. The Democrats fostered black migration because it made political sense to increase the roles of those most likely to vote Democratic. As the migration increased to floodtide, however, during the late '50s, the very migration which the Democratic party fostered was proving to be the undoing of the New Deal coalition in big cities like Philadelphia because it was putting inordinate pressure on the urban ethnic neighborhoods. During the '50s, the parishes of North Philadelphia bore the brunt of migratory pressure as one by one the blocks went black and the whites moved to either the suburbs or the suburb-like northeast section of the city.

Migration alone would have caused problems, but black migration brought with it serious ancillary problems as well, the most serious of which was the tenuous condition of the black family. Nicholas Lemann, in his study of migration from Mississippi to Chicago, points up the same dynamic that would cause problems in Philadelphia. The sharecroppers were the proletariat of the South, and they brought their not inconsiderable family problems with them when they came north, problems which were exacerbated by the overcrowding and lack of social control in the northern ghettoes. Lemann sees extraordinary similarities between the sharecropper culture of the South and the ghetto culture of the North:

It is clear that whatever the cause of its differentness, black share-cropper society on the eve of the introduction of the mechanical cotton picker was the equivalent of big-city ghetto society today in many ways. It was the national center of illegitimate childbearing and of the female-headed family. It had the worst public education system in the country, the one whose students were most likely to leave school before finishing and most likely to be illiterate even if they did finish. It had an extremely high rate of violent crime: in 1933, the six states with the highest murder rates were all in the South, and most of the murders were black-on-black. Sexually transmitted disease and substance abuse were nationally known as special problems of the black rural South; home-brew whiskey was much more physically perilous than crack cocaine is today, if less addictive, and David Cohn reported that blacks were using cocaine in the towns of the Delta before World War II.

Lemann argues convincingly that the major white fear in the South was fear of the Negro's unbridled sexuality. Segregation was the South's way of insuring that no black male would impregnate a white female. Whites in the north viewed the newly-arrived Negroes in virtually the same terms. The major factor blocking their assimilation was the disorder of black family life, and the fact that blacks were perceived as sexually uninhibited by whites. Dennis Clark, who worked on the Catholic Interracial council during the '50s, faced the attitude almost constantly in his attempts to defuse violent confrontations between blacks and ethnic whites in Philadelphia's changing neighborhoods. Along with the threat which black migration posed to housing, which was the biggest financial investment in most whites' lives, there was the fear of sexual aggression. The whites Clark came in contact with didn't want "niggers riding on the bus with my daughter."

The expanded liberal government might have contributed to a solution to the problem of black family pathology if it had been able to deal with the problem honestly. But this would have meant ignoring one of the constitutive elements of liberalism itself, namely its desire for sexual liberation. As the liberal government expanded, so did its constituents' desire for sexual liberation and the two in combination proved to be a deadly blow for the black family. At the same time that the liberal bureaucracy was casting about for solutions for the problem of black poverty, the liberal intelligentsia—people like Jack Kerouac, Paul Tillich, and Norman Mailer—looked to the Negro as a paradigm of sexual liberation. These two trends would converge and reach their culmination in the mid-'60s when the War on Poverty would become a front for the distribution of government-funded contraception.

Krol arrived in Philadelphia during the time when these forces were making an indelible mark on the life of cities throughout the nation. During this period, according to Lemann:

> The fabric of city life in the United States changed forever. Some of the bitterness of race relations leached into city politics. The ideal of high-quality universal public education began to disappear. Street crime became an obsessive concern for the first time in decades. The beginning of the modern rise of conservatism coincides exactly with the country's beginning to realize the true magnitude and consequences of the black migration, and the government's response to the migration provided the conservative movement with many of its issues. The idea that government programs don't work, and can't work, comes out of the Great Society, and particularly the war on poverty; all through his political career, one of Ronald Reagan's favorite sayings was, "in the 1960s we fought a war on poverty, and poverty won."

In Philadelphia, the Catholics arrived at their place in the political sun side by side with the Negroes from the South as part of the New Deal coalition. They arrived as liberals, as liberals were defined at that time, and found themselves increasingly uncomfortable as the terms of the agreement got changed to their disadvantage. As the first Irish Catholic mayor of the city, Mayor James H. J. Tate had to deal with the increasing tensions between blacks and whites, oftentimes in his own North Philadelphia neighborhood. Under the Clark/Dilworth and Tate administrations many blacks moved into high government posts previously unavailable to them. Yet the liberals proved powerless to address the problems racial migration were causing. At the same time that family life was becoming an imperative for successful integration into the city, the liberal regime was deliberately muzzling any institution which fostered the traditional rhetoric associated with sexual restraint, the *sine qua non* of successful family life. Prayer was no longer permitted in the schools, but pornography was permitted in the mails. Given an increasingly narrow philosophical and moral space within which to work, the liberals turned to poverty programs, which because they had to function in the same moral vacuum, more often than not just exacerbated the problems they purported to solve. Meanwhile, the white Catholic ethnics, most often Irish, who lived in the neighborhoods abutting the ghetto got to feel the brunt of family pathology first hand in the form of increasing crime and juvenile delinquency. The Irish found themselves tied to an alliance that was increasingly construed to their disadvantage. The spread of blacks beyond their neighborhoods need not have been the traumatic event that it was. However, that spread was exacerbated by liberal policies which made its bad aspects worse. As a result the New Deal alliance was just beginning to fall apart during the Tate administration when Krol took office. "Blacks," according to Dennis Clark

> were attempting to penetrate beyond their ghetto areas, and intermittent neighborhood disorders accompanied housing changes. Black rioting and militancy in the ghetto produced bitter confrontations with the police, a portion of the municipal service still strongly Irish in personnel and spirit. As the reform glow faded from the Democratic machine, racial polarization increased. Many white neighborhoods where the Irish had lived changed their populations in a few years and became totally black. Portraits of John and Robert Kennedy might appear beside that of Martin Luther King in ghetto windows, but the sneering racism of hard hat Irish blue collar workers left little room for inter-ethnic sentimentality in the age of the Black Panthers.

The consequences of these policies have proven to be a disaster from which the city of Philadelphia has yet to recover. During the almost three decades of Krol's tenure as archbishop the population of Philadelphia declined steadily. In 1960 Philadelphia had a population of 2,003,00, by 1970 that figure had dropped to 1,950,000, by 1980, the population had dropped to 1,688,000, and in 1990, three years after Krol retired and the last year figures are available, the figure stood at 1,586,000. The loss of almost half a million people is dramatic enough testimony to the failure of the program of the reform Democrats, but the figures tell only half the story. The flight out of the cities was mostly white, the migration into the city during the '50s and '60s was mostly black. Those who left were for the most part wage earners and tax payers, those who arrived to take their place lived overwhelmingly off of the largesse of government. What had been a Republican city, a city which had actually turned down a grant for federal housing in the '40s because accepting it smacked of "socialism," became a Democratic city at a time when the Democrats across the country were steadily broadening the role government played in people's lives and steadily redefining moral controls out of those very same government programs. As a result, Philadelphia was caught in an increasingly common vicious circle. As the tax base of the city shrank, the city increased taxes to pay for its ever-increasing menu of public services. As taxes increased, however, more people and, more importantly, more businesses left the city, necessitating more tax increases levied on an ever-decreasing number of people and businesses remaining to pay them. Beyond that, the liberal retreat from moral values along with the enabling agencies they established in place of intermediary structures like the Church, created an atmosphere in which crime throve. As crime increased, the city found itself increasingly unable to provide its citizens with the protection they needed to do business, further increasing the hemorrhage of jobs and wage earners from the city into the surrounding suburbs.

In a situation like this something had to give. What gave was the city itself. Throughout the period of Democratic hegemony, decay continued to spread in its dreary nonspectacular way. Graffiti spread across public space like a tetter on the skin indicating pathology inside. Black migration reached its culmination in the '80s with two related events. Wilson Goode, child of the migration from the South, became mayor. He will most probably be remembered for two things, both of which could serve as the culminating event of the decline of Philadelphia in the postwar period. First, Goode presided over the city as the city went broke, and second, Goode ordered a bomb dropped on a fanatical black religious sect in southwest Philadelphia, thereby touching off the most devastating fire in the city's history.

No one could have seen this as the culmination of the policies of the reform Democrats in 1951—or in 1961 for that matter—but both came about inexorably as liberalism followed its trajectory from being the party of the working class to the party of the sexually liberated. It was a trajectory which was the composite in many ways of the lives of the men who brought about the changes. Joseph S. Clark began his political career as a reform Democrat and founder of the ADA; he ended his political career as an increasingly strident pleader for Planned Parenthood and government-funded contraceptives. The middle term in Clark's transformation seems to have been his second wife, Noel Hall Clark, who was chairman of Planned Parenthood of Philadelphia for much of their marriage. Clark promised his wife that if he were re-elected to the United States Senate in 1962 that he would bring up the issue of contraception on the Senate floor, which he did in 1963 and continued to do until his exit from politics in 1968. Clark, whose cousin married Nelson Rockefeller in the '30s, divorced his first wife in 1934 to marry Noel Hall a year later. Clark's marriage to Noel Hall fell apart in 1967, after 31 years of marriage, when he divorced her to remarry Iris Cole Rickey, a woman 20 years his junior, in 1968.

Richardson Dilworth's life paralleled Clark's in many respects. Not only did they share the same patrician upbringing, in addition, Dilworth, who had known Clark from boyhood, was known as a ladies man during the '20s when he frequented parties on Long Island. Dilworth's first marriage also ended in divorce, in 1935, one year after Clark's first marriage ended.

Throughout the entire postwar period, the sexual subtext of liberalism gradually moved to center stage. The Republican opposition to Clark and Dilworth attempted to bring up the relationship between the personal and the political but more often than not the attempt was written off as *ad hominem* attacks at the time. During a televised debate held at the Academy of Music during the summer of 1949, Republican mayoral candidate Austin Meehan brought up Dilworth's divorce, as well as the fact of Dilworth and Clark's association with the ADA and Clark's wife's association with Planned Parenthood. but few if any saw the relevance of what he was saying to the office of mayor. Just to play it safe, though, Clark decided to keep play down his ties to Planned Parenthood and didn't mention contraception publicly until 1963, when it was no longer considered a political liability, largely because of the efforts of fellow cultural revolutionaries. Clark and Dilworth may well have been guilty of all the charges Sheriff Meehan levelled against them, but Dilworth, who was a handsome man of aristocratic bearing, had a stage presence which outweighed Meehan's, an important factor in the newly-dawning age of media politics. Beyond that, Dilworth stood for reform, and the city needed reform, even if it eventually got more than it bargained for. As a result, the reform team was elected bringing with it 17 members of the Philadelphia branch of Americans for Democratic Action and a new philosophy of activist local government which would bring about its own dissolution.

That activism meant more money for public projects and more money for social programs, both of which are neither good nor bad, but the fact remains that the activism of the liberals increased in inverse proportion to their commitment to the moral law and social order of the sort that had traditionally characterized the mainline Protestant churches. In this regard, Clark and Dilworth were really not so much traitors to their class as products of their class, and the decline in commitment to sexual morality that characterized mainline Protestant churches throughout the period following both world wars. Beginning with contraception, the mainline Protestant Churches began a step by step retreat along the whole front of sexual morality. The Episcopal church to which both Clark and Dilworth belonged was the first in this regard to break ranks.

In their 1908 Lambeth Conference Encyclical letter, the Anglican Church expressed grave concern over the fact "that there is a widespread prevalence amongst our peoples of the practice of resorting to artificial means for the avoidance or prevention of childbearing." The assembled delegates appealed "to the members of our own Churches to exert the whole force of their Christian character in condemnation of them." Finally, the conference adopted resolution #41 which "earnestly calls upon all Christian people to discountenance the use of all artificial means of restriction as demoralizing to character and hostile to national welfare."

By 1930, the Anglicans had evidently undergone a change of heart on the matter. At the Lambeth conference of that year, the Anglicans decided that artificial means of restricting births were no longer "demoralizing to character and hostile to national welfare." In fact, they now claimed in resolution #15, that "where there is a clearly felt moral obligation to limit or avoid parenthood," the couple could choose whatever method it desired; even artificial methods could be used "provided that this is done in the light of the same Christian principles." Then as if to cover all bases, the conference went on to express "its strong condemnation of the use of any methods of contraception-birth control from motives of selfishness, luxury, or mere convenience."

By 1958, the Anglicans were claiming that contraception was "a right and an important fact in Christian family life," provided of course that "such ways are mutually acceptable to husband and wife in Christian conscience and secure from the corruptions of sensuality and selfishness."

By the 1960s, the mainline Protestant churches had reached the conclusion that not using contraception was immoral. In late 1962, Richard M. Fagley, Executive Secretary of the Commission of Churches on International Affairs in New York City, described what he saw as "the emerging Protestant consensus regarding the concept of responsible parenthood within the doctrine of marriage." According to this consensus, "motives, rather than means form the primary moral issue." The couple can use whatever method it chooses as long as the motive is not selfishness, etc, etc. Fagley gives no indication of how to assess motives in his presentation. He does claim, however, that the consensus found "no inherent distinction between periodic continence or the use of contraceptives." He mentions the story of Onan, "the one biblical mention of an act with contraceptive intent," but finds the story ultimately "rather ambiguous." His reading of the history of the Protestant reformers on the issue takes a similar tack. They "did not reexamine the generally profertility teaching on parenthood" most probably because of "the underpopulated state of northwestern Europe at the time." As it that weren't reason enough to retard progressive views on contraception, "the emergence of the new Protestant consensus was long delayed by the expansion of Europe through the Industrial Revolution and immigration to the Americas and later by Puritanism and Victorian prudery. Its growth has been primarily a development of this century."

If all this sounds like special pleading, it might be helpful to elucidate the context of the document. Fagley is writing to Frank Notestein, who at the time was head of the Population Council, a tax-exempt foundation created by John D. Rockefeller, 3rd in 1952, when he became disenchanted with the reticence of his brothers in funding controversial issues like sexuality and population control. "Its goal" according to the Population Council's own description of itself, "has been to bring about a reduction in the number of births that occur in the world." The fact that the Rockefeller Foundation had funded Kinsey's sex surveys through out the '40s and early '50s give some indication of what JDR, 3rd construed as reticence. JDR, 3rd's father had subsidized Margaret Sanger and her Birth Control League as well, prompting one critic to say that the Rockefellers were to abortion and contraception in America what the Krupp family was to munitions in Germany. After converting to the religion of population control at the age of 28 and after doing some research on the topic, JDR, 3rd became convinced that population control was the source of all of the world's problems. John D. Rockefeller, 3rd, according to his biographers,

> never could explain exactly why he had developed such a strong interest in the population field long before it came into vogue or was generally recognized as an area of concern. He had seen the negative effects of too much population growth in his visit to China in 1929. He had chosen population as the subject for a reading course he took at Princeton, where he studied the works of Malthus and others. He had served on the board of an organization his father had created, the Bureau of Social Hygiene, which had supported a number of projects related to the population field, including aid to the clinics of the intrepid birth control pioneer Margaret Sanger.

> In fact ,it was Junior's decision to terminate the Bureau that led his oldest son to volunteer to make the population field a major focus of his interest and to do what he could to carry on the work. In a letter to his father in 1934, he expressed concern that the support of population studies and projects would not be picked up by any of the other Rockefeller organizations, including the foundation, because of "the element of propaganda and controversy which so often is attached to endeavors in birth control." JDR wrote: "I have come pretty definitely to the conclusion that [birth control] is the field in which I will be interested,

for the present at least, to concentrate my own giving, as I feel it is so fundamental and underlying" (Harr and Johnson, p. 24).

To state the case more precisely, population control including contraception and abortion was the *conditio sine qua non* of solving problems like hunger and development in the Third World. JDR, 3rd spent much of the late 1940s and early '50s travelling around the Far East at the behest of John Foster Dulles, so much so that his travels earned him the name Mr. Asia at the *New Yorker*. His travels there only reconfirmed what he had concluded in his late twenties as a student at Princeton. Population was the problem.

The Population Council considered the development of the IUD as one of its crowning achievements. Later to be driven off the market in the United States as a result of product liability lawsuits, the IUD, even more so than Pill, which the Pop Council also had a hand in developing, was Rockefeller's equivalent of the Holy Grail and the philosopher's stone all in one little piece of coiled plastic. Unlike the Pill, the IUD could be inserted and forgotten—unless, of course, it caused internal hemorrhaging and severe abdominal pain, which it oftentimes did. Because the element of choice was not played out on a daily basis as it was with pill, the IUD was the favored vehicle for population control for the people at the Population Council. If population was disease, then the IUD was the cure. While in Taiwan visiting a small provincial town where the Population Council was experimenting with the IUD, JDR, 3rd looked at the mass of people there and said, 'Well, that's the problem, isn't it?' Then he turned and headed off for his next meeting" (Horowitz and Collier, p. 291).

Fagley sent the above-cited paper to Notestein with a note adding that "any criticism or counsel would be welcome." The paper, as may be surmised from its content, was not really intended for Protestants; it was intended to explain Protestants to outsiders, in this particular instance Catholics. Fagley sent his paper to Notestein for approval because he was intending to present it at a conference to be held at the University of Notre Dame on population which was sponsored by a grant from the Population Council. As a final point in describing the Protestant Consensus in favor of contraception, Fagley added that "in the Protestant consensus abortion is strongly condemned as a method of family limitation, since it involves the destruction of human life." Time would show the Protestant Consensus flexible on this issue as well, primarily as a result of Rockefeller money going to the Methodist-sponsored Religious Coalition on Abortion Rights. But Notestein raised no objection at the time, probably because he felt the opposition to abortion would sit well with the Catholics convening at Notre Dame.

Rockefeller's interest in the Catholic Church awakened in the early '60s, primarily because, as a result of the defection of the mainline Protestants on sexual issues, Catholics were the main obstacle to the policies Rockefeller wanted implemented. JDR, 3rd was also intrigued by the news he was hearing about the impending Vatican Council. During the early '60s it had become virtually a foregone conclusion among liberal Catholics that the Church would change its teaching on birth control. Rockefeller's biographers, Harr and Johnson, mention that "the papacy of John XXIII, who was elevated in 1958, seemed to promise a liberalizing of Roman Catholic doctrine" on precisely this issue.

But the attraction was mutual. At the same time Rockefeller was looking for an opening in the Catholic Church's opposition to the modern world in the sexual arena, the Catholics were looking for more acceptance from the Protestant consensus, and the people who ran the foundations. Rene Wormser complained that Catholics were frozen out of social science research as a result of the conscious policy of the foundations. As of 1957, Wormser claims,

> there are 30 million Catholics in this country, who maintain scores of universities and colleges. Their institutions do not figure among the favored of the foundation complex, nor are academicians connected with them likely to receive research grants from the complex. Perhaps there is a good reason for this discrimination. If so, I cannot guess what it might be. True, Catholic institutions were included among the institutional donees to which The Ford Foundation recently donated a huge aggregate of money, a step which deserved the most enthusiastic approval of the general public. But when it comes to special, individual grants, to find a Catholic institution as a donee is a rarity indeed (Wormser, p. 235).

For some time during the late '50s, the Rev. Theodore M. Hesburgh, C.S.C., president of the University of Notre Dame, had been concerned about this lack of support from the foundations. Hesburgh, according to one source, went to the foundations, who told him that to qualify for money he would have to remove certain faculty members. Hesburgh proved amenable to the suggestion and as a result not only started to get grant money but also was appointed a trustee of the Rockefeller Foundation in 1961. He would later become its chairman during the years when Rockefeller money was heavily involved in abortion advocacy, an advocacy which culminated in the overturning of the country's abortion laws in 1973.

It was clear that in the early '60s both the Catholics and John D. Rockefeller, 3rd felt that they had something to gain by collaborating. What the Catholics wanted is obvious. They wanted money. They wanted an *entre* to the interlocking world of foundation respectability, where grantsmanship was in many respects an all or nothing proposition. Because of their interlocking nature, once you got money from one foundation you were in a position to get money from all of them. Beyond that, grants were an *entre* to the newly-burgeoning federal aid to education as well as an indication that Catholics had achieved a certain level of intellectual respectability, which the Catholic universities like Notre Dame evidently felt they lacked.

What the foundations wanted was just as specific: they wanted the Church to abandon her opposition to contraception. The history of the first Notre Dame conference on population goes a long way toward indicating what it is the foundations, specifically JDR, 3rd's Population Council wanted from amenable Catholics like the people at Notre Dame. On October 10, 1962, one day before the opening of the Second Vatican Council, the Population Council, "following discussions among leading Catholic authorities, representatives of Planned Parenthood, and the officers of the Population Council" granted $5,000 to the University of Notre Dame to host a "two-day meeting in December which would bring together representatives of different religious and other points of view to discuss problems of population growth, with particular interest in exploring areas of possible convergences in approaching these problems."

The conference would actually not take place until early 1963, but the groundwork preparing for it took place throughout the summer of 1962. The initial impetus for the conference came not from Hesburgh but from a CBS documentary "Birth Control and the Law," which aired on May 10, 1962. One of the participants was the Rev. John A. O'Brien, C.S.C., a Notre Dame theologian who had caught the eye of the pro-contraceptive crowd when an article of his entitled "Let's Take Birth Control Out of Politics" had appeared in the November 10, 1961 issue of *Look* magazine. The CBS documentary was widely denounced in the Catholic press as pro-contraceptive propaganda. Rev. John B. Sheehan criticized Moderator Eric Severeid's fawning attitude toward Planned Parenthood and called the documentary "an extended commercial for that organization."

The Rev. John C. Knott, family life director of the National Catholic Welfare Conference in Washington, claimed that "CBS gave evidence of having become a public relations medium for a particular philosophy of life with an oversimplified solution to human problems" and went on to wonder why CBS didn't allow Catholics equal time. Evidently he missed the contribution of Father O'Brien, or perhaps he didn't feel that Father O'Brien's suggestion that a group of Catholic and Protestant experts should get together to "try to iron out the problem" qualified as the Catholic position. Either way he was evidently not impressed with Father O'Brien's position.

Other people were, however. On July 6, 1962, Cass Canfield, Chairman of Planned Parenthood Foundation of America and a board member of the Population Council, wrote to Father O'Brien to tell him how he had been following his writings on birth control for a number of years and how impressed he had been with what O'Brien had to say on the recent CBS telecast "Birth Control and the Law." In the interest of fostering "dialogue" in this area among religious groups, Canfield invited O'Brien to take part in a "small discussion—primarily of Catholic, Protestant and Jewish clergymen" at a New York hotel on the morning of October 25 "to discuss fertility regulation in the context of responsible parenthood and population growth." In closing, Canfield added a few "very general questions" which might be discussed at the meeting, such as "what is the general thinking from various viewpoints on the 'population problem'" and "what are the opportunities—among religious groups themselves, and between religious groups and the Planned Parenthood Federation—for cooperative thought and action on these vital matters."

On July 24, Canfield received a response, not from Father O'Brien, but from George Shuster, personal assistant to Father Hesburgh at Notre Dame, informing him that O'Brien's attendance at the Planned Parenthood conference was out of the question. "It is impossible, as matters stand now," Shuster wrote

> for Catholic priests and laymen who follow directives (and this is the kind you doubtless want) to attend a meeting sponsored by Planned Parenthood. The time is not yet ripe for that. Those invited would have to secure permission from the New York Chancery Office to attend, and there would seem no possibility that the answer would be affirmative.

Shuster's objections, however, revolved more around form than substance. Instead of the New York meeting, Shuster proposed holding virtually the same venue at Notre Dame, implying that the name Notre Dame would some how purge the meeting of disagreeable associations as well as evade the watchful eye of Cardinal Spellman:

"This arrangement," according to Shuster,

> would enable prominent Catholics to attend without difficulty, for any problem involving participation in a meeting sponsored by Planned Parenthood would have been removed. The University has arranged and is currently doing so in a series of meetings in various fields at which important problems are being discussed on a basis of parity between Catholics and others.

In a letter to JDR 3rd on July 31, Canfield can hardly contain himself, calling Shuster's response "the answer to a maiden's prayer." An opening of some significance in influencing the Church's sexual morality had finally been found with the Catholics, the last roadblock to universal acceptance of contraception. During the '50s the Population Council had had contact with a Jesuit from Baltimore by the name of William J. Gibbons, who requested funding for a "New York Professional Sodality" from the Population Council which would attempt to study the problem of overpopulation as essentially a moral problem. The Population Council was underwhelmed by the proposal. Frederic

Osborn in a memo to Dudley Kirk opined that "it is hard to see how there could be much serious exchange of ideas on such premises," especially since Father Gibbons was proposing that each meeting start with a pledge "to respect the right of each parent to participate in the creation of life." If this was what the Catholics had in mind then the Population Council wasn't interested. What Shuster was proposing at Notre Dame, however, was a whole new ball game, and Canfield urged JDR, 3rd to fund it claiming that it "should serve a very useful purpose."

Frank Notestein, who was in on the discussion, seemed to concur with Canfield and listed a number of potential positive outcomes as resulting from it. To begin with the Population Council and the pro-contraception Protestants who were invited could exert pressure

> of the supportive sort on the liberal Catholics attending, to strengthen in the Church those elements which recognize a) the need for tolerance of non-Catholic views, b) the desirability for restraint on the part of Catholics seeking legal restrictions that prevent non-Catholics from following their own moral views, and c) the need for greater attention to parental responsibility in Catholic teaching.

Beyond that, the conference would provide

> an opportunity for the Catholics to educate non-Catholics in their position, particularly with a view to letting us see, in sophisticated form, the almost immutable constraints faced by the Church in certain parts of its position and the operations which are amenable to change.

Notestein felt that it was unrealistic to feel that a conference of this sort could get the church to change its teaching on birth control but it could help "to strengthen that element in the Church with which we have many common aspirations and a minimum of differences." With this in mind, "it would be pointless to publish the results of the conference because that would incur the wrath of episcopal authorities and harden the positions into two immutable fronts. The only influence the pro-contraceptive party can have is on those influential Catholics who attend the meeting." With this in mind, Notestein adds, "it is also important, on these premises, that we select for attendance not representative Catholics but Catholics who represent the position nearest our own. This is the group whose influence we would be endeavoring to enlarge." The Population Council would fund the Notre Dame meeting, in other words, on the condition that only "liberal" Catholics, i.e., those willing to work for a change in the Church's position on birth control, be invited. Notestein even suggests "leaving out people such as Father Zimmerman," evidently referring to the Rev. Anthony Zimmerman, S.V.D. a noted opponent of population control. In another letter to JDR, 3rd on August 2, Notestein reiterated his opposition to inviting "representative Catholics." The only people to be invited were Catholics "who represent the position nearest our own."

"Personally," Notestein added,

> I would like to reemphasize my opinion that an endeavor be made to have this group include only the liberal-minded Catholics. We will get simply nowhere if right-wing groups are involved. These conversations should be between the people on both sides who have minimum differences of opinion.

Notestein obviously feels that Father Hesburgh is precisely one of their kind of Catholic and nominates him as chairman of the conference in place of JDR, 3rd, whose connection with contraception and population control might prove too controversial. "My guess is that he," Notestein wrote referring to Hesburgh, "would be effective in blocking long-winded arguments in theology, which are useless once the positions are understood. No one is going to make converts at the theological level."

JDR, 3rd was evidently persuaded by Notestein's arguments. In a letter to Cass Canfield on August 6, JDR, 3rd characterized Shuster's proposal as "an encouraging next step in an important and sensitive area." He is also persuaded by Notestein's suggestion "that the individuals who might attend be selected from those who have liberal views; otherwise it would be difficult for the meetings to be very constructive."

By early August, the Notre Dame Conference was pretty much a done deal, at least in the higher echelons of the Population Council. Notre Dame, for its part, followed directives from the Population Council in a manner that can only be described as supine, a peculiar policy to be followed by a man like

Hesburgh, who five years later in his Land o' Lakes statement would claim that a "Catholic university must have true autonomy and academic freedom in face of authority of whatever kind, lay or clerical, external to the academic community itself."

By September of 1962, the Population Council was dictating not only who was to be invited but what books were to be displayed and discussed ("A Citizen's Perspective on Population" by J. D. Rockefeller and "Does Overpopulation Mean Poverty," by Joseph Jones) as well as the questions to be asked and, without too much stretching of the imagination, the conclusions they were to arrive at as well. Hesburgh went on to make a name for himself as a defender of academic freedom, receiving the AAUP's Meicklejohn award in the '70s. His and Notre Dame's supine behavior *vis a vis* Rockefeller money gives some indication that academic freedom was a one way street. It was used, as he did in the Land o' Lakes statement in 1967, to protect Catholic students from the interference of the Catholic Church. When it came to the stipulations the Population Council put on the 1962 conference at Notre Dame, it was not used at all.

"Conferees," Canfield writes in his memo "Some random suggestions about the Notre Dame conference," "should discuss the question of whether the adherents of any faith have a right to try and influence legislation, except as individuals expressing their own views." It didn't take a genius to figure out the right answer to a question phrased in that tendentious manner.

The fact of the matter is that at this point Rockefeller did not feel he could get the Church to change its teaching on contraception—at a later date he would be of another opinion on the matter. (Three years later, Hesburgh arranged an audience between Rockefeller and Pope Paul VI, at which Rockefeller offered to write the encyclical which eventually bore the name *Humanae Vitae*.) He did feel though that the Population Council might persuade liberal Catholics to persuade their less enlightened co-religionists that they as Catholics had no business trying to influence legislation concerning contraception in the United States. Planned Parenthood had already targeted the Connecticut contraception statute for overturning, as a prelude, Leo Pfeffer would say, for state-subsidized contraception aimed at primarily Negro welfare recipients. The main obstacle in the implementation of this design was the opposition of the Catholic Church.

Canfield kept hammering home the point that when it came to contraception, Catholics—good Catholics, according to the criteria of the Population Council—were supposed to keep their opinions to themselves. This was the purpose of the conference. The conferees were to understand that if "a religious group, as such, should try and influence legislation, [that] would bring up the question of tolerance." The reason, according to Canfield, the Population Council was putting up the money was in the "hope that the liberal views of certain Catholics will gain greater currency within the Church and that practical considerations in connection with limiting population (as well as biological research, partly or wholly sponsored by Catholics) will lead them to become less and less restrictive as to methods." To which view, neither Hesburgh nor Shuster expressed any objection.

Fred Jaffe, associate director of information and education at Planned Parenthood, took part in the memo dialogue and came to pretty much the same conclusions. The conference should "focus on objectives rather than methods." This would pare the differences down to size and also, although Jaffe doesn't state this explicitly, make the Church look unreasonable by its insistence that certain methods were illicit. The Population Council, on the other hand, could give the impression of being open to them all. Jaffe concluded by submitting his list of acceptable Catholics. These would include the already mentioned Father Gibbons, SJ., Father Joseph Gremillion of the National Catholic Welfare Conference, Father Hesburgh, and Father Walter Imbiorski of the Cana Conference in Chicago, later to become the author of a notorious sex ed program, and later still to leave the priesthood and to be denied a Catholic burial by the Archdiocese of Chicago.

On October 29, Shuster again wrote to Canfield discussing publicity and indicating that he was involved in not a little duplicity in this regard. He requests that no advance publicity be given to the conference lest the wrong people get wind of it, including perhaps the local bishop, but in the same letter he indicates that in the hope of "indirect benefits" he has invited "one or two editors of key Catholic periodicals." This echoes pretty much what Shuster said to Canfield in August when he claimed that "we are walking upon relatively difficult terrain and a measure of caution, in the hope of better things to follow is indicated." Shuster was not so much interested in keeping the symposium secret as he was in managing the way the information on it came out. News of the symposium would only be harmful if the wrong people showed up beforehand. Notestein in a note after the conference hopes that "there were no unfortunate leaks so far as publicity is concerned," and Shuster assures him that "there were no leaks, thank heavens."

"Hope of better things to follow" from Shuster and Hesburgh's point of view meant more money from more foundations for more conferences undermining the Church's position on contraception. On June 5, 1963, Shuster submitted a proposal asking for funding for virtually the same conference to the Ford Foundation. The conference was "to achieve a consensus which would first serve as a firm and clear basis for dialogue, and second point out areas for future study and discussion," which is pretty much what the first one had done. However, this time Shuster sweetens the pot by adding that "the objective is to prepare a final statement and distribute it widely." The statement would involve, it was understood, Catholic academe calling for a change in the Church's teaching, something that would most probably not change the teaching but something which would prove embarrassing to the Church nonetheless, especially if it were promoted by the media. "I am not going to stress further the obvious importance of this effort," Shuster wrote to Oscar Harkavy, head of the Ford Foundation. "The interest of *Cardinal Meyer* [Shuster's emphasis]— which is the only part of this letter which is at present confidential—suffices to indicate that these deliberations may find an echo far beyond the confines of the United States."

The Rockefeller crowd, who got the proposal through Harkavy, who asked their advice as to whether he should fund it or not, seemed less than enthused by the prospect of another conference at Notre Dame, much less a whole series of conferences. The boys at the Population Council had gone to bed with Notre Dame, and in the morning decided that they didn't respect her anymore. The Ford Foundation would eventually go on to sponsor a whole series of conferences which denounced in increasingly strident terms the Church's position on birth control. But the contempt in which the Pop Council held Notre Dame is evident in the tone of their memos. Dudley Kirk, after suggesting that they might "sponsor this and play it further by ear" goes on to wonder "whether to feel flattered or otherwise at being the only heretic proposed for inclusion in the first conference." Which prompts Marshall C. Balfour to add, "Hooray for the heretic: the cards are surely stacked against him! That is, unless, the way is being prepared for Pope Paul to change the rules of the game."

The wing of the Catholic Church whose conferences were sponsored by Rockefeller money were clearly planning for such an eventuality. Since most of the players were both old and ostensibly celibate, there is no reason to believe that they were hoping to benefit directly from such a change. But a change in the Church's teaching would mean that they as Catholic academics would be acceptable to the foundation powerbrokers and an acceptable member of the Protestant consensus, as well. They would be considered Americans in full standing, which has always been the aspiration of a certain kind of Catholic in this country. Effecting a change in the Church's teaching on contraception would show furthermore that they had considerable clout among their co-religionists. If they could show that they had delivered the vote on contraception, they might be valuable for wringing other concessions from the Church further down the line. Perhaps this is why people like Shuster and Hesburgh pursued the idea of the contraception conferences with such avidity throughout the mid-60s.

Their dedication in pursuing foundation money and the foundations' interest in changing the teaching of the Church on contraception shows just how outgunned the bishops were in opposing the forces arrayed against them. First of all, the bishops were unaware of what was taking place behind their backs. Beyond that, in addition to running their dioceses and the educational establishments in them, the bishops—almost at the very moment the negotiations between Notre Dame and the Population Council were being concluded—were being drawn into what would be a three-year commitment to the Vatican Council. In this regard Archbishop Krol was doubly handicapped.

Not only was he saddled with the tasks of a normal bishop, he was now ordinary of one of the biggest dioceses in the United States, and in terms of population in the world. Less than two years after assuming the reins as ordinary of Philadelphia, he would be called away to Rome to be one of the chief administrators of the Second Vatican Council while still in the process of learning the ropes in Philadelphia. From just about any way of looking at it, Krol was faced with a challenge that would have taxed three men in better times.

During the period beginning April 20, 1961, and ending March 1, 1966, Krol would spend a total of 372 days in Rome working on the Council. Krol began the autumn of 1962 faced with several major tasks all at once. While learning the ropes as ordinary of one of largest dioceses in the United States, he was also flying back and forth to Rome, at first as member of the preparatory commission and then as undersecretary for the Council itself, a task which would not end until four years into his tenure as archbishop. At the same time, he was left to deal with the outbreak of the Cultural Revolution which would sweep through virtually every institution in the West during the '60s, and the upheaval in the Church which ensued when the Cultural Revolution entered it following the Council. When the Church opened its windows, the Cultural Revolution blew in. At the same time, the whole parish structure of the Archdiocese of Philadelphia was suffering from the blows inflicted on it by the liberal-managed racial migration from the South. It was not only a series of tasks that any mortal would have found daunting. It was also a series of events from which any other institution would have suffered a mortal blow. It is quite simply a miracle that the Church survived any one of them. Even stranger to ponder was the fact that God chose a former manager of the meat department at Kroger's to guide the Church in Philadelphia through this period of its history. It was proof, once again to the ordinary of Philadelphia, that God not only existed, but that he had a sense of humor as well.

III
The Council Begins

The problem of procedure was very real. After all, a total of 2,900 fathers—bishops, auxiliary bishops, abbots and superiors of orders—were entitled to take part.

Joseph Cardinal Ratzinger

Theological Highlights of Vatican II

T oward the end of the summer of 1962, the Rev. Anthony Massamini arrived back in Rome after a summer of studying German at the Goethe Institute in Cochel am See in Bavaria. Father Massamini was a native of Philadelphia, ordained in 1959, and a student at the Gregorian in their program of ascetical or spiritual theology. He would go on to become the first professor of Italian extraction at Philadelphia's St. Charles Borromeo Seminary, but now he was in demand for other reasons. The Second Vatican Council was about to arrive in Rome within a matter of weeks, and in order to facilitate the exchange of ideas among the almost three thousand prelates planning to attend, the Church was dragooning all of its available manpower into service to help bring off an undertaking that the world's oldest institution had enacted roughly once a century during the past 20 centuries of her existence. It would prove to be quite an experience.

But then again Rome had already proven to be quite an experience for Father Massamini. Born in 1928, coming from Philadelphia's Italian ghetto, of immigrant stock, Father Massamini had been exposed to a religion that referred to itself as Catholic or universal but was in many respects radically discontinuous within its various phases, as Massamini came to learn them, so discontinuous in effect that 30 years after the Council, when Massamini was in his sixties, he would refer to the different phases of his life as different "gods."

"I grew up in South Philly," Massamini recounted from a point later in his life when he was neither functioning as a priest nor a practicing Catholic, although still a contributor on occasion to the *National Catholic Reporter*, "in an Italian neighborhood, and I had a family Italian god, a public school Italian god. It was a nice god. I went to Church. I didn't buy what the priests said, because the priests were Irish, and the Italians and the Irish priests were having problems with each other. That's why I was in public school. The few Irish kids I knew, were in Catholic school, and the Italian kids, which were the majority, were in public school because they didn't get along.

"When I went to the seminary, I met the Irish god. That's a whole different God—the strict keep-your-head-down, keep-your-hands-crossed, do-what-you're-told-you're-unworthy kind of a god. And after that I met the Italian god. And this was a whole different god. People running around Church, talking, mothers nursing their babies at the altar, and all the stuff which was so shocking till I realized: this is the way it was supposed to be. And then in my seminary studies, I met the apologetic, theological god. And of course the god of history, and the god of pre-Vatican II theology. And then in my doctoral studies, I met the psychological god. You know, the unconscious god, the god of the unconscious. And then I met the Evolutionary god. And my whole soul was expanding so tremendously, It was the most beautiful thing."

Thirty years after the Council, Cardinal Krol was fond of saying that if the Church hadn't convoked the Vatican Council, the Church would have broken into four warring factions, along the line of division among the Jews. If Tony Massamini is any indication of the divisions that were lurking just beneath the seemingly placid surface of Church life, Krol underestimated the divisions by at least half. Faced with what seemed like one radical discontinuity after another, Massamini eventually settled on an evolutionary "god" which incorporated all that had gone before it into an all-encompassing, if somewhat vague, synthesis. By the time Massamini was in his mid-sixties, he lived in a suburban-looking housing tract in Paradise, a small Amish town east of Lancaster, Pennsylvania and ran an organization known as the Institute of Wisdom Spirituality, which he described as "fine-tuning Matthew Fox." Fox was a Dominican who advocated pantheism, under the name of Panentheism and was expelled from his order during the early 1990s.

Massamini's evolutionary theology did not come solely as a result of extrapolating from his own experience of the disparate and discontinuous modes of Catholicism he imbibed while coming to his intellectual majority. It was also a direct result of what he was being taught at the Gregorian, one of the Church's own universities, in Rome in the early '60s. Massamini first met Archbishop Krol shortly after the latter had arrived to take over the archdiocese in 1961. Massamini had studied in Rome before being ordained, had returned to Philadelphia to teach at a diocesan high school just north of town, and then Krol called him down to the chancery office to discuss the possibility of further study for an advanced degree. Massamini was not thrilled with the prospect at the time because an advanced degree almost invariably meant a degree in canon law, and "being a lawyer was the last thing I wanted to be in my life, it wasn't even on the list." As a result, Massamini "was really concerned when he called me up."

During their interview Krol expressed concern about a drop in Massamini's grades during his third year in Rome. Massamini remembers a sense of dealing with two distinct people at the time and throughout his relationship with Archbishop Krol. John Krol the man was concerned about his health, but Archbishop Krol was concerned about his grades. After Massamini explained that the drop in grades came about because of time lost to his studies because of an appendicitis, Krol seemed reassured and urged Massamini to return to Rome even though the two of them had never really settled just what course of study Father Massamini was to pursue when he got there. And so beginning with the fall of '61 Father Massamini began to shop around. He did not want to study canon law because he did not want to be a lawyer, and he did not want to study moral theology because at the time, according to his view, moral theology was nothing but "baptized canon law," or "canon law with holy water sprinkled on it." In making up his mind about his course of study, Father Massamini also had in mind his year of pastoral experience in Philadelphia when no one seemed all that interested in intellectual approaches to God. When he arrived back in Rome in September of 1961 he told his professors that he had given all of his best dogmatic, theological sermons, but they didn't seem to have changed anyone. "That's because," one of his professors replied, "people's problems are not here (he pointed to his head) they're here (he pointed to his heart)." The explanation evidently resonated with Massamini's view of the world, so much so that he decided on the spot "That's what I wanna do" and signed up for a doctorate in ascetical or mystical theology.

It would prove to be spiritual theology in a highly qualified sense, qualified primarily by the thought of Sigmund Freud. During his time studying spiritual theology in Rome, Massamini imbibed deeply of the notion that spirituality was embedded in psychology. According to what he was being taught at the Gregorian at the time, the spiritual life was in effect a branch of depth psychology. In addition, he also learned that with regard to things psychological, the Church was hopelessly behind the times but trying as hard as it could to catch up. He remembers a quote from Bernard Lonergan, one of his teachers at the time, who used to say that "it's good the Church isn't a fire department because it always arrives on the scene late and out of breath."

"Spirituality in those days," Massamini recounts, "was heavily psychological. It was really a development and a maturing of the human personality in belief, in grace, in charity. We were studying depth psychology, about the unconscious, and this kind of stuff."

The Church, Massamini learned from Lonergan, was still trying to catch up to the twentieth century. When asked for specific thinkers from whom the Church might benefit, Massamini mentioned the name of Sigmund Freud without a moment's hesitation. In this he was being more forthright than his teachers who would give Freud as the unacknowledged content of their lectures, but without mentioning his name for fear of incurring the wrath of episcopal authority in Rome. Massamini found it often difficult to get his professors' notes for the same reason.

And so a sort of schizophrenia prevailed in the Church's universities on the eve of the Council. The mechanism of inquisition left over from the anti-Modernist crusade initiated by Pius X was still in place, but few if any people in authority had the heart to enforce it effectively because they were not convinced that the ideology of modernity was false. As a result young Father Massamini was exposed to an education in which his teachers believed and propagated things condemned by the Church. They did this not because they were part of some arcane conspiracy but because they felt that people like Sigmund Freud were in possession of the truth and because they felt the Church would benefit from making use of his insights. A dangerous dualism prevailed in the Church on the eve of the Council. Faith and reason were perilously out of sync. The people who should have forged those two elements into a Catholic synthesis, namely the professors at Catholic universities like the Gregorian, had developed the bad habit of nodding piously in the direction of faith and then with a sly wink to their priest students teaching that something the opposite of faith was the truth. As a result the people who were sent to Rome for study were confronted with a sort of dualism which had become virtually unbridgeable by the time the Council convened. Tony Massamini the priest would accept certain things on faith, especially when told to do so by episcopal authority; but Tony Massamini the thinker would accept what was tantamount to contradictions of those tenets of faith because he felt that science had shown them to be true, and not coincidentally because his teachers were telling him the same thing. It was Averroism all over again, and the Church had to admit in all candor that it had lost its intellectual class to the ideologies of modernity in spite of the oath and the crusade against it.

Freud wasn't the only modern in vogue at the Gregorian in the early '60s. In spite of the encyclical *Humani Generis*, Teilhard de Chardin, the French Jesuit paleontologist who would become one of the founding fathers of the New Age Movement, was also being taught in spite of an official *monitum* or warning against his teachings. Massamini remembers a Spanish theologian teaching evolutionary spirituality in Castilian-accented Latin. He also remembers being unable to obtain the professor's notes because the professor was afraid that if what he was teaching fell into the wrong hands he would end up fired, as had two Jesuits from the Biblicum across the street.

In the fall semester of 1960, the Archdiocese of Philadelphia had a student at the Biblicum too. His name was William Leahy. Leahy was a young priest who had just graduated from the North American College in Rome and had been ordained the same year as Tony Massamini. He remembers meeting Archbishop Krol in Rome shortly after Krol had been named ordinary of Philadelphia. Krol was in Rome working for the preparatory commission. Walking into a room of students from the Biblicum, he went up to Leahy and without introducing himself much less saying hello, asked him, "What's all this about mishmash?" Young Father Leahy was needless to say taken aback by the brash young bishop from Cleveland who spoke about the ancient rabbinical commentary on the Bible, or "Midrash" in such jocular terms. "At that time," Leahy recounted later, "in Biblical studies, Midrash was very important."

Leahy was very serious about his studies and such talk seemed strange from the man who was paying for them. Throughout the early period of the Council, Krol would blow into town for work on the preparatory commission and invite the priests of his archdiocese to dinner with him, during which time they would discuss "mish-mash" and whatever else was going on. From these discussions, Leahy got the impression that Krol was suspicious of Biblical studies. He does not, however, remember any resolution to the suspicions during this period or later. "We were all kind of on edge," Leahy said later of the dinner discussions. It was the same uneasiness conveyed by their professors. Priests like Leahy and Massamini were being taught things at the Greg and the Biblicum their bishops would have had to condemn had they known what was going on, and there seemed to be no way of building a bridge from one position to the other. At this point, it seemed doubtful that the Council was going to do this because, from the initial reports, the Council was supposed to involve little more than a rubber stamping of the commission reports. It is doubtful that Krol saw the Council in a different light himself. He was a friend of Cardinal Ottaviani, had spent time with him at his family's home in Trastevere and had visited his orphanages, the Oasi della Pace, as well. Krol was in many respects the quintessential American in this regard. He was interested in getting things done, and in effect had created a reputation for himself as someone who could do just that. Just what needed to be done, especially when it concerned something like the Council was not immediately apparent to him, nor something that overly concerned him. He was content to implement the mind of the Church. And if the Church proved to be of more than one mind on a matter, as would in fact be the case at the Council, he would construe his role as facilitating discussion rather than championing one position over the other.

As an indication of his growing reputation as a man who got things done and the clout at the Vatican that went along with it, Krol was in position to arrange audiences with the pope for the young priests of Philadelphia studying in Rome. Both Massamini and Leahy remember theirs vividly. In October of 1962, just before the beginning of the Council, Krol arrived in Rome and, as was his habit, took the Philadelphia priests there out to dinner. During the course of the dinner's conversation, Krol announced that he was going to see the pope and told them he would take them along. Massamini remembers the long trek through the part of the Vatican closed to tourists to get to the pope's private study as a prelude to meeting the famous Pope John XXIII himself, the one man who along with John F. Kennedy embodied the *Zeitgeist* of the early 1960s.

Massamini remembers the conversation as warm and cordial. The pope wanted to know what Massamini was studying, and then showed interest in him because of his Italian background, wanting to know which part of Italy his parents were from. Massamini remembers being awed by the meeting. That and the fact that he was studying spirituality, which was not considered particularly dangerous to the faith of those who studied it, kept the contradictions between what he was being taught and the teachings of the Church in abeyance.

The same cannot be said of the audience Krol arranged for Father Leahy. When Krol introduced Leahy as studying in the Biblicum, the pope stopped and in the course of what was supposed to be *pro forma* polite questions started to grill Leahy on what he was being taught at the Biblicum. "What are they teaching you over there," the Pope wanted to know. What are we going to say about the scriptures? Are they teaching you the right thing?"

Leahy was taken back by Pope John's vehemence.

"As far as I know, your holiness," he replied, "I'm being taught well."

But the pope was evidently not reassured. He was clearly upset about what was going on at the Biblicum and wanted to know how it was affecting this young impressionable priest from Philadelphia.

"Let's forget about the Old Testament," Pope John said pursuing a train of thought that had obviously been causing him concern for some time, "When it comes to the New Testament, what are we going to tell the pious women about the Virgin Birth, and about the star and the magi?"

Leahy was tongue-tied. He had come to the audience expecting to trade pleasantries with the pope and now he was put on the witness stand and cross-examined by a prosecutor who seemed skeptical of the entire Biblical critical enterprise. Finally, Leahy stammered out something to the effect that the religious message of the stories was intact and that all the details did was promote the person of Jesus as Savior. The pope seemed mollified. The cloud passed from his face and he became the cordial and jovial pope of pious legend once again.

"*Ah, va bene,*" he said. "*Va bene.*"

Leahy took the conclusion of their conversation as a sign of Pope John XXIII's openness to things new. Archbishop Krol, however, did not. Krol saw the little interlude as a warning against the dangers inherent in Biblical studies, proffered in Pope John's warm Mediterranean manner, but proffered nonetheless. The warning was something Leahy should take seriously. He should be on his guard against what was being taught at the Biblicum. "See?" Krol said after the audience, "even the pope is concerned about what is being taught at the Biblicum. Now you be careful."

Krol was ever the loyal Churchman in the matter of Biblical studies as in everything else, but his was a loyalty of institutions more than one of ideas. If the pope was concerned, then

John Krol was concerned as well, and he would express that concern to those under his authority in no uncertain terms. But the fact that the concern got expressed on such an *ad hoc* basis was something that those under him found disconcerting. Leahy remembers precisely this feeling as the dominant emotion coming out of his meeting with the pope. If it's so bad at the Biblicum, Leahy wondered, why was the archdiocese sending its priests to study there? It seemed clear from the encounter, and Krol's emphatic restatement of the case, that the pope's authority trumped that of the professors, but did his knowledge trump theirs as well? The authority of both the pope and the bishops was being challenged by what would come to be known as the magisterium of the professors, and at this point young Father Leahy and young Father Massamini found the challenge bewildering. Both men regarded Krol as above all else a canon lawyer and an administrator, someone who knew what to do when he had a law to follow. When things weren't so clear cut, they both found Krol's guidance confusing. He would seem to encourage them and then pull them up short when the direction they took was not in keeping with the thinking of the Church.

The conflict over Biblical studies, however, was quickly forgotten in the wake of the euphoria which came over the Church with the beginning of the Council. Pope John was in large measure responsible for this himself. First, there was the benevolent personality, but beyond that there was the famous "prophets of doom" speech which began the Council. Both Leahy and Massamini felt that the pope was referring to Cardinal Ottaviani, and both saw Krol as both personally close to the aging head of the Holy Office and sharing his views. Both Leahy and Massamini felt that their professors had been vindicated by the pope's speech. They felt further vindication when the Council, under the leadership of the German bishops, rejected the schema prepared for them by Ottaviani and the other preparatory commissions. By the time the Council got under way, Ottaviani, the man who was perhaps more than anyone else there, responsible for convoking the Council, had been stigmatized as a "prophet of doom" and would continue to labor under that label for the rest of the Council and, for that matter, for the rest of his life as well. Once this had been accomplished, the focus of the Council's interpreters shifted as well.

From now on the Council was seen to be an exercise in *aggiornamento*, or updating, which came to mean accommodation to the very ills it was convoked to combat. In regard to the Council, Krol remained the canon lawyer throughout. *"D'ove scritto?"* was his favorite response when confronted by an interpretation more inspired by the spirit than the law. "Where is it written?" Where it got written was often the more apposite question as the explication of the Council fell more and more into the hands of scribes who were incapable of interpreting it as anything other than the triumph of the liberal agenda over the forces of reaction. Through the assistance of the mass media, the Council very quickly became an Age of Enlightenment morality play, something not unlike Mozart's *Magic Flute*. Pope John XXIII was Zarastro; the Queen of the Night was, as before, the Church.

Tony Massamini remembers the "prophets of doom" speech vividly. It was a day which he would later claim changed his life. All of the concerns which had been building during his studies in Rome seemed to pass away like a cloud moving away from the sun revealing the radiance of the pope's optimism. "I said, this is great," Massamini recounted referring to the pope's opening speech at the Council. "This is going to be an age of grace. We have this pope who overcame some of his own concerns and is still going to open the windows." Massamini's job at the Council entailed checking the microphones and so he heard a good deal of the debate between the bishops, even debate in favor of Teilhard de Chardin, who according to Massamini, received more than one favorable mention at the Council. Massamini was to carry away from the experience the belief that Teilhard had been rehabilitated, and that the *monitum* had been lifted sometime during the pontificate of Paul VI. This wasn't true, but it seemed possible that it might have become true and more often than not in this era the wish became the father to the act. The prophets of doom were in full retreat.

Just who Massamini had in mind was clear: the curia in general and Cardinal Ottaviani in particular. When asked whether John Krol belonged to this group, Massamini was emphatic. "No, not John Krol. John Krol would have done whatever they said. John Krol is the loyal, loyal, loyal, obedient churchman." Instead of devoting his energies into debate, Archbishop Krol devoted his energies to seeing that the debate took place. "My impression of what John Krol did with the Council," Massamini said, "is that he ran it. He helped a lot; he made sure that it was efficiently run, that everything was done exactly right and on time."

Leahy concurs. When asked what part Krol took in the debates at the Council, Leahy opines that debate was not Krol's overriding concern.

> I don't think he was into the Council at that level. He's not a theologian. His interests were administrative. I don't think he got into any depth on the Council issues. He was there and not there. I don't think he listened to the speeches. His deepest interest was to see that it came off smoothly. I think that was his greatest concern. He would have supported the Ottaviani forces, but I did not see him politicking for that. I think he felt it was his role to be neutral. I was involved in politicking every night I would spend until the wee hours of the morning discussing John Courtney Murray and the political maneuverings that were going on, but Krol never involved himself in that.

Both men came away from their experiences with Archbishop Krol under the impression that he was in fact two different people: the man and the prelate. The man had opinions, perhaps sympathetic to those of Cardinal Ottaviani, but the Churchman felt that it was not his place to express those opinions publicly or to confuse them with the position of the Church. Both men shared a certain measure of warmth toward John Krol, the man, which did not carry over to John Krol, the Bishop. Tony Massamini remembers Krol making announcements on the council floor one day.

"I walked past him, and I gave him a "look-at-you-up-there" look, and he looked right back at me with a "look-at-me-up-here" look in return. This is John Krol, the humble John Krol, who was very much the priest, the humble Polish boy who worked in the butcher shop. He never lost that. That is very much a part of him. But when he gets official, he gets official, and he has very, very serious trouble, in my opinion, reconciling those two dimensions of his personality."

Leahy sensed the same dichotomy. He felt Krol clearly identified with Cardinal Ottaviani, but if the Council chose another direction, then Krol was with the Council and saw his task as primarily facilitating the Council's deliberations. "Once the documents were completed," Leahy said, "they got his support." Leahy's subsequent irregular position with the Church made disagreement on matters of law and discipline almost inevitable, but he still feels a certain fondness for Krol the man.

> On the personal level I have a real fondness for the man. I like his sense of humor, his wry smile. And he could kid you. He was just a warm, very friendly person. At the time and even now. I feel a kind of father-son/love-hate relationship. On the official level, though, as far as the church goes, it seems like he puts on a different aspect. When it comes to the Church, he is straight down the line, rigidly supportive of whatever the position of the Church is.

Once the preparatory schema had been rejected at the Council, it became apparent that the position of the Church on many important issues was a matter of debate. This almost guaranteed that John Krol would not have much to say, and this is the impression Leahy got of him during the Council. Leahy plunged into the debate and maneuvering surrounding it with a vengeance. "I was more exposed to the liberal side of the politicking, but I was exposed to the conservative side too, and I did not see Krol involved with either."

John Krol did not come to the Council with a lot of ideas about how the Church should be changed. He came in the *persona* of the classic American bishop, as a man who was there to get things done. He came as an administrator. Whenever he was asked to explicate the Council from the point of view of an insider, Krol invariably stressed the administrative challenges he faced and not the issue which were debated. When asked by Frank Morriss, then of the *National Register,* what the most significant accomplishment of the first session was, his answer was weighted heavily in favor of the administrative. The most significant achievement was "the very fact of setting up the organization for the Council." This in turn was followed by "the election and appointment of the members of the ten commissions, the wide freedom of discussions which took place, and the approval by the General Session of the preamble of the first chapter of the Liturgical Schema."

Krol was not alone in stressing the administrative challenges of the first session. Joseph Cardinal Ratzinger, certainly not shy when it came to explicating the meaning of the Council or entering into the debates which it spawned, in many ways gave the same assessment of the first session. He saw the rejection of the schema as an historical moment, but admitted that the logistical issues in achieving any debate whatsoever were formidable. "The problem of procedure was very real," he wrote shortly after the Council. "After all, a total of 2,900 fathers—bishops, auxiliary bishops, abbots and superiors of orders—were entitled to take part."

The sheer logistics involved in letting each of these prelates have his say were daunting indeed, but it was "precisely this real if slightly cumbersome catholicity of the assembly," according to Ratzinger, "which was, historically speaking to be so decisive." Perhaps more than anyone there, Krol was responsible for the smooth functioning catholicity of the assembly. It clearly preoccupied him more than the debates themselves. When the Lutherans in Philadelphia asked him to explain the Council in the spring of 1965, it is probably fair to say that the ins and outs of the Council's administration were not uppermost on their minds, but that is precisely what they got because it was the aspect of the Council with which Krol was most familiar and the arena in which he made his major contribution. "The time afforded to me," Krol told what must have been not a few disappointed Lutherans, "might be used in describing the complexities of organization and procedure in the day to day operation of the Council."

"You can appreciate," he continued, "the problems involved in assembling 2300 to 2400 Cardinals, Archbishops, Bishops and Religious Superiors from all parts of the world." John Krol was a Catholic bishop but he was also an American who felt most at ease in applying technology as the facilitator of some large enterprise: "Through a happy combination of the ancient and the modern thought," he told the Lutherans, "the ancient language Latin, and through jet-expressed airmail and computers, all subjects are studied and discussed and votes are taken and tabulated at a rapid pace."

Rather than discuss "the personalities of the Council, the points of view that were forcefully expressed and the unfolding fate of the various schema from their introduction on the floor until the final voting," something Krol considered "a task for the calm and sober gaze of history," Krol chose to focus on the unanimity which arose out of all this technologically managed diversity. "The record is clear," he told the Lutherans, there were "majorities of upwards of 95 percent on each issue that has been brought to resolution."

Given his view of the Council as the Holy Spirit speaking with the aid of modern technology, it was inevitable that Krol would look on much of what appeared in the press as not only inaccurate, but slightly effeminate, shall we say, in purveying gossip composed of "stories of factions and intrigue" which falsify "what is truly a committed effort at understanding and expressing the delicate tension between the ancient and the modern, the unchanging and the changeable, the truth and its modes of expression." Krol considered it bad form to talk about such things, and as a result his relations with the press were never particularly good. The press found Krol in general abrasive, and from their point of view an air of unreality hung over his discussion of the issues because he refused to see Church issues from the point of view of competing factions. Taking the long view on this sort of thing tended to seem like lack of candor to the press, or lack of contact with reality.

In his book on the Council, Michael Novak gives vent to just this sense of exasperation in dealing with Krol. After describing him as "one of the most powerful Americans in Rome," Novak faults him for his arrogant behavior *vis a vis* the fourth estate. Krol, Novak writes,

> began a press conference on October 30 [1963] with several remarks about his policy of not talking to the press during the council; he said he was present only as a favor to Bishop Zuroweste. The reporting of the council until then seemed to him like the work of "cub reporters" on an assignment beyond their powers. He pictured the Church as an anvil on which hostile forces beat in vain. And, no doubt because of nervousness rather than ill will, he let slip several insulting remarks to the reporter from the *New York Times.*

Novak has a difficult time deciding whether to patronize Krol for his Cleveland slang and hostility to the *New York Times* or to admire him for his parliamentary acumen. John Cogley found himself confronted by the same sort of ambivalence, although he clearly leaned to the latter alternative more than Novak. Cogley complained in the already maligned *New York Times* that "with some exceptions there has been strikingly little leadership at the council from the American archbishops," but saw Krol "the first Polish-American to reach the top levels of the hierarchy" as one of these exceptions. "He is one of the undersecretaries of the entire council, and in that position he plays a pivotal role." However, here again, his role was largely parliamentary and not theoretical. "It is known, for example," Cogley tells us, "that he helped his close friend Archbishop Hallinan of Atlanta, steer the historical Liturgical Decrees to a safe landing—no mean accomplishment in view of the powerful opposition to it."

Msgr. Vincent A. Yzermans, in a treatment that is less adversarial than Novak's, describes Krol as "the busiest American at the Council."

His specific duty as the under-secretary of the Council was to keep a record of all the voting and to coordinate the announcements of the votes, the distribution, collection and tabulation of the ballots. In the absence of Archbishop Pericle Felici for two days during the fourth session, Archbishop Krol acted as substitute for the General Secretary. "Archbishop Felici," wrote the Archbishop of Philadelphia, "had the most difficult, delicate and demanding assignment in the Council. I can speak of his work and his many responsibilities only in superlatives." As a member of the central coordinating commission, Archbishop Krol shared the responsibility of coordinating the work of all the conciliar commissions, keeping the progress of the Council on a projected time schedule and reducing to a minimum the objections of those who favored or opposed the passages of decrees."

Yzermans devotes some time to Krol's interventions at the Council all of which were written and all of which were submitted on July 5, 1963. Here again Krol's concerns are often procedural, and the fact that all of them were submitted on the same day highlights the fact that Krol was most probably put in a position where he could only participate in the Council by running it. It was obvious that he couldn't run the Council and participate in the debates at the same time, and the decision to function administratively was no small challenge given the number of participants as well as the barriers of language and culture they brought with them to Rome in a way unprecedented in the history of the Church.

Krol was also called upon to function as a diplomat. When speakers went on too long he was often called on to cut the speech short. It was in many ways his lack of ideological identification which made this possible, if not particularly palatable, to speakers who might otherwise have thought they were being cut short for ideological reasons.

It was this penchant for procedure over ideas that made Krol hard to place on anyone's ideological spectrum. Liberals considered him a conservative; however, conservatives invariably expressed disappointment when his name came up, and then would cite one instance or another where he let them down. When asked to describe Krol's contribution to the Council, Rev. Gommer de Pauw, founder of the first traditionalist group which arose to protest the excesses following Vatican II, claimed after a long pause that Krol "was an interesting American presence, but made no outstanding contribution." Then as if to sum things up from the conservative point of view, de Pauw added, "He's not my favorite cardinal. I expected great support from someone who was personally a conservative." Leahy, the liberal, responded in much the same way, claiming that Krol "was considered an influence because of his position. He would be considered to be prestigious in a political sense." In terms of the political maneuvering behind the scenes, "he'd be in a position to push a particular proposal. He made it well known that he was a great admirer of Ottaviani and he would have been identified with the ultraconservative branch." But as far as contributing to the doctrine of the Council, "Krol basically kept himself aloof from that and involved himself with the administration because he's a good administrator. He was always an imposing figure."

Krol was by conviction a man of conservative principles but someone who always felt that his vocation was to get a particular job done. In this he was in many ways the pragmatic American just as much as he was the problem-solving, technophilic American. When Philadelphia's Jews asked for an explication of the Council in 1964, what they got was an explication heavy on the quantitative side. It was the Council as seen from the point of view of the undersecretary's desk:

> The Council opened October 11, 1962 and closed December 8, 1965—a span of almost 38 months. During the four sessions, there were 168 general and 10 public meetings with an average attendance of 2,200—with a high of almost 2,400. At these meetings, 147 reports were made; 2,112 speeches were given 4,361 written observations submitted, 544 votes taken and more than one and a half million ballots and attendance cards distributed, collected, tallied and reported. In addition there were thousands of meetings by the various committees and subcommittees responsible for drafting the decrees. Procedure was governed by parliamentary rules, and any real or alleged failure to observe the rules was referred to an Administrative Tribunal for a decision.

"The fact of the matter is," Krol concluded to an audience of Jews who probably now felt that they knew more than they wanted to know about the workings of the Council, "that the procedure of the Council is governed by rules. It is the duty of the Council presidency and Council Moderators and others to make certain that the rules are observed."

In his personal correspondence, Krol showed the same predilection to discuss the Council in procedural terms that he showed in his public addresses. In a letter to Bishop Wright of Pittsburgh in 1965, Krol described the functioning of the Council in terms that make one aware of the enormity of the challenge and the complexity of bringing so many topics up for debate among so many bishops of such varying background. In each instance, the final result was a document which was binding on the faithful of the Roman Catholic Church as an expression of their faith. Ratzinger mentions as one of the accomplishments of the Council the fact that it was not captured by any one ideological faction, and the fact that large majorities eventually approved each of its documents. The realization of this goal was due in large measure to the administrative ability of John Krol, who described in detail to Bishop Wright the amount of work necessary to bring it about. When Bishop John Wright got a request from the Pittsburgh chapter of the American Society for Public Administration to speak on the topic of "Conducting a World Wide Conference: The Administrative and Procedural Framework" Wright had no doubts about where to turn for advice. He wrote to Krol, who told him once again probably more than he wanted to know about how the Council got run:

> In about a two-hour working session, the Secretariat takes and records the roll call and within an hour has a printed catalogue of all those present and all those absent. It makes all the necessary announcements and distributes all documents. It distributes correspondence, tablets and reports up to ten separate ballots among the 2300 to 2400 Council fathers.

> The recording department takes the minutes of every session. In addition, there are stenographers who take down each word of the speeches. In addition also there are two separate tapes made of the entire proceedings. By the end of the week transcriptions of the tapes are made and filed and copies of everything distributed are filed, and even copies of unauthorized distributions are made and filed. So if the file is opened for any one day of the Council Session, you can find therein a record of who said the Mass, the opening prayers, who chaired the meeting; a list of all the speakers, lists of all documents distributed, as well as medals, books, etc.—all can be found under the current date.

Things, however, did not always go smoothly, especially at the beginning of the Council, when many of the procedures were in the process of being worked out. On October 30, 1962, the Council fathers were discussing proposed changes in the Mass during the 10th general assembly. At this juncture, Cardinal Ottaviani rose to address the assembly. Ottaviani had grave reservations about the changes that were being proposed. Beyond that, he had already been labelled a "prophet of doom" by the media opinion-makers surrounding the Council. Beyond that, Ottaviani seemed older than his considerable years. The movements of his right eye were beyond his conscious control and as a result of his failing eyesight, he had memorized his speech in elegant ciceronian Latin. Perhaps because that required a good deal of concentration, or perhaps because his hearing was almost as impaired as his sight, Ottaviani exceeded the ten-minute time limited granted to the Council fathers and showed no signs of slowing down or of heeding the hints that he should step from the podium. As a result, Bernard Cardinal

Alfrink, the Council's presiding bishop that morning, gave the sign to switch off Ottaviani's microphone. Ottaviani was silenced at the Council he was so instrumental in convoking.

According to the unsympathetic Xavier Rynne, Ottaviani was asked "politely" by Alfrink to stop, but ignored the request. According to Gommer de Pauw, an admirer of Ottaviani and an eyewitness to the event, the act was malicious on Alfrink's part and ideologically motivated. Alfrink was enforcing a rule which had never been invoked against a cardinal before, and Ottaviani's humiliation, according to de Pauw's account, was followed by "cardinals and bishops," who "enjoyed every minute of it . . . applauding enthusiastically" Ottaviani's humiliation.

Thirty years later, Cardinal Krol remembered the incident well. "That was a damn shame," he said later, obviously feeling that Ottaviani had been treated shabbily.

"You have to understand," Krol continued, "that Ottaviani could not see. He was able to say his divine office from memory, but in this case he got up and held a paper in front of him even though he could only see the outline and started talking. A few turks who didn't show the normal courtesy and respect that should have been shown him kept saying that his time was up. When he went his 10 minutes without adverting to anything, the president told him his time had elapsed."

The issue at stake here was more than the feelings of one old cardinal. If there were even a hint of ideological manipulation during the Council proceedings, the documents the Council produced would be construed as worthless, and the whole three-year endeavor would have been viewed as the results more of politicking than the Holy Spirit. The fact that many conservative elements did in fact view the Council in just these terms (Ralph Wiltgen's *The Rhine Flows into the Tiber* comes to mind) in no way changes the fact that the situation would have been incalculably worse if the Ottaviani incident had become the rule rather than the exception.

That it did not was in large measure the result of the work of John Krol. The Ottaviani incident prompted Krol's major contribution to the Council. His innovation was, as one would expect, in the area of administration. It was an idea he got, however, not from theology or from his training in canon law, but from watching football games. Krol's major contribution to the Council was the institution of the two minute warning. "After 8 minutes," Krol wrote in a letter explaining the innovation to Bishop Wright of Pittsburgh, "the telephone alongside the microphone rings as a warning that two minutes are left. Incidentally, the two minute signal was copied from the two minute signal in our football games."

In his assessment of Vatican II, Joseph Cardinal Ratzinger found the rules restricting each speaker to ten (later eight) minutes "obviously an inadequate remedy." However, he does feel that the fact that no parties were formed at the Council was a tribute to the fathers' "sense of responsibility toward the truth." Yet this absence of faction could only have flourished in a council where the procedures were above the suspicion of political machination and that sense was in large measure the result of John Krol's doing—perhaps in equal parts because of his discomfort with the clash of ideas, but also because of his scrupulous sense of fairness, his American ingenuity, and his desire to be a facilitator when it came to the mind of the Church, no matter how multivalent that mind might appear in this particular context. When that sense of fairness is lacking, the results are disastrous for the Church. The manipulation behind the scenes of the various listening sessions put on by the American bishops recently are a good example of that. Following a secret meeting held at St. Mary's College on the eve of the synod on the laity in 1987, Germain Grisez exposed the behind the scenes manipulation to devastating effect. The listening sessions were simply misdirection in the sense of that term as used by magicians, diverting the faithful's attention away from an agenda already in existence according to which the American bishops were to go to Rome to lobby for altar girls. Had the Council itself succumbed to this ideological manipulation, the results would have been disastrous for the Church. That they did not was in large measure due to the procedural fairness established by John Krol.

In fact, it was, according to Ratzinger, only the free expression of ideas from the assembled bishops that allowed the Council as a whole to reject the already-written schema and engage in debate on the topics at hand rather than merely rubber stamp them as foregone conclusions. It was procedure which enabled the debate, no matter how cumbersome that debate turned out to be, and it was the debate, the bishops feeling free to speak their mind, which allowed the Church to break out of the paralysis in which it found itself during the end of the papacy of Pius XII. With the passage of the liturgy schema by such a wide margin (2,162 in favor, 46 opposed) on November 14, 1962, the Church had broken loose from its increasingly constricting and ineffectual mode of reacting to modernity.

"The passage of the liturgy schema," according to Ratzinger, "had given rise to a new possibility foreign to the old pattern of 'anti-ism' and negativity, the possibility of abandoning the defensive and really undertaking a Christian 'offensive.' They could now act and think in a positive manner."

The situation at both the Biblicum and the Gregorian universities was some indication that the anti-Modernist strategy was not working. The professors took an oath against something they believed to be true, and unless the Church could show that what they believed was false, the oath would continue to be meaningless. Worse than that it would create a sort of neo-Averroism at virtually all of the Church's institutes of higher learning. Anti-modernism was not working, and the first session of the Council provided a way of addressing the problem in a different way. "The real question behind the discussion," according to Ratzinger,

> could be put this way: Was the intellectual position of "anti-Modernism"—the old policy of exclusiveness, condemnation and defense leading to an almost neurotic denial of all that was new—to be continued? Or would the Church, after it had taken all the necessary precautions to protect the faith turn over a new leaf and move on into a new and positive encounter with its own origins, with its brothers and with the world of today? Since a clear majority of the fathers opted for the second alternative we may even speak of the Council as a new beginning. We may also say that with this decision there was a major advance over Vatican Council I. The Council had resolutely set itself against perpetuating a one-sided anti-Modernism and so had chose a new and positive approach. In this sense we may consider November 20 or November 21, 1962 as a real turning point. It was a

turning point too, in the sense that in contrast to Trent and
Vatican Council I, the pope had rejected curial dominance and
sided with the Council (Ratzinger, *Council*, pp. 25-6).

Ratzinger would go on to temper his feelings in the light of
subsequent history. He would go on to claim that it was "incon-
testable" that the ten years following the Council "have been
decidedly unfavorable for the Catholic Church." But he would
never claim that a *post hoc* relationship was also *propter hoc*. First
of all, Ratzinger would go on to claim that the damage was not
the result of the "true Council," but rather the result of "the
unleashing within the Church of latent polemical and centrifugal forces; and outside the Church it is due to the confrontation
with a cultural revolution in the West: the success of the upper
middle class, the new 'tertiary bourgeoisie,' with its liberal-
radical ideology of individualistic, rationalistic and hedonistic
stamp." Beyond that, he felt years after the Council had concluded that the Church would have had to face these forces
anyway, and that facing them without the doctrinal clarifica-
tions provided by the Council would have caused much more
damage than what in fact occurred.

> I am convinced that the damage that we have incurred in these
> twenty years is due, not to the 'true' council, but to some texts of
> Vatican II that at the moment of their proclamation seemed re-
> ally to be ahead of the times. Then came the cultural revolutions
> and the social convulsions that the Fathers in no way could have
> foreseen but which have shown how their answers—at the time
> anticipatory—were those that were needed in the future. Hence
> it is obvious that return to the documents is of special impor-
> tance at the present time: they give us the right instrument with
> which to face the problems of our day. We are summoned to
> reconstruct the Church, not despite, but thanks to the true coun-
> cil (*The Ratzinger Report*).

Ratzinger blames the misimplementation of the Council on
the fact that "its documents were quickly buried under a pile of
superficial or frankly inexact publications" and indicates that
the damage done by the cultural revolution would have been
much worse in a Church whose structures were unhealthily
rigid. The Council was in many ways the response to a problem
which was as yet still invisible over the horizon, but it was no
less a problem because of its position. In addition to that, the

Council "turned out to be an intensive theological education for the bishops."

It was proving to be educational for the nonbishops in attendance—people like Tony Massamini—as well. In fact, education would be too mild a term to describe his experience of the Council. Intoxication was a more apt expression. From the moment of the opening speech at the Council, when Pope John XXIII rebuked the "prophets of doom," to hearing Teilhard discussed on the Council floor, Massamini was swept away with the possibilities. One broker of possibility at the time was a German theologian by the name of Hans Kung. Massamini got to know him when the German theologian came to speak at the North American College. And during the Council period, his fame spread. Krol was to later claim that Kung was in fact not a *"peritus verus"* at the Council. But Massamini claims that Krol was just as enthused by his writings as he was. In the course of one of their discussions, Krol said to Massamini "this guy is great," referring to Kung, and suggested that Massamini write something about him. Massamini initially demurred but then complied and wrote a piece which he envisioned as eventually being published in the Philadelphia diocesan newspaper. There was evidently some miscommunication along the line because when Krol read the piece he was appalled at what he saw.

"I submitted it to John Krol first," Massamini said later, "and the next day, after the Council he comes home and says 'we're going to lunch,'" so I say, great, we're going to lunch. He had read the piece on Hans Kung, and he sat down—it was a little *trattoria* just a little down from St. Peters—and just tore the place up with me.

"'I don't want to hear about this guy Hans Kung," Krol said according to Massamini. "' I don't want to hear about every book the pope is reading. There are debates going on in the Council, and I don't want to hear any of this stuff.'

"He just tore me apart," Massamini said later. In the middle of a knock down drag out fight over Massamini's article on Hans Kung at a trattoria near St. Peter's, Krol also let it be known—almost as an afterthought—that he had appointed Massamini a professor at St. Charles Seminary. After the fight, Krol paid for Massamini's lunch and on the way home admonished him to write to his parents. Massamini took it as an indication of the duality of John Krol, the archbishop at war with the man and vice versa. It was more probably an indication of Krol's administrative style when confronted with the realm of ideas. He took the issues seriously but not personally. Beyond that he dealt with the intellectual issues in an administrative fashion. He ordered Massamini to destroy the manuscript, and Massamini the obedient priest did just that. The destruction of the manuscript, however, did not deal with the issues that were raised in it. Thirty years after that luncheon meeting, Massamini is unable to say what the issues were, and that fact itself is indicative of the impasse the Church had reached with its own intelligentsia. The Church could order them around, but it was having a difficult time convincing them. In this respect, modernity seemed to have it all over the Church in the intellectual sphere. It was another variation on watering the dry stick. There is doubtless a time for intellectual persuasion and a time for administrative action, but at this juncture the latter was serving as a substitute for the former, leaving people like Tony Massamini obedient but unconvinced, and prone to feeling that the Church believed what it did purely as a result of executive fiat and not because a particular thesis was true or false. Tony Massamini tore up his manuscript but he continued to believe what was written there, something that would cause him greater and greater problems as he returned to Philadelphia and took up his post as seminary professor.

Rev. Paul Mankowski, S.J., gives an especially acute analysis of the warped dynamic obedience had acquired even in the wake of the Council which was convoked to correct such things. According to his thesis,

> the Second Vatican Council in general and the document *Lumen Gentium* in particular restored an authentic Christian authority to its proper place in the life of the Church. In so doing it displaced a notion of authority that had gained ascendancy with post-Enlightenment liberalism, an authority marginal to Christian faith but imported by churchmen from secular society and limited ecclesiastical use into their own administration of the Church.

According to the Enlightenment view, a view shared incidentally by Leo Pfeffer, the exercise of authority entailed the imposition of one person's will on another. In the absence of an external framework which specified how this authority was to be exercised—which was of course the historical context of the whole post-Enlightenment period—authority became what Oliver Wendell Holmes said that it was: the will to power or the powerful inflicting their will on those too weak to resist. This view made its entry into ecclesial life through instances like the parable of the dry stick, whereby the monk is supposed to water a dead dry stick. Because of the monk's essentially irrational obedience, God intervenes and causes the stick to bear fruit. Mankowski cites an anecdote about a Connecticut priest in the mid-'70s who, upon hearing that women worshippers had pronounced the words of consecration at Mass, replied, "Gracious! they must have had to get a papal indult for that!" The priest, who would qualify as both traditional and conservative, had a notion of authority that was based on the purely arbitrary whim of the pope. "In the mind of this dutiful and obedient Catholic, this 'conservative,'" Mankowski writes, "we could start sacrificing bullocks to Isis tomorrow provided we got a papal receipt first. . . ." Authority, then, comes to mean the displacement of the will of the subject by the will of the superior, a displacement that occurs not because the subject sees the will of the superior as right but because he fears harm at his hands.

Authority in this instance comes not from reason apprehending the order of things placed there by God and conforming oneself to that overriding rationality, it becomes instead Nietzsche's will to power, according to which the powerful impose their will on those powerless to resist. "In every case," Mankowski continues, "the will of the superior is in some sense imposed on the subject; in every case the consent or obedience of the subject will be non-rational, prompted ultimately by love of safety rather than truth; in every case the will of the superior is self-ratifying—that is, it needs appeal to, or can be mitigated by, no standards outside itself (unless that standard itself be a sanction of a yet more powerful threat)."

From this notion of authority there will flow two separate reactions, depending on the personality of the person expected to obey. "Trained on one sort of personality," the post-Enlightenment idea of authority will "produce our Connecticut priest:

that is, the man for whom all authority can be reduced to the superior's *ipse dixit*, and who is thus relieved from any personal responsibility: I can bend the knee to Baal with the Pope's say so. Trained on another man, the system will engender a fierce and implacable hostility."

In the case of Tony Massamini, the post-Enlightenment idea of authority seems to have produced both reactions but at different times on a trajectory of steady alienation from the Church. It was precisely because he shredded his manuscript on Hans Kung, in other words because of an obedience that was not based on rational conviction, that the hostility began to grow. This is not to absolve him from responsibility in the matter, but simply to explain what at first glance seems puzzling, namely, the bewilderment of a man who felt he was getting in more and more trouble for doing what he thought the Church wanted him to do. Tony Massamini thought he was implementing the Second Vatican Council when he wrote the article which Krol disliked so vehemently. He would continue to interpret the Council when he came back to Philadelphia to teach at the seminary with equally unpleasant results.

When Archbishop Krol told Massamini that what he was doing was not consonant with Church teaching, Massamini obeyed and shredded the manuscript, but even while obeying he never quite understood why what he had written was wrong. Either Krol was unable to make the case clear to him, or Massamini was unable to understand. Whatever the case, the confusion gradually hardened into a position of rebellion. Tony Massamini had been taught at the Gregorian that Sigmund Freud and Teilhard de Chardin held the key to understanding the spiritual life. Long after he stopped functioning as a priest, he held on to this bit of information as if it were self-evidently true. "The Church is still trying to catch up to Sigmund Freud," Massamini opined 30 years after his run in with Krol. In many ways he was still being the docile and obedient student he must have been at the Gregorian during the early '60s. Tony Massamini was smart enough to pick up what the professors were saying, but not smart enough to see that what they were saying was wrong and why it was wrong. (In many ways, no one was smart enough at the time given the subterfuge that was practiced in Freud scholarship and the cover-ups surrounding

Freud's biography.) Massamini was educated into a system that was pulling him in two opposite directions: faith said one thing and reason contradicted it. Blind obedience could only go so far in patching over a situation like that. When the crisis came, as it did in the '60s, Church discipline broke under the strain. "In practical terms," Mankowski writes, "the justification for authority offered most Catholics in most circumstance of their lives, but preeminently to priests, in the mid-1960s was too brittle to withstand the shock of cultural change. The strain was showing throughout the '50s and early '60s, and when the dam broke, it broke with a vengeance."

The parable of the dry stick might have worked during the Middle Ages when the notion of authority most men imbibed was from a political system more embedded in the natural law tradition. However, when combined with a post-Enlightenment, Nietzschean, or legal positivist metaphysics it would prove disastrous to the Church. The individual priest was simply being asked to bridge an unbridgeable gap, and his frustration in this regard turned to anger against the Church and rebellion as soon as it seemed that the *ancien regime* was no longer willing or capable of enforcing the old rules. "All this," according to Mankowski,". . .was complicated by an episcopacy that was increasingly chosen from among men more accomplished in canon law than theology, and thus more at home with a juridical than a biblical view of authority."

Vatican II dealt with this problem, specifically in *Lumen Gentium* #25. Obedience was described in conciliar documents not so much as the annihilation of the subordinate's will as the willing conformity of that will to the order established by reasoned apprehension of revelation. As Mankowski puts it, "when the Church asks us to 'submit' to her authority on a point of doctrine, this submission is understood not (as in the ascetical tradition) as an annihilation of will, not (as in the liberal view) as a counter-rational suspension of will, but as a mature judgement informed by reason."

The fact remains, however, that the Council was not perceived that way at the time, certainly not by people like Tony Massamini who were swept away by the give and take of the various sessions, and most certainly not by people who learned about the Council through the writings of Robert Kaiser or

Xavier Rynne. In the popular mind the council had already been cast as an Enlightenment morality play, in which the forces of light would triumph over the Queen of the Night, i.e., the Catholic Church as the Enlightenment had always understood her. The Council was in the process of becoming "buried," as Cardinal Ratzinger would say later, "under a pile of superficial or frankly inexact publications." *Lumen Gentium* was, of course, yet to be written when Tony Massamini had his first run-in with Archbishop Krol, but this only underscored the fact that the Church was basing its actions on the presuppositions which made the Council necessary in the first place, long after the Council began, and—how could it be otherwise—until the documents got first understood and then implemented.

In many ways, the liberals rejected the Council in favor of the Enlightenment's view of authority. In such a world liberty leads to terror in a very short period of time. Mankowski cites Matthew Fox's curiously totalitarian views as an example. If everything is based on arbitrary will, the the only thing that will adjudicate competing wills is power, exercised in equally arbitrary fashion. After a while all liberals who follow this trajectory begin to "sound uncannily like Bismarck,"

> What is striking is Fox's implicit agreement with the great totalitarians that all authority is based on power and that all power must be irrational. His redistribution of power may have a certain sentimental appeal to those of like mind, but it appears that the Abbey of Theleme, whose motto is 'Do what Thou Wouldst,' always seems to have doors that lock form the outside only.

At around the same time that Tony Massamini and Bill Leahy were having their respective audiences with the pope, a newly professed Christian brother was beginning his career as a religion teacher at the newly constructed La Salle College High School, one of the two Philadelphia area high schools run by the Christian Brothers. Brother Paul Francis, F.S.C. was only 22 years old but looked about six years younger than that, and if it hadn't been for the floor length black robe and curious ten-commandment tablet-like collar the brothers wore, he might easily have been mistaken for one of the underclassmen he taught. For the first two years of his tenure at LaSalle, Brother Paul did what just about every other new teacher has to do in the same situation: he learned how to teach, which meant first of all learning how to control a class of thirty or so exuberant adolescents.

La Salle differed from the average diocesan high school in Philadelphia for a number of reasons. First of all it was a "prep" school, i.e., only for those who were destined for higher studies. Because of its entrance exam, La Salle got students who were in general more intelligent and more motivated, and as the price of tuition increased the motivation (at least from the parents' point of view) increased as well. Brother Paul, in other words, had roughly one half of the bright young Catholic kids in Philadelphia (the other half went to the Jesuit-run St. Joseph's Prep in the North Philadelphia ghetto). LaSalle High School was in many ways just what Brother Paul was looking for, because he too had the reputation of being bright. He began his studies at LaSalle College and by the time he graduated with a master's degree in theology he was number one in his class. Since he went as a brother from the brothers' college to teach at the brothers' high school, his reputation preceded him.

But as Tony Massamini was to find out at the Gregorian in Rome, being bright meant learning ideas of a specific content in 1962. It would not be accurate to say that Brother Paul was influenced by Vatican II in September of 1962, because the Council hadn't officially opened yet, but he was influenced by what the Council was influenced by and that was in general two things: biblical studies and the liturgical movement.

From his biblical studies courses, Brother Paul learned that the New Testament was the "product of a bunch of people who were called the early church and tradition and all that kind of thing." The gospels were, in other words, fictions created to suit the needs of the people who wrote them. From his participation in the liturgical movement Brother Paul learned of the importance of community. Putting both together, Brother Paul came up with a formulation of the *Weltanschauung* of the '60s as it would come to be implemented at La Salle High School: "the community creates its own texts." Since the early Christians had done it then, there was no reason that we should not do it now, especially since Vatican II was calling us back to precisely those sources.

"We saw Vatican II," Brother Paul would say in retrospect when he was no longer Brother Paul, but Richard Deasy, an education consultant living in Maryland, "as simply a confirmation of what we already felt. It wasn't as if we waited for Vatican II and were influenced by those decisions. We saw ourselves as part of the broad movement that forced Vatican II on everyone else. The liturgical and scriptural movements were what created the group that hit the Philadelphia schools with an entirely different attitude toward religion."

Deasy at one point described himself as the "star" of his class. It was precisely Deasy's status as the best and the brightest pupil that the Christian Brothers had to offer at the time which was to cause everyone concerned problems. Being a star at LaSalle College in 1960 meant pretty much what it means at any other college in any other time or place. The star is the one who can most successfully absorb the categories being proposed by the teacher and the one who can re-present them back to the teacher in the most cogent and imaginative fashion. As the mesh between Church teaching and Church university began to erode—as it had been eroding throughout the modernist crisis beginning in 1910—picking up what the teacher said meant more often than not picking up an ideology that was inimical to the Church's interests. As with Tony Massamini so with Dick Deasy: the brighter students were more often than not able to pick up what the teachers were saying, but not bright enough to understand that what the teachers were telling them might not be true or congruent with the Catholic faith. In general, they recognized that what they were being taught was in conflict with what the Church held. But that conflict was almost always resolved in favor of the teacher, who was there in the flesh—whereas the Magisterium, whatever that was— was far away in Rome. Beyond that, the teacher gave the student a grade at the end of the course: the Magisterium did not. Beyond that, the teacher could be charismatic and attractive and fill in the gaps of his theoretical system with large doses of attractive personality, which seems to have been the case with Deasy, both as a student and as a teacher himself.

As a result, the Church in general and the Christian Brothers in particular had reached a very dangerous situation on the eve of the Second Vatican Council. The people they denominated as their own best and brightest were characterized as such to the extent that they could master disciplines and ideologies which were undermining the Church's very intellectual credibility. The situation was compounded in the case of priests and religious. The more Deasy excelled in mastering the categories of modernity, the more authority he was given in the Christian Brothers to implement those ideas in the schools and curricula the brothers managed. That coupled with the *Zeitgeist* inspired by Vatican II and *aggiornamento* thrust Deasy very quickly into a position in which he, in the name of updating curricula in the Baltimore province of the Christian Brothers, would wreak havoc in catechetics throughout the Archdiocese of Philadelphia. By 1964, Brother Paul had learned what every teacher has to learn in terms of how to manage a classroom. Now he was in a position to implement his ideas in a way that seemed mandated by the spirit of the times.

Robert Rooney arrived as a freshman at La Salle High School in the fall of '64. He was placed in the brightest section of students in a high school of bright students and given Brother Paul as both his religion and English teacher. Religion instruction under Brother Paul was, according to Rooney, "very comparable to what would have been taught at LaSalle College in a freshman course." That entailed discussing the sourcing of the Gospels, including an explanation of Q, and a discussion of the difference between the synoptic gospels and the Gospel of John. Brother Paul also gave his class of bright 14-year olds hand outs by Martin Buber and Dietrich Bonhoeffer. They also read Rudolf Bultmann's "Demythologizing the Gospels."

The result of this on boys who the year before were learning the Baltimore Catechism at the hands of nuns in the parishes they came from was, in Rooney's phrase, "cultural shock."

"It took the top of my head off," said Rooney, who is no longer a practicing Catholic. "I'm sure for those engaged in it, it took the top of everybody's head off. It was exceedingly subversive from my parents' and my friends' parents' perspective."

Subversive is the word Rooney uses with the benefit of almost 30 years hindsight. "Bewildering" is the word Rooney uses to describe his and his classmates state of mind at the time.

"I don't think the students were afraid to admit that they were bewildered. I think they were far too busy being bewildered. In fairness, Deasy was not at all a threatening guy. It was not an effort to brainwash anybody. It certainly was an effort to challenge falsely held convictions. Or to challenge you to think about anything to do with religion which in my case wasn't a thing you thought about. You had done your Baltimore Catechism, and you didn't think about it. That's not how the system worked. So there was a challenge to think about religion but not in an overbearing or threatening fashion."

Rooney remembers Brother Paul as an "exceedingly charismatic" teacher, "as charismatic as any teacher I've ever had." This may have distracted the students from the fact that what Deasy was doing in class was—from a pedagogical point of view, without any consideration of its religious content—wildly inappropriate. The curriculum it turns out was simply the books Deasy had read as an undergraduate imported into a class of high school freshmen without any concern that they might not understand what they were reading, or that their misunderstanding might cause problems for them farther down life's road.

The impression one gets, however, is that the important thing was not pedagogic appropriateness any more than it was the transmission of the faith. The impression one gets was that the freshmen at La Salle High School were being given a crash course in the tropes and methods of modernity. The quicker they adopted them the better off they would be. It was most probably an educational mission which Deasy could embark on with complete sincerity. After all, mastery of the tropes of modernity had helped Deasy's career, and the people who went to La Salle High School shared the goal of upward mobility probably as avidly as he did. The important point, pedagogically speaking, was to throw as much modernity on the table at one time in the hopes that the students would absorb as much of it as possible. This is neither Rooney's nor Deasy's assessment, but the conclusion seems hard to avoid.

In addition to teaching Rooney religion, Deasy also taught him English. In retrospect, Rooney finds the two classes running together in his mind, perhaps because the pedagogy in the English class was as wildly inappropriate for 14-year-olds as what they got in religion. Rooney remembers that for the midterm exam of their freshman year they were given, sight unseen, without title or attribution, "The Journey of the Magi" by T.S. Eliot and told to explicate it. Again one is struck by how Deasy's pedagogy involved simply taking college level material and techniques and using them on high school freshman. The explication of the poem without title or author was a standard trope of the New Criticism, which had its vogue in the '50s. As with most honest critical schools, there was something to be said for its methods, especially when practiced by people like Cleanth Brooks or Rene Wellek, people with a huge store of erudition to draw on. In the hands of epigoni, the method degenerated quickly into the sort of thing Rooney experienced in his freshman English class, which was more indicative of the academic fads of the times than any well-thought out approach to literature. When asked what a 14-year-old was supposed to say under these circumstances, Rooney defended the assignment.

"In fairness to Deasy, you were supposed to do a rigorous New Critical attack of the poem. You were supposed to give that poem a reading based on the words and the meaning in it." However, the method seems to have included messages all its own which corresponded to what modernity was telling people to think at the time. "Presumably," Rooney continued, "if you could have argued that the poem was about a search that led to nothingness and could support it in the text and if the quality of the argument was good enough, that would have warranted an A."

Deasy himself was in much the same situation as his students. He was to say later that if the older brothers hadn't validated what he had to say, he probably would have dropped it and picked up on something else. But they did validate what he was saying, and at the time there was a whole network of validators who read the same books and went to the same movies and derived from the experience the feeling that great minds all must travel in the same circles. It was one of the quintessential illusions propagated by Cultural Revolution and it would cause the Church and the parents of kids like Bob Rooney innumerable heartaches as the decade progressed to its frenzied Dionysian conclusion.

IV
The Racial Front

During Labor Day weekend of 1963, a little over a month after the death of Pope John XXIII, and shortly after Tony Massamini had returned from Rome to take a teaching job at St. Charles Borromeo seminary, and just as Archbishop Krol was preparing to leave for Rome to be undersecretary to the Second Session of the Second Vatican Council, a Negro by the name of Horace Baker moved into the all-white suburb of Folcroft in Delaware county just southwest of the city's borders, touching off a series of demonstrations or riots, depending on one's point of view, which would eventually lead to a nervous breakdown on Mr. Baker's part and a lot of soul-searching on the part of thoughtful Catholics in the Archdiocese of Philadelphia. Folcroft was, as the press reports were fond of saying, an overwhelmingly Catholic area

The Catholic bishops of the United States had gone on record five years earlier opposing segregation, and here were local Catholics expressing their vociferous opposition to what their pastors were claiming was the right thing. Caught in the middle of it all was the parish priest, Father John I. Kane, the pastor of St. Gabriel's Parish in Folcroft (now Norwood), who seemed unequal to the task at hand and gave the impression of not so much malevolence as befuddlement. Kane agreed to let Miles Mahony, a local civil rights activist and a Catholic, read the 1958 statement of the U.S. bishops on discrimination and Christian conscience to the assembled parishioners. However, after the first few lines, the audience got up and walked out, causing bad feelings on the part of the civil rights activists, who felt that Father Kane had been instrumental in the walkout. The walkout was described in the local papers in terms that implied racism on the part of the Catholic Church. In many ways the incident set up a dynamic that would persist throughout the decade. The liberals would accuse the Catholic ethnics of prejudice; they, on the other hand, were the people who had experienced the brunt of black migration in their neighborhoods first hand. In fact, many of them were in places like Folcroft in Delaware County precisely because of what had happened to their neighborhoods across the border in Southwest Philadelphia.

The Catholic intelligentsia were caught in the middle in this battle. They kept urging solutions that in many ways had been tried and found wanting by the people they preached to. The liberal Catholic intellectuals eventually resolved the issue by becoming absorbed into liberalism in general and into the the civil rights movement in particular. For priests like Father Kane, the solution was not quite as simple. He was caught in the middle in many ways and simply could see no way out of an impossible situation. Should he support the lone Negro interloper who was probably not a Catholic or should he support his parishioners, most of whom had already seen first-hand what black migration did to a neighborhood? The local priests needed a moral calculus on racial matters more sophisticated than their training had provided. The statement of the U.S. bishops, written by Catholic intellectuals who had absorbed, for the most part uncritically, the categories of liberalism and the civil rights movement, provided little assistance to someone who was a pastor to refugees from neighborhoods which were destroyed by the unsocialized elements which the government programs were supposed to cure at some unspecified future date after the expenditure of large sums of taxpayers' money. With the benefit of 30 years' hindsight, it was possible to see that government programs weren't going to solve anything, but at the time this was not apparent and the Catholic ethnics were asked to place a large act of faith in an as yet unproven liberal axiom. They were being asked in effect to bet the farm on it. They were being asked to bet their house, the largest financial commitment these people would make in their lifetimes on the as yet unsubstantiated hope that Negro migration would not destroy property values as it had already done in the neighborhoods these people had just left. They were asked to believe that the social anomie which they had seen rising from the southern Negro's disordered family life would somehow cure itself by proximity to white neighbors. The request for this *auto da fe* on their part was put to them in the form of a non-negotiable demand. By the fall of 1963, the same year as the famous civil rights march in Washington to which Martin Luther King preached his famous "I have a dream" speech, integration had become a moral imperative having just about the same binding quality as the decalogue. To question a liberal's commitment to integration was like questioning a Thomist's adherence to the first principle of practical reason "Good is to be pursued and evil avoided," so deeply entrenched had integration become as an axiom of social behavior to the liberal consciousness. "I remember the march as one of the great events of my life," Paul Spike wrote describing the 1963 civil rights march on Washington (Spike, p. 24).

As Leo Pfeffer would indicate, the civil rights movement was the defining moment for the mainline Protestant churches in the 1960s; it was every bit as important to the liberal Protestants as the Vatican Council was for the Catholics and the 1967 Arab Israeli war was for the Jews. Spike's father, Robert W. Spike, who headed up the civil rights division for the National Council of Churches, felt much the same way. In fact the son picked up the feeling in large part from the father, who would say "I felt for the first time in my ministry that the church was where it belonged—in the middle of the street. There was an eschatological feeling about the whole day." Spike senior would eventually go on to torpedo the Moynihan Report, an essentially Catholic inspired initiative (Moynihan credits the papal social encyclicals and the work of Jesuit John LaFarge as his inspiration) to strengthen the black family, and one year after accomplishing that would be murdered at the hands of a homosexual he picked up in Columbus, Ohio. But in the halcyon days of 1963, there was hardly a cloud on the liberal horizon when it came to everyone's idea of what needed to be done on racial matters. Spike junior's poignant tribute to his father makes a number of things clear: For one, by the mid-'60s, the agenda of the mainline Protestant churches and that of the liberal left had become virtually indistinguishable; and 2) the civil rights movement was the essential middle term which lent this implausible marriage of convenience plausibility. "In certain ways," Spike junior recounts of his own youth experimenting with drugs, reading beat writers like Kerouac and Ginsburg, personal acquaintances of Spike senior, and listening to Bob Dylan records, and trying to make sense of why a Presbyterian minister would encourage all this, "my father encourages me to be a rebel." Then, as if discovering the answer, he adds that his father

> sees civil rights as only one part of a vast social, technological, sexual and moral revolution. . . . The civil rights struggle gives the church a new chance to act in a "Christian" way without that implying narrow-minded or prudish behavior. It may even be the last chance for the Protestant Church in America.

Thrust into the no-man's land between the bitter economic truths the Catholic ethnics—primarily Irish—had learned first hand and the crusading spirit of the mainline Protestant Churches whose moral fervor in supporting the civil rights movement was in direct proportion to their abandonment of the sexual morality that the disintegrating black family needed so desperately, stood the Catholic intellectual. It was he who would provide the rationale for the Catholic priests and in many respects for the Catholic bishops trying to mediate the struggle. Or it was he who would not provide it. For the most part the nation's bishops and priests would be dependent on him, but dependent in a qualified sense. There was among the clergy at the time a sense of what the Catholic faith was, in spite of the increasing upheaval the Council was causing, a sense of what the Church could do and what it could not do, and a sense that race was a problem. It was up to the intelligentsia to make the connection on all of those points. If they did not, the Church would continue to manifest the befuddlement it had shown in Folcroft.

One of Philadelphia's Catholic intelligentsia who was deeply concerned about what had happened at Folcroft was Dennis Clark, a Philadelphia native who had been born in the late '20s and had his consciousness formed in the crucible of economic tribulation that was the Great Depression. Clark was born into the blue-collar ethnic bulwark of Kensington, attended Northeast Catholic High School, where he studied the modern popes' social encyclicals, and then St. Joseph's University (then college) from 1947 to 1951 where he came under the influence of Father Dennis Comey, the Jesuit who had made a name for himself in labor relations in the city. Clark was a contemporary of Michael Harrington, author of *The Other America*, and Daniel Patrick Moynihan, now Senator from New York. In many ways the three men all shared the same intellectual trajectory. All three were Irish-Americans whose consciousness was deeply imbued with the social teaching of the Church; all three became involved in the racial issue in their separate ways, and all three gradually moved away from the faith as the categories of the social encyclicals gradually became replaced with the axioms of liberalism. Harrington became a socialist, Moynihan became a notorious supporter of abortion, and Clark eventually abandoned the faith—in face of what he claimed was the Church's disappointing response to social justice issues—in favor of Irish-American ethnicity. As the '60s progressed, Catholic intellectuals of this sort became increasingly unable to distinguish between the liberal agenda and the teaching of the Church. By the end of the '60s, the relationship had become clearer: the liberal agenda became the procrustean bed upon which things Catholic were laid and then trimmed to size.

This apostasy of the intellectuals would wreak havoc in the Church, but it also caused innumerable social problems as well, especially in a place like Philadelphia, which in 1963 was largely a Catholic city subjected to increasing pressures from racial migration from the South. The Catholic intellectuals were in many respects simply not plausible to the hierarchy and as this implausibility increased so did their hostility to the hierarchy and the Church they represented. They became largely an alien advocacy group within the Church and then when they failed to get what they wanted they oftentimes left in disgust. It was, in other words, a two-sided tragedy.

Dennis Clark graduated from college the same year that the Clark/Dilworth Democrats took over the city, and Clark soon found himself part of the liberal cadres that Clark/Dilworth had appointed to help make the city work. Long before Clark began civil rights advocacy with the Church, he was involved in the city's efforts to defuse the burgeoning racial crisis black migration had spawned in the city. He remembers one year of his life as part of the city's Commission on Human Relations, in which he spent over 300 nights away from home, for the most part visiting various racial hot spots in the city trying to defuse an increasingly explosive situation. For the most part, it was a labor of Sisyphus. He was later to describe the commission as "a lightning rod for both blacks and whites." It was the Clark/ Dilworth reform team's way of keeping things calm. Clark had met with Krol's predecessor John Cardinal O'Hara in the '50s and remembers him as old and tired and possessed of a very simple strategy: the black coming into the city would simply inherit the parishes that the whites vacated. It was a strategy that might have worked if the liberals hadn't been so intent on manipulating migration and the ensuing civil rights movement for their own ends.

First of all, since with the New Deal blacks tended to vote Democratic, every new Negro arrival in Philadelphia or any other northern city for that matter was one more voter for Democratic machines in place there. In this, Philadelphia was no different than Chicago. Secondly, black migration corresponded with the rise of the liberal welfare state, which guaranteed first of all that the problem of the black family would not be solved, and secondly, that the Catholic Church and its parishes and other welfare instrumentalities attached to its system of values would be equally hamstrung in bringing about a solution. The pullback from the moral order ratified by the Supreme Court on school prayer, on aid to Catholic schools, on obscenity, on criminals' rights, all took place at the same time, and each aspect exacerbated the other to make the type of orderly transition Cardinal O'Hara hoped for virtually impossible. And as it became apparent that the situation was out of control, the Catholic working class in Philadelphia, to use Lenin's term, voted with their feet. They panicked; they moved into the suburbs; they, in effect, left too much infrastructure behind to people who were, first of all, not Catholic to begin with, and beyond that, used to an economic system—the share-cropping system of the South—which did not foster responsibility, either personal, or familial, or economic, or civic.

As a result of the sheer magnitude of the transition, and as a result of the conditions under which it took place, Clark's work with the Philadelphia Human Relations commission was largely an exercise in frustration. When he bumped into incomprehension on the part of the Catholic hierarchy, Clark's frustration increased exponentially because he felt that his prime motivation in working for the Human Relations Commission was to implement the social teachings of the Church.

When Krol arrived in Philadelphia in early 1961, Clark felt more than a little optimistic at the change. First of all, Krol was a younger man, and secondly he was part of the "proletariat." Anyone who had worked as a butcher in Cleveland, Clark felt, would be sympathetic to the plight of the working man. On January 17, 1962, Clark wrote to Krol introducing himself and offering his services based on his experiences with the Philadelphia Human Relations Commission to the archdiocese. In his letter Clark was quite open about his distress at the situation in which Catholic ethnics, primarily the Irish, were involved in an ongoing series of confrontations with the newly-arrived blacks. The conflicts, he felt, "are damaging not only to racial harmony in the civil order, but to the the church as a symbol of spiritual leadership and as a mother to the afflicted." Because the Church had failed to exercise the necessary leadership in racial matters, whites were manifesting "irritation, confusion about future prospects and a vulnerability to exploitations by demagogues and sharp real estate operators." Clark's disappointment with his fellow Catholics on racial matters becomes more palpable as the letter continues. "Catholic leaders and pastors," he writes,

> when, indeed, they can be approached at all are either stolidly reserved or deeply suspicious in such situations. I am sensible of the desire of priests not to be victimized by special pleaders, but in cases where the physical safety of innocent families and the prevention of racial violence is in question, a somewhat more positive response could be looked for. Catholic lay leaders at the local level, are all too often, not only irresponsible about protecting the common good in racially changing areas, but openly hostile to inevitable change and, in some cases, militant in efforts to forestall it.

Clark had in mind the practices of real estate agents, oftentimes in collaboration with the pastors in white parishes like Most Blessed Sacrament Parish in the southwestern section of the city. MBS, as the parish was called, covered a geographic area roughly eight city blocks by eight city blocks of densely populated row homes. It was during the '50s overwhelmingly Irish, and in spite of its blue collar population and small geographical area a Catholic powerhouse for the archdiocese. During the '60s it had the largest Catholic grade school in the world, over 3,500 students in three buildings in a complex of granite structures that dominated the entire neighborhood. MBS was not a rich parish by any stretch of the imagination, and yet during virtually every diocesan-wide fund-raising appeal, they would invariably top other far richer parishes in contributions. When black encroachment into the parish became a critical issue at some time during the early '60s, the pastor in collaboration with a local real estate agent would allow the Church to be used as an ad hoc housing market after Mass. People would stand up and announce that a house on Conestoga St. was for sale and hope that a buyer could be found who would contribute to the preservation of the neighborhood as an Irish-Catholic enclave. In an age in which community action became a catchword which brought down untold millions of federal dollars, this was one sort of community action which the government did not smile upon. The pastor was told at one point that what he was doing was illegal and threatened with prosecution if he continued.

When the Irish Catholics in MBS realized that they could no longer defend their community, when they realized that they could no longer preserve it as they saw fit, when, in other words, they realized that they had been denied practical sovereignty over the area in which they lived, they voted with their feet. They abandoned MBS and moved to the suburbs or the northeast section of the city. The change did not take place overnight. But they did take place in a fairly dramatic fashion. Over the summer of 1966, the first dramatic change took place. Up until that time the enrollment at the parish school had remained fairly constant at about 3,400 children. Over the summer of 1966, the enrollment dropped by 600. It was the beginning of a hemorrhage that would end 10 years later when the population of the school and parish became almost 100 percent black at a fraction the numbers it had before. By the 1990s, the only whites left were those who could not afford to move. The Irish were replaced in large measure by single parent families led by black women with all of the problems that went with that social configuration. MBS with its huge buildings was in effect bequeathed to a group of people who lacked the skills to make use of what it had to offer. By the 1990s, the overwhelming majority of the neighborhood's population was unchurched; a small percentage attended MBS's school, a smaller percentage attended MBS church, and the rest of religious observance in the area was taken up by a smattering of storefront black Baptist churches with names like the "Church of God of the State of Michigan."

In 1962, the crack in this dam was invisible to the human eye. MBS was beleaguered but still holding its own, and much of what Clark was proposing made a lot of sense both in terms of Philadelphia politics and the teaching of the Catholic Church.

"The benefits of reasonably steady employment and decent housing," Clark wrote to Krol, echoing what Daniel Patrick Moynihan would say two years later

> are highly necessary if orderly and wholesome family living are to prevail among Negro families. Even among Negroes who in growing numbers are reaching middle class income levels, there are disturbing signs of confused standards of family life and moral tragedy. It is unfortunate that where job situations and civic contacts permit Catholics to encounter Negroes, the encounters are often stiff and unfriendly. Negro Catholics have often stated to me their disillusionment with contacts they have made in their parishes with white families.

Clark, in his 1962 letter to Krol, put his finger on an issue no one wanted to bring up in the early '60s, namely the sexual/moral issue. The main cause of social anomie in the black community was the dysfunctional family. In 1964, Daniel Patrick Moynihan, who like Clark had been influenced by the social encyclicals and Father John LaFarge (Clark concludes his letter to Krol by announcing that he is leaving Philadelphia to accept a job with LaFarge's interracial council in New York), made a convincing case that black economic welfare could only be improved by strengthening the black family. However, he made the announcement when the liberal Protestant establishment (people like Robert W. Spike) had decided that their goal was to "liberate" the nation from family ties. Clark remembers the Moynihan Report as "a work of penetrating intelligence." If so, his letter to Krol was even more prescient for he was proposing virtually the same program two years before Moynihan did.

"Stronger emphasis," Clark wrote,

> from Catholic quarters upon the need for job improvement and
> housing opportunity, and further penetration of the negro com-
> munity with Catholic influence on family life is dearly needed.
> Public agencies in welfare and education work do not feel that
> they have a mandate to impart family life standards to their
> clients. The root issues of family disorganization and the Chris-
> tian teachings that counter them are only dimly perceived in the
> Negro community.

It is true that Catholic social teaching as discussed here gets
cloaked in the raiment of government programs, programs
which invariably failed, but there is no indication that they
were necessarily doomed to failure in 1962, at a time when
Catholics occupied the mayor's office, the governor's mansion
and the White House, and the United States showed itself more
amenable to the contributions of Catholics than at any time in
its history.

In 1962, Catholics were in a unique position to contribute to
the solution of the country's racial crisis. To begin with they,
unlike the mainline churches and the social welfare bureaucracies, were still in contact with the rudiments of sexual morality
and, therefore, able to at least see the dimensions of the problems affecting the black family. Beyond that, the Church infrastructure in terms of schools and welfare agencies was stronger
than it had ever been in the past and ever would be in the
foreseeable future. Beyond that, the culture's openness to a
Catholic contribution to common problems was even greater.
Beyond that, the Catholics had a coherent, clearly articulated
tradition of social thought dating back to Pope Leo XIII's *Rerum
Novarum* which articulated the connection between the micro
and the macro in a way unrivalled by any other American
philosophy. Yet, in spite of all this, the Catholic contribution to
the racial issue was stillborn.

Tragically, and in spite of early efforts like Father LaFarge's
Interracial Council and Friendship House in Harlem, the necessary connections were never made. The specific connection between Krol and Clark was hindered most certainly by the other
things the archbishop had on his mind. The beginning of the
Council was less than a half a year away. It was most probably

also hindered by the fact that Clark announced that he was leaving Philadelphia in the same letter in which he proposed his suggestions to Krol. When Krol answered Clark's letter on February 1, 1962, his response was polite but formal and concluded with the regret that he was "sorry to hear that you and your wife will be soon moving to another city."

There is some indication that Clark was at fault in failing to make the connection as well. Recounting his experiences 30 years later, Clark recalls a meeting with a Rev. Peter McGarrity, an Irish-born priest at St. Francis of Assisi parish at Green and Upsal Sts. in Germantown, another racial hot spot during the '60s. When Clark proposed a program similar to what he had proposed to Krol, McGarrity could only reply that the blacks moving into the neighborhood were "barbarians," and that "their family life is chaotic." The latter assertion was the same thing Clark had said to Krol in the early 60s; however, as time went on the notion of proposing Catholic sexual morality as the cure for the ills of the ghetto was gradually replaced by the generic liberal reliance on tax money channeled through federal programs. Clark remembers McGarrity as a "dinosaur," and to be fair, Clark had suffered enough frustration on the issue to warrant intemperate language of a far stronger sort. Clark eventually wrote off McGarrity's response as "confused and dismissive." But the fact remains that the connection was not made. Clark could not make his case plausible in terms accessible to pastors like Peter McGarrity, and as the '60s progressed the frustration and estrangement increased on both sides.

In 1964, Clark's frustration spilled over into an article he wrote for *Commonweal* entitled "Philadelphia: Still Closed." Clark had worked with SNCC, and he had worked with Father LaFarge and as time went on the categories of the former group began to predominate over the latter in terms of his thought on racial matters. He had even arranged to have a meeting with Krol and two of his auxiliaries but the meeting only increased his sense of frustration. Clark felt that he was caught up in one of the most important social movements in this country's history and was hoping that Philadelphia's Catholics could contribute to the outcome, but at the same time he found the bishops "uncomprehending." Bishop Cletus Benjamin, one of Krol's auxiliaries, announced to Clark during their meeting that there was no such thing as a ghetto in the United States. Back in New York, Clark was arguing with James Baldwin over the latter's hatred of religion. Now he was dealing with bishops whom he felt were as tone deaf on race as Baldwin was on religion. Krol and his auxiliaries emphasized prudence; they would not pull the rug out from underneath their pastors, and Clark, with the Folcroft incident still fresh in his mind, came away from the meeting "thoroughly disheartened."

The state of mind comes through in "Philadelphia: Still Closed," which appeared in *Commonweal* on May 1, 1964 (pp. 167-70). Written perhaps with Clark's experiences in New York fresh in mind, the article comes across as a patronizing attack on Philadelphia as a bastion of stodginess. "When people say that nothing is going on in Philadelphia," Clark opines,

> they are right. Nothing goes on in the present; the city's past makes its events. . . . Philadelphia is stable. It has a high home-ownership rate, small immigrant proportion and a conscious class and status fixation. The Philadelphians are burghers who dug in long ago. . . . The Catholics of the Archdiocese are proper, quiescent and uncongenial to innovations. . . . Philadelphiaphobia. It consists of an exquisite sensitivity to criti-cism, a reserve bordering on the comatose and *a fear of drafts from open ecclesiastical windows.* [underlined by Krol] Philadelphia Catholics have pretty much been a world unto themselves.

Ironically what Clark lists as evidence of Philadelphia's stodginess could just as well have been seen as an indication of its social health. It is difficult to see how a high rate of home ownership is a vice, especially in light of later developments. Since widespread ownership of income producing property is applauded in the papal social encyclicals as a social good, it seems that in this instance Clark was more influenced by the liberal Zeitgeist in New York than what he learned from the Church. Clark mentions incidents in Levittown in 1957, in Fishtown in 1960, and in Folcroft in 1963, as indications of the hierarchy and clergy's failure to lead.

> In September,1963, a Negro named Horace Baker moved his family into a suburban village called Folcroft. The white neigh-bors hit the streets, stoned the house, and once again the news media had a home-town panorama of prejudice to display. *The*

Folcroft areas was heavily Catholic [a fact Krol underlined]. . . .
Rather quickly a number of Catholics chorused their concern
about the Folcroft incident. A group of university types met, and
typically wrung their spirits in disgust at the lack of official
Catholic leadership in race relations over the years that was felt
to be the major scandal. Catholics moving in articulate circles
have been the butt of honest criticism for years about the local
"church of silence" situation. It is indisputable that in Philadelphia, perhaps above anywhere, the priests and bishops are the
leadership of the laity.

Clark quite rightly claimed that Philadelphia "is not going
to see its way through the great racial revolution without a
powerful Catholic effort to make the transition possible," but he
failed to take into account the fact that at the same time that this
contribution was so necessary the Church was being robbed of
making any contribution of value in the area of religion or
morals by the agents of *Kulturkampf* operating under the banner
of separation of church and state. Because of fair housing laws,
it had become illegal for residents of ethnic neighborhoods to
preserve their ethnic character. Because religion had been driven
out of public schools and aid to parochial schools had been
proscribed, it was almost a foregone conclusion that the children of the Negro sharecroppers coming up from the South
would not be socialized in any effective manner, which in effect
accelerated the exodus of white ethnic Catholics from neighborhoods, which had become impossible to control and as a result
increasingly dangerous.

Significant by its absence from the *Commonweal* article is
any mention of the weakness of the black family and the role
the Church could play in strengthening it, all elements which
were included in Clark's letter to Krol two years previous.
Clark's frustration at a situation which was going from bad to
worse boils over into an attack on Krol himself. Krol is described as "an impressive figure" with "dignity, self-possession
and a relentlessly logical approach to issues." However, Clark
adds, "the Archdiocese has yet to hear personally from him on
race." Clark then gives a list of grievances which could only be
construed as such in light of the liberal ideological presuppositions of the time, both in and out of the Church. "No religious of
the Archdiocese," we are told,

felt free to participate in the march on Washington [Krol annotated that statement with a question mark.] Those who asked if it would be possible were discouraged. Most prelates who met with President Kennedy to discuss racial tensions last summer issued statements on their return home. Archbishop Krol did not. it was widely known in the Archdiocese that when the National Liturgical Conference met in the city last summer an attempt was made to issue a televised statement on the connection between worship and interracial justice, and the Archdiocese put the quietus upon the plan. Many bishops have spoken personally on racial problems within their localilties. Archbishop Krol has not seen fit to do this.

It is difficult to know what Clark means by speaking personally. Neither the fireside chat nor the warm tete a tete was part of Archbishop Krol's repertoire of interpersonal relations. He was more often than not unintentionally abrasive in personal contacts and prone to the wise crack as his preferred mode of expression in one-on-one conversations. Beyond that, he was deeply suspicious of ideologies of the Left, probably because of his experience with Poland. But beyond that, most of what Clark is complaining about is more the result of inattention than anything else. In May of 1964, when Clark's article appeared in *Commonweal*, the Vatican Council had yet to reach its midpoint, and Krol had been head of one of the largest archdioceses of the country for a little over three years. In a personal memo, Krol wrote on March 1, 1966, he calculated that from late winter of 1961, the time he took over the archdiocese, until the above mentioned date he had spent a total of 372 days in Rome working on the Council. That means that of his first five years in office, more than an entire year was spent out of the city in Rome. The 372 days includes only time spent in Rome, not work on the Council done while still in the United States. Given this drain on his attention, it is not difficult to understand that Krol would not have the time to speak personally on racial problems, no matter how pressing. In light of the other demands on Krol's time at the time, Clark's complaint was bound to be perceived as unfair carping.

Responding for the archdiocese in a subsequent issue of *Commonweal*, Msgr. Philip E. Donahue, vicar general of the archdiocese dismissed Clark's piece as "not only inaccurate—it was a rank distortion of the truth." Donahue accused Clark of ignoring "the impressive history of Catholic solicitude for the Negro in this Archdiocese going back over a century " and claimed that the article might have been more aptly titled "'Archdiocese of Philadelphia Disobeys Clark.'"

"We do not have to march in parades to proclaim our respect for these principles," Donahue continued and then went on to cite the work of Mother Katherine Drexel among the Negroes and the Indians as well as the fact that "the enrollment of several of our parochial schools is over 50 percent non-Catholic Negro."

> The thrust of Mr. Clark's article is that the Archbishop of Philadelphia has not adopted the kind of measure which Mr. Clark recommends. The *Commonweal* should know that the Ordinary of a Diocese has many considerations affecting the welfare of his entire flock which must be weighed against the importunities of any small group. . . . The *Commonweal* should not have permitted the sincerity of the Archbishops' intentions to be impugned without knowledge of the reasons for his actions.

The net result of the exchange was the retiring of the archbishop and liberals like Clark into two separate corners from which neither was to emerge. The tragedy therein consisted in the fact that an avenue for cooperation which would have benefited the city and the Church was closed off. Three years later Clark wrote another article on the racial situation in *Ave Maria* magazine, (Dennis Clark, "Philadelphia," *Ave Maria*, April 29, 1967, p. 10) which rehashed much of the same charges in language slightly more intemperate and more dominated by liberal categories of thought. "The archdiocese," Clark told *Ave Maria* readers, "has moved slowly on social issues in the wake of Vatican II. There has been a succession of disciplinary actions against innovators, expulsions of priests and obscurantist wheezings in the Catholic weekly." One innovation on racial matters which does get mentioned is the founding of the Archdiocesan Commission on Human Relations, but the Commission is dismissed almost as soon as it is mentioned as "ponderous and undramatic. Some would say ponderous and ineffective. The spirit of the effort is stolid and dutiful, rather than inspired or bold."

Clark was to claim later that the establishment of what came to be known as the Cardinal's Commission on Human Relations came as a result of his critique, and Msgr. Philip Dowling, the organization's first executive secretary, confirmed the essential truth of this statement. A large segment of the clergy and Catholic intelligentsia were clearly appalled at what they saw happen in Folcroft and felt that something needed to be done, especially to help the priests who seemed to be placed in an impossible situation and were reacting accordingly. In the wake of Folcroft, Msgr. Newton, the archdiocese's chancellor, called together a group of about six priests, the eldest of whom was Msgr. Dowling, and asked them to come up with a response to the racial situation in the archdiocese. Dowling in turn wrote a paper, in which he proposed the idea of having a single body for outreach to both the Negro and the non-Catholics of the archdiocese in light of what was being called for during the Vatican Council. One of the crucial linkages was the fact that most Negroes arriving from the South were non-Catholics and so racial relations were *ipso facto* ecumenical relations as well. Dowling wrote the paper, rang the bell, dropped it off at the Cardinal's residence and left. Within a short period of time, Krol had agreed to what was being proposed and in May of 1964, right around the time of Clark's *Commonweal* critique appeared, the Commission on Human Relations was launched.

Three years after its founding, Cardinal Krol praised the Commission for a number of achievements in racial relations in the city of Philadelphia. The commission was responsible for:

Clarification and promulgation of an admission policy that has opened the doors of city parochial schools to hundreds of non-Catholic Negro children

Institution of a continuing training program for parochial school teachers to show them how to present sound ideas about race

Putting almost all the seminarians of the archdiocese to work in inner city parishes one day a week to give them experience in interracial work

Placing priests with skills in interracial relations into special positions where these skills could be used

Encouraging students in diocesan high schools to work with deprived children—mostly Negroes—as tutors and as "foster brothers and sisters" and establishment of a Community Service corps to help coordinate this effort

Reviewing textbooks to insure their racial objectivity

Launching a program through which suburban parishes help inner city parishes and establishing a commission for inter- parochial cooperation to coordinate this effort

encouraging greater participation in community affairs by priests and lay people. Priests now serve on the advisory committee to the board of education, the antipoverty action committee, clergy associations, and neighborhood improvement committees and they cooperate with civil human relations agencies to relieve tension situations

It was an impressive list of accomplishments, but ultimately the commission did little to stop the decline in either black family morals or the collapse of the white ethnic parishes in the city. The two facts were intimately related, as Clark among others had found out through personal experience. The main fears on the part of whites were essentially sexual in nature. The blacks brought an uncontrolled sexuality into the neighborhoods that the whites found too threatening. As Clark himself related, the whites he talked to didn't want "niggers riding on the bus with my daughter." The more the Church and the state showed itself incapable of dealing with the problem of black family breakdown and its consequences, the less the whites were willing to stick around and wait for them to come up with a solution. Nicholas Lemann in his account of black migration from Mississippi to Chicago tells much the same story.

The heart of the matter was sex. . . . The idea that blacks possessed a powerful, uncontrolled sexuality was responsible for the rough edge of the white Delta ideal of benevolent paternalism: a certain harshness was necessary in order to protect white women from black men.

According to Lemann, the purpose of segregation was social and not economic and at the heart of its social purpose was

absolutely preventing the possibility of a black man's impregnating a white woman. Gunnar Myrdal, in *An American Dilemma*, written just before segregation began to crumble, provided a ranking of the various aspects of segregation in their importance to white Southerners. Whether blacks voted was only fourth most important, and the denial of good jobs was sixth; first was "the bar against intermarriage and sexual intercourse involving white women." David Cohn wrote: "We do not give the Negro civic equality because we are fearful that this will lead in turn to demands for social equality. And social equality will tend toward what we will never grant—the right of equal marriage. As a corollary to these propositions we enforce racial separation and segregation." And: "It is the sexual factor . . . from white social and physical segregation grows."

What the whites found unsettling was the liberals' inability to look the situation squarely in the face and stop pretending. What the ethnic Catholics found unsettling was the Church's penchant for adopting the categories of liberalism in formulating its racial policies. When Miles Mahoney read from the U.S. bishops 1958 statement on race, the parishioners at St. Gabriel's parish in Folcroft walked out to a man. On November 18, 1966 the U. S. Bishops issued another statement (*On Race Relations and Poverty: Pastoral Statement of the National Conference of Catholic Bishops*) in which they told the faithful that "comprehensive programs to eradicate poverty have been begun. We ask for strong and continuing support for them and constant efforts to improve." At another point the bishops ask "that a concentrated attack upon poverty be mounted upon many fronts" and call for "strong governmental intervention at appropriate levels."

The document does mention the importance of the family, but almost invariably as the recipient of some government program to strengthen it. It also claims that "most" poverty is the result of past or present discrimination. As one of their pastoral suggestions, the bishops opine that "We," presumably Catholics in general and not bishops in particular, "must learn, and learn first-hand, what it means to be poor, to be a poor Negro, a neglected Spanish-American or a disenfranchised Indian." The irony, of course, is that virtually all of the inhabitants of Philadelphia's ethnic neighborhoods knew what it meant first hand to be poor Irishmen, Italians, Germans and Poles in a hostile country and had used the Church and its subsidiary institutions as a vehicle out of that poverty. Now the Church, or at least the people who wrote the bishops' pastoral letters, were urging, along with expansion of the federal government's role at a time when the government had been cut loose from its

Christian moorings, "programs to assure equal housing opportunities for all, without discrimination based on race, creed, or
color," programs in other words which made it impossible for
Catholic ethnics to maintain the neighborhoods which were
their passage out of the grinding poverty of their immigrant
forebears.

Thus, in spite of the founding of the *Cardinal's Commission
on Human Relations* and the undoubtedly good intentions of
those who founded it, the Church was faced with two problems
which proved to be increasingly intractable. The liberal solutions they espoused proved in the course of time to be unworkable, and as a result of that the Church started to lose credibility
on the part of those who looked to it for support on these
matters. The walkout in Folcroft was indicative of something
that would only get worse with time. Delaware county would
continue to be populated with refugees from the city's failed
liberal social policies, and it would also spawn a large Lefebvrite
community of people who became disenchanted with the
Church's collaboration with the liberal agenda. Because of the
Church's inability to deal with the racial problem effectively,
because of her inability to defend the neighborhoods, many
Catholics lost faith in the Church as a viable agent of social
order.

In this the conservatives were not unlike liberals like Dennis
Clark who left the Church because of his disappointment over
her failure to exercise a more active social role. The cruel irony
in this equation was the fact that the Irish were most affected
because they put more trust in the Church. Unlike the Italians,
the Irish gravitated to jobs in the public sector. They became
cops and politicians and so lacked the independent financial
base the Italians had in South Philadelphia. When racial migration came to South Philadelphia, it was blocked primarily because the Italians refused to move, and they refused to move
because they oftentimes invested more money in their homes
than the Irish. They withstood the destruction of their neighborhood because they were Italian and incidentally Catholic
and were less dependent on Church-run institutions. The Irish,
on the other hand, spent more on their churches than they did
on their homes, which in the case of MBS, were nothing spectacular. When the Church was thwarted in its attempt to keep

the neighborhood Irish, Irish culture proved too brittle to withstand the change. It cracked and broke, and the inhabitants beat a path to the suburbs, where they, for the most part, did not regroup.

In an interview in the early '90s in a Philadelphia Irish newspaper, Clark claimed that the Irish in America "need to get unhooked from the automobile, break our addiction to this idiot mobility which has permitted people to move away from problems rather than solve them." In this, Clark is talking precisely about the post-World War II Irish diaspora that took place in Philadelphia. Ironically, it was liberals like Clark who were most prone to grasp at liberal platitudes about education and expanded government programs. The disillusionment of the Irish ethnic Clark in the '90s was almost palpable.

But beyond Clark's disillusionment, there were other problems which were more pressing for the Church. The Church, which could not face the racial issue squarely according to its own carefully articulated principles, was going to have a difficult time selling the changes that were coming from Vatican II as well. Taken together the two issues would create a major crisis of faith for a group of people who had received the Gospel though the medium of a European culture whose bulwark in the United States, a parish like MBS, was being whipsawed by the twin forces of assimilation and racial turmoil.

Msgr. Philip Dowling takes a considerably less sympathetic view of the Irish parish in post-World War II Philadelphia. Dowling was curate at Corpus Christi parish in North Philadelphia beginning in 1957 when the Irish diaspora was well underway in that section of the city. He also gave the last sermon at Corpus Christi when that parish closed its doors in 1987. Like other pastors in the parishes the Irish left behind, Dowling feels that the Irish neighborhoods did not survive because the culture supporting them was too brittle or too lacking in Christian concern. When change came, the neighborhood proved incapable of welcoming the stranger and what was brittle broke. The same was true of the Italian ethnic parish in North Philadelphia. It did not survive the way the Italian neighborhoods in South Philadelphia did, but in retrospect one wonders if it is fair to place this sort of burden on the Irish. First of all, they were of all the Catholic ethnics the most readily assimilable, and when the suburbs called they saw little reason not to answer. But beyond that, when it comes to race, we are not talking about just any problem. As the riots in Los Angeles in the early '90s showed, this country has shown itself singularly ineffective in dealing with the race issue. Individuals faced with the culture's failure will tend to seek individual solutions, and that is precisely what the Irish did, for the most part, voting with their feet.

If Dowling was disappointed in the Irish, there is some indication that the Irish were disappointed in him as well. In an article for NC News service done by Father John Foley in March of 1968, Dowling claimed that "the problem is that there are just too many people in one area." Dowling called for "the diffusion of Negro families throughout the city and suburban area," a proposal that is unlikely to have found favor with the recent refugees from the liberal racial policies which had just driven them across the city's border. Dowling, however, perhaps as a result of his experiences in Corpus Christi felt that it was unfair to make the people in changing neighborhoods bear the brunt of racial tension when they didn't cause the problem. "It is not that they are especially prejudiced," Dowling said, expressing a refreshing change from the normal point of view one found in the standard media portrayal of the Catholic neighborhoods, "but the confrontation happens to occur there." As if to add that the Church wasn't sitting on its hands when it came to racial matters, Dowling cited specific programs initiated by the Cardinal's commission, including one that brought together "2,000 students in Philadelphia and suburban Catholic high schools [to] cooperate in the work of the Community Service Corps which engages young people in direct contact and involvement with inner city youngsters through tutoring and foster brother and sister programs."

Archbishop Krol's major decision on racial matters was his decision to accept Dowling' proposal and to work with him on the matter. As some indication of the seriousness with which he viewed the issue, Krol asked Dowling to move into the cardinal's residence on City Avenue so that he could be kept apprised of the situation on a regular basis. But faced with an intractable problem, Krol seems to have decided that in delegating the responsibility he could devote his energies to where they might be more productive. His views on the racial situation were dominated by two considerations. First of all, he was skeptical of people like Clark and the civil rights movement Negroes Clark associated with because he suspected both of having an agenda that was in many ways inimical to the interests of the Church. This is in many ways born out in Clark's article in *Commonweal*. Clark describes the frustration of local Catholic Negroes, seven of whom met with Krol's staff in the wake of the Folcroft incident. What becomes clear from the meeting is that the blacks are becoming increasingly seduced by the rhetoric of the civil rights movement to the point of declaring in Clark's words, that "they would leave the Church if some change were not brought about in the local scene." What ensued was a vicious circle. In light of this sort of threat, Krol became wary of Negroes who seemed, in his words, "more black than Catholic." The Catholic Negroes on the other hand, sensing some sort of rebuff on Krol's part, had, In Clark's words, begun drifting out of the Council and joining CORE and SNCC. Dowling succeeded where the Catholic Negroes didn't because he had Krol's confidence and they did not. After the *Commonweal* article appeared, Krol would only feel that his misgivings had been confirmed. What Dowling had in terms of Krol's support, he lacked in terms of support in the black community, and given the increasing racial polarization of the '60s that was to prove a formidable obstacle to the Church's efforts.

The second principle which guided Krol's racial policies was simply his reading of demographic trends and his coming to the conclusion that "you can't prevent people from moving." Krol's experience with the racial situation in the United States began with his job at Kroger's, which was located in a black neighborhood. To him blacks were "God's children," but they possessed no special talismanic qualities. They were just another ethnic group, like the Germans in Cleveland with whom the Poles had a "stone throwing relationship," as Krol was to put it later in life.

Krol remembers spending a great deal of time preparing parishioners at St. Gregory's in West Philadelphia for the closing of their parish only to have his efforts "greeted with one great big yawn." Krol saw the issue of race and the parishes as one of demographic shift, which occurred with the impersonality of tectonic plates moving from one position to another. It was not the business of the archdiocese to tell people where they should live, and beyond that the shift was for the most part a zero sum game for the archdiocese. The Irish might move from the city to the suburbs, but they remained within boundaries of the archdiocese for the most part even when they did. Racial migration was more of a problem for the city of Philadelphia than it was for the archdiocese, and after so many years of watching the city rebuff the Church's efforts to strengthen the moral foundation of the social order, Krol gradually came to the conclusion that the city got pretty much what it deserved. The fiscal insolvency of the late '80s under the administration of the city's first black mayor was just the financial analogue to the moral policies the city had been pursuing since the advent of the Clark/Dilworth reform in 1951. The chickens had come home to roost, as Malcolm X once said.

Krol for the most part was busy with other things during 1963. Less than a month after the Folcroft incident he flew to Rome to attend the second session of the Second Vatican Council. On September 29, 1963, the second session convened at St. Peter's Basilica to see if the Church could hammer out a definition of itself that was something more relevant to the situation of the mid-twentieth century than the reaction to the Reformation's idea of the invisible Church which the Church had formulated at Trent. Emphasis on the institutional character of the Church had made it virtually impossible to deal with Christians separated from Rome and heal the breach brought about by the Reformation. It had become increasingly necessary to disentangle the Church's definition of itself from the political language current when that definition was last forged. The arguments of Cardinal Bellarmine, according to Ratzinger's assessment of the Council, were too dependent on late medieval political theory, too dependent on Aristotle and as a result increasingly incomprehensible to an age which drew its ideas of politics from other sources.

Beyond that, there was the unfinished business left over from Vatican I, which defined papal infallibility and then had to prorogue before defining the role of bishop, when the French withdrew their troops from Rome. That historical fact, com-

bined with the rise of the new media of communication, combined with the personality of Pius XII, led to a concentration of
power and governance in the hands of one man that was simply
not healthy for the Church. The Church had to redefine herself
in terms of her scriptural origins and redefine the role of bishop
in that light as the successor of the apostles and not, as had
often become the case under Pius XII, the employee of the pope.
On October 30, the bishops opted for collegiality, a ratification
of the idea that the bishops "as a college" continued the office of
the apostles. In the period following the Council this would
lead to abuses of its own, but in light of the paralysis which had
come over the Church during the latter days of Pius XII, it was
clear that some corrective in course was necessary.

Aside from an intervention on November 20, 1964 on the
incompatibility of the Church's matrimonial discipline with the
Council's Decree on Ecumenism and its Decree on Religious
Liberty, Archbishop Krol made all of his interventions in writing during the month of July 1963 before the second session
began. The reason should be obvious. Krol could not both run
the administrative machinery of the Council and intervene at
the same time. In keeping with his interests and aptitude, the
major suggestions in the written interventions of July 1963 were
procedural. He urged the Council fathers to consider submitting their proposals in writing rather than *viva voce*. "The right
of speaking in general congregation is an individual right," he
wrote, "and should not impede the right of the community."
The intervention was Krol's response to the often unwieldy
mechanism of the Council and his impatience at getting something accomplished in the face of what must have seemed an
interminable line of speeches. He also recommended "that an
automatic warning be given each speaker two minutes before
the end of his assigned time." Finally, he recommended that the
individual bishops be granted permission to address the individual commissions rather than the entire assembly of bishops.
Taken together his procedural interventions betray an impatience which some would describe as typically American. Krol
felt that there was too much talk and too little result and wanted
to streamline the procedures to correct that imbalance.

Beyond that, his interventions were for the most part technical and legal in scope. In reading the schema on the Church

he came up with ten grammatical errors. In addition to that, he felt that the word sacrament was used imprecisely and that the second chapter of the schema which dealt with the bishops as the successors of the apostles was "obscure." "The universal jurisdiction in the church," Krol wrote, "as it is given to the college of bishops is clearly affirmed; but perhaps the power of each of the bishops to teach should be stated with greater clarity." To rectify that lack of clarity, Krol proposed adding the following sentences to the schema: "We teach that the bishops united in college with their head, the successor of Peter succeed to the college of Apostles with a divine mandate. . . . . We teach that the bishops alone, in conformity with the divine establishment of the Church, exercise immediately and completely the apostolic ministry of doctrine, sacred worship, and government of the faithful, since it is the source of all the power and sanctification in the Church."

Archbishop Krol also praised the schema of the Blessed Virgin Mary for "its brevity, clarity, its derivation solely from Sacred Scripture and the previous declarations of the Church's magisterium." He thought too, that the schema was notable "because it rejects the errors of both the maximalists and of the minimalists." The discussion of the role of Mary in the Church, in redemption and in relation to the separated brethren was to prove to be one of the most protracted debates of the Council. The maximalists wanted a document devoted to her alone, a motion which was defeated on October 29, 1963 when the schema on Mary was incorporated into the document on the Church as a way of taming what had become in many council father's eyes a kind of Mariolatry. Ratzinger said that much of the discussion on Mary gave more indication of the bishops' piety than it did their theological acumen and felt that the discussion during September 16 to 18, 1964 "scarcely rose to the level of the average devotional treatise." Ratzinger is adamant, however, in claiming that the Church did not want to "dismantle Marian devotion and through this to gradually adjust to Protestantism." Rather, it was his contention that the devotion to Mary had taken on a life of its own, independent of and often in contradiction to the the life of the Church, and that the time had come for the two to be integrated in some rational, scripturally cogent fashion. As was often the case, Krol could see both sides of the issue and proposed a middle way, which he felt incorporated the best points of both positions.

Krol felt that ecumenism was an inspiration of the Holy Spirit, but he was troubled by what he saw as an indiscriminate opening to positions that might undermine the teaching of the Church. As he did with some of the other schema, he felt that the schema on ecumenism suffered from lack of precise language, showing his penchant for legal precision. Krol applauded the desire to express the doctrines of the faith in a more biblical and patristic fashion, but wondered if this amounted to a *de facto* demotion of Thomistic theology and an imprudent opening to existential and Kantian philosophy without recognition of the doctrinal pitfalls involved in this openness.

Archbishop Krol's contribution to the Council was mainly administrative. When he had something substantive to propose it was generally either technical, i.e., a criticism of the imprecise use of the ablative case, or legal, generally betraying the distress of a canon lawyer at terms he found legally imprecise. If he found the documents themselves often imprecise, it is clear that he was going to be unhappy with the accounts of the Council which began appearing in the press at that time. By the end of the second session, it was becoming increasingly apparent to Krol that what went on in St. Peter's and what got reported in the press were two separate things. Being a canon lawyer, an administrator and a linguist of sorts meant that Krol was a stickler when it came to precision in Council documents. This also meant that Krol was by temperament not favorably disposed to journalism in general even under the best of circumstances. And as experience would show, the journalistic coverage of the Council was far from journalism's finest moment. The journalists, in this regard, had plenty to complain about as well. The Council sessions were not open to the press, and as a result they had to depend on inside sources, sources who all too often used the press to push for a particular agenda.

On the plane returning from the recently concluded second session in December 1963, Krol happened to pick up the December 6, 1963 copy of *Time* magazine and turned to an article on the Council by *Time's* Vatican correspondent Robert Kaiser. What he saw did not please him. Krol found Kaiser's account full of inaccuracies and decided to write a letter exposing them which would be signed by Bishop Albert R. Zuroweste of Belleville, Illinois, the chairman of the United States delegation's press panel. The letter to the editors of *Time*, even if it didn't go out under Krol's name, was classic John Krol, beginning with his wise guy expression of "sincere sympathy to *Time* readers who at best got an incomplete and distorted account of the Council." Krol chides *Time*'s Kaiser, who "seems to approach his task with the attitude: 'Please, my mind is made up—don't confuse me with facts.'"

The allegation was, of course, essentially true. Virtually all of the major media covering the Council had turned it into an Enlightenment morality play before it had even begun, and *Time* was no exception (it never is). In fact, in many ways because of the curious character of the magazine itself, which often did stories that were simply rewrites of other news accounts with a spin that was hoped would appeal to the conventional wisdom, *Time* was worse than most. Alfredo Cardinal Ottaviani was predictably cast in the role of stock villain because he was "dead set against Murray's ideas on liberty of conscience." (Theodore Hesburgh gave a further example of this genre in his autobiography when he pitted Ottaviani against Murray once again, Hesburgh of course siding with Murray on the side of "academic freedom.")

The bishops, on the other hand, were praised because they "overwhelmingly approved the democratic notion of collegiality." In general, the accounts of the Council emanating from the American press took on a singularly nationalistic cast, with progressive Americans battling obscurantist Italian cardinals in an an attempt to bring the Church into the realms of light and modernity. It was like a sort of flatfooted Henry James novel, all American-European conflict and no nuance.

Krol took special exception to Kaiser's statement that the second session was a "parliament of stalemate, compromise and delay" and countered with a barrage of statistics:

> The facts are: in the 43 meetings of the second session six schemata were discussed—as compared with two in the first session, and two were approved and promulgated—as compared with none in the first session. . . . In the second session there were 1471

oral and written interventions as compared with about 650 in the first session. . . . Is this increase of more than 100 percent a slow down?

Krol then ripped into Kaiser's terminology. It was the same sort of thing he had criticized in the Council documents but here Krol felt no need for rhetorical restraint. "There is no such thing as a "'standpat schemata,'" he informed the editors of *Time*. "A 'schema' is a draft or proposal, submitted for acceptance or rejection. If accepted, it is accepted for discussion, revision and further revision, until the Council Fathers vote final approval."

Krol then proceeded to list one error after another in Kaiser's article:

The "schema' on the Liturgy was never rejected—not in its entirety nor in any part, as your reporter alleges.

No "schema" was ever proposed by the conservative Roman Curia." The Curia has no right or opportunity to propose any schema.

Neither Pope John nor Pope Paul were ever called upon "to mediate a dispute" or "to intervene," nor did either of them volunteer to mediate such alleged dispute. Pope John intervened only once and that was to give consideration to the views of a substantial minority.

Your reporter talks about "the twelve council commissions." There are only ten such commissions, and one Secretariat.

Your reporter alleges that the chapter on religious liberty was composed in part by a U.S. Jesuit, and that "Pope Paul intends to have it revised by the Theological Commission and its president who is dead set against . . . [the Jesuit's] ideals on liberty of conscience ." The fact is that the initial draft of the chapter was prepared by the Secretariat for Christian Unity and was then discussed and revised by a joint Commission consisting of members of both the Secretariat and the Theological Commission, and was then voted out of the Theological Commission for submission to the Council Fathers.

On the last point Krol is being somewhat legalistic, proposing a false dichotomy between the people who wrote the schema and the people who influenced them, but in general the critique is fairly devastating. "These FACTS," Krol concluded, "may take some of the steam out of your reporter's campaign against his favorite 'bad guys,' but they will also correct the distorted picture of the Council he gave to your readers. *Time* readers deserve better than they received from your Council reporter."

In early January, Bishop Zuroweste released the letter under his name to the National Catholic News Service which did a short article on it that appeared in diocesan papers throughout the country on January 11, 1964. However, it was now over a month since the original article appeared and Krol's letter still hadn't appeared in *Time*'s letters column. Then in early February, Bishop Zuroweste received a letter from Marylois Purdy of *Time* dated February 4, in which she attempted to reduce the distortions in Kaiser's piece to issues of "semantics" and "matters of opinion." To bolster her latter point Miss Purdy informed Bishop Zuroweste that "the *Christian Century* editorialist, and Michael Novak of the *New Republic* reached similar conclusions" to those reached by Kaiser. In addition to that impressive bit of information, Miss Purdy wrote that "various writers in *Commonweal* and *America* indicated that the session did not meet their expectations."

Miss Purdy concluded by saying, in effect, that everyone was right. "It's apparent that you would have submitted a very different evaluation of Vatican Council II had this been your assignment—but this difference of opinion does not negate *Time*'s stand, nor your own." Miss Purdy also opined that "we are glad to discuss this reporting with you and we respect your stand on the subject," but she gave no indication that *Time* was going to run the letter in its letters column. Two days after receiving the letter, Zuroweste wrote to Krol elated at Purdy's response. "We finally smoked *Time* out of its cover," he crowed to Krol. "In my opinion, the answer was written by Kaiser himself with the help of some of his Jesuit friends and members of *Commonweal*'s staff." In addition to showing the mistrust the bishops were beginning to feel toward certain elements in the Church, i.e., *Commonweal* and the Jesuits, the response showed that when it came to logomachy, the bishops hardly had the killer instinct. Both Krol and Zuroweste felt vindicated by a response that left the misconceptions still firmly in place in the minds of *Time* readers, which it seems safe to assume involved not a few Catholics.

In a letter dated February 20, Krol in essence agreed with Zuroweste's assessment. "We could cut up *Time*'s attempt to reply, but I doubt whether it would now serve any good purpose." Krol concludes on a note of chivalry indicating that "there are so many gratuitous statements, and such weak attempts at justification that it might be cruel to expose the author of the letter." Krol proposes letting the matter drop, believing that "our purposes were accomplished. The author may be more careful, and our people will not be inclined to accept as authoritative, *Time*'s reports on the Council." In a letter written at the end of February, Zuroweste concurs and the matter was dropped. In retrospect, though it's difficult to see that much was accomplished. The letter never got to *Time* readers, the people most immediately affected by the article's inaccuracies. Beyond that, the exchange does not seem to have tempered either *Time*'s or Kaiser's view of the Council, and may have contributed to their impression that the Church was not willing to pursue the issue. The misrepresentation of the Council was to continue unabated, and the Catholic laity, many of whom subscribed to secular organs like *Time* magazine, were its first victims, as what the Council attempted to do receded behind a bewildering maze of media-erected misrepresentations.

On Friday, August 28, 1964, roughly one year after the Folcroft incident, two Philadelphia police officers, one white and the other black, arrived at the corner of 22nd and Columbia Aves. in the heart of Philadelphia's Negro ghetto in answer to a complaint that a car was blocking the intersection. Sitting at the wheel of the car standing in the middle of the intersection was a woman by the name of Odessa Bradford, 34 years of age and obviously intoxicated, in the middle of a heavy domestic dispute with her husband, Rush, also the same age and also intoxicated. After attempts to persuade Mrs. Bradford to move her car failed, the two police officers attempted to remove her from the car forcibly, which because of her resistance—she hit the officers repeatedly—and shouting, attracted a rather sizeable crowd in a short period of time. Before long the crowd joined in the struggle. A man later identified as James Mettles, 41 years old, attacked Officer Hoff, and in response to the attack Officer Wells, his partner, radioed an "assist officer" call. By the time police reinforcements arrived the crowd had spread to the roofs of neighboring buildings, and as Mrs. Bradford and Mr. Mettles were taken away, the crowd showed its disapproval by unleashing a barrage of rocks and bottles which smashed the windshield of one police car and of ten other parked cars in the vicinity. The Philadelphia riots of 1964 had begun.

What happened in Philadelphia was the beginning of a chain reaction of racial events that began in Harlem on July 18, 1964 and ended in the Watts section of Los Angeles one year later. It was a series of events which would cause the liberal mind a great deal of anguish and perplexity. Nineteen sixty-four marked the tenth anniversary of the modern civil rights struggle born out of the landmark *Brown v. Board of Education* decision. During that decade of legislative progress culminating in the Civil Rights Bill of 1964, the legal framework of segregation was dismantled law by law, and the federal government put the full weight of its financial might and moral influence behind an effort that would attempt to erase the legacy of race discrimination and bring the Negro up to a par with his white fellow citizens. Perplexing to the liberal was the fact that each new legislative breakthrough was followed by outbreaks of random and seemingly pointless violence that no one could explain. If things were getting better, why were the Negroes so upset? It was the question the liberals were having a hard time answering.

One man who pondered this paradox over the fall of 1964 in the wake of both the landmark civil rights bill and the riots it seemed to inexplicably spawn was Daniel Patrick Moynihan, an undersecretary in the Department of Transportation in the Johnson Administration. In an interoffice memo that subsequently came to be known as the "Moynihan Report," Moynihan posited a correlation between family breakdown and economic well being. No progress would be made in raising the economic standard of blacks until something was done to strengthen the black family. In order to solve the nation's race problem, something would first have to be done to roll back the black illegitimacy rate which stood at the then appalling figure of 20 percent. The liberals would have their own say on the idea of strengthening the family—any family—during the summer of 1965, when the whole idea was torpedoed in favor of something more congenial to liberal interests than strong families—things like heavily funded government programs that would distribute information on contraceptive use.

But in the summer of 1964, it looked as if the conservatives' worst fears were about to come true. The cities became engulfed in flames as hordes of anarchic Negroes pillaged their own neighborhoods in what many thought was a prelude to their pillaging other people's neighborhoods as well. Moynihan was more prescient than any one knew at the time. For days after the riots in North Philadelphia, the papers were full of speculation about possible conspirators. A shadowy group called the "Blood Brothers" was named, but no evidence was produced linking the initial people arrested other than the severely strained marital bond linking Mr. and Mrs. Bradford. The spark that set off the Philadelphia riots was a domestic quarrel, which provided a symbolism of the beleaguered state of family life among Negroes that no one could understand or wanted to acknowledge at the time.

After a momentary lull in the course of events following the initial arrests on the evening of August 28, the calm was broken by a Negro agitator from the area by the name of Raymond Hall, 25 years of age, who stood on the corner of 23rd and Columbia Avenues and shouted to anyone in his vicinity that white policemen had just beaten a pregnant black woman to death. Hall wasn't the only agitator apprehended that night. Also arrested was a local activist by the name of Shakykh Muhammud Ali Hussan (also known as Abyssinia Hayes), who operated out of a combination dry cleaning shop and "African-Asian Culture Center" at 23rd and Columbia. Hayes was arrested while jumping up and down alternately screaming obscenities and "We want freedom," and had previously been arrested for assaulting a Negro reporter for the local black radio station, WDAS, which had run accounts critical of Hussan's racial views. Hussan or Hayes' choice of slogans was instructive. Like the rest of the residents of North Philadelphia, most of whom had come from the South as recent migrants, Hayes had watched the civil rights movement on television as it confronted Jim Crow in the south. The experience was transposed to the cities of the north in ways that mystified many, including Martin Luther King, Jr. To begin with, Jim Crow was not in force in the North. The neighborhoods were "segregated," if by that one meant racially homogeneous, but that was the result of the ethnic colonization of the city, whose neighborhoods and parishes were often ethnically homogeneous as well. That was simply the way immigrants settled in Philadelphia and the fact that it had nothing to do with the system of segregation erected in the defeated South after the Civil War should have been apparent to people more acute than Abyssinia Hayes.

Beyond that, the other dissimilarity had to do with the fact that protest in the North was not nonviolent, and in many ways was so diffuse as not to merit the term protest at all. The Negro in Philadelphia, the overwhelming majority of whom had come up from the South or whose parents had, clearly identified with what was going on down there, but implemented it in a way that liberals found baffling. The same gap between image and reality afflicted the white ethnics as well. The image of the long-suffering, nonviolent vaguely intellectual Church-going Negro they saw on television was not being replicated by the mob marching down Columbia Avenue smashing store windows, or the gangs that would fight pitched battles in their campaign to take over the city's playgrounds. In 1964, no one was capable of bringing these two discordant images into intellectual alignment. The culture suffered from a bad case of cognitive dissonance: the racial theories did not fit the racial facts.

By 11:00 P.M. on that Friday night the original crowd had multiplied in size and greeted anything it did not like with a hail of rocks and bottles. When a patrol car arrived on the scene at around that time, its rear window was smashed in by something the crowd threw. As if on cue, while the damaged patrol car was radioing for reinforcements, the mob started marching east on Columbia Avenue, smashing store windows and looting the stores. The mob also radiated out north along Ridge Avenue with the same effect on that street's stores. By 2:30 A.M. the mob had reached 15th St., one block west of Broad St. (there is no 14th street in Philadelphia) the city's main north-south artery. If the disruption were allowed to cross Broad St, it would have disrupted traffic on that thoroughfare and virtually cut the city in half.

One of the first casualties of this cognitive dissonance was the police department. The Clark/Dilworth reform tradition was not going to foster black migration and then turn around play Bull Connor. By 1964, the Mayor of Philadelphia, James H. J. Tate, however, was only a distant relative of Clark/Dilworth, and oftentimes not on particularly good terms with them. Tate was an Irish Catholic and a Democrat at a time when the New Deal coalition of Blacks and Catholic ethnics was showing considerable signs of strain. Black migration was one of the main causes of the strain. When blacks came to Philadelphia, they did not end up in either Dick Dilworth's or Joe Clark's neighborhood. They did end up only a stone's throw—if you'll pardon the metaphor—from where Mayor Tate lived in St. Veronica's parish in North Philadelphia, and the mayor was hard pressed to keep the coalition together when he saw the ravages of black migration first hand.

In order not to end up on TV with hoses and German shepherds, Police commissioner Howard Leary evolved the strategy one year before the riots of applying maximal manpower but minimal force. By the morning of Saturday, August 29, there were 600 policemen on the scene, but the police were not allowed to draw their guns. Commissioner O'Leary, probably with images of the civil rights marches in the South still fresh in his mind, had also proscribed the use of fire hoses, dogs and police on horseback. There were to be no pitched battles between the police and the roving mobs. The looters and rioters were to be arrested one by one, a tactic which entailed a number of footraces and wrestling matches until the police became too exhausted to proceed. The results of this strategy were apparent in the 1964 riots. On the positive side human casualties were kept to a minimum. On the negative side, the mob, sensing that it had nothing to fear, inflicted maximal property damage. "It was like being in a war," one officer recounted later. 'We couldn't do anything. There were so many rioters. Most of them women, teenagers or even younger. The situation was completely out of hand. We'd chase them one way, and another group would come at us from another direction throwing bricks, trash cans, and anything."

One of the first groups to complain about Leary's strategy were the black property owners in the ghetto, specifically some of the ministers of the area's largest black churches. Rev. Leon Sullivan, minister of a large Baptist church in the area, requested that the National Guard be called in. Sullivan would go on to become a major broker of federal money through his Opportunity's Industrialization Corps later in the '60s. At the time of the riots, he was upset at being called to bear the brunt of the police department's nonviolent crowd control strategies.

In the end, other Negro leaders would have no more success with the crowd than Sullivan had with the Guard. Cecil Moore, the local head of the NAACP, took to the streets urging the people to return to their homes only to be taunted by looters with arms full of booty, who shouted back "See this Cecil? See this? What are you going to do about this?" When a police car arrived at the corner where Moore was speaking, the crowd deserted Moore and surrounded the car shouting "We want freedom." When black disk jockey Georgie Woods arrived on the scene in an automobile equipped with a public address system he received the same treatment Moore had. Dick Gregory, who was then known as a "comedian," arrived on the scene and had some success in dispersing the crowd. When he tried the same thing one year later in Watts, he got shot for his pains. The mob acknowledged no leaders black or white; it had become a law unto itself.

By daybreak of Saturday, August 29, the number of police in the neighborhood had doubled to 1,200 but the police were fatally handicapped by the tactics imposed on them by Commissioner Leary. As a result the situation was completely out of control. At 6:00 PM one eyewitness watched as a band of looters invaded five stores with impunity; the police stood by and watched but made no attempt to stop them. "The hell with it," one police officer was overheard saying. "Let them do what they want." Eventually the number of police would triple to 1,800 by Saturday night when the looting reached its peak, but by Saturday morning it was apparent to virtually everyone that the mob and not the police were in control of the situation. There were simply not enough policemen to run down the alleys of North Philadelphia to tackle looters one by one. The riot would continue until it burned itself out. The rioting ended in effect when the weekend did. Gradually the crowds began to thin over Sunday afternoon, perhaps because people were tiring, perhaps because the stores had been picked clean.

By Monday morning it was over. North Philadelphia went back to a state of affairs similar to that which prevailed before the riots; the storefronts of the looted buildings were boarded over, but for the most part the Jewish merchants who owned them never returned. The net result for the ghetto was a loss of infrastructure, compensated somewhat by an increase in federal programs. The pattern established would persist for the next 30 years. "Pay up or the cities will burn," was Moynihan's formulation of the general rule which was still being applied some 30 years later after the Rodney King riots in Los Angeles in the early '90s.

At a press conference on Sunday afternoon, Mayor Tate invoked an 1850 state law, ironically spawned by the Nativist Riots, and placed a curfew on a 410 square block area which included the southernmost segment of his own parish. All bars and liquor stores and movie houses in the area were closed and those who violated the dawn to dusk curfew were subject to immediate arrest. In the end, two people were killed, 339 wounded (including 100 policemen), 308 arrested, and property damage was estimated at $3,000,000.

The other casualties resulting from the riot were not as easy to quantify. Foremost among them was the New Deal Democratic coalition in the city of Philadelphia. The ineffectiveness of Leary's tactics contributed to the rise of Frank Rizzo, who became the champion of the city's blue collar ethnics, and within a short time a police commissioner who wanted to buy armored vehicles as a precaution against the next riot. Rizzo also made a name for himself by inviting the press to a police raid on Black Panther headquarters in Philadelphia, inviting the Black Panthers to take off their clothes and be photographed by an obliging press. Rizzo also was photographed with a nightstick protruding from his cummerbund when he was called from a formal dinner to give leadership to a police raid. When Tate chose Rizzo as his heir apparent, it was the final nail in the coffin for the Clark/Dilworth coalition of blacks and ethnics. From then on, one chose one side or the other in an ongoing urban conflict: the Catholics (although the issue was never framed in these terms) or the blacks. Lest anyone doubt where they stood, both Clark and Dilworth came out against both Tate and Rizzo. Being liberal and being Catholic in Philadelphia became as the '60s progressed an increasingly self-contradictory proposition.

Archbishop Krol was to find this out in his own fashion. Krol did not feel compelled to make a personal appearance at every natural disaster which occurred in the city, but he did go to some. He would be on the scene if a Catholic church caught on fire and his secretary of the time, Msgr. James Connelly, remembers the archbishop possessing a certain charismatic following among the police and firemen, most of whom were Catholic at the time. "The firemen on the scene would go down on one knee to kiss his ring in a street full of water," Connelly remembers. He also remembers four motorcycle cops crying as they carried Krol to a waiting patrol car when he was stricken with pleurisy at a local banquet in honor of Cardinal Wyszynsky of Poland. And Krol reciprocated in his attitude toward the police and firemen. It was he who instituted the annual police and fireman's Mass at which police and firemen serve Mass in their uniforms, a tradition which is still in existence in the Archdiocese.

With Connolly at the wheel, Krol toured the riot area by car on the night of Sunday, August 30, driving first to the police staging area at Broad and Columbia, where Krol was debriefed by Commissioner Leary. Krol may have been archbishop of the entire Archdiocese, but his sympathies were clearly not with the rioters, a fact he made clear in his statement on the riots which appeared in the archdiocesan newspaper:

> The effects of the widespread vandalism and violence, which we saw at first hand, may well have an adverse impact on some to the just aspirations of our good Negro people. If the outburst was planned, it could not have been planned by true friends of the Negro people. It is most regrettable that some of the people in the area followed such false leadership to the extremes of plunder and violence.

Krol then focused his attention on the civil rights movement and the effect it was having on social order throughout the country.

> For some months we have been apprehensive about the repeated appeals for civil disobedience. Those who recklessly incite to civil disobedience must not ignore the full impact of their action especially upon the young. Civil disobedience is a volatile instrument even in the pursuit of a just objective. Grave responsibility is shared by those whose reckless appeals for civil disobedience result in violence and disorder and even hampers the attainment of a just cause. The courageous restraint of the police in the face of such grave provocation deserves highest commendation.

After meeting with commissioner O'Leary, Krol went to the police station at 17th and Montgomery, where he discussed the situation with the chief inspector there, also an Irish Catholic. Krol liked the police, and they liked him, so much so they gave him a light blue riot control helmet with his name on it. In accepting the helmet, Krol was to learn that taking sides was often no easier for prelates that it was for politicians. A number of the priests involved in the civil rights movement accused Krol of racial insensitivity for accepting it.

In conjunction with the curfew imposed by Mayor Tate, Krol dispensed Catholics in the riot area from any obligation to attend Mass on Sunday, August 30. This, in turn, earned him the ire of a local representative of the Quakers, Richmond Miller, of the American Friends Service Committee, who accused Krol of a racial double standard.

Krol responded in typical fashion. "Richmond," he responded, "Let me ask you a question. How many Quakers are in that area?"

Connelly, whose father was a Philadelphia policeman, feels that the riots were a turning point of sorts for Krol. "I think at that particular time he realized that the Church had to become involved more in the civil life of the city."

In the aftermath of the riots, various groups, one by one, came forward and levelled the finger of blame. On November 24, Mayor Tate claimed that "the civil disorders in North Philadelphia were greatly intensified, if not actually caused, by the heavy concentration of taprooms, taverns, barrooms, and similar establishments." It was an explanation more sensible than many. Cecil Moore, in the midst of the riots on August 29, claimed that police brutality was the cause. The liberals claimed that it was the Negro's lack of education that caused the riot, or at least the frustration at being inadequate to urban life that flowed from that lack. A pamphlet on the riots commissioned by the American Jewish Congress tended to see lack of education as the cause and called for "a crash program of education, penetrating every age group from the pre-school child to the retrainable adult. . . . What is needed is a program so massive that many will dismiss it as visionary—a program that will deeply engage all the public and private sectors of American life." They went on to quote Michael Harrington's suggestion "that the Federal government pay the children of the poor to go to school." The AJC would soon get its wish in the form of the War on Poverty, but with dubious results.

Conspicuous by its absence from all of the proposals was any treatment of the actual cause of the riot, namely, a domestic squabble. The notion that domesticity gone bad could fuel such a conflagration was simply a notion invisible to the categories of the time. As a result the problem got worse. In fact the money poured into solving it proved all too often—given the secularization of government agencies at the time and the penchant for sexual liberation among the agents—to be gasoline poured on the fire. The report of the AJC concludes with a plethora of platitudes common to the time: "These demands upon whites and negroes will not be easy to meet since it is difficult, if not impossible, for anyone growing up in America to escape from some form of racist contamination." At the same time, the AJC report gives some evidence that racism may not be the source of the problem after all in the form of perplexity concerning the "significant" fact "that the recent eruptions in Negro communities have not occurred in areas dominated by more flagrant forms of racism, by the Klan and other institutions of Southern bigotry."

The riots followed by four months the founding of the Commission on Human Relations which came into existence as a result of Folcroft. Krol was convinced by the confluence of events that year that something had to be done; however, he was realistic enough to know that he was not in a position to do anything himself. The importation of Msgr. Dowling into the Cardinal's residence was Krol's way of keeping apprised of a critical situation. However, knowing what the problem is and knowing a solution to it are two different things, and in the issue of race Krol was probably more dependent on his lieutenants than in other areas. His lieutenants, for their part, were coming up with solutions that sounded a lot like what the federal government was proposing. As a result, the Catholic Church lost the sense that it had something unique to provide and as a result of that, Krol and the Church in general gradually slipped to an attitude of tacit discouragement in the face of what seemed to be such an intractable problem. The seminary gradually phased out its program of sending seminarians to work in the inner city, a fact which Dowling regretted.

By the early '90s, the Church had all but admitted that the social breakdown which racial migration occasioned in Philadelphia was beyond its power to resolve. By the early '90s, no one in the archdiocesan chain of command had much to say on the race issue anymore. Krol had the sense that the problem was moral at root and involved breakdown of society in general, but at the same time the government was emphasizing the urgency of the racial problem, it was doing everything within its power to prevent the Church from bringing her peculiar moral and spiritual gifts to bear as part of the solution. As a result, Krol over a period of time began to view the problem as essentially one of demography. Whites were abandoning the city, largely as a result of liberal policies which made their neighborhoods uninhabitable. Krol had no authority over city policy, nor did he have the right to tell Catholics where to live. He did institute a policy whereby suburban diocesan parishes shared their financial resources with parishes in the inner city, but that was in many ways closing the barn door after the horse had escaped. In 1963, MBS was a thriving Catholic powerhouse which found itself faced with a problem which threatened its very existence as a community. In 1993, MBS was a remnant parish of single parent families whose children often went through the parish school and were often baptized into the Church but thereafter seemed to drift back to living according to the default settings of ghetto culture. The seed of the gospel was falling on the cultural equivalent of very hard ground. In retrospect, it is difficult to see that anyone benefited from the policies which brought about the change. The blacks got some mean row houses at bargain basement prices; the real estate agents made a killing; but the neighborhood is no more integrated than it was 30 years ago and in the process something vibrant which went against the liberal agenda was replaced by something sick which conformed to it.

Looking back on his tenure as the first executive secretary of the Cardinal's Commission on Human Relations and Krol's right hand man on racial matters with the benefit of 30 years' hindsight, Msgr. Philip Dowling is not prone to fits of revisionism in reviewing the Church's policy in dealing with racial migration in the post-World War II period. The 1964 riots happened four months after the commission was formed and in many respects Dowling still holds the views he held then. The main problem was racism, exacerbated by overcrowding in poor sections of Philadelphia, which two factors were in their turn exacerbated by television's coverage of the civil rights movement.

"The consciousness-raising," Dowling claimed with the benefit of almost 30 years hindsight, "took place among blacks mostly because of what was seen on TV and what was read in the papers, and looking at their own situation they felt more angry about it and reacted. Then also at that time was the great civil rights movement on the part of the federal government. So it was very much in the air, it was very much talked about, what was happening. You had laws being passed that had to do with voting rights, that had to do with where people could live. Fair housing laws were being passed, so it was very much a part of everyday awareness. And with that came reactions to it."

Dowling feels that it was unfair to blame Catholics for what happened, but that is more often than not how the scenario got played because Catholics happened to be in the neighborhoods that were changing. Oftentimes the people reacting in the neighborhoods were not Catholic, as was the case of a number of incidents in Kensington, but since the neighborhood was perceived as Catholic, Catholics got the blame.

Fair housing laws were one of the pillars of the Clark/ Dilworth reform movement throughout the '50s. Dowling, as head of the Cardinal's Commission, supported them then and still supports them now. He admits that they may have had a devastating effect on the inner city parishes only reluctantly.

"It didn't really mean the destruction of the parish," Dowling responded, "except in regard to the psychological response. People feared what would be the result. The history of Philadelphia has been strong neighborhoods. Philadelphia is a city of very strong neighborhoods with tremendous cohesion and identity." The real story of the destruction of those neighborhoods, according to Dowling, is still untold and that involves explaining how "that tremendous, entrenched cohesiveness was overcome by fear."

Dowling saw the devastation first hand. Beginning in 1957, he was curate at Corpus Christi parish which abutted the northern boundary of the martial law zone imposed by Mayor Tate during the 1964 riots. In 1987, he preached the last sermon at Corpus Christi parish when it ceased to exist.

"In 1957, Corpus Christi was still a very strong parish," Dowling continued. "I went on the block collection from '57 through the early '60s house to house. Maybe one person on the block might be non-Catholic. The whole neighborhood was an entrenched, powerfully Catholic thing."

During the '60s, Dowling began to notice a change among Corpus Christi parishioners who would seek him out for advice about how the neighborhood was changing. "They would say," he continued, "'I have daughters; I have to be concerned about raising my daughters,'" or "'Our bicycles are being stolen off our porches.' This sort of thing."

The people of Corpus Christi were hurting and when they turned to the Church for help, the Church didn't know what to say. In many ways the situation was beyond the Church's control. Fair housing laws had made it impossible to maintain the character of the neighborhood; but the Church in many ways added insult to injury by supporting the laws that were destroying Catholic neighborhoods throughout the city. Were the people of Corpus Christi being asked to make an *auto da fe* in the liberal *Zeitgeist* that was tantamount to an act of self-immolation? Dowling answers a question with a question.

"What did destroy the neighborhoods?" Dowling responds as if to say he's thought it over himself many times and still hasn't come up with a satisfactory answer. "What was the factor that destroyed the neighborhoods? It was the exodus, the exodus of people to the suburbs. When it comes to moral pressure, I never felt with the work that I was doing that I was ever any kind of agent of the government. I felt from day one throughout the total experience that I was an agent of the Church and that whatever moral persuasion I was involved in was the teachings of the Church. So that's the whole thrust of everything we were involved in. Now simultaneously, of course, you had civil rights activity going on, but all of our activity was to be based on what is the Catholic Church all about."

In retrospect, it seems that there was a lot of overlap between the civil rights movement and the Church's program. In fact, in retrospect, it's difficult to see the difference. The Church's categories in dealing with the matter were derived in large measure from what was presented to them by liberal racial strategies. The Church was forever being chastised by people like Dennis Clark for not doing enough when in reality it seemed to be doing everything it could to foster the same agenda. The Church did not accept everything the civil rights movement proposed uncritically, but it seemed incapable of formulating the problem in terms other than those which the civil rights movement proposed.

A good example of this sort of thinking can be seen in the "Bishops Statement on National Race Crisis," issued on April 25, 1968, on the tenth anniversary of their 1958 statement condemning racism, the statement which was read at St. Gabriel's parish in Folcroft, prompting the parishioners to walk out of the church.

"Now ten years later," the bishops opine, "it is evident that we did not do enough. We have much more to do." What that entails is pretty much the same as before. Part of the "unfinished business" left over from 1958 entails throwing the power of the Church behind "a breakthrough in our educational system," as well as "continuing interfaith efforts to push for the enactment of critically needed legislation in the fields of employment, housing, health and welfare which comprise what the late Martin Luther King, Jr. called the 'Poor Man's bill of rights.'" In their 1968 statement, the bishops urge the further creation of "jobs programs," as well as "strict implementation, nationally and locally, of both the letter and the spirit of the recently enacted federal open-housing act."

If the Church had a unique role to play in solving the nation's racial crisis, it is difficult to discern it in the bishops' 1968 statement, which relegates the Church to the role of cheerleader for the liberal agenda of expanded government. The bishops' statement comes close to making just that statement explicitly. After informing Catholics that "the National Advisory Commission on Civil Disorders concluded last month that white racism was a key factor in creating and maintaining the explosive ghettoes of our cities," it goes on to tell Catholics that "it would be futile to deny what the Commission on Civil Disorders has told America—a white segregationist mentality is largely responsible for the present crisis."

The bishops statement was read in all of the churches of the Archdiocese of Philadelphia when it appeared along with a "suggested homily prepared by Msgr. Dowling, executive director of the Office of the Cardinal's Commission on Human Relations," which told the faithful that "Christian freedom means involvement."

Was there at very least a sort of ambiguity about what role the Church was playing in the minds of beleaguered white inner city parishioners? If we take the fiction of LaSalle University professor emeritus Claude Koch as evidence, it seems that there was. His short stories are populated by Philadelphia Catholics bewildered by the changes of the '60s, and disappointed at the response of the Church, or in the case of the priest characters disappointed in themselves at not being able to mount a better response. Throughout all of the human weakness arises a dominant note of bewilderment. What we are trying doesn't work, his characters seem to be saying, and we don't know what else to try.

When asked if the Cardinal's Commission on Human Relations had to choose between fostering the civil rights movement or preserving Catholic parishes, Msgr. Dowling finds both alternatives repugnant. Dowling was trying to do something else entirely, but it is a something he finds difficult to articulate.

"The priority that I operated under and the priority that I thought I had received a mandate from the Cardinal to pursue was 'What is the Church all about?' What is the Catholic Church all about in the context of this situation, and, therefore, what kind of response should we be making?' Part of showing to the diocese that this was a serious effort was that when it was established in May, shortly thereafter I was asked to come and live in the Cardinal's residence. So that gave among the priests a very strong signal that this is to be taken seriously."

"Did the Cardinal have a strategy here?"

"The strategy," according to Dowling,

> would be really try to bring out the deepest strengths that the Church has to be a force for good in this situation, across the board. At one point, with regard to housing, the question arose: Where should public housing be located within the city? And this was a major issue. The federal government was supplying cities with a good bit of money in order to promote public housing. That public housing was being concentrated only in the poor sections of the city so that they were overburdened really with public housing. At one point the federal government says it should be distributed across the city so that public housing will not be concentrated in one area of poor people, but should be shared across the city. Now this was discussed very carefully by the commission and a policy was developed that we would agree with that. We felt this was a fair thing to do that public housing was something that should be shared by—across the city and not just concentrated in one area.

Needless to say, the public housing did not go up in Chestnut Hill near Senator Clark's home. If it didn't end up in the ghetto either, there was only one other alternative, namely, Catholic ethnic neighborhoods. One such high rise project was built in East Falls, with devastating consequences to the neighborhood. It's darkened skeleton now stands 100 per cent vacant and can be viewed from the Schuylkill Expressway. It is one of many monuments that dot the Philadelphia landscape to failed government policies, but no one seems in a hurry to acknowledge it as such.

Given the categories with which he operated, as stated in the bishops statement of 1968, did Dowling feel constrained to work to the detriment of parishes like Corpus Christi?

"No," he says, "I never did."

"But it did go out of existence."

"People left," Dowling added as if trying to reduce a complicated issue to its simplest formulation. "People moved away. And when people moved away the parish was no longer there. It was just the buildings left. And then you would send in priests and try to maintain a school for a whole new population and with the burden of taking care of the parish of those buildings, we couldn't do it."

Dowling seems to have difficulty making up his mind on the matter of Corpus Christi parish. On the one hand, he seems to imply some moral flaw on the part of parishioners. If the Irish Catholic enclave in North Philadelphia had really been as great as people said it was in retrospect, it should have had the inner spiritual resources to withstand the onslaught. The fact that it didn't means *ipso facto* that the resources weren't there. "Corpus Christi," Dowling concludes at one point, "never really made the effort of welcoming black people into the parish. That was the downfall."

So it was moral flaw, *hamartia*, a hidden cancer? But then Dowling changes his mind and says

> the main thing that happened was a demographic shift. People left where they had been living and moved elsewhere. That was the basic fact of the change. How you interpret that, or how you analyze that, that's where there can be some differences of opinion. It's in the ordinary course of events that people have upward mobility. People want to move on to something better. The suburbs were very attractive. There was a lot to that. Only the Lord knows the internal motivation of people. So there were positive reasons why many people moved: because of their work, because of their desire to have their own home with some ground around it, they went to the suburbs. There was a lot of that there. There was also a lot of fear. And I heard this personally from a

lot of people prior to the beginning of the commission and certainly afterwards. We have a responsibility to take care of our family. We have a fear of what's going to happen. We don't want to live under these circumstances so we're going to move. There was a mixture of motivations but the result was a complete change of the region.

In discussing the situation at MBS which occurred later than that in Corpus Christi, and almost completely under Krol and Dowling's respective tenures, Dowling shifts back to the moral view of things. MBS was, in Dowling's words, a "powerful, powerful parish, but as John XXIII said about historical movements we judge the movement by its fruits."

If MBS didn't survive, in other words, it couldn't have been that strong to begin with. "All of the power of the Catholic parish," Dowling continued, "went to naught because the people couldn't resolve the knot of racial hatred that had formed within them."

According to Dowling, the real loser was not the Catholic Church; it was the city of Philadelphia. The result of fair housing has been "a worse kind of segregation than there was before. And judging from North Philadelphia where I have my experience, before it was black, but you had a mixture economically. You had professional people, teachers and policemen, living together in a much stronger neighborhood. That has been ruined. Because now through mobility and fair housing and open employment, many, many blacks have moved elsewhere who are able to leave these areas now in a much worse situation where you have the underclass with the hopelessness and drugs really rampant."

In addition to losing its tax base of working families, the city also lost its manufacturing base as a result of the high taxes needed to pay for expanding the welfare bureaucracy, which in turn took money from the police who were needed to provide the protection those businesses needed to do business. "It's happening today," Dowling continued. "Whitman's Chocolate, Mrs. Paul's, they're all leaving. Out of the Northeast [a traditionally all white area], out of the Northeast. I'd say it's the biggest disaster for urban areas in the country."

The Church had been maneuvered into a position in which it had become morally impossible for its people to defend their parishes. In her altruism —a misapplied altruism perhaps—the Church wanted to make its contribution to solving the premier social issue of the mid-twentieth century in this country. That altruism entailed supporting open housing laws which made it illegal for Irish Catholics to maintain the ethnic identity of their neighborhoods. When the Irish decided that the only alternative was to move, the Church construed the issue in strictly demographic terms.

When asked if he or Krol ever held a meeting to discuss what could be done to save MBS, one of the archdiocese's major resources, Dowling mentioned "meetings where we tried to project the demographics and see what might happen as you looked ten years down the line. There was never the feeling the the archdiocese by fiat could halt or alter the migration of people." Dowling couldn't go against open housing because it would have been illegal, and besides the bishops were urging compliance in their pastorals. The Church had put Catholics in a position where it seemed as if it were immoral to defend their neighborhoods.

"I'd say it is immoral," Dowling said,

> for a Catholic, for anyone, to make a decision with regard to another person purely based on that person's race and not on other factors. That's what's immoral about the whole thing. I attended a meeting of the priests, a priests' conference, at St. Charles way back, and Bishop McDevitt was up on the stage, and the question about what should we do, and from the stage he picked me out and said, you know, "Answer the question." From the floor, my answer was that when it comes to morality the whole point is that we don't make a judgment on the basis of a person's race. We make it on the basis of the facts of the situation. If the person coming in is a person who is not going to be keeping their home up, if they're not going to be taking care of paying their mortgage, if they're going to be a destructive force, they are factors on which you'd make a decision. You don't make a decision just purely on the basis of a person's race. That's wrong. The Church has taught that it is wrong, and the Church teaches that it is wrong. And that's not only in the way of housing but across the board. Race cannot be a criterion for

making decisions affecting other people, where they live, where they go to school.

Of course, it had been precisely the experience of the parishioners of Corpus Christi and MBS that race did correlate with behavior on a number of relevant points. When blacks moved in crime went up. Undersecretary Moynihan discovered a correlation between race and illegitimacy in 1964. But his experience is apropos here too. If he was shouted down after having gotten the ear of Lyndon Johnson and the approval of Martin Luther King, what chance did a factory worker from North Philadelphia have in making the same points in considerably less elegant fashion. Not much. As a result, the complaints of the Catholics got drowned out by the media din over civil rights and the ethnic Catholics took the only course left to them: they voted with their feet. Once the process was underway, Dowling looked upon it as possessing a sort of geological inevitability.

> The Church does not have that kind of power to force people to stay wherever. Added to that, however, a lot of positive motivation was being spoken of. People, I mean, first want to have the right, and secondly it's very understandable that people want to have upward mobility. Now after World War II a lot of that was happening. The whole development of Levittown . . . So only God can judge the motivation of a person. There was a mixture of motivation. It could very well have been primarily "we're moving because we have an opportunity of living in a much nicer house with ground around it closer to where I work" or other motives. But along with that, however, because of the mass movement of people, there obviously was the factor of fleeing living close to blacks. And that remains with people 'til this day.

How to get beyond that attitude was how Dowling construed his task as head of the Cardinal's Commission on Human Relations. Catholics, according to Dowling, should be above all, "free of hatred, free of bitterness based on hate and racial attitudes, and if the past was this or that, now we'll try our best to be free."

With the gift of hindsight, it is possible to see that the forces at work in the destruction of the neighborhoods were less impersonal than they seemed at the time. When Rev. Hugh Campbell was chaplain at the archdiocesan Newman Center at West Chester University, he received a visit from a man whose conscience was bothering him. "My father broke the blocks in West Philadelphia," the man said as he handed Father Campbell a check made out to the Church for a significant amount of money. The man in question was a professor in the university's education department by the name of Scott Dunlap. His father Alex O. Dunlap had inherited a thriving real estate business from his father, which he proceeded to run into the ground during his lifetime as a result of his twin obsessions with 1) tennis and 2) hatred of the Catholic Church. As the result of listening to Protestant missionaries describing their experiences in South America in the 1930s, the elder Dunlap became obsessed with the Catholic Church as the root of all evil in the world. In order to combat this evil, he founded the "Priest's Conversion Center" on Eagle Road in Delaware county. On December 9, 1964, Dunlap wrote to Archbishop Krol wishing for, among other things, Krol's "early conversion from the Roman Catholic Church to Jesus Christ as your only, personal and all-sufficient Saviour." Dunlap would send what he claimed were consecrated hosts to priests through the mail, referring to them as "pieces of toast." His son remembered seeing his father dress up as a priest at a church the Dunlaps attended, and then take a host and drop it on the floor and step on it. The younger Dunlap was scandalized by such behavior, which he considered blasphemous, and broke with his father, who ended up disinheriting both him and his wife. When Dunlap died all his money went to the Priests' Conversion Center.

Perhaps because of the break with his father, the younger Dunlap is hazy about his father's real estate practices. "I don't know of him trying to wreck parishes," Scott Dunlap said. "I'm not saying he didn't. I split with him about the year 1960."

By the mid-'60s Alex O. Dunlap, according to his son, was spending most of his time either playing tennis or attacking the Catholic Church, often in conjunction with the Rev. Ian Paisley of Northern Ireland and the Rev. Carl McIntyre of Cape May, New Jersey. What Scott Dunlap does remember was that many people were involved in breaking the blocks in Southwest Philadelphia. He can also give a fairly detailed account of how block-busting works.

"It worked in this way," Scott Dunlap recounted. "A realtor could buy a property at a sheriff's sale and then sell it to a black. Putting a black family on the block would make the people next door unhappy and then they would put their house for sale. But now the only people who would buy it were other blacks. Suppose some unscrupulous person buys a house near you. You would then want to get out. The unscrupulous guy offers you a dirt cheap price, but it's cash right away. Otherwise you think if I don't sell right away it might take ten years to sell this place. So you sell it dirt cheap. He then turns around and sells it to someone else but for slightly more than dirt cheap. All you've got to do is make $500 bucks. "

The real estate agent could profit doubly from this by driving the prices down by causing panic in the neighborhood and then buying up the houses themselves at bargain basement prices. He could then sell to other blacks at a significant profit. Even if the amount involved was a low as $500, the real estate agent could oftentimes make handsome profits on sheer volume in changing neighborhoods.

However, profit was not the only motivation in the housing market in Southwest Philadelphia. In addition to real estate agents out to make a quick buck, and anti-Catholic bigots like the elder Dunlap using blockbusting as a way to destabilize Catholic neighborhoods as part of his campaign against the Catholic Church itself, Dunlap remembers that the Quakers were heavily involved in the housing market in both Southwest Philadelphia and Delaware County. Dunlap, who has his own real estate license, remembers "that some Quakers, trying to be do-gooders," would "buy a house in a white community and put a black in there to change the community from white to black."

"The American Friends Service Committee?" I ask.

"Yeah," Dunlap replied, "they do that kind of thing to try to find housing for blacks. They were always thinking that they were doing the right thing. They weren't trying to make money or anything. They were helping poor people get housing. In the process they mainly wrecked housing for other people."

Dunlap traces the decline in the neighborhoods of Southwest Philadelphia to the efforts of the Clark/Dilworth reform machine of the '50s to turn Philadelphia into a permanently Democratic city. "If you wrote about it," Dunlap opined, "they would probably call you racist." Dunlap's prophecy is fulfilled when I call fellow West Chester University Professor Charles Hardy, an expert on black migration, when I mention the proposition that Clark/Dilworth fostered racial migration as a way of building up the Democratic machine in Philadelphia, he immediately denounces the proposition as racist, ending the discussion.

Another factor in the equation, according to Dunlap, was bussing. Taken together, the combination of greed, bigotry and liberal altruism would prove devastating to the city's Catholic neighborhoods. When contacted for their side of the story, the American Friends' Service Committee gives the name of Morris Milgrim, president of Fund for an Open Society, a group which has been building integrated housing for the past 30 years. When asked if the Quakers had bought Horace Baker's house in Folcroft, the incident which set off the riot, Milgrim says, "I can't recall any of the details of it" and changes the subject. When asked if there were groups working on bringing blacks into white neighborhoods at this time, Milgrim replied, "Sure. Sure," but added that "the idea of my integrated housing was not to bring blacks into white neighborhoods but to strengthen integration. It's not a one way street."

The Quakers themselves were much more forthcoming about their efforts to bring blacks into Philadelphia area neighborhoods, at least in the material they were publishing in the early '60s. In the American Friends' Service Committee consolidated budget for the year 1962-63 (the fiscal year ending September 30, 1963), a total of $97,137 was allotted to their "Integrated Housing Program." In the AFSC annual report for 1962, the Quakers explain just what this program entails:

> In areas surrounding our cities, housing opportunities for minority group members have become increasingly restricted. To respond to this problem in their area, a group of citizens from

Burlington County, New Jersey, organized four years ago with the requested aid of the AFSC. Educational and action programs have been designed to bring about more democratic living patterns. Upwards of 50 minority families have moved into various locations throughout Burlington County, without incident, and the new Levittown community there has been successfully integrated. As this program is devolved, AFSC staff continue working on problems of discrimination in housing elsewhere [RBF #5].

The Quakers never get around to defining what "democratic living patterns" entail, but it was clear from the context that it did not entail the self-determination of the people living in Philadelphia's neighborhoods. The Quakers had taken it upon themselves to teach Philadelphians a lesson. "Diversified neighborhoods," the AFSC wrote in its 1961 pamphlet *Homes and Community*,

have "built-in" lessons in democracy—lessons in the dignity of the individual and respect for his contributions to society. Such communities build citizens more secure in their knowledge of democracy and better able to share its responsibilities.

The use of the word "democracy" is especially ironic since the Quakers were operating what was first of all, an essentially clandestine operation, and secondly, one that would hardly have gained the approval of the majority of the residents of the area which received the benefit of their ministrations. But by the time their program was in effect, democracy had become in effect congruent with whatever the liberal agenda was at the time. In terms of the people whose neighborhoods were targeted for change by the Quakers, this meant that "prior judgments against unknown persons can perpetuate stereotypes which should be replaced by open-minded acceptance." Again, ironies abound here. If we take Folcroft as a sample case, ignorance was not the issue. The people who were there had fled across the city's borders for the most part because of first-hand experiences about the effect of black migration in their neighborhoods. If they voted with their feet once, the Quaker program was to ensure that they would not have that option again. "Valid decisions on personal relationships," the Quakers opine dogmatically, "can then be made after the newcomers and their neighbors have had a chance to know each other in a neighborly atmosphere." In addition to judging the validity of the decisions Philadelphians might make on personal relationships, the Friends opine that "new Negro owners have improved properties they purchased from white owners." Now all of this may or may not be true, but none of it was proposed as a topic for open discussion and then eventual ratification by the democratic process. Catholics, for the most part unbeknownst to them, had had their neighborhoods targeted for restructuring by another religious group, operating in a completely clandestine fashion. The biggest investment these people would ever make was being jeopardized by a group bent on manipulating the housing market to make a social point at their expense.

"Many people around the world," the AFSC continued, "heard of the rioting which marked the move of the first Negro family into Levittown, Pa, but few of them have heard of the success in integrating the other mammoth Levittown development in New Jersey." The account continued with an appeal for support for the Friends' program.

One of the people who responded to the appeal was the Rockefeller Brothers Fund, which contributed steadily to the AFSC's request for funds throughout the '60s. On November 17, 1965, Earle Edwards of the AFSC wrote to Dana S. Creel of the Rockefeller Brothers Fund for financial assistance for the fiscal year 1965-66. As part of their appeal to the Rockefellers, Edwards cited the AFSC's "on-going housing opportunities programs in other Northern cities" whose budget by fiscal '65-66 had grown to $276,300.

But the housing program was not the only thing the Quakers were doing that was of interest to the Rockefellers. On the international scene, the Quakers were using their international family planning programs as a conduit for contraceptives. In Mexico, "this work includes greatly expanded use of intrauterine contraceptive devices in clinics in Mexico City. . . . In Hong Kong AFSC is engaged in a major undertaking with the Hong Kong Family Planning Association, the goal of which is to equip with intrauterine devices 30,000 women each year for a period of five years." The IUD was an invention of John D. Rockefeller, 3rd's Population Council, and Rockefeller saw it as the prime vehicle of international population control because of the fact that it was inexpensive and that once it was installed, women had a tough time removing it.

If the Quakers included the IUD programs in Mexico and Hong Kong as a way of currying favor with the head of the Population Council, they were successful. The AFSC was a steady recipient of grants throughout the '60s while many other organizations were turned away empty-handed. One group that went away empty handed was Philadelphia Minister Leon Sullivan's OICs of America. Another group was the Catholic Church. In the fall of 1967, Catholic Relief Services applied for a grant to solve the problem of malnutrition among African children, only to learn that "this is not a matter which the fund could take up with view to being helpful." When a grant application was submitted to help Archbishop Sales of Brazil in 1966, Yorke Allen of the Rockefeller Brothers Fund wrote that "the Fund usually seeks to avoid having to select one or another from among the large number of missionary and church-supported activities in foreign countries." Especially, it seems, if the Church in question does not dispense IUDs as part of its missionary efforts, as the Quakers did.

It is difficult to establish cause and effect here. Because the Quakers were willing to proselytize for contraception as part of their missionary program, they were favored by the Rockefellers when it came to requests for other funding. Part of what the Quakers wanted was money for their housing program. The net result of this complicated interaction was that the Rockefellers were in effect paying the Quakers to be blockbusters throughout the Philadelphia area. The net effect of blockbusting was the destruction of many of Philadelphia's strongest Catholic neighborhoods. Whether the Rockefellers knew this or whether they intended it is beside the point. The breakup of the neighborhoods weakened the hold the Catholic Church had on social mores and sexual morals in this country. And if this fact had been brought to the attention of the people in charge of the Rockefeller Brothers Fund, it is doubtful that they would have seen this fact in a negative light.

The breakup of the neighborhoods would have a doubly demoralizing effect on the Catholics of the area. Not only were they dispersed throughout the suburbs and their political power, as a result, diminished, the transmission of the faith was affected as well, although this was in part due to the turmoil of the times in general and the misimplementation of the Vatican Council in particular. The Church became in effect the weak mother, and many of the people raised under this regime came to make a separate peace as Catholics with the secular establishment.

Born in 1950, Anna Quindlen grew up in Drexel Hill as part of an Italo-Irish family of refugees from Southwest Philadelphia. Quindlen would go on to graduate from Barnard and get a job as a columnist with the *New York Times*, where she would proclaim loudly her identity as a Catholic, but at the same time undercut the Church's position on virtually every point where it came into disagreement with the policies seen as good by the *New York Times*. Abortion and contraception were two notable examples where the Catholic Quindlen sided with the *Times*. She was undoubtedly orthodox in her views on the hypostatic union and the *filioque* clause, but these issues were of minimal concern to her employer.

In May of 1992, on a swing through Philadelphia to endorse a local proabortion candidate for the senate, Quindlen visited her father's old neighborhood in Southwest Philadelphia and described "the block on which my father grew up half a century ago," as "a truncated little street that leads nowhere." In addition to being an undoubtedly accurate description of the street where her father lived, the description was as well an apt description of the career prospects of Catholics who chose not to make their separate peace with cultural revolution as well.

What Quindlen finds on her return does not please her. The house her family grew up in is in ruins: "The small setback porch is still covered with debris from the fire that gutted the building several years ago. There is plywood nailed over the glassless windows and the doorless doorway." The moral she draws from the ruin of her former neighborhood is as predictable as most of her columns. The persons responsible for this devastation are the people who left it, in other words Quindlen's family, who presumably did not live in it in its present condition and, for good measure, Ronald Reagan and George Bush.

"Since LA burst into flames," she opines,

we have cast a net of blame in our search for who abandoned America's cities. The answer is simple. We did. . . . Ronald Reagan and George Bush did, too, and so did many Democrats, truth be told. And they're going to have to ante up now. . . . I've walked many times down blocks like the one on which my father grew up. I've been a poverty tourist with a notebook, but I never felt ashamed of it until now.

Watching Ms. Quindlen beat her breast for her parents' alleged "sins" leaves a faintly bad taste in the mouth, even if it does allow her to curry favor with the mandarins of her class. Blaming the victim is how the case would have been judged in the parlance of the civil rights movement. It wouldn't be the first time this happened in Philadelphia, nor would it be the last.

"I was born in Philadelphia," she wrote in another column for the *Times*, "a city where if you can't dance you might as well stay home, and I was raised on rock-and-roll." What she learned during this tumultuous period was that mastering the vocabulary of upward mobility meant trimming her Catholicism to what the secular establishment found acceptable. The only good Catholic, as someone put it, was a bad Catholic. The breakup of the neighborhoods under the liberals' management of black migration was one of the major battles of America's *Kulturkampf*, and, as Ms. Quindlen indicated, the music playing in the background when it happened was rock'n'roll, in many ways the main vehicle of cultural revolution. As Nicholas Lemann said,

> Most of the substantial changes in the folkways of the white middle class during and after the 1960s had their roots in black life. Rock-and-roll music was an outgrowth of the Mississippi blues; the Rolling Stones named themselves after a song by Muddy Waters. The white protest movements—antiwar feminist, environmental, gay rights—were modeled on the civil rights movement. The founders of the SDS learned their techniques in Mississippi. A seminal event in the feminist movement was a rebellion by the women in SNCC at the Waveland, Mississippi, meeting in the fall of 1964.

"Unquestionably," Charles Reich writes in his hymn to cultural revolution, *The Greening of America*, "the blacks made a substantial contribution to the writings of the new consciousness."

Rock'n'roll, opines Ms Quindlen, the alumna of Southwest Philadelphia, is "one of the few things left in my life that makes me feel good without even thinking about it."

V

The Catholic Counterattack

In early 1961, William Bentley Ball sat in the elegant sitting room just west of the main entrance to the Cardinal's mansion on City Avenue, referred to in general as City Line by Philadelphians, with a preoccupied look on his face. Ball was legal counsel for the newly formed Pennsylvania Catholic Council, a Navy veteran of World War II, and a lawyer from Harrisburg, Pennsylvania, the state's capital. Ball was in Philadelphia to meet the city's new archbishop. He was preoccupied for a number of reasons, but these can be reduced in this instance to two of significance. He was concerned about the direction Church leadership was taking in this country, and he was concerned about the challenge the Church was facing from forces he would define as inimical to the Church's interests. In many ways, these two concerns were simply two sides of the same coin. The bishops of the United States were faced with a direct challenge from the burgeoning welfare state throughout the country at all levels of government. In the United States, education and public welfare had traditionally been the domain of the churches in the United States. As the Catholic Church grew in importance in the country, her role as a provider of education and public welfare increased correspondingly.

By the early '60s, however, government on all levels was expanding its role into spheres traditionally dominated by voluntary organizations like the Church. All of this would in all likelihood have been a matter of indifference to the Church in a more benign age, but concomitant with the expansion of the role of government came the suffusion of those government agencies with the spirit of secular humanism. The government not only wanted to expand its role and power, it wanted to move into areas that the churches in general and the Catholic Church in particular regarded as off limits. The state wanted to be not only the major player in the administration of education and welfare; the state wanted hegemony over the definitions of those terms as well. Looming on the horizon was a crisis of definition. The state wanted to define education and welfare in ways congenial to the secular *Zeitgeist*, and the Church, as one of the major providers of these services, was slowly but surely being drawn into a conflict over precisely these definitions and who had the final say in determining them. It was a crucial period for Catholic leadership in this country. Not only were the bishops faced with increasingly truculent manifestations of the secular spirit in the areas of education and welfare, they were increasingly outmanned in the fight as well. Government bureaucracy was expanding on all levels at rates out of all proportion to the government's ability to cover those expenditures by tax revenue. This expansion of government's role would lead to ruinous deficits at all levels. Eventually the city of Philadelphia would go into *de facto* state receivership, and its bond rating would sink to junk bond level as a result. In the early '60s, all of this was far over the horizon—in fact, it was virtually inconceivable—but Ball was increasingly concerned at how quickly the government was expanding its reach at the time and how handicapped the bishops were in defining just what welfare was and how it was to be provided. Law in this area was often a bureaucratic invention and as the bureaucracies proliferated, the Church found it increasingly difficult to keep up.

Perhaps that was why Bill Ball had a look of preoccupation on his face. If so, it was a look the newly appointed archbishop noticed as well.

"What are you looking so worried for?" Archbishop Krol said as he entered the room. Ball was slightly taken aback by what he would describe as the archbishop's "point blank" attitude. Krol was cordial but blunt in a Cleveland sort of way. Ball, like most of Pennsylvania, had never heard of him as auxiliary in Cleveland, and since Philadelphia played a leading role in Catholic affairs in Pennsylvania, Ball was interested in the kind of leadership the Church was going to get. The times, Ball would say later, required two leadership qualities in particular: perception and courage. Ball would rate Krol highly in both areas, although he would not give him perfect marks in either. Perception was necessary because on its surface the threat oftentimes looked so benign. This was complicated by the fact that the Catholic hierarchy of the time, on the verge of plunging into the Council and a newly discovered age of ecumenism, was expected to be more than normally irenic in their dealings with other religious and social groups. "The Church," they would eventually say, in union with the pope, "had nothing to fear from the modern world."

Well, maybe not. But the modern world had its own notions of the arrangement it wanted with the Catholic Church and those terms included a secular spirit of increasing stridency. At the same time the Catholic bishops were opening the windows for more effective dialogue with Protestants and Jews, those very same Protestants and Jews were becoming increasingly compliant fellow travellers in the secularization of American culture. So a certain schizophrenia could develop on the local level, in places like Pennsylvania, where the official above-the-table demeanor bespoke nothing but ecumenical cooperation, while beneath the table there was an increasingly nasty amount of kicking and scuffling going on over things like school prayer, aid to parochial schools, and whether welfare agencies should be allowed to give out information on contraceptives and eventually contraceptives themselves. In this struggle the Catholic Church was finding itself increasing alone in its struggle to preserve the practice of religion and social mores in the face of the ostensibly benign but increasingly imperious liberal regime and its religious Amen corner. That, it was becoming increasingly clear, was why the new archbishop would need courage.

As the relationship continued, Ball increasingly liked what he saw. Krol was "a strong-minded individual" who closely reflected the mind of the Church on family issues, which were the issues most relevant to *Kulturkampf* in Pennsylvania during the '60s. Krol was also not afraid to use the Pennsylvania Catholic Conference to apply political pressure to the levers of power in the state. The result was an especially fruitful period of cooperation. Krol was to say later in his life that the more diverse the subjects the bishops became involved in, the more they became dependent on the people who advised them. Krol was no exception to this rule. In many instances throughout his tenure as archbishop of Philadelphia, Krol was a general without troops. He could not be expected to come up with solutions to all of the problems the Church faced, and when his subordinates either misunderstood the issue or were unwittingly drawn into supporting a position inimical to the Church's interests, the general lost the battle.

In Ball, however, Krol found a collaborator who possessed both perception and the tenacity to carry that perception into completion. The results of that collaboration are obvious if we compare the performance of the PCC with the national version of the same thing, the USCC. The PCC has had its setbacks, but it has also had an important influence on the Pennsylvania legislature, which continues to be an ongoing source of prolife legal initiative which regularly reaches the Supreme Court challenging the tenets of abortion culture in a way that is unprecedented and surprising considering the part of country it represents. If Krol was not as effective on the national level as he was on the state level, it may be due to the fact that the USCC was dealing with an operation of necessarily larger scope, but it also may be the result of the the the fact that he never found a collaborator with Ball's acumen on the national level. More often than not, the staff at the National Catholic Welfare Conference, and later the USCC, felt that it had a mandate to make policy on its own independently of the bishops. Oftentimes, they took the posture of dictating to the bishops what their policy should be. It was, in many ways, a classic case of the tail wagging the dog, and Ball and Krol would complain bitterly about this division as they became more deeply embroiled in the various battles that the PCC had to fight oftentimes not only without assistance from the people in Washington, but also guarding themselves from subversion on this flank as well.

As a result of the increasing confidence which Ball felt in Krol, he proposed in June of 1964 what amounted to a counterattack against the forces of secular humanism in the country on a state by state level. Ball's initiative found its impetus in the school prayer decisions of the early '60s, in *Engel* and the *Schempp-Murray* cases which banned prayer from public schools.

These decisions, coupled with the school desegregation decisions in the South, effectively destroyed the public school
system's metaphysical underpinning as a an instrument of pan-
Protestant enculturation. As a result, two forces were set in
motion. The secularists, fresh from a series of stunning victories, had no desire to rest on their laurels and allow the private
schools *carte blanche* in implementing what had been banned in
the public. On the other side of the coin, increasingly large
numbers of America's religious-minded citizenry would become alienated from a system which prohibited the expression
of their values and so would turn to private schools as a result.
The urban blacks were a good case in point. As Philadelphia's
public schools showed themselves increasingly under the spell
of the secular *Zeitgeist* and as a result increasingly unable to
educate or even maintain a semblance of order in the schools
without the assistance of armed policemen, blacks began to see
the Catholic schools in the emptying ethnic neighborhoods as
an increasingly attractive alternative. As a result of that, the
secularists found themselves shifting attention from the battles
they had already won in the public schools and confronting the
Catholics directly on the issue of aid to non-public schools. The
schools, of course, were only one area of conflict. Catholic social
services, Catholic hospitals, and Catholic welfare organizations
in general were another. In each instance, the expansion of the
role of the state and secularism went hand in hand. The state, in
other words, was not simply interested in supplying services,
or even interested in competing with the Church in supplying
services; the state rather was interested in redefining the idea of
service to something more compatible with the secularist view
of the world. That was the crux of the issue.

As would often be the case, it was up to Leo Pfeffer to frame
the issue with a clarity which many of his fellow secular humanists would find embarrassingly candid. In the November
1963 number of the *Journal of the Separation of Church and State*,
Pfeffer declared victory on the school prayer issue. Citing the
Schempp decision, Pfeffer claimed that "the controversy regarding the role of religion in the public schools will begin to disap-
pear as a major national issue." The war, however, was far from
over. With the Protestants defeated in the public schools, the
front shifted into a direct conflict with the Catholics:

> The field of battle will now shift to the question of government aid to religion in the form of Federal aid, shared time, tax benefits, etc. Indeed, this is already indicated by the Catholic reactions to the *Schempp-Murray* decision, reactions which emphasize that since religion may not enter the public school, the only way to assure religious liberty is to finance religious instruction in parochial schools. During the next decade the major national issue in Church-state relations will most probably be around the question of government funds for parochial schools.

The secularists were involved in a two-pronged campaign against the expression of religion in the field of education. Phase I culminated in the *Schempp-Murray* decisions of 1963, which eliminated religious exercises and practices from public schools. Phase II would reach its culmination seven years later in *Lemon v. Kurtzman*, which prohibited the use of public money in assisting Catholic parochial schools, and *Tilton v. Richardson*, in which the Catholic colleges and universities proved to the court's satisfaction that they were sufficiently secular in purpose to receive government money. Since the courts could not very well ban religion in parochial school, the secularists achieved their goal by making religious education as difficult as possible to fund. Success in the school prayer issue not only emboldened the secularists, it threw them in direct conflict with the Church on a number of related issues as well.

Ball's counterattack against the forces of secularism began as a confidential memo to Krol, entitled "Legal Challenges of the Coming Decade: A Step Toward Protection of the Church." Eventually this document would be sent to all of the country's bishops and the apostolic delegate as well. Since the forces of secularism were using the courts to undermine both the standing of the Church and the democratic institutions of the republic, Ball was proposing a legal strategy in response.

"The Church," according to Ball,

> has watched with an anxious eye certain trends in the law— trends toward narrowing the definition of what is private in the fields of welfare and education; trends toward sanctioning an immense expansion of governmental regulatory power over individuals and over voluntary welfare agencies; and a body of judicial opinion which is being widely interpreted as opening the door to total secularization of our society. . . . Profound

changes are also being felt in the areas of the law concerned with public morals and crime and in the entire field of law pertaining to marriage and the family. These changes have reflected a marked departure from traditionally accepted Christian principles.

The courts, according to Ball, were demonstrating an increasingly militant insistence to broaden the power of the state and "to recognize government as the solely competent agent in the fields of education and welfare." There were even indications at the time that the Church's tax-exempt status was being threatened. All of this was being accomplished on two fronts by two agents seemingly unrelated to each other. The courts worked hand in hand with the secularist interest groups by striking down the laws those interest groups opposed, and then government agencies would move in and colonize the newly cleared territory. Oftentimes the connection was causal. The Supreme Court, to give an example we will deal with in depth, struck down a Connecticut law banning the sale of contraceptives in a case engineered by Planned Parenthood and the Yale Law School. Once the law had been struck down, government quickly moved into the business of disseminating contraceptives. Indeed, according to Leo Pfeffer, the law had to go precisely because the government wanted to get into the contraceptive business.

Ball's "Legal Challenges" paper presents one of the clearest explications of how *Kulturkampf* worked in the United States during the 1960s. Thirty years after the fact, it is still common for people to view the revolutionary changes of the '60s as something that just "happened." As Ball makes clear to Archbishop Krol, the happening was preceded by a large amount of planning and behind-the-scenes manipulation of public opinion. According to Ball,

> A high percentage of the most important church-state litigations which have arisen lately in the nation have been the result of campaigns by interested groups or by individuals who are crusading for doctrinaire ends. The recent Supreme Court cases dealing with school prayer and Bible reading have been the products of such deliberate campaigns of so-called "associational jurisprudence." Key features of these campaigns are the seeking out of "soft" situations for the bringing of suit and the creating

(through public relations techniques) of a climate of opinion in the community and state, favorable to such litigation.

One aspect of this *Kulturkampf* which Ball finds most disturbing is the penchant of these revolutionary groups to bypass the democratic process. "Causes disapproved of by overwhelming majorities of the American people, but vigorously pushed by pressure groups, have been established as the law of the land." Their success in achieving their goals outside of the democratic process has been, according to Ball, nothing short of "astounding" and now "the legal guns of many of the same pressure groups are . . . being trained, with singleness of purpose, upon church-related institutions."

The paradigmatic example of this subversion of the democratic process was accomplished in the *Schempp-Murray* cases of 1963. What seemed to the untrained eye a simple interpretation of the constitution was in reality the result of a campaign "formally launched in 1959 by representatives of major Jewish organizations in the United States for eliminating religious teaching and observances in the public schools."

To illustrate his point Ball quotes extensively from a document published in June 1961 entitled "Report of a Conference for a Reassessment of Strategy and Approaches in Implementing Policies on Religion and the Public School." Both the conference and the report emanating from it were sponsored by a wide-ranging coalition of Jewish organizations, including the Synagogue Council of America (consisting of the Central Conference of Rabbis, the Rabbinical Assembly of America, the Rabinnical Council of America, the Union of American Hebrew Congregations, the Union of Orthodox Jewish Congregations of America and the United Synagogues of America) and the National Community Relations Advisory Council (consisting of *inter alia* the American Jewish Congress, the Jewish War Veterans and 53 state and local Jewish Community Relations councils.)

The 1961 Report distilled its experience in the school prayer front into a a quasi-science of bringing about social change through manipulation of public opinion and, if necessary, litigation. The information was valuable not only for future reference for the Jews, for example in gaining support for Israel in the aftermath of the 1967 Arab-Israeli war, but also for any other group which shared the same goals. Leo Pfeffer, it should be remembered, was not only legal counsel for the American Jewish Congress, but a member of and the recipient of awards from virtually the entire spectrum of cultural revolutionary groups from the ACLU to the Unitarian Universalists. Pfeffer, in recounting the history of the *McCollum* case, stated quite frankly that "the Courts' decisions reflected fully the arguments presented in our brief." Pfeffer was not the exception in this regard, and the overlap in memberships shared by the cultural revolutionary groups meant that the same strategy, the one Ball was explicating in his brief, was available to them all. "How," Ball asks,

> do the pressure groups in question achieve their ends? The technique is essentially threefold: a) planning, b) public relations (sometimes called "education"), c) litigation.

Under the heading "Specific Means and Methods," the 1961 Report lists the strategy which was transforming the social landscape in the United States. The procedure is described specifically in terms of Jewish interests, but it is easy to see how these tactics could be generalized for use by other like-minded groups. The push for social change begins with "education," an effort "to interpret and win acceptance for our positions both within the Jewish community and in the general community and among special groups." After the public opinion of the community has been reconfigured in favor of the proposed changes, phase two begins, which entails "negotiation" or "face to face confrontation." This phase is "designed to bring about, directly or indirectly, changes in actual practice in the public schools."

According to the "Report,"

> the term "negotiation" as used in this statement designates a basically different process. In the sense used here, "negotiation" typically takes the form of discussion between a school authority and a Jewish representative concerning a Jewish appeal or demand for change in an existing school practice deemed objectionable from the Jewish position. The element of *quid pro quo*, which plays a major role in classic negotiations is largely missing here. And equity is not involved at all; for the Jewish posture is not one of seeking equal treatment but rather of urging compli-

ance with a moral and constitutional principle. The Jewish nego-
tiator cannot, in any strict sense, compromise with this principle.

Litigation was the threat that made negotiation seem like a
plausible way of achieving a solution, and, of course, the more
their anti-prayer cases succeeded at the Supreme Court level,
the more clout the individual negotiators had. Beyond that, the
Report goes on to specify that "it is of first importance that the
Jewish representative or representations be in a position to as-
sert with confidence and accuracy that their representatives
have substantial support in the Jewish community. This may
involve considerable advance negotiation within the Jewish
community. . . . "

This was important for two reasons: first of all, because
simply accepted at face value it was their strategy, but more
importantly, the converse of this position was also important in
weakening the cultural revolutionaries' opponents. We have
already shown, for example, how important it was for John D.
Rockefeller, 3rd to gain a foothold in Catholic academe to undermine the Catholic position on birth control. Throughout the
'60s, the cultural revolutionaries bankrolled dissent in the
Church as their way of giving the impression that the Church
was divided whenever it spoke.

Interesting in this regard is the role that Bernard Berelson
played. Although he had been trained as a librarian, by the late
'50s, Berelson had established a name for himself as an expert in
the manipulation of public opinion. In 1963, Berelson was re-
cruited by Rockefeller to become a vice-president of the Population Council and by the mid-'60s he was recognized as "a major
figure in the population field" [John Ensor Harr and Peter J.
Johnson, *The Rockefeller Conscience: An American Family in Public
and Private* (New York: Charles Scribner's Sons 1991)]. In 1964,
Berelson and JDR, 3rd met privately with President Johnson
and eventually succeeded in getting mention of overpopulation
as an issue of serious concern for the world in the state of the
union address following Johnson's 1964 landslide victory. By
the mid-'60s, however, Berelson had gone far beyond measuring public opinion on the issue of birth control; he was deeply
involved in creating public opinion in accord with the views of
the Population Council. In a memo to Pop Council staff dated

October 18, 1965, Berelson reports on the survey he has commissioned from the Gallup Poll people. The questions were of the generally tendentious sort, e.g., "Do you feel that the United States Government should give aid to states and cities for birth control programs if they request it?" The tendentious nature of the questions in this "opinion poll" was not surprising. What was surprising was the interest Berelson and Co. took in the position of the Catholic Church. Question number 8 of the survey commissioned by Berelson states: "The Roman Catholic Church does not approve many methods of birth control. Do you believe that the Church should change its position on this matter?" (The response, incidentally, was: Yes, 55% No 22%, Don't know 23%)

The surveys were clearly intended to insinuate the idea that the Church ought to change her teachings into the mind of the population in general. But beyond that, they were also designed to show that the mind of Catholics was divided on the issue—a fact that was just as favorable to the agents of change as the sense that the Jews were united on the issues they wanted to have implemented. "The Catholics strongly favor a change, by 2 to 1 and . . . they are far less undecided" than the population at large, Berelson concludes in his report to John D. Rockefeller, 3rd. Berelson is obviously pleased by the conclusions the poll has reached and plans further study of a similarly specific nature on the thoughts of Catholics on the issue. "Did the Pope's statement at the UN," for example, "affect this distribution? Tune in next time," Berelson writes, indicating he intends to devote a good deal of time to what people think of Pope Paul VI. In a piece he did on population control in 1967, Ball singles out the efforts of Berelson by name as the strategist behind "'Madison Avenue' advertising agencies' tactics" that could be brought to bear in changing people's attitude toward contraception."

By the mid-'50s, Berelson's theories had gained wide currency among groups which were interested in bringing about social change without recourse to the democratic process. The Jews were especially interested in this regard because they were 1) hopelessly underrepresented in the population as a whole and therefore unable to change social mores by recourse to the ballot box and 2) significantly overrepresented in the media.

This would include publishing and TV but also film. The resentment which Hollywood felt toward the Legion of Decency was a scenario with an unmistakable Jewish/Catholic subtext, which would be the source of a story all to itself. In his presentation to Krol, Ball cites the "findings of the Reassessment Conference of May 1956," a convocation of the groups already mentioned as sponsoring the above-mentioned report, which was held to plot the "use of the mass Media of Communications for Community Relations Purposes." What resulted from the meeting of these Jewish groups was in effect an anatomy of the mass media and how the various organs of public opinion could be used to effect specific ends.

"Those media," for example, according to the findings of the Reassessment Conference, "concerned primarily with the dissemination of current news, such as newspapers, weekly magazines, certain radio broadcasts, and the like seem best adapted to use in pursuit of immediate objectives." The media of entertainment, on the other hand, best lend themselves to "long range efforts" which involve "modification of attitudes."

In fine, the Reassessment Conference on Mass Media recommends that "communications be directed toward specific target audiences," that it "be concrete, and have meaning for the individuals to whom they are addressed rather than being abstract, hortatory, and impersonal." Some of those "specific target audiences" were "teachers," a group "who may be expected to be most responsive to arguments that religious practices in the public schools create conflicts in children's minds." Religious practices, the teachers were to learn, "tend to undermine rather than strengthen all religious commitment." Religious leaders, however, are also to be targeted because they can be expected to "be most responsive to the arguments that religion in the public school creates confusion as to true religious values and thus undermine all genuine religious commitment, and that elaborate holiday programs in the schools detract from attendance at church services."

One of the strategies the Jewish groups found most effective was the creation of "news." The purpose of this creation was, of course, to get their point across. But the fact that the information was packaged as "news" made the proselytizing element involved in its creation all but invisible to the media consumer. Rather than ask point blank for the removal of religious elements from the schools—the goal of the campaign—the Jewish groups found that it made news more often if they publicly called for the removal of any observance of Channukah from public school programs without any reference to Christmas.

In order to facilitate the dissemination of "news" favorable to their cause, the ACLU instituted a weekly bulletin entitled "Feature Press Service" as well as *Civil Liberties*, a monthly national newsletter which is a feeder to the general press throughout the United States. The most sophisticated public relations agency in the entire field of church-state relations, according to Ball, was the Institute of Human Relations, established by the American Jewish Committee in the fall of 1961. As part of the AJC's push in 1962 to create a climate of public opinion favorable to banning prayer and Bible reading in public schools, the Institute issued a series of pamphlets entitled "Facts at Your Fingertips" as well as fact sheets, discussion guides and reprints of articles and editorials. Virtually all of what got disseminated contained material attacking the Catholic position on prayer and aid to education. In waging the war of the polls, Berelson and the Pop Council were just implementing the converse of the strategy employed by the Jewish groups. If the Catholics could be shown to be disunited, that was just as good as showing that the revolutionaries were united.

If Phase Two succeeds, according to the Report, the Jewish groups have accomplished what they set out to do and no further action is necessary. If it does not succeed, the Jewish groups move onto Phase 3 or "litigation." However one divides up the phases, the Jewish groups make clear that they are all part of one coherent strategy and are to be "employed in combination" because "it is not possible to distinguish with precision the contribution each has made." The main point to understand here is that all three phases are to be used in conjunction with each other as part of a coherent strategy because each phase is "generally mutually reinforcing to a very great degree." "Litigation is wisely regarded as a last resort," the report states but the more successful previous litigation has been, the less one had to have recourse to it specifically to attain the aforementioned ends in the future.

In essence, Ball's position paper was a declaration of cultural counter-revolution, and he was asking first Krol and then the nation's bishops to endorse it. Perhaps because of his own training, Ball proposed the establishment in each state of a Catholic conference whose main purpose would be to monitor the regulations emanating from the ever-burgeoning welfare and education bureaucracies for trends inimical to the welfare of the Church. Even at the outset, it was clear that Ball was not proposing a step by step imitation of what the Jewish groups had done. Steps one and two, those specifying the manipulation of public opinion, were largely missing from Ball's proposal, which was primarily conceived of as creating the legal arm of the bishops. This may have been an omission on Ball's part, or he may simply have been making a virtue of necessity by confining his resources, which were largely legal in scope, to where they would do the most good.

The Catholics, unlike the Jews, had hardly a toehold in the media, and the little they had would be shortly stripped away from them as Catholic academe went into apostasy and took its publishing houses with it. The Church, in other words, had a legal army of sorts, under the direction of people like Ball, but it lacked protective air support from the media. As a result, it would be forever fighting last ditch efforts, because, as the Jewish groups said, "litigation is wisely regarded as a last resort." In the Catholic counterattack, it was the only resort, and as a result suffered accordingly. This is not to say that, in many instances, it wasn't effective. It is only to say that at the outset and even under the best of circumstances, Ball's counter-attack was a matter of one versus three, and as a result the Catholic bishops were constantly outgunned when it came to the manipulation of public opinion in which favorable court cases throve.

On July 20, 1964, copies of Ball's confidential report were sent to the apostolic delegate and all of the bishops of the United States accompanied by a cover letter from Archbishop Krol recommending the implementation of what it proposed. "The maxim *'leges serviunt vigilantibus non dormientibus,'"* Krol wrote, "impelled me to submit a documented report to the NCWC administrative board at its April 1st meeting. The report concerned the planned and relentless efforts toward total secularization of our society principally through legislation and litigation. The board unanimously resolved that my report be circulated among all the bishops, and I am happy to oblige."

Krol concluded his endorsement of Ball's report by claiming that "the issues are gravely important; the stakes staggeringly high and the need for greater vigilance imperative." The response of the United States bishops indicated that they shared Krol's view of the urgency of the situation facing them. Bishop Joseph H. Albers, ordinary of the Diocese of Lansing, Michigan, wrote back to Krol a week later calling Ball's proposal "a splendid presentation of the need for the establishment, on the state level of a Catholic conference for every . . . state in the country." At the time the Krol letter arrived, Albers was involved in a battle over the Michigan Bus Law, a bill enacted in 1963, which provided transportation for Catholic students to Catholic schools. The bill was being contested as unconstitutional by the ACLU, which had retained as counsel none other than Leo Pfeffer, then of the Anti-Semitic League of New York. Albers placed much of his hopes for the bill on the fact that four of the seven Michigan Supreme Court justices were Catholic, but experience was beginning to show that by 1964, the judge's religion was not a reliable criterion of how he would vote on matters considered important by the hierarchy.

Bishop Karl J. Alter of Cincinnati responded by claiming that the "big problem always is one of finance. We find it difficult to interest our Catholic laity in raising the funds necessary for a purpose of this nature—largely because they do not see the immediate need, as do those of us who are constantly engaged in administrative work for the Church." Bishop Floyd L. Begin of Oakland, California, responded by saying that "we are being attacked from so many angles and so efficiently that it leaves one breathless. Only when these matters are put together in one brief do we recognize the need for concerted and consistent action."

Bishop John P. Cody, at the time Apostolic Administrator of the archdiocese of New Orleans but soon to be Cardinal Archbishop of Chicago, responded by sharing his experience in setting up the Louisiana Catholic Conference, which was influential in getting a birth control bill tabled, and in getting compulsory education re-enacted after it was abolished as a result of integration. The LCC was also instrumental in having "put to death" several "punitive measures which would have hurt our Catholic schools . . . —the assassins were excellent Catholics who received some suggestions from their ordinaries," Cody stated.

In general, though, Bishop's Cody's optimistic account was not echoed by the other bishops, who felt, in the words of the bishop of Yakima, Washington, that the Church was "missing the boat time and again because we are not keeping abreast of the challenges." The Church for the most part is "going around with BB guns to stop the onslaught of the big guns aimed against us. . . . Old lady Murray's campaign against our tax exemption is taking hold all over the country."

Archbishop Fulton J. Sheen was similarly pessimistic. The Church was losing the battle to the interest groups who were using terms like "separation of Church and state" in a way that distorted the meaning of the words.

"Almost all of the arguments used by the opposition," Sheen opined, "are based upon the separation of Church and State. Why are we so hampered by history that we do not publicly affirm the separation of church and state? It might be well for the bishops at the Rome meeting to make a declaration that we believe in the separation of the Church and State. It is in our Constitution."

Archbishop Sheen was evidently unaware that the term "separation of Church and state" was not in the constitution, but he was adamant in insisting that the Catholics did not want an established religion, nor did they want special privileges, nor did they want "religion to be a test for public office." Sheen was proposing something that he felt was completely consonant with both the teaching of the Church and the American political system. His complaints go a long way toward explaining the Council fathers' deliberations over *Dignitatis Humanae*, the Council document on religious freedom, which were going on in Rome at the time. "As long as we are silent about the separation of Church and State," Sheen concluded, "the opposition can use the Constitution against us. Although we are opposed to the union of Church and State, we are not opposed to the State and religion, which is also very basic in our constitution."

Bishop John Mark Gannon of Erie responded by complaining of the generally increasing secularization of the culture with specific regard to the state of Pennsylvania and its "out-of-date Quaker constitution." The Protestants secured special favors for themselves before the Catholics knew what was going on, Gannon complained. Now they were reluctant to share with the Catholics the same benefits they arrogated to themselves. "During our sleepy period of poverty and ignorance when we were poor immigrants," Gannon wrote to Krol, "Protestant organizations secured preferences from our government. I think the time has arrived for Catholics to receive similar treatment. Just to mention one, the school bus problem. You are wise in broadening the purpose and work of the Pennsylvania Catholic Welfare Committee."

One of Gannon's priests in the Erie diocese expanded on the problem. Not only were the Catholics frozen out when the Protestants divided up the pie to their own benefit, they are still frozen out as the Protestant exclusion of Catholic beliefs got revised at the hands of the cultural revolutionaries into a secularist version of the same thing.

> Over the years we have relaxed our vigilance because we have been protected by exemptive and protected statutes. Suddenly we realize that we are living in changing times. . . . Almost daily we read of the activities of such groups as the American Civil Liberties Union, the Planned Parenthood group, or the NEA. These organizations are making great inroads in helping draft future laws that could be very harmful to us. . . . Their attack is very well planned and expertly publicized. We should and must make use of the very same procedures in defending our position (Msgr. Thomas F. Griffin to Gannon 8/28/64).

James Francis Cardinal McIntyre of Los Angeles responded by claiming that "the NEA is perhaps the paramount offender and source that will activate against us," and Bishop Stephen S.

Woznicki of Saginaw claimed that the Ball proposal was "the correct and only thing to do, irrespective of the costs."

In all, Krol received 64 acknowledgements, all of them favorable. When they were allowed to express themselves candidly, the bishops showed a remarkable unanimity in expressing dismay at the increasingly militant forces arrayed against them. Some bishops clearly saw a continuity between the efforts of the secularists of the 1960s and the nativists of the 1920s and the previous century. The fact that the age was supposed to be one of ecumenical sweetness and light created an all but universal sense of irony among the bishops. In a report on Ball's proposal which Krol filed with Egidio Vagnozzi, the apostolic delegate, Krol claimed that the climate of legislation unfavorable to Catholic interests was "promoted according to planned strategy" and that the goal of that strategy was the "total secularization of our society through legislation, litigation and administrative regulations." Krol is quick to point out that ecumenism is often more form than substance, and that "some of our ecumenical friends are wittingly or otherwise supporting programs detrimental to the interests of religion and Church."

If Krol were looking for allies in an upcoming fight, sending out Ball's Legal Challenges Report pretty much achieved its desired effect. Krol was heartened both by the response of the American bishops and that of Rome. If he were looking for a fight, he didn't have to wait long either. The first engagement was over the issue of birth control. In January of 1964, Planned Parenthood of Pennsylvania launched a major publicity campaign urging the "liberalization" of regulations governing what social workers could and could not say about birth control to clients of Pennsylvania's Department of Welfare. Planned Parenthood was essentially lobbying for state funding of "family planning," with itself foreseen as the major beneficiary of the newly opened area of public service. True to to the trajectory described in the report of the various Jewish agencies, various newspapers throughout the state began to echo the demands of Planned Parenthood as the carefully orchestrated plan took on all the aspects of a groundswell of popular demand in the matter. Another major supporter of the change in welfare policy was the Pennsylvania Council of Churches, a fact which might have prompted Krol's remarks about "our ecumenical friends" to Vagnozzi.

If opposition to the change in the 1964 birth control regs was a major challenge to the newly-discovered political consciousness of the Catholic Church in Pennsylvania, the Church won the battle hands down. By May of 1964, the issue had been dropped. Ball had contacted a number of influential Republicans throughout the state, who approached administration officials claiming not so much that birth control was wrong, but that the introduction of funding it would prove to be explosively divisive. It would re-open old religious wounds in an age that put a premium on irenic ecumenical relations.

On May 22, 1964 Ball wrote to Krol that "the birth control battle has been won for the time being."

"It occurs to me also," Ball continued, "that any future efforts to 'liberalize' birth control in Pennsylvania should prove more difficult after this defeat, because we have gotten the state government into a position of opposing change, and we have given quite a number of key persons arguments why a liberalized policy would be undesirable."

It was good that Ball added the caveat "for the time being" after his declaration of victory. The peace after that victory would last roughly 18 months, until December of 1965, when the Pennsylvania Department of Welfare announced that, once again, it was changing its policy so that social workers could bring up the issue of birth control to their clients. The relatively short-lived peace after the May '64 victory showed that the major disadvantage under which Catholics labored was not influencing state legislatures but rather in coping with media-enhanced publicity campaigns which led to changes in bureaucratic regulations. Over the summer of 1965, Ernest Gruening held hearings on the so-called population explosion with dire predictions of catastrophe unless the government got involved in distributing contraceptives. The media, likewise, continued their drumbeat in support. In an atmosphere like this, it was only a matter of time before the bureaucrats felt that the forces of progress and enlightenment were on their side, and the regs got changed again. In this regard, there was little the Church could do but fight the fire once it had already broken out.

Influencing the culture through the media of persuasion was simply not an avenue open to the Church in any extensive fashion.

There is some indication that on the issue of birth control the Church's disadvantage was more than simply a question of being outgunned by media bias. The problem was compounded by a policy emanating from Rome. On June 3, 1964, Krol received a confidential memo from Vagnozzi *"Sub Secreto Sancti Officii,"* which in effect prevented him from engaging in public discourse on the issue of contraception. "For some time now," the Vatican communique began,

> the Holy See has been greatly disturbed by the fact that Catholic scholars as well as some members of the hierarchy have been making statements or have been expressing judgments on birth control, which are not always in accord with the traditional teaching of the church. These assertions have frequently gained much attention, not only because of the authority of the persons making them, but also because of the wide publicity they have received through the modern media of communication. They have thus given rise to the impression that there is serious divergence in understanding this important and delicate question. The result has been great confusion, if not bewilderment, among the faithful.

> Therefore, the Holy See invites the members of the Hierarchy to refrain from making public statements in this vein and requests, moreover, that greater vigilance be exercised over the publications of theologians and other scholars so that theories which deviate from the teaching of the Church and cause anxiety in the souls of the faithful will not be proposed. Likewise, for the same reasons, the Holy See desires that the bishops of individual countries avoid taking positions on this question, which concerns the whole Catholic world, without due consideration of the teaching of the bishops of other countries and especially of the Holy See.

The purpose of the letter was obviously to silence the dissenters. The net effect, however, was to silence only those who were obedient to the Church's position. Since those interested in changing the Church's position on contraception could hardly be termed solicitous of Church teaching in general, the directive emanating from Rome gave the dissenters in effect unencumbered freedom to speak for the Church in their attempt to undermine the Church's position. It was an unfortunate state of affairs which would recur many times in the coming years, and Krol complained about it bitterly, but being a man who valued foremost the mind of the Church, he did what he was told.

Ball, for his part, was probably not privy to the directive from Rome, nor was he in all probability hampered by it, although at the back of the minds of all those engaged in the birth control battles of the times was the nagging feeling that the Church might pull the rug out from beneath the feet of her defenders and approve contraception as morally licit. Ball was not hampered primarily because his strategy entailed working behind the scenes as a lawyer fighting bureaucratic regulations on constitutional grounds. In response to a query from the executive director of the Michigan Catholic Conference dated October 5, 1964, Ball remained optimistic about the battles looming over birth control that were to be fought in state legislatures throughout the country, until *Griswold v. Connecticut*, in effect, made the whole matter moot. Ball was convinced that the Catholics could fight fire with fire and still end up winning the contraception battle. Ball was convinced that "constitutional arguments . . . stressing rights of privacy, etc." could "furnish the tools by which it is just possible that a bloodless victory can be won."

"The language of American liberties," Ball continued, "has far better currency among the non-Catholic majority than does the theological vocabulary which has been employed in some of these crises."

In formulating a legal strategy for the Church, Ball, like Krol, had to work with a number of handicaps. Foremost among these was the fairly widespread notion that a change in the Church's teaching was imminent. This was, of course, fostered by those within the Church who wanted such a change and those without who were oftentimes willing to subsidize those within in their efforts. The newly-convened Vatican Council added to the sense that age old prohibitions were suddenly debatable and that the debate could be steered in directions the party of change found amenable by the techniques of manipulation we have already mentioned, i.e., the conference, the poll, the study, the "news" story run by a sympathetic reporter, etc.

John D. Rockefeller, 3rd and his subordinates at the Population Council felt that the '60s provided them with a window of opportunity. And one major opening was the cracks in the Catholic monolith caused by the new pope and the Council. Population control measures were stalled in the '50s for a number of reasons. One was the fact that the communists and the Church opposed them to such an extent that sustained technical assistance to countries under their respective spheres of influence were simply not possible (Harr, p. 43). The Catholic sphere of influence extended to the United States as well, particularly to the cities dominated by ethnic Catholic Democratic machines. When General William H. Draper decided in 1959 to promote birth control from the unlikely platform of the President's Committee to Study the United States Military Assistance Program, the reaction of the Catholic bishops was uniform and forceful, so forceful in fact that it prompted then President Eisenhower to issue a statement of his own, in which he let it be known that he could not "imagine anything more emphatically a subject that is not a proper political or governmental activity or function or responsibility" than birth control.

President Eisenhower's imaginative powers would be tested considerably over the next few years as Rockefeller, through the Population Council, pushed relentlessly for government involvement in population control and the legitimization of contraception, sterilization and abortion. By the early '60s, there had been a technological breakthrough as well. The Population Council had been instrumental in the development of both the pill and the IUD, and the two were destined for consumption both at home (primarily the former) and abroad (primarily the latter because its use was not a matter of daily decision).

Emboldened by the sense that they now had a combination of state of the art contraceptive devices at their disposal, Rockefeller and the Pop Council began to press their advantage. Within days of Johnson's landslide victory in November of 1964, Rockefeller and Berelson travelled to Washington seeking an audience with LBJ. What they got was a meeting with Dean Rusk, secretary of state under John F. Kennedy, but a Rockefeller alumnus as well, having headed the Rockefeller Foundation in the early '50s. It was Dean Rusk who pulled the plug on Kinsey, when Kinsey's sex surveys became a matter of public embarrassment in the wake of the Reece hearings. Through Rusk's ministrations, a sentence was inserted into Johnson's January 4, 1965 State of the Union message, in which the president announced to the world that he would "seek new ways to use our knowledge to help deal with the explosion in world population and the growing scarcity in world resources." Rockefeller's biographers see the statement as "a decisive turning point" in changing the public's aversion to contraception and paving the way for the government's involvement in disseminating at first information about contraception and then the contraceptives themselves.

Griswold v. Connecticut, handed down in the early summer of 1965, was another crucial step in this process. Writing after the victory had been safely won, Leo Pfeffer was completely candid in explaining why a law prohibiting the sale of contraceptives which never got enforced had to be struck down. This was so "because their presence made it impossible for the state to encourage contraception, something it now increasingly deems necessary to do. The middle income and the affluent, married and unmarried, use contraceptives; the poor have babies. When the poor, often racial minorities, are on the welfare rolls, taxpaying Americans rebel and expect the state to do something about it. . . . The national government already established this policy as part of its program of aid to underdeveloped countries, but the States could hardly follow suit as long as their own laws forbade the practice" (Pfeffer, *God, Caesar,* p. 96).

The liberals were, in effect, playing a double game here. They were using race to overturn the notion that the social order was somehow dependent on the moral order, as embodied in Christian moral teaching. The South had condoned segregation, and they were all Christians; therefore, Christianity had been discredited as a force with anything to say about how this society should be structured. The mainline Protestant denominations were completely in agreement with this strategy even if it seemed on the surface to be to their detriment, because they were just as avid for sexual liberation. To the extent that the mainline Protestants capitulated on the sexual front, they sought to compensate by increasing their efforts for racial justice.

Part II of the double game had to do with eugenics. Once the social order had been weakened by the liberals using race as a cover for sexual liberation, contraceptives were prescribed as the cure for welfare, by cutting back on the number of blacks, i.e., welfare recipients that were being born. The blacks, who were used as the pretext to change social mores, became the first victims of the change as they were targeted by the population controllers as the "beneficiaries" of expanded government services which were more often than not just a pretext for the legitimization of contraceptive eugenics. *Griswold v. Connecticut* was the major breakthrough in this regard. Now the government could push forward with its population control programs without coming into conflict with state laws.

Perhaps emboldened by this string of stunning successes, JDR, 3rd decided to take his struggle for contraception a step further. He decided to confront the enemy in his own lair. With the help of Father Theodore Hesburgh, president of the University of Notre Dame and board member of the Rockefeller Foundation, JDR, 3rd arranged an audience with Pope Paul VI, who was mulling over the issue of birth control at the time and, it was hoped according to the Enlightenment view of history, might prove to be even more liberal than John XXIII, who was as different from his predecessor as day was from night. Hesburgh, who is described by Rockefeller's biographers Ensor and Johnson as "decidedly liberal in his own views on population although he would not go as far as JDR on some aspects" (p. 169) was only too happy to oblige. After being briefed by a number of Jesuit professors from Georgetown University on "the complexities of the Catholic Church that curtailed the freedom of any Pope," Rockefeller met with Pope Paul VI for 45 minutes in mid-July of 1965.

Years later in a letter to Henry Cabot Lodge, when the latter was appointed U. S. emissary to the Vatican, Rockefeller described the meeting as "warm and friendly," but at the same time "not too meaningful or constructive in terms of the population question as I did not feel that I could push too hard and he obviously could not be entirely frank with me as to his own personal views when he had the major decision on birth control pending." The decision in question, as expressed in the papal document which would eventually come out under the name

Humanae Vitae in 1968, must have been a bitter disappointment for JDR. Five years after his meeting with the pope and two years after the appearance of *Humane Vitae*, Rockefeller was still obsessed with the Church's opposition to birth control. So much so that he was willing to trade on his friendship with Lodge as a way of getting his point across to the same pope who had so pointedly ignored his views in the summer of '65. "The population question," JDR, 3rd wrote to Lodge, "is the most important subject which you would have to discuss with his Holiness, assuming that you have a close and informal relationship." One gets the impression that Rockefeller never got over the fact that the pope never took him up on his offer to help co-author *Humane Vitae*. Because JDR, 3rd never got over the fact that the pope turned him down, he wrote to Lodge in 1970 explaining that "still today the Church could make a major contribution if it were willing to make a positive statement."

The Church's failure to make what Rockefeller considered a "positive" statement could hardly be ascribed to lack of zeal on the part of Mr. Rockefeller. Within minutes of his brief meeting with the pope in July of 1965, Rockefeller was reproaching himself out loud for not having expressed his case forcefully enough. In an attempt to calm him down, Msgr. Paul Marcinkus, later head of the Vatican bank, suggested that JDR write the pope a letter expressing any points which might not have been made during the meeting. A day later on July 16, 1965, JDR duly sent off his letter on "the importance of the population problem . . .and the role that the Church might assume in its solution."

The incident read like a chapter out of an unpublished Henry James novel. The earnest Protestant American with his two newly invented contraceptives and a boundless faith that technology and progress will solve all of the world's ills confronts the head of the old world's seminal institution, an Italian gentleman by the name of Montini. "There is no problem more important facing mankind today," Mr. Rockefeller informed the pope earnestly. If the pope fails to heed Mr. Rockefeller's advice "we will face disaster of an unprecedented magnitude."

Mr. Rockefeller then goes on to explain his invention to the pope, calling the IUD "a breakthrough of truly major proportions, making available a method which is safe, effective, inexpensive and feasible under the most difficult living conditions. Experience with its use to date indicates that it will prove highly acceptable to great masses of people everywhere."

The IUD, as we have already indicated, was driven off the markct in the United States within a matter of years as a result of product liability lawsuits. Those who claim that the Church missed an historic opportunity by issuing *Humanae Vitae* would do well to ponder the consequences for papal credibility, much less infallibility, if Paul VI had taken Mr. Rockefeller's advice and endorsed the IUD as a means of Catholic-approved birth control. When it came to giving advice, JDR was used to the undivided attention of religious leaders, who in general seemed to benefit financially in direct proportion to how avidly they implemented his agenda through the agencies of their denomination. The Quakers, whose idea of missionary work included installing IUDs in Mexican women, are a good example in point. It was perhaps the accommodating nature of the mainline Protestants which led JDR to dispense with niceties and get blunt with the pope and point out to His Holiness what might happen if the pope failed to see things JDR's way. "As I see it," Rockefeller wrote to the pope,

> if the Church does not supply this leadership, there will be two consequences: one, the present accelerating pace toward population stabilization will proceed, country by country, without overall guidance or direction, particularly on the moral side: on the other, if I may speak perfectly frankly, the Church will be bypassed on an issue of fundamental importance to its people and to the well-being of all mankind. The flooding tide cannot be stopped or even slowed, but it can be guided. Because I believe so keenly in the importance of the role which your church has to play in our troubled world of today, I am deeply concerned to see a situation developing which in the long run, it seems to me, inevitably will be harmful to the Church's position around the world.

One wonders what was going through the pope's mind as he read these lines. Was he supposed to feel a sense of gratitude at being saved, along with his Church, from being swept aside by the flooding tide of progress and history? Or was it something more like the Italian version of "If you're so damn rich, why aren't you smart?" Either way, history shows that the pope passed on JDR's suggestion.

History shows just as conclusively that many liberal Catholics in the United States were much more willing to accommodate JDR's wishes than the pope was, especially if the institutions they ran might benefit from the largesse of Rockefeller funding or that of other foundations. Father Hesburgh, who arranged the meeting between Rockefeller and the pope, is a good case in point.

In his letter to the pope, Rockefeller wanted to know if it were possible "to shift the focus of this concern from the method itself to the uses to which the method will be put. Would it be feasible to state that the Church will leave to the discretion of the individual family its choice as to the method it will use to determine the number of its children provided the method is not harmful to the user and provided it does not interfere with the meaning and importance of sexual union in marriage?" This, of course, was the position the Population Council took as the condition for sponsoring its conference on population at Notre Dame. Father Hesburgh had proved to be as amenable on this point as the pope would later prove intractable.

Since sex was simply an instrument—something like a knife—according to the Rockefeller view of things, "could not the full weight and prestige of the Church be brought to bear on prescribing the circumstances under which the chosen method will be used? . . . To express the above more concisely, what I am suggesting is that specific methods be regarded as merely instruments, like knives, whose use is morally good or bad depending on the intentions of those who employ them." It was the sort of consequentialism which Father Charles Curran would advocate roughly two years later in a book published by the University of Notre Dame. The Church was, however, not buying. It did not buy the view implicitly in 1968 with the issuance of *Humanae Vitae*, and it still did not buy it 25 years later, this time explicitly, with the issuance of *Veritatis Splendor*. Of course, the Catholic universities and theologians bought into the Rockefeller view at around the same time that Father Hesburgh did. They made their break with the Church explicit when Hesburgh issued his Land o' Lakes statement in the summer of

1967, two years after he arranged the meeting between Rockefeller and the pope.

Rockefeller went on to add that dissemination of contraceptives would diminish recourse to abortion, implying that he opposed the practice, when in fact he was already involved in funding abortion advocacy in the United States. What he was proposing as his contribution to the pope's birth control encyclical would later come to be known as consequentialism, the notion that the good or evil of any action is ontologically free of its essence and solely determined by the intentions of the moral agent. This would become a prominent feature of Catholic dissent as the decade progressed. It would be the cornerstone of Charles Curran's position, the man who would mount the most effect protest against *Humanae Vitae* in the United States, and it could be picked up at any number of conferences being sponsored by foundation money in the United States. JDR didn't succeed with the pope, but his arguments were heard with increasing frequency coming from the mouths of liberal Catholics.

In October of 1965, the whole series of conferences on contraception at Notre Dame which began under the aegis of the Population Council in 1962, and whose continued funding was provided by the Ford Foundation, finally emerged from the secrecy under which they were held with the issuance of what George Shuster had promised Rockefeller three years earlier, namely, a statement by Catholic academics contesting the Church's position on birth control. In October 1965, Religious News Service announced the publication of a "remarkable statement on birth control prepared this Spring by 37 American scholars, the very existence of which was not revealed" until seven months after it had been written. Catholic scholars, at least 37 of them, were now on record in calling the Church's position on contraception "unconvincing." The statement had been delivered personally by Rev. Theodore Hesburgh to the Rev. Henri De Riedmatten, secretary of the papal commission on birth control. The story broke in the Paris edition of the *New York Times*, in an article written by John Cogley which included the text Hesburgh carried to the birth control commission as well.

Not surprisingly, the Notre Dame Statement, which was hammered out from March 17 to March 21, 1965, claimed that "the crisis of world population" was the main reason that the Church's teaching had become "unconvincing." The statement went on to list a number of propositions endorsed by the members of the conference, specifically:

> * The members of the conference, respectful of the authority of the Church, are convinced that the norms established in the past are not definitive but remain open for further development. (Point # 2)

> * The members of the conference do not find convincing the arguments from reason customarily adduced to support the conventional position. These arguments do not manifest an adequate appreciation of the findings of physiology, psychology, sociology, and demography, nor do they reveal a sufficient grasp of the complexity and the inherent value of sexuality in human life. (Point #3)

> * The majority of the members were of the opinion that there is dependable evidence that contraception is not intrinsically immoral, and that therefore there are certain circumstances in which it may be permitted or indeed even recommended. (Point #5)

> * The members were persuaded that in matters of public policy in a morally pluralistic society, Catholics while rendering witness to their beliefs need not for reasons of private morality oppose governmental programs of assistance in family limitation, provided that the consciences of all citizens are respected. (Point #7)

The last point was especially important. It was one of the suggestions laid down by the Population Council as a condition for funding the 1962 Notre Dame conference. Now, *mirabile dictu*, it appeared as if a group of "responsible" Catholic scholars had arrived at the same conclusion all by themselves, simply by pondering the exigencies of Catholic theology. With all of the crucial links in terms of funding and personnel tucked invisible behind the scenes, the fact that the same ideas kept cropping up in such seemingly unrelated places was simply ascribed to the fact that great minds always travelled in the same circles. As we shall see, the notion that Catholics should not oppose government funding of contraceptives would rear its head at the Greuning Hearings before the summer of '65 was out.

The ideas which came out of the '65 conference were, of course, not the sole property of Rockefeller and the Population Council. By the summer of '65 a consensus was emerging which had a number of interested parties involved. One of the signers of the Notre Dame statement, for example, was Notre Dame graduate and trustee, Thomas P. Carney. Carney was at the time of the conference vice-president in charge of research and development for G.D. Searle Co. of Chicago, a major pharmaceutical house.

Bill Ball, who, while working at Krol's behest, found himself fighting the move toward Catholic approval of contraception almost single-handedly, wrote to Krol to express his outrage at the havoc events like the Notre Dame conference were wreaking in his efforts. Claiming that the conference at Notre Dame "does not make my task any easier," Ball related the experience of a Catholic physician who attended the conference "and was sickened by what he heard" which "involved a unified attack on the position which Your Excellencies have taken, even to the point of referring to me in a prepared paper."

"The conference," Ball continued, "was chaired by a Notre Dame graduate named Carney, who is vice president of Searle, perhaps the leading manufacturer of contraceptives in the USA."

When it came to the discussion of birth control at Notre Dame, the field was hardly level, nor were the observers disinterested. In addition to academics eager for grants, pharmaceutical companies like Searle had representatives at the conference to insure a favorable outcome from their point of view. Notre Dame seems to have been happy with the collaboration as well. In 1967, Carney, who graduated from Notre Dame 30 years earlier with a degree in chemistry, was appointed to the board of trustees; in 1969, he was given an honorary degree; in May of 1971, he was awarded the Edward Frederick Sorin Award, the highest award granted by the Notre Dame Alumni Association.

The Catholic Press for the most part took the belated announcement of the secret Notre Dame conference as if it were an encyclical from the pope. "For the first time in my reading experience at least," wrote Msgr. George W. Casey in *The Boston Pilot*, "a committee of responsible moral theologians and sociologists meeting under Catholic auspices have made a public declaration giving endorsement, however, qualified, to contraception" (Rt. Rev. George W. Casey, "Birth Control is Waiting in the Wings," *The Boston Pilot*, 10/9/65). Msgr. Casey was much taken with the boldness of the Notre Dame statement even if it had been issued in secret seven months before. The fact that it was being publicized in the fall of '65 meant for him that a change was in the offing. The fact that people could say things like this and suffer no consequences meant that the teaching must be in doubt. In other words, the monsignor was reacting more to how the statement was propagated and how it was disseminated through the media and how the Church reacted to that dissemination than to the content of the document itself or the reasoning behind its assertions. The fact that the statement was signed by experts who claimed to be Catholic in effect took care of the problem of content, since most people would not presume to call themselves experts. The reaction to the Notre Dame statement was also a tribute to the loyalty which Catholics had toward institutions sponsored by the Church. In the minds of most people at the time, there was little difference between Notre Dame and the Church, a fact which the foundations sponsoring the conference used to maximal effect. The combination of residual trust in Catholic institutions along with a sense that the Church was changing as a result of the Council, along with the population explosion drumbeat that Rockefeller and others were orchestrating in the media all contributed to the sense that some sort of glacial unstoppable movement was in progress, and that one's attitude toward contraception was some indication of whether one sailed with the tide or got swept away in the flood. "Signs are mounting," Msgr. Casey opined with specific reference to contraception, "that the reform and the renewal instituted by Pope John will be best remembered for what it does or doesn't do with regard to this agonizing problem."

"It seems to me," he concluded, "that it is waiting in the wings to come on the stage front and center."

By the latter half of 1965, Archbishop Krol was feeling an increasing sense of exasperation at the way Catholics in general and the clergy in particular were drawn into opposing the Church's position on contraception. "Kindly note list of scholars," he wrote in a memo to himself on the Notre Dame conference and statement. It was obvious to Krol that the scholarship was dubious at best and the credentials of the scholars equally so, but all of this got ignored by the naive Msgr. Casey simply because of how the information had been portrayed in the media. "Thus opinion is made," Krol concluded grimly. There were traitors enough in this struggle. But even more disconcerting were those who seemed to stumble off in the wrong direction because they weren't clever enough to see how the information was being manipulated. If this were the case with the clergy who wrote for official Catholic newspapers, one could imagine the effect it was having on the rank and file. Krol had reason to be grim.

One indication that the efforts of Rockefeller and the Population Council were having their effect was the fact that the government was starting to get involved on their side of the issue. Johnson's endorsement of population control in the 1965 State of the Union message was followed six months later in June of 1965 with *Griswold v. Connecticut*. Then following Griswold, throughout the summer of 1965, Sen. Ernest Gruening of Alaska chaired a senate committee which held hearings on what was coming to be termed the "population explosion." The hearings were orchestrated with two major effects in mind: first of all, the populace was to have the dangers of overpopulation impressed on it in the direst terms possible, and secondly, there was to be virtual unanimity among those addressing the Gruening committee. The fact that there were no dissenting voices was to give the impression that a consensus of the best and the brightest already existed on the issue and that the only thing left for the Senate to do was to put the recommendations of the population control solons into action.

The predictions were nothing if not dire. The teeming masses were portrayed as an imminent disaster, something on the level of nuclear war. Deluge was a term frequently heard. Senator Gruening himself was of the opinion that "if our population growth does not stabilize, we may reasonably assume that we will lose the freedoms, privileges, and good life we enjoy today." Senator Joseph S. Clark of Pennsylvania, bringer of New Deal politics to Philadelphia, whose second wife was on the board of Planned Parenthood of Philadelphia, had become by the mid-'60s a tireless proselytizer for government-funded contraceptives. "In my opinion," said Senator Clark before the Gruening hearings, "with the exception of the problem of war and peace, this is the most critical matter which confronts our country today." Robert C. Cook, president of the Population Reference Bureau, told the Gruening hearings that "the point of demographic no return" was "not far in the future." For the uninitiated, the point of demographic no return was "that moment when mushrooming population growth makes disintegration and despair unavoidable." General William H. Draper, Jr. vice chairman of Planned Parenthood—World Population, told the committee that he conceived of population as a "bomb" which must be defused "so that mankind does not multiply itself into oblivion."

"Like cancer cells multiplying in the human body," Draper continued changing his metaphor but not the pathological condition it hoped to portray, "it will, unless slowed down, destroy our present day civilization just as surely as would a nuclear conflict."

Not surprisingly, given the attitude that Gruening was trying to foster, John D. Rockefeller, 3rd, chairman of the board of the Population Council, was called to testify as well. And just as unsurprisingly, JDR told the Senator from Alaska that "no problem is more urgently important to the well-being of mankind than the limitation of population growth. As a threat to our future, it is often compared with nuclear warfare."

Well, it was certainly being compared to that at the Gruening hearings often enough. And if people were becoming alarmed, that was not surprising either. Two people who were becoming alarmed as well, although not in the sense that Senator Gruening intended, were William Ball and John Krol. On the evening of August 10, Ball watched the NBC evening news with Huntley and Brinkley and listened to Stuart Udall, formerly of the department of the Interior, and Alan Guttmacher of Planned Parenthood, announce that the hearings were proceeding smoothly and that so far no opposition had surfaced. That, of course, was precisely the point of orchestrating the hearings so that only the pro-population control side got heard.

But Ball, who was responsible for representing the Church in the state of Pennsylvania was wondering if the people at the National Catholic Welfare Conference in Washington hadn't fallen asleep at the switch. Was it really true that the Catholics were planning to sit this one out? Ball wondered. A few phone calls indicated that this was precisely the case, and he was taking the time to register his alarm with Archbishop Krol. Ball had contacted William "Bud" Consedine, the legal counsel for the NCWC in Washington only to find out that the NCWC was "staying out of this" because they felt, so Consedine said to Ball, that the bill wasn't going to pass anyway. Ball was dismayed at what he heard. With the summer drawing to a close, it looked as if the hearings would conclude with not one voice expressing any opposition, and not one representative of the Church allowed to testify, not so much because Gruening refused to permit such testimony but rather because the National Catholic Welfare Conference decided that it had nothing to say on the matter.

The more Ball probed for answers on this perplexing matter the more alarmed he became. After his initial contact with Krol and after receiving permission to testify on behalf of the PCC, Ball contacted Msgr. Francis Hurley, who attempted to discourage Ball from following through with his intention to testify. Speaking as a representative of the Pennsylvania Ordinaries, according to Hurley, would create friction in other states where welfare departments had already instituted birth control programs under the anti-poverty program with the express consent of bishops in those areas. Hurley felt that the position Ball was planning to take would be an embarrassment to those bishops.

As the date set for Ball's testimony neared, it became clear that Hurley's objections were more than just procedural. The procedural maneuvering, i.e., Hurley telling Ball that the NCWC wanted to pick its own time and place to take a stand on birth control, was complicated by the fact that they claimed to be waiting for "directives from Rome" on the matter. Behind both procedural objections there was the matter of substance. Hurley in particular and the NCWC in general did not agree with Ball's confrontational attitude on government involvement in contraception. The sticking point was again racial, or at least this was the excuse given for not opposing what was going on at the Gruening hearings. Hurley wondered if it were right to kill the anti-poverty program just because it included elements that promoted birth control. Hurley, in other words, accepted the poverty programs at face value, whereas Ball saw them as a front for expanding the power of the secular state at the expense of the Church, and beyond that, something inspired by the even darker motivation of eugenic suppression of the Negro birth rate.

The impasse was never resolved. Ball continued to think of Hurley as an intelligent dupe who was out of his depth because he wasn't trained in the law. As a result, he should not have been negotiating for the Church. Because the impasse never got resolved, mistrust started to build on both sides. Hurley and the NCWC put forward their own candidate as a spokesman for the Church, a Jesuit at Georgetown by the name of Dexter Hanley. Ball and Krol, for their part, began to feel that the NCWC was working to undermine their position.

On the eve of Ball's testimony as a spokesman for the Catholics bishops, before the Gruening Commission in August of 1965, Ball announced to Krol that on August 12 the Economic Opportunity Act had been amended to include, at Senator Clark's request, specific authorization for birth control projects. Ball used the rest of his letter to complain bitterly to Krol about how the NCWC was handling (or failing to handle) the whole issue of government funding for contraceptives, a policy whose blame he lays at the feet of Msgr. Hurley point by point. According to Ball,

> 1) the NCWC never opposed the introduction of birth control into the anti-poverty program
>
> 2) Msgr. Hurley's personal position (which appears to be carried out in NCWC policy) is that the Church should not oppose publicly financed birth control

3) he approves the enclosed family planning statement by Father Hanley et. al.

4) he expressly disapproved the view against family planning expressed by me in *Commonweal*

5) he thinks that I should not testify at the Gruening hearings upon behalf of any bishops, but solely as an individual

6) the NCWC has taken no position at the Gruening hearings

During the time in which the NCWC did nothing, ostensibly while "awaiting further indications from Rome," the Gruening commission spent the entire summer giving the impression that the case in favor of government-funded contraception was virtually unanimous. As the summer passed day by day, with no response from the Catholics, Ball can hardly contain his amazement.

"I cannot believe," he told Krol, "that after 50 years of preaching against birth control, the bishops of the USA have handed Planned Parenthood a total triumph. . . . Yet that is the fact. There is little point in protesting the use of state funds for birth control by the Pennsylvania Department of Health when national Catholic policy has sanctioned such use."

Ball was scheduled to testify before the Gruening Commission on August 24, but it is clear that he felt demoralized by the lack of support coming from the NCWC in Washington.

"I am woefully tired of being a self-starter insofar as the NCWC is concerned," he told Krol. "The basic weakness, of course, lies in the fact that the horse seems to have gotten out of the barn already."

On August 17, Krol wrote to Archbishop O'Boyle, ordinary of Washington, D.C., expressing many of the same concerns. Krol was upset at the lack of activity emanating from the NCWC, which did not oppose the introduction of birth control in the anti-poverty bill, had no plans to testify before Gruening's committee, and did nothing to protest Clark's amendment to the Economic Opportunity Act. More important than any one issue, however, was the cumulative effect all of this inactivity was having on public opinion. The press was beginning to suggest that "Church leaders have gone underground on this issue."

"Others," Krol continued, "interpret it as capitulation. All consider it 'significant that there has been no great protest by the Roman Catholic Church in the United States against President Johnson and the Congress for their programs of using public funds for birth control programs.'" Krol concluded his letter to O'Boyle with the sincere "hope that Your Excellency will break this silence."

In a letter to Apostolic Delegate Egidio Vagnozzi, Krol complained bitterly not only about the tendency of the NCWC to undermine what he and the bishops of Pennsylvania were trying to do, but also about the directive from Rome to hold in abeyance any discussion of birth control until the Holy See published its decision.

"The loyal and devoted Catholics," Krol complained "observe the directive scrupulously." And as a result they are taken out of the discussion and leave only disloyal Catholics as the spokesmen for the Church. The Catholics who do continue to speak in spite of the ban "are giving the impression that the Church has no choice but to reverse its teachings. Some of the faithful and many non-Catholics assume from this one-sided presentation that it is simply a matter of time and the Church must reverse its teachings."

"I don't want to sound like an alarmist," Krol continued,

> but I do believe the problem merits serious consideration. While the so-called experts are conditioning public opinion by denigrating the Church's traditional teaching on birth control and by extolling the rights of conscience we dutifully obey the Holy Father's directives to avoid public discussion. Perhaps some are apprehensive that, if they reaffirm the Church's traditional teachings today, they might possibly be wrong when the Holy See will eventually come out with the statement. Personally, I am concerned that in this age of confused ecumenism, and exaggerated individualism, some of the faithful have been conditioned to reject any decision which displeases them.

"I don't know the solution to this problem," Krol concludes, "but I believe that it is a serious problem."

On the eve of Ball's testimony before the Gruening committee, Krol wrote to Vagnozzi again complaining specifically this time about "Father Hanley, S.J." who had testified on August 9 before the family law section of the American Bar Association on "Problems of Public Policy Arising out of Tax-Supported Family Planning." As Krol had come to expect, Hanley's position, which was sympathetic to the idea of tax-supported family planning programs, was widely publicized and was as a result widely regarded as the Catholic position on the issue. Krol went on to complain to Vagnozzi that this sort of misinformation was making dramatic inroads on the way Catholics viewed the issue. He cited a Gallup poll in 1953 which claimed that 53 percent of Catholics said that birth control information should be available to anyone who wanted it. In January of 1965, 78 percent of Catholics polled expressed the same view. Similarly, 60 percent of Catholics felt that the Church would approve some method of birth control like the birth control pill, and 81 percent believed that that approval would come within the next ten years.

Vagnozzi, for his part, can only respond by sharing "Your Excellency's concern about the attitude of some individuals with regards to the Holy Father's directive on birth control discussions. Unfortunately, these persons or self-styled experts are succeeding in creating a false impression as to the Church's position on this subject. Frankly, I think that there should be more concern."

"As you say," Vagnozzi concluded, "this is a serious problem."

It was clear from their correspondence, that both Krol and Vagnozzi felt that the misrepresentation of the position of the Church and the ban on discussion, which was, in effect, only being followed by those who adhered to Church teaching, was having serious repercussions among the faithful because of the malformation of public opinion by the pro-contraceptive media. This in turn was having serious ramifications in the realm of public policy. The only countermeasure which the Church was able to mount during an entire summer of contraceptive propaganda, Krol told Vagnozzi, would be Bill Ball's testimony, which was scheduled for the morning of August 24.

When Ball finally arrived at the subcommittee hearing room at the capitol on the morning of August 24, he was surprised to find that he was no longer to testify as scheduled. After overcoming some initial disinclination on the part of Gruening's staffers, Ball was scheduled to testify as the first witness on the morning of August 24. When he arrived, he found to his surprise that he had been replaced in the line-up by none than the Rev. Dexter Hanley, S.J. A look at Father Hanley's testimony gives some indication of why Gruening found his views more congenial than Ball's.

Father Hanley began his testimony on a note that was Catholic enough. He claimed that "the only morally acceptable form of voluntary family regulation is through continence, either total or periodic. Any public program which will either directly or indirectly challenge these premises will meet opposition from Catholics." But after saying that, Hanley effectively took the teeth out of the Catholic position by claiming that it affected them alone and that in a pluralistic society the good Catholic would not seek to impose his will on society as a whole. Hanley's idea of "a practical and political accord" meant in effect the marginalization of the Catholic Church on the issue of birth control and the further secularization of culture with its concomitant decline in social order. Catholic opposition to contraception was portrayed as the moral analogue to their refusal to eat meat on Fridays. While "it would be ideal," Father Hanley opined, "if all citizens could share the same basic moral codes and convictions," the fact that they don't somehow means that the Catholics should withdraw their objections to anything which the secular state wants, but which the Church opposes. "Government," Hanley claimed, "is not the proper organ to decide the truth of conflicting views."

> Hence, while firmly maintaining my basic moral positions as a Catholic, I believe that I can support a government program which, in its legitimate concern about education, health and welfare in a rapidly expanding population, permits each citizen a fully free moral choice in matters of family planning and aids him in implementing this choice.

Now it may be that Father Hanley hammered out his position in his room all by himself with nothing but an open copy of Denzinger before him, but the fact remains that there are remarkable similarites between his position and the position Mr. Rockefeller and the Population Council specified as the necessary condition for the grant he gave for the Notre Dame conference in 1962. The other fact which remains is that Hanley was invited to precisely these conferences, so in all likelihood he knew the "progressive" position on the matter of birth control, and he knew the position that would insure Catholics a welcome response from people like Rockefeller on the matter. It didn't take a genius to figure things like this out; in fact, it would take a moron not to figure them out, and Father Hanley was not a moron. Beyond that, Hanley's position had the blessing of Msgr. Hurley and the bureaucrats at the NCWC, who were increasingly inclined to push their own agenda at the expense of the teaching of the Church and beyond that, inclined to make policy behind the bishops' backs. The insertion of Hanley into the line-up at the Gruening hearings was just one indication of them pursuing their policies at the expense of their employers, the bishops.

Bill Ball did eventually get to testify on August 24, but as the last speaker of the day. As if that weren't bad enough, the fact that the Church's position was, in effect, represented as two different points of view—his and Hanley's—gave the impression that the Church was of two minds on the issue of government-sponsored birth control. In the face of an artificially orchestrated unanimity of opinion on the part of the secularists on the dangers of a population "bomb" which was about to go off momentarily, the Church's position seemed vacillating and unsure by comparison.

Of course, that was only the case if one ignored Ball's actual testimony, which was a powerful indictment of government sponsored birth control plans as both detrimental to the citizens' freedoms and covertly eugenical as well. Hamstrung by both the Vatican's prohibition on the one hand and an increasingly prohibitive notion of the separation of Church and state proposed by the secularists on the other, Ball did a brilliant job of portraying government-sponsored birth control as a threat to civil freedoms. Ball's argument was based on two Supreme Court cases of recent memory. From *Griswold* he established the right to privacy and from the *Engel* and *Schempp* cases, he talked about the freedom from government coercion when religious issues were concerned. If the Supreme Court could argue that prayer or Bible reading being offered in school was intrinsically coercive to those who did not share the Judeo-Christian view and, therefore, an impermissible infringement on the separation of Church and state, then a social worker probing his client's views on sexuality and procreation could hardly be construed as less invasive or less of a breach of that separation. This was true of anyone on welfare, according to Ball, but it was especially true of Catholics on welfare, or in any other capacity affected by a public entity.

According to Ball's testimony, "the main features of the bill pose serious dangers to civil liberty while offering no genuine prospect of relieving the problems of poverty, crowding and disease which they purport to solve." Beyond that, these programs are necessarily coercive, as that term was defined in the recent school prayer decisions. This is so because the main target group in birth control programs had always been the poor. Telling a person he is free to reject the proffered birth control is not ameliorated by adding that he is free to refuse. The very fact that the government, which is the source of the person's livelihood, is offering the services means that the government feels that the contraceptive is a good thing to offer, and by extension that the welfare recipient would do well to accept. The exchange is by its nature coercive. For the Catholic, the state is intruding into a sphere around which it just erected a very high wall of separation.

If the Court were sincere in its concern over the separation of Church and State, they doubtless would have accepted Ball's argument. With the benefit of hindsight, however, it is difficult to see how the government was being sincere in the matter. The doctrine of privacy, invoked by Justice Douglas in 1965, seven years later was used to justify the decriminalization of abortion, but it was not used to stop the government's ever-deepening involvement in funding contraceptives. The lesson seems plain enough in retrospect. Privacy meant in effect the protection of sexual liberation against the threats posed to it by organized religion. Eventually, the doctrine of privacy would be invoked to protect two homosexuals caught *in flagrante dilectu* in an automobile parked on a street in Albany, New York. The doctrine of privacy in this instance was used to strike down that state's law prohibiting sodomy. It was just one more example of how the terms the secular state used to widen the acceptance of sexual liberation could never be used at face value to threaten the aforementioned expansion.

In this regard, one could fault Ball for naivete, but that would invite undue cynicism, especially in light of the evidence of the time. In 1965, it was not apparent that Justice Douglas was not sincere when he referred to marriage as something sacred and private in *Griswold*. Ball was simply using the language available to him as a lawyer, in a country that ostensibly placed great regard in the notion of rule by law.

Ball also mentioned the fact that in recent times both the courts and the legislatures had simultaneously broadened the definition of social welfare and narrowed the power of government over individuals. Common to both features was a "concern for the weaker members of society . . . most recently this concern has been more emphatically extended to the criminally accused, the alien, the Negro and the poor." Gruening's bill was calling for something which went contrary to both trends. "S. 1676," according to Ball, "is, plainly and simply, a bill for the establishing of a domestic and international birth control program and for the creating of permanent federal governmental organs for the carrying out of the same." Ball complained that not only would such an entity be of its nature intrusive and coercive, he went on to say that the onus of its intent would fall on the Negro.

"The note of racial eugenicism," Ball continued, ". . . . is inescapable in the proposal of S. 1676. . . . In this hour of the painful emergence of our Negro brothers into the American society, surely this consideration should be weighted in the balance with the assumed but unproved benefits of S. 1676's birth control proposal." Ball concluded by saying the whole bill reflected the psychology of "the White Man's Burden" and should be rejected as a result.

Ball's approach to the birth control issue seems to have taken the secular establishment and its Catholic Amen Corner by surprise. John Cogley, who can safely be categorized as representing both bodies in his capacity as religion writer for the *New York Times*, was favorably impressed by Ball's testimony—at least at first. In an article which appeared two days after Ball's testimony, Cogley not only mentioned that Ball "heavily relied on decisions of the Supreme Court" in his presentation, he also gave the impression that the argument about the intrinsically coercive nature of government-funded birth control was persuasive. Ball's decision to fight fire with fire, seemed to be bearing fruit, at least in the impression it made on Cogley at the *New York Times*, who seconded the notion that someone's rights were bound to be violated and that that someone would invariably be the "client":

"The fact that the citizen," Cogley opined, "was in the position of 'client' of an all-powerful government put him in the danger of being 'susceptible to subtle pressure.'" One gets the impression that Cogley was expecting a frontal attack on the morality of birth control conducted by Ball in the name of the bishops, and that when this did not occur he was caught a bit off balance.

Within a matter of days, however, Cogley changed his mind about Ball's testimony and went on the offensive by accusing Ball of making it under false pretenses. Since he couldn't very well go back on what he said about the content of Ball's presentation, Cogley decided instead to attack the auspices under which he spoke (John Cogley, "Bishops' Unanimity on Birth control Bill in doubt," *NYT*, Monday August 30, 1965). Cogley intimated that Ball was lying when he claimed that he had spoken on behalf of the American hierarchy. Cogley's article was full of innuendo and unnamed sources, but the intent was clear. Discredit the messenger by claiming that he did not represent the Catholic position.

"At least one member of the administrative board of the National Catholic Welfare Conference," Cogley wrote without naming names, "the only body that can speak for the American bishops, had no knowledge that the statement was to be made with the conference's authorization."

"The argument advanced by Mr. Ball," Cogley continued, "was legal and juridical. But since he announced that he had the authorization of the National Catholic Welfare Conference for it, the statement committed the Roman Catholic bishops of the

United States. . . . Consequently he gave the impression that the hierarchy was united on a single juridical position and constitutional interpretation of a proposed bill." Cogley then quoted an unnamed bishop who couldn't "imagine all of us agreeing on anything but the Apostles' Creed."

The reason for Cogley's *volta face* on Ball's testimony is not clear. One plausible explanation is that Cogley was, in fact, persuaded by Ball's argument and then filled with the fear that it might have its desired effect. He could have reached this conclusion on his own, or he could have been helped in this regard by others. In a letter to Vagnozzi in early September, Krol gave some indication that Cogley was reacting to pressure from the *New York Times* as well as being "prompted by someone within our own camp." Either way, Krol felt that it was "a standard technique of Planned Parenthood, which was used successfully in dividing and conquering Protestant and Jewish leadership."

Krol goes on to say that Ball, in any juridical sense of the word, did speak for the hierarchy in the United States when he addressed the Gruening committee, a fact born out not only by Krol's meticulous nature as a canon lawyer but also by the reception Ball's testimony received from other bishops. Archbishop O'Boyle was so enthused by Ball's testimony that he urged that it be made in the name of all of the United States bishops.

On September 2, Krol wrote to O'Boyle to say how "intrigued" he was by "the changing tone of Cogley's three reports on the Birth Control Statement."

"The first was good," Krol continued, "The second raised the question. The third deliberately challenged. In the last article he casts some reflections on both Your Excellency and on Bill Ball. He tried real hard to get Mr. Ball to say that he was speaking for all the bishops. Bill Ball repeated what he had said in the testimony—the statement which was prepared by Msgr. Tanner.

Krol concludes by suspecting that "it was some of the boys in the NCWC or in the Hanley camp who might have given

Cogley the nod." He suspected the same sort of thing in the circumstances surrounding Hanley's testimony.

"We are still puzzled," he continued in the same vein, "how it happened that Father Hanley, who made a statement on August 9, gave his testimony on August 24, the day on which Mr. Ball was scheduled to testify. Mr. Ball was supposed to have been first on the list for that day. Father Hanley was first and Mr. Ball was placed last. We have recently heard that Father Hanley's statement was in the hands of some people at the NCWC even before he delivered it on August 9. . . . All of this, of course, seems relevant to your observation that perhaps some of the boys in the NCWC, who should be serving and briefing the bishops, may be working at cross purposes, even by giving Cogley a nod or two."

The loyalty of the NCWC staff was an open question in the minds of many bishops. Yet, none of them seemed to know how to deal with the situation without causing more division than the division they sought to heal. So for the most part, the suspicions were expressed *sub rosa* in private communications. As time went on, bishops like Krol would react to their suspicions by freezing NCWC staffers out of their deliberations, something which was hardly conducive to the type of effort that was needed at the time.

Ball's testimony clearly ruffled feathers at the NCWC, first of all because they disagreed with Ball's approach in deference to that of Father Hanley, but also because they felt their turf had been invaded by an interloper from Pennsylvania. Krol felt that Ball's arguments were effective claiming that "even our confirmed enemies—Protestants and and other Americans United—recognize the validity of Mr. Ball's arguments based on the decisions of the Supreme Court" (Krol to Vagnozzi 9/2/65). What Krol found especially annoying was the fact that Ball's arguments got watered down by having Dexter Hanley testify in his place on the same day, thus giving the impression that the Church was of two minds on the issue. Ball could have had the wisdom of Solomon and the eloquence of Demosthenes, but the fact remains that there were two spokesmen representing two opposing views instead of the one that had been scheduled that day. And that fact led Krol to believe that the Church had been the victim of foul play, probably instigated by the NCWC itself.

He also felt that Hanley's testimony was full of flaws, notably

1) He assumes as factual the claims of Planned Parenthood that this program is a solution to so many problems. The fact is there is no conclusive evidence that such a program has or is capable of solving the many problems.

2) Father Hanley talks about procedures to safeguard liberty of conscience. [But] He fails to indicate what procedures would safeguard liberty of conscience of those who depend upon the favor of the case worker to continue receiving financial help.

3) Father Hanley says he is against sterilization and abortion. [Yet] He did not ask that the Gruening Bill be amended specifically to exclude these norms of population control. Father Hanley is not taking into account that the Birth Control (Gruening) Bill is primarily the fruit of high pressure from Planned Parenthood leadership.

The Catholic Amen Corner was quick to close ranks behind Cogley, Hanley, and the staffers as the NCWC. Within days of Ball's testimony, Daniel Callahan wrote in the *National Catholic Reporter* that "there are no facts to support Mr. Ball's assumption" that government birth control programs would be coercive. Callahan also dismisses the charges of "racial eugenicism," claiming that the Negro is on welfare not because of "the racist's claim of Negro immorality and irresponsibility. On the contrary, it is a direct consequence of the inferior education imposed on Negroes by the white man." The response causes one to wonder if Callahan understood the term. Ball wasn't responding to why Negroes were on welfare. The charge of eugenics was in response to how the secular state wanted to get them off welfare, not on it.

In addition to dismissing Ball's concerns about coercion and eugenicism, Callahan also dismisses the notion that any private agency (e.g., the Catholic Church) could take on a social welfare burden of the magnitude needed in the United States at the time. Callahan knows this because Planned Parenthood had "barely been able to scratch the surface." It is difficult to know which surface Mr. Callahan thinks need to be scratched. But again there seems to be a difference of opinion about just what needs to be done. Like Dexter Hanley, Callahan accepts the arguments of the secular state at face value. His only disagreement is with the size of the operation.

> At one time, it might have been realistic to argue that private organizations could sufficiently cope with problems of social welfare. If there ever was such a day, it has now passed. In a mass society, nothing less than massive, carefully planned and carefully directed programs will do much good.

As a result, "the response of the bishops, through Mr. Ball, is anachronistic." The two positions, of course, go hand in hand, and their relationship to each other is a bit like the chicken's to the egg. Callahan is using the need for birth control to justify an expansion of the role of federal government, and he is also using the moral mandate in things like the racial issue, which was used to expand government's scope, as justification for the legitimacy of birth control.

The role of the Church, in Callahan's view, is to give the government pointers on how it can do its work without infringing on personal freedom. "What can work," he opines, "is for the Church to use its moral prestige—even its political power—to insist upon the necessity of a free choice on the part of those affected by birth control programs." Callahan closes his article with the same appeal to historical inevitability which John D. Rockefeller used on the pope. "The nation," Callahan writes, "desperately needs effective and accessible family planning services. These services are bound to come. The only remaining question is whether the bishops, and beyond them other Catholics, will have something constructive to say while they are still mainly in the planning stages." Again the similarities in thought and expression are not surprising. Callahan attended the Notre Dame conferences as well. JDR's strategy of reaching "liberal" Catholics was bearing fruit. The same ideas were coming from so many ostensibly different sources that an unformed observer would have to conclude that great minds were at work.

In the immediate aftermath of his testimony, Ball was happy with the results. "For the first time," he wrote to Krol three days after the appearance before the committee, "the nation's attention is being focussed on government birth control as a civil liberties problem. The bishops have presented a case for freedom and now have gained the initiative in a great public controversy." Ball felt that Father Hanley's statement was "both confused and harmful." Beyond that he is "puzzled over the fact that the NCWC office did not tell me that Father Hanley was scheduled to appear the same day I was to appear."

By the time he got a chance to read Cogley's column attacking him for speaking in the name of the U.S. bishops, Ball's mood had changed. He was by then concerned about the effect of the Cogley article on his reputation and the standing of the Pennsylvania Catholic Conference. Even if Ball felt upset at the attack on his reputation though, the Cogley attack was still a perverse recognition of the strength of his argument. "The big point," he concludes in his letter to Krol, "is that the opposition cannot discredit their arguments and therefore seek to discredit the authorization."

Krol for his part is of much the same opinion. Ball's testimony in conjunction with Archbishop O'Boyle's sermon at around the same time on the same topic, "produced the desired impact."

> It put Gruening's committee on notice. It made Father [Dexter] Hanley's group react strongly. It reversed the trend of a few people in the NCWC who presumed to make policy instead of briefing the bishops on a critical issue. It is possible that Cogley's shift to a challenging posture may have been inspired by some of the people who were reversed.

Krol's remarks then take a personal turn that is not characteristic of his correspondence, but which indicates as a result all the more the fact that he felt that both men were personally involved in a high-stakes game with opponents that would stop at nothing to thwart what the Church held valuable. "You said," he wrote to Ball,

> our opponents are ruthless and resourceful. We must take for granted that they will lash out at us. You have rendered a valuable service to the church and even to the NCWC. Please don't retreat to lick your bruises, or to feel sorry for yourself. Such action is not worthy of you. Although my name has not been publicized—for which I am grateful—I have been in this battle

up to my neck, and I propose to stay in it regardless of the consequences.

Ball's testimony may have had more tangible consequences than either he or Krol saw at the time. Roughly three weeks after Ball's testimony, Senator Joseph Clark's amendment calling for the dissemination of birth control was eliminated from the Johnson Administration's $1.7 billion anti-poverty legislation. In the article reporting the change in the *Philadelphia Bulletin*, anonymous Capitol Hill sources laid the blame at the feet of the National Catholic Welfare Conference, a remark which both Ball and Krol must have found mordantly amusing. The article also mentioned the fear of members of Congress that the whole poverty program might be adversely affected as a result of opposition from the Catholic Church. So the battle was still on. And the Church, even in its divided state, was still having an impact.

Ball for his part was often placed in the position of exhorting some of the less stalwart bishops to stand up to their increasingly liberal staffs. Shortly after his testimony before the Gruening hearings, Ball complained to Lawrence Cardinal Shehan that the bishops were being forced to fight a war on two fronts because of the behavior of the NCWC. Ball had been fighting what he called a "full scale public birth control program" in Pennsylvania for two years and in conversations with the Secretary of Public Welfare was constantly having the position of the NCWC thrown back in his face. "If the NCWC has gone along" on public birth control programs, Ball was told, "who are the bishops of Pennsylvania to object?" The bureaucrats in Washington were setting a policy that was undermining the ability of the local bishops to maintain their own position at the local level. The NCWC gave its tacit approval to the birth control provisions of the Anti-Poverty Act when the advocates of the provisions themselves knew that an objection from the Catholics could have killed the bill, as they in fact did within weeks of Ball's communication with Shehan.

Shehan, in spite of Ball's prodding on the matter, seemed incapable of 1) understanding the magnitude of the problem, and 2) disagreeing with the advice of his subordinates, who invariably took the accommodationist position. Ball related how Senator Gruening informed him that "all human progress is based on experimentation, and we've got to start experimenting on population control." By accepting "the factual assumptions of Planned Parenthood lock, stock and barrel," Father Hanley and his supporters were in effect condoning medical experimentation on the poor on a massive scale. According to the language of the Gruening bill, this sort of experimentation even then would not preclude sterilization and abortion. "Father Hanley," Ball complains, "says that he is against sterilization and abortion. Yet he did not ask that the Gruening bill be amended specifically to exclude these forms of population control." Shehan for his part seems preoccupied with the fear that aggressive opposition to government birth control programs will offend the "ecumenical spirit." Ball tries to allay his fears by explaining that the introduction of birth control into the poverty program was "essentially the fruit of high pressure from Planned Parenthood leadership."

Shehan's timidity on this and other issues would remove him from any effective role of leadership in the matter. Shehan was quite simply intimidated by the experts. In the week following his testimony, Ball received a call from Francis X. Gallagher, Shehan's attorney, who relayed the information that Shehan had been shocked by Ball's testimony. Many of the people who had signed the Hanley statement, it turns out, were from the Archdiocese of Baltimore, and Shehan was worried that the aggressive nature of Ball's statement, coupled with the fact that it was made in the name of the bishops, of which Shehan was a prominent example, would cause a division in the ranks: in the words of Gallagher echoing Shehan, "the bishops will now be in one corner and the academic community in another." Shehan especially feared the power of the Jesuits and of the Jesuit law schools, and the prestige that Father Hanley, who was both a Jesuit and a law school professor at Georgetown, had among that group. Hanley's statement, it turns out, had enjoyed wide circulation among the lawyers and scholars at the NCWC for months before he gave it as a talk at the ABA. It should come as no surprise then, that outrage on the part of the NCWC should come as the major result of Ball's testimony before the Gruening hearings. Ball had, in effect, destroyed the NCWC's carefully worked out position of accommodation, a position which had the backing of the Jesuits and virtually all of the apparatus of Catholic academe.

What Ball was proposing was war on birth control in the bishops' name, as a proxy for Krol and other hardliners on the issue, at the very same time that the image of acceptance by the secular powers that be, with all of the funding that would go with that, was being dangled enticingly in front of the eyes of the people who were in charge of the Catholic universities and other intellectual organs. The Catholic intellectuals of the day craved acceptance by the secular authorities of the time. In a book published in 1964, *A New Generation: American and Catholic*, Michael Novak, who, along with his wife, signed the Hanley statement, displays this craving in a way that was perhaps exaggerated but not untypical. "The secular university," Novak wrote, "seems in fact to promote, through the method of liberty, the achievement of a profound personal synthesis in a remarkable number of its graduates," whereas "Catholic pastoral theory seems clearly to favor the weak, the slow, [and] the undiscerning." Novak, who was a student at Harvard at the time and would eventually come to revise his attitude toward secular education, even finds good things to say about "secular" cocktail parties: "a cocktail party in a secular environment is open on the world, more pluralistic, more respectful, more favorable to the individual talent."

Cardinal Shehan of Baltimore was in effect caught in the middle. He was intellectually incapable of dealing with "experts" like Novak and Hanley and the staffers at the NCWC, but he was, because of his irenic nature, constitutionally incapable of siding with Ball and Krol and the bishops who wanted to pursue a policy of confronting the expansion of the welfare state head on. As a result, all he could do was register his discomfort, and Ball and Krol were forced to look elsewhere for allies in the fight who would take a more active and aggressive position.

One of those allies was Archbishop Patrick O'Boyle of Washington. On the Sunday (August 29, 1965) immediately following Ball's testimony before the Gruening Hearings, O'Boyle delivered a sermon on "Birth Control and Public Policy" at St. Matthew's Cathedral in Washington. The sermon got widespread coverage in the press, and its influence was felt in Washington. The Church in the person of Archbishop O'Boyle was taking a stand on the poverty program and the attempt by the government to deal with the plight of the poor in general and the negro poor in particular through eugenic means. The sermon was a clear attempt on O'Boyle's part to draw a line in the sand, and the line had to do with the insinuation of birth control programs into the budget of the War on Poverty.

"In the United States," O'Boyle began, "progress in the field of racial and social justice has been nothing short of phenomenal." O'Boyle's sermon was intended to put Washington on notice that no matter how phenomenal, nor no matter how "holy" a cause the civil rights movement had become, the Church was not going to tolerate it as a front for advancing public acceptance of birth control.

Implicit in O'Boyle's challenge was a rebuke of the accommodationist polices of the NCWC up 'til that time. "Committees of the Congress and other public bodies," O'Boyle said, "hearing no official expression to the contrary, have assumed that 'silence gives consent' and have initiated programs intruding on the private lives of citizens—programs in which, to put it bluntly, the government has no business." In addition to breaking with the policies of the NCWC, O'Boyle called into question the whole notion of a "population explosion," conceding at the very most that "there may well be at this moment areas of relative overpopulation in certain parts of this country—the so-called Negro ghettos of some of our northern cities, for example." Even if this were the case on a widespread basis, O'Boyle made it clear that birth control, especially in programs sponsored by the government, was not going to alleviate social problems.

A program of such dubious benefit is clearly outweighed by its negative side, which involves a threat to the American family, specifically as a result of "the gradual intrusion of government into the private lives of its citizens." Taking his cue from Ball, O'Boyle cited Supreme Court cases to bolster his arguments. Justice Brandeis's "right to be left alone" was given modern application in *Griswold v. Connecticut*: "Now," concluded O'Boyle, "if the government is enjoined by this decision from forbidding the practice of birth control, it logically follows that it is likewise forbidden to promote it." O'Boyle then went on to attack the Gruening bill specifically, if not by name.

> In spite of these unmistakable constitutional roadblocks, a bill is now before the Senate sub-committee on Foreign Aid expenditures that would formally and directly involve the federal government in birth prevention programs, including he dissemination of information and materials at public expense. . . . . In a number of cities, there have been attempts to link promotion of birth control with the new antipoverty program, on the theory that, as one senator put it, "the poor are more likely than any other group to have large families."

"That," O'Boyle thundered from the pulpit, "is not the government's business. The choice of how many children a couple should have is the sole, personal responsibility of the spouses. It is not less their responsibility if they happen to be poor."

The line in the sand was clear. The Church would support the War on Poverty and the concomitant expansion of the welfare state only if that expansion remained within the bounds of the moral law. Once that line was crossed, the government could expect opposition from the Catholics. This, of course, is precisely what the secularists had feared all along. Rockefeller and his minions at the Pop Council were only interested in Catholics who were willing to relegate their moral beliefs to the realm of personal predilection. This had been the *sine qua non* for funding the contraception conferences at Notre Dame, and it was the heart of Hanley's position in front of the ABA and the Gruening hearings. It was also at the heart of the NCWC's strategy, which, Krol suspected, had gone out of its way to insinuate Hanley and his position into the Gruening hearing lineup in place of Bill Ball.

O'Boyle was, in effect, arguing for an honest interpretation of the separation of church and state, and on sexual matters this is precisely what the Church would never get, because, in virtually all important aspects, the separation of church and state was nothing more than a pretext for the establishment of the secular agenda as the law of the land, and sexual liberation was, as time would show with increasing clarity, one of the secularists' non-negotiable demands.

"For a government agent," O'Boyle stated, "to inquire respecting details of their sexual life, or in any way to suggest to them practices respecting sex which may do violence to their religious beliefs, is a clear violation of the sacred right of privacy which the Supreme Court held to be inviolate." O'Boyle was arguing, in other words, that it was inconsistent to ban prayer as a violation of religious beliefs but at the same time promote contraception. This was, of course, true, but it was also true that this self-contradiction lay at the heart of the secular agenda.

"In great issues of this kind," O'Boyle continued, "where opinion is sharply divided the first and most important consideration in searching for a solution is the preservation of the God-given right of conscience. Catholics, for example, have no right to impose their own moral code upon the rest of the country by civil legislation. By the same reasoning, they are obliged in conscience to oppose any regulation which would elevate to the status of public policy a philosophy or practice which violates rights of privacy or liberty of conscience. The citizen's freedom cuts both ways. . . .In situations, like this, involving serious moral issues in which people strive to form a right conscience, the role of government is clear—strict neutrality. . . . The moment the government presumes to "give advice" in this delicate area, it opens the door to influencing the free decision of its citizens. And from influence it is only a short step to coercion."

Unfortunately, Archbishop O'Boyle, like all the bishops, was fighting a war on two fronts on this issue. In addition to warning the government away from funding birth control programs, he had to admonish the Catholics to adhere to the Church's position. "A Catholic," O'Boyle claimed turning his direction to the second front for a moment, "accepts voluntarily, by the very fact of his membership the official teaching of the Church in matters of faith and morals. And, my dear good people, the Church's teaching with regard to contraception has been both clear and consistent." As an indication that that teaching was not going to change, O'Boyle quotes the statement of Pope Paul

VI that "we do not have a sufficient reason to regard the norms given by Pope Pius XII in this matter as surpassed and therefore not binding."

"If next week," O'Boyle asks in concluding his homily, "you were asked to sacrifice one of your children to ease the 'population explosion,' which one would you choose? . . . Surely in the glorious history of this great nation, we have found better guides to the Great Society than the four horsemen of artificial birth control, abortion, sterilization and euthanasia. . . . This is the philosophy of defeatism and despair."

In a letter expressing satisfaction over the reception of his sermon, O'Boyle mentioned the outrage his mentioning the Great Society in a negative light caused. The light, of course, was only contingently negative. If the Johnson Administration continued on its current course, it would have to deal with the Church casting doubts on its moral *bona fides*. But O'Boyle nonetheless decided to take the criticism to heart and in future publications backed off any mention of the Great Society. The message was clear without it anyway.

Over the fall of '65 Ball, Krol, and O'Boyle collaborated on a policy designed to thwart the entrance of the United States government into the field of birth control. On October 29, Ball had a four and a half hour meeting with O'Boyle in Washington during which he laid out three possible responses to the birth control issue. The first response was "peaceful coexistence," which Ball characterized as the position advocated by Msgr. Hurley and the NCWC. The arguments in favor of this policy were the ones the liberals found most congenial, namely, ecumenical cooperation, civil peace, and avoiding jeopardy to the antipoverty program. Pursuing this policy would cause minimal damage to the interest of the liberals in benefits from the welfare state because it in effect would remove the Catholic Church from the fight. Option number two was the policy of limited opposition advocated by Father Hanley. This policy would resist government birth control programs unless provisions were made banning coercion, protecting privacy, and excluding abortion and sterilization. Ball was skeptical about both strategies, feeling that the birth control movement was already gaining power to the point of being uncontrollable by any means, and that government funding would make them so powerful that they would effectively be beyond any legal apparatus designed to control them. His objection to limited opposition policy was of the same sort. And he cited his experiences with Planned Parenthood as an indication that legal controls of the sort Hanley was urging, even if accepted on paper, would prove worthless in practice. In applying for a $90,000 grant in Philadelphia under the Economic Opportunity Program, Planned Parenthood targeted the plan for a 100 percent Negro area in the North Central part of the city. In addition to that, the people staffing the program were not medically trained but had been trained to pursue Planned Parenthood's social program. According to the grant application, the "home visitors" trained by Planned Parenthood go to the houses of their "clients" to "note the conditions under which the family lives and [to] seek the information necessary for effective future programming." If grants were funded under those conditions, it seemed foolish, according to Ball's reasoning, to expect such programs to be neither intrusive nor coercive no matter what the safeguards.

As a result, Ball advocated a policy of "full opposition," but not without first adding a few caveats. Full opposition was going to be uphill work because birth control had become a billion dollar industry which was willing to spend a considerable amount of time and money to create a mentality in favor of government funding for its services.

Beyond that, any campaign that the Church would wage must appear to be both reasonable and not arbitrary. This campaign should be both knowledgeable in its use of constitutional law and sparing in its use of ecclesial and moral fiat. If the Church could convince a large segment of the population of the reasonableness of its position, another probably equally large segment of the population would go along out of simple political expediency.

The campaign would also have to be pursued on federal, state, and local levels simultaneously, to avoid the sort of whipsawing that occurred when Ball was confronted by the Secretary of Welfare in Pennsylvania, who the NCWC's policies against him. One of the main government agencies that needed to be targeted was the Office of Economic Opportunity, a task

Ball himself would tackle before long with mixed success. Above all, Ball encouraged the bishops, O'Boyle and Krol in particular, to count the cost before becoming involved.

"I feel," Ball wrote to O'Boyle on October 28,

> that no opposition should be mounted unless it is very thorough and planned step by step. The contraceptive manufacturers see an enormous bonanza in government-underwritten birth control. Already at their disposal are Planned Parenthood's well devised propaganda techniques. A partial or ad *hoc* opposition by the Church will create far more bitterness than a thorough campaign and that will be its main result. Better silence than a half-hearted effort.

In urging caution before proceeding with a policy of full opposition, Ball had two things in mind. First of all, the magnitude of what was at stake in terms of sheer dollars was staggering. Ball compared government funding for birth control as a financial windfall that was on a par with the cold war defense contracts, "so to mount a one horse campaign against government birth control would be a very foolish thing." Secondly, in addition to having a very formidable enemy, the bishops also had a very weak bunch of troops. The NCWC, according to Ball, "is pitiably poor in staff work," capable of nothing more than a "terribly *ad hoc* effort" and a "hit or miss approach to serious public questions." In addition to making their own policy behind the bishops backs, the NCWC withheld important documentation from the bishops that caused crucial delays in areas like the funding of birth control in the OEO. If the situation had been dealt with promptly in 1964, the issue would have long since been defeated. The blame for the fact that it wasn't Ball lays unambiguously at the feet of the NCWC.

Krol, who had serious doubts of his own about both the effectiveness and the loyalty of the NCWC staff, seemed undeterred by the grim picture Ball painted. Without hesitation, he opted for the strategy of full opposition. In a letter dated November 2, 1965, responding to Ball's description of his meeting with Archbishop O'Boyle, Krol agrees that "the policy of peaceful co-existence and even the policy of limited opposition would be a waste of time and effort, and implicitly conceding victory to our opponents. Full opposition is the only reasonable course left open."

Within two weeks of Krol's decision, Ball was in Rome giving a confidential briefing to the general body of bishops there on the dangers of government-funded birth control and the best strategy in dealing with it. Perhaps because he could speak his mind without fear of reproach from the media, Ball sketched out a very cynical picture of the War on Poverty. The Economic Opportunity Act, the main funding vehicle for anti-poverty programs had become, according to Ball, "a major artery for government birth control in the United States." This money was directed exclusively to the poor and would be used against them in ways both coercive and intrusive. Ball cited the $90,000 program proposed by Planned Parenthood for the North Philadelphia ghetto as an example. The Church, in terms of opposing such measures, was now almost a year behind the efforts of those who wanted them implemented, primarily as a result of the inaction of the NCWC in early 1965 when

> officials of the Department of Health, Education and Welfare moved . . . to encourage birth-control programs as part of the War on Poverty. This they did in two ways: 1) by publishing in March a policy statement entitled "Family Planning and Birth control Activities and community Action Programs" 2) by beginning to approve grants for funding of birth control programs by local anti-poverty councils. . . . These programs have been drafted by Planned Parenthood, which has organized in each instance the public campaign to get the program adopted.

Ball felt it was urgent in this campaign to avoid any appearance that the Church was somehow attempting to exercise a "veto" in our pluralistic society. This was important for two reasons: first of all there was enough anti-Catholicism in the United States to make such an approach the kiss of death for any effort, but secondly, Ball had to deal realistically with the possibility that the Church might reverse its teaching on contraception:

> unless it would be made absolutely clear to the American public that the civil liberties issue was the focal point of opposition, a new teaching from Rome on contraception could leave a campaign of opposition out on a very public limb.

In dealing with the situation, the bishops would have to take into account two very important factors. First of all, the gigantic financial stake the pharmaceutical industry had in thwarting the Church's opposition to contraception, and secondly, "the anger of American taxpayers over the mounting cost of public assistance and their accompanying belief that birth control is licit and that government should actively promote it in order not only to reduce the cost of public assistance but at the same time to slow down the proliferating of 'undesirables.'" The Church could increase its credibility in this area, Ball felt, by increasing its commitment to "jobs, housing, distribution of goods, food supply and—of major importance—civil rights of Negroes, Puerto Ricans and other distressed American minorities."

When Ball returned from Rome, he had not only the support of key bishops but the blessing of the Holy See as well. Dealing with Catholics in the Johnson Administration was to prove more difficult, though, than getting a blessing from Rome. On December 13, 1965, at 3:45 p.m. Ball met with Sargent Shriver, head of the Office of Economic Opportunity, to discuss the bishops' concerns. Ball got immediately to the point. There was, he said, strong support among the bishops for the antipoverty program, but deep dissatisfaction over the use of the program to promote birth control. Ball then challenged the legal authority of the birth control funding directly. There was, Ball said, no legal authority to use the program to fund birth control in terms of statutory interpretation and construction. Shriver, in other words, was acting illegally and had been acting so all along. Implicit in the statement was the threat that Ball, acting on behalf of the bishops, might take the OEO to court if Shriver did not prove amenable to less contentious means of persuasion.

Shriver responded by dismissing the threat from the Church and making it clear that he felt he faced an even more potent threat from the Left. As a result he "could not venture to defer even for a moment the approval of pending applications." Shriver made it clear that the OEO would approve any birth control project that had been recommended by a local antipoverty council. Because of the inaction of the NCWC at the program's inception, a precedent had been set, and Shriver could not now go back on that precedent without indicating that he had been acting illegally all along. Shriver continued by saying that he was anxious to "make a good record" by funding as many applications "of every sort possible" prior to the end of the year.

When asked by Ball if he could hold off until February 1, Shriver replied in the negative, and then indicated that he was "under pressure" from Dr. Guttmacher of Planned Parenthood and others who wanted funding for projects which involved financing for abortion and sterilization. In addition to that, Shriver informed Ball that he was under pressure from Protestants and other Americans United for the Separation of Church and State to defund any project sponsored by the Catholic Church. POAU felt that any involvement of the Church in welfare activity supported by the government was a violation of the separation of church and state. Shriver refused to accede to POAU's demands and tried throughout the interview with Ball to portray himself as a man who was trying to tread the reasonable middle ground on the issue. But it was just as evident that he was defining the middle in terms of the political forces being brought to bear on him at the time, and in the absence of a strong policy on the part of the NCWC he was being pushed considerably to the left of what the Catholic bishops found acceptable.

As a final attempt to sway Shriver, Ball brought up the fact that the Congress had refused to adopt the Clark birth control amendment that September, and that this reflected Congress's intention to exclude birth control from the poverty program, but Shriver was not only unmoved, he also went on the offensive by warning Ball that the more the Church raised a fuss over the birth control issue, the more unlikely it would be that her agencies would be included in poverty projects. On that not-so-veiled threat, the meeting ended.

Ball left the meeting convinced of two things: first of all, after talking to Shriver and his assistant, Ball was convinced that the authorization for birth control was lacking, and secondly, that Shriver and the OEO would continue to fund birth control programs because reversing themselves on the matter would expose them to greater legal and political jeopardy than continuing would. As a result, Ball drew a number of conclusions. Most significantly, he concluded that further attempts at persuasion were pointless and that the bishops should look into the possibility of litigation as a way of making their point.

Given the Congress's veto of the Clark amendment, this approach stood a good chance of success. Beyond that, Ball concluded that the bishops missed a golden opportunity in the beginning of 1964, but that even with that as the case, they had no choice but to take a stand on the OEO birth control programs because "if no resistance is offered to the OEO programs, Planned Parenthood should soon be 'in business' at public expense throughout the U.S.A." Once programs like that got rolling they would only increase in scope to include abortion, sterilization, and "birth rationing," the idea that everyone should be made sterile unless otherwise permitted by the government to have children. It was an idea that was making its way through the media through the efforts of people like William Shockley, who received the Nobel Prize for inventing the transistor and then promptly used that as a platform for increasingly strident calls for racial eugenics. As before, the Church was outgunned on just about every front, but Congress's reaction to Ball's testimony and O'Boyle's sermon gave reason for hope.

The hope proved to be shortlived. Less than a week after his meeting with Shriver in Washington, Ball and Krol's attention was diverted away from the national scene back to Pennsylvania when the state's Department of Welfare announced that it was reversing its 1959 policy of only responding to queries by clients about birth control. As of December 1965, the social worker could initiate discussion of birth control. Archbishop Krol reacted almost immediately denouncing the proposed change in a statement that was picked up by the AP wire as "a dangerous experiment with the lives of the poor."

"These activities," Krol continued, speaking on behalf of Pennsylvania's bishops, "are not the business of the state, and they are serious threats to civil liberties."

The crisis had been precipitated by money being made available from the department of Health Education and Welfare, increasing the scope of the federal government into what had been traditionally the state's concern for welfare . State health officials were able to use federal funds for birth control programs at the end of January 1966, and Pennsylvania, reacting to the new opportunity to get money, liberalized its regs. The change in Pennsylvania meant that Ball had to postpone his plans to contest the legality of OEO funding in order to put out a fire in Pennsylvania.

The NCWC, for its part, continued to plead for a policy of limited opposition in spite of the decision of bishops like O'Boyle and Krol. The NCWC was for accepting government birth control programs provided that the programs were modified to protect Catholics, but the bishops in question saw no way to guarantee this legally. As a result, efforts were divided further.

Ball's demeanor was beginning to show the strain, as he found himself increasingly isolated and overburdened in fighting so many battles with so little help. In January of 1966, he wrote to Krol complaining about the fact that his efforts were being spread so thin largely as a result of the negligence and incompetence of the NCWC legal staff, whose opinion on the government birth control issue "must be held responsible for having opened the floodgates to birth control under OEO and resultantly rendering it easy for Cohen now to say that HEW will follow suit. Archbishop O'Boyle . . . stated that Frank Gallagher (Cardinal Shehan's attorney) had separately stated that OEO had full power to finance birth control under the Act."

"I cannot be unmindful," Ball continued, "of the implacable opposition of Father Charles Whelan, Mr. Gallagher, and others closely involved with NCWC to the position which has been taken, nor of Monsignor Knott's frequent remarks that cooperation "within the building" is lacking. Kindly understand that I am perfectly ready to take the whole crowd on. On the other hand, I can see great tactical advantage to the entrenched opposition in managing to isolate this to 'Mr. Ball's case.'"

In May of 1966, Ball was still complaining about the subversion of the bishops' position that had become endemic at the NCWC. As far as birth control is concerned, Ball wrote in a letter to Krol dated May 26, 1966, "the horse is now well out of the barn." Ball's main concern is that those at the NCWC who saw to it that the barn doors were left open, are going to continue to frustrate his efforts.

"All of this has not been by accident," Ball continued.

Nothing can change what is written down in the notes of my conversations with Monsignor Hurley at the three crucial moments in this sinister development: the opening of 1965 when OEO was making its first move, the weeks just preceding my Gruening testimony, and December 1965, when I was told: "You'll have to prove to me that Shriver hasn't got legal authority." . . . If this determined posture (the promotion of Fathers Hanley, Vizzard, and Whelan [who has gone on the national board of directors of the American Civil Liberties Union]) has been largely responsible for the historic default which is now evident, the paralysis of your non-advocate attorneys has accounted for the balance.

According to Ball, the bishops had an historic opportunity in the fall of 1965. But largely as a result of the footdragging of the NCWC legal staff, the winter months passed and the Church has "taken an historic non-step." By May of 1966, Ball felt that "many will look back with horror upon what can only be described as an historic default." Especially galling from Ball's point of view was the fact that the NCWC was fleeing from a very beatable opponent, from "a legion of kapok dragons," as he put it in a letter to Krol. If the Church were able to present the case that government birth control created a threat to the right of privacy, Ball felt that a large segment of public opinion might be won over. But Ball found himself more often than not engaged in a one-man campaign, while at the same time Father Charles Whelan, S.J., with the backing of the NCWC, was claiming that it was absurd to fear government's involvement in the birth control issue. The Hanley-Whelan faction, Ball complained, was so fearful of "imposing Catholic morality" on others, that they were opening the door to abortion, sterilization, and racial eugenics—all in the name of making peace with the liberal social agenda. Disbelief is the characteristic emotion of Ball's increasingly exasperated correspondence with Krol. "This whole question of government birth control has become to me a thing like death," he writes. "You look at it and you can't believe it's so."

Krol, for his part, could do little more than commiserate. "I share your convictions that they are creating a good bit of mischief," he wrote on June 2. Krol attaches significance to the fact that Hanley, Vizzard and Whelan are all Jesuits; Vizzard, he feels, is the ringleader of the group, but in spite of the fact that he has obviously been plagued by the interference of the Jesuits and the NCWC, he proposes no solution to the impasse.

Meanwhile the battle over birth control continued to rage outside the Church throughout the entire first half of 1966. Within a month of the Pennsylvania Secretary of Welfare's announcement, the head of Philadelphia's Planned Parenthood called a press conference to urge that the city's public health clinics provide birth control. One day later, Cecil Moore, head of Philadelphia's NAACP, counterattacked by calling the local birth control proposal a plan for Negro "racial suicide." Alan F. Guttmacher, then national president of the Planned Parenthood Federation, responded by saying that the accusation "gives me serious concern." Ultimately, the Negro response would be co-opted as one by one Negro leaders were bought off with increasingly lucrative grants to administer the Birth Control programs.

This of course had been Margaret Sanger's explicit intention all along. Sanger even specified which Negroes to target, namely, the black ministers, and, true to form, Planned Parenthood's first eugenic beachhead in North Philadelphia was at the Bright Hope Baptist Church of Rev. William Gray, Sr., father of the congressman of the same name. Jesse Jackson's about-face on abortion much later is only one instance of the co-opting of black leadership on the question of sexual liberation, and a good explanation of why so much money did nothing to alleviate the problem of black poverty. Because the money was spent in ways that weakened the already weak black family further, government grants were analogous to gasoline being poured on the fire. Since the poverty programs were established to help blacks primarily, their voice objecting to them as a front for racial eugenics would have been a powerful force in thwarting the trend toward government's ever deeper involvement, especially if combined with that of the Catholic Church. But the voice of black indignation over the eugenic intent behind the War on Poverty got raised once and then went quickly silent as the money from federal programs started to roll in.

In early February of 1966, Senator Joseph S. Clark was in Philadelphia addressing a Planned Parenthood benefit and telling the world that "I have no hesitation in telling you that espousal of the cause of Planned Parenthood is, in my judgment, today a political asset and not a liability." In one of its editorials (2/1/66) the *Bulletin* opined that "what he is saying may be an exaggeration today, but if so, it is less of an exaggeration than it would have been a few years ago. And from every sign it will be the exact reality soon."

By June of 1966, what began as a disagreement over welfare regs concerning who could bring up the issue of birth control in the encounter between social worker and client had grown into a full-scale media war. It had also become the cause of a state fiscal crisis as well. State Representative Martin P. Mullen, chairman of the House Appropriations Committee, was threatening to hold up the entire budget for the coming fiscal year unless the birth control provisions were returned to their status as of 1959. Mullen was born in 1921 and raised in West Philadelphia, attending Most Blessed Sacrament grade school and West Catholic High. He served with distinction in the Air Force in the Pacific during World War II, and in the summer of 1966, he had suddenly become the most important man in the state of Pennsylvania. If there were any question about why the liberals hated the ethnic neighborhoods, Martin Mullen was the answer. Mullen was a product of the Catholic school system—a product in fact of MBS, the biggest parish in the city, which in the summer of 1966 was going through the racial crisis that would eventually destroy it. Mullen had been elected by Catholics from a Catholic district, and he was now giving the state a lesson in Catholic social teaching by refusing to release the state budget from his committee in the Pennsylvania House of Representatives. Martin Mullen was Leo Pfeffer's worst nightmare come true, and the rage of Pfeffer's fellow believers in contraception as the benchmark of social progress was palpable throughout the state, but most acutely among liberal circles in Philadelphia.

KYW TV and radio, the NBC affiliate in Philadelphia, ran an editorial denouncing him on June 15, 1966. Mullen, the people at KYW announced, "has told us he personally does not believe in birth control." From the liberal point of view, it was hard to imagine a more damning instance of self-incrimination. The enlightened folk at KYW, on the other hand, "believe the birth control program should be continued," primarily because "the Federal government encourages it through the anti-poverty program." But there is more to it than that. The folk at KYW "believe birth control is a personal matter, to be decided individually on the basis of private beliefs and religious convictions." But wasn't that, after all, what Mullen was doing? Evidently not. In the parlance of the day, the attitude toward contraception was ultimately what determined whether what one held was a "personal belief" or not. If one opposed government funding of contraception, that was *ipso facto* a "personal belief." KYW's position in particular, and the liberal position in general, is difficult to discern otherwise, since it was arguing, in effect, that contraception was such a personal matter that it should be funded by the government. If it was a personal, religious matter, then that on the face of it was reason the government should not get involved. That was in effect the position of the Catholic Church, but since it was expressed by Catholics, it became in the parlance of the time a "personal, religious belief."

Other denominations did not labor under this constraint. When the Rt. Rev. Robert L. DeWitt, Episcopal bishop of Pennsylvania, signed a full page ad in the *Philadelphia Inquirer* on June 29 urging public funding of contraceptive services, no one objected that he was imposing his "personal, religious beliefs" on the Commonwealth of Pennsylvania. That was because support for contraception was not a "personal, religious belief," only opposition to it was, especially if expressed by Catholics. KYW concluded its appeal by urging "approval of the necessary appropriations so that all of our citizens —rich or poor— can decided for themselves whether or not they want to practice birth control." Evidently, the citizens of Pennsylvania were incapable of making a decision on this weighty matter unless the government funded the programs for them. Such was the logic of the day. Birth control had taken on a mantra-like quality. The more it got chanted the less it possessed any meaning. It became a conjuring device, a shibboleth for separating those worthy of entering the brave new welfare state from those who were not.

The radio stations battled it out over the summer as the legislative logjam seemed more and more unavoidable. WIBG, ironically the rock 'n' roll station in Philadelphia, came out in favor of Mullen and the Church's position. WFLN, the classical music station, launched a vicious attack on Mullen and Krol and would continue in that vein for years afterward. "William Ball, attorney for the Pennsylvania Catholic Conference," opined Philadelphia's premier AM rock'n'roll station,

> says that this program is an effort to change the definition of health from one relating to the physical and mental well-being of the individual to one relating to the well-being of society... thus paving the way for government birth control as a social program aimed, not at health, but at population control. . . . The case worker can ask the welfare recipient: "Do you have a religious objection to this matter?" In either case, opponents argue that the state is wrongfully involving itself in a question of religion.

Actually, the battle of the radio stations had more to do with demographics than music. WFLN appealed to the people who shopped at "the extraordinary shops of Chestnut Hill," Senator Clark's neighborhood, and other bastions of the WASP establishment in Philadelphia. When Ralph Collier, the WFLN talk show host who ran the attack in late June, attacked Mullen for his intransigence he did so with the help of a number of Protestant ministers. Since they came out in support of government funding of contraceptives, their views were ipso facto sanitized of any taint of religion or personality.

The letters Krol was receiving on the issue ran heavily against both him and the Church. After running a full page ad in late June opposing the change in welfare policy, Krol was informed by one Philadelphian that

> the Catholic hierarchy never intends to let anyone alone. Rather in most egregious fashion it seeks to impose its authoritarian will on parishioners and non-parishioners alike. This is especially bad taste in areas of personal choice where one's choosing has little or no effect on others. And that is one reason why the

existence of a Catholic hierarchy is inconsistent in and inharmonious with a democratic society.

It was a letter Otto von Bismarck could have written himself, or Paul Blanshard. Krol was also blasted by one letter writer from Narberth for "being a celibate" and as a result "it is not within your experience to know that man indulges in sex largely for pleasure and to satisfy his passion and not for the purpose of begetting children." This correspondent concluded by "sincerely" hoping that "the Catholic hierarchy will someday soon take a realistic position on this great 20th century problem."

As in the past, the Church was both outgunned on the media front and undermined by the Catholic intelligentsia. As part of their efforts to educate the public on their position, the PCC issued a pamphlet entitled "Betty and Jack Talk About Government Birth Control." It was a sort of Socratic dialogue aimed at explaining the Church's position to the average citizen of average reading ability and average intelligence. No one was claiming that it was high art, but it was immediately ridiculed by the secularist Amen Corner at *Commonweal*. In an unsigned editorial which appeared on July 22, writer John Leo, who would later go on to become a columnist of conservative leanings, described the fictional Jack as someone "who apparently has been reading articles by William Ball, the secretary of the Pennsylvania Catholic Welfare Conference." Leo goes on to describe Betty as "a loser by casting," and so dumb that she "does not think to reply that no civil rights group in the nation sees a necessary civil-rights problem in the privacy argument." Nor has Betty "read the specific safeguards in the Welfare Department's policy statement."

On July 20, the *National Catholic Reporter* took much the same tack in attacking "Betty and Jack" ("Tell it to Betty like it is, Jack" *NCR* 7/20/66) by claiming that the pamphlet "offers a very clerical picture of conjugal conversation" and "seems at times aimed at the high school dropout crowd." The *NCR* also accused the pamphlet of being "disingenuous" for using the privacy issue as a smokescreen for opposition to contraception *per se*. Once again the same double standard emerged. The bishops were biased because they felt contraception was wrong, but those who approved of it and urged government funds for widespread dissemination had no such biases. Bias was simply another word for opposition to sexual liberation. Those who did not oppose it were free of bias.

The dissension within the Catholic ranks was having its effect on public opinion as well. *Commonweal* was cited as a quasi-official Church publication in the WFLN Ralph Collier show attacking Mullen and Krol. But it was not having an effect on the one person who counted in the matter at the moment, Martin Mullen, who continued to hold firm in his insistence that the regs be changed as the fiscal showdown came day by day closer. In late June, Governor William Scranton said that the entire welfare program depended on getting state funding, and that if the funding were not approved the program would go down the drain. Meanwhile, the head of Philadelphia's Planned Parenthood was claiming that support for birth control was "in the same public interest category as fluoridization of drinking water and the use of insecticides for mosquito control which 'have been programmed despite great opposition by segments of the community.'"

On July 26, Mullen was still standing firm. "If they buy this provision," he told the *Philadelphia Inquirer*, referring to a reversal of the DPW birth control regs, "we can get the whole budget out of the way tonight. The rest of it will fall in line." The provision in question was the following statement: "No part of any funds appropriated hereunder shall be expended for the support of any birth control program adopted after 1959 by any department of the Commonwealth."

One day later, the Liberal-Protestant alliance launched its counterattack against the Catholics. At a public hearing on federal aid to city programs, a group of 20 church and civic organizations asked the Philadelphia Board of Education to cut off all federally funded education programs being conducted at Catholic parochial schools because such services offered by parochial schools violated the Constitution and encouraged segregation. The counter-attack was sponsored by the Greater Philadelphia Council of Churches, the Episcopal Diocese of Pennsylvania, representatives of the Lutherans, Methodists, Baptists, and the United Church of Christ, as well as the American Civil Liberties

Union, the Philadelphia Home and School Council, the Philadelphia Teachers Association and a number of Jewish community action groups. Given the make-up of the group, it is not surprising that Krol would refer to them as "our so-called ecumenical friends." With ecumenism like this, the Church had no need to look around for anti-Catholic bigotry. The alliance was, *mutatis mutandis*, a lot like the alliance which Bismarck had put together against the Church in Germany one hundred years before. Both the mainline Protestants and the liberals found common ground in their newly-discovered zeal for sexual liberation. The neo-Nativism of the 1960s would have a distinctly sexual tinge to it. As the letters to Krol indicated, one was suspected of being less than 100 percent American if one did not support the government-funded distribution of contraceptives. In addition to being labelled un-American, by opposing Planned Parenthood's eugenical excursions into North Philadelphia, the Church was also being publicly tarred as supporting segregation.

On July 26, a group of Protestant clergymen led by Bishop Robert L. DeWitt of the Episcopal Diocese of Pennsylvania sent a telegram to all of the Democrats of the Pennsylvania House of Representatives asking them to pressure Mullen into backing down. "This tactic, if successful," DeWitt wrote of Mullen's refusal to let the appropriations bill out of committee, "would make the moral standards of one religious group public policy even though most citizens of the Commonwealth dissent from that position." Neither DeWitt nor Richmond P. Miller, associate secretary of the Philadelphia Yearly Meeting of the Religious Society of Friends, who also signed the statement, seems to have noticed any irony in their statement. Weren't they trying "to make the moral standards of one religious group public policy" as well? The conclusion seems inescapable. Yet, no one was willing to draw it because in the parlance of the times, imposing one's views had become synonymous with opposing sexual liberation.

To say that no one noticed the irony may be overreaching, for the House Democrats along with Mullen remained firm. Two days later they were still standing firm when Democratic Gubernatorial Candidate Milton Shapp attempted to undermine fellow Democrat Mullen's position. Ball was outraged at the stab in the back and wrote to Krol that "Shapp's wire openly flaunts our concerns and gives an indication of what might be expected from the Pennsylvania president of American Jewish Congress if elected governor."

On the same day as the Shapp telegram, Mullen and the Democratic caucus were attacked from another quarter within the party as well. On August 27, Senator Joseph S. Clark called a press conference to announce that the Senate subcommittee on Employment, Manpower and Poverty, which Clark chaired had just approved a bill, submitted on February 28 by Sen. Joseph Tydings of Maryland, which would make federal grants available to both public and nonprofit private agencies engaged in providing birth control. This meant that both city and state agencies, as well as groups like Planned Parenthood, could collect government money to dispense contraceptives. The timing of the announcement, released on the eve of the Pennsylvania house vote, seemed calculated to cut even more ground out from underneath Mullen. Not only did it undermine Mullen's standing within the party, coming on the heels of the Shapp statement, it also made clear that the federal government would provide what the state legislature had deemed illegal. For the especially dimwitted, the *Philadelphia Bulletin* explained that Clark's actions

> meant, in Pennsylvania, that the action of State Sen. Martin P. Mullen (D PA) in restricting family planning services of the Welfare Department to married couples living together would be circumvented. Such people could seek help from another agency, not controlled by the Welfare Department (David M. Cleary, "Sen. Clark tells of Backing for Birth Control," *Bulletin* 8/28/66).

When asked whether the bills he proposed would provide funding for sterilizations, Clark responded by saying, "I don't think I'd better comment on that."

In a related article in *The Sunday Bulletin*, Hugh E. Flaherty, later legislative aide to Governor Raymond P. Shafer, described how "a quiet revolution in the attitude of Congress and the Federal Government toward establishing birth-control programs is reaching Philadelphia and other major urban areas."

"Millions of federal dollars," according to Flaherty, "now are being made available for birth-control programs through medical research programs, the war on poverty and health care programs. . . . For the first time in Philadelphia's history, federal funds are available to local hospitals through the Philadelphia Department of Public Health for maternity and infant care programs that include giving patients birth control information and contraceptive devices. . . . The significance of the Clark amendment is that for the first time the Senate has been bold enough to state clearly it is permitting the use of federal monies for birth control in a broad, domestic, social welfare program."

If the announcement was intended to demoralize Rep. Mullen, it did not succeed. Mullen and the Democratic Caucus continued to stand firm. By July 30, Governor Scranton realized that he did not have the clout to override Mullen, and so he called Ball in to negotiate the matter. Scranton led off with a concession—he would remove the power of initiation and references to Planned Parenthood from the regs—but he quickly followed that up with a threat. If Mullen's amendment cutting off funds passed, the Secretary of Public Welfare would ignore it as unconstitutional and go on using welfare funds to support it until told by the courts to cease. Ball replied by saying that he could not believe that any governor would flaunt Pennsylvania's statutes on fornication and adultery so flagrantly, or that he would defy the expressed will of legislature in such a flagrant manner. Ball left the meeting with the idea of calling a press conference as the best response to Scranton's challenge. At the conference, he would present Republican candidate for governor Raymond P. Shafer with what he felt was a "golden political opportunity," phrased as a series of questions:

> 1) we all know the views of one candidate for Governor [Ball said in reference to Milton Shapp, the Democrat] but where does Mr. Shafer stand on supplying contraceptives to unmarried persons, in the face of Pennsylvania's public policy as expressed in our criminal statutes?

> 2) If Mr. Shafer becomes Governor, will he permit his Secretary of Public Welfare to flaunt the expressed will of the general assembly?

3) Does Mr. Shafer believe that two or three people in the Department of Public Welfare should legislate on the vital matter for all the people of Pennsylvania?

Ball concluded his account of the meeting with Governor Scranton by telling Krol that he was in "one very hard fight," but that "so far we have kept the initiative." Ball also mentioned in closing the chairman of the House appropriations committee: "Mr. Mullen," he said, "is a truly courageous man."

By August 2, the battle was over, and with the exception of a few minor concessions, the Church had won. In face of Mullen's intransigence, the state backed down and decided to revert to the 1959 regs. At 12:30 A.M. on the morning of August 1, the Democratic caucus accepted an agreement drafted by Ball which rolled back the Planned Parenthood position on everything except the termination of a strictly medical program limited to married women on relief. "Pennsylvania," Ball announced to Krol,

> now becomes the first state in which Planned Parenthood has suffered a reversal. Two months ago, they were looking forward to expansion of the December 17th program to include the other unmarrieds, "voluntary " sterilization and their own sex education program. Now these hopes are dashed. They have been severely set back, and will have great trouble even in trying to get back to the December 17th program.

"Representative Mullen," Ball continued, "carried through this fight with no strong assistance from any other member of the legislature. He has been the soul of courage and deserves the greatest praise for the magnificent battle he has waged. . . . For the first time anywhere, great numbers of people have been focused on such matters as the privacy issue, the nature and aims of Planned Parenthood, persuasion by initiation, whether Pennsylvania has a population explosion, the sterilization and abortion issues."

One day later Krol wrote back to express to Ball his "sincere congratulations." Krol was pleased with the accounts he had seen thus far in the press, but expected a reaction from "some of our ecumenical friends," who will probably "scream 'foul' and accuse legislators of yielding to pressures from the Church."

According to Krol, the Pennsylvania Birth Control Battle of the summer of 1966 "proved a very important point," namely, that "government adoption of the Family Planning Program is resistible and to some extent reversible. As you said on a number of occasions, there is no sense of capitulating. If we are to go down, let's do so fighting." Krol ended his letter by extending his congratulations to Ball.

If the battle of '66 was successful, the war between the Church and the Liberal-Protestant alliance over sexual liberation was far from over. On the evening of August 1, just before the state capitulated to Mullen, Ball received a phone call from the Pennsylvania attorney general. After a perfunctory discussion of constitutional issues involved in the case, Attorney General Friedman got down to business.

"It's a strange thing," he told Ball, "how sometimes a judge lets his judgment in one matter be affected by some other matter. For example, this birth control thing could possibly upset a justice's thinking in the school bus case." Ball knew immediately that the Church was being offered a deal, a *quid pro quo*. If the Church went along on birth control, the state might find it easier to come up with financial support for parochial schools. Ball responded by playing dumb, claiming that the justices would simply have to call the shots as they saw them. Ball was in no mood to make a deal at the moment. Besides he and Krol had other concerns at the time.

The Church was being offered *sub rosa* the carrot of state aid to parochial schools in exchange for support of government-funded contraceptive programs, but no one knew what that meant because both Ball and Krol had the nagging fear that a victory on the state level would be undone at the federal level through the funding available for the War on Poverty. But as the drumbeat for government-funded contraceptive services increased, and as local efforts were subverted by the introduction of federal programs, and as the cost of maintaining Catholic schools increased with the defection of increasing numbers of Religious from their teaching posts, the deal would look increasingly attractive as time went by.

VI
The Hollywood Front

What the exhibitors and manufacturers want more than anything else," Mankiewicz said, "is for people to believe that they
are on the side of morality, that some how those same writers
and directors who used to sneak "communist plots" into pictures
are now sneaking naked tits into pictures. They want people to
understand that they too are fathers—that therefore, it is inconceivable that they would appeal to adolescent pruriency simply
to make a buck.

Joseph L. Mankiewicz,

quoted in *Ramparts*, September 1965

In December of 1964, right around the same time that the
War on Poverty was funding the first government-sponsored
birth control centers, and right around the time that Senator
Moynihan was hard at work on the analysis of the black family
which would eventually bear his name, the episcopal committee of the Legion of Decency under the chairmanship of Archbishop John Krol of Philadelphia issued a report condemning
what he termed the "moral brinksmanship of 1964." The film
industry had sent one movie containing nudity after another to
the people at the production code in what was to become a full
frontal assault on the Legion's influence over Hollywood and
the hegemony of the production code established by the
Legion's clout.

In mid-April 1964, the Legion of Decency celebrated its thir-
tieth anniversary, but judging from the tone of the statement
the bishops issued under Krol's chairmanship, there seemed to

be little cause for celebration. The bishops were in the middle of a battle that had been virtually constant since the end of World War II but which had intensified as a result of recent Supreme Court decisions and a growing unwillingness on Hollywood's part to adhere to standards which it deemed morally unrealistic and, not coincidentally, financially less remunerative. In mid-April, the bishops denounced "a laxity in standards displayed during the last six months, instigated by powerful factions in Hollywood" as well as the attempt "to attract an audience by directly stimulating base emotional responses of an erotic and violent nature." They also deplored a "growing tendency to challenge the Judeo-Christian vision of man."

The cutting edge trend was, of course, sexuality. Hollywood was bent on introducing nudity into the first-run, big budget films that eventually trickled down to the neighborhood theaters, and 1964 was the year the war on the code's restrictions began in earnest. What followed was a series of battles, in which, as in the case of contraception, the Catholic Church stood alone in defending standards not really of their own making but which had been abandoned by the Protestant denominations which had given birth to them. Within two years the battle was over, and the Church, outgunned and out-maneuvered, settled for film classification as the consolation prize. Within ten years, virtually all of the barriers had fallen. Two of the top ten grossing films of 1973 were *Deep Throat* and *The Devil in Miss Jones*, pornography by anyone's definition other than that of the Warren Court which muzzled the forces which had been holding Hollywood at bay since the days of Mae West.

Judging the films of 1964 is difficult for two reasons. First of all, they invariably seem tame by comparison with what followed. As a result, it is virtually impossible to judge the effect they had on the people and mores of the time. Community standards are, in effect, just that—relative judgements about matters of absolute importance. In retrospect it is difficult to understand the furor created by Howard Hughes over Jane Russell's breasts in *The Outlaw*, but that is simply because the boundary situation of the time, that threshold of public toleration, has long since been transgressed and replaced by any number of other thresholds in a continuing downward spiral involving the coarsening of public taste.

Judging the films of 1964 is difficult for another reason as well. Most of the offending material ended up on the cutting room floor, as Hollywood tested the limits of what they could get away with and then backed off so as not to jeopardize the film's profitability. In 1964 Kim Novak appeared nude in *Of Human Bondage*, as did Carroll Baker in *The Carpetbaggers*, Natalie Wood in *Splendor in the Grass*, and Elizabeth Taylor in *The Sandpipers*. All of those scenes, as well as nude scenes from *The Cincinnati Kid* and *The Americanization of Emily* ended up on the cutting room floor. Monsignor Thomas Little, executive director of the Legion of Decency, would claim in that organization's 1965 report that "in the last two years 34 films, of which 20 were major American productions, would have been released with scenes employing nudity had not the producers realized that they would then have been condemned."

Hollywood, however, had a sense that the times were changing. The Protestants no longer supported what the Catholics were doing. Geoff Shurlock, the main enforcer of the production code during the '60s, described a meeting with two Protestant ministers on a trip to New York. Instead of criticizing Hollywood's efforts to break the codes, Shurlock listened in disbelief as they complained about the code's "pruriently impure" rules prohibiting nudity.

Hollywood's reaction to the Legion of Decency's 1964 blast was in general defensive and attempted to deflect the blame onto foreign films. "I'm sorry they did it," said Jimmy Stewart of the bishops' report. "I think all that stuff started by the great influx of foreign films is dying down. I don't think we deserve this blast they gave. We're trying and I think we're getting better." With six months to think over Hollywood's response, Archbishop Krol remained unimpressed. Citing both Pope Pius XII and Nikita Khrushchev, Krol described film as an invention of unparalleled power in influencing people for good or evil. The Production Code, with the backing of the Legion of Decency, had proven to be a voluntary way of keeping this power, certainly not without problems, within the purview of the moral law. Beginning with the late '50s, the Supreme Court took it upon itself to disrupt that *modus operandi* by, in Krol's words, "providing obscenity with a high wall of constitutional protection."

In the 1957 Roth-Albers decision, the Court upheld a conviction, establishing as a test: "whether to the average person, applying contemporary community standards, the dominant theme of the material take as a whole appeals to prurient interest.". . . On this basis of "contemporary community standards," the Ohio Supreme Court convicted Nico Jacobellis—operator of a so-called "art theater" —for showing the French movie "The Lovers." On June 22, 1964, the Supreme court reversed the decision, invoking a national rather than a local standard, ruling: "It is, after all, a national constitution we are expounding." Chief Justice Warren dissented, arguing "there is no provable national standard."

In the *Roth* and *Jacobellis* cases, the Court was situating itself just to the right of Justices Black and Douglas, who were of the opinion that all censorship was unconstitutional. "I would put an end to all forms and types of censorship," Justice Douglas opined in the mid-'60s, "and give full literal meaning to the command of the First Amendment—guaranteeing freedom of speech and the press." The fact that the freedom of the press was being applied to films in the first place was an innovation on the part of the Warren Court. In 1915, a different Supreme Court had decreed that "the exhibition of motion pictures is a business pure and simple, originated and conducted for profit, like other spectacles, not to be regarded, nor intended to be regarded . . . as a part of the press of the country or as organs of public opinion." The change in outlook at the Supreme Court could be ascribed in large measure to changes in film technology, but those had occurred long before 1957. More persuasive was the argument that the Court, in film, as in contraception as well as school prayer and aid to parochial schools, simply wanted to readjust the mores of the country to settings more congenial to the secularist, sexually liberated mind.

Whatever the motivation, the net result was an increase in the amount of protection accorded to what was previously termed obscene material. Beyond that, because the issue was seen as one under the purview of the first amendment to the Constitution, local communities were, in effect, stripped of their right to regulate this material. Although they probably would have disagreed about the desirability of the changes brought about by the Supreme Court, both Archbishop Krol and Leo Pfeffer would have agreed on the consequences. In *God, Caesar and the Constitution*, Pfeffer's peaen to secularism, the counsel for the ACLU and the American Jewish Congress claimed that "the net effect of these decisions. . . was to accord constitutional protection to almost anything short of the hardest of hard-core pornography" (Pfeffer, *God, Caesar*, p. 312). In the Legion's 1964 report, Krol cited the winning lawyer in the case which reversed Florida's ban on Henry Miller's novel *The Tropic of Cancer*, who claimed that the decision "spells the doom of all obscenity laws." Stanley Fleischman, the attorney in question, went on to say that "to be obscene, a book has to go significantly beyond what has already been declared not obscene and that is impossible. You can't talk about sex any more frankly than is being done now."

The *Roth* decision also put the Supreme Court in the pornography business for the next fifteen years. "This meant," according to Pfeffer, "that the Court, in every case in which it accepted an appeal, would have to read the particular book or magazine or sit through a showing of the film." Pfeffer would go on to claim that the "Supreme Court decisions did not cause the sexual revolution of the 1960s and '70s; it is closer to the truth to say that they reflected it." Still closer to the truth would it be to say that the Court enabled the sexual revolution. There is no question that the justices were men of their time, and some of the chief architects of sexual absolutism on the bench—William O. Douglas comes immediately to mind—reflected the loosening of social mores from the moral law more faithfully than others. But the fact remains that the Court played a crucial role in changing the American attitude toward sex and marriage. The dynamics of cultural revolution were such that laws did not need to be imposed. Only the restraints against powerful instinctual forces needed to be removed to achieve the social effect that the revolutionaries had in mind. In this sense, libido was akin to the force of gravity. Things fell not because there were occult forces behind them propelling them in a certain direction, but rather because barriers to natural motions had been removed. In the sexual realm, behavior would continue in a straight line, a trajectory fairly apparent to those who had studied history, unless acted on by a force which would conform that behavior to the moral law. In this regard, what Pfeffer *et. al.* were proposing was Enlightenment morality based on an analogy to Newtonian physics. There was precedent for this in American cultural history. Jonathan Edwards had done much the same thing in his famous sermon "Sinners in the Hand of an Angry God." Natural forces, i.e., things like libido, would provide the cover for the secularist agenda. In this regard no imposition was needed for this social program anymore than angels were needed to move the planets in Newtonian physics. Once set in motion, things continue to move unless they are stopped. Pfeffer's Deism was Newtonian in its approach to the social order. What was needed was not the heavy-handed direction from the top which characterized the German and Russian and Italian modern regimes. What was needed was simply the removal of barriers. What Pfeffer and co. were proposing was simply Edwards' Newtonian morality in a world from which the concept of original sin had been abolished. In this regard, Pfeffer was acting in a direct line of influence established by Ralph Waldo Emerson and Oliver Wendell Holmes.

In this regard both the Legion of Decency and the Hollywood production code were anachronisms, but since they were voluntary on the part of Hollywood, they were beyond the reach of the law and therefore beyond the reach of the Supreme Court's ability to manipulate the law to its own ends. The Legion could no more force Hollywood to edit its films than it could order the police to arrest those who attended those films. But the Legion could urge Catholics not to attend those films, which is precisely what it did in increasingly specific terms following the establishment of the code and the Legion in the mid-'30s. The key to the Legion's power was, as Leo Pfeffer might have said, the "monolithity" of the Catholic Church. The thought of fifty million people (or any significant percentage of that figure) not going to see a particular movie (and this figure doesn't take into account the significant amount of influence the Legion's ratings had among the Protestant rank and file) was enough bring even the most hard-boiled producer into the editing room. But with the advent of Vatican II, the "monolithity" of the Church was being called into question more and more.

Actually, the Council was in many ways analogous to the Supreme Court decisions in this regard. The Council did not mandate dissent, but it provided an occasion for the forces which had been up 'til that time kept in check to break loose and oppose one another. Once they broke loose, the illusion of

Catholic unity disappeared, and once that disappeared, the Church lost its clout with Hollywood, and Hollywood, emboldened by the green light from the Supreme Court and the general desire on the part of the American public in the period following World War II to disconnect the pleasures of sex from the responsibilities of marriage, decided to make its move.

Krol's problems in this regard began shortly after he became chairman of the Legion of Decency Committee in late 1961. In June of 1962, Martin Quigley, Sr. wrote to Krol complaining about "the moral and philosophical viewpoint which has been imposed upon the work of the Legion of Decency in recent years." The occasion for Quigley's complaint was a Moira Walsh review of the film *A Taste of Honey* which had appeared in the Jesuit magazine *America*. Particularly offensive from Quigley's point of view was Walsh's reference to the provision in the production code prohibiting reference to sexual perversion. "Miss Walsh and her Jesuit advisors" called the provision "bad law," a phrasing which Quigley found particularly offensive because he, along with Rev. Daniel Lord, S.J., had written the production code some 30 years earlier.

Martin Quigley was the publisher of *Motion Picture Herald*, a magazine he founded with money he came into after marrying an heiress. Quigley was instrumental in bringing Hollywood and the Catholic Church together for the filming of the Eucharistic Congress in Chicago in the '20s, and it was out of that collaboration that the idea of harnessing the movies' power over American culture and morals grew. One of the speakers at the congress was Will Hays, Postmaster General under the Harding administration and an ardent Presbyterian. When Hollywood finally found itself backed into a corner during the early '30s as a result of economic pressures resulting from the stock market crash and the social pressure for censorship which resulted from Hollywood's ever increasing penchant to exploit human flesh for financial gain during the '20s, Quigley stepped in and proposed a *modus operandi* which would last for over 30 years.

Part of the *modus operandi* entailed having Catholic principles invisible as such, and Catholics as removed from the positions of authority as possible. This is why the Presbyterian

Hays was appointed as the Code's first director. The Code was essentially an intermediary organization between the industry and the Legion of Decency, the specifically Catholic organization whose ratings were almost without exception mirrored in code recommendations throughout the next three decades. Still smarting from the KKK anti-Catholic demonstrations during the Al Smith campaign of 1928, the Church was reluctant to get too involved in policing Hollywood. As a result of Quigley's maneuvering, an ideal solution was found. When Quigley assured George Cardinal Mundelein of Chicago that the code would ban from movies "things inimical to the Catholic Church," the Cardinal allowed Father Lord and Quigley to proceed.

The Hollywood Production Code specified, among other things, that:

> 1. No picture should lower the moral standards of those who see it.

> 2. Law, natural or divine, must not be belittled, ridiculed, nor must a sentiment be created against it.

> 3. As far as possible, life should not be misrepresented, at least not in such a way as to place in the mind of youth false values on life.

As administered by Joseph Breen, Quigley's appointee in Hollywood, the code was never an instrument which had an exclusively Catholic character. It was always something which took into account both the mores of the country as Breen found them and the interests of Hollywood. Breen, the Catholic, for example, forbade the sign of the cross in *Gone With the Wind* because it would offend English viewers. Similarly, he opposed fraternization between blacks and whites because that would offend movie-goers from the South. Had he been simply in Hollywood to represent the interests of the Catholic bishops of the United States and, to use of the term of the separationists, "impose" the will of the Church on the United States at large, Breen's job would have been much simpler. As it was, the code was in essence one Catholic's attempt to preserve the mores of the country, no matter how contradictory they happened to appear to him at the time. As with the laws on contraception, the Catholics stepped in to administer a code which was not of their making, and which in many respects made no sense to them. No one was aware of this more than Breen himself, who told *Q* Magazine during the summer of 1940 that "to satisfy everyone, every movie villain should be a native-born white American—with no college, no fraternal, no political affiliations. He must be a member of no church. He must belong to no lodge. He must have no profession. And no job."

The Church was put in the unenviable position of protecting taboos which were not of its own making at a time when the originators of those taboos, namely, the mainline Protestant denominations, no longer believed in them. As a result, the code tried to adapt to the times, and proved itself remarkably flexible in this regard, but its flexibility was intimately tied to the flexibility of the Legion of Decency, which provided the teeth for the Code's enforcement.

Martin Quigley was in many respects not only the author of the code; he was a fixer as well, a broker who could act as an intermediary between the people in Hollywood and the Legion of Decency. If Quigley spoke for the Legion, he was obviously a man with some stature in Hollywood. However, the gist of Quigley's complaint to Krol had to do with the fact that the reasoning behind the Legion's rulings was becoming increasingly opaque to Quigley. The influence that the Legion had over Hollywood was in large measure the result of the united front the Church could present, and Quigley was becoming increasingly dismayed at the tendency on the part of Catholic intellectuals like Walsh to undermine what the Code and the Legion stood for.

"What changes," Quigley wanted to know in his letter to Krol, "can anyone argue have there been in recent years in the moral law and in its correct application and in the nature of man to warrant such a judgment?" The syntax was a bit opaque, but the message was clear. Sexual perversion was still morally wrong; therefore, the provision in the code proscribing treatment of it was still valid. What bothered Quigley was the fact that the rules of the game were being changed on him without his consultation. The production code was erected on the foundation of the moral law, to insure that the films that got produced remained within its purview. Now Moira Walsh and her

"Jesuit advisors" were redefining the code to take into account "supposed artistic values." This, Quigley warned Krol, was "a course fraught with grave danger to the Catholic interest in motion pictures and to the moral welfare of the Catholic people, particularly youth."

Krol, for his part, was noncommital in response. He recommended that Quigley contact Miss Walsh directly and enclosed the U. S. bishops' statement on censorship along with the explanation that the "above published statements of the Bishops contain an answer to your questions about the viewpoints and policies of the Legion of Decency." Krol was noncommittal for a reason. This was not Quigley's first attack on the Legion. In September of 1961, shortly before Krol took over the reins of the committee, Quigley had written to Archbishop Karl J. Alter of Cincinnati with much the same complaint. The Legion had adopted a new course, subordinating moral to cultural and artistic considerations and the changed policy of "extreme liberalism" was leading to the bewilderment of the faithful. According to Quigley's formulation of the Legion's new policy, "the Legion . . . contended that any theme whatsoever—including sex perversion . . . could provide subject matter of acceptable motion pictures provided that such subjects were treated in 'good taste.'"

Quigley laid the blame for this "radically altered philosophy" at the feet of Rev. Patrick J. Sullivan, S. J., the Legion's new assistant to Msgr. Little. The result, according to Quigley, is that the Legion was no longer able to "hold the line" in Hollywood. Just when the Legion needed to get tougher, it turned soft on the very issues, i.e., the sexual issues, that Hollywood was determined to press. One of the policy changes that was being recommended at the time was film classification, a position which both Hollywood and Quigley opposed. Hollywood claimed that classification would be tantamount to censorship. Quigley, on the other hand, felt that classification was harmful "because it would tend to legitimatize subjects of a kind that had no rightful place in mass entertainment." As a result Quigley urged "a thoroughgoing change in philosophy, policies, procedures and personnel" so that the Legion could "be returned to a position of substantial influence."

Alter for his part shared Quigley's misgivings about the way the Legion was classifying films. "I share your opinion with regard to the liberalistic viewpoint which has been adopted in our New York Office," Alter said in a response to Quigley dated October 3, 1961, "I trust that this viewpoint can be corrected and that we can return once more to the criteria and evaluation which give primary, if not exclusive, emphasis and attention to the moral considerations."

On the same day, Alter sent off a letter expressing the same concerns to Msgr. Paul F. Tanner, General Secretary of the National Catholic Welfare Conference. "The group in New York," wrote Alter referring to the Legion, "now seems to use artistic value as its measuring rod rather than moral influence of the pictures in reaching a judgment." Alter felt that so much tension was arising out of the liberal bias of the Legion's reviewers that the matter needed to be discussed at the next meeting of the administrative board.

In preparation for that meeting, Tanner circulated the letter expressing Alter's concerns to members of the episcopal committee. By mid-October he received a response from Bishop James McNulty, Krol's immediate predecessor as chairman of the Legion of Decency committee. It was a letter which circulated among committee members and eventually made its way into the hands of Krol himself as McNulty's successor. McNulty responded to the charge of liberal bias by attacking Quigley, whose "trouble with the Legion developed when he tried to derive more prestige, power and profit than he was entitled to."

"Because," McNulty continued, "of his established reputation of being able to save a producer whose film had been subject to condemnation by the Legion of Decency, Mr. Quigley's own commercial interests are alleged to have been handsomely enhanced through special advertising given to his trade journals in preference to those of his competitors. His Catholic competitors have not been pleased with the reasons for the preferences given to Mr. Quigley. . . . Mr. Paul Greenbalgh, a Catholic and general manager of *Motion Picture Exhibitor* was vehement in his accusation that Mr. Quigley was given preferential treatment in his advertising as a payoff for his Legion activities."

McNulty went on to claim that in the Spring of 1959 alone Quigley received $50,000 in consulting fees from the major production companies. His consulting involved delivering Legion approval for films of dubious moral value. In his letter, McNulty claims that Quigley's financial well-being was in direct proportion to his ability to convince Hollywood of his influence with the Legion. As his influence at the Legion waned, so did his earning capabilities with the producers.

"Bishop Ready of Columbus, Ohio," McNulty continued,"

> former chairman of the Episcopal Committee for Motion Pictures on the front page of the diocesan paper publicly accused Mr. Quigley of exploiting his position of influence over the Legion of Decency for personal aggrandizement and of being guilty of flagrant violations of decency in the advertising copy which he accepted for his journals, at the same time that he was publicly espousing the cause of decency in the Motion Picture medium. . . . In 1956 Bishop Scully, my predecessor as chairman of the Episcopal Committee. . . instructed the executive secretary of the Legion to undo the reputation which Mr. Quigley enjoyed in the Motion Picture industry as being the "Legion of Decency" . . . During the last four years Mr. Quigley has lost personal power and prestige and has suffered financial reverses because of the complete break of the Legion with Mr. Quigley which prudence and the good name of the Church demanded.

McNulty then went on to relate the details of a meeting which took place on July 21, 1959 between Quigley, Cardinal Spellman, and Bishops Scully and McNulty. During the course of the meeting, Quigley claimed that there was a "Jesuit conspiracy to control the Catholic communications media in America." When Bishop Scully challenged Quigley to substantiate this allegation, McNulty continued, Quigley "had no answer." McNulty intimated that Quigley's "obsession" with the Jesuits had two causes. The first had to do with the appointment of Father Sullivan. "Shortly after his appointment at the Legion," McNulty wrote,

> Father Sullivan was invited to the home of Mr. Quigley . There he was told that if he did not conform to Mr. Quigley, who was responsible for his appointment to the Legion, he would see to his dismissal from that office. Father Sullivan's refusal to conform has brought him public ridicule from Mr. Quigley.

In addition to that, McNulty claimed that Quigley's animus toward the Jesuits was based on the fact that his son suffered a mental breakdown while at a Jesuit seminary, and as a result was never ordained. As if this weren't enough, McNulty felt that Quigley had lost all credibility in acting as a consultant for the Seven Arts Associated Corporation, the producers of the film version of *Lolita*, which had been condemned by the Legion. By the time Krol assumed his duties as chairman of the episcopal committee on the legion of Decency, Quigley had been discredited in the eyes of all those on the committee, most certainly in Krol's eyes, who said as much to Egidio Vagnozzi in early December of 1961, when Quigley approached the Apostolic Delegate with similar complaints.

Quigley's reputation for hypocrisy was widespread among the bishops. Primarily as the result of the experience of previous chairmen of the episcopal committee, Quigley got nowhere in his complaints with Krol. Bishop McNulty did such an effective job in discrediting the messenger, however, that virtually no one at the Legion or the Legion's episcopal committee spent anytime dealing with the message that he brought, which was discredited as well. Quigley may have been a hypocrite, but did that mean that the Legion was not changing its criteria in judging films? Was the Legion becoming too liberal? Was their policy of weighing artistic along with moral considerations well thought out or well executed? Had the Legion compromised itself by rigidity in the past? Was it now overcompensating in the opposite direction? None of these questions ever got raised in dealing with Martin Quigley, who undercut not only his own effectiveness but the Legion's as well by profiting too much from the fact that he had authored the code. By the beginning of Krol's term as chairman of the Legion, Quigley was a discredited figure in the bishops' eyes, and it is difficult not to conclude that the Legion and the code suffered as a result.

The Legion with its posture of "I condemn" had become a victim of *aggiornamento*. The bishops were uncomfortable with Quigley and they were uncomfortable with Quigley's legacy. They were looking for collaboration with the people who staffed the Legion, which had always been the case, but the people who staffed the Legion were coming more and more under the sway of the culture, which saw film more as art than entertainment and more to be judged as a piece of sculpture than as Exhibit A in a pornography trial.

Time Magazine, ever limping behind what it saw as progressive opinion on matters of taste, did a piece on September 20, 1963 entitled "A Religion of Film," which captured the new attitude toward the new films as evidenced at the First New York Film Festival, held at Lincoln Center's Philharmonic Hall. Citing the work of "a hardy little band of inspired pioneers . . . Kurosawa, Bergman, Resnais, Truffaut, Fellini, Antonioni, Visconti, Tony Richardson, Andrezj Wajda, Polanski," *Time* opined that "the movies have suddenly and powerfully emerged as a new and brilliant international art, indeed as perhaps the central and characteristic art of the age." Of especial interest to Archbishop Krol, whose job now included keeping abreast of such trends, was the quote by Francois Truffaut, who effused that :

> A revolution of intentions is beginning. No longer do we trust in the old labels, the established themes. To express ourselves! To be free, free of prejudice, free of the old cult of technique, free of everything, to be madly ambitious and madly sincere!

Time concluded that "rage and the revolution are rising everywhere," and henceforth the above-mentioned directors would be "able to say what they want to say and not what some banker thinks the public wants to be told."

The bankers, it should come as no surprise, never really lost their interest in Hollywood, nor was there that much conflict of interest between bankers and directors once the issue of nudity in film had been laid to rest and it had been established that pretty much the only people who were interested in fighting that battle were the Catholics. It is doubtful, in this regard, that Hollywood could have ever succeeded with a frontal assault on the code. But they tried in 1964, when the Code people approved a sex farce directed by Billy Wilder entitled, *Kiss Me, Stupid!*

Kiss Me, Stupid! was a two-hour-long dirty joke. Its leering prurience was a good indication of the forces Hollywood hoped to harness for its own financial benefit, but in this respect Hollywood jumped the gun and created something that virtually no one could stomach. The Legion promptly condemned the film, and the first encounter was resolved in favor of the Legion, as the secular reviewers dismissed *Kiss Me* as an advanced case of bad taste.

Had Hollywood continued its assault with films of this sort, they probably would have strengthened the Legion rather than weakening it. In its press release denouncing the film, the Legion expressed its "astonishment that a film which is so patently indecent and immoral should have received the seal of approval from the Production Code Authority of the Motion Picture Association of America." In a memo to Krol dated December 4, 1964, just before the bishops issued their moral brinksmanship statement, Msgr. Little informed Krol that "the Production Code people informed me that unofficially they welcomed the condemnation of the film [*Kiss Me, Stupid!*] since they are having trouble holding their own position with the industry."

The secret to marketing sex, as Hugh Hefner found out when he invented the *Playboy* philosophy, was providing a rationalization that made the purchaser of one-handed magazines a protagonist in a Promethean struggle against Puritanism. The Left fell for *Playboy* in this regard just as much as the junior executive. In its September 1965 issue, *Ramparts*, the left-wing quondam Catholic magazine, compared *Playboy* and the civil rights movement and then sat back and listened as Hugh Hefner declared with a straight face that

> People who think that the sexual revolution represents sexual decadence and that the new morality this generation is searching for is really immorality, completely misunderstand what is really happening: in truth our society is coming alive for the first time—it is really beginning to put an emphasis on the things that this country in its best sense is based upon—that life can be an adventure—that the individual is important.

In this regard Hollywood would eventually take its cue from Hefner by proposing, as their second attempt to break the code, a film that would not offend the sensibilities of the intellectuals, particularly the Catholic intellectuals. As the '60s would show repeatedly as the cultural revolution gained ground, the Catholic intellectual was vulnerable to manipulation on any number of fronts. Film was one of the most obvious. This is not to say that there were not Catholic intellectuals of superior perspicacity when it came to things like the culture in general and film in particular, but for the most part such intellectuals were not American. The Catholic intellectual in America at this time was in many ways blinded by the experience of the Kennedy era. He thought he had arrived on the scene at the moment American culture was eager to embrace his contribution, when in fact the exact opposite was the case. It took people like Michael Novak thirty years to wake up to that fact. And in this regard he was exceptional only in the fact that he finally woke up. For the most part, the Catholic intellectual dove head first into the enticing but murky waters of liberalism never to emerge as either a Catholic or an intellectual.

The American bishops, for the most part not noted for their intellectual accomplishments, generally made one of two mistakes with regard to the intellectuals. They made the mistake of taking their advice; and they made the mistake of ignoring it. This is not to say that there was not good advice to take. But for the most part it wasn't coming from Americans.

On July 2, 1962, Fordham University awarded an honorary degree to Jean Bernard, president of the International Office of the Film. Bernard's analysis of the medium was exceptionally acute in seeing the moral consequences of the new media of film and television. Bernard rivals Bernard Berelson as a student of the media and an especially perceptive observer of its effects. "By distracting a person," Bernard said in his acceptance speech,

> by engaging his attention with a recital, by astounding him with an artistic production, by making the attack at the moment of his least resistance, namely at his bedtime hour after a wearisome day, by using as an accomplice—where there is a question of films or TV—darkness and the peculiar atmosphere that derives from a spectacle which has been experienced in common, the mass media encourage the beginning of a semi-conscious state and of a receptivity which opens wide the door for any and every suggestion from what we can call "clandestine persuasion."

By making information easily available, those who control the media control the flow of information and thereby increase the powers of manipulation inherent in that exchange. The lessons Berelson and others learned from the use of propaganda during the Second World War had, by the early '60s, been incorporated into the cultural life of all of the major western countries, with what Bernard saw as devastating consequences, especially for moral life of the young "whose intellectual sloth," he continued,

> is already inclined thereto in its passive receptivity. This danger consists in seeing our intelligence, our will, our conscience, in a word, our person invaded and helplessly surrounded, violated, subdued by ideas and concepts that can be imposed on us almost against our will if such is the intent of those who have control of the means of communication. Confronted by the fascination of a moving picture man no longer enjoys his full liberty.

The thing Bernard railed against was, of course, the essence of what we might call the Politics of the Enlightenment. The goal, according to people like Pfeffer, was not to control by imposing restrictions from the top, rather the goal was to remove moral barriers and then channel the events which flowed from that removal. Enlightenment Politics was based on the Invisible Hand. It entailed the ability to harness libido through the manipulation of the media, to get people to choose things which they found unnnatural—contraception and abortion, for example—as if the choice came from the people themselves. This was the essence of America's regime of modernity, and in this regard the liberal regime born after World War II and out of Roosevelt's New Deal was the most sophisticated modern regime and destined to outlast all of its competitors—Nazism, Fascism and Communism. Essential to this regime was what Bernard termed "the industrialization of information." This means that information "is less esteemed for its truth content than for its market-value, which in return is measured by its power to 'hook' the reader." Once information is "industrialized," once it becomes concentrated in the hands of the few—the case with TV and film as opposed to print media—the more that power is likely to be manipulated by the most powerful interests in society according to their view of the good.

Bernard as a result is confronted by a dilemma: "on the one hand there is no liberty without mass media; on the other, there is no liberty when confronted by these same mass media left to themselves." His solution? Echoing *Miranda Prorsus* of Pius XII, he calls for increased education: "to develop with great care the critical sense of young people when they are about to enter the life of state and society."

In the area of film, especially in the United States, the Church had been having problems with its intelligentsia ever since the Second World War when films began claiming that they were something more than entertainment. Allen Tate and Carolyn Gordon disagreed with Cardinal Spellman's view of *The Miracle*. The biggest debacle for the Church in this regard came in the mid-'50s over the Otto Preminger film *The Moon is Blue. Moon* was a low budget independent film that got to the weaknesses of the Code in an especially effective manner. There was neither nudity nor profanity in the film, but code approval was withheld because of the sexual situation, William Holden trying to seduce an innocent young woman. Joe Breen, who had already complained about the Code's rigidity, was bound by the code to condemn the film. Once he did, the Legion was bound to condemn it as well to shore up Breen's diminishing authority in Hollywood.

What followed was a chain of interlocking events whose net result was to undermine the authority of both the code and the Legion as the Catholics once again manned the barricades against a film which even the morally sensitized considered no big deal. In a confidential memo to the Legion's diocesan directors, Msgr. Thomas P. Little, then assistant director of the Legion, explained that the Legion had to condemn the film because its commercial success "would be used to destroy the Code operation." Breen needed the Legion to back him up so that the Production code could continue being "the first bastion of strength in preserving proper moral standards motion pictures" (*Kimono*, p. 199). The Production Code was never something based on purely Catholic principles. It was always a reading of the Protestant culture as of 1934 in a way that was congruent with Catholic principles. As a result, the code needed to change with the times. Catholic principles would have allowed this change, and in fact did allow it, but each individual adjustment was a sophisticated and complicated operation that did not always succeed. When the Legion people felt the need to update the criteria they used, there was always the danger that Hollywood would consider it a retreat of the sort the Protestants had already made. If the Legion did not attempt to move with the times, they would end up squandering their authority on films like *Moon*, which hardly seemed worth the effort that was expended on them, especially when one considered the heavy canonical and moral machinery that was brought to bear in keeping Catholics away from them.

When Krol took over as chairman of the Legion's episcopal oversight committee, Catholics were still expected to take the original pledge on what came to be know as Pledge Sunday in early December every year. In 1961, the original pledge began with the sign of the cross and proceeded with the faithful saying in unison:

> I condemn indecent and immoral motion pictures and those which glorify crime or criminals.

> I promise to do all that I can to strengthen public opinion against the production of indecent and immoral films, and to unite with all who protest against them.

> I acknowledge my obligation to form a right conscience about pictures that are dangerous to my moral life. As a member of the Legion of Decency, I pledge myself to remain away from them. I promise, further, to stay away altogether from places of amusement which show them as a matter of policy.

On December 10, 1961, the "Suggested Outline for the Instruction of the Faithful" which served as the basis for homilies on Pledge Sunday throughout the Archdiocese of Philadelphia made it clear that "for ourselves individually and for our children there is no better solution than an habitual consultation of the classifications of the Legion of Decency." This meant, among other things, that "B films (morally objectionable in part for all) should not be patronized by any Catholic who has a love for his Christian faith and for the common welfare of his fellow citizens." In addition, " unrated films should be ignored." C films were considered an occasion of sin.

When levelled against a film like *The Moon Is Blue*, the C rating seemed like a case of overkill to many Catholics, and most especially many of the Catholic intelligentsia who were always sensitive to the gibes of their secular peers when it came to the idea of culture and intellectual inquiry. The result was that going to the barricades over *Moon* alienated many of the people the Church needed as troops in the upcoming cultural wars. The Church won the battle but lost the war on this one. The Catholics flexed their muscle at the box office, and receipts were limited, but in the process they came off sounding unreasonable to the very people they needed as allies.

"The Moon Is Blue ," wrote Leff and Simmons in their history of the Production Code

> sounded the death rattle of the Legion of Decency and the Production Code. The film was "totally innocuous," one prominent Catholic later observed; Catholics who saw it puzzled over the "Condemned" rating, and the dialogue that followed seriously undermined the Legion.. . . It seemed to demonstrate that the mighty Production Code Administration and Legion of Decency had withered, that courageous filmmakers could now afford to probe once-taboo subjects without concessions to Breen and the Catholic fathers (*Kimono*, p. 203).

During the late '50s and early '60s, the Legion was having a difficult time making a number of crucial distinctions. To begin with the Code had difficulty distinguishing between treatment of a subject and advocating the subject under treatment. According to the Code it was impermissible to discuss adultery, a prohibition which eliminated from consideration most of the literature of the West, beginning with *The Iliad* and the Bible. Secondly, the Legion was having a difficult incorporating morality into its consideration of art, or art into the consideration of morality. The liberals wanted to make the Legion into the religious equivalent of the Academy Awards, whereas the conservatives wanted to prohibit from discussion much of what literature had discussed for the past 3,000 years. Faced with this impasse, Krol often brought the full weight of his episcopal authority to bear on instances that might have called for more education and finesse.

On January 17, 1963, Krol wrote to Edward Rice, editor of the Catholic magazine *Jubilee*, complaining about a review that magazine ran of the Jules Dassin film *Phaedra*, starring Merlina Mercouri. "The film," Krol informed Rice in no uncertain terms, "was condemned by the National Legion of Decency on October 11, 1962 because it 'attempts to elicit audience sympathy for the immoral character and behavior of its heroine. . . .'" Krol went on to cite the statement of Pope Pius XII that the faithful were bound to "fulfill the grave obligation of acquainting themselves with the decision issued by ecclesiastical authority on matters connected with motion pictures and faithfully obeying them." Krol concluded by bringing the full weight of episcopal authority down on Rice: "I am sure that you can appreciate the import of such a favorable review in a Catholic magazine of a film which was condemned by the National Legion of Decency, which operates in accordance with the directives of the Holy See and by authority and approval of the Hierarchy of the United States," he concluded.

Rice for his part responded meekly a week later by saying that "we have no desire to violate the Legion of Decency Code, and I hope you will understand our embarrassment." On the surface, it looked as if the situation had been resolved in favor of the Church. But beneath the surface, Rice and his peers (Rice was a friend of Thomas Merton) continued to seethe in incipient rebellion at what they considered unreasonable restrictions and ecclesiastical overkill. *Phaedra* was, after all, based on Euripedes' play *Hippolytus*, which had been around for a long time, and which most probably would not have been approved by the production code because it treated the subject of adultery. Burdened with a code whose tenets were not of their own making, the Catholics began looking for a way to bring the Legion's proscriptions more in contact with reality without opening the floodgates of pornography. *Hippolytus* was hardly, after all, *Kiss Me, Stupid!* but both the Code and the Legion were having a difficult time telling the difference in a way that was plausible to both their own troops and the culture at large. Hollywood, it should come as no surprise, noticed their difficulty and decided to exploit it to its own advantage. The next attempt to break the code would not be a leering dirty joke like *Kiss Me, Stupid!* It would be arty. It would exploit the Church's intellectual flank by coming up with something they would be too embarrassed to condemn.

The Legion had, of course, changed over time, especially during the late '50s. This was precisely the basis of Martin Quigley's complaint to Krol. But with the onslaught following *Jacobellis* in 1964, Krol was faced with an even graver situation. "In 1964," Krol wrote in that year's annual report of the Episcopal Committee, "the Legion condemned the greatest number (16) and the highest percentage (5.93) of films in its recorded history." In addition to the actual condemnations, 24 films slated for condemnation were re-edited according to the Legion's specifications to get an acceptable rating. Krol considered this "an eloquent tribute to the respect which the Legion merits from the film industry, and to the effectiveness of its work."

But the fact remained that the world had changed, and Krol knew it. To begin with, the nation's mores, which were just as much the basis of the Code as Catholic morality, had steadily eroded in the wake of, and as a result of, the dislocations following World War II. Beyond that, the Church didn't have the backing of the Protestants anymore in enforcing the Code. Beyond that, the Council was in the process of changing the Church, and no one was quite sure in 1964 where that process of change was going to lead. *Inter Mirifica*, the document on communication, was generally conceded to be the Council's weakest document, so there seemed to be little help coming from that corner. Beyond that, there was the increasing willingness on the part of the Supreme Court, as the then recent *Jacobellis* decision had shown, to tear down any semblance of protection against obscenity. "Justices Douglas and Black," Krol said in his 1964 statement, "implied that all censorship of any sort is unconstitutional." And Black and Douglas were the intellectual powers behind the throne for the Warren Court.

Krol concludes his report by opining that "these trends call for the greatest possible vigilance and effort by the Legion of Decency," but it is clear by the end of his statement that the changing times demanded a different response than the one that was possible in 1934 and in the succeeding 30 years. To begin with, "the judicial sanction and protection of obscenity by the Supreme Court progressively reduces the possibility of fighting obscenity by legal control." Evidently influenced by Bernard's speech at Fordham, Krol implicitly called for a deemphasis on controlling what Hollywood produced, since that situation wasn't going to last anyway. Instead the Legion under Krol endorsed a program of educating Catholics to be more sophisticated viewers. "There seems to be no alternative," he wrote, except to concentrate efforts in line with the directives of the Decree on the Media of Social Communication—on the social acceptance factor. This calls for a high-powered program of film education, beamed to all levels of schools, seminaries, religious institutions, parishes and organizations . . . .The diminishing prospects of protecting decency by legislative and judiciary means, as well as the directives of the Decree on the Media of Social Communication, make the need for an educative program imperative.

To accomplish this end, Krol announced that the Chicago Center for Film Study under Cardinal Meyer was affiliating with the National Legion of Decency to facilitate the new educational approach. Krol also renewed his call for film classification, something he had been asking for since 1963. "A free and well-ordered society," Krol said then, "should not place such a burden of research upon parent, but should provide them with a readily available source of guidance." What the Catholics did not count on was Hollywood's determination to overturn the Code. Resentment had been smoldering for years.

"The Legion of Decency," claimed Otto Preminger, director of *The Moon is Blue*, the first successful challenge to the Code, "has assumed an undue position of power because of the cowardice of some major motion picture companies. They're scared of the Legion; scared of losing money; I don't know what the hell they're scared of."

Much of the bitterness in Hollywood over the Code took on the language of *Kulturkampf* as waged by the courts. Even though the Legion was a private organization and the Code was a purely voluntary arrangement, the Catholics were being accused of something akin to violating the separation of Church and state. By the very fact that it existed and had been so successful, the Legion of Decency was guilty of imposing its views, according to those who wanted nudity in films. It was a charge normally reserved for religious groups who are successful at what they do. One history of film written during the mid-60s called the code, "one of the most restrictive, unrealistic and hypocritically observed codes of conduct ever clamped on creative people."

"I don't care if the Legion of Decency makes it a sin for Catholics to see my films," one anonymous Hollywood insider said, echoing the Church/state argument, "but it has no right to prevent others from seeing them and boycotting the theaters. Their dogma is not the world's dogma and yet, they have the temerity to proclaim themselves responsible for the morality of mankind." Just why the Catholics had no right to boycott theaters was never explained. But it was a common practice to accuse the Church of "censorship" any time the Catholics made a concerted effort not to go to the movies.

Much of the resentment had a religious undercurrent. The people who ran Hollywood were Jewish; the people who ran the code were Catholic. As the Jews became more and more liberal, and as liberalism defined itself more and more as defiance of traditional morality, the conflict became more and more difficult to avoid.

On March 29, 1965, roughly three months after Archbishop Krol chided Hollywood for practicing "moral brinksmanship," Hollywood launched another attack on the code with the release of *The Pawnbroker*. During the course of the film a woman playing a black prostitute opened her blouse and exposed her breasts to the camera, breaking as a result, Section Seven, subsection two of the Motion Picture Production code and one of Hollywood's last remaining taboos. As was the case less than a year earlier with the release of *Kiss Me, Stupid!*, the production code approved the film and the Legion condemned it. However, because of the nature of the film, *The Pawnbroker* would prove to be a much more serious challenge to the Code and the Legion than Dean Martin leering at Kim Novak, the main characters in *Kiss Me*.

One reason the challenge was so serious this time was the serious artistic intent of the film. *The Pawnbroker* was not Dean Martin telling dirty jokes. It was an account of a Holocaust survivor whose memories of his dead wife are reawakened by the sight of the prostitute's bare breasts. The breasts, in other words, served a function in the plot. They were artistically justified breasts—the Legion's worst nightmare. Because the Legion had only one category for condemned films, the Catholics were put in the unenviable position of lumping *The Pawnbroker* in the same category with *Kiss Me, Stupid!* or *The Carpetbaggers*. They were also put in the position of criticizing a film that had an immediate connection with an important event in recent Jewish history. They were also put in a position where they were obviously throwing out the art baby with the nudity bath.

Hollywood's position was clear. *The Pawnbroker*, according to Joseph L. Mankiewicz, was "a golden opportunity to demonstrate that the morality of the motion picture 'industry' was a shining and untarnished force for the public good." Since it was serious art, and since it was about the Holocaust, an event having a numinous quality for most Jews of this time and place, to suggest that *The Pawnbroker* was a vehicle for "sneaking naked tits into pictures," to use Mankiewicz's colorful phrase, was not only impious according to the canons of liberal discourse, it was also downright unecumenical, especially since the debate over *Nostra Aetate*, the Second Vatican Council's Declaration on the Relation of the Church to Non-Christian Religions, had just been recently concluded.

"What the exhibitors and manufacturers want more than anything else," Mankiewicz continued, "is for people to believe that they are on the side of morality. . . . They want people to understand that they too are fathers—that therefore, it is inconceivable that they would appeal to adolescent pruriency simply to make a buck." In terms of challenging the Code, *The Pawnbroker* was the ideal vehicle. It was art. It was about the Holocaust, and it had naked tits to boot. When the Legion objected to the tits, it came across as a pack of Philistines ignoring serious art. The Legion also came across as vaguely anti-Semitic because it failed to genuflect before the Holocaust. All the Church seemed to be interested in was bare breasts, and as a result it had lost the high moral ground. Any organization, Mankiewicz sniffed, "that would condemn *The Pawnbroker* rather than *The Carpetbaggers* cannot expect its standards or reasons for its decisions to be taken seriously by adults."

The Legion's position was just as clear. It may be art, they said of *The Pawnbroker*, but it was also the proverbial foot in the door. In the April 4, 1965 issue of *Variety*, Msgr. Little was quoted as saying that the exception made for *The Pawnbroker* would "open the flood gates to a host of unscrupulous operators out to make a quick buck."

"*The Pawnbroker*," Msgr. Little told Judy Stone of *Ramparts Magazine*, "is a foot in the door. If we were to agree to that, how could we hold back the next one? Nudity would become just as common as blowing your nose."

On June 9, 1965, the Episcopal Committee For Motion Pictures, Radio, and Television issued a statement "on the subject of nudity in Film Treatment" occasioned by *The Pawnbroker* controversy. "In itself," the committee claimed, "nudity is not immoral and has long been recognized as a legitimate subject in painting and sculpture. However, in the very different medium of the motion picture it is never an artistic necessity. . . .The temptation for film-makers to exploit the prurient appeal of the nudity in this mass medium is so great that any concession to its use, even for otherwise valid reasons of art, would lead to wide abuse."

Pretty much the same line of argumentation emerged from correspondence between Ely A. Landau, the producer of *The Pawnbroker*, and Archbishop Krol. On April 21, 1965, Landau wrote to Krol complaining of a meeting with Msgr. Little and Father Sullivan, who told him that *The Pawnbroker* would have to be condemned by the Legion of Decency because "only in that way could the flood of nudity on the screen be stopped."

Landau felt that the decision was unfair on two counts. First of all, the film was being judged for potential effects flowing from it and not its own merits, and, secondly, it was unfair to single out nudity as "the sole justification for the Legion of Decency's condemnation." This condemnation, Landau continued, "will undoubtedly cause many uninformed people to consider *The Pawnbroker* (a picture of unquestioned high moral intent and purpose) to be a dirty or salacious film. Not even the most violent of its critics can, in fairness, call it that." Landau concluded by offering to come to Philadelphia to hold a screening for Krol and his staff.

Krol demurred. In a letter dated, May 10, 1965, he stood by the Legion's condemned rating. Making an exception would open the floodgates. On the same day, the Legion issued a statement from its New York office stating that "the acceptable classification is denied to this film for the sole reason that nudity has been used in its treatment."

"Such treatment of nudity in film," the Legion continued, " is open to the gravest of abuse."

Aside from his letter to Landau, Krol never really got into the fray. But Msgr. Little did. Little felt that the nudity was cinematically gratuitous as well. "They could have had the same scene," he said at the time, "and shot it from the back." He then went on the offensive by wondering how Landau, if he were so interested in cinematic realism, could justify the act of simulated sexual intercourse between the prostitute and her boyfriend.

History has shown that *The Pawnbroker* was less the harbinger of great cinematic art, than, just what Krol and Little feared it would be, namely, the first trickle of what would become a deluge of naked flesh that would pour onto the movie screens, culminating in any number of moments. The mid-'70s could serve as a high water mark of the trend Krol and Little feared. In addition to *Deep Throat* and *The Devil in Miss Jones* with their unknown stars, Hollywood's big names got into the act with Marlon Brando simulating various forms of sexual activity in *The Last Tango in Paris.* By that time, flesh had become its own justification. By the mid-70s, no one needed the Holocaust anymore to justify showing naked tits on the big screen.

As with contraception, the Catholics had to fight this battle alone. In his annual report for 1964, Little saw the handwriting on the wall. "For various reasons," he wrote,

> such as a pseudo-pretense at artistic integrity or a craving to exploit nudity for commercial gain there has been a very evident effort this year on the part of some American producers to introduce nudity into the treatment of American films. In a visit to Hollywood during January of this year [1964] the Executive Secretary informed studio executives and producers that in the treatment of films the Legion would not accept nudity or the illusion thereof, no matter what the alleged artistic reason might be. This policy has been adopted, not because in the judgment of the Legion all nudity is per se obscene, but because the common good demands it. Once nudity was permitted for any valid reason, there would be no control of its abuse. This policy was welcomed by the administrators of the Production Code Authority and also by the more responsible American producers.

"The Legion," Little concluded with admirable understatement, "is not of the opinion that the fight against the introduction of nudity has been won."

The strain of distinguishing art and morality proved to be too much for the Catholic intellectuals, who defected almost to a man in the ensuing conflict. On June 5, 1965, Moira Walsh published her review of *The Pawnbroker* in *America*, in which she claimed that "whatever their intention, the Production Code and the Legion . . . inhibit the serious artist who might have raised the level of the screen." When it came to the issue of nudity, Walsh simply refused to discuss the issue, and took instead a virtually absolutist position in favor of artistic license: "The only really appropriate regulator of a work of art," she opined, "is the artistic conscience of the skilled and responsible practitioner." Walsh suggests that the Legion keep revising its code "so that they can in the future take a stand on principle without resorting to the misleading and damaging course of condemning a film like *The Pawnbroker*" (pp. 838-9). To its credit, *America* came out in support of the bishops in its June 26, 1965 issue: "No one," they opined in favor of the bishops' position, "who has watched the miserable performance of the publishing industry and the courts of law in dealing with the problem of printed pornography will be quick to say that they are wrong. "

Six months later, on December 8, 1965, the Legion of Decency issued a press release announcing that "effective immediately the name of this organization has been changed from The National Legion of Decency to the National Catholic Office for Motion Pictures." The change was described elsewhere as the fruit of an eight year "aggiornamento" which began in 1957 with the issuance of Pope Pius XII's document on film and television, *Miranda Prorsus*. The major reason given for the change in title was that "the old title no longer accurately reflected this broad transformation." Whereas the work of the Legion was "once limited to the moral classification of films," the work of NCOMP "now also embraces the positive endorsement of outstanding films and concentrates more and more upon the promotion of film education."

Nomen est omen, the Romans used to say. In exchange for what *Time* magazine would call its "rather arrogant and muscular name," the Legion chose for itself a vague and bureaucratic title which invariably got reduced to a string of letters which no one could remember. In the official announcement of the title change, Archbishop Krol announced that by adopting a new name, "the American bishops hope that the National Catholic Office for Motion Pictures will be better able to encourage interfaith collaboration in the promotion of films whose artistic vision and expression reflect authentic human values."

It was, as time would show, a misplaced hope. The infelicitous title mirrored a similarly infelicitous change in focus. Or, more accurately, it mirrored a blurring of focus. By incorporating artistic values as part of the criteria by which the bishops and the Legion judged a film, they set the rating system hopelessly adrift by placing it at the mercy of people who couldn't define their terms, and as a result the Legion viewers were all the more susceptible to pressure to ratify whatever was being proposed as "artistic" by the dominant culture. The bishops were put in a similar position. A bishop like the Ordinary of Philadelphia had a pretty good idea of what was moral and what was not. But he was completely adrift if asked whether a certain film had "artistic" merit or not. In instances like this, he was completely at the mercy of his advisors, and that state of affairs, as time would show, would have disastrous consequences for both the Legion and the moral state of the country at large.

The conservatives defenders of the Legion had been hammering away at this point for years. In early 1965, just on the eve of the fight over *The Pawnbroker*, Cardinal Spellman received a letter from Charlie Reagan, a Catholic film exhibitor "who has never exhibited a film condemned by the Legion." Reagan wrote to complain about the Legion's policy over the past several years, but most particularly over what had been happening during the last two. The Code, according to Reagan, was being undermined by the Legion's repeated approval of films it previously would have condemned. As a result, "the Legion has lost completely the respect of the well-meaning people in the motion picture industry" because it "is now more interested in approving the 'art' content of the films, rather than the disapproval of their immoral content, which was understood to be the original purpose of the Legion." Reagan concluded by urging Spellman to "take a more militant stand in favor of that which we have been taught to believe." Martin Quigley, Jr., echoing his father had been making the same point. "The great tragedy for the cause of screen decency," he wrote shortly after the Legion had changed its name, "is that the NCOMP in recent years has failed to support the film industry's Production Code Administration. The result has been the destruction of the Production Code. Don't take my word for this —ask any one of the qualified film industry leaders who are Catholic, such as James Mulvey . . . or Charles Reagan. . . or Spyros Skouras (who is Greek Orthodox, married to a Roman Catholic.)"

No one, least of all Archbishop Krol, felt that the change in name and corresponding change in focus was without peril. As early as late 1963, Krol wrote to one priest that he was pushing for the adoption of a new form of the pledge because his predecessor had recommended it. In his dealings with the Code and the Legion, Krol gave the impression, more than in other instances, of pressing for things his subordinates wanted. When the agenda he pursued ran into trouble, Krol, more often than not, would find himself at a loss for words and would respond by asking his subordinates to respond for him.

In an article which appeared in *Sign* magazine in 1963, Francis Cormac described the soul searching and the attempt to redefine itself that was taking place in the Legion at the time. Cormac's description, like most of the time, is more one-sided than the situation it purported to describe. In articles of this sort, the Legion was described as being "viewed by many sophisticated Catholics as an outdated encumbrance, when it is actually very much part of the aggiornamento."

"The Legion," Cormac continued, "would like to shed its reputation in some circles as a censor." This was, of course, only half the story. At the same time that it was engaging in *aggiornamento* according to the criteria of "sophisticated Catholics," i.e., those in sync with the dominant culture, it was losing its support among those who saw increasing danger from the films Hollywood was producing. Little and Sullivan were bent on "modernizing the Legion," but that was a course fraught with danger. "The process," according to Cormac, had to be handled discretely because it meant relaxing the rating system at the very time objectionable films were increasing. . . . It could not alienate those Catholics who clung to the view that the Legion was only a means of personal sanctification and rejected out of hand any "liberalizing" of the Legion's standards.

"Msgr. Little," Cormac concluded, "has had to steer a deft course."

By December of 1965, when Little's description of the theory behind the name change appeared in *America* Magazine, it seemed that the course had been tacking to the Left. Virtually every point Little raises has to do with objections that had or would be raised by "sophisticated Catholics," who were interested in the primacy of art over morals. The concerns of the old line supporters of the Legion were prominent by their absence. This may have been in reaction to Little and Sullivan's unhappy experiences with Martin Quigley, Sr. but the approach showed little understanding that the position Quigley represented, whether motivated by financial gain or not, had a significant constituency among the most powerful bishops and cardinals in the United States hierarchy. That position was also, no matter what Quigley's motives in proposing it, the position of the "unsophisticated Catholics," which is to say the overwhelming majority of Catholics in the country who had grown up saying the old pledge every December for the past thirty years. Because it seemed so focussed on one side of the discussion, Little's description of the program did not inspire confidence that the change would work.

"There are those," Little began,

who see this ecclesiastical office [Legion of Decency] as the very antithesis of aggiornamento. To them it appears no more than a stubborn, antiquarian, unrealistic defender of Catholic moviegoers against moral corruption—a group of censors who pass moral judgment on films they cannot begin to understand, and operate by arbitrary rules of thumb that are insulting to intelligent Catholics (Rt. Rev. Thomas A Little, "The Modern Legion and Its Modern Outlook," *America*, December 11, 1965, pp. 744-746).

To begin with, Little began his description of the reasons for the change on the defensive, which was bad enough, but what was worse, he spent the rest of his article on the defensive against only one faction. The concerns of the "unsophisticated Catholics" got virtually ignored or, worse still, patronized.

"From the time of its establishment in 1934," Little continued, "the Legion's primary attitude toward the motion picture medium had been largely one of defensiveness, of caution, of treating films as merely a form of escapist entertainment that must never shock or upset or confuse the average movie-goer."

This approach, according to Little, bespoke "an arrogant disregard of conscience." Then almost as an afterthought, Little added that this was not "to say that we will approve films that preach a philosophy of life opposed to the Judeo-Christian view of man. The key word here is preach. There is world of difference between a film that holds up to view a situation that is obviously reprehensible morally and a film that says such a situation is desirable and worthy of emulation. Movie-goers must learn to tell the difference."

The changes were predicated on a number of assumptions. First that the Church "faced a new generation of Catholics." This group of people "because of their higher level of education. . . were much better fitted to cope with the content of films than their parents were." What went unaddressed in the assumption about increased education on the part of American Catholics was the quality of that education. As with the theologians, so with the laity. Becoming more educated meant for the most part becoming more receptive to the categories proposed by the dominant culture. Thus, since the culture entailed in increasingly detailed and uniform fashion what education meant, the more educated Catholics became, the more they were willing to side with the dominant culture when a conflict arose with the Church. The secularization of education in general, both public and Catholic, meant that in reality the "sophisticated Catholics" were less able to appreciate the fact that the areas where the culture contradicted the faith were increasing. By ignoring this fact, the Legion simply set Catholics adrift when they were more than ever in need of guidance. It is true that more education was needed, but the reformed Legion was less and less in a position to do the educating. They expanded the ratings to include a "think film" category, but the ratings never explained adequately why these films were included. As a result, Catholics became more and more bewildered at the ratings films were receiving. The Legions' censors, it is true, had become more educated, but they had become more liberal in the process as well (since that was to a large extent the goal of education), and more willing to side with the dominant culture when it came in conflict with the Church. The original code may have been too rigid. It may not have changed sufficiently to meet the new challenges Hollywood was throwing its way, but rigidity was not the only problem the Legion faced. It was, however, virtually the only problem that got addressed in all of the peaens to the "new" Legion and its new name and new approach.

The new pledge bespoke *aggiornamento*. It was positive. It didn't condemn anything. It attempted to deal with both morality and art, but it never specified how those two things related to each other, or if there was a conflict, which had priority over the other. Whereas the old pledge—"I condemn indecent and immoral motion pictures and those which glorify crime or criminals"—was undoubtedly negative, it was at least clear in its thrust, especially in a culture which shared a consensus about what was indecent and immoral. In the new pledge, however, Catholics promised "to promote by word and deed what is morally and artistically good in motion picture entertainment" without being told how the moral related to the artistic. The omission was reminiscent of the scholastic discussion of a "good thief." Was the thief to be praised because he was so clever that he never got caught? Similarly, how did the new pledge relate to the decision six months previously to give *The Pawnbroker* a condemned rating? Everyone conceded that *The Pawnbroker* was a serious, artistic movie. Was the new pledge an admission that the Legion had erred? To some "sophisticate Catholics" it meant just that. "Many people," opined *Time* Magazine in its piece on the Legion's name change, "agree with *America*'s film critic Moira Walsh, herself a Legion consultor, who argues that something is wrong with a rating system that can condemn a serious attempt at cinema art like *The Pawnbroker* for the sole reason that it shows a young woman baring her bosom."

Little's point that films could deal with moral evil without advocating that evil was well taken, but it is not clear that that was situation that needed to be addressed at the time. The actual situation was much closer to the one the Church found itself in *vis a vis The Pawnbroker*, where Hollywood was using the vehicle of serious art to break down prohibitions surrounding nudity. Hollywood was willing to use the Holocaust to smuggle bare breasts into the films it produced because it found that high seriousness was the best vehicle to achieve that end. It had tried Dean Martin and failed. It would continue to use the high art excuse until the barrier had been torn down irrevocably. Then, when art had become synonymous with bare breasts, the justification was no longer needed and Hollywood could do whatever it wanted as long as it was profitable.

The Legion was so busy listening to *Time* praise it for its sophistication that it lost sight of the fact that its new direction and new pledge had been approved with serious reservations on the part of a number of bishops. One of the skeptics was Bishop Timothy Manning, auxiliary of Los Angeles, a crucial diocese because of the simple fact that Hollywood was located within its boundaries. In preliminary discussions on the new pledge six months before it was unveiled, Manning expressed reservation at the confusing effect that adding the term "artistic" would cause.

"I think it would be better to leave that door closed," he wrote to Krol. Archbishop Hoban, Krol's former boss in Cleveland, wrote to say that he was not satisfied with either pledge. The old one "seems negative in these days of positive pastoral spirit," but the new one was "vague."

The new pledge went into effect as well as the new policy of *aggiornamento* that it bespoke without much thought to how the vagueness was going to be resolved. However, Hollywood, like the ACLU in the legal realm, was determined not to let the vagueness pass unnoticed, especially when it could be contested to its advantage. On September 28, 1966, less than a year after the "little *aggiornamento*" at the former Legion, *Variety*, the Hollywood trade magazine, announced that "for the first time in its history, the National Catholic Office for Motion Pictures has given a favorable rating to a non-documentary film containing what it refers to as 'bare-breasted nudity.'" The picture in question was *Hawaii*, and the nudity in question concerned the performers representing the island's natives. NCOMP explained that "we have always made exceptions for films in a native setting," but *Variety* countered by bringing up the apparent contradiction between the okay for *Hawaii* and the condemned rating for *The Pawnbroker*, arguing that many people at NCOMP felt "that the girls in *Hawaii* are younger and more attractive than the femmes in *The Pawnbroker*, and that the scenes in question are more not less likely to 'arouse prurient interest.'"

In other words, the Catholics were contradicting themselves. In addition to bare breasts on native girls, *Hawaii* also carried a not so subtle anti-Christian message that was not lost on the people at *Variety*. Max von Sydow played a Protestant minister who was uniformly unsympathetic. The Hawaiian royalty, whose customs included incest, were portrayed as just the opposite. As a result, the film "in effect leaves it up to the audience to decide whether incest was 'right' for the Hawaiian ruling family for whom it was a sacred institution." The "the uninformed viewer of *Hawaii*" according to *Variety*, "might seriously question whether 'converting the heathen' was such a good idea after all."

Aggiornamento at the Legion was turning out to have some fairly unpleasant fallout. Chastised by the dominant media culture for being rigid and puritanical, the Legion suddenly found itself being patronized by the same people when they tried to be sophisticated. In the process they also caused increasing bewilderment on the part of the faithful, for whom the newfound connection between art and morality was neither comprehensible nor persuasive.

In a letter to Krol after the *Variety* article appeared, Father Sullivan attempted to explain the seeming contradiction between the *Pawnbroker* and *Hawaii* decisions. The Legion had always exempted "documentary-type treatment of primitive people," and in this particular instance "almost every reviewer and consultor whatever may have been his reservations on the subject of the religious element, was of the opinion that the nudity was essential to the treatment, that it was handled with admirable restraint and that it should be no moral problem to the average viewer. "

The president of United Artists, Arthur Krim, had contacted Msgr. Little on June 9, 1965, the same day on which the Legion had issued its statement on nudity in response to the uproar caused by the condemnation of *The Pawnbroker*. With all of the major photography almost completed on *Hawaii*, United Artists had a lot of money at stake, and Krim wanted to know if the same rules applied to *The Pawnbroker* would apply to *Hawaii*. The Legion assured Krim that he would have no problems "provided that the nudity was limited to presenting a verisimilitude of the conditions which faced the missionaries upon their arrival in Hawaii; that no major or minor character would appear nude; that every trace of sensationalism or exploitation would be avoided."

"Mr. Krim," Sullivan assured Krol, "kept his agreement to the letter." "*The Bible* and *Hawaii* are clear exceptions," he continued, "there is no danger that these exceptions will become a rule."

As part of their attempt to accentuate the positive and eliminate the negative, NCOMP decided to institute a series of film awards. On February 16, 1966, The NCOMP took out a full page ad in the *Film Daily* announcing the winners for 1965. Not surprisingly, *The Sound of Music* won the NCOMP's first film award for the category of family film. More surprising was the fact that best film for mature audiences went to the Julie Christie film *Darling*. Even more surprising was the fact that a film about an affair between emotionally disturbed teenagers (*Nobody Waved Good-bye*) received the award for best film for young audiences. To round out the surprises, the biblical epic, *The Greatest Story Ever Told*, received not even an honorable mention in any category.

To underscore their commitment to the new Legion's new course, NCOMP held a Catholic version of the Academy Awards on February 2, 1966 at the Lotos Club in New York. Krol got wind of the idea in late December of 1965 and was so taken with the idea of rewarding Hollywood for producing films the Catholics thought were of merit that he wrote Little and announced that he would be willing to cut short his annual Florida vacation in order to present the awards in person. On the evening of the awards, Archbishop Krol expressed "gratitude for what the motion picture industry is doing for young people" and then declared "the role of the church has changed from the area of a critic of the motion picture industry to the area of a partner." Krol then handed out, to the delight of the industry, the first of what Catholics hoped would be a series of annual awards for "films whose artistic vision and expression best embody authentic human values." The film industry then sat back in amazement and listened as it was praised for the films of 1965, "whose artistic vision and expression best embody authentic human values." The picture of the evening's events which got the widest circulation was one of Krol in full episcopal regalia presenting the award for the producer of *Darling*, the best film "for adult audiences," to Joseph E. Levine. Mr. Levine's head is bowed reverently as would be befitting such a religiously charged occasion, but his face is turned at the same time toward the camera and the smile of satisfaction and gratitude on his face seems perilously close to a smirk.

If so, it would be with good reason, for probably no one in Hollywood during the decade preceding his reception of the first Catholic film award had done more to undermine the effectiveness of the Code and the influence of the Legion of Decency than Joseph E. Levine. If the first annual Catholic film awards were supposed to send a message to the industry, they succeeded beyond the NCOMP's wildest dreams. However, the message they sent is probably not the one that NCOMP intended. The Legion's giving an award to Levine was *aggiornamento* with a vengeance. It was a bit like B'nai B'rith praising Hitler for getting the German economy back on its feet again. In 1960, Levine had been named Hollywood's Motion Picture Pioneer of the Year for hyping Italian sex and action epics like *Hercules Unchained* and thereby making a lot of money and skirting code restrictions at the same time. The character Franky who plays Anita Eckberg's husband in *La Dolce Vita* is based on Steve Reeves, the muscle-man star of the Italian Hercules movies which were being turned out at Cinecitta at the time.

In 1964, the year of Hollywood's moral brinksmanship, Levine produced *The Carpetbaggers*, the film version of the sleazy Harold Robbins novel, which featured what Alexander Walker, in his anti-Legion history, *Sex in the Movies*, called "Auditory

Sex," i.e., "putting into the dialogue the sexual implications that the censors would not allow to be put explicitly into the visuals." Walker, who is no friend of the Legion or the Code, gives Levine credit for subverting both, arguing that

> the enormous commercial success which Joseph E. Levine made of promoting his films helped precipitate the morality crisis that Hollywood found itself in at the end of 1964. High-pressure salesmanship of the Levine brand, and its envious imitators, put the emphasis on the sexy tone of the films. Inflammatory titles, advertising copy with a built-in leer, and magazine photo-spreads of nude or near-nude scenes, said to have been shot for the films but somehow not included in the released version: these were the commonest ways of making the mass of movie-goers imagine that a films' sex content was higher than it in fact was.

If the Catholics were interested in rewarding anyone in 1965, it's hard to imagine a candidate who had been working more assiduously to subvert their interests and the interest of morality in film than Joseph E. Levine. It would also be difficult to imagine a more inappropriate vehicle than *Darling*, which tells the story of a young lady from swinging England who wearies of decadence and marries an Italian nobleman widower with seven children. Thus far the film seemed at least something like *The Sound of Music*, but then Julie Christie tires of family life and returns to decadent swinging England to renew her affair with an old flame there. In terms of the moral law, it is difficult to imagine a more confusing film than *Darling*. By rewarding someone like Joseph E. Levine, the Legion wanted to show how broadminded it had become; what it did in reality was show the industry that either Catholics were running up the white flag or so incredibly stupid that they they didn't know the difference.

Krol, for his part, felt that the awards were the culmination of the mandate for updating which had received when he took over the chairmanship in 1961, but his role as episcopal overseer was attenuated to the point of rubber-stamping the decisions of his subordinates. Incredibly, Krol never saw *Darling*; in fact it is doubtful that he saw any of the films that received awards that night. In the case of *The Pawnbroker*, the viewing of the film was not really an issue. Krol was right in assuming that the Legion viewers could recognize bare breasts when they saw `them. But in the case of the awards, more guidance was necessary. Since Krol did not see the film, he was not in a position to provide any leadership in dealing with it, and when the negative reaction came in after the award ceremony he was powerless to respond in any effective fashion. Krol, it should also be remembered, was in the middle of a full scale war over birth control in the State of Pennsylvania at the time. The Pennsylvania Department of Welfare announced the change in its contraception policy at virtually the exact same time that the Legion unveiled its new name, its new policy and its intention to give its first annual film awards. Beyond that, Krol had spent the entire fall working on the conclusion of the Second Vatican Council, and work on the post-Conciliar sessions still stood before him. But even with all of these caveats, the fact remains that he didn't see the film, and as a result had no input in the awards selection, nor did he have a defense when the reaction to the awards turned sour.

Initial reaction from the industry was favorable to the point of disbelief. On February 3, and in the week following for the non-daily press, article after article appeared oftentimes with a picture of Krol in full episcopal regalia presenting the "first in history" awards to the motion picture industry. The press reports were, for the most part, full of wonderment at the direction that the Catholic Church had taken. In its February 3 edition *Film Daily* quoted Krol as saying that "these awards are in keeping with a broad program of positive support for worthy films which the national office has adopted in recent years." In the same day's edition of the *New York Times*, Vincent Canby wondered whether the awards to *Darling* and *Juliet of the Spirits*, "may cause some debate among conservative Roman Catholics who have fought the increasingly liberal policies of the film-evaluating agency."

The February 9 issue of *Variety* could hardly believe its ears: "What this means is that the Church no longer expects the film industry to provide nothing but easily digested pablum, designed just for entertainment or for profit." The fact that *Nobody Waved Good-bye* got an award and *The Greatest Story Ever Told* did not "would have been beyond imagining. . . . a few years ago."

"What brought about the change?" *Variety* wondered. "The basic answer. . . can be traced to the overall 'updating' of the Church since the rule of Pope John. "

Initial reaction at NCOMP was just as effusive as what appeared in the press. On February 8, Msgr. Little wrote to Krol, exclaiming that "the trade press coverage of the affair was wonderful and the reaction of the industry was most favorable." Krol's reaction was more tempered. In a letter he wrote to Msgr. Little giving his impressions, Krol called the awards ceremony an "historical event" and a "gratifying experience." Yet for all the positive response in the press, Krol still possessed a number of nagging doubts. First of all, he wondered about the appropriateness of a number of the selections, especially the film for mature audiences. Why, he wondered, should not the Catholic Office "in addition to authentic human values also pass their judgment on the moral content. It seems to me that this question is a valid one and that it merits consideration. . . . If our judgment is limited to human values, then we are at best giving a 'poor man's Oscar,' but if we include moral values, then ours is a distinctive type of award and then would have reason for continued existence."

Krol's misgivings were not misplaced. Before long the negative reaction to the decision started pouring in. "I suppose you are aware of the fact," Krol wrote to Little on February 10, "that there has also been some unfavorable reaction to the award given to the picture *Darling*." By the end of the month, the unfavorable reaction had increased considerably. The rank and file Catholics who were supposed to turn to NCOMP for guidance were shocked at what they were seeing at the movies. This fact was compounded by the fact that NCOMP had gotten into the awards business. Before the 1965 change in name and philosophy, the Legion ratings would have specified that it was permissible to go to a film like *Darling* without moral danger; after the awards ceremony. the Church had put itself into the business of recommending films, and the people who took the Church's recommendation on matters like this seriously were shocked. A housewife from Drexel Hill, Pennsylvania, in the Philadelphia archdiocese related to Krol the story of a friend who was invited to see *Darling* "by another couple who have

[sic] gone to condemned movies." The lady at first demurred but then agreed to go when she was told "this is not a condemned movie. This has a special rating and was given an award by Archbishop Krol." When the lady did go to see the movie with her husband she came away "completely shocked" and, what is worse, "the couple who invited them said it was worse than any condemned movies they had seen." This fact not only led the lady to wonder about why the Church recommended *Darling*; it also led her to wonder about all the condemned films she had not seen. In a similar vein, R. L. Bennet of Newark, New Jersey writing into the diocesan newspaper on February 24, called *Darling* "one of the most degrading pictures I have ever seen. "

> The female star portrays a prostitute who is repeatedly called just that by the male star. She is pictured in bed with several different men, in such a state of undress that very little is left to the imagination. During a game they called "Truth," shown with a group of depraved degenerates in reply to a question what she would most like to be, she replies, "A pimp in the royal household." In another scene she is depicted stealing various items in a food market. Later in the film, finding herself pregnant she submits to an abortion.

The NCOMP could argue that all that took place before the Julie Christie character's conversion to Catholicism and marriage in the movie. But how was one to explain her subsequent de-conversion other than as a repudiation of Catholicism? "Is that," Mr. Bennet wanted to know, "what NCOMP considers worthy of an award "given to films, the artistic vision and expression of which embody authentic human values?"

On this front, NCOMP had no answer to give to the Catholics it was commissioned to guide. The questions that people like Mr. Bennet raised were for the most part ignored as symptomatic of people who were uncomfortable with the changes flowing from Vatican II and destined for the ecclesial equivalent of the dustbin of history. Krol was in a special bind in this regard because he hadn't seen the film and as a result couldn't respond to the people who were writing to him for guidance without casting into doubt the competence of the whole NCOMP operation. Hollywood for its part seems to have concluded that the former Legion had either lost its nerve or had lost its mind and decided to waste no time in pressing for a complete revision and *de facto* abolition of the Code.

On June 10, 1966, an article appeared in *Life* Magazine on a new film starring Richard Burton and Elizabeth Taylor, *Who's Afraid of Virginia Woolf?*, the film version of the play by Edward Albee, which was described as "an honest, corrosive film of great power and final poignancy." Of course, since the film was still months away from release, the reader had to take *Life's* word on that matter. Either that, or make his own judgments from the accompanying still photos of a chubby Miss Taylor doing what the article described as a "sexy frug." The point of the article, for the especially slow-witted, was that *Virginia Woolf* was causing "a showdown in the movie industry over its anti-quated code of conduct ." At issue was not bare breasts this time as it had been in the case of *The Pawnbroker* one year before, but rather the films' language, which *Life* characterized as "raw and even obscene." There were, for the numerically-minded, "11 goddamns, seven bastards, five sons of bitches" in the film, any one of which would have violated the code as it then stood and prohibited the film from being shown in indus-try-sanctioned theaters.

When Warner Brothers went to NCOMP to find out what it thought, it was both surprised and relieved to learn that the film earned an A-IV rating and was not condemned. "We put *Virginia Woolf* in what we call our 'think film' category," Monsi-gnor Little explained to the people at *Life*. "This is the category we used for *Darling, 81/2* and *La Dolce Vita*."

"We have judged VW in its totality," concluded Msgr Little.

One group that did not agree with NCOMP was the industry's own Motion Picture Association itself, i.e., the Code itself. Shortly after NCOMP, the successor to the Legion of Decency approved the film, Geoffrey Shurlock, Joe Breen's suc-cessor as chief censor at the Code announced that *Virginia Woolf* would not receive the industry's code seal of approval. This was *aggiornamento* with a vengeance. The Legion, which was formed to put teeth into Code enforcement, was now more liberal than the Code it was formed to enforce.

"I could not give it the seal with that language," Shurlock told *Life*. "It clearly violates the code."

The message was clear. If even the Catholics were to the left of the Code, the Code was clearly "antiquated" and in need of being scrapped. Industry President William Valenti was said to be considering, as a result, "a massive overhaul of the Code to accommodate such films as *Virginia Woolf*." Within a period of two years, the moral brinksmanship position had been reversed. In 1964, the Legion condemned *Kiss Me, Stupid!* after the Code approved it. In 1966, NCOMP approved *Virginia Woolf* but the Code condemned it. The two contradictions were enough to weaken the average person's confidence in both the Code and the Legion, no matter what the people at the Legion said to defend their actions. Speaking to *Life*, Father Sullivan admitted that *Virginia Woolf* would have been condemned a few years ago. "But what would have happened," he wondered, "had a girl appeared on a beach in a bikini not in 1966 but in 1800?" Since *Virginia Woolf's* release was still months in the future, however, no one could know if what he had to say was a judicious accommodation to Hollywood's new found high seriousness or just plain old accommodation.

The pundits were quick to draw their own conclusions. Art, so it was claimed, transcended the "narrow" limitations of morality. If it was art, then what was normally immoral was now okay. In this regard the pundits were taking their cue from the Supreme Court's *Roth* decision which used "redeeming social value" as the yardstick. This measuring rod would not only put the Supreme Court in the pornography business for the next 15 years, it would also spawn movies like *I Am Curious (Yellow)*, the next challenge to the Hollywood taboos, which achieved "redeeming social value" by interspersing shots of Martin Luther King and interviews with Olaf Palme between the sex scenes.

By the beginning of the summer of 1966, Krol was receiving a flood of letters from people in the archdiocese who had read the article in *Life* and were upset about it. One 40 year old man with three children wrote from St. Martin of Tours Church, a blue collar parish in Northeast Philadelphia, explaining that he accepted the changes flowing from Vatican II, but was just as convinced that he had no intention of "accepting filth like this as one of our changes."

"The thing that has me upset," the man continued, "is the fact that our church censors approved it, and the movie industry censors would not approve it." This prompted him to go to his parish priest, who was hard-pressed to give an explanation of why the NCOMP had approved the film. "I got the impression," he continued, "that they were at a loss as to why the church would put any kind of approval on such filth ."

The man from St. Martin of Tours, as a result, felt that his authority with his children was being eroded by NCOMP's policy of *aggiornamento*, and as a result, a crisis of faith ensued:

"How am I to tell my children this sort of thing is completely wrong," the man asked Archbishop Krol, "if the Church says it's okay. They'll soon be telling me 'don't be holier than the Church,' Pop. How am I to cope with a situation like that? . . . It's hard enough raising kids right today, but if you don't get support from your Church, then the time is coming for me to wonder whether or not I need a Church that's thinking like this. . . . I'm beginning to wonder whether I'm in the right religion (after 40 years) or should I just stop going to Church and talk directly to God on my knees every night?"

The man, who had been a seminarian 20 years before, closed his letter by asking for a personal response from Krol. Krol, however, forwarded the letter to Father Sullivan and asked him to respond. "The mail is beginning to come in from my subjects," Krol wrote to Sullivan on June 14, 1966, "one of whom says if this is what priests are doing today, he wonders whether he should continue to be a Catholic."

On June 11, Vincent Canby announced in the *New York Times* that Industry Association President Valenti had overruled Shurlock's decision to withhold the Code's seal of approval and was planning to re-examine "the entire philosophy of self-censorship" as represented by the code. By mid-June, Sullivan was feeling the heat himself.

"Yes," he responded in a letter to Krol, dated June 16, "the executive secretary and his assistant are drawing fire."Sullivan, however, seemed reluctant to go on the offensive against either

Life or the trade papers. The new policy of working with the industry was based on good will, but it was becoming quickly apparent that the only thing that purchased good will in Hollywood was the clout that the former Legion had used to threaten economic reprisal. "Short of an open declaration of war," Sullivan continued, "there is no effective way to control the hostile treatment which *Variety* has so frequently accorded this office over many years."

Whenever Krol would receive flak for NCOMP's decisions, he would ask either Sullivan or Little to respond for him. In early 1967, after *Who's Afraid of Virginia Woolf* had finally been released, Mrs. Joseph E. Penzkofer, Secretary Treasurer of the Inter-Faith Citizens Committee for Decency, wrote to Krol complaining that under NCOMP, Catholics were "condoning the abuse of God's name —being repeated millions of times. Shame!"

"We Catholics," Mrs. Penzkofer continued, "have really taken it because of the decision and article in *Life* Magazine. We have gotten intellectual and sophisticated—watered down our standards. Sin isn't sin anymore."

Father Sullivan, who received the letter from Krol with instructions to respond, deplored "the patently sensational" *Life* magazine article. "Not only," Sullivan responded "was it full of inaccuracies and distortions of the film itself, but both Msgr. Thomas P. Little, then Executive Secretary of NCOMP and I were misquoted." Sullivan then goes on to give NCOMP's rationale for the A-IV classification:

> We have never said that this is a film for all adults nor that we had not reservations about it. . . . We have also made it abundantly clear that any other film attempting to use the same language or behavior to sensational and prurient effect would be harshly dealt with by this office. Since we operate as a guidance service, it is difficult to see how our position with regard to *Virginia Woolf* could have been improved upon.

> If the classifications of films are more "liberal" than they were a few years ago, it is at the urging and direction of Our Bishops and the Holy Father himself. Please consider the fact that this Office once had no alternative but to list as objectionable some essentially unobjectionable films only because they could not be

said to be suitable for every last member of any audience. This was patently unfair and unrealistic.

Sullivan concluded his letter by claiming that NCOMP's decision approving (or at least not condemning)*Who's Afraid of Virginia Woolf* was "consistent with the Decrees of Vatican II."

The Catholic Intelligentsia would eventually side with NCOMP and Krol in the controversy which followed the publication of the *Life* magazine article on *Virginia Woolf*. In its September 24, 1966 issue *America* ran an article by Marist brother, George Wead, who also served as their film critic. Wead reviewed the summer's furor over the NCOMP rating of Virginia Woolf, including the attempt of "21 "outraged (not merely 'offended')" Catholic laymen" who "petitioned bishops, newspapers and Catholic organizations to help them get rid of the NCOMP, "to clean house." Wead dismissed the 21 as " the voice of the fearful . . . crying that Christian morality is succumbing to obscenity, blasphemy, and godlessness."

This was, according to Wead, a "sterile game" because "most Catholics do not yet understand the role of the professional film critic in the Catholic press."

"Too few," he continued, "will consider critically whether the film is always as well-paced as it might be. . . . " By now, the intelligentsia were playing a dangerous game of their own. The first fault lines of the split between the liberal intellectual and the orthodox but beleaguered faithful that would plague the post-conciliar Church until the end of the millennium were beginning to show. The faithful for the most part could care less how well-paced a movie like *Virginia Woolf* was; the important thing was that it, more than *The Pawnbroker*, violated their moral sensibilities. What was worse, the Church approved *Virginia Woolf* whereas it had condemned *The Pawnbroker*. The intelligentsia, for its part, was gradually reorienting itself away from being a guide to the ordinary faithful, and becoming more aligned with the liberal opinion makers of their class. The hierarchy, as one might suspect, was caught in the middle of this split with one foot on either side of an ever-widening opening between two rapidly diverging tectonic plates.

Wead concludes his piece by calling on Catholics to "trust the value of human ferment, despite the attractiveness of simple rules of thumb." But by the end September 1966 when the article came out, no one in the opposite camp was listening. The Intelligentsia had lost the ear of the faithful every bit as much as NCOMP had.

More to the point in that regard was the response of Martin Quigley, Jr. in *Motion Picture Daily* at the end of June. "The Code," Quigley opined, "is Dead." It died "because of *Who's Afraid of Virginia Woolf?" The Pawnbroker* may have included nudity, he continued, but the nudity was not prurient, and besides the Legion had condemned *The Pawnbroker*. There may be such a thing as good taste when it comes to nudity but "there is no such thing as 'good taste' in blasphemy, profanity and obscenity," the situation in *Virginia Woolf*. If the bare breasts in *The Pawnbroker* were the beginning of a deluge, the case was even more aggravated in *Virginia Woolf*, primarily because the Catholics approved the film. "When producers rush in to imitate the verbal excesses of the film," Quigley wondered, "who or what can stop them?"

In addition to publishing his editorial in *Motion Picture Daily*, sent a letter to Francis Cardinal Spellman protesting NCOMP's rating of *Virginia Woolf* and accusing NCOMP, in effect, of subverting the Code.

"The code," according to Quigley, "has provisions forbidding blasphemy, profanity and obscenity. Those provisions represented Catholic thought—as well as that of all of the major religions—when written in 1929 by my father and Rev. Daniel A. Lord, S.J. . . . When NCOMP rated *Virginia Woolf* as 'unobjectionable for Adults,' it was inevitable that the Motion Picture Association's code review board would approve the picture, despite the fact that it had been rejected by the Production Code Administration."

"The catholic film office," Quigley concluded ", . . . has been a powerful force in making the industry self-regulation machinery ineffective."

On the same day he received the letter, Archbishop Krol rerouted the letter to NCOMP's headquarters in New York with instructions to Msgr. Little to "direct to His Eminence an adequate reply to Mr. Quigley's letter." Since Little was on vacation, the task fell to Father Sullivan, who replied that "in the judgment of this office and of the Episcopal Committee for Motion Pictures, the Code has been dead for some time now. Any doubt about the matter was resolved in December of 1964 when the seal of approval was given to *Kiss Me, Stupid!*, a film condemned by this office and subsequently rejected by even secular critics on moral grounds."

NCOMP, according to Sullivan, was simply reacting to the realities of the situation as it actually existed. The exhibitors had lost confidence in the Code's seal in 1964. Since that time, they relied on NCOMP's ratings, which had concentrated its efforts on encouraging self-regulation on the part of the industry and film classification.

The Quigleys, according to Sullivan, were calling for a response it was within no one's power to give, certainly not the within the power of the Code. Sullivan then provided Cardinal Spellman with a whole laundry list of complaints against the Quigleys. The Quigleys did not support the episcopal committee when it called for voluntary film classification. The Quigleys offered no support during the fracas over *The Pawnbroker*. The Quigleys ran ads for *The Blue Max* in their magazine, a film which contained two explicit lovemaking scenes.

"Quigley Publications" Sullivan continued, "thrived in the days when Mr. Quigley Sr. controlled the code and had producers convinced that he also controlled the decision of the Legion of Decency. This was a scandal to me and, for the sake of the Church's good name, I extended every cooperation to Msgr. Little in his successful efforts to make our office the guidance agency of the Church which the Bishops intended it to be rather than a pawn in the building of an empire."

Once again, the Quigleys were taken to task for their venality, but the underlying issue, as before, remained unresolved. The fact remained that NCOMP had serious credibility problems with the rank and file, or at the very least a severe problem in communicating the reasons for its decisions to the ordinary Catholics it was commissioned to serve. By focusing their attention on the Quigleys, Sullivan and NCOMP once again ignored the bigger issue of how the competing and distinct demands of morality and art were to be combined in a rating system possessing a very limited number of categories and options.

Krol, more than ever, was caught in the middle. He did not view the films; he did not make the decisions, yet as head of the episcopal committee he was called to task when the decisions caused controversy, and he found it difficult to find maneuvering room without attacking his subordinates. Feeling the heat of a controversy which looked as if it were not going to go away any time soon, Krol wrote to Msgr. Little on July 5 and expressed the fear that "the reaction of those who protest the classification will be re-echoed at higher levels."

"Would it be well," he wondered, "to have a standard explanation that might be sent to all such complaints?"

Before too long, Krol's fears had become reality. In the middle of July, Krol received a letter from Cardinal McIntyre of Los Angeles registering a formal protest against NCOMP's rating of *Virginia Woolf*. The decision, he informed Krol, was causing "scandal"; it constituted in the opinion of many bishops "a danger to the faith of many,"

"We feel," McIntyre continued, "that some action should be taken by your commission or some other agency to explain or withdraw this grave error that has been made in placing the Church and the bishops in such an embarrassing position. We cannot defend ourselves." McIntyre, who not only outranked Krol because he was a cardinal but also outranked him because of his position as ordinary of Hollywood, in a manner of speaking, demanded that "immediate action. . . be taken."

"I present my protest in this form," he concluded, "because it would be entirely ineffective if it were delayed until the meeting of the bishops in the fall."

One day later, on July 14, 1966, McIntyre sent Krol the text of a letter repudiating NCOMP's decision that was scheduled to appear in the July 22 edition of the LA diocesan newspaper. Basing his judgment on the "comments of those who represent the average motion picture-goer," McIntyre concluded that "NCOMP has made a very grave error of judgment and manifest imprudence in presenting a verdict on the picture that is subject to adverse interpretation. . . . It is indeed to be lamented that an attempt has been made to accommodate truths to varying and degrading language and circumstances. The result can only be condemned."

In a world in which one ordinary only spoke of another in public in the most laudatory of terms, this serious breech of protocol indicated the gravity with which McIntyre and many other bishops viewed the *Virginia Woolf* affair. Krol for his part, when he got over the shock, was galvanized into action. At 12 noon on July 19, he sent a telegram to McIntyre indicating that "public declaration of opposition will promote injurious discord—stimulate interest in the production and be interpreted as censure of the more than 120 volunteers who for years have viewed and classified over 250 productions." Krol stated that he had called for an emergency meeting of NCOMP staff on that coming Friday and pleaded with McIntyre not to release the letter to the diocesan newspaper.

One day after sending his open letter, McIntyre showed signs that he was reconsidering the option of going public, primarily as a result of a telephone conversation he had had the night before with Cardinal Spellman, who, while also embarrassed by NCOMP's decision, predicted "the possibility of injurious discord that might ensue from a public declaration of opposition from Los Angeles."

"For myself," McIntyre concluded, "I still adhere to the opinion that something should be done to place us on record in the proper light. Since we do not go to press until Thursday, I shall have time to reform and cool off."

On July 19, McIntyre wrote to Krol in response to Krol's telegram of the same day, which arrived early that morning, Los Angeles time. McIntyre had decided not to go public, "largely due to my respect for yourself," he told Krol. However, he was still of the opinion that NCOMP was seriously wrong and that the volunteers who work for it "were sold out by the administration in the ultimate decision." The fact that 44 reviewers had expressed reservations in rating *Virginia Woolf* could easily have changed the majority decision.

Within the breathing space created by the decision of the ordinary of Los Angeles to keep his objections within in the confines of the American episcopacy, Krol had the opportunity to write back on August 4 and explain his role in the whole affair.

"My role as chairman," Krol began by way of explanation, "has taken far more time than I could normally spare, but I felt that I owed this time and service to the Bishops and to the Catholic Church." The whole thrust of the updating at the Legion was to make a distinction between depicting evil and advocating it. This had been the Achilles Heel of the Legion and the reason it lacked credibility in condemning films like *Phaedra*. According to Krol,

> the II Vatican Council's Communication Decree says: "to depict evil is not necessarily to advocate it—that evil is a part of life." In line with the Papal teachings of Pius XII, John XXIII and the Council, the NCOMP has increased the categories. The A-4 rating finds justification in the precise word of an Encyclical which talks about some pictures being for "adults with reservations." Such a rating by no means approves everything in the picture. . . . May I respectfully add that I have some strong personal convictions about film productions. However, I have not ventured to substitute my personal conviction for directives and norms indicated in Papal teaching.

McIntyre for his part remained unimpressed. "I can find nothing in Papal documents," he responded, "that would modify the morality of this picture. Basic norms confirm the presentation of the picture as immoral in speech and action, and I feel the Bishops of the country have an obligation to protest in some manner this rating."

Krol concluded his letter by adding "that it will be a pleasure to say that the 1966 report will be my fifth and final one as Chairman of the committee."

If so, it was one of the only pleasures the two bishops shared during their exchange of correspondence. On August 16, McIntyre wrote back to Krol that he was still "shocked and scandalized" by the whole affair. "The mother of a family," McIntyre continued, would find "little guidance, if not confusion, from a designation of 'unobjectionable, with reservations.' In reality, this terminology is contradictory."

Beyond that, McIntyre felt that "in light of the universal acknowledgment of all critics that the picture is sacrilegious, lewd and disgusting," rating it as "unobjectionable" made no sense. To say that the rating was derivable from papal authority struck McIntyre "as irreverent, inaccurate and not factual." It seemed especially hollow to McIntyre, who was privy to Hollywood gossip in a way that Krol was not. To say that papal teaching condoned the picture, when McIntyre knew that Jack Warner condemned it was too much for the cardinal archbishop of Los Angeles to take.

"It is indeed deplorable that the Bishops of the country are obliged to accept the responsibility for such misinterpretation. I definitely challenge the interpretation." The only moment of congratulations that McIntyre could summon in the letter was conditional: "I congratulate you if this be your last year on the committee." McIntyre closed by promising to be "vocally critical" at the bishops meeting in that coming November.

Krol, for his part was only to happy to have done with an assignment that he never really wanted in the first place, and one which he only accepted—foolishly, perhaps—out of a sense of episcopal duty. In a letter he wrote on October 7, 1966, Krol described the job to Bishop Walter W. Curtis of Bridgeport as being asked "five years ago to expose my thick skin to the stream of criticism that was directed against my predecessor."

The main difference was that the years 1961 to 1966 were much more tumultuous than those during which his predecessor served. They were, one can say without a trace of exaggeration, the five most important years not only in the history of the Legion of Decency, but also in the history of film thus far. The Catholics, befuddled by mistaken notions of renewal, dropped the ball, and the whole country suffered as a result. Hollywood got what it wanted, but as in the case of the liberal fostering of racial migration in Philadelphia, one small group profited at the expense of the common good. Krol and Little were proven right in a very short period of time. The bare breasts in *The Pawnbroker* were the first drop in what was soon to become a flood of pornography flowing out of the nation's movie theaters and into the minds of the nation's populace causing untold misery.

In December of 1983, Linda Marchiano (aka, Lovelace) testified before the Meese Pornography Commission about her life as the star of the first run pornography hit of 1973, *Deep Throat*. It was a tale of sexual sadism and beatings and an escape from a world which nearly killed her. Untold still is the story of how her actions on the screen affected the people who paid money to see her. It remains untold because the cultural revolutionaries have thwarted most attempts to tell it. "We find it difficult to understand," the Meese commission concluded after listening to the testimony of Linda Marchiano and many others, "how much of the material we have seen can be considered to be even remotely related to an exchange of views in the marketplace of ideas, to an attempt to articulate a point of view, to an attempt to persuade or to an attempt seriously to convey through literary or artistic means a different vision of humanity or the world."

"At bottom," the Meese commission concluded, "the predominant use of such material is as a masturbatory aid."

This may not be what Ely Landau had in mind when he produced *The Pawnbroker*, but it is what the country got nonetheless. When Krol retired from his position as chairman of the episcopal committee, the battle was largely lost. The Catholics were once again excluded from bringing the moral law to bear on public life, and once again it was the country at large which suffered as a result.

VII
The Council Comes Home

T he Reverend Anthony Massamini returned from Rome during the summer of 1963, at around the same time that Pope John XXIII died and right before the racial disturbance broke out in Folcroft. Father Massamini had attended only one session of the Council, which was to continue for another three years, but that was enough to qualify him as an expert in the eyes of a world hungry for news that the Catholic Church was finally conforming to the modern world. Massamimi returned to Philadelphia to a job at the archdiocesan seminary full of what he would later characterize as "naive exuberance that a new age of grace was dawning that matched the Age of Aquarius."

Given that sort of attitude it is not surprising that he soon ran into trouble with his immediate superiors at the seminary as well as the ordinary of the archdiocese, Archbishop John Krol. Massamini's stature as an expert was even greater among the seminarians than it was in the Philadelphia community at large. His reputation, however, soon put him in a difficult situation. To begin with, it is doubtful that even someone who had attended the whole Council in Massamini's capacity could have anything like the overview that was needed to explain it to seminarians. Beyond that, the end of the Council was still two years away when Massamini began teaching courses on it, and so he was in effect reduced to expounding on his one year there, which since it was one year more than most people spent there, seemed like qualifications enough in an age so avid for information. Tony Massamini, however, was forced to bridge the gaps in his personal experience of the Council by going to the journalistic accounts we have already mentioned—Kaiser, Rynne, Novak, et al.—and so in effect what the seminarians were getting were the newspaper accounts, most of which were of dubious accuracy, but all of which shared the liberal bias of the age. In addition to that, Massamini was in contact with Bill Leahy who would remain at the Council until 1965. The expert, in other words, was reading the papers like every one else, and forced to fall back on them to fill in the gaps of his knowledge.

Massamini's account of the Council was so similar to Xavier Rynne's, in fact, that many seminarians thought that Massamini was the pseudonymous Rynne. The rumor, which made the rounds at the seminary, only enhanced Massamini's reputation. And since the seminarians were forbidden at the time to read the newspapers, much less watch television, Massamini as the source of information on not only what was happening there but what it all meant was enhanced as the Council continued. The seminarians, for their part, were longing for a change in a system that for some time lost the respect of the people it purported to form. St. Charles Borromeo Seminary, in spite of being named after an Italian saint and being designed in the Italian style, had virtually no Italian presence when Tony Massamini began teaching there in the fall of 1963. Massamini was conscious of the fact that he was the first and only teacher of Italian extraction at a seminary which was dominated almost exclusively by Irish Americans.

At the turn of the century, the seminary was dominated by Germans, but as the Germans assimilated and lost their cohesiveness, the Irish began to fill the vacuum they left behind. During Dennis Cardinal Dougherty's tenure as archbishop from 1918 to 1951, the faculty of the seminary gradually lost its German character, and with the German culture went German scholarship, which was in its turn replaced by an Irish American culture that was, depending on whom you ask, somewhere between resolutely and coincidentally anti-intellectual. The enculturation of the gospel had taken place with a vengeance among Philadelphia's Irish immigrants; it was so successful, in fact, that by the time of the Council, the tail was pretty much wagging the dog and the training at the seminary had become intellectually suspect by those who were there to be formed by it and heavily dependent on rote recapitulation of notes (and jokes) that seemed hundreds of years old.

In addition to being hailed as an "expert" on the Council, Massamini and his standing at the seminary were enhanced by the fact that he had an advanced degree from Rome in what was seen as an exciting new field that had many connections (too many, some would argue) with the "science" of psychology which by the early '60s was just coming to be recognized by many Catholics. In fact by the late '60s, catechesis would be considered by many educators as nothing more than a branch of psychology. "Many who glance through this book will be perplexed," Brother Andrew Panzarella, F.S.C. wrote in the teacher's introduction to his 1968 high school religion text published by Sadlier, *Growth in Christ*, "at first anyway, by the amount of psychology in it. They will be asking: What has all this got to do with religion?"

By the late '60s, irate parents were asking just that as *Growth in Christ* wreaked havoc among the students at West Catholic, one of the two schools in the archdiocese run by the Christian Brothers, and elsewhere. Catechetical texts were the *causus belli* in the conservative reaction to the excesses following the Council. And texts like Bro. Panzarella's gave every indication that what the parents pursued qualified as a just war. "Only recently," Panzarella continued to the teachers using his book, "has theology, like a cautious housewife sizing up a salesman, opened the door slightly to hear what modern psychology and sociology have to offer."

If caution was prescribed here, Panzarella seems not to have noticed. Of the three books teachers are recommended to read before commencing teaching his course, all are texts of psychology: *"Man's Search for Meaning; A Primer of Freudian Psychology,* and *Man for Himself."* The main source of inspiration for *Growth in Christ*, according to Panzarella's own account, was "the viewpoint which Erich Fromm has stated so well in his book *Man for Himself: An Inquiry into the Psychology of Ethics.* " That Fromm's combining of the insights of Freud and Marx might be somehow incompatible with the teaching of the Catholic Church is an issue which never gets raised. What Bro. Panzarella does tell us, though, is that the perennial philosophy, the one recommended by virtually every modern pope beginning with Leo XIII, was hopelessly out of date and superseded by more recent insights.

"There is no reason," Panzarella opined to prospective teachers, "why we should continue to settle for the psychology of the thirteenth century. In our own times psychology has developed in scope and depth to a degree unimagined by St. Thomas." Panzarella in this regard was no different that the typical Catholic intellectual of his place and time. He, like Massamini, was handicapped first of all by an inadequate understanding of Freud, perhaps because it was refracted through popularizers like Fromm, but beyond that, handicapped as well by an almost constitutional inability to detect the ideological African-American in the psychological woodpile. Liberalism was for the denizens of that age stealth ideology. Catholic radar was incapable of detecting it until it was too late and the damage had already been done. It differed from its military analogue only in that most Catholic liberals would refuse to concede that what had been done constituted damage. With the Church's educational system in Philadelphia a shambles by the late '60s, Catholic educators were still willing to go on record and call the devastation progress.

"They're more liberal in the good sense," Father Francis X. Schmidt, director of the archdiocese's Catholic Youth Organization, explained to a reporter from *Philadelphia Magazine* in 1967. The "they" in this instance referred to students at West Catholic, one of the two schools in the archdiocese run by the Christian Brothers (Bernard McCormick, "The Troubled See: The Church is being renewed here, as elsewhere, it is a time of painful uncertainty," *Philadelphia Magazine*, 1967, pp. 52ff).

"They seem more up on Vatican II," Schmidt continued, "more willing to talk about their religion and more aware of the role of the laity and willing to sacrifice. I think the Brothers are really reaching kids out there. I think the other kids marvel at their spirit and motivation." Another brother, who went unnamed in the article, equated sacramentals like the rosary with "religious voodoo," and explained that "we've gotten completely away from that." Catechesis, as defined by the Christian Brothers not only entailed viewing sacramentals as "religious voodoo." It put the sacraments themselves in pretty much the same light. "This may be shocking," the same brother continued, "but about 60 percent of our kids don't receive the sacraments regularly." By way of explanation, the brother claimed that "we try to impress on the kids that they should do things because they feel they have meaning."

The Church was in a dangerous situation. Its rules had become incomprehensible to those who were supposed to enforce them. Beyond that, the culture seemed to be proposing programs and branches of science that were not only more attractive, they also made much of what the Church held seem unreasonable. After plumbing the depths of Sigmund Freud and Teilhard de Chardin in Rome under people like Bernard Lonergan, and after hearing the irreverence of Xavier Rynne and Hans Kueng, Tony Massamini was being called on the carpet at St. Charles Seminary for bringing a "foreign" priest, i.e., one from the Camden archdiocese directly across the Delaware river, to a lecture without permission from his superiors. This rule-ridden paternalism probably never made much sense, but now in the light of the aggiornamento emanating from Rome, it was becoming intolerable.

Massamini felt constrained by the strictures of the regime at the seminary and the seminarians felt pretty much the same way, so it was no surprise that Massamini and the seminarians would gravitate toward each other in an alliance of the progressives. The Council provided these people with a leverage which they otherwise would not have had. Without the Council there would have been no focal point for their discontent. With the Council, the burden of proof was placed on those who impeded "change," and both Massamini and the seminarians intended to press the issue.

The progressive forces at the seminary were strengthened in the fall of '65 when Father William Leahy was called back from his stint at the Council to teach at the seminary as well. The combination of two young *"periti"* along with a lot of unhappy seminarians was to prove volatile indeed.

Massamini's stature as a "peritus" was magnified by the fact that he was being asked to explain the Council to non-Catholic organizations throughout the Delaware Valley, often with the media present to ask pointed and sometimes tendentious questions. One group had the curious name of "the 12." It was a group of Protestant ministers which met every Thursday at the cafeteria of the Philadelphia Gas Works at 12:12 P.M. to discuss topics of interest. For the uninitiated, the Gas Company was the citadel of WASP influence over the affairs of the city. Because the mainline denominations had become virtually indistinguishable from groups like the ACLU, this meant that the Gas Company and "the 12" were at the center of the Liberal/Protestant network that was at the time working so hard to change the city's attitude toward contraception.

Throughout the '60s, the Gas Company sponsored a radio commentary show on WFLN, Philadelphia's classical music station, hosted by Taylor Grant. Grant was a liberal's liberal, who went out of his way to praise people like Senators Clark and Gruening and criticize people like Martin Mullen. He probably would have gone to his grave doing the same sort of thing, but during the early '70s, Lennox Moak, city controller under Mayor Frank Rizzo heard something he didn't like and the city pressured the Gas Company to drop its sponsorship of the program. Taylor Grant became a local celebrity for a while as a result of being "moaked," as he was fond of saying. Ralph Collier, another WFLN commentator at the time, was hosting Protestant ministers who attacked the Church's position on birth control at around the same time that Massamini was explaining the Council to the ministers at the Gas Works.

Massamini comes across as a warm-hearted and sincere Italian from South Philadelphia. He has an enviable capacity for empathy. What he lacked, however, as an explicator of the Council to both seminarians and the non-Catholic world in Philadelphia was a firm sense of what was orthodox and what was not, as well as a firm sense of its converse, what was historically conditioned and what was not. Taken together, the sense of empathy along with the intellectual inability to come to grips with modernity would provide a deadly combination in an age which put a premium on "ecumenism," as defined by the liberal *Zeitgeist*. In addition to that, Massamini fell into the unfortunate trap of explaining the Council without sufficient data at his disposal, which led to the even more unfortunate situation of making up in empathy what he lacked in expertise.

Like many experts, he ended up telling the people what they wanted to hear.

Massamini remembers addressing "the 12" during a week when there was a convention of ministers in town. "I got up in front of them and started talking," he recounted almost 30 years later. "It was first time they had heard a priest talk, and I said major changes have taken place, and are still taking place in Rome right now. And I remember two things. I said, 'up until now, I would say to you, you and I are different, although we have some things in common. Now, I'm going to say to you, we are now brothers. Although we have some differences.' And that hit them. And I kept talking about Pope John, ecumenism, and the bigger church of Christ. And in closing I said, gentlemen, the last thing I want to say to you today is, 'hello.' And they went nuts. They went nuts. And they invited me to talk all over the area. I started going to all the Protestant churches, doing this kind of thing."

One of the groups involved in "the 12"'s network was Planned Parenthood, who invited Father Massamini to speak, not surprisingly, on birth control. Massamini, who would pass on a chance to object to *Humanae Vitae* when contacted by the dissident theologians who were organizing their protest during the summer of 1968, took the same irenic line with Planned Parenthood that he had taken with the ministers, giving some indication that the organization that Margaret Sanger founded was a religion, and not only that, a religion indistinguishable from mainline Protestantism as well. Massamini spoke on the morality of birth control, explaining that "we," i.e. the Catholic Church, "were a little biased ourselves." It was just the sort of thing Planned Parenthood was avid to hear at the time. Massamini went on to say that he didn't think that the Church should be "giving anatomy lessons," but should focus on "moral insights that we have to try to protect here and to wrestle with and work out," presumably with the help of Planned Parenthood. After the talk, the woman representing Planned Parenthood thanked Massamini."We really appreciate your focussing on the moral like that," she said. "We really appreciate that very much."

After a similar talk on the Council sponsored by a Presbyterian Church in Swarthmore, a Quaker stronghold southwest of Philadelphia, Massamini was asked by a woman in the audience if the Church were going to change its teaching on birth control.

"Pope Paul," Massamini responded, "is in the process right now of writing an encyclical on the question on birth control." Massamini had just finished speaking about collegiality. The Church, according to his explication of collegiality, "as a church, as a unity, has the spirit within it to help itself make decisions."

As a result, Massamini assumed "that the Pope is going to consult with the whole church on this. And especially he's going to consult with people who have something that he hasn't got. He's going to consult with our married people who have a sacrament that he hasn't got. See, they have a particular insight into the meaning of marriage. And he's gonna consult with them. And then he is going to make his decision."

The lady in question turned out to be a reporter for the *Philadelphia Bulletin*, who reported Massamini's response— "pretty accurately," he would later say—in the next day's paper. Not long after the article appeared Massamini got a call from Father Philip Dowling, head of the Commission on Human Relations, one of whose responsibilities in the diocese was ecumenism. Dowling had gotten a complaint from "some priest outside the archdiocese" and wanted to know what exactly Massamini was telling everyone about the Church's teaching on birth control. Massamini, for his part, claimed that he was not seeking the spotlight, but was only responding to what he felt was widespread curiosity about what was happening in the Church. He would often feel that he was out of his depth in responding to so many questions from so many groups

"I kept saying," he recounted later, "'wait, this is over my head. This is beyond me.' And I would take this and I would write back to the chancery office. And I would say, they are asking me this; they're asking me that. I think we should have some kind of official way to respond, I'm telling them its beyond my authority to answer these questions. But I kept getting back: 'Don't you say anything. You just teach the teachings of the church.' They were especially uncomfortable that I went to the Planned Parenthood thing. I went with their okay, but they were very uncomfortable with that."

Massamini was eventually to feel that the chancery was being a dog in a manger. "They were kind of pushing me back," he claimed. They would send him to speak, but without guidelines more specific than "the teachings of the Church." Then they would criticize what he had said. A spokesman with a better sense of the Church's teaching might have given a better response. But Massamini, with all his inadequacies, was the man of the hour. He was the expert; he had attended one session of the Council, and since the chancery wasn't forthcoming with any more specific guidelines, conflict was bound to recur.

Given the parameters of the situation, when conflict came, it came on a number of fronts. Bill Leahy would later say that he had returned from the Council with "unrealistic expectations." Beginning in the fall of '65, both he and Massamini as the young turks in the seminary began to spread these expectations among the seminarians. Vatican II, Massamini would tell the seminarians, "is gonna change the Church. We're gonna have a new kind of Church when we finish. Its going to be open; [the title of Michael Novak's book on the Council]; it's going to be more in tune with the times. It was a sign of the times. It was going to be a New Pentecost. I was really booming this kind of thing out."

Looking back, Massamini feels that his attitude toward change may have "polarized the students." There was a great deal of unrest at the seminary anyway. The curriculum had become ossified; the seminarians had a sense of intellectual inferiority because the seminary was not accredited and because their bachelor's degrees were not recognized elsewhere. The library was full of outdated science books and had no regular professional staff, resulting in among other things, comic misfilings of books. *The Changing Tides*, a book on politics, was shelved in the geography section. In addition to the legitimate complaints, there were those which savored more of the spirit of the times. Open, as in Michael Novak's book *The Open Church*, was a key word in this regard. Students wanted "open" discussions, as well as an "open" education, even if few people could define the word with any precision.

During the '65-'66 academic year, Massamini moved into a room in the student dormitory at the seminary. "This was a '60s type of thing," he explained, "you know, have your pad in among the students." Even if the move was somehow condoned by the *Zeitgeist*, it was a move that was destined to alienate the older faculty members, who began to feel that Leahy and Massamini were undermining their authority. Authority, either way, was being undermined at an extremely rapid pace. By the '65-'66 academic year, the seminary found itself encumbered with rules that no one had the will to enforce. As a result there was a widespread contempt for authority in general, fostered by the spirit of the times, specifically the cries of "freedom" emanating from the Protestant-sanctioned civil rights movement. The Church had reached an extremely dangerous situation. The seminary was for all practical purposes out of control. Insubordination was rife. The prefects of discipline refused to discipline anyone, leading in the words of an official report on the state of the seminary, to "collapse of discipline in the seminary."

"The seminary rulebook," the report continued, "certainly needs to be revamped. A number of the rules are obsolete. The committee believes that the rules should be reduced, but that any rule which is in effect should be strictly enforced. It appears that the observance of silence is almost completely neglected."

On October 28, 1965 the Council passed its Decree on Priestly Formation. News of its passage combined with lack of details on what the Decree specified made a bad situation at the seminary even worse. By the end of 1965, Archbishop Krol was up to his neck in a number of crises occurring simultaneously. In early December the Legion of Decency announced its name change and awards dinner, precipitating the crisis which would arrive six months later with the publication of the *Life* Magazine article on *Who's Afraid of Virginia Woolf?* On December 19, 1965, the Pennsylvania Department of Welfare, following the steady drumbeat of that summer initiated by the Gruening hearings on government-funded birth control, announced that it was changing its regulations, a move that would precipitate a battle that would only be resolved, and then only temporarily, when Martin Mullen held firm on the state's budget in August of 1966.

Beyond all that, Krol still wasn't finished with the Council. On January 30, 1966 he was scheduled to fly back to Rome for some concluding deliberations.

In the midst of all this, Krol wrote to Monsignor George O'Donnell, of the seminary faculty on March 7, 1966 announcing that Bishop Gerald V. McDevitt, one of Phildelphia's auxiliary bishops, along with Msgrs. John J. Daly and Henry A. McCracken, would conduct a canonical visitation on the seminary from March 26 to March 30 as the first step in implementing *Optatam Totius*, the decree on seminary training. Before the visitation could take place, however, 31 students walked out of their Scripture class. The students claimed that their action was unpremediated and occurred in protest against the unfair treatment of one of their peers, who was asked to leave the classroom. At an emergency meeting called to deal with the incident one day later, the seminary faculty concluded that "no further action was necessary prior to the arrival of the visitation team."

As part of their own evaluation of the seminary, the students issued a 51 page paper, which they presented to the evaluation team on March 30. In it they produced a list of complaints some of which would be implemented as part of the seminary reform, some of which were more indicative of the spirit of the times. Among other things, the students wanted "'Mass facing the people to be the rule not the exception." In discussing discipline at the seminary, the students complained of "an imbalance between an overly cautious authority and individual freedom," and asked that the "compulsory 'lights out'" policy be abolished. They also complained of a pervasive feeling of "academic inferiority" among the college students and "requested that the professors teach only those courses in which they had their degrees." The library facilities had "serious defects." Rounding out their complaints was an appeal for "better athletic facilities" (although Cardinal Dougherty had installed an Olympic size pool during his tenure) as well as "permission to attend sporting events, art exhibits, and cultural activities off campus" and "more freedom in their personal contacts outside the Seminary; in receiving visitors in the Seminary; and in visiting the homes of families and friends."

On the whole, the requests were not unreasonable, and the authorities were inclined to go along with them, even before the walkout. On April 24, 1966, however, the student petition appeared on the front page of the Sunday *Bulletin*. Under the headline "Seminarians at St. Charles Ask for Greater Personal Freedom," the *Bulletin* article went on to criticize the "stifling paternalism" of the seminary discipline, the "grave deficiencies" of the academic program, and the Seminary's "glaring lack of spiritual direction." With the reform of the seminary threatening to become a captive of the media, Krol decided to act.

On May 1, 1966, one week after the story appeared in the *Bulletin*, Krol arrived unannounced at the Vesper services in St. Martin's chapel on the seminary grounds. Under normal circumstances the archbishop did not appear at the seminary unannounced. His presence there on that Sunday night announced even before a word was spoken that circumstances were no longer normal. Nor had they been normal, although this was neither announced nor implied, since Krol had taken over the reins of the diocese more than five years before. The Council had been an enormous drain on his energy and time, and now it looked as if the Council were in the process of getting away from the one man in the archdiocese who knew its workings most intimately. Any changes in the seminary, he announced after a dramatic hush had fallen over the seminarians, who sat facing each other in rows of hardwood pews beneath the imposing gilt ceiling of the Italianate chapel that in another place might have done service as a Cathedral, would be made in strict conformity with the directives of the Church. The leaking of the student evaluation constituted scandal and had caused resentment and disunity. Equally clear from the presentation was the fact that Archbishop Krol was the person in Philadelphia who determined what was in conformity with the Council and what was not. Those who disagreed with his interpretations were free to leave.

"If any of you," Krol announced by way of conclusion, "students or faculty, entertain any ideas that the renewal must follow your directives, rather than those of ecclesiastical authorities, then you had better reconsider. If in conscience you are willing and able to accept the authorized directives of renewal, I shall thank God. If, in conscience, you feel that you cannot comply, then in conscience you should leave. You have a choice of staying and obeying or of leaving. *Non datur tertium.*"

Non datur tertium—"there is no third possibility"—became the short hand expression among the priests of the archdiocese of Krol's attitude toward the renewal. Combined with his other favorite, *"D'ove scritto?*—"where is it written"—these dicta would provide the parameters between which the updating following the Council got channeled. This is not to say that Krol had the power to hold whatever happened between the boundaries implied by these epigrams, but if he felt the stream of renewal was threatening to leap its bounds, these were the rules that got applied. Many people would begin to wonder, especially within the realm of Catholic education in the archdiocese, if Krol wasn't turning a blind eye on what was happening. But the seminary incident made clear that no matter what Krol could tolerate at the archdiocesan high schools and the Catholic colleges and universities in the area, he could not afford to give the same latitude to the seminary. And he did not. As a result, the reform of the seminary went fairly quickly, and within a decade St. Charles had overcome the identity crisis that continued to plague the rest of the country's Catholic colleges and universities.

Tony Massamini would claim to have had nothing to do, at least directly, with the student walkout and the leaking of the student evaluation to the newspaper. In fact, he would claim that were it not for his efforts the crisis at the seminary would have been much worse. No one was denying that the seminary was in need of a change, but in the aftermath of the student walkout and *Bulletin* article, nobody believed Massamini's claims that he was an innocent bystander either. In the official report submitted to Krol by the visitation team, the possibility was mooted "that the students had received direction from some of the younger professors." The younger professors in question were listed as Fathers Leahy and Massamini explicitly. "There is a definite cleavage in the faculty between the older and some of the younger members," the report continued, "and in this matter Father Leahy and Father Massamini seem to be the source to a great extent of this cleavage."

As a result the committee recommended that both Massamini and Leahy be removed from the faculty because "it was the impression that they are responsible for the division among the faculty and also that through their close association with the students they may well have been the cause of the unrest and antagonism of the students toward the professors. It is very noticeable in the papers submitted from the students that there was never a condemnatory word but only praise for these two."

In addition to that, one faculty member accused

> some of the younger faculty members . . . of stirring [the semi-narians] up to a spirit of disrespect and contempt for some of the older members of the faculty. This is an intolerable situation. If any of the senior members of the faculty are not qualified to teach the subjects to which they are assigned, they should be assigned to a parish. And if any of the junior members of the faculty are guilty of inflaming the students with disrespect and lack of confidence in the senior professors, they should be dismissed.

Once again Massamini was called down to the archbishop's office. Once again the same impasse occurred that had taken place in Rome when Krol took Massamini out to a trattoria and told him to destroy his article on the Council. In the interaction between the Italian theologian and the Polish prelate, the respective minds seemed incapable of finding any middle ground. Krol kept wanting to exert his authority in a way that Massamini found intellectually opaque, and Massamini, while accepting Krol's decision, was incapable or unwilling to understand the reasons behind the decision. The meeting, as a result, quickly degenerated into a shouting match.

"I kept yelling at him," Massamini recalled. "'Tell me what I'm doing wrong and I'll change, but I 'm not going to change until you tell me what I've done wrong.'" The confrontation reminded Massamini of two boxers who would sally forth from their corners to land a few punches and then retire back to their separate corners. Krol would reel off a list of complaints he had heard about Massamini from various sources, and Massamini would ask him to explain what he had done wrong, thinking that he was simply following the mandate set for him by the Church at the Council.

When they finished arguing, Massamini got up and both men walked to the center of the room. Massamini then knelt down to kiss Krol's ring and Krol took his hand in his and remarked that his hands were cold.

"Calm down," Krol said, as if the fight, now over, should be forgotten as well.

"I never felt excluded from his care," Massamini said in retrospect. "He was mad at me and I was mad at him, but it was never on account of cold exclusion. All the time, I kept saying, 'If I'm wrong, tell me where I was wrong.'"

"We liked each other," Massamini said of his relationship with Archbishop Krol. Then correcting himself, he added. "No, we loved each other; we didn't like each other. We loved each other. And I could always tell that when he talked to me. A lot of times, it was, 'my dear son, what the hell are you doing now? I'm gonna kill ya. Cause you're my son, and I love you.' I always had that feeling with him. Always. And it made me free. Therefore, I argued back with him. If not, I wouldn't. And, he would have probably done the same things. Again. I'm a free spirited type of person. I'm, Italian. And the entire seminary was heavily Irish at the time."

The two minds never met effectively on the issue of who was right on the Council. Massamini never felt that there was a trace of personal animosity on Krol's part no matter how vehement the shouting match between them became. He would later feel that there were two John Krols—John Krol, the churchman, and John Krol, the person—and that the two were never really in sync, but neither John Krol did what he did out of spite or vindictiveness.

However, if John Krol, the person, felt powerless to persuade Tony Massamini of the error of his ways, John Krol, the Churchman, still felt constrained to act, and the upshot of the conversation was that Massamini was out of a job as of the fall of 1966. Beyond that, he was forbidden to talk to anyone but Catholics on issues like the Council and birth control.

The enforced leisure gave Massamini time for some serious soul-searching. In many ways, animosity on Krol's part might have been easier to take. However, Massamini went away from his encounters with the archbishop convinced that Krol was doing what he thought he had to do, both in the best interests of Tony Massamini and the Catholic Church. As a result of his trust in Krol's character if not his theology, Tony Massamini began to undergo a crisis of faith. He became convinced that his vocation to the priesthood was a "magnificent error."

"My idea of what a priest was," Massamini explained, "and the Church's idea at that time of what a priest was, were incompatible." Massamini didn't arrive at this idea on his own though. To begin with, once he was released from his courses at the seminary, he began teaching at St. Joseph's College, now university, run by the Jesuits just about a mile down the road from the seminary. There his contacts with the Catholic counterculture deepened along with the liberal left milieu that that counterculture inhabited. Along with John Malinowski, a theology instructor at St. Joseph's and a student of Paul van Buren, the Death of God theologian at Temple University, Massamini helped organized the Death of God symposium at St. Joseph's in the fall of '67. Death of God was a theological fad that received whatever credibility it had at the time by appearing on the cover of *Time* Magazine. After every one else lost interest, it made its way through the backwaters of Catholic academe, to the confusion of the students and the consternation of the parents of those students.

Like Tony Massamini, Bill Leahy also found himself without a job in the fall of 1966. The news came to Leahy in a distinctly less personal fashion. After returning from a trip he took at the end of the 1966 spring semester, Leahy met a friend who offered his condolences "I'm sorry to hear you've been removed from the seminary," Leahy was told. The announcement was news to Leahy, who was furious at Krol for the way his job got terminated. Leahy eventually expressed his anger in a meeting with the archbishop, during which Krol apologized for the way the news reached him.

But Krol did not rescind the order, and Leahy was assigned to a parish in suburban Warminster which he found oppressive and which he left, going the ecclesial equivalent of AWOL within a short period of time. Leahy was eventually reassigned to an inner city, i.e, black parish, Mother of Sorrows at 48th and Wyalusing, which suited his idea of what he wanted to do more, but in the process of getting what he thought he wanted, Leahy, like Massamini, got caught up in the trammels of the Catholic counter-culture. The chain of events went something like this: black parish meant civil rights movement, and that at the time meant antiwar movement, and that at the time meant an entree into the whole spectrum of left-wing causes which were at work attacking the Church's influence on the social order in Philadelphia at the time.

As a result, both Massamini and Leahy began drifting farther and farther away from the Church. There were other factors at work as well. Leahy was suspended from the priesthood by Rome in 1969 for officiating at his priest brother's wedding. Leahy had a drinking problem as well which eventually caused him to lose his job at St. Joseph's College. In 1977, he ended up in a rehab after losing his last job, which was as a bartender so that he could support his drinking habit. Massamini got involved in something even more pernicious; he ended up seeing a psychiatrist. Once again, Massamini seemed incapable of seeing the ideological underpinnings of the therapy that was gradually maneuvering him into a position where he would abandon the priesthood. Eventually Massamini would get a certificate in psychological counseling himself, but in the interim he would pour out his feelings to a psychiatrist, whose role in the matter seemed to be an enabler that would free him from the vows he had made to the Church.

In the meantime, he tried to deal with the way the Church had treated him as best he could. "I was silenced until further notice," he said giving his assessment of the situation at the time. "Give it a little bit of time, something like that," he thought, "So I cancelled a lot of speaking engagements." And after that he tried to make sense of what had happened to him. "I remember thinking at the time, 'Number one, I'm a priest, and I've been ordered to be quiet, so I'll obey. I'll be quiet. Number two, I asked for the reasons why this is happening and I haven't got any. And nobody's giving me any. And number three, I think you're dead wrong.' That was my understanding, and that was all I could say."

The turmoil at the seminary did not end with the departure of Fathers Massamini and Leahy. On September 20, 1966, at 11 PM, two priests and 11 seminarians were discovered celebrating mass in a storeroom next to the gym in the theology division. The two priest celebrants had been recently ordained and according to one account had just spent a marathon counseling session with the seminarians attempting to persuade them not to drop out in frustration at the slow pace of change at the seminary. In order to put a sort of sacramental seal of approval on the moment, the priests and seminarians spontaneously decided to celebrate a mass according to their own norms. At another time, the authorities might have looked on the gesture a bit more indulgently as a sign of youthful enthusiasm more than anything else, but the times were what they were, which is to say, extremely tense as a result of the walkout and the leaking of the student white paper to the *Bulletin*. By the same token, at another time, in a less tumultuous age, priests and seminarians probably would not have felt compelled to celebrate mass in a storeroom next to the gym. Because of the times, Krol was in no mood to view the situation indulgently. As the 1966 academic year began, seminaries throughout the world were shaken by the ecclesial equivalent of student revolt. The situation was serious enough to close seminaries in Barcelona, Spain, in Mariana, Brazil, and even at the North American College in Rome. At St. John's Seminary in Brighton, Massachusetts, the seminarians actually marched in protest in front of Cardinal Cushing's residence.

Krol was determined that the same thing was not going to happen in Philadelphia and reacted with alacrity; the two priests were sent off to a retreat house in what seemed to the lay group that was urging reform at the seminary an overreaction and a denial of due process to the priests involved. When the *Bulletin* refused to do a follow-up story on the illicit mass, ICTHUS (Interested Catholics to Help Upgrade the Seminary) took out an ad in that paper to keep the issue before the public eye. All of this was heady stuff for a diocese like Philadelphia, but Krol by his reaction gave evidence that he could not afford to either compromise or do nothing on an issue as vital to the health of the archdiocese as the seminary.

He also could not afford to pretend that nothing was wrong with the way the seminary was run either. On September 29, 1966, he arrived personally to announce the personnel changes that he made following the proposals advanced by the visitation team. Leahy and Massamini were out, but gone too was the seminary rector, Msgr. John P. Connery, D.D., P.A. The seminary's official historian was later to advance the proposition that Msgr. Connery died of a broken heart after having been relieved of his duties. Whatever the reason for Connery's death four years later, Krol seemed determined to pursue his own course at the seminary. It was clear that St. Charles was not going to get the *laissez faire* treatment that the area's Catholic colleges got. This was a battle that Krol could not afford to lose.

The turmoil at the seminary, however, did not abate as a result of the personnel changes. Five days after the new rector assumed office, he discovered two seminarians going through confidential student records. In addition to that, several students were also caught secretly taping a faculty meeting during which faculty members at the seminary discussed whether the students would be ordained or not. Because of the times, something that was probably burglary and certainly conduct unbecoming a priest got absorbed into the efforts of the liberals to modify the Church to a position more in keeping with that of the dominant culture. ICTHUS began calling for optional celibacy in addition to reform at the seminary. The liberals were trying to portray the break-in as a form of protest and then to use the unrest the incident generated to push for their own agenda. In order to clarify the situation, the chancery issued a statement on November 25, 1966, which was published in the diocesan newspaper.

"Any effort," the chancery statement concluded, "to sublimate the incidents or to involve other issues are neither honest nor in accord with the full truth."

The incidents which occurred during the fall of 1966 were in many respects a vindication of Leahy and Massamini's claims of innocence. The fact that the protest continued without them indicated that it was not simply a device of their own making. It was, instead, an expression of the times and of the ability of the media to disseminate the issues it wanted disseminated. People were seeing the same thing repeated from what seemed to be so many independent sources that the ideas took on a life of their own. The seminary revolts of 1966 also pointed up just how badly the Church in general and the seminaries in particular were in need of reform. The people who were the Church's future priests had reached the point—partially as the result of media manipulation, it must be admitted—where the rules they were to enforce made no sense to them. The most obvious shortcomings were then used by certain groups as the thin end of the wedge which would push for substantial changes in Church doctrine, things like the abolition of celibacy and the approval of contraception. In 1966, the sky was the limit, and rules that no one could defend any more were the tinder that fueled the revolutionaries' flames. It was clear that the Church had to remove this combustible material itself or suffer the greater and unforeseen consequences when it ignited as a result of the conflagration going on around it.

To say that everyone who got caught up into the fervor of the times was a revolutionary, or that they even understood what they were doing, would be to misread the times completely. Tony Massamini was, to a large extent, caught up in something which he did not understand. It is is difficult if not impossible to judge another's motives, but according to his own recounting of the story of those times, Tony Massamini kept asking the Church what he was doing wrong and never got an answer that made any sense to him. He, at least, felt that all he was doing was implementing what the Council told the Church to do. With any job of that magnitude there are bound to be differences of opinion, and when they occurred, as in the arguments he had with Krol, nothing seemed to get resolved. According to his own version of the story, Tony Massamini kept trying to do what he thought the Council wanted the Church to do and kept getting in trouble as a result, until finally he began to feel that he was part of the wrong Church.

When the revolution broke out in earnest in the Church, during the summer of 1968, when Pope Paul VI issued *Humanae Vitae*, Massamini in spite of his unpleasant experiences found that he could not sign on as a footsoldier. He remembers "being in touch in those days with Charlie Curran or Dan Maguire."

"One of those guys called me" to sign the protest against *Humanae Vitae*, but Massamini decided not to sign.

"One of those guys," Massamini related, "said to me: 'This is a question of authority.' And I said: 'I have no argument about who is in charge of the church.'" Massamini did not agree with *Humanae Vitae*, explaining in incoherent fashion that it was "a development of Platonic theology." But at the same time, "the South Philly kid," as he described himself, felt that "maybe the Pope had some kind of a spiritual insight of some sort, that I'm not getting."

Massamini, as a result, did not sign the protest against *Humanae Vitae*. "These guys are in charge," he said, broadening his notion of authority to include people like Krol. "We may not agree with them, but these guys are in charge. I'm not a bishop. I really believed all that. So I didn't sign it."

VIII
The Gate Opens from Within

On September 21, 1966, one day after the illicit mass at St. Charles Seminary in Philadelphia and just about two weeks before the break in there, an article appeared in the *National Catholic Reporter* about a 32-year old assistant professor at Catholic University who had some startling things to say about the moral law and what he claimed was the Church's changing attitude toward it. Father Charles E. Curran, the focus of the NCR story, predicted that "moral theology as now understood in seminary manuals will be gone within five years" to be replaced, he felt, by an ethics that was to be based on "the experience of the Christian people.'"

In the autobiographical account of his ultimately unsuccessful attempt to retain his position as a professor of moral theology at Catholic University, Curran mentioned that "the protocol number they assigned to me" was 48/66, the latter number referring to the year that the Vatican started compiling its dossier on him. The Vatican, however, was not the only group of people who were showing an interest in Father Curran's theories. Throughout the fall of 1966, the bishop trustees of Catholic University had been receiving a number of disquieting reports from a number of different sources, including sympathetic accounts in the NCR about what Father Curran was teaching in both his classes at Catholic U. and his lectures on the road. According to one report emanating from Oklahoma, Curran announced to a group of nuns there "now that we have covered the male semen, after the break we will enter the vagina." Curran's comment, according to the report, which landed in the hands of the bishops, elicited "much laughter and squeals from the 'religious' audience."

The bishop trustees in general and Archbishop Krol in particular were well aware that this was not the first time that someone had questioned Curran's orthodoxy. Indeed, the very fact that he was teaching at Catholic U. at all came about as a result of being asked to leave St. Bernard's, the diocesan seminary in Rochester, New York. In early 1965, Hugo Maria Kellner had complained about the sermons Curran was giving in a parish in Caledonia in the Rochester archdiocese, feeling that "the unrestrained language he used in his lecture, seems to indicate that Fr. Curran's imagination is unduly preoccupied with the sphere of sex." In both his 1976 and 1986 autobiographical accounts of his teaching, Curran likes to stress the scholarly nature of his lectures. The complaints arriving from other people at the time, however, indicated a certain prurience, a certain undue preoccupation with details which were seen as inappropriate for a priest in such circumstances. Beyond that, the complainers felt that Curran was clearly contradicting Church teaching, and Curran's account of what he believed in both *Commonweal* in late 1964 and the *NCR* in 1966 gave every indication that there was a prima facie case against him.

According to his own account of his early intellectual development, Curran was a priest whose situation was not unlike that of Tony Massamini and Bill Leahy. In his 1986 autobiography, he describes himself as "the intelligent, dutiful and unquestioning seminarian" and as "a typical product of United States Roman Catholicism of the pre-Vatican II times" (Curran, p. 4). Curran was ordained in 1958 and then sent to Rome to study moral theology so that he could return and teach that subject at the seminary in Rochester.

Like Massamini, and Leahy, Curran seems to have been bowled over by his experience of the Church's system of higher education in Rome. Going to Rome was to prove both a seductive and demoralizing experience for many Americans of this generation. The American seminarians of this period went to Rome thinking that they were going to the heart of the Church only to be exposed to the corrosive theories of one or the other professors whose teaching was at odds with the Catholic faith. Like Tony Massamini, Curran was exposed to Bernard Lonergan's course in dogmatic theology. Like Massamini, Curran probably heard Lonergan's famous statement that it was a good thing that the Church wasn't a fire department because it always arrived late and out of breath. The sense that the Church was hopelessly outdated was the main if not the only impression Massamini retained from Lonergan's course.

Because he was studying moral theology, Curran made the acquaintance of Joseph Fuchs, S.J. and Bernard Haering, C.SS.P., both of whom would prove influential in reorienting Curran's thinking away from moral absolutes and toward a system which he described euphemistically in the September 1966 *NCR* article as "somewhat 'situationist.'" Curran is effusive in his praise of Haering in the 1986 autobiography—probably because Haering had just accompanied him to his hearings in front of Cardinal Ratzinger—but somewhat dismissive in the 1976 autobiography, where one gets the impression that the teacher benefited more from association with the student than the other way around. Curran claims that he helped set up Haering's first theology course in Buffalo in 1962, but "as the 1960s moved on and the post-conciliar period of the Church opened, I was somewhat disappointed to realize that Haering's publications were no longer breaking new ground in a systematic way." Ten years later, though, Curran called Haering's three volume work, *The Law of Christ*, "a new approach to moral theology" that "broke away from the format and approach of the traditional manuals of moral theology." Curran claimed that he found both Haering and Joseph Fuchs " intellectually stimulating and spiritually inspiring" and laid the credit (or blame) for the development of his own theology at their feet.

However, even in his own account of his intellectual development, Curran gives some indication that he was not as naive as Leahy and Massamini—nor, for that matter, as naive as he portrays himself in his own autobiographies. There was a slyness to Curran that even his own self-serving account of his struggles fails to camouflage. One of the people he met during the early '60s was a Redemptorist priest by the name of Francis X. Murphy. Father Murphy would go on to become famous, under the *nom de plume* of Xavier Rynne, as probably the most famous chronicler of Vatican II. Curran as the American naif was both scandalized and intrigued by the Vatican gossip he was hearing from Rynne—scandalized in the sense that his faith in the intellectual and decision making machinery of the Church was shaken, but also intrigued about how this type of manipulation might have a beneficial effect on his own career. In order to make what Murphy must have recognized as Curran's already subversive theology palatable to the seminary authorities in Rochester, Murphy suggested that Curran begin by teaching his courses in Latin. The ruse worked like a charm. The students couldn't understand Latin, and so Curran "relented" after a few days and switched to English, but by then he had established his impeccably "traditionalist" credentials, and could teach pretty much whatever he wanted after that, no matter how subversive.

No matter how much Curran attempts to portray himself as the American naif in Rome, a certain calculating slyness intrudes. Unlike many of his contemporaries, Curran would prove adept at manipulating the forces that were sweeping through the Church at the time to serve his own ends. Curran announced the change in his position on the liceity of contraception in December of 1964, in the midst of the ongoing series of conferences at Notre Dame sponsored by the Ford and Rockefeller foundations aimed at changing the Church's teaching on contraception. His transition from St. Bernard's Seminary to Catholic University took place over the summer of 1965, the time of the Gruening Hearings, in the immediate wake of *Griswold v. Connecticut*, and in the aftermath of the Notre Dame conference which finally went public with its call for the Church to change its teaching. Since Curran's field of expertise at the time had to do with contraception, he would have had to have been particularly obtuse to miss what was going on, and as his conversation with Xavier Rynne showed, Curran was anything but obtuse when it came to manipulating public opinion in his favor. Curran's genius lay in his ability to harness the forces which wanted a change in the Church's teaching on contraception to his own benefit. In 1965, he was a young man just barely out of graduate school; by 1968, he was the undisputed leader of dissent in this country. Like Lenin, his genius lay in his ability to act on an unstable historical situation and mobilize the forces of revolution. In 1967, he saw a window of historic opportunity and knew that it would not last forever. In his 1976 memoir, Curran stressed the historical contingency surrounding the strike at Catholic U. that followed his denial of tenure. By implication he also stressed his own astuteness in marshalling the forces of the moment, and the fact that those historical forces would not be available to be marshalled forever.

"The timing was fortunate," he wrote referring to the strike,

> —who wants to picket in the middle of winter? Or who wants to go on strike the week before final examinations are to begin? In my judgment, all those facts would never again come together to make possible a strike by the entire university community. For one thing, after ten years on the same campus and having been scarred in many battles, I am sure that I could never get the type of unanimous support which I obtained at that time. Such are the contingencies of history.

Curran was, of course, righter than he knew at the time. In 1986, when he finally was dismissed from his position at Catholic University, there was hardly a whimper of protest from the students. The only people who complained were the professional theologians, but that was understandable simply from the point of view of their own self-interest. If Rome could do such things to Curran, it could do such things to his peers as well.

In the summer of 1965, in the deliberations surrounding the Gruening Hearings, Curran's name was nowhere to be seen. It was people like Dexter Hanley, S.J. and other Jesuits at Georgetown who carried the banner of the Catholic accomodationists on contraception. That he could leap to such a position of prominence on the matter within a period of three short years bespoke first of all, the power of the forces within society and the Church which were longing for a change in the Church's position on contraception and secondly, Curran's ability to manipulate these forces for his own ends. Curran acted with a decisiveness which left the bishops dumfounded. In a sense, the American bishops were never his equal in the fight and it would take Rome, and someone of the stature of Cardinal Ratzinger to bring him to bay some 20 years after the dossier on him began to be assembled.

Curran would prove to be a master at manipulating the press, something that is no small accomplishment in a cultural war. And of course a major part of the manipulation was his *persona* as the boyish, slightly abstracted professor who was dragged reluctantly from the ivory tower to defend academic freedom from the predations of Catholic bishops. "On the lecture platform," the *NCR* informed its readers in the famous September 1966 article, "the tall slender priest is a mixture of the boyish and the classroom manner."

The *New York Times* account of the 1967 strike would make much of the fact that he drove a Falcon without a muffler: "one of the worst looking cars on campus," readers were told. As if that weren't sign enough that the priest in question was one of the good guys, the *Times* informed its readers that "in the confessional, [Curran] has told women to bake their husband's favorite cake as a penance." In keeping with the age, "the students call" this "eminently approachable" professor "Charlie." In fact many agree that he is "one of the greatest Christians on campus," being not only "dynamic and tense" but "extremely considerate" as well. By the end of the *New York Times* account, it was hard not to see the halo of secular sanctity hovering over his head. In another article published around the same time, ("Father Curran: Symbol of the bishops' problem," *NCR* 4/26/67), the *NCR* gave some indication of the preferential treatment Curran was receiving from the press. "Admirers," the *NCR* reported,

> spoke of him as one of the brightest young American theologians around, but discouraged publicity about his talks. "Take it easy on Charley; we need him," was the response of one priest asked by a newsman for tapes of some Curran talks.

The glowing reports in the secular press, no matter how one-sided, (we never learned, for example, whether the muffler on Cardinal O'Boyle's car was in good repair or not, or whether many people considered him "one of the greatest Christians" in Washington, D.C.) did much to sway public opinion in favor of Curran's cause. The bishops who were privy to the growing dossier on Father Curran, however, with its reports about him entering the vagina after the break, took it as a sign that Curran was a dissembler who couldn't be trusted, and as the evidence mounted Archbishop Krol, as bishop trustee of Catholic University, began to formulate his strategy in dealing with Curran accordingly.

At the bishops' CU board meeting on October 20, 1966, Rector McDonald presented a detailed report on the case of Father Curran, recounting the main events in his short but already controversial career at Catholic University. According to McDonald, both Msgr. McAllister, CU's vice rector at the time, and Father Walter J. Schmitz, dean of the School of Theology, made it clear to Curran that complaints had been received about his teaching and that in light of those complaints, that he must be especially "careful to teach only orthodox views."

When McDonald brought up the subject of the *NCR* article on Curran which appeared that September, Curran claimed that his views were not accurately reported. When asked for his position on certain controversial subjects in his recently published book, *Christian Morality Today*, Curran became evasive. Instead of responding directly to the question, he informed his interlocutors that the book had an *imprimatur*. At the conclusion of the presentation, Archbishop O'Boyle asked McDonald to make clear to Father Curran that he was to make no further statements on birth control until the Holy Father had issued his paper on the subject.

In retrospect, the statement was fraught with irony. Curran did, of course, not stop disseminating views on contraception contrary to the teaching of the Church, but he did in a way wait for the pope. Within hours of the release of *Humanae Vitae*, Curran's dissent along with the signatures of the those who agreed with him was coursing through the country's mass communications network giving the impression that Catholics could disagree with their Church on matters of moral import. It would take the Church 20 years to catch up with Curran himself, and 25 years to deal formally with the issues he raised. Whether the Church ever corrects the misimpression he created during the summer of '68 in the minds of the faithful is still an open question.

On November 13, 1966, the board of trustees of the Catholic University of America met again, and the subject of Father Curran's future status at the university came up once more. After some discussion and following a motion made by Archbishop O'Boyle, "it was unanimously resolved," according to the minutes of the meeting "that a committee consisting of the

Most Reverend Rector, Archbishop Hannan and Archbishop Krol be formed, and it is hereby established to determine in whatever way the committee deems feasible, the exact views of Father Charles Curran, and to recommend appropriate action."

Acting on the former mandate was, as already indicated, more difficult than one would initially imagine. In addition to simply referring all questions about his views to the *imprimatur* on his book, Curran also claimed that he had been misrepresented in the *NCR* article. At this point, it is doubtful that any of the bishops believed him. To begin with, there was the significant fact that the book and the *NCR* article contained essentially the same views. There was, in other words, a good bit of corroborating evidence for what was in the *NCR* article. Beyond that, the *NCR* itself disputed Curran's claim that they had misrepresented his views. In the heat of the controversy, the *NCR* gave its version of the story behind the article in the September 1966 issue:

> When Father Curran was asked to cooperate in an article on his views in September of last year, he did so. The article—based on tapes of five of his talks at a theology institute in Shawness, Oklahoma, and on a telephone interview—was read to him before publication and he pronounced it fine, with a few minor changes.

Father Curran, in other words, was either lying to the *NCR* or to the bishop trustees of Catholic University. Either way, his agenda seemed to include something other than disinterested scholarship, and the bishops' committee formed to deal with his situation began to mull over the possibilities of how to deal with him in accord with what they could garner about his character.

On January 16, 1967, Rector McDonald received a letter from the Theology Faculty informing him that they were recommending that Father Curran be promoted to the rank of associate professor, which was the same thing as granting him tenure. According to the canons of American academe, a professor once granted tenure would no longer be subject to dismissal except for the gravest of reasons. No one knew precisely how the notion of academic tenure fitted in with the role which the bishop trustees played at Catholic University as guardians of the faith, and in light of the increasingly unfavorable impression Curran's writings were making on the bishops, no one wanted to find out.

On January 19, 1967, after reading Curran's book, Archbishop Hannan came to the conclusion that the views expressed in that book would disqualify Curran from holding a position at Catholic University. On March 17, Archbishop Krol, Bishop McDonald and Archbishop Hannan met to discuss Curran's situation once again. Most of their deliberations were based on his book *Christian Morality Today*, which, according to Krol, left "little doubt that Father Curran advocates some form of situationism." According to Krol, Curran "says as a confessor and guide he must continue to uphold the present teaching of the Church. But before he completes this section, he states: 'there are times when contraception might be necessary for an individual couple. I have counselled couples along these lines.'"

"Throughout the book," Krol continued, "Father Curran artfully jumps from one to a contrary position." Curran, in other words, could not be trusted to give an honest exposition of his beliefs.

As a result of this fact, Krol made a fateful decision. All three bishops agreed that certain propositions in Curran's book were contrary to Catholic teaching. In addition, Krol at least was convinced that Curran "artfully" attempted to disguise the true nature of his views. As a result of the first premise, all three bishops decided that Curran would have to go, but as a result of the second, they decided not to contest his orthodoxy. The episcopal committee concluded that Father Curran was not being honest with them, and as a result they decided to deal with him accordingly. "For these reasons," Krol wrote later, referring to Curran's artful dodging on doctrinal issues, "I recommended that we do not introduce the question of orthodoxy" in the matter of Curran's dismissal. In fact, from a legal point of view, Krol maintained that Curran was not being dismissed at all. His contract as a non-tenured assistant professor at the university would lapse on August 31. All that the university needed to do, Krol concluded, was to allow the contract to expire at the end of August. Curran was not being fired; his contract was simply not being renewed.

Krol took note of the fact that Curran strove to cultivate student and faculty "popularity," but he seems to have underestimated what Curran was cultivating simply by the term he used to express it. "Popularity" seemed to indicate a contest which a teenage girl might win for her senior yearbook. What Curran cultivated was concerted action among committed revolutionaries. This became apparent in a letter from a student at Catholic University which eventually became part of Curran's dossier circulating among the bishops and in Rome.

"Having been closely associated with Father Curran both as a friend and as a student," the student/priest began, "I can tell you that the situation is much more serious than is actually known." The priest informant made it clear that Curran, in spite of his protestations to the contrary, was "not in sympathy with Rome on many matters." Curran was an outspoken opponent of Church teaching both to colleagues and to students who would come to visit him after class. Since most of the students were either priests or religious, the multiplier effect was significant because Curran in effect was educating the Church's educators, just as he had been educated by Haering, Fuchs, "Xavier Rynne," and Lonergan during his stay in Rome. Curran, the priest/student continued, was "exceptionally vehement in attacking the Church's stand on birth control and especially so in relation to Cardinal Ottaviani, whom he referred to on my last visit with him as 'that old bastard of the Vatican.'"

According to the same informant, Curran was planning to widen his rebellion against the teaching of the Church once he got tenure. He had written several "lengthy articles" on birth control which he planned to publish once he was assured that the bishops could no longer threaten his position.

On April 10, 1967, the board of trustees at Catholic University met once again to discuss the Curran affair, this time to hear a report on a meeting of the special committee which was held on March 17. The special committee meeting was chaired by Archbishop Krol, and he gave the report at the April 10 meeting. Krol began by claiming that he was not questioning the orthodoxy of Curran's views, but he continued, somewhat undercutting what he had just said, that "the statements, writings and views of Father Curran in matters of moral theology are not clear but are open to serious question." Krol felt that during the two years in which Curran had been employed as a professor at Catholic U. that he had had ample opportunity to clarify his views, but had not done so. As a result his contract should be allowed to lapse and no new contract given. In the discussion that followed, the major issue was not whether Curran's contract should be renewed—virtually everyone agreed that it shouldn't—but rather whether the reasons for the bishops' action should be given to Father Curran and/or made public. Krol maintained that this was not necessary. Archbishop Hallinan, however, disagreed and continued to disagree throughout the discussion. Bishop McDonald, for his part, reminded the bishops that Curran had the unanimous recommendation of the Faculty of the School of Theology for promotion to the rank of associate professor and that the recommendation had been ratified by the academic senate and that disregarding these recommendations, especially when no reasons were given, "may result in serious Campus repercussions."

When it came to a vote, however, Krol's position held the day. On a motion of Archbishop Krol, seconded by Archbishop Cody, it was resolved that "the most Reverend Rector of the University inform Reverend Charles E. Curran that by formal action of the Board of Trustees of the University his appointment as member of the faculty will not be continued beyond August 31, 1967." The motion passed would have passed unanimously were it not for one dissenting vote. Archbishop Hallinan maintained his opposition to the "don't tell" strategy to the end. He voted against it, and when it passed over his objection he asked that his dissent be recorded in the minutes of the meeting. According to Hallinan, Father Curran "should be informed precisely of the reasons for this action."

"It was obvious that he was a controversial person—" Krol said summarizing his own feelings and those of a good number of the bishop trustees, and "that he came to the University because his own diocese found him troublesome." One of the bishops most reluctant to move on Curran was Rector McDonald, perhaps because it was he who would have to tell him face to face that his contract would not be renewed. Beyond that, McDonald was the one bishop most familiar with the situation since he was the bishop running the university. He was also the one bishop who seemed most impressed by the fact that the theology faculty and the academic senate had given their unconditional endorsement to Curran as a teacher. When the outcome of the vote was clear, McDonald indicated that since he was the one who would have to notify Curran, he would like explicit instructions on what he should say and do since he suspected that Curran might "react strongly." If it was an attempt to change the vote, and it seems to have been perceived that way by Archbishop O'Boyle, it failed. O'Boyle stated that McDonald should simply inform Curran that he was acting on a mandate of the bishop trustees, and that furthermore the bishops should be guided by what was right and not by fear of reaction. After Hallinan's dissent was duly noted, the bishops commissioned Rector McDonald to act on their behalf.

On Monday, April 17, 1967, Rector McDonald called Father Curran into his office and announced in presence of the executive officers of the university and Dean Schmitz that the board of trustees voted not to renew his contract. McDonald was quick to add, according to Curran, "that he was not speaking in his own name but as an agent for the board of trustees." No reasons were given for the action.

Curran's reaction to the announcement varies according to the source. According to his own account ten written years after the fact, he accepted the news calmly and left the room agreeing to keep the whole situation quiet for 24 hours. He even claims that he left the Rector's office and returned to teach an 11:00 AM class "as if nothing had happened."

Krol, however, received a different version of the meeting from McDonald, who called him on Monday, April 17, shortly after the meeting was terminated. According to McDonald, "Father Curran's reaction was strong" when he heard the news. Curran threatened to go public immediately and continued by saying that once the newspapers got the information "that he would open the way to a real storm," unless he got word by the following noon that the order had been rescinded. Curran was, in fact, so enraged that he informed McDonald that even if the order were rescinded, he could give no assurance that he would not disclose the matter to the newspapers. In response to

McDonald's report, Krol suggested that the university alert its public relations department and prepare a statement stating the facts of the case in advance. According to Krol, the statement should make the point that "there was no dismissal and there was no tenure—it was simply allowing a contract to lapse—and there was no charge of unorthodoxy or any question of academic freedom."

Krol seems not to have realized at the time that his strategy put the Catholic University trustees and the bishops in general into a situation where the only source of information on the case would be the dissenters. If the bishops had held their ground, the strategy might have worked, but the relentless pressure from the press followed by silence from the bishops and CU almost ensured that the bishops would not hold their ground. If there was no charge of unorthodoxy, people wanted to know, then why was Father Curran being relieved of his duties, especially since he had received the unanimous support of his academic peers? The university public relations department could issue a statement, but it is doubtful that anyone at the university, including Rector McDonald, could have defended the statement. By failing to charge Curran with unorthodoxy and proving their case, the bishops left themselves wide open to the charges, being levelled by Curran, that their actions were authoritarian and arbitrary and ultimately irrational. It looked as if the bishops were simply jealous of their prerogatives and this is exactly how the decision got portrayed in the press.

On Wednesday, April 19, Catholic University's students and faculty, with the exception of the school of religious education, voted to strike. At 10 A.M. after a story describing Curran's failure to get tenure appeared on the front page of the *Washington Post*, 2000 faculty and students assembled in front of the rector's quarters and listened to various faculty members move the crowd to urge the university to rescind the order. The demonstration was immediately subsumed into the *Zeitgeist*. Young and ostensibly downtrodden Catholics were demanding their rights from the bishops, just as the young black civil rights workers had done in the South earlier in the decade. In an AP article which appeared the next day, the reader was told that many of the demonstrators "joined in a rally in front of the administration building blocking traffic while singing folk songs readily identified with the civil rights demonstrations" (AP April 20, 1967, "Catholic U shut down by strike of Faculty until Priest is rehired").

On April 19, the day of the rally and strike, the School of Theology issued a statement "unanimously reaffirm[ing] our confidence in the professional competence and the doctrinal and personal integrity of our Colleague, Father Charles E. Curran, which was attested to by our unanimous recommendation on November 16, 1966." The School of Theology claimed that its "professional judgment and integrity " had been impugned by the action of the bishop trustees, especially since "no charges have been brought against Father Curran and no reasons have been given for this action of the Trustees."

When Father Curran issued his own statement on the same day, he harped on the same theme, claiming that "in the whole procedure I have never been given any specific charges." According to Curran, the bishops' action violated not only academic freedom, it also violated a *motu proprio* issued by Pope Paul VI. Curran claimed he "in no way" denied "the direction and guidance of the Church by the Bishops," something which he considered "absolutely necessary." Father Curran concluded by claiming, "I deeply regret the need to bring this matter to the public forum".

Deep regret was not the precise emotion which one priest remembers as uppermost in Curran's mind at the time. He remembers being contacted by Curran on both the 19th and 20th and asked "to meet with him and other friends of his who were formulating plans to act against his dismissal of the University. "

"At this meeting," the priest continued, "students from surrounding colleges and universities were called and asked to send delegations of students to help fill the ranks of those from Catholic University so that the action would have the appearance of being larger than it really was. In order to induce more students to participate it was agreed with the members of other departments, among them the History and Philosophy departments, to insure the students that they would not be required to take comprehensive exams or other final examinations if they would cooperate with the strike. I am a student of theology and when I expressed concern about my examinations he assured me that I would receive a high grade for my efforts to help him."

The priest wrote his letter to Krol out of frustration at seeing only the Curran side of the story being portrayed in the press. The issue went well beyond due process or academic freedom, the strategy which Curran used so effectively against the bishops. The priest informant was scandalized not only by an attempt to redefine Church teaching and the authority structure of the Church, he was also scandalized by the personal lives of the people who were involved in the lobbying for change.

"Father Curran," the priest continued,

> features greatly in the so-called "Action Masses" which are held here at the university. These masses are a mockery to the Church and are held under conditions which are anything but wholesome. They are frequently held jointly with Protestant Church Clergymen who are allowed to participate in the Holy Sacrifice of the Mass to the same degree as is the Catholic priest who allows them to he held. The aftermath of these services is usually that of over indulgence in liquor, etc.

Father never got around to specifying what the "etc." covered, but he did given a pretty clear indication that the revolutionaries were not being honest with the bishops, and that the bishops would do well to understand the extent of the conspiracy arrayed against them. When two of Curran's supporters were called to Archbishop O'Boyle's residence for questioning, they first met at the Marist house of studies on campus to coordinate their stories.

"They were aware," he continued, "of the fact that Father Curran was under investigation, and all agreed not to mention him in regards to these matters. They purposely kept from the Archbishop most of the vital information concerning the action masses. In fact they boasted on their return of having 'pulled the wool over his eyes.'" Part of this priest's frustration resulted from his inability to see anything but the official Curran line in the newspaper account of the strike, something which was directly related to Krol's strategy of refusing to explain why Curran's contract was not renewed.

By refusing to prove that Curran was unorthodox, the bishops played right into the anti-authoritarian bias of the press and the age in general. Krol's strategy ensured that the press would fan the flames to a white hot heat, and when things got that hot it was inevitable that one bishop or the other would break ranks, especially since they were in effect prohibited from explaining their actions. Everyone had been rendered so uncertain by the changes flowing from the Council, and more importantly, by the possibility that the Church actually might change its teaching on contraception, that a united front was impossible. Hallinan's demurral at at the meeting of the board of trustees was in this respect only the tip of the iceberg.

On Friday, April 21, an article appeared in the *New York Times* ("Catholic U. Board Polled on Priest by John D. Morrisan, *New York Times*, April 21 1967) which intimated that cracks were showing in the facade of episcopal opposition to Curran's position. Archbishop Paul J. Hallinan of Atlanta was represented, now not simply in opposition to Krol's don't-tell policy, but as opposing the firing altogether. The *Times* article had uncanny similarities to the article written by John Cogley which tried to undercut Bill Ball's testimony opposing government-funded contraception before the Gruening Committee. In the summer of '65, Cogley mentioned certain unnamed bishops questioning Ball's credentials as a way of implying that the bishops were divided on the issue of contraception. In the spring of '67, the *Times* went further in its divide and conquer approach by citing certain bishops by name, most notably Cardinal Cushing of Boston, who was quoted from an interview in the *Boston Pilot* as saying, "I would not condemn this man. He must teach all sides."

A perceptive observer would have recognized that Father Curran was hardly teaching all sides of the contraceptive issue, but Cardinal Cushing, who had not attended the CU board meetings, was not a perceptive observer. The reason he did not attend, he told Boston's Catholics, is because "I know nothing about running a university"—a lacuna which did not prevent him from criticizing those bishops who felt they had the duty to do just that. Cushing felt that the bishops should adopt a *laissez faire* attitude toward the university and let it be governed by professionals, i.e., people like the theology department.

"I am absolutely opposed," Cushing claimed, "to the method the trustees pursue in regard to the curriculum and professors. . . . It makes no sense to appoint people to a board who know nothing about running a university. "

Curran himself was acutely aware that the response of the bishops was crucial. When he became aware that Cardinal Dearden, the liberal prelate from Detroit, might issue a statement condemning his actions, Curran immediately proposed a 30-day truce. However, when it became apparent that the rumor was just that, and that other bishops were beginning to waver, he became emboldened to press his case. Curran was originally scheduled to meet with Krol and a delegation of bishops on Monday, April 26, but when the cracks in episcopal solidarity began to show and when the condemnation from Cardinal Dearden failed to materialize, Curran suddenly lost interest in the meeting.

On Monday, April 26, Krol called Hannan in New Orleans to find out if the meeting with Curran was still scheduled to take place only to find that Hannan was already in Washington and that a meeting was going on at that very moment, without his knowledge. Just why the other bishops of the committee felt obliged to exclude Krol from their deliberations is not clear. But Krol was shocked to hear about it and even more shocked when he got the gist of the deliberations that had gone on without him. Present at the meeting were Archbishop O'Boyle, ordinary of Washington, D.C. and *ex officio* president of the university, Archbishop Hannan, Rector McDonald and Father Schmitz of the theology department. When Krol finally got through to O'Boyle, the issue had already been decided. The bishops had decided to rescind the order getting rid of Father Curran.

"After talking with Archbishop O'Boyle and Archbishop Hannan," Krol related later,

> it appeared that they and Bishop McDonald felt that the decision of the Trustees had to be rescinded. At this point I repeated the argument that if the Board of Trustees was obliged to follow the recommendations of the Academic Senate, then it no longer had any authority; that if it could not even allow a contract of a professor who lacked tenure to lapse, then it was no longer a Board of Trustees. I also explained that in a brief meeting with

Cardinal Spellman and Archbishop Dearden on the previous Friday, there was a consensus of opinion that time was on the side of the University and of the Trustees. One of the reasons for this was that two of the priest friends of Father Curran had called the USCC offices alleging that Father Curran was worried and that if Archbishop Dearden would enter into the controversy on behalf of the Conference of Bishops, Father Curran was willing to declare a thirty day truce or moratorium. Nevertheless, it was clear that those attending the meeting in Washington felt there was no alternative. It was the lesser of two evils. I again said that I believed that the greater evil would be to yield, since it would only invite a constant flow of similar problems. Nevertheless, I agreed that I would not take any exception to the decision of the majority and I would not express public dissent.

Two days later, on April 26, 1967, Rector William J. McDonald called a press conference to announce that the bishops had not only rescinded their action, they had also promoted Father Curran to the rank of associate professor with tenure. One day previous to the rector's announcement, Archbishop O'Boyle issued a statement of his own in the course of which he attempted to "emphasize that the present action must not be interpreted as in any way affecting the theological issues injected by the news media. In particular, this decision in no way derogates from the teachings of the Church and statements by the popes and bishops on birth control. As with every appointment to a teaching position in Catholic schools, statements in the field of doctrine are subject finally to the teaching authority of the Church."

In terms of hollow gestures, Archbishop O'Boyle's statement was the perfect foil to Father Curran's claim that he was not disputing the teaching authority of the bishops. In the narrowest sense of the term, the teaching authority of the bishops would be contested one year later, when the same people who organized the strike at Catholic University would organize the opposition to *Humanae Vitae*, the Church's encyclical reiterating its opposition to contraception. In the Spring of '67 what the Bishops lost was their control over their universities. The first to go was Catholic University. What Archbishop Krol said was essentially true. If the bishop trustees could not override the recommendation of the faculty senate, then they no longer were in control of the university which billed itself as a pontifical institution.

Seeing his opportunity, Father Theodore Hesburgh, president of the University of Notre Dame, a non-pontifically chartered Catholic university, promptly assembled a number of other Catholic university presidents at a retreat house in Wisconsin owned by the priests of the Holy Cross in July of 1967 and pushed through his "Land o' Lakes" statement, which effectively severed universities run by religious orders from the control of the Church. Twenty-five years after the fact, Cardinal Krol, the canon lawyer, would call Hesburgh's move "alienation of Church property," the ecclesial equivalent of an indictable offense. But by then he was too old to do anything about it, and at the time, he was too preoccupied with other more pressing matters. Krol, however much he acquiesced with the decision rescinding Curran's termination in order to preserve episcopal solidarity on the matter, never wavered in his belief that the Church had made one costly mistake in backing down in the Curran case.

In the short run, however, Krol seemed more interested in repairing fences with the fellow bishops involved rather than claiming some sort of vindication. Two weeks after the decision to rescind, Krol wrote to O'Boyle on May 5, 1967, apologizing for "my seeming intransigence."

> In the present disturbance it was my deep conviction that the decision of the Trustees had to be upheld. There was principle at stake: the principle of the right of decision by the Trustees. They cannot be bound by the recommendations of the Faculty or even of the Academic Senate. In this case the professor had not tenure. If they lacked authority to allow the contract to lapse, then they simply lacked authority. I was also convinced that yielding would only encourage a repetition of demands of every type, shape and form. I was also afraid that yielding would encourage similar tactics in other Catholic institutions; and for that reason I was reluctant to agree with the majority that yielding was the lesser of two evils. However, since this was the judgment of yourself, of Archbishop Hannan and Bishop McDonald, I assured them I would not express my dissent in any public fashion at all.

> I regretted that my seeming intransigence was a source of added annoyance to you. While I still have great reservations about the solution of the problem, I have no reservations about Your Excellency's total dedication and total efforts in behalf of the University.

One week later, Krol was still convinced that his position was right. Krol was convinced that the the board would regret having backed down, but he was also still defending the more contestable proposition, that it was neither necessary nor advisable for the bishops to give reasons for their actions.

"Father Curran," Krol continued, "was not being accused of unorthodoxy; he was not being fired or dismissed; he had no tenure; this was merely a matter of allowing his services to lapse-without renewal. Since he had no claim or right to employment by the university, there was no need to offer any explanations to him."

From a legal point of view, Krol was undoubtedly right, but his strategy could only succeed if the bishops remained firmly behind him, something they proved incapable of doing. Knowing how the bishops were going to react was either the matter for a crystal ball or a prudent exercise in counting the cost, depending on one's point of view. But the don't-explain strategy was an unmitigated disaster from the point of view of public relations because it left the defenders of the faith with nothing to say. The strategy showed a clear preference for the role of bishop as an administrator according to the tenets of canon law rather than that of the bishops as primary teacher in their respective dioceses and at the institutions they ran.

In a post mortem written two weeks after the bishops rescinded their decision, Archbishop Hannan wrote to Archbishop O'Boyle claiming that Krol felt compelled to take the "don't explain" position "as a result of his contacts with priests in the Archdiocese of Philadelphia." Because of his experience with Father Daniel Maguire, a priest of the Archdiocese of Philadelphia who was Curran's right hand man in organizing the rebellion at Catholic U., Krol was convinced that Curran was looking for controversy, and that a public dispute over his beliefs would play right into the hands of the dissenters. Krol, according to Hannan's assessment, felt that controversy of this sort was to be avoided at all costs, and Krol, "therefore, urged that he be dealt with in administrative manner simply by allowing his appointment to expire." Archbishop Krol, according to Hannan,

> was convinced that it was sufficient to state if asked, that Father Curran had failed to teach and write with clarity. We discussed

the lack of clarity in his writings. It should be noted that semantically he avoids a direct denial of some of the practices and teachings of the Church but manages to convey easily that he disapproves them. It was decided that the least controversial manner of handling the matter was simply to notify him that his appointment would not be renewed.

In this respect, Archbishop Hallinan, in spite of how he was portrayed as a Curran supporter in the *New York Times*, advocated a middle position. He quite definitely supported Curran's termination, but he also proposed informing Father Curran of the reasons his contract was not being renewed. Those reasons, if rejected by Father Curran, then could have been passed on to the public at large, and the bishops could have defended them to the best of their ability and thereby have prevented defections from their own ranks. Even if that were not the case, it is difficult to see how any defense, no matter how poorly prosecuted, would have been worse than no defense at all, followed by the sort of supine capitulation entailed in promoting the man who had gone out of his way to undermine the bishops' authority. In their handling of the Curran case, the bishops showed themselves first as underhanded, then intellectually feckless, then vacillating, then weak, a course of action that was bound to embolden the bishops' adversaries into feeling that the only way one could deal with them was by calling their bluff and forcing the issue. Once the revolutionaries got what they wanted they showed no sign of resting on their laurels. They quickly set about securing various strategic positions in the university, to insure that the bishops' wouldn't attempt the same thing twice. They also set out to punish those who had dared to cross them.

On April 26, 1967, on the same day that Rector McDonald claimed that he was "happy" to announce that Father Curran had just been promoted to the position of associate professor with tenure, the victorious faculty revolutionaries announced that they were going to "press additional demands for academic freedom after the university's backdown that ended a five-day campus boycott."

"The immediate battle is won," one faculty member told the *New York Times*, "but the war is still far from over. What we must do now is prevent a recurrence of this"("Catholic U Faculty To Press Demands for a Wider Role," *NYT*, April 26, 1967, p. 16C).

What "this" meant, of course, was the purging of anyone who didn't support the campus strike. The first order of business was the elimination of any counter-revolutionary elements from campus, which is to say, anyone who felt that the bishops and not the theologians had the final say when it came to expounding Catholic doctrine. One of the first people to feel the wrath of the revolutionaries was Msgr. Eugene Kevane, then head of the newly formed School of Education. During 1965 Kevane had been instrumental in upgrading the department of education at Catholic University to the point where it became a school in its own right. Then when the bishops moved against Curran and the faculty voted to strike, the School of Education had stood alone in opposing the action.

For Msgr. Kevane, opposition to the strike was a matter of principle. On April 20, four days before the bishops capitulated to Father Curran's demands, Kevane and the School of Education passed a resolution in support of the bishops, claiming "the embodiment of knowledge and wisdom on religious matters is not to be found in the group of scholars and specialists in the sacred sciences, but rather in the successors of the Apostles." The CU School of Theology reacted with outrage, claiming that the School of Education statement implied "serious deficiency on the part of the School of Theology. In context these statements are nothing short of libelous." According to William Ryan, who filed an account of the dispute for National Catholic News Service on May 20, Msgr. Kevane "believes that loyalty to the bishops, who make up the majority of the university's board of trustees, is more important than other aspects of the dispute." Three days before, the School of Theology passed a unanimous resolution claiming that it had been libeled by Msgr. Kevane, who was instrumental in persuading School of Education faculty members to continue teaching during the strike out of "loyalty to the Holy See and to the United States Bishops' Conference."

Msgr. Kevane was to learn that loyalty to the pope and bishops would exact a high price. The same bishops who capitulated to Father Curran would show no stomach for supporting the people who had supported them when a campaign was mounted to bring about Kevane's ouster from the university. Kevane also waged the campaign the bishops declined to wage by claiming that Curran's teachings were unorthodox. Kevane in this regard would be vindicated almost 20 years later when Rome would say the same thing. But by then, Kevane was no longer teaching at Catholic University. In the aftermath following Curran's victory over the bishops, the revolutionaries at Catholic University turned on Kevane as a traitor to his class and gave him the dubious distinction of becoming the revolution's first victim. Academic freedom was now defined as the revolutionaries saw fit. It included the right of people like Father Curran to dissent from the Church's position on sexual morality, but it did not include any right on Msgr. Kevane's part to dissent from the dissenters. When Kevane accused Curran of doctrinal deviations, the theologians, according to Ryan's already-mentioned account, were "not able to be equally indulgent to Msgr. Kevane."

On May 17, 1967 Msgr. Kevane wrote to Archbishop Krol to enlist his help. As one of their first actions after the Curran debacle, the faculty revolutionaries had gotten a Rev. Thomas J. Taylor appointed to fill Kevane's still-occupied post. Taylor, Kevane complained to Krol, "was neither elected by the Faculty of the School of Education nor appointed by its elected dean. Apparently he qualified in the eyes of the hidden managers of this list because he voted against me and the majority of my faculty in our recent refusal to strike in support of Father Curran." Kevane closed his letter to Krol by complaining of the "terror" that has taken over the university. Members of the School of Theology were afraid to say anything critical of the revolutionaries because their jobs were in jeopardy. "They would only talk freely," Kevane concluded, " if there were the privacy of a canonical visitation," hinting that something of that magnitude was appropriate to the crisis which had overtaken the university. Krol responded by saying that "the final chapter on the disturbance has not, in my judgment been written," but seemed reluctant to get involved in rescuing the School of Religious Education from the people who had just defeated him in the Curran case. Krol suggested instead that market forces might have the final word; "the people who have been contributing their nickels, dimes and quarters and dollars annually for the support of the University" might find themselves so appalled at what was happening there that they could no longer contribute. By 1970, Catholic University was, in fact, in the grip of a financial crisis, and Krol, the man to whom people inevitably turned when they needed money, showed little sympathy for the plight of the people who had sided with Father Curran. But that crisis was still in the future and it seems doubtful that Msgr. Kevane derived much consolation from so contingent an event when faced with a fight for his own survival at the university.

After a lull over the summer vacation, the campaign to remove Msgr. Kevane was reinaugurated in the fall with increased intensity. Throughout the period, both the administration and the bishop trustees received correspondence from members of the department of education in support of Kevane, but neither the bishops nor the administration seemed interested in pursuing any concerted course of action.

On October 16, 1967, two professors of the School of Education wrote to acting rector John P. Whalen stating that "it is no secret that tremendous opposition has been waged against Dean Eugene Kevane." Both professors stated explicitly in their letter that it was also no secret that Kevane was being punished for the stand the School of Education took in opposition to the Curran strike the previous Spring. Kevane was also singled out for punishment for his "unflinching allegiance to what is regarded as traditional Catholic thinking." The two professors were outraged at the call for Kevane's removal since "nobody accuses him of incompetence, immorality or abuse of any kind."

On October 10, 1967 Kevane was re-elected Dean of the School of Education in spite of "highly unethical and irregular procedures [that] were used to apparently intimidate certain faculty members prior to the election" (letter from Jose A. Baquero, professor of education, and Gabriel D. Ofiesh, to John P. Whalen, October 16, 1967). The professors were appealing to the administration and the bishops for help because "we are convinced . . . that there has been a concerted effort launched to wreck both the School of Education and the programs which Dean Kevane stands for and represents."

On November 6, Kevane wrote to Krol again, again trying to enlist his support. In spite of being reelected by his own school, Kevane's position still was not secure. "There are powerful organized forces here that are determined to set me aside," he told Krol.

> Personally I shall accept quietly whatever eventuates. . . . *Nihil sine episcopo.* But I believe that some of the larger issues of our time are involved. . . . .I have been almost "alone" here for some time,. and have to do everything in the face of an ongoing campaign of harassment and obstructionism. Realistically, I have to wonder whether I can continue to function academically in this atmosphere and under these conditions. The Catholic University of America no longer enjoys peace and freedom for academic research and education planning . . . . I do need therefore some sign of support and some effective clarification from the US bishops conference.

Kevane was in need of support, but he was far from alone. He enjoyed the support of a large number of people in the School of Education who were perplexed and bewildered by the actions of the administration and the bishops in ignoring the plight of their supporters among the CU faculty. On December 12, 1967, Sister Mary Verone, SND, a nun from Cleveland who was a colleague of Kevane's, wrote to Krol to enlist his support for Kevane in particular but also for the well-being of Catholic University in general, which she had served since 1939, and at the time of her letter, as director of elementary education. "Unless the hierarchy detects the insidious undercurrent of a group of five or six ambitious priests," she wrote, "the School of Education will collapse." In addition to support from colleagues, students from the School of Education had written to acting Rector Whalen in support of Msgr. Kevane, but without any effect.

In a letter to the Most Rev. Clarence E. Elwell, episcopal vicar for Education, of the Archdiocese of Cleveland, copies of which were sent to Krol, Verone went into the situation in still greater detail. Msgr. Kevane, according to this account, "is literally enduring a persecution and a martyrdom" at the hands of a "clique of ambitious priests who are positively intolerable." Sister Verone emphasized the fact that the people out to get Kevane were priests, the laymen in the school being with one or two exceptions on Kevane's side. The priest conspirators were attempting to discredit Kevane by disrupting as much as possible the functioning of the School of Education. This entailed disrupting department meetings with repeated arguing and questioning and the referring of points to Robert's Rules of Order to see if the motions in question could be made. It also included stalling meetings so that the projected topics for doctoral dissertations could not be discussed. It was hoped that when the graduate students found that their topics had not been approved, they would become disgruntled and hold the delay against Kevane. The laymen, with one or two exceptions, were siding with Monsignor Kevane, but with little effect. "We are sick and tired of their conniving," said Verone in reference to the clique of priests.

In addition to disrupting faculty meetings and holding the students' dissertations hostage to their delaying tactics, the clique of priests threatened faculty members with reprisals if they voted for Kevane in the upcoming election. Sister Verone herself got a call from a Father Duffy, a new faculty member, who "got as far as the third sentence when I told him in no uncertain terms that he was calling the wrong woman." In her letter to Krol and Ellwell, Verone characterized the tactics as "below human dignity, not only communistic in their tendency to undermine authority, but diabolical. The devil has a hand in stirring up this unrest."

Virtually all of the letters pouring into the bishops' after Curran's coup at Catholic University stressed the irony of the situation. The people who complained loudest about due process and academic freedom in the Curran case were the same people who were denying it to people like Msgr. Kevane. The fact that Kevane could demonstrate the overwhelming approval and support of his colleagues in the School of Education, the fact that he won election to his post by these peers was all swept aside as irrelevant to the one fact which counted: he had supported the bishops and opposed the strike. The clique of priests described by Sister Verone simply refused to accept the fact that Kevane had been re-elected to his post, and beyond that gave the impression that the administration was on its side in this matter. One young priest from Youngstown, who according to Sister Verone should have been one of Kevane's supporters in the matter, told her that: "No matter how it turns out, the new rector will not appoint Msgr. Kevane." This incident involving

the persecution of Msgr. Kevane, and the bishops unwillingness to become involved in rectifying the situation at the university they were charged by the Church to govern led her to
conclude that "this University is sick."

"When you find your people losing their faith," she continued, "sisters going home from here who refuse to teach Original Sin and Eternal Punishment, and priests who question the
Real Presence, it is frightening." Msgr. Kevane "stands as a
solid teacher of truth," but "unless we get strong support from
the Cardinals and Bishops the university is going to collapse."

Bishop Ellwell echoed the urgency of Sister Verone's letter
in his response to Krol. "It would be a tragedy," he wrote three
days after Sister Verone wrote her letter, "if the Graduate School
of Education at Catholic University were to be wrecked or dis-
banded or placed in the hands of men inimical to the teachings
of the Church."

The Curranites, who seemed assured of a sympathetic hearing from acting rector Whalen, pursued the matter in the spring
semester of 1968. In November of 1967, the charges against
Kevane were taken seriously enough to establish a committee
of bishop trustees to look into them. On November 12, the
committee under the chairmanship of Cardinal Shehan decided
that "there is insufficient evidence to conclude that Msgr.
Kevane's administration as Dean of the School of Education has
been either inadequate or incompetent." But characteristically,
the bishops' committee, in spite of finding that the charges
against him were baseless, refused to endorse his continued
tenure in the position as well. Kevane was cleared of the charges
trumped up against him, but his job was no more secure than
before the committee held its deliberations.

On February 13, 1968, Acting Rector Whalen wrote a memo
to all the members of the board of Trustees recommending "an
immediate change of leadership" in the School of Religious
Education, even though Kevane had been reelected to his post
and had been found guilty of no wrong doing. To justify his
decision, Whalen claimed that "the faculty is clearly divided
into two groups with no strength of leadership in between."
Rather than side with the people at Catholic University who

supported them and the teaching of the Church, the bishops decided to attempt a compromise by getting rid of the man the revolutionaries found offensive and appointing someone inoffensive to both parties instead. In his memo of February 13, Whalen announced that he was appointing Rev. Aubert J. Clark, OFM Conv., as acting dean of the School of Education. The revolutionaries had won again, simply by being more outrageous and overreaching and unscrupulous than those they opposed.

Kevane took the decision philosophically. In a letter to Krol, written two weeks after the decision ousting him was handed down, he thanked Krol for his efforts in getting his name cleared. "The action of the board of trustees," he told Krol, "has saved my academic and professional standing, and I am grateful for it." Even though he had been replaced in the deanship by Acting Rector Whalen, Kevane concluded by saying that he owed Krol a "debt of gratitude." Krol responded by claiming that Kevane's response reflected on "the high calibre of your own priestly character." Sister Mary Verone, however, received the decision of the administration with considerably less equanimity, and characterized the resulting atmosphere at the School of Education as "an unsettled state of confusion."

On April 9, she wrote to Krol wondering what had happened. "Monsignor Kevane was found competent and adequate," she wrote, "so the rector replaced him. It just does not make sense." The group of priests who had been so diabolical in disrupting the functions of the School of Education had won out after all, in spite of the fact that the bishops themselves had decided that their charges were baseless. Why, she wondered, were the bishops so intent on collaborating with people who did "not want the bishops running this university."

"Once the strength of the bishops is removed ," she concluded, "they [the clique] will secularize it. That seems inevitable. We are more concerned than we can say."

The pattern established at Catholic University would spread throughout the Church, and it would continue for years. As might have been expected, the revolutionaries were not satisfied with their ouster of Msgr. Kevane either. Writing to Krol almost a year after he had been removed as dean, Kevane described the atmosphere on campus as "beyond description."

"A priest who is loyal to the Church," he continued, "must live in silence. Priests dominate the dining room who are loud and angry against the Holy See and the hierarchy in our country."

For the most part, the loyalists in the struggle found the position of the bishops impossible to defend as well as impossible to understand. However, a communique issued by Acting Rector Whalen issued in September of 1968, in the aftermath of both Kevane's ouster and the protest which Curran and his clique organized against *Humanae Vitae* sheds some light on his motivation in the case and, as a result, the motivation of the bishops who let him determine policy at CU.

"When I first learned of the statement of dissent," Whalen wrote to the bishops hoping evidently to reassure them that the situation was well in hand, "I realized that the problem was wider than the campus of this university, and my immediate fear was that there would be a hardening of sides on the issue and a cessation of discussion. I frankly feared that there was enough division manifest and sufficient emotional content in the two positions for a schism to occur."

Whalen's fear is evident enough in his statement. The administration of Catholic University had never experienced something like the Curran tenure strike or the protest over *Humanae Vitae* in its entire history, and both of these landmark events happened within a year of each other. The idea that a man who was a priest could also be a revolutionary was a concept which had never existed in the Church in the United States, and for a referent within the Catholic Church as a whole one would have to return to the outbreak of the Reformation in Germany. As a result, it is not surprising that the bishops and administrators at Catholic University were filled with both fear and perplexity. But the word schism connotes something else as well. First of all, it indicates the magnitude of the threat as Whalen perceived it. Whalen was evidently acting on the assumption that the revolutionaries at Catholic University represented a large segment of the Catholic Church in the United States and that that

segment was at the time willing to follow Curran and his colleagues out of the Church if they did not get their own way.
Both assumptions were of dubious validity. The dissenters were
never organized along the hierarchical lines of the group that
finally did go into schism, the Society of St. Pius X. It is difficult
to believe that the academy at the time spoke for anything other
than itself and the interests of its class, and perhaps most importantly, the interests of the cultural revolutionaries. The revolutionaries understood the interests of the dominant culture
quite well and acted accordingly. These groups included the
foundations, like Rockefeller's Population Council, which
wanted to legitimatize the use of contraceptives; they included
as well modernity's intellectual class—the publishing industry,
the film industry, academe, the media—who had converted to
the values of sexual liberation *en masse* during the course of the
century and had gradually colonized the nation's cultural institutions.

Catholicism was the last great roadblock to universal acceptance of the dionysian transvaluation of all values which this
class espoused, especially when it came to sexual mores, and as
Father Hesburgh discovered during the course of his association with the Rockefellers, the cultural revolutionaries were
willing to pay the fifth column within the Catholic Church
handsomely for giving the impression that the Church was
divided on the issue. Curran was simply an astute young late-
comer in a process of subversion which had been going on for
some time.

There were undoubtedly Catholic laymen whose businesses
would profit handsomely from a change in Church teaching—
Mr. Carney of Notre Dame comes immediately to mind. There
were, in addition to that, a significant number of Catholic intellectuals who felt embarrassed by the Church's refusal to go
along with the modern *Zeitgeist* on sexual issues, but by and
large the issue in the United States was analogous to what it
was in England and Germany during the Reformation. The
revolution was the creation of a clique of influentially placed
clerics who saw an opportunity of historic proportions and who
acted on that opportunity. To call what could have resulted
from it a schism, as Whalen did, shows more than anything
else, the fact that this particular academic was impressed by the

media circus the dissenters were able to evoke. What Whalen failed to see was that behind the media orchestrated events there was little more than more media orchestration. Curran was able at that moment in history to read the signs of the times and to mobilize those forces to his own benefit against a Church which was incapable of marshaling its forces because it was unable to perceive the type of threat that was arrayed against it. Father Curran was astute enough to recognize that all of the most influential forces in the country, from the Supreme Court on down, had decreed that the culture should be restructured without regard to its Christian heritage, and that the cutting edge of that restructuring was birth control. The courts were in the process of redefining those who believed what the Church held into the position of a tolerated minority with citizenship of a qualified sort.

When Curran pushed to the head of the line of dissenters in this country, the cultural revolutionaries came to his aid with a publicity campaign that gave people like Acting Rector Whalen the impression that millions of Catholics stood behind him ready to follow him out of the Church if the bishops pursued anything other than a policy of appeasement. The fact that a firm like Cravath, Moore and Swain, the firm whose liberal advocacy stretched from the days when William O. Douglas worked for them in the '30s to the defense of the homosexuals against the Ancient Order of Hibernians in the '90s battle over New York's St. Patrick's Day Parade, was willing to defend Curran *pro bono* only made it clearer that the power of the dominant culture stood behind Curran's efforts.

But there was a sense in which Acting Rector Whalen was correct in his choice of words. The policy of appeasement did result in a split. Catholic Academe split with the Catholic Church. In 1980 Rosemary Ruether, noted Catholic revolutionary, described the split 13 years after it happened as a *fait accompli* but in terms remarkably reminiscent of those Whalen used in appealing to the United States bishops in September of 1968. In an article which appeared in the winter 1980 issue of the *Journal of Ecumenical Studies*, Ruether described the status quo in Catholic academe at the time as "in effect, an internal schism." In an article remarkable for its frankness, she described what had happened in the Catholic Church not in the terms which Curran used when talking with bishops, but in the terms he used when lobbying for support among his priest student constituents at Catholic University as the man who created the cultural revolution's first major beachhead in the Catholic Church. "The lack of consensus in the Catholic church on basic theological and exegetical matters," according to Ruether, "has nothing to do with academic disagreement and cannot be resolved on that basis. Fundamentally, it is a schism between two magisteria, the magisterium of the professors and the magisterium of the pope and the hierarchy. It is a power struggle not an intellectual debate."

By the time Ruether wrote her article, the papacy of John Paul II was two years underway and showing signs of rolling back the gains the revolutionaries had won over the past 13 years. As a result, a clarity in strategic thinking was in order. The Revolution had to come up with a strategy which would safeguard its victories over the hierarchy. "This cannot be accomplished," Ruether continued, "by the academy itself. It entails the equivalent of the French Revolution in the Church, the deposing of a monarchical for a democratic constitution of the Church."

The strategy she proposes, however, is nothing new. It is virtually a repeat of the same strategy that succeeded for Curran a few years before, namely, by promoting "pluralism." As Msgr. Kevane found out, pluralism meant not what it claimed to mean, i.e., the toleration of differing points of view, one of which was hopefully the Catholic position. What it entailed in reality was the use of the organs of government and culture already colonized by the forces of sexual liberation against the hierarchical governance of the Church. These forces included both the media and the courts, as well as the increasingly intrusive bureaucratic management of education dominated by groups like the feminists, of whom Ruether was notable example.

"Pluralism," Ruether continued, explaining the revolutionary strategy against the Church which had proven so successful, "can be defended only by making sure that this hierarchical power structure is not strong enough to repress successfully the independent institutional bases of conciliar and liberation theology."

She then obligingly goes on to list the institutions within the Church which the revolutionaries have succeeded in colonizing. These are above all, "Catholic academic institutions," but they also include "Catholic faculties of theology at colleges and universities, seminaries (primarily order rather than diocesan seminaries), renewed religious orders, lay-run base communities, independent study and action centers and movements concerned with social justice, and the independent Catholic media." The reason these institutions can be characterized as independent is very simple. It is "primarily because the hierarchy has lost control" over them. Defense of the revolution means, in Ruether's terms, defense of the revolutionaries' hegemony over "these independent bases of Catholic thought and life."

> Catholics must learn to fight in new and more political ways to defend the freedom they have achieved. When the faculty of the Catholic University is threatened by the bishops with withdrawal of funds if they don't conform to a certain doctrinal line, one must do more than appeal to Church authority. One must demonstrate the large amount of funding of this university that comes from American governmental sources. One must threaten the possible loss of this American funding if investigation turns up serious violations of academic freedom.

"In short," Ruether concludes, "one must use the liberal institutions of the secular society against the illiberal practices of the monarchical church to limit the latter's power."

Four years later in June of 1984, Thomas Sheehan, a professor of philosophy at Loyola University in Chicago, caused a furor by saying pretty much the same thing in the *New York Review of Books*. "The dismantling of traditional Roman Catholic theology by Catholics themselves," Sheehan wrote, " is a *fait accompli*." More important for our purpose than the developments in exegesis which Sheehan claimed as the cause of this "revolution in the Church" is the extent to which "the liberal consensus" which subscribes to these views has colonized the Church's educational system. The people who "hold the chairs, get the grants, publish the books and define the limits of scientific exegesis and theology in the Catholic church today" are all at odds, according to Sheehan, with the teaching of the Catholic Church, and the event which led to this revolutionary state of affairs happened in a one year period at Catholic University beginning in the spring of 1967.

In the light of this zeal and determination on the part of Catholic revolutionaries, Acting Rector Whalen's assessment of the situation at Catholic University in the wake of the *Humanae Vitae* uprising seems ludicrously inadequate.

"I can tell you," he wrote in his September 1968 communique to the bishops, "that I sincerely believe that no harm will come to the faith of your seminarians and students who are enrolled here." If he felt there were such a danger, "I would do all in my power to close the University, and if I failed to do that, I would resign."

"Academic respectability," he continued, "is essential for a university if it is to serve the Church. . . . I often think that if we believe we have problems because we have an educational system, we should stop to think of the problems we would have without them. There can be no real conflict between our faith and the intellectual enterprise. We need a university as the forum in which seeming differences are reconciled."

Whalen saw his role as that of mediator, and as a result the revolutionaries were always assured of achieving half a loaf in any demand that they made. Whalen's acquiescence in the ouster of Msgr. Kevane was a good case in point. No matter how outrageous or baseless the demand, the administration was determined to meet the revolutionaries half way, and as a result, *de facto* control of the university fell into their hands, a fact attested to by both Ruether and Sheehan.

"Despite its occasional vagaries—theological or otherwise—" Whalen assured the bishops, "the University is in basic health as is evidenced by how well it has done this year even with inexperienced leadership."

In her book *The Desolate City*, Anne Muggeridge describes the promulgation of *Humanae Vitae* as the date on which the liberal revolution broke out into the open in the Catholic Church. "The appearance of *Humanae Vitae*," she wrote, "was, in fact, the turning point of the revolution, on the one side the throwing off of all the pretense of moderation and legitimate development, on the other hand the birth of counter-revolution."

> The release of *Humanae Vitae* on July 29, 1968, touched off the full
> public emergence of the present revolution in the Catholic
> Church. . . . *Humanae Vitae* is the touchstone of orthodoxy, just as
> it is the symbol of rebellion. The encyclical acted as the catalyst
> for the revolution because it identified with shattering clarity
> that the real subject matter of the struggle going on in the Church
> was the basic religious and political question of moral authority:
> Whose? If the Church's account of its authority was correct, then
> it would not find itself in a position in which it had to change a
> teaching consistently and authoritatively put forward since its
> foundation. If the Church were to accept a different account of
> authority, that of the autonomous and authoritative individual
> conscience, it would have to vacate its claim to have been di-
> vinely inspired and appointed to interpret both the Scriptures
> and the natural moral law.

On the evening of Sunday, July 28, 1968, Father Charles
Curran received word that the long-awaited encyclical on birth
control would be issued on the following day. He also claims to
have received a copy of the encyclical itself. In this regard he
was more fortunate than the bishops of the United States, who,
because of an unaccountable mishap concerning the diplomatic
mailpouch out of the Vatican did not receive their copies until
the end of the first week of August. Making use of a plane
reservation he had made for just this contingency, Curran flew
to Washington and organized his attempt to redefine not only
the Church's position on contraception, but the notion of who
possessed what sort of authority in the Church.

"Our quick, forceful response supported by so many theologians," he wrote in 1976, "accomplished its purpose. The day
after the encyclical was promulgated American Catholics could
read in their morning papers about their right to dissent and the
fact that Catholics could in theory and practice disagree with
the papal teaching and still be loyal Roman Catholics." Curran's
action, magnified by sympathetic media coverage, following so
closely on the heels of so many disorienting changes flowing
from Vatican II, in effect redefined the structure of authority in
the Catholic Church for many American Catholics. "The dispute over contraception," he continued, "would be paradigmatic of a growing pluralism in the Roman Catholic Church on
such issues as abortion, divorce, medical ethics, and some questions of sexuality. . . . The Church must learn that its unity is not

to be found in terms of absolute agreement on such specific moral teachings." Curran ratified the forces in the dominant culture which wanted to condone sexual liberation, and those forces rallied to his defense when the Church tried to discipline him. In the same memoir, Curran mentions "the generosity of the law firm of Cravath, Swaine, and Moore of New York" as one of the major deterrents to any effective action on the part of either Catholic U. or Archbishop O'Boyle in disciplining him.

But beyond that, the major thing Curran had working in his favor was the element of surprise. Not only did he act decisively before the bishops had received their copies of the document, he also acted from behind the *persona* of the loyal priest who claimed to be nothing more than a disinterested professor. Churchmen in general perceived neither *persona* as particularly threatening, and Curran strove to exploit that fact. That, coupled with a large amount of doctrinal insecurity on the part of bishops who were chosen for their administrative ability rather than their theological or intellectual acumen, guaranteed that the response to Father Curran would be divided and half-hearted. The bishops always seemed to harbor the hope that what they saw before their eyes wasn't really happening. And when Father Curran told them the very same thing, they seem to have accepted his version of the story with a sigh of relief. So eager were the bishops in this regard that they even issued a statement condoning dissent during the very same academic year in which the rebellion took place. It was a document which proved unworkable from the start and was eventually rescinded by Rome, if not *de jure* then by the simple fact that Curran's ouster from Catholic U. contradicted its letter as well as its spirit.

In their July 30, 1968 statement, Curran and the dissenters repudiated *Humanae Vitae* for a number of reasons, one of which was that the birth control encyclical "pays insufficient attention to the ethical import of modern science." Taken at face value the statement was preposterous; taken in the context of the times it meant that the dissenting theologians accepted the eugenic assumption of the people who claimed that the earth was in the grips of a population explosion. Paul Ehrlich's tract, *The Population Bomb*, appeared in the same year as *Humanae Vitae*, and is full of all sorts of dire predictions of mass starvation and exhaustion of natural resources, none of which came true. The pope evinced, according to the dissenters, "an almost total disregard for the dignity of millions of human beings brought into the world without the slightest possibility of being fed and educated decently." The dissenters likewise excoriated *Humanae Vitae* for its "unfounded assumptions about 'the evil consequences of methods of artificial birth control,'" virtually all of which have come true, including the fact that birth control led to abortion, which it was supposed to replace according to the conventional wisdom of the time.

"Therefore," the dissenters concluded, "as Roman Catholic theologians, conscious of our duty and limitations, we concluded that spouses may responsibly decide according to their conscience that artificial contraception in some circumstances is permissible and indeed necessary to preserve and foster the value and sacredness of marriage."

The mentioning of the "sacredness of marriage" in the same breath as artificial contraception was one of the most deeply held aspirations of the age—William O. Douglas had attempted the same thing in *Griswold v. Connecticut*—and about as chimerical as the population bomb, which never did go off. Contraception was supposed to improve marriage, according to the conventional wisdom of the time, and by the time it became apparent that it did not, the cultural revolutionaries were into different things. The critics of the dissenters who claimed that the severing the procreative and unitive aspects of sexuality would make marital intercourse no different than homosexual relations were hooted down with derision. By the time that prophecy came true and homosexuality was the *cause celebre* of the '90s, the proponents of contraception no longer considered homosexuality so bad. One by one, Paul VI's prophecies came true, and one by one the claims of the dissenters about the benefits of contraception went down the memory hole. Rev. Daniel Maguire, along with Father Curran, one the the architects of the rebellion, would eventually become an advocate of abortion, and would sample the sacredness of marriage himself with a former nun he met while hearing confessions at Catholic University—for a while at least. The marriage to the nun ended in divorce, but Maguire continued to teach theology at the Jesuit-run Marquette University in Milwaukee, where he achieved a modicum of fame as the house theologian for a number of proabortion groups, including Catholics for Free Choice, a front group which got its money from pharmaceutical firms which made contraceptives.

A little over two weeks after the dissenters issued their statement, Acting Rector Whalen, in his self-appointed role as mediator, arranged a meeting between the main dissenters and a delegation of Catholic bishops at the Statler Hilton Hotel in New York City on the evening of Sunday, August 18, 1968. As a result of the meeting a number of points became clear to Bishop Joseph Bernardin, who later wrote a memo which was circulated among the trustees of Catholic University. To begin with, Father Curran announced quite openly at the meeting that his purpose was precisely "to cause confusion and tension" among the Catholics of the United States. Father Curran, according to Bernardin's account, "said that such confusion and tension is necessary for proper growth and development within the Church."

Beyond that, Bernardin felt that

> the real issue at stake is the magisterium. The contraception problem is simply the occasion for bringing the much broader problem of the teaching authority of the Church, and specifically the Holy Father out into the open. All four bishops present, after listening to the discussion, concluded that the ecclesiology of the dissenters is, in fact, different from our traditional understanding of the Church, as updated and specifically set forth by Vatican II. When asked if their ecclesiology was new, some [of the dissenters] replied that it was, but they hastened to add that it was in line with Vatican II.

"It was Father Maguire," Bernardin noted, "who best articulated their position."

When, after hearing the dissenters present their case, Bishop John Wright of Pittsburgh opined that the theologians were arrogating to themselves a magisterial role which they did not possess, no one rushed to contradict him. With that matter out of the way, the question was raised of how to solve the present pastoral crisis. At this point Father Curran's teacher, the Rev. Bernard Haering, took the floor and articulated the dissenters' position on the matter. Since, he admitted, it was asking too much to expect the pope to rescind the encyclical, the bishops should side with the theologians. The crisis, in other words, would not be resolved unless and until the bishops took a stand which would allow for "theological pluralism."

Haering's suggestion evoked strenuous objection on the part of the non-dissenters present at the meeting. And at this point Bishop Bernardin made it clear to Haering that the bishops in conscience could not take this course of action. Then, the notion of ecclesial penalties was broached. At which point, Haering again took the floor and announced that if the bishops resorted to penalties, thousands of priests (as many as 20,000 he stated) and even sisters would go on strike immediately, and many people would leave the Church.

The bishops, who were not used to being talked to in such fashion by their own priests, much less their own theologians, much less theologians employed at a pontifical faculty in Rome, were taken aback by the threat. Bernardin records them as responding "by simply stating that these ideas would be conveyed to Archbishop Dearden and, through him, to the other Bishops."

> Regarding penalties, they assured the theologians that no bishop wants to use them. But what alternative, it was asked, does a Bishop have if, after much dialogue, a priest tells him that he intends to teach in a way which is contrary to the doctrine of the encyclical .

Curran in one of his memoirs would describe the meeting as "cordial." (With cordiality like this, who needs rancor?) One wonders how much more explicit the threats would have to get before cordiality suffered. But neither he nor Bernardin felt that anything got resolved. "The dissenters," according to Bernardin, "showed no willingness to move away from or to modify in any way the original position they had taken. " The best he can say about the fact that the meeting was held at all is that "no one can say now that the Bishops were unwilling to speak with the theologians."

In order to encourage this willingness, the ever-irenic Acting Rector Whalen arranged another meeting two days later, this time with Archbishop O'Boyle, chancellor of the university, at Caldwell Hall on the CU campus. The meeting is significant for our purposes because a stenographic transcript was made of the talks between the dissenters and the Chancellor. The tenor of the conversation gives a good indication of the strategy of the dissenters and the unwillingness of Archbishop O'Boyle to treat them as anything other than loyal—if somewhat misguided— members of the Catholic priesthood, whose theology was a bit beyond his ken, partially as a result of the changes emanating from Vatican II.

Father Curran began the discussion by emphasizing again "the fact of the responsible action taken on the part of the theologians who signed this statement."

"There can be no doubt whatsoever," he continued belaboring his own point, "about the orthodoxy and Catholic faith commitment of the people who have signed this particular statement. This statement involves no disrespect whatsoever for the Papal Office or hierarchical magisterium of the Catholic Church. The people who subscribed made that clear in their opening sentence. We believe our position is in total conformity with the document of Vatican II."

As a result Curran can "list authors who prove that dissent to such teachings of the authoritative magisterium of the Holy Father is possible by theologians, and even necessary at times."

Archbishop Krol, who received a copy of the transcript from the apostolic delegate, found Curran's claim about the necessity of dissent particularly amusing. When O'Boyle asked Curran for a citation proving his point, Curran responded by asking "Do you want Latin or English?" indicating that the lesson urged on him by Xavier Rynne had made a lasting impression. Whenever Curran's orthodoxy was being questioned, he felt a strong desire to speak in Latin.

When Archbishop O'Boyle replied, "You better use English," Father Curran indicated that "our position is in total conformity with orthodox Catholic teaching as enunciated in all the documents of the Roman Catholic church and as interpreted by respected theologians," a proposition he might have done better to articulate in Latin.

Perhaps feeling that Curran's statement needed some nuancing, Father Daniel Maguire joined the conversation by claiming that dissent "would not be problem for persons who are familiar with the history of Theology, especially for persons who are familiar with the role of universities, especially in the 13th, 14th, 15th Centuries; it would also, what we have done, not be a problem for those who are keeping abreast of the very subtle debate on the nature of religious assent, and the nature of dissent in the church. It is understandable that many would not be aware or up to date on the theology of the judisterium [sic]. Magisteriumogy is very immature at this time and underdeveloped."

When asked if he considered how his dissent might have an adverse effect on Catholic University's reputation, Rev. Carl Peter responded by saying that "it is not my business to worry about supporting the University."

Rev. Bernard Marthaler, who would later become a force in the catechetical movement in the United States "felt that for too long we theologians in a place like CU have been silent while journalists have been doing theology in the vacuum of our silence, and I felt that for that reason we had to speak out, and had to show that there was another view within the church. We are in a position to help explain what Christian Doctrine is, and that we help to make them understand what the magisterium is."

This in turn inspired Rev. Peter to expound on his own loyalty to the Holy See. "When I have a papal encyclical," he informed Archbishop O'Boyle, "I accept it as coming form the Pope, and I pay much more attention to it than I do other things that cross my desk."

"On the other hand," he continued perhaps feeling that he had gone too far in the direction of papalatry, "the pope even when speaking infallibly is involved in time and space and all the laws of time and space, and encyclicals need interpretation."

The Rev. Robert Hunt claimed that "to have remained silent, or simply to quote material blankly without adequate pastoral explanation—for us that would have been irresponsibility. A grave scandal and disedification would have been committed by the theological community had it not spoken loudly, clearly and publicly."

Rev. Russell Ruffino, of the department of philosophy, claimed to be motivated by "a concern for the Church, for the Office of the Holy Father and the bishops as the Church moves on its incarnate pilgrim way . . . and I speak as one who lived seven years in the shadow of the cupola of St. Peter's and felt a personal affection for the Holy Father."

Rev. Ruffino not only did not see the dissenters' statement as destructive, he saw it as "manifesting the vitality of the church, the vitality of this university, and if anyone, or any statement, would call into question these motives or this faith, speaking for myself, this would be the greatest pain that I could bear."

When Archbishop O'Boyle asked Sister Mary Charles Bryce if she had a comment she was so overcome by Father Ruffino's effusions that all she could add was that "I think Father Ruffino expressed my sentiments most clearly, more clearly than any other single person."

At this point Father Curran, who gave the impression that the meeting according to his understanding would be limited to the dissenting priests giving testimonies of their loyalty to the Holy See and the bishops, announced that "in my name and the name of the others I would like to express my gratitude for the Chancellor of the University for this opportunity he has given to us to expose our views in this particular period of time."

In other words, the meeting was over.

Acting Rector Whalen, the man who brought everyone together seemed relieved first of all that the dissenters were so effusively loyal and secondly that the meeting was almost over.

"One thing about this meeting that rejoices my heart," Whalen stated, "is the good spirit that has prevailed here that pleases me no end. And the second is that Religious Education and Theology are talking with each other on a substantial issue. I do think with a theological resource of this kind existing on the same campus, it should not be split."

One can imagine everyone gathering up their papers at this point, the brief case latches popping open and then shut again and in general smiles of congratulation on everyone's faces. But one person was not quite ready to conclude the meeting, and that person, unfortunately for the dissenters and Acting Rector Whalen, was Archbishop O'Boyle. Now that the professions of loyalty were out of the way, O'Boyle wanted the theologians to defend what they had written especially the two paragraphs beginning "It is common teaching in the Church. . . . "

It seemed like a reasonable enough request, but the theologians were dumbstruck by O'Boyle's effrontery in asking.

"This is hardly time for a serious, full, amply documented research paper," Father Hunt sniffed, "if you want the reasons for concurring, because the reasons are enormous for some quantitatively and qualitatively."

The issue, of course, was under what conditions it was licit to use contraceptives. The statutes of the university specified that a three bishop panel should be formed to judge whether what the theologians were espousing was congruent with Catholic teaching. The theologians would eventually have to defend themselves in front of the panel, and so O'Boyle was giving them the opportunity to begin by answering his questions then and there. The theologians, however, were in no mood to respond.

Father Hunt described the response to O'Boyle's request as "an enormous labor."

"I have commitments until the Tuesday after Labor Day," he continued, "and could not participate in that proposal." Beyond that, Hunt wanted to know "the title or basis on which that is being requested explained."

"Let me put it this way," O'Boyle responded, "these two paragraphs struck me as being very important. They could be addressed to me as Chancellor, as part of this meeting."

"Your eminence," Father Curran responded, "I would submit that I don't think I could do that because I think it goes beyond the bounds of the statutes themselves, and I see no grounds on which you can ask for this to be done. It seems to be against the statutes of the University." Father Curran, who was known for his opposition to legalism when it came to the

Church's position on contraception, seemed quite at home arguing legal technicalities with the chancellor of the university.

"Let this be part of the record," O'Boyle said, "I am not demanding, I am asking if it could be done."

"Then we will put into the record," Curran responded, "that it is acknowledged it is not in the statutes of university, and therefore there is no obligation on the part of the people to respond as such to this."

At this point Father Daniel Maguire claimed that "I would be in a difficult position if I were asked to judge the activities, say, of three bishops or more, and I am very uneasy about committing the existing three bishops to judging a theological explanation. Not that I am saying that bishops don't know theology . . . "

Maguire was, of course, saying just that. His inadvertent comment was corroboration of what Bishop Wright had claimed in the meeting two days before. The Magisterium was now in the hands of the theologians and not the bishops. But even it that were the case, the theologians were proving reluctant to give any justification for their own statement of dissent. The statement was proving to be a sort of the ukase from the new magisterium which could only be interpreted by the media. Taken out of that context, it was proving surprising lifeless even under the benign, common sense scrutiny directed at it by Archbishop O'Boyle.

The most Father Hunt was willing to concede was "that further amplification as theology and in the theological idiom, be given in the proper theological forum at this point, and if and when it appears a copy be sent to you."

"What do you mean by 'in the theological forum,'" O'Boyle wanted to know, "are you referring to a periodical or what?"

"Whatever would be the means that university professors would use to communicate to the educated laity of this country who would be interested in what university professors have to say," Hunt responded.

"Is this the feeling of all here?" O'Boyle asked.

"It is my feeling," Father Maguire chimed in.

By now the irenic glow had worn off the meeting. One can imagine large beads of perspiration forming on the forehead of Acting Rector Whalen. Everything was fine as long as the dissenters were allowed to confine themselves to protestations of loyalty to the Holy See. When they were asked to justify their position, they proved either unwilling or incapable of doing anything other than parrot what they had handed to the media.

By now O'Boyle was beginning to show annoyance.

"I think what I am asking is a very simple request," he continued, "and that is that if I had signed the document, I would certainly know what theologically lies behind these two paragraphs."

Father Hunt, however, was of another mind on the matter.

"Frankly, I think it is a very dangerous request. Respectfully, I say that, from the standpoint of a member of the academic community, as I am. It is dangerous, I think, when this is a relationship so clearly and beautifully established in this meeting between yourself as Chancellor, and ourselves as professors, when there is something not provided for and ambiguously justified. . .

"Look," O'Boyle responded, "you wrote, 'Therefore as Roman Catholic theologians. . . ' I would like to see the theological reasons for that statement."

"Would you accept then," Father Hunt wondered a little lamely, "sending you a bibliography which would elucidate the background of this?"

O'Boyle clearly had the theologians on the ropes, but at this point he made a fatal mistake. "If you send a bibliography," he added, perhaps out of humility, "—I will be frank—I have not the time, nor, I will admit, the competency to go through it."

This was just what the dissenters wanted to hear. It played right into their contention that they, because they had the advanced degrees and were academics, were the real magisterium and the bishops just a front for their prompting.

"Well," Hunt responded seizing the opportunity O'Boyle just handed him on a silver platter, "if you lack the competence to go through the theological presentation, then to what end would a personally written one be?"

The moment of opportunity for O'Boyle passed. The rest of the discussion was taken up with the professors saying how busy they were with much more important stuff than responding to the Chancellor's request. Fathers Peter and Marthaler announced that they "were going to the Midwest," where they would " find it extremely difficult to do anything before Labor Day because of the lack of libraries and so on. "

"Look," O'Boyle said, finally reaching the end of his patience, "just talking man to man, supposing I am a married man and I read this, and I meet you and I say, 'Father, you are one of the signatories of this document. Would you mind telling me in what circumstances artificial contraception can be used?'"

"I would ask you," Father Hunt responded by way of answer, "what your circumstances are. I feel that under that title I would not have to give a documented professional reckoning and rationale of it all. I would simply say that as a pastoral minister of the Sacrament of Penance, or in general pastoral ministry as in the Rectory parlor, I would respect your responsibly formed conclusions if you should follow this opinion. I don't think I would have to write a theological tract under those circumstances."

By this point it must have been apparent to the theologians that O'Boyle was honestly wondering if there were some theological justification for their claims. O'Boyle, however, continued to treat the dissenters as men of good will and continued to be frustrated by their evasiveness.

"I am no theologian," he responded at one point. "but I think you would have to go a little further and tell him how these are responsible conclusions."

The theologians, however, were in no mood to prove themselves to a mere bishop, even if he was chancellor of the university which employed them. The employment issue had been settled a little over a year ago when O'Boyle backed down in face of the strike. The best that father Curran can do is promise to send Archbishop O'Boyle a copy of his forthcoming book as soon as it is published. The meeting concluded at 1:20.

As Curran said, "the meeting achieved no tangible results."

"Velit Eminentia Tua Reverendissima," wrote Gabriel M. Card. Garrone, Prefect for Seminaries and University Studies in a cover letter to Cardinal Krol along with a transcript of the conversation cited above, *"hunc fasciculum nostri Commentarii libenter accipere, qui argumentum pertractata magni momenti pro instituione sacerdotali."*

On July 31, 1968, one day after Curran and the other theologians had issued their Statement of Dissent, Cardinal Krol issued a statement of his own in which he claimed that "the Church is not a mere echo of religious consciousness of the community, nor an expression of the opinions of the faithful." Krol traced the history of the commission examining the "extremely complex and delicate problem " which was the focus of the encyclical, an issue which "touches the sources of human life."

"At no time" he continued, "—certainly not during the interval of study—was there a vacuum in the official teaching of the Church. Pope Paul VI made it clear that the traditional teaching was not suppressed. It continued to be valid and binding." One detects here a large sigh of relief. As of the Gruening Hearings during the summer of 1965, Krol and Ball were forced to plan their strategy of opposition to government-funded birth control on the contingency that the Church might change its teaching. The fact that it didn't vindicated their efforts, if not their strategy. If the Church did not bend on birth control, in the face of virtually universal clamoring for its legitimization, then it was clear that the dissenters were wrong, and the bishops had a much clearer mandate in front of them.

"Others," Krol continued, "erroneously assumed that the study introduced a period of doubt about the validity of the doctrinal teaching." The encyclical proved them wrong, but beyond that, *Humanae Vitae* showed that

The truth cannot be distorted for the sake of secular relevancy to the values of the world or suitability to the temper of the times. To a society which insists on options in everything, but fears decisions—especially those which require fidelity and restrict spontaneity on behavior, the Church must echo Christ's words: "He who does not take up his cross and follow Me is not worthy of Me" (Matt. 10,38).

On the day after he made his public statement of support for *Humanae Vitae*, Cardinal Krol sent a cablegram to Pope Paul VI informing him that "we offer thanks to God for His guidance and to Your Holiness for the courage and wisdom of the Encyclical to which we respond with enthusiastic devotion." Krol, however, was not the only one with reason to be happy. On the day before he made his public statement, he received a telegram from Bill Ball, who announced that "His Holiness's encyclical makes me 'feel like a Catholic again.'" Ball also had words of praise for Krol and his leadership of the Pennsylvania bishops: "In what you called the 'final outcome of the battle,' those reactionary, antediluvian, non-progressive Pennsylvania Ordinaries, led by yourself, suddenly stand forth, on a pinnacle, in the sunlight."

On August 9, ten days after the dissenters had issued their statement, Cardinal Krol received a copy of the encyclical itself along with a note of apology from Bishop Bernardin, who explained that the delay was "due to an oversight of some kind on the part of the airline responsible for transmitting the diplomatic pouch." As a result the documents didn't reach the apostolic delegation in Washington until August 8.

Krol, however, had received his copy of the encyclical two weeks before it appeared at the specific behest of Paul VI. In a cover letter accompanying the document, Amleto Cardinal Cicognani wrote to say that "his holiness strongly recommended that I draw your attention to the importance and to the necessity of a concerted effort on the part of the entire Catholic episcopate, in order that the doctrine it contains be explained with care and in full to the Christian people. "

According to Cicognani, the pope after years of agonized deliberation had concluded that the greatest service he could render to the Church in particular and mankind in general was to "re-propose in all its purity. . . the constant teaching of the Church, for, seeking only the true good of man and of the family, she gives the problem in question its only true and profound solution."

The Holy Father, according to Cicognani, was well aware of "the bitterness that this reply may cause many unmarried persons who were expecting a different solution for their difficulties." He is, therefore, more dependent than ever on "his brothers, the bishops of the Catholic world, asking them to stand beside him more firmly than ever in this circumstance and to help present this delicate point of the Church's teaching to the Christian people." The pope wanted to be sure that "no ambiguity exists among the faithful or in public opinion concerning the Church's position in this serious matter."

What Tony Massamini construed as Krol's dual personality could be construed in another light as the personality of a man who was always willing to conform his personal desires and preferences to the will of the Church. Cardinal Krol was in many ways hostage to the complexity of the situations he found himself in. When his subordinates misread the situation, he often times followed their recommendations with unhappy results. When the mind of the Church was not clear on a particular situation, Krol did not flourish either as a thinker or as an administrator. However, with the issuance of *Humanae Vitae*, this was no longer the case with regard to the Church's position on contraception. Rome had spoken; the case was finished, and Cardinal Krol was going to do whatever was within his power to respond to the Pope's call for assistance.

By Tuesday, July 30, 87 theologians, many of whom were teaching at Catholic University, had signed the statement of dissent. On August 5, at a regional meeting of the United States Catholic Conference, the post-Vatican II successor of the National Catholic Welfare Conference, was convened in Washington to discuss the responsibility of the bishops and the board of trustees in handling the matter. Eventually, Catholic University would come up with no better response to the *Humanae Vitae* crisis than they had in the Curran tenure battle. The best the university could muster was a statement by Acting Rector Whalen's successor, Carroll Hochwalt that "those members of the faculty of the Catholic University who recently signed with others a statement of dissent from the teachings of the pope in his encyclical *Humanae Vitae* do not speak for the university."

The bishops evidently had something more forceful in mind. As a result, an episcopal delegation comprised of Cardinals O'Boyle of Washington, Cody of Chicago, McIntyre of Los Angeles, and Krol of Philadelphia, (Cardinal Shehan of Baltimore backed out at the last minute because of the intensity of dissent in his own archdiocese) resolved to meet with the pope himself to discuss the encyclical and their response. And so when the delegation was assured of an audience on August 13, they packed their bags. Eventually the "secret" visit would end up in the newspapers ("4 U. S. Prelates make Secret Visit to Pope," *NYT* News Service 8/15/68) as an attempt to deal with the situation at Catholic University as well as the theological misrepresentations of conscience being disseminated by the dissenters.

Shortly after their arrival in Rome, the American cardinals were informed that there was to be a preliminary meeting with Cardinal Cicognani on August 12 at 5:30 PM. At that conference, it was made clear that the delegation did not officially represent the hierarchy in the United States. Why this was necessary would become apparent in the light of subsequent developments, particularly when the bishop trustees of Catholic University refused to endorse any action against Curran or any of the other dissenters employed there.

Bishop John Wright, who was Prefect of the Congregation for Higher Education at the time, then addressed the delegation concerning the specific problems the American bishops faced. Wright emphasized that the issue of birth control was only a vehicle for challenging the authority of the magisterium and that the real issue was who speaks for the Church, the bishops or the theologians? Wright then conferred on the plan the delegation had developed to deal with the dissenters. During the meeting it became immediately clear to Cardinal Krol that the Vatican was convinced that the bishops had no choice but to proceed to discipline the dissenters and that the Vatican would in no way consider these proceedings an embarrassment.

"Because of the immediately clear reaction and assurance," Krol wrote later, "and partially because in England and Canada there were reported instances of suspension of priests, the American delegation was satisfied that we can and should proceed as planned [disciplining the theologians] and that it would be better if the delegation did not meet with his Holiness—to preclude any suspicion or suggestion that the Bishops here would be acting under order rather than in compliance with their own pastoral responsibility."

Cardinal Krol eventually did meet with the pope on that trip, but not as the representative of any delegation. Since Cardinal McIntyre was the senior member of the delegation it was agreed that he should meet with the pope, but then it was also agreed that Cardinal Krol should meet with him as well. After Cardinal McIntyre left the audience, Krol later wrote,

> I was alone with His Holiness, who took great pains to show me of his deep appreciation of our concern, of our analysis of the nub of the problem and our plans to face it. He respected our desire to meet the responsibilities of our office independent of any specific directions or guidance from him. However, he said he could not assume the role of a bystander and that he wanted to make it clear that he was available not only to strengthen and support the bishops, but also to take any active part that might be indicated at whatever cost to him. He urged that we preach, teach, talk and write in order to balance or counterbalance the articulate, highly vociferous voices of the minority; that we make special appeals and approaches to our priests and that we do everything possible to help families.

Krol was later to characterize the "total impact of the meeting" as "encouraging and gratifying." It was clear that the pope was willing to accept martyrdom for the truth, no matter how much the age raged against him; it was also clear that the delegation had its work cut out for them fulfilling the pope's mandate in the face of such a divided episcopate, but rather than be daunted by his own personal feelings on the matter Krol ended his analysis in a way that was as anticlimactic, as it was business-like and typical of the man he was. "On the 14th," he concluded his summary of the meeting, "I was back in Philadelphia at 5:15 pm."

IX
The Conservative Reaction

O n May 28, 1967, Archbishop Krol received word from Egidio Vagnozzi, the Apostolic Delegate to the United States, that Pope Paul VI planned to elevate him to the College of Cardinals at the next consistory. Coming as it did, precisely one month after the Curran tenure debacle, the appointment could be taken either as an indication that the Vatican approved of Krol's failed attempt to discipline Father Curran and their way of sending a message to the less stalwart American bishops, or as an indication that Rome had no idea what was going on in the United States. Given the amount of correspondence between Krol and Vagnozzi on the Curran affair and good relations that existed between Krol and Vagnozzi's predecessor, Amleto Cardinal Cicognani, who was now back in Rome, the former seems the more likely possibility.

Krol received his red hat along with 26 other prelates, among whom was Archbishop O'Boyle of Washington. If in rewarding both Krol and O'Boyle, the Vatican intended to send a message to the American hierarchy, it was a message of some nuance, and one which Pope Paul VI must have formulated in light of his own situation, as he watched the Church beginning to shake apart as a result of the imbalances introduced into its engines in the wake of Vatican II. "No one is perfect," Rome seemed to be saying, "but the man who perseveres to the end will receive a red hat." Rome was not going to second-guess the strategies of the American bishops. No one could be guaranteed of success in a situation as grave and fluid as the one which now faced the Church. If success were measured by the ability to persuade every recalcitrant sinner of the error of his ways, certainly Paul VI was a failure, but in that regard so was Jesus Christ. If success were to be measured by the ability to formulate a winning strategy in dealing with an overwhelmingly hostile culture, then, in the short run at least, St. Peter was a failure as well. But in spite of the fact that Krol's strategy of no explanations in the Curran tenure battle had backfired because the bishops refused to hold the line, Krol had shown Rome that he was able to recognize a challenge to the authority of the Church when he saw it and to act on it to the best of his ability.

But even if Rome had decided to reward intentions more than performance, a difficult situation remained. Within the period of little over a year, Father Curran had not only risen from relative obscurity to a position of leadership among the dissenters in the Church, he had also split the Church in the United States into two mutually hostile camps by his bold and decisive action on the part of the cultural revolutionaries. As a result of Curran's victory over the trustees in the tenure battle, followed by Theodore Hesburgh's Land o' Lakes statement, followed by Curran's successful defiance of the Church on *Humanae Vitae*, the Catholic wing of the cultural revolution succeeded in capturing Catholic academe.

Curran's actions established a liberal beachhead in the Church from which the revolutionaries could proselytize for liberal ideals while using the resources of the Church to do so. Since the institutions the liberals captured were for the most part educational institutions, the liberal victory was bound to cause an equally violent reaction, not for the most part from the bishops, who were more often than not befuddled by what was happening around them, and not from the bishops' clerical staffs, who were often sympathetic to the revolutionaries' cause, but from the parents of the children who were exposed to what the liberal revolutionaries were teaching at institutions which still called themselves Catholic.

Father Curran's action split the Church into liberal and conservative factions, a division which would characterize its existence throughout the post-Conciliar period. Curran's rebellion first of all brought the revolutionaries out in the open in the institutions they controlled, but it also galvanized the conservatives who felt that as a result of the rebellion, Vatican II had shown its true colors. Many conservatives also felt that the bishops had forfeited their position of leadership in the Church as well.

In June of 1967, in the same month that Krol received his cardinal's hat and ring from Pope Paul VI, the newly-founded counter-revolutionary journal, *Triumph* magazine, delivered a blistering attack on the bishops' mishandling of the Curran tenure affair entitled "Collapse at Catholic U." *Triumph* grew out of an aggressively anti-Modernist group which wanted, among other things, to restore the monarchy in Spain. In this, they were eventually more successful than in other endeavors. The magazine, edited by Brent Bozell, brother-in-law of conservative pundit William F. Buckley, took its aggressively anti-Modernist, anti-Americanist line for the nine years of its existence, and eventually succumbed to a combination of insufficient funds, personal illness and direct action assaults on abortion clinics that were either prophetic of the the later Operatior Rescue or misguided kamikaze attacks, depending on one's point of view.

"Collapse at Catholic U." is significant for a number of reasons, but most significantly because it sets the tone of virtually all of the conservative counter-revolutionary crusades which would follow by finding two villains in the affair: first of all, Vatican II and secondly, the bishops. With a few notable exceptions—Catholics United for the Faith springs to mind— this would be the metaphysics of counter-revolution for the next 25 years, and this approach, coupled with a nostalgia for the Tridentine Mass, would all but guarantee that the conservatives would never integrate into anything bigger than a political faction which the bishops would invariably view with suspicion.

Triumph began its critique by indicating, with not a little irony, that out of the Curran debacle, they could discern "some signs of hope." "Could it be," they continued letting the other shoe drop, "that the revolution in the Church, officially launched by Vatican II, has at last begun to reveal for human eyes a divine purpose?"

Throughout the post-conciliar period, the conservatives showed themselves incapable of a coherent reading of the Council. The definitive text for the conservatives became Divine Word Father Ralph Wiltgen's *The Rhine Flows into the Tiber*, which intimated, without any recognition of the theological problems that this position entailed, that the Council had been "hijacked" by its Germanophone delegates. Archbishop Marcel Lefebvre would eventually follow this position to its logical conclusion somewhere outside the Church when he consecrated four bishops in 1988, thereby taking his Society of St. Pius X into schism. Other conservative groups would struggle with variations on the same theme, but none of them could come up with a plausible explanation of how the Church—and by implication the Holy Spirit—had erred by convoking the Council. Beyond that, the same groups were plagued by the "if it ain't broke, don't fix it mentality" with regard to the Church, an attitude which overlooked the shortcomings of the papacy of Pius XII which grew worse with the passage of time. By the time Anne Roche Muggeridge wrote her book describing the revolution that hit the Church following Vatican II, she could write without a trace of irony that "there had been no weakness or tremor in Pius XII's strong papacy" (Muggeridge, p. 70).

This attitude was in large measure the result of the difference between America and Europe. The maxim "if it ain't broke, don't fix it" also became more compelling in direct proportion to the amount of time which passed since the time of Pius XII and also to the amount of disruption which followed in the wake of Vatican II. The conservatives were on the whole incapable of seeing that the revolution was in large degree the result of the situation which arose during the post-war period of Pius XII's papacy, when the Church showed itself incapable of dealing with the defection of its own intellectuals in its own institutions, throughout Europe but in Rome as well. The experience of young priests like Charles Curran and Tony Massamini and Bill Leahy could only go on for so long before some effect was felt, and Vatican II was, in the eyes of people like Cardinal Ottaviani, a preemptive strike against just those positions. That the Council and, more importantly, the Council's aftermath turned out differently than Ottaviani expected is a fact of history. That things might have turned out worse is a matter for speculation, but Cardinal Ottaviani's successor, Joseph Cardinal Ratzinger, raised precisely that point as a way of defending the Council's achievements 20 years after its conclusion.

By the late '60s, the conservatives were plagued by a "blame the victim" attitude with regard to the Council. The Council was held responsible for what it hoped to cure in an orgy of *post hoc ergo propter hoc* thinking that to a large extent prevented the laity from linking up with the bishops who were working for the same ends. The Curran rebellion not only brought the revolution out in the open by putting academe into the hands of the revolutionaries, it also caused the conservatives to lose faith in the bishops in a way that would play right into the revolutionaries' hands.

"Charles Curran and his message," *Triumph* opined, "presented a striking case of the disruptive and rebellious influences that have plagued the Church since the Vatican Council and that during the past year especially have called down increasingly urgent remonstrances from the Holy See. . . . . Curran was doing a demolition job on the whole body of the moral law by arguing that the concept of an objective moral order had outlived its usefulness and must henceforth be subordinated to considerations of 'conscience' and 'the situation.'"

The gravamen of the *Triumph* critique, however, falls on how the bishops handled the case at Catholic University. The bishops were faulted for being unaware of the magnitude of the forces arrayed against them and for backing down when the reaction was stronger than they had anticipated. Once the bishops backed down at their own university, it was inevitable that the rebellion would spread to Catholic universities and colleges not directly under their control, and by mid-summer Hesburgh's Land O' Lakes declaration of independence would prove them right. "If heresy could not be be effectively combatted at [Catholic University]," *Triumph* wondered, "which operated under the direct administrative control of the corporate American Church, where could it be combatted?"

The bishops, in other words, "could have shut it down themselves" rather than let the students and faculty do it for them. But there was another alternative as well. "The other alternative was to take to the public forum, and teach. It might not have worked, but, curiously, it was not even tried."

"Not once," the argument in *Triumph* continued,

> did the bishops undertake to explain their position—why they had felt obliged to do what they had done. Not one of the bishops stepped forward to tell the country. . . that the teaching authority of the Church was at stake, and that the removal of Fr.

Curran had been a necessary step in asserting and defending that authority. . . . Against this background, the silence of the bishops seemed to mean only one thing: they had been caught *in flagrante* in a pre-Vatican II witch-hunt about which (they now felt) the less said the better.

The conclusion to be drawn from all this was clear. "The American bishops," *Triumph* opined,

> are simply not equipped to deal with the menace confronting them. They do not know how to fight because their unique talents, talents for which they were made bishops, fit them to administer a huge financial and economic empire rather than minister to the spiritual needs of a church.

As a result, the bishops, according to *Triumph*, should "turn over the administration of the diocese to laymen" and concentrate on their role as teachers. There was an element of truth in what *Triumph* said, but their critique in many ways simply exacerbated the problem. The reason the bishops delegated their teaching role so readily was because they had been as unsettled by the changes emanating from Vatican II as everyone else, and in many respects felt inadequate to the task of proposing a public defense of the faith which might have been in the process of changing. This was especially true of the Church's position on contraception, which wasn't reaffirmed until one year after the Curran tenure battle. Instead of providing the bishops with a critique that would arm them against the dissenters, the conservatives spent their time urging them into the breach without weapons, a prospect no one finds congenial. The bishops, who had been weakened by the defection of their own intellectual troops, were now being urged into battle against the defectors with virtually no intellectual or cultural weapons at all in a battle they never felt comfortable engaging in the first place. Beyond that, the revolutionaries were for the most part priests, and the bishops by and large found it incomprehensible that they should do battle with people who they had been raised as viewing on their own side, nay, even more than that, their peers and their own spiritual children.

Beyond that, in the not too distant memory of every Philadelphia ordinary at least, stood the specter of lay trusteeship and the lessons the hierarchy had learned from that battle. Here were the conservative defenders of the faith urging the creation of what seemed like a Church without bishops, which struck the hierarchy, and in this they had the recently minted documents of Vatican II to back them up, as a car without wheels. The *Triumph* article was in this regard a particularly inauspicious beginning in a relationship that only got worse as time went on. The bishops were naturally more inclined to trust their own priests before they would trust laymen, and as the attacks from the right grew more strident, the bishops tended to follow their natural inclinations rather than figure out what was bugging the conservative laity. When the conservatives sensed this reversion to natural inclination, they oftentimes increased the intensity of the attack, resulting in what, without too much exaggeration, might be termed a vicious circle. The more alienated the conservative laity became as a result of the revolutionaries extending power through the Church's educational system, the more vocally the conservatives called upon the bishops to correct the situation. And the more vocal their complaints, the less likely the bishop was to lend a sympathetic ear to what they said, and the more he was inclined to take the side of the dissenters, or at least to view them with more sympathy than they deserved.

Coupled with this misreading of the bishops, the conservatives were involved in a similar misreading of the apparatus of cultural revolution, most notably the courts and the media. As with Operation Rescue some 20 years later, there was a point of view in some circles that the conservatives could simply imitate the power politics that the revolutionaries had used so effectively. The conservatives could "go public," and the bishops would react to the pressure. The strategy never worked because the conservatives never understood that the revolution was not procedural, as the revolutionaries liked to portray it. It was content-based. The separation of Church and state was a myth created by people like Leo Pfeffer to implement the liberal world view in general and a sexually liberated society in particular. Cravath, Swaine, and Moore, to give just one example, was not going to come to the aid of a conservative group wishing to block sex education simply out of love of judicial procedure. As a result, the conservatives' attempts to fight fire with fire invariably failed. The revolution was not about procedure, legal or otherwise; it was result-oriented and the main result the revolutionaries strove to achieve was sexual. Using the courts to fight sexual liberation was a bit like using Beelzebub to cast out devils. It was a lesson the conservatives would have to learn the hard way.

The Curran debacle meant that the split in the Catholic Church between liberals and conservatives, which would characterize it during the entire post-Conciliar period, was out in the open and that both sides felt that there was little point in softening their respective positions. Just as the conservatives were becoming more vocal in telling the bishops how to run the Church, the liberals were throwing off all caution in saying that they and not the bishops were in charge, at least in charge of certain critical areas like liturgy and catechesis.

For John Krol, the revolution and the red hat arrived simultaneously. The applause had hardly died down from a formal dinner which the city held in his honor at Convention Hall on July 6, 1967 when an article appeared in *Philadelphia Magazine*, the local organ of what would later come to be termed yuppie culture, criticizing Krol's six-year tenure in Philadelphia.

"It has not been officially announced," *Philadelphia* announced in its breathless way, "but the Roman Catholic Church is no longer the Church that it was" (Bernard McCormick, "The Troubled See: The Church is being renewed here, as elsewhere, and it is a time of painful uncertainty," *Philadelphia Magazine* 1967, pp. 52ff). *Philadelphia*, which was aimed at an upscale audience whose views were in keeping with the dominant national liberal culture, spent a good deal of time patronizing the city whose name it bore on its masthead as a hopeless backwater. (One often got the impression that the really successful could only demonstrate that fact by moving to New York, which seemed to be a curious marketing strategy for a regional magazine, but it evidently struck some sort of chord with *Philadelphia* readers.)

Conservative Philadelphia, i.e., the bad Philadelphia against which the magazine crusaded in its pages, was not the Main Line, nor was it Chestnut Hill. Bad Philadelphia was the Philadelphia of the neighborhoods, which was another way of saying Catholic Philadelphia. Many of the writers for the magazine were Catholics of the upwardly mobile sort, who were willing to use their writing as an indication of how far they had come from their benighted childhoods.

By the '60s, the genre had become widespread in style sections across the country. Anna Quindlen, at a later date, would refine the local-Catholic-makes-good-by-arriving-in-New-York-and-adopting-the-mores-of-the-upwardly-mobile *persona* in her columns in the *New York Times*. During the '60s, people like this were characterized as "thinking Catholics," thinking being generally defined as congruity with the worldview of the *New York Times*. Evidence of disruption in the neighborhoods as well as evidence of disruption in the Catholic school system was taken as a sign of hope for liberals like Leo Pfeffer but also for Catholics whose past associations were a hindrance to upward mobility. By the late '60s, the disruption of neighborhood life in Philadelphia caused by the liberal regime's manipulation of racial migration was beginning to take its toll, and it was difficult not to detect a note of *Schadenfreude* in the account in *Philadelphia Magazine*.

"The Catholic world," readers were told,

> has been hit with a torrent of theological speculation and pressure for change. . . and the people in the parishes, nourished on a religion whose salient characteristic was unchanging truth, suddenly find the flood of renewal dislodging their old familiar rocks. . . . . The blacks and whites of basic dogma are rapidly turning gray. The deeds and misdeeds that made the difference between eternal happiness with God in heaven or fire unending in hell are no longer poles apart. . . . Unchanging truth is changing. . . . Confusion reigns. In Philadelphia the confusion is greater than in most places. . . . Philadelphia Catholics may be the most thoroughly indoctrinated Catholics in the whole wide world. Certainly they are the most indoctrinated Catholics in the United states.

Not surprisingly, one of the areas in which *Philadelphia Magazine* applauds change most vigorously is in the area of sexual morality. Liberal culture had always found this the chief sticking point in its relations with the Church, and when the cultural assault on the Church's sexual teaching began to find adherents in places of significance in the archdiocese, *Philadelphia Magazine* was there to egg them on. "The Catholic Church's obsession with sexual sin as the chief propellant to Hell," readers were told, " is being replaced by a set of moral values which urges Catholics to stay cool on sex and transfer the force of their consciences to all human relationships, many of which take priority over sex."

Also not surprisingly, race was used as the counterweight to transvalue traditional sexual morality. Unlike the liberal Catholics praised in the pages of *Philadelphia Magazine*, "the considerably larger body of traditional Catholics . . . are hard-pressed to see a relation between the Ten Commandments and Negro Blockbusters." Dennis Clark is quoted as saying, "Let's face it. This is a conservative town," and is cited as one of the liberal new breed, the type of Catholic who attacks the archdiocese, but is "decidedly comfortable with God."

Liberal Catholics, we are told, "have already made their religion a matter of personal conscience. Confident that theirs is the Catholic Church of the future, they are mostly unworried about such matters as the Church's stand on birth control. . . . They feel that involvement is the definition of the modern Church, and they are often active in civil rights work and the peace effort."

Once again *Philadelphia* made clear the role that race played in overthrowing sexual morality. "Already," the reporter continued, "there are kids out there who are learning that an act of racial hatred is a more serious matter than a little dark street dallying with one's girl friend, provided one has deep feelings for one's girl friend. In this respect some Philadelphia high schools are considerably more progressive than the diocesan seminary."

Caught in the middle was John Cardinal Krol, whose unenviable task was "guiding a deeply traditional Diocese though the uncertain period of renewal." Krol's task, according to *Philadelphia*, "is to implement the spirit of Vatican II without destroying the solidarity of the Archdiocese," and that "is a seemingly impossible job." As would become customary in articles of this sort, Cardinal Krol was portrayed as the conservative who "probably would have been just as happy had there never been a Vatican Council." The author of the article had the impression that Krol was not really answering his questions when he tried to pin the newly named cardinal down on his view of the revolutionary changes that were taking place in the Church in Philadelphia. The seminary crisis was followed by the Curran tenure battle, which in turn was followed by the catechetical crisis in the Archdiocese. Each in its way was the result of the Second Vatican Council. In each instance, a group had appointed itself the authentic interpreter of the Council, and was corroborated as such by the media, whose values were in many ways the same as the group they anointed. The real challenge which the *Philadelphia Magazine* article brought to the fore was the challenge of the catechists in the archdiocese. If Cardinal Krol had been too busy before to notice—and in many respects this was precisely the case—*Philadelphia Magazine* was determined to bring to his attention "one of the most significant things happening right under his nose," namely ,the revolution in catechesis, particularly on the high school level.

According to *Philadelphia*,

> the humanistic theological approach, which shifts the emphasis from man-to-God to man-to-man—an approach the Cardinal calls a "distortion"—is already being strongly felt in the catechetical instruction in at least two high schools in the Archdiocese and to a lesser extent in practically all of them. The two schools using the new catechetics are West Catholic and LaSalle High, both run by the Christian Brothers. The Christian Brothers, like all the religious orders working in the diocese, theoretically fall under the authority of the Cardinal, but by tradition the orders have pretty much run their own shows. The Christian Brothers have an excellent reputation as educators and when the order decided to revise its theology course in all its schools throughout the country, the Brothers in the local schools conformed.

As one has come to expect in articles of this sort, the only reason that this particular "reform" was deemed significant by the secular press had to do with the fact that "the Christian Brothers have greatly reduced the old Catholic preoccupation with sexual sin." The article then went on to announce that "the word sin is rarely mentioned" in the new catechetical approaches. It also went on to quote one particular brother at length.

"Sex just isn't that important," this unnamed brother explained to *Philadelphia Magazine*.

"We try to put it in perspective," he continued. "Don't get the impression that we tell the kids to go out and do anything they want. We don't. But we're trying to make them more personally aware of relationships. We have no real dogmatic approach at all. We're not interested in how much they can recite back. We're trying hopefully to mold attitudes and to stress positive Christianity."

Positive Christianity meant the elimination of the use of not only sacramentals like the rosary, but also extended to frequenting of the sacraments as well, both of which were termed "religious voodoo."

"The Brothers," the article continued,

> as late as 10 years ago, made a big thing of students constantly carrying the rosary. It was supposed to be a guarantee that you couldn't die without the opportunity to confess. "We've gotten completely away from that," said one Brother with a slightly embarrassed grin. "In fact we try to impress on the kids that they should do things because they feel they have meaning. This may be shocking, but about 60 percent of our kids don't receive the sacraments regularly."

One person who agreed that what the brother said was shocking was Cardinal Krol himself. Like the incident at the seminary, this was a challenge he could not afford to ignore. A delegation was dispatched from the chancery to LaSalle High School to discuss things with Dick Deasy, then Bro. Paul Francis, chairman of the religion department, but nothing came of the investigation. Just why that was the case is not difficult to understand. The chancery officials were just as imbued with the *Zeitgeist* as the catechists, and a liberal deformation of the gospels was as invisible to the one as to the other. One such chancery official was even quoted in *Philadelphia Magazine* as saying of the Catholic high school students in the archdiocese, "They're more liberal in the good sense. They seem more up on Vatican II, more willing to talk about their religion and more aware of the role of the laity and willing to sacrifice. I think the Brothers are really reaching kids out there. I think the other kids marvel at their spirit and motivation."

With inquisitors like this, it is not surprising that Deasy and LaSalle were given a clean bill of health. However, the problem would not go away. Krol, who felt bound to support the Church even when he disagreed with the direction those under him were taking, gave the impression of not being aware of things happening right under his nose. *Philadelphia Magazine* quoted him as claiming, "They're trying to take God out of the picture."

Philadelphia was intrigued by Krol's use of the third person plural, opining that he referred to "'they' as if they were on another planet." *Philadelphia*'s point was that "this stuff," i.e., the liberal transvaluation of values, "is being taught in Philadelphia" at schools under Krol's jurisdiction.

The fact that this was the case was in no small measure due to the efforts of Dick Deasy or, as he was known at the time, Brother Paul Francis, F.S.C. Deasy was not only the anonymous brother quoted in the *Philadelphia Magazine* article, he had also been commissioned by the Christian Brothers to "force change," to use his formulation of his mandate, throughout the Baltimore province, which included all of Philadelphia. By 1967, "forcing change" had precipitated a deep catechetical crisis at both of the schools run by the brothers in the archdiocese. Both West Catholic and LaSalle High School were experiencing the turmoil which was attributed to the times, but more often than not had to do with the importation of the spirit of the times into those schools' religion courses.

LaSalle High School, because it was a prep school and not part of the archdiocesan system, was more dramatically affected by the changes. During the '67-68 academic year, when Robert Rooney was a junior at LaSalle the full force of the curriculum changes there began to take effect. By the time Rooney was a senior, during the '68-69 academic year, it was clear to him that what he was being taught was incompatible with the Catholic faith, but by that time, he wasn't sure he wanted to be a Catholic anymore. Deasy's situation continued to evolve as well, one step ahead of the curricular changes he was forcing throughout the archdiocese. When he graduated from college as a brother with a master's degree in theology in 1962, Deasy held that the Church's liturgical life was the product of historical evolution and therefore subject to further modification at pretty much the whim of those who chose to implement the changes. He felt this because of what he had learned in a biblical studies class at LaSalle College taught by a Franciscan priest.

"The community creates its own texts," is how he formulated this position thirty years after the fact. By that time, Deasy was not only no longer a brother, but also no longer a Catholic either. When asked when he had ceased being either, he claimed that he had stopped being a Catholic before he had stopped being a brother. Since, according to the tenets of the theology he had learned in formation, the role of community was paramount, being a brother was more important that professing what the Catholic faith espoused. Deasy, as a result, felt no immediate need to leave the brothers when he stopped being a Catholic. Nor, since he was still a brother, did the fact that he was no longer a Catholic create in him any need to desist from his reform of the catechetical programs in the archdiocese.

Deasy was, however, not just any old brother. He was considered the star of his class and given roles within the brothers commensurate with that exalted position. During the '68-'69 academic year, Deasy was at Princeton studying philosophy, a career move which undoubtedly enhanced his reputation as a *Wunderkind* among the brothers. Deasy was undoubtedly an intelligent man, but no one in the brothers at the time seemed to question to what extent intelligence meant simply adopting in an astute but essentially uncritical fashion the tenets of the dominant liberal culture. As Deasy progressed in accumulating prestige, the brothers gave him roles fraught with more and more responsibility in the order, apparently without anyone in the order having noticed that Deasy was gradually transforming Catholic catechesis into an Introduction to Liberalism.

The most crucial transaction in this regard, as we have already mentioned, had to do with the Church's teaching on sexuality. This continued to be the bone which stuck in the liberal's throat, and Catholics who aspired to upward mobility found it increasingly unpalatable as well. "Sex just isn't that important," was how Deasy framed the issue in the *Philadelphia Magazine* article. The statement is comparative. "That important compared to what?" one is tempted to ask. Sex, however, was playing an increasingly important role in the life of Brother Paul Francis and at LaSalle High School as well throughout the late '60s. In the aftermath of the '68-'69 school year, Gerald Tremblay, an English teacher at LaSalle and along with Deasy, co-reformer of the curriculum there, left his wife and children and would eventually marry the wife of a prominent high school alumnus. Deasy, who no longer considered himself a Catholic but was still involved in reforming the catechetical curricula for the Christian Brothers, then moved in with Tremblay's wife. Once the situation became known at LaSalle, it caused an enormous amount of scandal and made a student body already unruly because of the times (and, of course, Deasy's reading of the times) virtually unteachable and to all practical purposes unmanageable as students. Rebellion ensued and the school administration, feeling itself compromised by the actions of two of its most notable curriculum reformers, could do little but give in to the demands of the students. The students were not superior to the master, nor in this instance were the masters superior to the students. The Dionysian curriculum was beginning to bear its antisocial fruit.

When asked at a later date why he left the brothers, Deasy would reply that it was "a complicated story." When pressed, he claims that he left the Church "because I came to believe that Catholicism and the Roman Catholic Church was a historical evolution. And so I no longer accorded it any kind of primacy."

When he learned at Princeton that "Christianity and Catholicism were really cultural artifacts," he was faced with a "real dilemma because I was being asked to teach the brothers" something he himself no longer believed.

"So I left," Deasy continued. "Not for any other reason other than I concluded that the life they were living was a historically conditioned moment that was wonderful, but I couldn't empower it with transcendence and absolute significance. It was just a lovely way to live. And I wasn't prepared to challenge them, and so I left" roughly three years after he stopped being a Catholic.

One of Deasy's students at LaSalle remembers the summer of 1969, the summer between his senior year in high school and his freshman year in college, as the time when "the wheels came off the wagon."

"Tremblay's marriage was over, and Deasy had moved in with his wife," and the impressionable young students who had been told that the curriculum changes bespoke a revitalization of the Gospel message began to feel that, first of all, what was being promoted as the spirit of Vatican II was really not Catholicism at all, and, secondly, that they were the victims of a vaguely manipulative scheme whose ends had less to do with the goals of Catholic education and more to do with the personal agendas of the teachers who were managing curriculum change. In retrospect, the student claimed some 25 years later, "we had the sense this wasn't Catholic. It was subversive. There was nothing in what we're learning that corresponded to Catholicism."

The realization "was real slow in coming," which is to say that it didn't arrive until this student's senior year. "By the time I was a senior, I already knew there was this gulf between Catholicism and the religious instruction I'd had for at least half of those four years of my life." Deasy's former student characterized that religious instruction as "Christian existentialism. It's about being a Christian in the ethical sense without necessarily believing in a god."

If the Catholic Church was one circle and the cultural revolution was another, catechesis was the part of the two circles which overlapped. Beginning in 1967, but with increasing frequency in the years following, Catholic parents were getting the uncanny sense that what their children were being taught did not correspond to the Catholic faith. Of course, the feeling was rarely formulated with that sort of precision. The thesis was often cast in terms that refuted itself by its very formulation. "That's not the way I was was taught" was just one of many ineffectual ways of drawing attention to what was becoming an increasingly serious problem in the archdiocese. "That's not what I learned in the Baltimore Catechism" was another. Professional catechists loved to hear the problem cast in those terms. It allowed them to wrap the mantle of Vatican II more effectively around their shoulders.

Therese Ickinger remembers having the same sort of feeling at some time during 1967 and then with increasing frequency in the years following. By 1969, she had become a figure of some significance in the conservative reaction to the excesses of the catechetical establishment in Philadelphia. By 1969, she had become spokesman for a group known as P.O.P.E. (Parents for

Orthodoxy in Parochial Education). In a few years she would gain a national reputation after a fiery speech against the new catechetics which she delivered at a meeting of the Wanderer Forum.

"What!" wondered Mrs. Ickinger in the florid style which came to characterize both her speeches and writings, "Shall the Christian Brothers at West Catholic be permitted to teach that "Christ and Mary Magdalene were lovers" and no one challenge them?" ("'Religion' Texts: An Indictment" by Therese Ickinger, published by POPE, May 30, 1970 as an open letter to all of the pastors of the Archdiocese of Philadelphia). As early as the late '60s, the pattern of interaction between the conservative reaction and the hierarchy had been pretty much established. People like Mrs. Ickinger would bring up one abuse after another and be criticized, not so much for the content of of her criticism, but the way in which she presented it.

Mrs. Ickinger even makes note of the reaction in her talk. "We have been advised by diocesan officials," she explains, "that 'abrasive criticism' will get us nowhere." After making that concession, Mrs. Ickinger goes out of her way to be abrasive: "May we ask you then, Fathers," she continues, "to bear in mind that this is not a criticism. It is an indictment. "

The indictment then continues in the same tone established at the beginning of the talk: "Shall their student publication," she continues referring specifically to West Catholic, one of the two Christian Brothers schools in the archdiocese,

> be permitted to openly boast of the sale of drugs on the premises, warn pushers to watch out for narcotics agents, advise the reader that there are more kicks in this than in "juicing" on weekends; solicit fornication; encourage all to attend an obscene film, while publicly revealing in a student letter that most of the boys are attending the dances drunk (*West Catholic News*, October 16, 1969). In the face of this, Fathers, shall we call silence charity?

"Shall the books used at fully half a dozen high schools," she continues, citing the Sadlier Light and Life series, "say that abortion is all right once in a while and mercy killing once in a while and suicide occasionally; that there are no extrinsic moral values?"

"We are indignant at the insult," Mrs. Ickinger continued, speaking for a growing number of concerned parents in the Philadelphia area, "not only to our morality but to our intelligence. We know these things are being done! We cannot believe that the authorities do not know it—or could not know it—or should not know it."

Ickinger's critique included not only what was in the textbooks but also the type of spiritual formation the students were getting at retreats that made use of, as she put it, "the seductive arms of sensitivity training."

"Shall mauling touch and go sessions," she wondered, "be-ins, live-ins, paw-ins, and sin-ins be permitted to deceive Catholic parents who think that their children are being given spiritual guidance when in reality they are being fanned into a delirious erotic frenzy?"

Behind the rhetorical overkill were complaints that should have been taken seriously, but were often brushed aside, perhaps because of the rhetoric. Before long, an understandable frustration becomes evident in her writings.

"For a period of almost two years," Mrs. Ickinger complained

> as a group of concerned mothers and fathers we have respectfully appealed to those in authority to give us Catholic orthodoxy in our religious programs. In reply we have been ignored, criticized, rebuked; called "witch-hunters," "slanderers," "emotional fanatics," "hot-air merchants "; in their more generous moments our critics dismiss us as a coterie of little old ladies in tennis shoes who are disturbed because the fans have been moved. Over all, we are accused of lacking charity, showing anything but how Christians should love one another, preaching hate instead of love. . . . Well, Fathers, in part this is true; hate is certainly the word. We hate the "new" catechisms; we hate the erosion of faith and morality which they spawn; we hate the treason which calls itself Catholic while ravishing the very soul of Catholic truth.

Mrs. Ickinger may have gotten nowhere with the educational establishment in the archdiocese of Philadelphia, but she did get support of a sort from an unanticipated quarter. In an article entitled "Catechetics, RIP," Gabriel Moran, one of the major gurus in the catechetical movement at the time and also a Christian Brother (at the time), opined that "I not only could enjoy, but also agree with much of the speech on textbooks given at the Wanderer Forum by the lady whose rhetoric left Spiro Agnew in the dust."

Moran was not only a Christian Brother at the time, he was president of the Christian Brothers. In his book *Catechisms and Controversies*, Msgr. Michael J. Wrenn describes Moran as "one of the biggest 'names' in catechesis in the United States"(Wrenn, p. 118). The 1983 Sourcebook for Modern Catechetics claims that with the publication of his 1966 Catholic University doctoral dissertation in two volumes, *Theology of Revelation* and *Catechesis of Revelation*, Moran "influenced catechesis worldwide." When "Catechetics, RIP" appeared in *Commonweal* in 1970, the same editors opine that it "created something of a sensation."

Dick Deasy remembers Moran not so much as a leader as much as "just a colleague at a distance," in other words someone who was reacting to the same pressures which motivated Deasy and other members of the cutting edge of change in the Christian Brothers. "The fundamental transformation," Deasy said, situating himself and Moran as peers in the same movement, "that occurred in the late '50s and early '60s was community. Because out of liturgy came the concept of the communal celebration. Out of biblical studies came the sense that the community created its own texts."

Moran's agreement, however, is probably not the sort that Mrs. Ickinger would find consoling. The whole thrust of his article is to admit that the new catechesis arising out of Vatican II has caused dissension and chaos—Ickinger's point—but that this is not necessarily bad, and that an "ecumenical" Church in an ecumenical age in a sense demanded just this sort of catechesis. "There is something very peculiar about a field which disappears as it improves," Moran opined. And parents were finding his pedagogy increasingly peculiar as its impact on high schools in Philadelphia increased.

"The improvement to theology and education did not improve catechetics," Moran concluded, "it blew the field apart" (Moran, pp. 299-300).

This, of course, was precisely Therese Ickinger's point as well, although she might cavil at the word "improvements." What Moran had in mind by "improvements" becomes discernible without too much intellectual effort. The educational theory behind catechesis improved after the Council, according to Moran, because of the importation of the theories of John Dewey. In other words, catechesis in the name of improving technique became secularized, and its proponents became secularized as well by their naive adoption of categories inimical to the the Catholic faith. The proponents of the new catechesis became so secularized in fact that they failed to see that process as something bad, even when the self-destruction of their own enterprise became too obvious to ignore.

"When religion courses are improved," Moran claimed, giving expression to the already mentioned process of secularization, "they gradually come to look like something other than religion." Catechesis in an ecumenical age, in other words, meant self-destruction for the Church. Moran's equanimity in facing this prospect may have been due in large measure to the fact that he, like Deasy, was on his way out of the brothers and out of the Church. Catechesis, as a result, was nothing more that his own personal trajectory of secularization writ large on the screen of the school system where thousands of parents were undergoing financial sacrifice to have their children learn the Catholic faith.

Catechesis, in Moran's formulation, had become synonymous with the destruction of the Church. Moran's own words indicate that this formulation is far from an exaggeration of what he saw himself doing. "What should be clear today," he continues, "is that we do not have a catechetical problem but we do have a crisis in the existence, form and function of the Christian Church. . . . The catechetical movement found that when people really began to explore religious possibilities, the process inevitably undermined the existing church." Moran and the catechetical movement in which he found prominence started out by taking the mandate of the Council and adapting the gospel to the modern world. Before long that ambiguous project became something else again. The Gospel got laid on the procrustean bed of modernity and everything which protruded, everything which the modernist sensibility found offensive, got lopped off, and once the process was complete the catechetical reformers found that the only thing left was the ideology of modernity. The minds of the reformers were, furthermore, such captives of the categories of the dominant culture of the time that when the process of autodemolition was complete, they failed to see that anything was amiss.

"Catechetics is unworkable because the present church is unworkable," Moran opined. The council had brought "many people to the realization that the Church walls had to come down and a new form of community had to be developed" and "to the extent that a catechetical movement succeeded in knocking down the walls" it eliminated itself in the process.

"Anyone who sets out to educate in the field of religion," Moran continued, showing that he had the courage to pursue this train of thinking to its logical, self-destructive conclusion, "has to put scripture, liturgy and Christian theology into a broader context that does not afford Christianity a normative role. I think that this step should be taken and must be taken."

Therese Ickinger's point was that the step had already been taken in the Archdiocese of Philadelphia, but she was having a tough time convincing the catechetical establishment there that Moran's principles were the road map they were following. Moran would claim "that the right wing adversaries of catechetics have no workable alternatives," which is precisely the difficulty Mrs. Ickinger was having in Philadelphia. Moran had a credibility because of his position as president of the Christian Brothers, even when he was advocating the destruction of the faith in the name of updating it. Ickinger was viewed with suspicion, one suspects, because she lacked clerical standing and credentials.

By 1969, the complaints had become loud enough to come to the ears of the pastors in Philadelphia, and since Mrs. Ickinger had risen to the status of spokesman for the complainers, she was given a hearing. On Thursday, April 24, 1969, Ickinger, as a representative of P.O.P.E., spoke to a gathering of concerned parents and teachers at St. Martin of Tours parish in northeast Philadelphia at the invitation of the pastor there, Monsignor Walter Bowers. One of the people in audience was Msgr. Thomas B. Falls, a friend of Cardinal Krol's who had addressed the

Vatican Council and spent time in Rome with Krol during its sessions. Falls sent a detailed report of the meeting to Krol one week after it happened. Considering the lack of headway Ickinger was making with the clerical establishment in the archdiocese, the report was notably sympathetic. Ickinger, according to Falls, "presented a documented criticism of some textbooks currently being used in elementary and secondary religion courses. The speaker made it clear that she was not criticizing individual teachers —just textbooks. "

Before Ickinger could make her point, however, a group of hecklers in the audience began shouting her down. The hecklers were for the most part "long-haired students," but Falls makes clear that they were being encouraged by a number of brothers and priests, one wearing a turtle-neck sweater. In spite of the moderator of the program requesting order, the heckling continued. The behavior of the students and their clerical accomplices was, according to Falls, "a perfect example of the 'liberals' refusing to listen to another side of a controversy, and trying to deny concerned parents the freedom to express their concerns."

Eventually the tactics of the protestors began to get on the nerves of the audience, who began to boo the hecklers when they disrupted the talk. Only when a number of men in the audience threatened to take the situation into their own hands was Ickinger able to finish her talk, at the end of which she received a standing ovation.

In the question and answer period which followed, Falls noted that "not one of the questioners even attempted to refute her specific charges of errors in the textbooks she criticized." At one point one of the questioners brought up the fact that the books in question had *imprimaturs*, but Falls, when he was called to give his opinion reminded the audience that the notoriously unreliable Dutch catechism also had an *imprimatur*. The hostility failed to abate during the question and answer period, according to Falls, because "most of those who opposed the talk really misunderstood it, for they understood it as an attack upon the teachers instead of the textbooks."

When Falls took the floor during the question and answer period, he had suggestions for both sides in the controversy.

The offending textbooks should be sent to the Superintendent of the Diocesan Schools "to be studied calmly by competent persons" and P.O.P.E. should "proceed in a moderate way if they wanted to become a respected and worthwhile organization in the Archdiocese."

Falls' advice seems eminently reasonable and looked to be a way of bringing some officially sanctioned sanity to a situation which threatened to spin out of control. But his was not the last word at the meeting. In the middle of his presentation, Falls noticed a priest approaching the stage uninvited. The priest in question was Msgr. Philip Dowling, head of the Cardinal's Commission on Human Relations, and as such responsible for race relations and ecumenism in the archdiocese, but with no particular competence or responsibility in catechetics or Catholic education. Before Falls had finished speaking, Dowling took the microphone out of Falls' hand, and announced to the crowd who he was, that he taught at the seminary, and that he had personally examined the textbooks in question. Before anyone could notice that Dowling did not say that he found no errors in the controversial texts, he announced to the crowd that "I have a sister who is a nun," and before he could explain the significance of that fact, he began to cry.

"I would hate to think that she is a heretic," Dowling continued. With tears streaming down his face, Dowling ended his presentation as abruptly as he had begun it and walked to the back of the hall.

Dowling's performance was so unexpected and so emotionally overwrought that Falls wondered about his mental stability and worried in his letter to Krol "about the possibility of Monsignor Dowling over-working himself."

The incident was taken up in the May 23, 1969 issue of the *Catholic Standard and Times*, the archdiocesan newspaper. One reader wrote into the paper to complain that Msgr. Dowling's emotional outburst "completely seemed to neglect the nucleus of the problem," which had to do with serious deficiencies in the catechetical texts in use in the archdiocese and not whether Msgr. Dowling's sister was a heretic or not.

"Parents are frantic," the letter writer continued. "In order to keep the child from growing weak in his faith or from losing it, the parent must keep his offspring away from some Religious who seem to be indoctrinated to this new morality, situation ethics, existentialist philosophical pseudo-religion."

"So please," he concluded, "give the parent a little more consideration. Would anyone dare admit there is no confusion?"

Falls' letter was a clear warning to Krol from a messenger he could trust in language that he could understand. While admitting that P.O.P.E.'s methods often "can get out of hand" and that "some of their accusations can be unfounded," Falls felt that the parents' reaction was justified "when their children come home and tell them that there is no original sin or that hell does not exist." The fact that P.O.P.E. existed at all was a sign that something was seriously wrong and that the chain of command in the archdiocese had broken down. Parents had been complaining to their pastors for years about faulty catechetical texts, but the pastors seemed incapable of responding to their complaints in any coherent fashion. The pastors and the catechetical establishment at the chancery office seemed incapable of comprehending that the texts were not orthodox. It was an indication of the decline in intellectual standards which prompted the Council in the first place. The Church had reached the point where whatever the clergy did was *ipso facto* to be considered Catholic. This had been the case before the Council with results that were not particularly healthy but not spectacularly deleterious either. When catechesis fell into the hands of the cultural revolutionaries in the post-Conciliar period, the changes became too dramatic to be ignored. What resulted was an explosion of indignation on the part of parents, and the clergy, which had been conditioned by years of hearing that change was imminent and the implication that all change was for the better, simply didn't know how to respond. Instead of examining the texts, they decided to attack the messengers who were bringing the bad news. The concerned parents, according to Falls, replied that when they brought the texts to the attention of the authorities, "they were given the 'brush-off' and were treated as 'crack-pots.' Some parents thought that the only way they could get a full and fair hearing was to organize. Hence P.O.P.E., an organization which with proper handling might be of some service to our schools."

Falls' endorsement was unmistakable, but Krol's reaction was instructive. The cardinal began by reassuring Falls of Msgr. Dowling's mental and emotional stability. His response, Krol felt, was more the result of "the vicious nature of the remarks, accusations and recriminations which flew across the hall" than attributable to being "overwrought or overworked." Krol then turned his attention to P.O.P.E., and it then became apparent that he did not share Falls' essentially sympathetic view of the organization.

"I should observe," Krol began, a bit defensively perhaps, "that I too am genuinely interested in orthodoxy and am in fact responsible for orthodoxy in the Archdiocese. I regret very much that the organization known as P.O.P.E. by the methods and tactics of some of its members is not enlisting the co-operation of others similarly interested. For the organization to be successful its members will have to seek orthodoxy in its objectives and to be orthodox in its methods."

Krol's defensive reaction is understandable in a way. The accusations of people like P.O.P.E got much closer to the essence of his role as bishop in the archdiocese than the complaints of the Left that he was dragging his feet on civil rights or the war in Vietnam. Beyond that, Krol was caught in the middle of a struggle over the Catholic educational system. As defections from the religious life increased in the wake of Vatican II, the cost of running the archdiocesan schools increased astronomically, forcing Krol to turn to the possibility of state funding as a solution. At the same time that the cost of Catholic education was going up, the quality of catechesis was going down, causing a potentially dangerous defection of Catholic children to the public schools. At the same time that he was trying to assure Catholic parents that they could trust the religious education in the schools under his care, Krol was also having to assure the state authorities that religious views did not spill over into otherwise secular subjects. Added to all of that, there was the simple confusion of people who thought that what they were doing was mandated by the Council and were incapable of seeing the bad results that were resulting from that implementation.

Brother Fidelis of Jesus, now known as Joe Schmidt, F.S.C., remembers going to a meeting in northeast Philadelphia around the same time Therese Ickinger spoke at St. Martin of Tours. Schmidt was one of the four-brother team which included Dick Deasy and had been commissioned to "force change" throughout the schools of the Baltimore province. Schmidt, unlike Deasy and Moran, is still a brother. The group whose talk he attended may have been P.O.P.E., but he remembers it as Catholics United for the Faith. The talk was advertised as a discussion of religious issues which was to involve parents, and since Brother Fidelis was involved in precisely that enterprise, he decided to take two of his students and attend the meeting.

Once again, however, there was no meeting of the minds. Schmidt remembers the students as "really surprised at what was being said." They kept turning to Schmidt during the talk and saying, "We don't do that in this school, do we, brother?" Schmidt construed the anger of the parents as more in reaction to Vatican II than to what he was doing at West Catholic. Schmidt was also involved in dealing with the increasing explosive racial situation in West Philadelphia at the time. His response was to take an equal number of black and white students to a retreat house in Elkins Park, a northern suburb, where the students were subjected to the techniques of sensitivity training as orchestrated by two professors from Temple University. These were, of course, the very techniques which Therese Ickinger found so offensive, but to Joe Schmidt they were simply a means of fostering communication between two polarized racial groups.

The frustration of two groups talking at cross purposes is never far from the surface in the archdiocese's dealings with the conservative reaction caused by the outbreak of cultural revolution in the Church. Deasy would claim later that Krol was constitutionally incapable of understanding the "seismic" sort of transformations which were occurring in society at the time.

"Not only his personal training," Deasy said of Krol, "but his affinity with Polish movements and cold war ideologies and his own intellectual perspectives and training would have made it very difficult for him not only to comprehend—which would imply that he was stupid, which he wasn't—but to intuit what this whole business was about. There was fundamental and profound cultural conflict going on for which the institutions of the Catholic Church were ill-equipped to respond. That's what

I said to you when I said that to people like me, who were very much on the cultural side of that change, institutionalized formulations weren't of very much interest to us. It's like saying to a young person today that's listening to Grunge music, 'gosh, you don't realize that there used to be something called Guy Lombardo.' They don't know what you're talking about."

Deasy, in other words, was saying that Krol had lost control of the educational institutions under his authority. "The institution was floating," said Deasy, formulating the idea in his way, "The institution that they were in charge of was grounded in a culture and tradition and a set of intellectual points of view that had simply changed. It's geology. The tectonic plates had moved, and they didn't even know it. I think Vatican II was simply trying to come to grips belatedly with cultural and intellectual movements that had begun 25 years before. And many of us thought it did a wonderful and remarkable job."

Deasy spoke with the confidence of a victor in the cultural wars. He had exchanged his Catholic identity for something more compatible with the secular world view and had done well in terms of his career—better, let's say, than Therese Ickinger, who ended up getting straight-armed by the Church she set out to defend. After leaving Princeton before getting his degree in 1969, Deasy applied unsuccessfully for a job with *Philadelphia Magazine*, but eventually did land a job with the *Philadelphia Inquirer* after Walter Annenberg sold his interest in the paper. Deasy takes credit for the famous Mayor Frank Rizzo lie detector test and seems to have found the editorial ideals of the *Inquirer* congenial. He was nominated for a Pulitzer Prize, and eventually made his way back into education, initially as undersecretary to the the Department of Education in the ill-fated Shapp administration in Pennsylvania and then as part of an educational exchange firm in Maryland.

Deasy was also able to network with like-minded clergy in a way that would prove beneficial to his career later on. In '65 and 66, he was associated with the Metropolitan Alliance for Philadelphia, which he describes as "a reformist group in the Clark /Dilworth mode." When the two priests who celebrated the illicit storage room Mass were expelled from the seminary in September of 1966, they came to Deasy for assistance ("What they wanted to do was develop a library of catechetical materials"), and one of them even ended up living at the brothers' residence at LaSalle High School. Deasy also organized alternative religious communities for the Christian Brothers known as "six-packs." When asked if these experiments in small group living were successful, Deasy remains uncertain because the attrition rate of the brothers at the time was over 50 percent under normal conditions.

Because they were working at cross-purposes with the dominant culture, the counter-revolutionaries did not fare as well as Dick Deasy or Gabe Moran. Nor did the groups they founded. In the wake of the Curran challenge to *Humanae Vitae,* a group of conservative Catholic laymen under the leadership of Lyman Stebbins founded Catholics United for the Faith. Eventually a CUF Chapter was inaugurated in Philadelphia, but it met with no greater success than P.O.P.E. In a letter to Stebbins written on August 21, 1984, then assistant to the Vicar of the Archdiocese of Philadelphia Thomas P. Forkin, wrote to complain about something he had recently read in the newsletter of Philadelphia's second CUF chapter. In the letter, Forkin adverted to CUF's early unhappy history in the Archdiocese, which involved, in Forkin's words, "some right-wing politicists and some fundamentalist quacks." In response, Stebbins is quick to agree with Forkin's analysis of CUF's ill-fated and then defunct first chapter in Philadelphia.

"The Philadelphia Chapter," according to Stebbins, "early fell under the influence of several firebrands who had not yet had time (even if they had the disposition) to be formed by the CUF spirit."

The first Philadelphia CUF chapter was formed in December of 1971 and lost no time in attacking the archdiocesan catechetics program. On January 19, 1972, Mary Diamond, head of the newly formed chapter, wrote a letter to Rev. Francis X. Meehan, head of the archdiocesan department of education, challenging him "to a public debate on the subject of the New Catechetics in general and the Sadlier series in particular." Defending CUF's position in the debate was John J. Mulloy, then a teacher at Central High School, and later a columnist for *The Wanderer.* In *CUF-Links,* the chapter's newsletter, Mrs. Diamond expanded on the theme she broached with Father Meehan.

"If there is so much merit in these texts," she wrote, "let Fr. Meehan or Msgr. Schulte or Dowling step forth and uphold them. In large measure we have built these schools, our children people them, and we pay the salaries of the educators. In justice then, we request an airing in public of the differences of opinion on this critical subject. Mr. Mulloy is waiting." Diamond goes on to urge her constituents to write to the archdiocese and seize the advantage which has been presented to them: "If they continue to refuse to debate, they are suspect. If they do debate, Mr. Mulloy will devastate them."

The tone was hardly irenic, and the result of the query was predictable. The archdiocese refused to debate. The tactics of the counter-revolutionaries had once again forced the catechetical establishment to circle the wagons and defend texts, over which they were willing in private to express some doubt. In an article in the *Philadelphia Inquirer* reporting the challenge to debate, Father Meehan was quoted as saying that "public debate politicizes issues," and allows "the best demagogue" to win.

"The Holy Spirit," he concluded, "is not concerned about such things."

In responding to the charges that the texts in question were doctrinally deficient, Meehan responded by saying that the education series was attempting to give children "the proper teaching at the proper time." The existence of hell, Meehan explained "cannot be fully developed for children of 5 to 9 years of age."

"I can't imagine Jesus threatening little children with the fires of hell," he concluded.

Lyman Stebbins was adamant about not alienating bishops throughout his tenure as president of CUF and so it is not surprising that he would pull the plug on a group which decided to use the above-mentioned tactics. However, even more glaring than the strategic mistakes of the counter-revolutionaries was the doctrinal myopia of the archdiocesan catechetical establishment. By the early 1970s, the post-Conciliar pattern in this regard was fairly well established. Irate parents would object to doctrinal heterodoxy, and the education departments would circle the wagons and attack the mode in which the parents stated their objections. Mrs. Ickinger's relations with Cardinal Krol were no exception to this rule.

In response to the charges Ickinger levelled against the archdiocese at her meeting at St. Martin of Tours parish in April, Msgr. Edward T. Hughes, Superintendent of Schools for the Archdiocese of Philadelphia, wrote to Ickinger trying to express his fears that "efforts to preserve doctrinal orthodoxy [might] be converted into unwarranted charges of heresy and condemnations of reasonable pedagogical methods employed by experienced and sound teachers."

"Quite frankly," Hughes continued, "some of our teachers felt that the atmosphere at the meeting was more conducive to inflammatory charges than to full and reasonable discussion. . . .We do not believe that your charge of heretical statements is warranted." At the end of the year, Hughes wrote to Krol about complaints about inappropriate psychological testing being given at Father Judge High School. Hughes admitted to Krol in his letter that 1) the "test was given at Father Judge," 2) that the "test had not been authorized by the school administration, 3) that "such a test and such a sex education program are opposed to our diocesan policy and procedure, 4) that "a test of this type appears educationally and psychologically unsound," 5) that "the teachers were unanimous in their conclusion that such a test did not belong in the program," and 6) that "it is rather unusual to find it at Father Judge High School. Generally such incidents occur at several other high schools which seem to lean more to this type of approach."

In October 1969, Rev. Francis X. Meehan, superintendent of schools, wrote to Krol to express his misgivings about the Sadlier series, particularly a phrase in the text referring to Jesus as a "fully human person."

"No one is particularly happy with those phrases," Meehan told Krol. He felt justified, however, in retaining the texts because Sadlier had given him notice that the offending phrase would be removed in the next printing. Meehan concluded that it seemed "rash to read into the Sadlier phrase any reference to such theological speculation. Rather it seems to be a simple oversight, that we easily fall into in our current English use of the word human."

On November 10, 1969, Krol wrote to Ickinger to say that the charges she raised were under investigation. He also took the opportunity to criticize her tactics in raising the issues, suggesting that in future meetings "the discussion instead of being hostile and adversary [sic] should be Christian and charitable dialogue."

"It is regrettable," Krol continued, "that in your sincere efforts to promote integrity and orthodoxy of doctrine you seem to operate in an un-Christian atmosphere of hostility which shows anything but how Christians should love one another. . . . Abrasive criticism, emotionally charged accusations and condemnations are self-defeating. It is sincerely hoped that you will continue your interest in promoting integrity and orthodoxy of doctrine, but that in the future you will adopt measures which are Christian and charitable."

Ickinger responded by claiming that she and her group "want only the magisterium of the Church taught to our children." She goes on to say, "Quite honestly, we are not getting it. We are mothers and fathers, frightened and horrified at the materials that are given to our children under the name 'religion.' We want it to stop. . . . We are obedient to the Pope, obedient to you; we respect our pastors. We defer to authority; we appeal to it. . . It is rude to shout, but is it rude to call loudly for help when you are drowning . . . You put the tigers in our tanks you confirmed us" (Ickinger to Krol November 12, 1969).

One year later, Krol was still directing his superintendent of schools, now Msgr. Francis B. Schulte, to investigate the charges Ickinger was levelling against the school system .

"I want you or someone in your office," Krol wrote to Schulte on October 9, 1970, "to take all the time necessary to investigate these charges that she makes and to prepare an explanation or refutation of them. . . . I do not question her sincerity, and I may not approve her methods; but I cannot ignore the fact that such charges often repeated without a reply at least for the sake of the record will permeate the climate and erode the confidence of our own people in our Catholic educational system."

As time progressed with little change in the texts in the schools, Ickinger's tactics became increasingly confrontational. In the *Philadelphia Inquirer* of September 16, 1970, she was quoted as urging a "'limited boycott' of textbooks by parents, asking them not to buy offensive material." Ickinger said that P.O.P.E. "simply wanted John Cardinal Krol to 'exercise his authority' in controlling the dissemination of religious literature teaching 'heresy and immorality.'"

"This is not an attack on the cardinal, " Ickinger said. "POPE has tried unsuccessfully for two years to gain an interview with him," she added. In the same article, Schulte countered by claiming that attacks of this sort "are discouraging to the teachers by questioning their orthodoxy, their good judgment and their dedication."

On December 30, 1970, Cardinal Krol directed Father Meehan to respond to Mrs. Ickinger's latest charges. As part of the response, Krol asked that a paragraph be added "that would indicate that in addition to the criticism coming from Catholics, the schools are also rocked from the outside by people who oppose government aid to Education." If the letter was Krol's way of asking for help, Mrs. Ickinger seems not to have gotten the message.

A little over a month later, Ickinger under the auspices of a group known as Families for the Faith announced that it had filed a canon law suit against the archdiocese charging that the religious education in Philadelphia was "heretical and immoral from a Catholic standpoint." Ickinger named as defendants in the suit John Cardinal Krol, Archbishop of Philadelphia; Msgr Francis B. Schulte, superintendent of Catholic schools, the Rev. Francis X. Meehan, coordinator of religious education, the Rev. Raymond Teller, CCD director. The brief requested that the new catechetics be put on trial and that the trial be held before the Pope.

Nine months later, Krol received notice from Luigi Raimondi, the apostolic delegate, that Mrs. Ickinger was circulating a petition throughout the country which had been signed by almost 500 people requesting the establishment of a lay order directly under the protection of the Holy See and "removed from the jurisdiction of their present bishop." The ecclesial lawsuit was also mentioned in the communication and along with it was enclosed a copy of Ickinger's "Petition to his Holiness, Pope Paul VI."

"In practically every diocese in the United States," Ickinger complained to the pope, "the religious education programs imposed upon us and our children by our bishops . . . are, in fact, so heretical and immoral that we are compelled in conscience to avoid them and to withdraw our children from them."

"Practically every sacred doctrine and discipline of the Church," she continued, "is either denied, attacked or insulted. . . . It is our bishops who hold the stirrup for this pale horse whose rider is death. It is our bishops whose *imprimaturs* appear on these deadly textbooks . . . The night is upon us. Our enemies are all about us."

"In Christ's Holy name," Ickinger continued, "through Mary's Immaculate heart, we appeal to the Father of all Christians, to appoint us and establish us as his own spiritual wards, his special cavalry to defend and spread the teachings of the Apostolic See, to preach a spiritual crusade, to effect the Will of Christ that every human person be subject to the Roman Pontiff; to give glory to God, freedom to man and saints to the Church."

On November 23, 1971, Krol responded to Raimondi's letter by documenting the archdiocese's dealings with Mrs. Ickinger beginning in 1969. "In one of her first meetings with Monsignor Hughes of the School Superintendent's Office," Krol complained, "she was surreptitiously recording the conversation on tape. At the next meeting she disclosed what she had done and was convinced that she had trapped the Superintendent's office. They told her she was free to play the tape and that they had nothing to conceal."

In addition to that, "Mrs. Ickinger was extremely critical using her *ad hominem* arguments to ridicule and discredit any priests, sisters or lay people who disagreed with her." Krol also attempted to justify not meeting with her personally by claiming that "those who have more experience in such matters take for granted that she would attempt to bait the Cardinal with the 'have you stopped beating your mother?' type of questions in order to be able to write another article which she could possibly sell to those interested in publishing such material."

Krol was also not surprised that Mrs. Ickinger appealed to the pope, claiming that the action "follows a pattern of direct approach to the top man." But he ends by being at a loss as to what suggestions to offer. "I think she is well-meaning and well-intentioned. She writes well and speaks well, but she is almost heartless in deprecating anyone who disagrees with her. The best advice that I have had was that it would be quite unproductive for me to give her any time of my own."

One week later Raimondi wrote back to Krol to say that he "concur[red] in your approach to this good woman and her organization" and for the time being the matter was laid to rest. The catechetical revolution was still pretty much in place and all the counter-revolution had succeeded in doing was alienating the people who had any power to change things.

X
The Education Front

As part of his last ditch efforts to rescue the state budget from the grip of Rep. Martin Mullen's budget committee and placate the forces that wanted to use the Commonwealth of Pennsylvania as a conduit for sexual revolution, Governor William Scranton called William Bentley Ball into his office for a conference in late July of 1966. Scranton wanted to make a deal, but, feeling that he was arguing from a position of strength, or, perhaps just feeling angry and frustrated at Mullen's tenacity, Scranton decided to try the stick rather than the carrot. He was willing to remove the power of initiation and references to Planned Parenthood from the Department of Public Welfare's 1965 regs, but that was all he was willing to concede. If Mullen's amendment passed, he warned Ball, the Secretary of Public Welfare would ignore it as unconstitutional and the state would continue to use welfare money to promote contraception until the court ordered them to stop.

"I cannot believe," Ball replied undaunted, "that any governor of Pennsylvania would flaunt our statutes on adultery and fornication." Moreover, Ball found especially reprehensible the idea that the Department of Public Welfare would use public funds in defiance of the express wishes of the legislature. But that was precisely what the Republican Scranton administration had in mind. One hour after the meeting, Ball was informed that Norman Lourie of the DPW had precisely such a secret plan in mind.

If Governor Scranton expected Ball to be intimidated by his willingness to flout the wishes of the democratically elected representatives of the commonwealth of Pennsylvania, he was mistaken. Mullen held firm on the appropriations bill, and Ball left the meeting with Scranton feeling that the standoff would provide someone with "a golden political opportunity." Ball had two people in particular in mind. William Scranton was a lame duck governor unable to succeed himself. The two people Ball had in mind were the two men vying for his office in the upcoming fall election—Milton Shapp, the Democrat and Raymond P. Shafer, the Republican candidate.

Of the two Shapp was the least likely candidate to seize Ball's "golden opportunity." Shapp had made his money as the head of a Philadelphia-area electronics firm and had made a name for himself as the president of the local branch of the American Jewish Committee, the agency which had been instrumental in *Schempp v. Abington* case, also of the Philadelphia area, which had removed prayer from public schools. Shapp's liberal credentials were evident from the start and when Ball, along with Matthew McCloskey, a prominent Philadelphia businessman and Catholic philanthropist, met with Shapp, he did nothing to disabuse them of their notion of him as a carrier of the liberal standard. When asked if he supported programs beneficial to children in non-public schools, Shapp replied that "ideally" there should only be one school system, but since we all lived in a mixed society it was proper that our schools reflect that fact.

Needless to say, the contingent representing the Catholic bishops of Pennsylvania was not impressed with Shapp's answer. The one school system approach was one of the main tenets of *Kulturkampf* and had been so as far back as President Grant's attempt to impose a national version of the Blaine amendment on the country's schools. Krol deemed the proposition "dangerous." When Shapp was asked about the state's position on birth control, he was evasive, but eventually admitted that he favored the December 17, 1965 revision of DPW regs. Interestingly enough, the conversation at that point shaded off into the race issue. Here Shapp claimed that there were only two solutions: either open housing or beefing up the police departments to keep blacks in the ghetto. Not surprisingly the Catholics were unimpressed by the Democratic candidate for governor. "Shapp's promises and commitments are legion!" Krol commented later, "Some are contradictory. We seek performance as well as promises."

As a way of prodding the Republican candidate in the right direction, Ball considered calling a press conference at which he would pose the following questions:

> 1) we all know the views of one candidate for Governor but where does Mr. Shafer stand on supplying contraceptives to unmarried persons, in the face of Pennsylvania's public policy as expressed in our criminal statutes?

> 2) If Mr. Shafer becomes Governor, will he permit his Secretary of Public Welfare to flaunt the expressed will of the general assembly?

> 3) Does Mr. Shafer believe that two or three people in the Department of Public Welfare should legislate on this vital matter for all the people of Pennsylvania?

Eventually Ball and the PCC would get to pose the same questions, perhaps not as provocatively phrased, to the Republican gubernatorial candidate in person. Specifically Ball asked Shafer whether the state's Catholic schools would be an object of his concern if he were elected.

"You know where I stand on the bus bill," was Mr. Shafer's response. Unfortunately neither Ball nor any of the other Catholic delegates at the meeting had the faintest idea where Shafer stood on the bus bill. When Msgr. Lohmuller pressed Shafer on the same issue, the candidate responded that, "You have my assurance of my interest in private schools. "

It was hardly a reassuring response. Equally equivocal was Shafer's stand on government funded contraceptives and abortion. Shafer claimed that he would not favor expansion of the program in the former instance and expressed a desire to "hold the line" on the latter.

Mr. Shafer then said off the record that he had misgivings over some people in the Department of Public Welfare and felt, as a result, that the department should be reorganized. When informed that the Pennsylvania Medical Society was pressing for liberalization of the state's abortion laws, Shafer said that his administration "will have to take a look at the total picture before coming to any final decision." He then changed the subject to a topic he evidently considered more pressing. "Do you know about Shapp's wife?" he asked the representatives of the

Pennsylvania Catholic Conference. When no one responded, the subject was changed.

Needless to say, the delegation was not overly impressed with Mr. Shafer either. Ball felt later that Shafer was rushing to get through the meeting. In his view Shafer radiated impatience, and his answers were for the most part unsatisfactory except on colleges and welfare. On birth control, abortion, and aid to parochial schools, Ball felt his position was little different than that that of of the avowedly liberal Shapp. Shafer was neither "deeply informed" nor did he "convey the impression of a person who is warmly sympathetic to us," Ball concluded.

The future, in other words, did not seem promising on issues of concern to the Pennsylvania Catholic Conference. Nor, for that matter, did the soon to expire Scranton administration give any indication it was about to act like the lame duck that it, in fact, was. One day after Governor Scranton wielded the stick at the PCC, Bill Ball got a call from Scranton's attorney general, who proffered this time a carrot.

"Attorney General Friedmen telephoned," Ball informed Krol on August 1, 1966, "ostensibly to discuss the so-called 'constitutional' issue. After some time he remarked: 'It's a strange thing, how sometimes a judge lets his judgment in one matter be affected by some other matter. For example, this birth control thing could possibly upset a justice's thinking in the school bus case.' This was, of course, a hint respecting Justice Roberts."

"I replied," Ball concluded, "that the Justices would simply have to call things as they saw them."

The Republican administration was still in the mood to make a deal with the Catholics. However, since Mullen had held firm, the administration was no longer in a position to issue threats. Instead, they proffered what they knew was close to the heart of the state's Catholics, namely, state aid for parochial schools. A number of forces were converging at the time to make this an issue of some importance to those whose responsibility it was to run the schools. To begin with, the cusp of the baby boom was now passing through the Catholic school system. If we take the years 1946 to 1962 as the birth date boundaries of the baby boom, the oldest boomers were in their last year of college and the youngest were entering kindergarten. Beyond that, Catholics had proportionally more children than the population at large and were at the time accustomed to sending them to Catholic schools. Coupled with the enormous number of children that needed to be educated, there were the defections from the religious life which followed the misguided implementation of Vatican II. The Religious hardest hit were the nuns and brothers, who predominated in the teaching profession. As a result of their defection, lay people had to be hired, and lay people cost the Church considerably more money than Religious did. In addition to that, the financial expectations of the teaching profession in general were rising because of the involvement of liberal government both on the national and the local level. Krol was nothing if not astute when it came to managing money and in the face of increasingly clear handwriting on the wall, he was filled with the gravest concern about the prospects of the parochial school system. He quite literally felt that the school system was in a do or die situation. In the light of the enormous burden the Church was facing, with troops that showed a propensity to defect for the slightest of reasons or no reason at all, Krol felt that the very existence of parochial schools was on the line.

Beyond that, Krol had the St. Charles Seminary battle just behind him. The professorate was not only increasingly unreliable; they were getting increasingly rebellious as well. Then there was the Curran tenure battle just over the horizon. If the bishops could not allow the contract of one untenured assistant professor to lapse at a university that was canonically and juridically under their explicit control, how were they supposed to provide the financial sustenance for an educational empire that never had more students with an ever-dwindling number of religious willing to teach them?

When Raymond P. Shafer was elected governor in the fall of '66, the Republican administration under Governor Scranton was guaranteed an element of continuity, which meant of course that they persisted in their attempts to get the DPW regs changed so that their case workers could bring up the issue of contraception to their clients. There was a certain continuity of personnel as well. In the Spring of '67, Bill Ball was still wran-

gling with Max Rosenn over the DPW regs. According to
Rosenn's account, the impasse ended when Rosenn imposed a
"compromise" on both parties. However, the "compromise"
did not come out of the blue. What became evident to the
Pennsylvania Catholic Conference was the fact that Mullen's
victory had proven short-lived in the face of a bureaucracy that
was determined to override the decisions of the state's democratically elected members. The bureaucracy had remained basically in place and basically unscathed in spite of the
legislature's rejection of their policies. In addition to that, the
battle for school funding was not going well. Instead of defeating one enemy and moving on to another, the PCC found itself
increasingly involved in a war on two fronts with what were
proving to be recalcitrant troops in their own trenches. On
April 21, 1967, in the same memo in which he announced that
he was going to have yet another meeting with Secretary
Rosenn, Ball announced that the ESEA (Elementary School Education Act) battle in the Pennsylvania legislature was not going
well either. Ball characterized the PCC's position as "both weak
and one of reaction rather than of action." Once again the Catholics were plagued by an internal dissension that made it virtually impossible for them to speak with one voice on matters of
concern to the Church and to be perceived as such by those
whose opinion was swayed by united fronts.

"Last summer," Ball continued referring to the time when
all of his energies were devoted to holding the line on government-funded contraception in Pennsylvania,

> our opponents managed to rewrite the ESEA regulations. While
> many of us believe that 1967 is a year of crisis for Catholic
> schools, no one at the NCEA convention sounded an affirmative
> note, expressing pride in our schools and signaling a campaign
> for public aid. Instead, there was an extensive public laundering
> of our internal faults and problems, including a speech by Mon-
> signor Donohue about our need to do better in racially integrat-
> ing the inner city. . . . Whereas all of this passes for ecumenical
> humility and fearless objectivity, it gets us not an inch farther
> along in solving our financial problems. Publicly, it sets us back.

The Bible tells Christians to count the cost before becoming
involved in any enterprise of pith and moment, and the Catholic bishops of Pennsylvania seem to have taken the message to

heart. Rather than continue a war on two fronts with uncertain, unpredictable and in many respects undependable troops under them, the Pennsylvania bishops decided to consolidate their position by dropping their opposition to government-funded contraception. Ball received word from Archbishops Krol and Wright simultaneously via teleconference. The bishops were evidently willing to take Attorney General Friedmen at his word, and the Commonwealth of Pennsylvania seemed intent on upholding its end of the bargain. Within a year, PNESEA, the Pennsylvania version of the national bill lending support to non-public education, was signed into law in Pennsylvania. On June 19, 1968, Act 109, authorizing state funding for the teaching of subjects with a secular purpose, became law. On July 12, Governor Raymond P. Shafer wrote to Krol congratulating him on their collaboration in the passage of the bill and indicating that it was "of great importance to the future of the Commonwealth and its children."

As anyone could have predicted, PNESEA was challenged almost immediately in the courts. The American Jewish Committee, the ACLU of Pennsylvania and the Pennsylvania Council of Churches all filed briefs contesting the law's constitutionality, which they won in the state's district courts. The stage was then set for a showdown at the Supreme Court. Given both the Warren and Burger Court's track record on matters of this sort, the prospects for vindication did not look particularly sanguine. But Bill Ball was not deterred. In fact, he had drafted the PNESEA bill with the Supreme Court in mind. PNESEA was based on the *Schempp* decision which had been handed down not five years before. *Schempp* declared that the establishment clause of the Constitution prevented subsidy of anything but subjects with a secular purpose, and could not have the primary effect of either advancing or inhibiting religion. The Pennsylvania aid statute was written with just this provision in mind. The Catholic schools would be, in effect, subcontractors of the state, which would pay the state's nonpublic schools to teach subjects that had secular purpose. No state money would be used to advance or inhibit religion. The Pennsylvania state legislature was persuaded by Ball's argument, but that was not the crucial issue. The Church had never had much problem convincing democratically elected legislatures. It was the courts that had become the bastion of secular humanism, as Leo Pfeffer himself had noted, and the courts were unlikely to allow Bill Ball or anyone else to fight fire with fire. If the objection of the courts, most specifically the Supreme Court, had been on procedural grounds, if, in other words, they were concerned about the principles they enunciated in their own decisions, it is doubtful whether they would have invalidated a law that was explicitly based on one of the their own decisions, as PNESEA had been based on *Schempp*. But subsequent history was to show that the court was more interested in *Kulturkampf* than in juridical procedure, and one of the main tenets of *Kulturkampf* both in Germany in the 19th century, and America in the 20th, was that the state should have as close to a monopoly position as possible when it came to the eduction of the nation's children. And if the public schools could not have a *de jure* monopoly, as the Court had decided in *Pierce v. School Sisters*, they could have the next best thing, a monopoly on state funding.

By early 1970, the Pennsylvania aid case had a name. It was known as *Lemon v. Kurtzman*, and as some indication of how seriously the opposition took it as a threat to the secular humanist hegemony over the country's educational system, Leo Pfeffer was named chief legal strategist for the plaintiff. By early 1970, Bill Ball was having difficulty pursuing his own legal strategy in the case because of the constant interference by people ostensibly on his side. To begin with, the *DiCenso* case, contesting benefits for parochial schools in Rhode Island, was also making its way toward the Supreme Court at the same time. Ball from the start had nothing but disdain for the *DiCenso* case because he felt that its provision to pay what were exclusively the salaries of Catholic teachers was indefensible in light of recent Supreme Court decisions. Ball never had any doubt that *DiCenso* was doomed to failure, and wanted to keep as much distance between it and the *Lemon* case as possible. Leo Pfeffer, for obvious reasons, had the exact opposite strategy.

In addition to *DiCenso*, there was also what would come to be known as the *Tilton v. Richardson* decision, which had to do with Catholic higher education. Ball wanted as much distance from this case as well, because Hesburgh and the rest of the *amici* in the case had taken the tack of proving that they were secular institutions. Hesburgh's Land o' Lakes declaration was written with just this end in mind. In mid-February, Ball wrote to another lawyer involved in the *Lemon* case that "we must in these cases, pursue our own theory and our own style, and not open ourselves up to the sorts of defense which Pfeffer and ACLU would trigger us into mounting." In addition to attempting to create confusion about the meaning of certain crucial terms in the case, Pfeffer and the ACLU

> seek to make us respond to the Horace Mann League theory thus seeking to make us come forward with voluminous exculpatory testimony, driving us, in the school cases to the absolutely contradictory point of saying that we are not religious, not religiously controlled, etc., when in fact we are. We would be very foolish to go down into the alley of Horace Mann League with these opponents. We ought to seize our own ground, and the most favorable and most effective ground in argument devoted to the logical extension of constitutional principles established in *Allen*.

According to Ball, there was only one defensible position. "The fundamental theory upon which these defenses must rest," he claimed, "is this, and nothing but this: that religiously affiliated and controlled agencies, which have a sacred, sectarian and religious function, also have a secular function, and that secular or public welfare function is publicly supportable." *DiCenso* was flawed because "the Act really contains no limitation to 'secular' teaching in the nonpublic schools." The approach in *Tilton* was flawed because it essentially claimed that the Catholic universities were secular in purpose in their entirety. Ball was faced with the unenviable prospect of sailing between a case like *DiCenso* which he felt subsidized religion and therefore demanded too much, and a case like *Tilton* which capitulated to secularism and, therefore, demanded too little.

"We are all of us, now," Ball concluded,

> starting to step out on a very dangerous bridge. The hopes, not merely of the Church, but of a great population of parents and Catholic people, are pinned on what we are doing in these cases. Beyond that, I feel, almost in my bones, the obligation which we have to a long, often bitter, often heroic past—going back a century and a half—in which so many people made such sacrifices for the parochial school. The least that we can do is to think together and to be candid with one another in attempting to advance the common cause.

Thinking together on this matter was to prove more easily said than done. By the summer of 1970, the situation had gotten no better; in fact, the dissension among the ranks of the Catholic attorneys had reached the point where it threatened the successful prosecution of the cases they were representing. Not only could the nation's bishops not come up with a common strategy on the funding for the nation's Catholic schools, not only had they divided their efforts between two major cases, *Lemon* and *DiCenso*, the most serious problem was that the one case was undermining the other. The USCC, the bureaucratic arm of the United States bishops, following the advice of its legal council William "Bud" Consedine, was throwing its support behind *DiCenso*. Ball and his supporters wanted the appeal in *DiCenso* dropped altogether, or at the very least they did not want the two appeals confused. If the attorneys in *Lemon* were having a hard time persuading the bishops to go along with their strategy; they were having an impossible time with the bureaucrats at the USCC.

In order to align the various strategies in the various states where state funding was being contested, a meeting was held on July 1, 1970 at the USCC offices in Washington. In order to bring about the unity the Catholics so desperately needed on this issue, and in order to set the strategic disagreements of the moment in their proper perspective, Ball tried to give a broad overview of the fight which was now reaching its culmination in the cases proceeding to judgment at the Supreme Court. The Catholics of the United States, according to Ball, were "now coming to the final answer to an historic question."

"For at least 140 years," Ball began, taking as his starting date the emergence of Archbishop Hughes in New York,

> there has been a struggle in this country for freedom of choice in education. Not a decade nor a year since the high tide of the Know Nothing Party in 1853 has been without manifestations of a searing controversy over whether public funds may be used in aid of education taking place in parochial schools. This controversy raged intensively for two decades before the Civil War. It figured prominently during the Grant Administration which proposed the federal Blaine Amendment. In the last quarter of the nineteenth century it exploded in state after state where constitu-

tions were shackled with copies of that amendment. The twentieth century saw no remission of the collision caused by the upward thrust of freedom and the the downward thrust of oppressive law relating to justice to parents and children in education.
In recent decades it was the Barden bill and the start of the
federal aid controversy. Now it is alive in most of the fifty states.

"What is present in this room today," Ball continued,

> is the awful weight of history. I refer not only to the struggles —
> and the savage rebuffs suffered by so many of our ancestors—
> but also to the equity of the savings plowed into Catholic schools,
> to the sacrifices of untold numbers of people who have now
> passed on, to the hopes of generations of immigrants and still
> today, of parents who believe that the state should not monopo-
> lize education but indeed should and can play a limited but
> meaningful role as an enabler of educational freedom. . . . From
> 1960 forward, those who favor reasonable aid to parochial edu-
> cation have at last managed to form some kind of battle line and
> cooperative front.

At this point Ball got to the heart of his argument, namely,
"that it is constitutionally permissible for government to finance the achieving of public objectives through religiously
affiliated institutions." This was the heart of the issue. If Pfeffer
and the rest of the secular humanists had really been interested
in the separation of Church and State, they would have had no
argument with Ball, who went out of his way to craft the
PNESEA bill precisely according to their specifications, as articulated in *Schempp*. What was at issue here was precisely the
nature of the "public objectives" which both sides desired. What
the Left wanted was a culture liberated from the moral law. The
great liberal illusion was that the destructive forces unleashed
by that liberation could be somehow managed by technology—
by positive laws, by condoms, by penicillin, by government
funded programs, by metal detectors—the list goes on and on
as one liberal illusion after another fell by the wayside as social
mores became involved in an increasingly vicious cycle of moral
and social degeneration. What the two sides wanted was pretty
much what Leo Pfeffer said they wanted: Catholics

> hope for an America in which, if not all will be Catholics, all will
> adhere to Catholic values: no divorce, no contraception, no abor-
> tion, no obscene books or pictures, no homosexuality, everybody

worshipping God in his own way, government solicitous of and helpful to religion, and children and adults equally obedient to their parents and lawful authority (Pfeffer, *God, Caesar*, p. 20).

Whereas the secular humanists seek an America

in which individuals enjoy maximum freedom of thought and expression, contraception is used and encouraged to control population and avoid the birth of babies that are unwanted or cannot adequately be cared for, women's right to control their own bodies is recognized and respected, the sexual practices of adults, whether of the same or of different sexes, are of no concern to anyone but themselves, governmental institutions avoid manifestations of religiosity, public schools are free of sectarianism, and citizens are not forced to fight in a war they deem immoral or in any war (Pfeffer, *God, Caesar*, pp. 20-1).

What both groups got was social chaos and moral anarchy, *volens nolens*. The principle of the separation of Church and state was simply a pretext people like Pfeffer used to bring about the sexually liberated society they so deeply desired. Ball's point, which was the same as Krol's, and the same, for that matter as George Washington's, was that religious institutions served a secular purpose—with no primary effect of advancing religion—and as such could be subsidized. In fact, the health of the state depended precisely on fostering the virtues whose natural support was religion. Outside of these virtues there was no possibility of social welfare, prosperity, or progress. "Of all the dispositions and habits, which lead to political prosperity, " Washington told the country in his farewell address, "Religion and morality are indispensable supports. . . . . Reason and experience both forbid us to expect that national morality can prevail in exclusion of religious principle."

In his attempt to foster the virtues which the country needed to prosper, Ball saw the *Schempp* decision as a "fortunate coincidence." The task at hand was to persuade his fellow Catholic attorneys as well as their handlers at the USCC that this was the case. It was to prove no easy undertaking for a number of reasons, but one which was never far from the surface of this and other similar discussions was the nagging suspicion that many Catholics sided more with Pfeffer's vision of America than they did with George Washington's. Liberalism was nothing if not an incredibly seductive philosophy, and the word is used advisedly in reference to liberalism's willingness to use sexual desire as a means to achieve its own political ends. As Leo Pfeffer made clear, libido was the engine that pulled the liberal train, and because Catholics were as libidinous as anyone else they were hardly immune to liberalism's blandishments. Libido was the avenue of defection for more than one priest and Religious. Libido was the energy behind the questions which made liberalism sound plausible to a mind full of revulsion at moral constraint. Liberalism was the philosophy which made libido sound respectable, and more often than not libido was the unspoken subtext in otherwise theoretical debates about things like constitutional theory and legal strategy.

When Ball finished his appeal, the meeting descended from the sublime to the mundane, from the theoretical to the practical, and the main issue in need of resolution was the fact that "the law firm which was retained by the diocese of Providence has moved to appeal the case of *DiCenso v. Robinson*, without consultation with Catholic attorneys in other vitally affected states as to the national interest involved" (Joseph Skelly to Krol, confidential Memo July 6, 1970). Worse than that, the Williams firm, the firm defending *DiCenso*, "had announced its determination to take similar steps to have *DiCenso* argued with the *Lemon* case." This step, according to Joe Skelly's recollection of the meeting, "had caused great alarm to all five counsel in *Lemon*."

"Why the hurry in Rhode Island?" Ball asked when he finished his presentation. It was a question that haunted the counsel for *Lemon* throughout the history of the case. Like a scene out of a nightmare which happens with a slow motion inevitability, Ball and his supporters saw *DiCenso* appear and then bear down on *Lemon* in a collision course whose inevitability no one could seem to avert.

Mr. Collins of the Williams firm of Rhode Island responded to Ball's question by claiming that "when the case was discovered, a trial date had already been set. In order to be granted intervention by the court, it was necessary to assure the court that there would be an early trial. With respect to the rush in the appeal, this was necessitated so there would be no lapse of the appropriation for the one payment. "

Paul McMahon, attorney for the diocese of Providence, the defendant in the *DiCenso* case, added that "for political reasons," neither the governor nor the attorney general would tolerate withdrawal of the appeal. The state, McMahon continued, would proceed with or without the interveners, and if the state proceeded alone, the man from the attorney general's office "who is being paid $1.00 a year to handle this appeal," would not do a competent job.

Both Ball and Skelly and the rest of the *Lemon* attorneys found the explanation of the *DiCenso* people hard to fathom, especially the "political reasons" part of the explanation. As McMahon himself stated, the population of Rhode Island was 60 to 65 percent Catholic. If the diocese expressed a desire to drop the appeal, it would certainly have enough political clout to make its will known to the politicians who were ostensibly doing its bidding for the sum of $1.00 a year. Ball pointed out repeatedly that *DiCenso* was not a good test case for school funding and as the discussion progressed around the room, the consensus of opinion seemed to support Ball's position. Beyond that, one of the attorneys pointed out the fact that a classic mark of Leo Pfeffer's strategy is "to start several suits and then advance those suits which appear favorable to him and letting those which are unfavorable lay dormant." Which is precisely what was happening in the *DiCenso* case. Because of their lack of unity (or worse), the Catholics were playing right into Pfeffer's hands. Thomas Rayer of Louisiana made the point that *DiCenso* not only disregarded *Schempp* and *Allen*, it was contrary to their holdings and as a result had little chance for success. Clark Hodgson of Pennsylvania made the point that "constitutional law is made in little steps."

"It has taken us decades to get this far," he continued. "*Lemon* is a little step. *DiCenso* is a very big step. *Lemon* is the best case."

"It is incredible to think," responded Joe Skelly, Ball's law partner, "that the whole question of nonpublic school aid in this country should be governed by the political situation in Rhode Island. I cannot fathom a state which has a Catholic population of 65 percent not being able to effectively deal with the political situation. The appeal in *DiCenso* must be withdrawn. The Court on its own motion and with the certain urging of Mr. Pfeffer will likely schedule *DiCenso* with *Tilton* and *Lemon*."

"Pfeffer is leading the waltz," Skelly concluded, "and we are dancing to his tune."

At this point Bishop William E. McManus, chairman of the meeting, interjected that he had a "dreadful fear," namely, "that the Supreme Court will rule that aid to colleges is permissible but that aid to parochial schools is not."

Ball then decided to press the issue. He asked Collins whether the Williams firm would desist from trying to get the Supreme Court to hear *DiCenso* with *Lemon*. If Ball was hoping for some concessions, he got none. Collins informed the meeting that his firm would not only not desist but that they would also do everything within their power to get *DiCenso* argued at the same time as *Lemon*. The most he would concede is that his firm would do nothing until the end of the month.

As a way of resolving the impasse, the chairman approved a vote on two questions: "Is *Lemon* a better vehicle than *DiCenso*?" and "Should the *DiCenso* appeal be delayed? " The response in favor of Ball's position was decisive. Those present approved the first proposition by a vote of 11 to 4, and the second by a similar margin (yes 13, no 6). The vote, unfortunately for Ball, was not binding and the meeting as a result adjourned without coming to any resolution of differences.

In the aftermath of the meeting, the consensus of opinion once again favored Ball's position that *Lemon* was the better vehicle to bring before the Supreme Court. On July 7, 1970, David J. Young of Ohio wrote to USCC legal counsel Bud Consedine to say that he and his colleagues in Ohio considered *Lemon* "the preferred test vehicle for legislation providing funds either directly to nonpublic schools or to non-public school teachers."

"The record in that case is clean," he continued, "The statute is well drafted. I join Bill Ball in being greatly disturbed over the fact that counsel (Edward Bennett Williams firm) in the *Tilton v. Finch* case . . . requested the Supreme Court to hear it along with the *Lemon* case. Since the *Tilton* case involves higher education, it is not in my opinion going to establish a particularly favorable precedent for our efforts at the elementary and secondary level. The courts and legislative bodies have traditionally shown a different attitude toward institutions of higher education. They realize that these institutions aren't considered as vital to us as are elementary and secondary schools. I see the *DiCenso* statute as a bad statute."

Young concluded by agreeing with Ball "that it could be disastrous to schedule the *DiCenso* arguments along with the *Lemon* arguments. I request that you and the executive authorities of the USCC do all in your power to prevent this from happening."

Throughout the month of July, Bud Consedine was bombarded with letters from Catholic lawyers across the country urging that he and the USCC bring pressure to bear on the Williams firm to abandon the *DiCenso* appeal. Ball himself wrote to Consedine on July 7. On July 8, C. Clark Hodgson Jr. wrote to Consedine claiming that "the absence of a record in *Lemon*, which means that only the merits of the Pennsylvania legislation will be considered in a major Constitutional test, presents the most favorable posture in which the court can decide the basic question of aid to nonpublic schools." On July 10, Charles Tobin of the New York State Catholic Committee wrote to Consedine to express his "strong conviction that every possible step should be taken to assure that the appeal in the *DiCenso* case is not perfected in Supreme Court." Tobin urged Consedine and the USCC to seek assurances from the Rhode Island Archdiocese that the appeal not go forward. On the same day, Ball mentioned to Krol Tobin's alarm over the determination of the Williams firm to proceed with the DiCenso appeal.

"I have seen ruthless tactics like this in big business," Ball explained to Krol, "but never before in law."

On July 14, James E. Gallagher of Philadelphia wrote to Consedine after reviewing Leo Pfeffer's most recent *amicus* brief in the case, explaining that the brief "reveals the eagerness with which he has seized upon the *DiCenso* decision to weaken the *Lemon* appeal."

"I strongly urge you," Gallagher concluded, "to use your best efforts to persuade the appellants in the *DiCenso* case to withdraw their appeal. Counsel in the Rhode Island case will recognize that in their eagerness to win a battle, they may cause us the loss of the war. "

Eventually, Krol, frustrated by the intransigence of Consedine and the USCC, decided to appeal to the bishop of Providence, Russell McVinney, directly. On July 27, Krol wrote to McVinney explaining "the urgency of delaying the appeal of the State of Rhode Island of the *DiCenso* case to he Supreme Court." Three days later, Krol wrote to McVinney again explaining that "we shall have a very difficult task in obtaining a favorable decision in the *Lemon* case—not so much because of merit, but because we have discovered personal antipathy and bias at an extremely high level."

Krol was referring to a recent meeting between Ball and Solicitor General Erwin Griswold, during the course of which Griswold announced that he had no intention of submitting a brief in support of *Lemon* because he was in favor of a single school system. The most he would do, Griswold informed Ball, was to try not to hurt the case. When Ball expressed his disappointment at Griswold's intransigence and opined that "it appears that you adhere to the public schools only philosophy," Griswold replied, "That is exactly right."

Griswold, according to Krol's assessment, had

> the old Protestant view of public schools. He spoke out against the Supreme Court decision against Bible reading and in the prayer case. He believes the Court was wrong. It seems that he wants the public school at which a peculiar branch of Protestant religion and practice may obtain. It is obvious that Griswold has his own point of view and that he intends to use this view as the voice of the United States even though it is his own voice.

Krol was deeply upset by the information because it was a clear contradiction of the position of support taken by President Richard Nixon. At the time he received the news, Krol was unsure whether Griswold was acting on his own without Nixon's knowledge, or whether the Catholics had been double-crossed once more by a politician who promised one thing to get elected and then reneged on the promise as soon as he got in a position of power. All Krol knew at the time was that Nixon's public record in the matter was clear, and that Griswold's position was a clear contradiction of it.

Eventually the mystery was resolved when U. S. Senator Hugh Scott, (R. PA) at Krol's request, brought up the matter after a breakfast meeting with Nixon on August 18. Nixon, according to Scott's account, was profoundly disturbed by the news that Griswold wouldn't sign on the *Lemon* case. Nixon said, *expressis verbis*, that he was "inexpressibly shocked" at Griswold's attitude.

"I am furious that Erwin N. Griswold is anti-Catholic," Nixon continued. "What does he mean substituting his own views for those of the president. I meant everything I've said. I want an *amicus* brief filed and I want his agreement today. If not, I want him fired tomorrow."

Krol adverted to the Griswold incident to spur McVinney into action in postponing the *DiCenso* appeal, but he met with only partial success. McVinney persuaded the governor and attorney general of Rhode Island to delay the filing of the *DiCenso* appeal until the 25th of August, but for some reason he could not persuade them to withdraw the appeal entirely. He felt that it was "his duty to proceed with the *DiCenso* case," McVinney explained referring to the governor. "Indeed, he and the lawyers who are handling the case feel sincerely that they have a better case than the *Lemon* case."

"I think," the bishop of Providence concluded a bit lamely, "I have done all that can be expected of me in this matter."

By mid-July of 1970, Ball had become convinced that the people at the USCC were deliberately subverting his efforts, and in the course of making his point to Krol, Krol began to share his views as well. On July 17, Ball complained to Krol that since the USCC General Counsel's office had done nothing on *Lemon*'s behalf, "we decided we would have to do the job of organizing this effort ourselves." Gradually the outlines of a USCC strategy against him began to take shape in Ball's mind. The essence of this strategy was the conflation of three related but separate cases—*Lemon, DiCenso,* and *Tilton*. Pfeffer and his allies on the Supreme Court clearly considered *Lemon* the most threatening case. The strategy behind associating all three was clear. *Lemon* could be conflated with *DiCenso* and disallowed on the latter's lack of merit, but if *Tilton* passed at the same time, the Court could evade any suspicion that it had acted out of anti-Catholic bias. Beyond that, the secularists would have strengthened their strongest ally, the fifth column within the Catholic Church, the Catholic colleges and universities, which since the summer of '67 following the dual attack of the Curran tenure battle and Hesburgh's Land O' Lakes statement were firmly in the hands of the liberal cultural revolutionaries. Ball was concerned that *Tilton* was getting all the *amicus* support from the Catholics, but why this should have been the case is not surprising. It was so because the liberal Catholics wanted it so.

On July 10, Bud Consedine admitted to Ball that the USCC had done nothing since the July 1 meeting to get *amicus* briefs supporting *Lemon*. Consedine claimed too much other work as the reason, but when pressed by Ball to explain why *Tilton* was nevertheless garnering so much prestigious support, Consedine admitted that the "NCEA has a greater interest in higher education than do the Bishops." Ball, needless to say, found the response "most discouraging" and shared his discouragement with Krol, who was getting confirming testimony from other sources as well. When one priest contacted Father Raymond Lucker, later bishop of New Ulm, Minnesota, but at the time a staff member of the Department of Christian Education at the USCC, to express dismay at the way *Lemon* was being handled, Lucker expressed with some annoyance that "the matter had been resolved by the legal department of the USCC" and that "there was nothing wrong with having the *DiCenso* case tied in with the *Lemon*."

If the matter had been resolved, no one had taken the time to inform either Mr. Ball or Cardinal Krol, two people who certainly had a right to know. The message, however, was clear. The USCC was making policy over the heads of the bishops. Or, perhaps, behind their backs might be a better description. Just as the Department of Public Welfare in Pennsylvania had *de facto* veto power over that state's democratically elected legislature, so the USCC was determining policy in the aid to public school issue over the head of Cardinal Krol and his legal strategist.

By the end of July, Krol's frustration could be contained no longer. On July 29, he wrote an attack on the way the USCC was handling the *Lemon* case. "Frankly," he explained to Bishop Bernardin, "I have been looking for some evidence of the full appreciation of what is involved. This is the culmination of over half-century of effort. If the *Lemon* case is sustained, all the moves in various states to get aid to non-public schools are viable. If *Lemon* fails—it will be disaster. It may take years and decades to get back –if possible—to the point at which we stand now.

"I am not speaking from ignorance and not exaggerating," Krol continued "when I say we are in a do or die—not in a business as usual situation. We simply cannot afford risks. If risks are taken which could have been precluded, we better all run for cover. Should we—God forbid—lose without taking needless risks, we shall at least be in a position to tell the story to our people and hopefully retain their confidence and support." Even under the best of conditions, *Lemon* would have been a tough fight because of "clear evidence at certain levels of personal bias and antipathy, and a very real danger that such bias may be manifested" when the Supreme Court hands down its decision."

Bishop Joseph Bernardin, later to become cardinal arch-bishop of Chicago, was not unaware of Krol's dissatisfaction with the handling of the Lemon case by the USCC general counsel. On July 22, Bernardin wrote a confidential memoran-dum to Krol admitting that "Mr. Consedine does not agree with the strategy recommended by Mr. Ball and the others who have been working on the *Lemon* case." Bernardin went on to add that he felt that Skelly's analysis of the July 1 meeting was "not shared by two other persons who were present at the meeting." A week earlier Consedine had written to Bernardin expressing his belief that the convergence of *Lemon, DiCenso* and *Tilton* before the Supreme Court was "more a fortuity than a master design of the opposition and in any event it was a reasonable probability for some time."

It is difficult to know whether Mr. Consedine is being naive or disingenuous here. In June, Joe Skelly had met with one of Leo Pfeffer's associates, who had told Skelly at the time that Pfeffer preferred to litigate against *DiCenso* because in *DiCenso*, Pfeffer "has everything he wants." Since the purpose of the July 1 meeting which both Consedine and Skelly attended was precisely to share information of this sort, it is difficult to believe that Consedine was unaware of what Skelly had heard, unless of course Skelly by then had lost so much confidence in the USCC that he had decided not to share information with them. This is, of course, equally unlikely since on that premise Skelly would most probably not have attended the meeting. The evidence points to the fact that Consedine either knew about Pfeffer's strategy from Skelly but did not take it seriously as a threat to the case or that he in some way wanted to push *DiCenso*, even though the majority of the lawyers present at the July 1 meeting felt that *Lemon* was the better legal vehicle. Either way, by mid-July Consedine viewed the convergence which Ball dreaded with an eerie kind of equanimity.

"I favor letting the cases take their normal course," he wrote to Bernardin on July 14.

Throughout the middle of August, both Krol and Ball tried to pursue their legal strategy independently of the USCC. Krol continued to write to McVinney asking him to pressure the Williams firm to drop the appeal. McVinney kept giving the impression that the case, which was supposedly to benefit the Catholic Church was beyond the control of the leader of the Catholic Church in the area to call it off, even if he were convinced that it was harming the Church. Ball, for his part, approached the Williams firm directly to make his case. On August 20, he rote to Edward Bennett Williams Esq. of Williams & Connolly in the aggrieved tone of someone who has been double-crossed.

"I thought we had a clear understanding that you were going to leave us alone," Ball wrote. Ball felt that the Williams firm either misunderstood *Lemon* or was deliberately misrepresenting it to put *DiCenso* in a more favorable light by claiming that in *Lemon* public money went to institutions while in *DiCenso* it did not. Ball's message was clear: Leave *Lemon* alone. This meant specifically refraining from the suggestion that the constitutional basis for *Lemon* was unclear as a way of bolstering *DiCenso*'s chances.

Ball did not have to wait long for an answer for his request. One day later, Jeremiah C. Collins, the man who had represented the Williams firm at the July 1 meeting, wrote back to

Ball informing him that "in good conscience we could not further drop those references we had made to *Tilton* and *Lemon*." To add insult to injury, the Williams firm, along with the Rhode Island attorney general, filed its jurisdictional statement one day after Ball made his request. Three days later, Ball wrote to Krol claiming that "the recitations in the Williams Jurisdictional Statement are both gratuitous and damaging to the defense in *Lemon*."

As a result of being stonewalled by the Williams firm, Ball began to feel that something more than unfortunate coincidence was afoot. After being rebuffed so repeatedly and consistently, Ball began to feel that the USCC and the Williams firm were colluding to the detriment of *Lemon*. Beyond that, by the end of August, he had become convinced that he and Krol would have to go it alone. Not only could they expect no help from the USCC and the Williams firm, Ball began to suspect that both of those groups were actively opposing his efforts and that any sharing of information with them would be detrimental to the success of *Lemon*'s cause.

Krol, according to Ball, should tell Bernardin to "very carefully and very flatly instruct Mr. Consedine that the Williams firm do nothing—but nothing—directly or indirectly, even by suggestion (to anyone whomsoever, including law clerks)—to attempt to get the Court to hear *DiCenso* at the same time that it hears *Lemon* and *Tilton*." Beyond that, Ball added, "we would be well-advised not to disclose to Bishop Bernardine [sic] or to Mr. Consedine the prospective favorable filing by Mr. Griswold. This will get leaked back to the Williams firm." Ball ended his memo by praising Krol's forceful leadership in the matter.

Krol, as was often the case, found himself in the middle of a fight that was diverting him from the real fight, and which was threatening, in fact, to become the fight which eclipsed the real fight. On August 31, he wrote back to Ball to say that withholding information of Griswold's promise to file a sympathetic *amicus* brief in *Lemon* and not one which damned it with faint praise, was "hardly possible." *Lemon* was proving to be a repeat of the previous battles Krol had fought on the cultural front. The main similarity, of course, was the inability to mount a unified front in the battle. As with the contraception battle five years earlier, as with the Legion of Decency battle, Krol was being thwarted by powerful interests within the Church bureaucracy which had decided to pursue a course of action at cross purposes with his own.

However, in spite of telling Ball that it was impossible not to share information with the USCC, Krol had clearly been listening to Ball's complaints, and in fact had come to Ball's very same conclusion one month earlier, at the end of July. Mulling things over in a July 29 memo written to document his involvement in the case, Krol mentions the feelings of the *Lemon* team "that further efforts should be made without consulting or informing the USCC." The reason the USCC was formed was precisely for this sort of united effort against an enemy which could function across the country to the detriment of the Church. However, it was becoming fast apparent that the instrument could only bring about what the ideological unanimity of the members permitted. And in the post-Vatican II period it was becoming equally apparent that many of the people in key positions at the USCC were more persuaded by the arguments of the Liberal Regime than by their Catholic coreligionists. As a result, the USCC became an administrative colossus which rested on the philosophical and religious equivalent of clay feet. The instrument was only as powerful as the unanimity of its members, and when that unanimity was lacking, the instrument became a hindrance to the individual bishops who strove to make policy. In this regard, no organization at all would have been better than one that worked at cross-purposes with the bishops.

Once again, the Church had failed to educate its own troops. Liberalism was in many ways, stealth ideology. It did not confront the Church directly, as say Communism was doing at the time. Rather it seemed to be proposing a different means of achieving the same end. The case of Mr. Consedine is instructive. The USCC seemed either naive in their inability to understand Pfeffer's strategy, or their naivete was feigned and what the disingenuousness expressed was the fact that the USCC secretly agreed with the program Pfeffer was proposing. In the case of contraception, the case was clear. There was an active fifth column in the Church working to overturn the teaching of the Church, active to the point of accepting money from the foundations who sought to bring about that end. With *Lemon*, the similarities were there, but the evidence was not as clear. Either way the Church, once again, was subverted by the inadequacy of its own intellectuals—either by the inadequacy of their intelligence or their character. Krol, who was constitutionally averse to any sort of utterance that would divide the Church, and most especially averse to those which would give the appearance of dividing the bishops, nevertheless, was forced by the circumstances to certain conclusions:

"From the reactions," Krol wrote, "of Father Rausch, Bishop Bernardin, Bishop McManus and Father Lucker, and from the fact that some of the clear views of the July 1st meeting were modified in the submitted briefs, and from the fact that the position which Consedine now favors is the same as that which he was said to have favored at the meeting, it appears that Consedine has a controlling influence on various people connected with the USCC, that he is not aware of the extreme danger involved, or the disaster that we face."

"Everything considered," Krol concluded, "it was best that he and his Department be by-passed."

Krol felt that Consedine had inordinate influence at the USCC, but also felt he was not acting alone. One of the strategists Krol mentioned in this regard was the Rev. Charles Whelan, SJ, of both the USCC and the Georgetown Law School. Whelan, like Dexter Hanley, had played a major role in derailing Ball's attempt to counter the increasing push for government-funded contraception at the Gruening hearings. Whelan had also been involved in the contraception conferences at Notre Dame. In addition to that, before John D. Rockefeller, 3rd met with the pope he was briefed by a group of Jesuits from the Georgetown University Law School which probably included both Hanley and Whelan. Whelan, according to Krol's suspicions, was now calling the shots in the *Lemon* case, and Krol saw similar disaster on the horizon flowing from his involvement here as well.

In late August, in the course of a phone call initiated by Bishop Bernardin, Krol could no longer keep his suspicions to himself. He accused the USCC staff of working to subvert *Lemon*. Specifically, he accused Bud Consedine of jeopardizing *Lemon* because of his relationship with the Williams firm. Krol wanted Bernardin as executive secretary to do something because if *Lemon* failed, Krol felt compelled to bring the matter before the entire body of American bishops. If *Lemon* failed, Krol was going to hold Consedine in particular and the USCC in general responsible.

Bernardin was deeply upset by the allegations. On September 4, 1970, he wrote back to Krol explaining his concern, not just for Consedine, whose actions he defended, but also because the accusations "have serious implications for the Conference." Bernardin's response centered around his assessment of Consedine's character.

"I am convinced," he wrote to Krol, "that whatever Bud did was done in good faith because he is as concerned about the survival of Catholic schools as anyone else."

Beyond that, Consedine, according Bernardin, was not setting policy, but simply following decisions made by the administration of the USCC "because he understands that he cannot determine policy for the conference." This statement was, of course, in direct contradiction to what Krol had heard about Lucker in terms of explicit policy, but it also does not deal with the fact that the official policy could be thwarted just as effectively, perhaps more effectively, by bureaucratic footdragging than it could by overt disagreement. By making sure that nothing got done the USCC allowed Pfeffer and the Supreme Court to win by default.

In his correspondence with Krol, Bernardin professed to be upset no matter what the outcome in the *Lemon* case. Even if Consedine hadn't acted improperly, there was serious breakdown of communication in the Conference which was instituted to facilitate just this sort of communication and united effort. If Krol, however, wanted Consedine's head to roll, as the result of an executive action taken by Bernardin, Bernardin indicated no willingness to go along. If Krol pressed the issue, Bernardin informed him that he would take the matter to all of the country's bishops by instituting a formal inquiry. This, of course, was precisely what Krol did not want to happen. He had seen the bishops cave in on the Curran case, a case which had only gotten worse as time went on, and he most probably feared that sort of inquiry more than he feared the further actions of what he considered the Consedine cabal at the USCC. As a result he seems to have settled on a two-pronged middle course. He would respond to Bernardin's call for documentation, but at the same time he would also tacitly follow Ball's recommendation that the USCC be kept in the dark as to what counsel was doing on the *Lemon* case.

On September 10, Ball informed Krol that Bernardin was planning a conference call. As part of his recommendations to Krol, Ball asked him to "leave all contact with the Justice Department to principal counsel in the case (Ball and Skelly)."

"We do not want Mr. Consedine involved," Ball continued, "or Father Whelan or the Williams firm. We do not want to risk anything along those lines."

One day later, Ball responded to Krol's request for "irrefutable" documentation of "the cavalier behavior of the USCC" in their handling of the *DiCenso* case and in their approach to Solicitor General Griswold. Ball cited memoranda of telephone conversations which established that in July of 1969, Consedine recommended that the Williams firm handle the *Lemon* case. On June 23, 1970, Consedine also conferred with Jeremiah Collins of the Williams firm in arranging a meeting with Supreme Court Justice William Brennan, which the latter perceived as an improper attempt to influence the outcome of the case and in addition to the embarrassment to the cause of *Lemon* seems to have prejudiced Brennan against it.

"It was the actions between June 23 and June 26," Ball wrote to Krol,

> which were the culmination of the power play: As of June 23, Bishop McVinney was still holding up any move on Justice Brennan. We left for Hartford the next day to argue the Connecticut case, with agreement that the USCC meeting would take place July 1 and assured that nothing would happen in that short interval. The USCC and the Williams people knew we would be tied up in argument in Hartford on the 25th. On that day, Williams went to Justice Brennan and cast the fateful die, rendering very difficult any attempt thereafter to withdraw. This could and should have been controlled and prevented by the USCC. Here the hand of the general interest of the Church was plainly forced.

On the same day that Ball furnished the evidence of collusion to Krol, he received the news he had been dreading all along. On September 9, 1970, Leo Pfeffer, representing the appellees in the *DiCenso* case, filed a memorandum with the U.S. Supreme Court urging the court to take jurisdiction of the case and to schedule oral argument at the same time as *Tilton* and *Lemon*. If the USCC was still convinced of the "fortuity" of these events, there was also further testimony from Joe Skelly, who ran into one of Pfeffer's allies while arguing the Connecticut school aid case. "Leo is in his glory," this lawyer told Skelly. "He has everything he wants now in the Rhode Island case."

Two days later, Ball wrote to Krol expressing his dismay. The unrolling of events had a nightmare quality of inevitability about it. Throughout the course of the entire case, it seemed that the very thing Ball feared most invariably ended up happening. Since he expressed these fears at the July 1 USCC meeting, it was not surprising that he felt the need to restrict the flow of information in that direction. There was too much unpleasant confirmation of his fears to allow him to feel that mere coincidence was at work.

"Exactly what we had feared has come about," Ball wrote to Krol on September 11, two days after the filing. "We must somehow get the Solicitor General to file a memorandum with the Court contra to the Pfeffer-Williams position." Leo Pfeffer now had the Catholics filing briefs against each other.

By this point, Ball was convinced that recent events were not fortuitous, but the result of a conspiracy hatched and carried out by the USCC. In coming to this conclusion, he was not simply reacting to events in the *Lemon* case. *Lemon* was simply the culmination of a whole series of events which had taken place over the past few years.

"What has happened these past few months," he wrote to Krol on September 11,

> is only a repetition of what happened on the great question of government birth control five years ago. At that time the interests of the Church (and a consensus among the bishops) were simply derailed—and almost by the same individuals. Then, as now, the effort was organized. Then, as now, a well meaning man allowed himself to be led by well meaning but plainly ill-

informed activists who pushed their own views and allowed no due process to any other views.

As the result of these repeated betrayals, Ball felt that drastic action needed to be taken at the USCC. "There needs to be a clean break," Ball complains, "from that group which we identify with the Horace Mann League case, a soft approach on federal aid, the frustration of the resistance to government birth control (1965-67), the "liberalizing" of college charters (Catholic University, etc.), the *DiCenso* affair, etc." Ball identifies "that group" as "the palace guard at the USCC," which he identified elsewhere as including Msgr. Francis Hurley, later bishop of Anchorage, Alaska, Father Whelan, and Consedine.

In mid-September, Ball took a much-needed vacation trip to Rome, where he reminisced about the time when Krol, then presiding at the Council, took him to see the sights. When Ball returned in mid-October, the pleasant memories were quickly forgotten in the light of more unpleasant developments emanating from the USCC. On September 11, Bud Consedine had issued a memo to all public relations entities associated with the USCC informing them that "it would be totally improper and unprofessional for the USCC to join in efforts to attempt to influence the pending court considerations of the case through the public media."

On October 17, shortly after his return from Rome, Ball wrote a note to Bishop Bernardin informing him how "dismayed" he was to hear the news. Consedine's action meant in effect that the ACLU and The American Jewish Congress would have virtually a monopoly in the press in presenting its case to the American public and drumming up public opinion support in the matter. Consedine's opinion in the case, Ball informed Bernardin, was "palpably erroneous. The canons govern attorneys, and they do not and cannot inhibit companies." Beyond that, when a Father Lewellis approached the USCC to volunteer to help drum up favorable publicity, the USCC not only turned him down, but Consedine, according to a source available to Ball, "left word that Father Lewellis' proposal is 'extremely dangerous.'"

Ball found Consedine's attitude mind-boggling. "To me," he complained to Bernardin, "it is unimaginable that the USCC

Department of Communications is to have its hands tied at this critical juncture during which Catholic education is undergoing what may be a supreme test. . . . I can only thank God that the efforts of Father Lewellis . . . have resulted in the splendid articles nationally syndicated by Russell Kirk, Charles Bartlett and Kevin Phillips."

Joe Skelly was of the same opinion. "Once again," he complained in a memo that he wrote to Krol, "the Office of the General Counsel has taken action which deals unfavorably with *Lemon* and thus with the whole school aid issue. This time the action is in the form of a very erroneous legal opinion which has inhibited NC News Service and USCC's other informational services from playing an effective role in disseminating proper items of information to the general public concerning the issues of our case. (This is in sharp contrast to all the press releases by ACLU and the lot.)"

By mid-October, it was becoming apparent to other attorneys across the country that the Catholics were fighting among themselves as much as they were fighting Leo Pfeffer. "It appears," one attorney wrote to Joe Skelly on October 13, "that you are being forced to undermine the *DiCenso* case (and future similar cases) in much the same way that *Tilton* is undermining yours." On the same day David J. Young wrote to Theodore N. Staudt, executive director of the Ohio Catholic conference, to complain that "counsel in the higher education case and in the Pennsylvania case seem to have as many disputes among themselves as they do with opposition counsel. Now that the Rhode Island *DiCenso* case has been filed, we find counsel who should be on our team criticizing each other's statutes."

"Our opponents," Young concluded, "are getting their way. We are fighting each other at the national level."

A few days later, Ball got more bad news. The Louisiana Supreme Court was hearing argument on a case attacking Louisiana's purchase of service act mounted by the ACLU and the NAACP. Now in addition to competing with what Ball considered a bad bill from Rhode Island, the doubly explosive issue of race was being added to the equation in Louisiana. The Church was going to be portrayed as circumventing efforts at integration, and once again *Lemon* would be tarred by the same brush. The loser in the Louisiana case would have the opportunity to appeal to the Supreme Court, and given "fortuity" and the desires of Leo Pfeffer, there was a good chance that that case would also converge with *Lemon*. But Ball reserved the brunt of his fury for the USCC and the way they handled the case.

"The USCC," Ball complained to Krol, "had the plain obligation to apprise us of these developments as fast as they occurred, and to send us copies of the Complaints and all relevant documents. We have received nothing. . . Once again, due process and due consultation have been omitted."

Ball was still convinced that they had a strong case in *Lemon*. *DiCenso* dealt only with Catholic Schools as they were operated in the State of Rhode Island, whereas Lemon represented a broad mix of schools whose only common denominator was that they had not previously received government funding. Beyond that, Ball had assisted in drafting a law which expressly excluded from reimbursement by the state "any subject matter expressing religious teaching, or the morals or forms of worship of any sect." Secular purpose was, in effect, written into the law. This, of course, made Pfeffer's strategy of confusing the cases all the more necessary, yet it was in precisely this area that Ball was experiencing maximal frustration. The USCC seemed to be doing everything within its power to assure convergence.

The Nixon Administration wasn't proving very helpful here either. In spite of the assurances of President Nixon, October rolled around and Solicitor General Griswold still hadn't signed his *amicus* brief. The best the Nixon administration could produce was a "Hamlet-like" document (Ball's term) whose style was equivocal and whose content was plagued by errors respecting the law. Ball conferred with William D. Ruckelshaus, head of the civil division in the Department of Justice, in mid-October stressing the absolutely essential nature of the changes that needed to be made.

On October 22, Ball got a call from the Nixon Administration informing him that Griswold still refused to sign the *amicus* brief. The best they could do was get Attorney General Mitchell to sign in his place. Ball considered this unacceptable. The Supreme Court was bound to notice that Griswold not only signed the government's brief in *Tilton*, but that he also presented oral argument in that case. The fact that his signature was conspicuous by its absence would only indicate that the government was not supporting *Lemon*.

Ball was of the opinion that no brief was better than the defective one the government planned to submit. "If the Government files its present brief," Ball told Krol,

> this would seem an arrogant move. Although this is the Government of the United States, it is not a party to the case. We know of no instance in which an *amicus* thrust himself upon a party, against the party's wishes. We trusted that the government would not try that kind of power play. Here, however, we could not rid ourselves of the view that Messrs. Friedman, Horowitz, Handleman or Zener (all in the Solicitor General's Office) appear ideologically hostile to aid to our schools and that "an enemy hath done this."

One week later, the government filed the *Lemon* brief without Griswold's signature. To make matters worse, the USCC issued a brief of its own with an asterisk and following note prominently displayed explaining that Solicitor General Griswold would not sign the brief "for personal reasons." Rather than defusing the issue, the USCC brief drew attention to its inadequacies. Then in early November Bill Ball's worst nightmare came true. The Supreme Court announced that it had decided to consolidate *Lemon, Tilton,* and *DiCenso* for oral argument. With uncharacteristic understatement, Ball termed the juxtaposition "unfortunate." He then went on to relate a new challenge on the horizon. The ACLU was suing a high school in Harrisburg over the length of a student's hair. Since the school was receiving public money, it had no grounds for imposing a dress or appearance code based on Catholic principles. The lawsuit was a harbinger of a whole second wave of lawsuits which were waiting in the wings if Pfeffer's attack on funding through *Lemon* were to prove unsuccessful.

On December 22, 1970, the USCC finally broke its self-imposed media blackout on the *Lemon* case. Russell Shaw of the USCC wrote an article giving the outline of the case for the national Catholic News Service. "One out of every five elementary and secondary school pupils in Pennsylvania," Shaw informed his readers, "attends a nonpublic school. At present, 1,181 schools with an enrollment of some 535,000 pupils are under contract with the state to provide educational services under PNESEA"("School Case Seen as Precedent Setter," Russell Shaw, NC News 12/22/70).

"At the moment," Shaw concluded, a little over a week after the three bills had been consolidated by the Supreme Court, "most of the portents for the outcome of the case look good."

Two days later, on Christmas eve, Shaw filed another story on *Lemon* in which he opined that "the outcome of the Pennsylvania case will have a profound impact on nonpublic education in the United States for years to come" ("Friend of Court Briefs Cite Free Choice Argument," by Russell Shaw, NC News, 12/24/70). It was a fitting culmination to the do-nothing campaign the USCC had waged on the media front throughout the entire history of the *Lemon* case. It was a classic instance of too little, too late, so uncoordinated with the actual needs of the Church at the time that it inspired the suspicion that it was intentional.

On June 28, 1971, the Supreme Court finally handed down its *Lemon v. Kurtzman* decision. The Court admitted that the Pennsylvania law, Act 109, was written expressly for the funding of subjects with a secular purpose, thereby evading a violation of the establishment clause. But in order to insure that that was in fact the case, the Court opined that the state authorities would have to police private education, thereby running afoul of the constitution's prohibition against "an excessive government entanglement with religion."

"We conclude," wrote Justice Burger, speaking for the majority of the court, "that the cumulative impact of the entire relationship arising under the statutes in each state involves excessive entanglement between government and religion."

"Ordinary political debate and division," Burger continued, "however vigorous or even partisan, are normal and healthy manifestations of our democratic system of government, but political division along religious lines was one of the principal evils against which the First Amendment was intended to protect." Once again, the court had rewritten history to find a right to be free from religion in the Constitution. As was the case throughout the *Kulturkampf* of the 60s, the conservatives and the liberals were of one mind on the issue. The liberals were simply more overt in their anti-Catholic bigotry.

In his concurring opinion, Justice William O. Douglas claimed that "if that surveillance or supervision does not occur, the zeal of religious proselytizers promises to carry the day and make a shambles of the Establishment Clause." And how did Justice Douglas know that the non-public schools in Pennsylvania were in the grip of "religious proselytizers"? He discovered this by reading a notoriously anti-Catholic tract entitled *Roman Catholicism* written by Loraine Boettner, in which he learned that

> in the parochial schools Roman Catholic indoctrination is included in every subject. . . . The whole education of the child is filled with propaganda. That, of course, is the very purpose of such schools, the very reason for going to all of the work and expense of maintaining a dual school system. Their purpose is not so much to educate, but to indoctrinate and train, not to teach Scripture truths and Americanism, but to make loyal Roman Catholics. The children are regimented and are told what to wear, what to do and what to think.

Douglas, who heretofore was not known for his zeal in promoting "Scripture Truths and Americanism," was nonetheless persuaded by Boettner's argument and cited him in his concurring opinion in *Lemon* and, as if this weren't enough, added that "one can imagine what a religious zealot, as contrasted to a civil libertarian, can do with the Reformation or with the Inquisition. Much history can be given the gloss of a particular religion."

There are many ironies here. The secular humanist caviling at the speck in the eye of the religious, ignoring the ideological plank in his own eye is the one which comes most immediately to mind. This was tantamount to the establishment of the religion of secular humanism which has had its day with parlous effects in both school and society for almost a quarter of a century. But another irony had to do with the actual situation of the schools. The court declared them bastions of religious indoctrination at the very moment during which they had been taken over by liberalism's cultural revolutionaries within the Church. At roughly the same time that William O. Douglas was saying that church schools were hotbeds of religious indoctrination, Dick Deasy was emptying the religion courses at LaSalle and West Catholic of virtually all Catholic content. In virtually the same year that *Lemon v. Kurtzman* was handed down, Therese Ickinger was accusing the Philadelphia Archdiocesan school system of having sold out to secularism. At some point, Krol must have wondered whether the schools weren't the victims of a severe case of mistaken identity. As if all this weren't bad enough, Douglas went on to insinuate that another major reason for the existence of private schools was the perpetuation of segregation. All in all, the *Lemon* decision was a virtuoso performance which combined the attributes of nativism and the Know Nothing Party with the liberal antinomian animus against anyone who crossed them on sexual issues. It also showed just how central the bias against Catholicism was in American's intellectual life and to what extent the liberal social engineers were willing to make use of it to achieve their own ends.

On the day the decision was handed down, Bill Ball and Joe Skelly were in Washington. As soon as he heard that the Court had handed down the *Lemon* decision, Ball called Krol on the way home to share the bad news. He remembers Krol as being philosophical in defeat. "You've done the best you can," Krol told Ball over the phone. "Let's go for another day." Ball found the response comforting, especially in light of the fact that two years of work had just gone down the drain. By the time he ended up submitting his postmortem report to Krol, however, he was feeling more angry than philosophical.

To begin with, the justices based their fear that surveillance would lead to "excessive entanglement between government and religion" on nothing factual and nothing more than a hypothesis about the future. "The Court," according to Ball, "has contented itself with unfounded reference to history and to pure speculation about the future." Beyond that the decision was self-contradictory. It says that "our decisions from *Everson* to *Allen* have permitted the state to provide church-related schools with secular, neutral or non-ideological services, facilities, or materials," but then in midstream the Court changes horses and goes on to say that it is the nature of the benefit, not the nature of the institution, which is the determinative factor.

Beyond that, the Court singles out the teacher in a religiously affiliated school as "compulsively unable to obey [the] law" at the same time that it assumes that the pubic school teacher is devoid of all "ideological character." Especially gall-

ing to Ball was the damned-if-you-do damned-if-you-don't character of the decision. If the law does not specify the funding of
secular subjects alone, the establishment clause is violated. If it
does specify that funding is to be used for secular subjects
alone, it creates "entanglements" and violates the constitution
because the state has to police the prohibitions.

"This whole idea," Ball wrote to Krol, "is the handiwork of
Professor Paul A. Freund and Leo Pfeffer and the Supreme
Court of this land has bought it lock stock and barrel." Also
attributable to Freund is the notion that aid to non-public schools
is unconstitutional because it may involve "religious controversy," a notion Chief Justice Burger, one of the court's "conservatives" imported into the decision almost verbatim from
Freund's writings. Burger's redaction of Freund, according to
Ball, "constitutes a mortally dangerous foreclosure of the political rights of citizens who support parochial schools."

Worse than the lack of any factual foundation in the case
was the fact that the Court relied only on the testimony of
people hostile to the Church and its schools as their basis in
evaluating parochial schools. Catholicism, according to the
Court, was what Loraine Boettner said it was. The Church was
not even allowed to define itself or what it does, the Court
obviously assuming that any description of that sort would be
obvious mendacious and self-serving. It was a bit like calling in
the SS as a character witness for the residents of the Warsaw
Ghetto.

Ultimately the motivation of the court remains opaque. Was
secularism really a front for Know Nothing Nativism, i.e, animus against the Church? Or was the Court using the patina of
anti-Catholicism as a way of disarming Protestant opposition to
their attempt to remove all religion from public life? The latter
suspicion comes to the fore when the court opines that "the
constitution decrees that religion must be a private matter for
the individual, the family and the institutions of private choice.
. . ."

Where, Bill Ball wanted to know, did the constitution decree
that? "This gratuitous pronouncement," he continued, "is open
to serious question (and should be publicly questioned). . . . It is
language disturbingly reminiscent of the *Kulturkampf* and the

French laic decrees of the late 19th century." Beyond that, the
wholesale re-writing of the past which the court submitted in
Lemon presented a "totally false picture of American history."

> What is shamefully lacking is the true account, which would
> show that Protestant institutions were state-aided through most
> of the 19th century, and that the "no aid" idea was nothing other
> than a bigoted response to the (mainly Catholic) immigrants
> from the 1830s forward.

Ball saw *Lemon* as a harbinger of increased anti-Catholic
bigotry. "It is again evident," he wrote to Krol,

> that the Catholic Church carries little political weight in the na-
> tion. What the Court has essentially reflected are the attitudes of
> the larger Protestant bodies and especially of the largest segment
> of the Jewish community as represented by B'nai B'rith, Ameri-
> can Jewish Committee and American Jewish Congress. . . . While
> we realize that the press and media have been holding open
> season on every failing and defection discoverable in the Church,
> we are freshly appalled at the spectacle of the Court's blithe
> ignoring of so numerous a part of the American community as
> the Catholic and, even more, by the Court's readiness to charac-
> terize our schools and our teachers and to rely exclusively upon
> caricatures of Catholic education and a mass of erroneous infor-
> mation ascribed to the Church, its people and its schools by our
> opponents. . . . As with much of the media, so now with the
> Supreme Court: the Catholic Church is the good natured fat boy
> on the block whom all are free to push about.

But the threat of increased anti-Catholicism was in reality
only half the story. By ignoring "the positive contribution which
the Church-related schools make at a time when the nation is
severely threatened and when every resource for stability should
be availed of," the Court made a major contribution to social
decline. Twenty-three years after *Lemon*, the notion of support
for non-public schools, this time in the form of vouchers and
under the term privatization, was more relevant than ever and
increasingly popular with parents who watched the secular
humanists—the people the court claimed were devoid of ideological taint—plunder the public school system for their own
benefit. As school budgets became more and more bloated and
less sustainable by a declining tax base, the people in control of
the schools recklessly pursued the secular agenda by pushing
things like condom distribution and the "rainbow curriculum,"

which proselytized for homosexual behavior. The more money spent on public education, the greater the resulting social chaos. It was a lesson the country had to learn the hard way, primarily because of the tutelage of the Supreme Court.

The animus against the Church on the court went deep, even deeper than the labels "liberal" and "conservative." Common to both was a commitment to *Kulturkampf*.

"The 'conservatives' on the Court," according to Ball, "are quite apparently so little aware of that contribution that they have willingly dealt with a grievous social problem in terms of the sterile abstractions put before them by the supposed 'liberals,' Freund and Pfeffer." It was, all in all, an uncanny replication of what happened in Prussia one hundred years before.

"The court in *Lemon-DiCenso*," Ball told Krol, "is plainly saying: 'Don't try this again.'"

> The above clearly forecasts the willingness of the Court to see a state monopoly of education in this nation. The supposedly anti-socialists, pro-private enterprise "conservatives" on the Court (Burger, Blackmun, Harlan and Stewart) as well as the avowed "liberals" join in a sense of horror at suffering a controlled, moderate partial program of state aid to religiously affiliated schools (on completely specious and unsupportable grounds.). These Justices plainly have no love for diversity, competition, and freedom in education.

Ball also saw more serious challenges on the horizon. Now that Pfeffer was victorious in *Lemon*, Ball expected him to expand his contestation of state funding of services from religious institutions to include Catholic hospitals. Pfeffer, Ball wrote, "has already written extensively on this subject, asserting that no hospital should receive public aid which a) preserves any vestige of religious atmosphere or control or refuses to engage in "modern" medical practices (specifically mentioning abortion)."

Roe v. Wade was still two years in the future, but already Ball could see the conflict on the horizon. By the end of his brief, the full magnitude of the changes that have occurred during the past decade breaks through. "It is astounding," writes the man who proposed the Church's response to the liberal *Kulturkampf* in the early '60s, "to realize that the ACLU, POAU, AJC, B'nai

B'rith, etc, have achieved so complete a victory as now is plainly theirs."

Cardinal Krol was left to contemplate, in silence for the most part, the victory of the cultural revolutionaries and depth of animus against the Catholic Church in the country his father had chosen so recently for his home. One notable exception to Krol's silence occurred on national television just about a year after *Lemon* was handed down. Krol complained about anti-Catholic bigotry in public life and as a specific example gave Justice William O. Douglas opinion in *Lemon* based on Loraine Boettner's book.

"It is the lowest form of a bigoted publication there can be, and this man," Krol said referring to Douglas, "is using it as a reading of the norm about Catholics."

"Is this a symptom of 'bigotry' on the part of Justice Douglas in your view?" wondered George Cornell of the Associated Press.

"All I can say," Krol responded, "is that he used this book which no respectable Protestant would recognize or would acknowledge as a responsible book, and he is quoting from that. It's a sad day when a Justice of the Supreme Court has to reach for a book of that type to get a view of the Catholic Church."

Almost a quarter of a century later, the Catholic school system, in spite of dire statements predicting its demise, was still in existence, in spite of massive defection from the teaching profession by Religious across the country. The public schools, on the other hand, were struggling in spite of the infusion of billions of dollars with a myriad of problems that money could not solve but which it could, and in fact did, make worse.

Thirteen years after *Lemon*, Ball attempted to put the relationship between schools and money in some sort of perspective. "I have heard some distressing comment that Catholic education's future depends on governmental aid.," Ball wrote to Krol. "No, Your Eminence, the cure for Catholic education lies in Catholic fervor and Catholic religious certainty."

Epilogue:
The Desolate City

According to Msgr. John Noons, its present pastor, Most Blessed Sacrament Parish in Southwest Philadelphia went out of existence as a viable, self-sustaining diocesan entity some time during the summer of 1972. In place of the parish, which in spite of its decidedly lower middle class economic status used to top all of the diocesan fund-raising appeals, in place of the parish from which the Irish contributed vocations to the arch-diocese out of all proportion to their numbers and resources, a new parish arose. The newcomers were overwhelmingly black and overwhelmingly not Catholic, but the Church refused to cut its losses and instead converted MBS to an outpost, a mis-sion Church which could only exist in the future as the result of being on a financial life support system designed by Cardinal Krol and run by the archdiocese.

The migration of the Irish out of the neighborhood began in earnest over the summer of 1966 when the full effect of the liberal agenda began to take effect in the neighborhoods of Philadelphia. Over the next six years virtually everyone who could move out did move out, for the most part to the suburbs of Delaware County, the political entity adjacent to but not under the immediate control of the regime in Philadelphia which had rendered their ability to control their own neighborhood virtually illegal. Filling up the tiny row houses the Irish left behind were wave after wave of blacks, blacks from the already overcrowded sections of North Philadelphia, but also blacks straight up from the South, lured North by ever increasing welfare benefits, now orchestrated from Washington as much as from Harrisburg. If they were especially upwardly mobile, the newly arrived blacks could aspire to a job in the increas-ingly expanding, increasingly unwieldy, increasingly expensive government bureaucracy which administered those benefits. The transition in the neighborhood did not stop when it went from white to black. The social disintegration continued apace, and the original black families in the neighborhood began to look back with nostalgia to the relatively manageable turmoil of the '60s. The turmoil that entered Southwest Philadelphia was not the result of race; it was the result of the liberal manipulation of race for its own ends. Race was the cover the liberals used to undermine the social order and the moral law, and they were successful beyond their wildest imaginings. In the period following 1972, the color of the neighborhood stayed constant, but the mores disintegrated with the times, as they did in white neighborhoods throughout the city during the same period of time. The color of the people at MBS remained the same after the neighborhood changed in the early 70s, but the disintegration brought about by the liberal transvaluation of all values continued apace with increasingly destructive results. Illegitimacy increased, as it did in the nation in general; as a result, the use of drugs increased, and as a result of increased use of drugs, especially with the arrival of crack cocaine in the mid-80s, violence increased as well. No wonder the blacks were caught up in feelings of nostalgia. The liberal promised land had become a very dangerous place. Caught in the middle of this twentieth century *Voelkerwanderung* were the priests who staffed MBS during its period of crisis and transition.

Getting a job at MBS in 1970 was a little bit like auditioning for a crucifixion. The Church was being held responsible for everything that was going wrong in the neighborhood, and for the most part all it could do was look on and suffer. Father Joseph Meehan arrived as a curate at Most Blessed Sacrament Parish in the summer of 1971 shortly after the Supreme Court handed down its decision in *Lemon v. Kurtzman*. In a memoir he wrote four years later ("Changing Priest and Changing parish: The Land of Jacob's Ladder" by Joseph J. Meehan, *Dimensions*, 1975), he described what it was like to be a Catholic priest in that place and at that time.

"In 1964," he began, giving statistics that could be replicated in urban centers across the country, "there were 3,210 students enrolled in the parish school: 3,198 of them white and 12 black." By the fall of 1975, there were

532 students: 147 white, 378 black and a few orientals. That's an average rate of 200 plus white students leaving per year over a ten year span. From an almost 100 percent white school in 1964, [MBS] has become 71 percent black in 1975. Once an extremely overcrowded school it now has numerous empty classrooms.

In the time since Meehan wrote his memoir the situation has progressed to the point where the parish is now almost 100 percent black, with considerably fewer Catholics than it had when it was a white Irish parish. "MBS," wrote Meehan in 1975 searching for a formulation that borders on euphemism, "has moved into a new era."

The transition to that new era, however, was fraught with conflict and violence, both physical and psychic. "In the summer of 1971 when I entered the parish," Meehan wrote,

racial unrest was peaking in the neighborhood. Battles of all kinds took place and within a two-year period three young men lost their lives in race-related incidents. It seemed that MBS was living future shock to the fullest. As I met the parishioners, I heard the common greeting: 'Welcome to the parish, Father. It's a shame what's happening, isn't it? Too bad you weren't here when . . . ' And then the litany began: when the neighborhood was wall to wall Catholic; when we had Masses almost every hour in both the upstairs and downstairs church, and both were bulging—people standing in the aisles and even in the street; when they had about four funerals a week and marriages had to be arranged about a year ahead of time; when 25 priests came at Christmas to hear confessions; when our school was probably the biggest Catholic elementary school in the world.

The changes brought about by racial migration in Philadelphia, and exacerbated by the liberal manipulation of that migration, were profound. A whole generation of Irish Catholic families was uprooted and dispersed to various suburbs and the Northeast section of the city, and the life they led was, for the most part, dispersed with them. This was to have a profound effect on the transmission of the faith. Since Bishop John Neumann, Philadelphia's first saint, the city had been divided up into ethnic neighborhoods and parishes which ministered to those ethnic groups, through the language and customs—in short, the culture—those people brought with them from Europe. The faith, in other words, was mediated through a particular ethnic group, and when that ethnic group was dispersed the transmission of the faith suffered. The already-mentioned case of *New York Times* columnist Anna Quindlen is instructive in this regard. Quindlen grew up the oldest of five children in an Irish-Italian family in Drexel Hill, a suburb immediately adjacent to Southwest Philadelphia. Her parents were refugees from the racial migration that hit that area in general and MBS in particular. In 1992, Quindlen returned to Southwest Philadelphia, and, predictably, blamed Ronald Reagan and George Bush for the decline in what was once her father's neighborhood.

I say predictably, because on just about every issue, Quindlen takes the liberal party line. She is also adamant in referring to herself as a Catholic even though, in true liberal fashion, she disagrees with the Church every time it deviates from the sexual agenda of the *New York Times*. Liberalism is, in other words, the procrustean bed upon which her Catholicism gets trimmed to a point where it deviates from the editorial policy of the *New York Times* only on issues on which the *Times* has no policy. Abortion, it is no secret, is one instance in which the Church disagrees with the *Times,* and on a crucial issue like that Quindlen is safely within the liberal pale. The same is true of her stance on contraception, the cutting edge cultural revolution issue of the 1960s. Reading her autobiographical novel, *Object Lessons*, it is difficult to avoid the impression that the '60s were the time when something happened that made the transfer of allegiance possible, or more than possible, necessary for survival.

In *Object Lessons*, Quindlen describes the '60s as "the years which set one sort of America apart from another." Those two Americas could be denominated MBS and the *New York Times*, the Catholic ethnic and the liberal secularist Americas respectively. Quindlen remembers the story of her father being reprimanded with a slap by three people in the neighborhood—the cop, the nun, and a neighbor—for the same offense, so seamless was the social fabric in MBS during the pre-World War II period. Then came racial migration and the cultural revolution which fostered it and its deleterious effects for its own ends.

As a child growing up, Quindlen watched her father's neighborhood get devastated as the Church stood helplessly by, and the lesson was not lost on someone of her intelligence. The Church was impotent. "The Roman Catholic Church is going to hell in a handbasket," opines the grandfather of the Quindlen character in *Object Lessons*. The lesson was not lost on Anna either. Gradually she began to act on what she saw. Attending Barnard in the early '70s, she describes how her generation was swept overboard by the sexual revolution. Gradually, the categories of the liberal dominant culture win out over the values she left behind when MBS, as the locus of her father's values, fell apart. In *Object Lessons*, the Quindlen character says of her parents that "their own fecundity had laid waste to that dream" (Quindlen, p. 29). It seems a curious way to refer to oneself and one's brothers and sisters. But perhaps not so curious if the purpose is to assure others (and oneself perhaps) that her primary allegiance is to sexual liberation and the culture which guarantees its "rights" and not to the neighborhood which failed, and the Church which stood by helplessly when this transpired.

The transition at MBS was traumatic for everyone involved but especially so for the priests who were supposed to steer the Church through these turbulent waters. For them the experience amounted to a crisis of faith.

"The '60s," Father Meehan explained, "brought to my life a re-evaluation of my convictions; my life was changing and how should I meet it?. . . . I was plagued with doubts about my input regarding my future. . . . My answer was akin to the stuttering, stammering of Moses: 'Who am I . . . ?'"

The cultural revolution was causing an identity crisis among the clergy. Their image of parish life was taken from what they had experienced when the culture of the neighborhoods was intact. When the culture broke down, it seemed as if the efficacy of religious practice taken from that culture were breaking down as well. This resulted, of course, from the often imprudent liturgical experimentation that masqueraded as the implementation of the recently concluded Second Vatican Council. The result was confusion, which the priest often articulated as a personal crisis in his vocation.

"The prevailing feeling in my initial stages at MBS," Meehan wrote, was confusion and shock. It did not take long to find that the changing parish was a world of smashing glass, barking guard dogs, multiple locks. Now, what had I gotten myself into! I had been trained for the MBS of 1964, and only rationally and abstractly by way of my religion course for high school seniors had I dealt with the urban social phenomenon of a changing parish. I was not only in an unfamiliar land, but a land filled with violence and racial battles among the youth. As I have reflected on the lonely "Who am I" question, I have been led to a greater appreciation of so many older priests who for many years have courageously walked this unfamiliar land of urban ministry in a changing parish. . . . Fear began to plague me. the front steps of the Church, the schoolyard, the playgrounds, the neighboring streets saw many young children at war. The evenings found them marching in attack, and running in retreat. Even the daytime had its threatening moments: once when I was crossing the street, I was barraged by light bulbs thrown from a third-floor window. A man standing nearby explained simply: "Looks like someone just doesn't want you around here."

What was I afraid of? Was it the confusion and shock of it all, or the fear of getting hurt in the street? Was it just the tension: responding to people who had been robbed or mugged; nervous irate parents; high strung apprehensive kids? Was it the atmosphere: the dogs, the locks the iron gates protecting the stores, the "for sale" signs, youths walking with sticks, the police sirens, the continuous "We're leaving, Father; we just bought a house."

Since the priest identified with his flock, he also internalized their cultural crisis and made it his crisis. Or perhaps he made it his crisis, because he was unable to externalize it, unable to get the perspective on the broad forces brought to bear on one small neighborhood.

Strange as it may seem, these external threats were not so acute as the fear of internal isolation—isolation that came, I think from two sources: from being in the middle between the races, and from the collapsing of previous images of myself and my role as priest. . . . Processing up the aisle before Mass on a Sunday I might pat the head of a black child. That afternoon an indignant white parent would berate me for my favoritism toward blacks. . . . I would respond to action in the schoolyard or gym and while blacks would accuse me of being a racist and refuge for whites who had injured blacks, whites would accuse me of catering to the blacks by letting them move into the school facilities and take over. At parish affairs, I mixed too much with the whites or with the blacks. One group wanted me to express appreciation to the police; another group wanted me to protest police negligence. It seemed that in the changing parish one was always in the middle.

The cultural revolution had become a personal crisis, primarily because no one was articulating in a coherent fashion what was going on. Philadelphia, like the rest of the country, viewed racial matters through the lens of the civil rights movement, according to which downtrodden non-violent blacks were shaking off the chains of segregation created by white racism, which was the root of the problem. The liberal solution was simply the elimination of segregation. After that everything would be fine.

When viewed from the perspective of MBS, however, none of this made any sense. From the point of view of the blue collar Irish who were sitting at home minding their own business, the blacks were a violent lawless group of foreign invaders who threatened the very fabric of community life with their unstable marriages, random unions, and the unruly children that sprang from these unions without fathers and ended up congregating in gangs and wreaking havoc on anything in their path.

Since the clergy were as dependent on the media for their view of the world as anyone else, they too adopted the civil rights view of racial migration and as a result they weren't able to make sense out of what was happening either. As the problem proved more and more intractable to the social solutions the liberals were proposing, the clergy descended deeper and deeper into identity crisis. The priest was the man in the middle. To the whites who were being driven from their homes he was an impotent "nigger lover." To the blacks who were often the victims of white backlash he was the "honkey priest."

"In this no man's land," Meehan wrote, "with its being in the middle and its isolation, many images of myself as well as many images of the priesthood collapsed: didn't these people realize that I was a nice guy, a priest, a very special person? After all, I had come with peace and unity. There was a very logical explanation for all the racial unrest, and the Christian solution was feasible."

The Christian solution is always feasible, but just how it gets applied in a particular cultural context, particularly one in such a violent state of flux, is never self-evident. As a result, the blame tends to get passed on to Christianity itself, in which case the man leaves the priesthood, or to the man himself, in which case the man also leaves the priesthood. Vocations crisis and cultural flux go hand in hand, as Joe Meehan found out.

> I found out that logic and Christian moralism were certainly not the approach, and that Mr. Nice Guy was worth nothing so long as he might be part of the enemy. People rejected me, and even hated me. Although rationally I told myself not to expect to bridge the gaps, emotionally and traditionally I was anticipating order and peace. And there was no peace.

> Where then was the new mission, the new ministry? Crowded masses, sick calls, confessions, novenas, parish societies—all were diminishing. Along with other urban ministers, I had to ask: What do I do today? And tomorrow? Is it hospitals and communion calls and waiting? Is it rejuvenating traditional parish societies and events? Or is the ministry to be community organizer and people's advocate? Is it sacramental; non-sacramental; parish priest or social worker? Is one the other? Anguish, loneliness. Am I losing my faith? What is this? Do I have a "vocation crisis"?

Meehan's overriding memory of the MBS of 1971-72 was "powerlessness" and frustration.

"Many things attempted are failures," he continued,

> Meetings are called, notices sent out and only two or three people come. Eucharist, indulgences, confession, Holy Name, novenas, First Fridays are all strange terms to a new culture and environment. . . . The changing parish often brings a kind of brokenness or death. Or is this a beginning to new life?

As of the early '70s the jury was still out on that question. Certainly from Meehan's point of view there were individual victories, but both the parish and the city were succumbing in these years to something which seemed terminal. In fact, there is no evidence that things have changed in this regard. The city may die the same death that its neighborhoods did. The city is, after all, nothing more than the sum of its parts. In allowing parishes like MBS to die, the regime in Philadelphia allowed the neighborhoods these parishes served to die, and in allowing that, the city embarked on a program of installment-plan suicide.

Joseph Alulis is now a university professor. From 1963 to 1967 he was a student at West Catholic High School and a pupil of Brother Fidelis of Jesus, now known as Joe Schmidt, Dick Deasy's collaborator in the reform or demolition (depending on your point of view) of the religion curriculum in the Christian Brothers' schools in Philadelphia. In late 1971, Alulis was home on vacation from college, walking down Chester avenue, in fact to add to the symbolism of the encounter, right in front of Most Blessed Sacrament Church, with his 12-year-old sister to pick up a pizza when he noticed a gang of black youths crossing the street heading in his direction. The next thing he knew he was on the receiving end of a piece of lead pipe wielded by one of the black gang members.

That was how Alulis discovered that the neighborhood was changing and that the change was not benign.

"We were aware of increases in violence, of deterioration. By deterioration of the neighborhood I mean rats appearing in the alley. These were the alleys where we had caught fireflies when we were kids."

"Not to wax nostalgic," Alulis added, waxing a bit nostalgic.

There was also a proliferation of abandoned cars. In short, all of the classic signs of urban blight appeared all at once with the suddenness, let us say, of getting hit over the head with a lead pipe.

"Catty-corner to us the man moved in and opened up a saloon. I mean it was some kind of speakeasy; it wasn't a saloon. It was his private residence into which people went for booze. Neighbors began shooting guns which was never a part of my childhood. So it was a very stressful time and my mother left the property; she moved out of the city entirely in 1973."

When asked for his assessment of how the Church dealt with the situation, Alulis is quick to respond that MBS as a parish had virtually no response at all. By the early '70s, the days of the real estate market after mass were long gone. West

Catholic, on the other hand, responded by becoming heavily involved in "consciousness-raising."

"Today it would be termed political correctness," Alulis continued. In a phrase, what West Catholic and the Christian Brothers were offering as the solution to the racial crisis was "bleeding-heart liberalism." To be fair, this is Alulis's term after the fact, a conclusion drawn with the benefit of hindsight, and with the secure feeling that the attempt had failed. At the time, the solution the Brothers proposed to the cultural crisis which racial migration had precipitated was "sensitivity training." Equal numbers of black and white students from West Catholic would be shipped up to the Dominican Retreat house in Elkins Park for intensive sessions of blind milling and "sharing."

It is easy to slip into condescension or ridicule when looking back on the Christian Brothers' efforts. The incongruity of it all almost demands that sort of response. It was a bit like offering love beads and bell bottoms as the solution to the Serbian policy of ethnic cleansing in Bosnia. But at the time, Brothers like Joe Schmidt were sincerely attempting to make the best use of the cultural tools available to them. And if that was a bit like opposing tanks with water pistols, it was not completely the fault of people like Brother Fidelis. The Church had simply adopted the categories of the civil rights movement and the human potential movement and virtually all of the other movements at the time, and attempted to solve a problem with a Robinson Crusoe-like fervor but with less than Robinson Crusoe-like results.

The problem was also exacerbated by the media, which sought to portray the dissolution of parishes like MBS as the triumph of the Negro Dionysian and a harbinger of the greening of Philadelphia. In the same *Philadelphia Magazine* article in which Dick Deasy announced that for Catholics like himself, sex was no big deal, author Bernard McCormick described how Father Eugene Dick had transformed St. Rose of Lima parish in northwest Philadelphia into a place which, on Sundays, "really rocks."

According to McCormick's breathless account, Father Dick ("he introduces himself as Gene Dick," we are told),

> has turned the parish, a former heavily Irish parish which is now almost entirely Negro, into a mecca for the disenchanted. Like

many of the Negro parishes, St. Rose of Lima does not draw very heavily from the parishioners on Sunday, but it does a booming trade with those who are dissatisfied with their own parishes.

"We're going to give them a meaningful worship," Gene opined, presumably referring to the "disenchanted" who flocked to St. Rose of Lima to escape the tedium of bourgeois life.

The passage is instructive for a number of reasons. It shows first of all how the inner city parish was seen as a "mecca for the disenchanted" rather than as a place for providing spiritual sustenance to the natives. One gets the impression that the whites went to the ghetto with a sort of Ku Klux Klan-inspired prurience. The "disenchanted" went to the Negro parish to find authenticity, which was invariably associated with the family pathology the Catholic Church was supposed to oppose. The white liberals in other words went to the ghetto to imitate the mores that the Catholic Negroes already living there were trying to escape. The comedy of errors implicit in the cultural politics surrounding race would be the material of slapstick if the results for both blacks and whites weren't so tragic.

One of the disaffected who got profiled in McCormick's *Philadelphia Magazine* article was Bill Leahy, who, as of 1967, had just been dismissed from his position as professor at the seminary and granted the status of cultural hero as a result. ("Father Leahy," McCormick informs his readers, "has become a hero to the malcontents because he rebelled against the Cardinal.") Soon thereafter Leahy walked out of his assignment in suburban Warminster, but his suspension was short-lived and he was granted his request to be assigned to an inner city, i.e., Negro, parish like St. Rose of Lima.

"I just couldn't take the traditional parish life," Leahy explained to a sympathetic McCormick, "I wanted to teach but they wouldn't let me, so I asked to be assigned to a Negro parish. I had no other choice but to get out of the archdiocese. So they gave me this (Our Mother of Sorrows, a predominantly Negro parish in West Philadelphia). . . . I've been in eight previous parishes and this is one of the few where they don't have a neurotic concern about picayune matters like making sure somebody was always here for sick calls."

Race had become an escape hatch from traditional Catholicism. Priests who could drape the mantle of the civil rights movement around their shoulders were exempt from picayune stuff like being around for sick calls, and presumably other corporal works of mercy. One wonders how consoling sick black Catholics from Our Mother of Sorrows found this attitude.

Leahy, who grew up in West Philadelphia when it was Irish and graduated from the now defunct St. Thomas More High School, would eventually be suspended from the priesthood for good roughly one year after the *Philadelphia Magazine* article appeared when he went to California to preside at the wedding of his priest brother. When he returned to Philadelphia, he found his name surrounded in black in the diocesan newspaper along with the notice that he had been suspended. Leahy's apostolate to the Negroes of West Philadelphia lasted a little over a year. During this time he circulated with what counted as the Catholic counterculture of the time—Dennis Clark, Jack Malinowski who taught at St. Joseph's college and was active in the draft resistance movement, which eventually led him to become a Quaker, and Father Jack McNamee, who is still active in a parish in a black area.

By 1973, Leahy's drinking problem eventually caught up to him and he was fired from his job at St. Joseph's College. Thereafter he became a bartender and after hitting bottom in 1977 entered a rehab run by the Paracletes in New Mexico. He is still suspended. Since 1987 he has wanted to get back into the priesthood. In 1989 he met with Cardinal Krol, whom he characterized as supportive, but as of 1993 the best he can manage is collaboration with Corpus, the federation of men who left the priesthood to get married but still miss their old jobs.

The inner city parish was very emphatically "a mecca for the disenchanted," but as such it was doing neither the priests who succumbed to the Philadelphia version of the noble savage fantasy nor the Negro Catholics they were ostensibly there to serve much good. As the situation deteriorated, the people in the neighborhoods began to take the situation into their own hands, and racial migration quickly degenerated into racial warfare.

On April 9, 1971, Russell Peed, a black 14-year-old honor student was struck on the head and killed by a white 14-year-old. A little over a month later, on May 10, 20-year-old Tyrone Dunbar was stabbed to death by four white youths who belonged to a gang called the "Dirty Annies". Abandoned by a Church which could propose nothing better than sensitivity sessions as the remedy for racial war and a State which seemed determined to reward lawlessness, the white youths formed gangs to protect both themselves and their neighborhood. The Dirty Annies took their name from a small candy store at the corner of Alden St. and Chester ave, not far from MBS.

"If we don't stick together, we're going to get killed," averred Michael, a 17-year-old Dirty Annie who was also a senior at West Catholic. "It's their neighborhood now," he continued, referring, to the blacks who had moved in (Thomas J. Madden, "White Gang is Resentful of 'Takeover' in Area," *The Philadelphia Inquirer*, May 16, 1971). Michael, according to the account in the *Inquirer* at least, blamed MBS for the racial strife in the neighborhood. According to Michael the only thing that would have kept the peace at MBS was racial segregation—"they don't do anything to keep us apart. It's a little late now to get us together. We don't like each other because we've been fighting each other for so long"—a solution, which for obvious ideological reasons was considered taboo, but one which was consonant, nonetheless, with the neighborhood structure of Philadelphia since the mid-19th century.

"White parents," he concluded, "are starting to realize they've got to help us out. We're the last white gang," Michael concluded by informing the reporter that "many whites called the church campaigning [sic, complaining] about its recent censure of the Annies."

The *Inquirer*, of course, went out of its way to emphasize the Catholicism of the gang members. Bill, who is identified as a junior at West Catholic, has a father who is a policeman, "and he don't like those guys," i.e., the Annies, but Bill, bad grammar and all, feels that someone has to defend the neighborhood.

"All these niggers coming in and taking over the neighborhood," says Bill, "That gets me mad. They stroll by, act real bad and stare at you."

"I hang around with the Annies because there's no one else I'd like to hang with. I just can't get along with the niggers. They're black, and we're white. There will never be peace until you separate us."

The blacks quoted in another article were pretty much in complete agreement with Bill. "All I can say," a 16-year-old by the name of Rim-ski said smacking his fist into his hand, "is that when I catch one of these white boys, he's going to get this" (Acel Moore and Gerald McKelvey, "Blacks Developing A 'Siege Mentality,'", *Inquirer*, May 16, 1971).

"For years," said Moon, a 20-year-old black youth, "I went to school with them at Most Blessed Sacrament. One day one of the white kids I was hanging with told me his parents didn't want him playing with niggers. After that we fought," Moon said.

Throughout the series of articles the Church was portrayed as at best doing nothing to stop the violence. "The Catholic Church has not involved itself in the social aspects of a changing neighborhood," Brother Mark Lowery, who was then vice principal of West Catholic High at 49th and Chestnut Sts, was quoted as saying. "Any active white Catholic who has tried to do something about this situation has been turned off by the church. There are no young priests, none who can really relate to the white kids."

Interestingly enough, Lowery, who is still a Christian Brother and now teaching in Pittsburgh, denies having ever said any such thing to the *Inquirer*. The Catholic Church in Philadelphia has long complained about the anti-Catholic bias of the *Inquirer*. As recently as the summer of 1993 there was an editorial in the *Catholic Standard and Times,* the diocesan newspaper, repeating the charge. But at the time everyone seemed bent on "blaming the victim," to use the phrase used against Daniel Patrick Moynihan. In another *Inquirer* article which appeared in 1971, John Ricchini, vice president of the Southwest Coordinating Committee [of the City Human Relations commission] "was especially critical of Most Blessed Sacrament parish, at 56th and Kingsessing Aves, because it has done little about the 'Dirty Annies,' a white street gang in the area."

In the same article, Margaret Prendergast, who is cited as "speaking for parents of Most Blessed Sacrament School," said "tearfully, 'I realize there is tension in the neighborhood and that things are bad. . . . We have done really everything to integrate," she said, but added that black parents have only recently become involved."

Once again the Catholics fell back on the remedies which the liberals were proposing and the liberals held them in contempt for falling back on them.

In the same year that the Dirty Annies were organizing their last ditch effort to save the neighborhood around MBS, and in the same year that the Supreme Court handed down its *Lemon* decision insuring that the government funds would not go to MBS or any other private school in the nation, Bantam issued the paperback edition of Charles Reich's best-seller of the previous year, *The Greening of America*. Reich had been a professor at Yale Law School, a clerk for Hugo Black, and a confidant and admirer of William O. Douglas, and in 1970 he became the official philosopher of the cultural revolutionaries. *Rolling Stone Magazine* sat at his feet and asked him to expound on the future, which as the title of the book indicated was going to be one long flowering of hitherto repressed natural forces.

Greening became the the classic expression of decadent art, namely, the point at which the final refinements are placed on an art form no one is interested in anymore. *Greening* proclaimed the dawning of the Aquarian age just as many of its major cult figures were succumbing to drug overdoses and the whole movement was descending to random violence and anomie. Nonetheless, in November of 1970 *Newsweek* called *Greening* "the chic conversation piece of the fall cocktail season." Twenty-two years later Reich was back in law school after having tuned in, turned on and dropped out. In December 1971, at the age of 43, Reich moved to San Francisco and after a sexual encounter with a male prostitute, decided that he was gay. Suddenly all of the effusion in *Greening* about the younger generation made sense in a way it hadn't in 1970. But 22 years later, Reich's law school colleagues found *Greening* more an embarrassment than anything else. "Even now," wrote Laurel Leff in *Legal Times*, "there doesn't seem to be much enthusiasm among his colleagues for *The Greening of America*, many preferring not to discuss it."

Even now? Even then someone described it as "such a tissue of impressions, contradictions and generalizations, not to mention unsubstantiated predictions and prophecies of the most apocalyptic kind, that it is difficult indeed to associate it with an outstanding legal mind" (Leff, Laurel, "Reich's Return: What a Long, Strange Trip It's Been," *Legal Times*, 20 April, 1992).

Perhaps the legal scholars had passages like the following in mind:

> Bell bottoms have to be worn to be understood. They express the body, as jeans do, but they say much more. They give the ankles a special kind of freedom as if to invite dancing right on the street. They bring dance back into our sober lives. . . . No one can take himself entirely seriously in bell bottoms.

Maybe not, but Reich sure tried. The book has the breathless quality of a manifesto, and the public reaction at the time indicates that everyone took Reich's pronouncements at face value, even what he had to say about bell bottoms. That is because, perhaps, Reich was in large measure correct about what he was describing.

"There is a revolution coming," he wrote in *Greening*. "It will not be like revolutions of the past. It will originate with the individual and with the culture, and it will change the political structure only as its final act. It will not require violence to succeed, and it cannot be successfully resisted by violence.

Reich felt that everything from "beads and bell bottoms to the Woodstock Festival" was part of a "consistent philosophy" which would overwhelm the traditional mores of the United States and replace them with a culture that was individualistic, most importantly in the sexual sense of the term. The revolution would begin with the nation's young people and spread to include everyone else in America.

This revolution had a curious relationship to technology. It both blamed and celebrated technology. The ambivalence was expressed by William O. Douglas who opined that *Greening* was "a book about Revolution—not in the Marxist sense, but

Revolution against many of the values which Technology has thrust upon us."

"Modern living," Reich stated in a passage which had special relevance to the turmoil raging in cities like Philadelphia at the time, "has obliterated place, locality and neighborhood, and given us the anonymous separateness of our existence. The family, the most basic social system, has been ruthlessly stripped to its functional essentials."

As an antidote to this "anonymous separateness of our existence," Reich proposed weakening the family further by espousing in predictable liberal fashion all of the technology of sexual liberation, most notably the pill. The book's ambivalence about technology is resolved when it is seen, as in the Douglas quote, as something bad, but also something that necessitates our current rebellious behavior.

The rebellion, of course, was directed at the moral order. "Consciousness I," Reich's code word for the more or less traditional values of his grandfather's generation, "insisted on seeing the evils of industrialism not for what they were, but as moral problems. If a given number of automobiles are crowded onto a highway, there will be a predictable number of accidents. The moral approach tries to deal with this as a question of individual driver responsibility. It stresses safe driving and criminal penalties. Yet reduction of the accident rate is demonstrably a problem in engineering. Similarly, urban crime is seen as a moral and law enforcement problem, although crime is a product of identifiable environment factors. The moralistic approach to public welfare is similar. Over and over again Consciousness I sought scapegoats rather than face the forces of industrialism directly."

Reich's vision was classic Liberal Gnostic. Man's nature was seen as a set of "limitations," i.e. "the job, the working day, the part one can play in life, the limits of sex, love and relationships, the limits of knowledge and experience," which were, as of 1970, all in the process of vanishing, leaving man "open to live a life that can be lived without the guideposts of the past."

"In the world that now exists," Reich continued, "a life of surfing is now possible, not as an escape from work, a recreation or a phase, but as a life—if one chooses. The fact that this choice is actually available is the truth that the younger generation knows and the older generation cannot know."

The experiences of the Dirty Annies, as representative young people in 1971, were probably not included in Reich's expansive picture of the younger generation. What both Reich and the Dirty Annies did share, however, was a vision of the Negro as subverter of the social order. The Dirty Annies, being on the receiving end of this revolutionary violence, were not happy with the changes, but Reich, removed from the locus of racial violence, was. In fact, Reich sees the nation's blacks as the avant garde of the cultural revolution. As in the already-mentioned article in *Philadelphia Magazine,* the blacks in *Greening* were drafted into the cultural revolution as part of the fantasy life of its main proponents.

The revolution began, Reich opines at another point, when white people started singing the blues. "So long as whites in America did not realize that their own identity was also oppressed and denied, so long as whites failed to search for their own selves, there could be no white "soul," no white blues to sing" (p. 270).

Given an attitude like Reich's and the fact that it was pervading the cultural elite at the time, it was inevitable that the music, film and publishing industries would produce and promote a series of Negro spokesmen who would tell the whites who wanted out from under the moral order just what they wanted to hear. Eldridge Cleaver, as Reich indicates, was a notable example. In *Soul on Ice,* he tittilated people like Reich with paeans to rape and the joys of sniffing white women's dirty drawers. When Cleaver returned to the United States and announced that as a result of staying married to the same woman for all those years, he was repudiating revolutionary ideology, the Left pretended that he had ceased to exist.

Philadelphia was no exception in this regard. Throughout the '60s and '70s, a series of increasingly strident Negro agitators or shake down men appeared on the scene with increasingly outrageous demands, virtually all of which were taken seriously by the media and the city's liberal establishment. This tradition reached its bizarre apogee in the two police sieges on

MOVE headquarters, the second of which resulting in a fire which devastated blocks of West Philadelphia when Mayor Wilson Goode ordered a bomb dropped on the cult's fortress-like hideout.

In 1971 the standard bearer of this tradition was a man who called himself Muhammad Kenyatta. Kenyatta, who was born in Chester under the name of Donald Brooks or Donald Jackson, depending on which report you read, was a product of Black migration to the North. His parents moved to North Philadelphia from the South between the wars, and he graduated from Edison High School there at the age of 16. At the age of fourteen, Brooks-Jackson-Kenyatta was a devout fundamentalist Christian, who often preached at Chester's Calvary Baptist Church. In 1964, Kenyatta dropped out of college to become involved full-time in the civil rights movement and eventually returned to Chester to join up with another local organizer, Stanley Branche, in a short-lived organization called Chester Citizens for Freedom Now. Kenyatta eventually broke with Branche, who denounced both him and his tactics.

On April 26, 1969, the 25-year-old Kenyatta attended the National Black Economic Development Conference in Detroit, at which he heard James Foreman, one of the founders of the Student Non-violent Coordinating Committee read the Black Manifesto, which was either a call to revolution or an especially ambitious fund-raising appeal, depending on how you looked at it. The manifesto was full of the Marxist boilerplate so typical of the times. According to Foreman, the United States was "the most barbaric county in the world and we have a chance to help bring this government down." This would involve a "revolution which will be an armed confrontation and long years of sustained guerilla warfare inside this country," in order to create "a socialist society inside the United States where the total means of production and distribution are in the hands of the United States and must be led by black people, by revolutionary blacks who are concerned about the total humanity of this world."

In the meantime, and in order to pay the bills while waiting for Armageddon, Foreman announced that he was sending a bill for reparations payments to the country's Churches and synagogues. The bill was for $500,000,000, and since Forman was black, the check could be made out to him.

"We are demanding $500,000,000 from the Christian white churches and the Jewish synagogues," Forman told the black militants assembled in Detroit. "This total comes to 15 dollars per nigger. This is a low estimate for we maintain there are probably more than 30,000,000 black people in this country. $15 a nigger is not a large sum of money."

"We call upon all black people throughout the United States," Foreman continued, "to consider themselves as members of the National Black Economic Development Conference and to act in unity to help force the racist white Christian churches and Jewish synagogues to implement these demands. . . . Black workers. . . are encouraged to seize the offices, telephones and printing apparatus of all church-sponsored agencies and to hold these in trusteeship until our demands are met. . . . On May 4, 1969, or a date thereafter depending on local conditions, we call upon black people to commence the disruption of the racist churches and synagogues throughout the United States.

"Brothers and sisters," Forman concluded, "we are no longer shuffling our feet and scratching our heads. We are tall, black and proud."

One of the people in the audience evidently moved by Foreman's manifesto was 25-year-old Muhammad Kenyatta. Returning from Detroit on fire with revolutionary fervor, Kenyatta and his followers organized a sit-in at Cookman Memorial Methodist Church at 12th and Lehigh, demanding that the church be turned over to the community, he being evidently their representative. On June 4, Kenyatta "liberated" an electric typewriter from the Presbyterian owned Westminster Press at Juniper and Walnut Streets.

On June 12, Kenyatta and his friends attempted something a bit more ambitious by occupying the former Robert Wade House and Concord Day Center at 217 Concord Ave. in Chester. The building was owned by the Society of Friends or Quakers, and for the next two months the liberal religious group agonized over what it should do in response. Eventually, on the night of

August 13 after a three hour meeting, the Quakers agreed to hand the building over to Kenyatta and his supporters. As part of the agreement, the Quakers issued a statement characterizing the occupiers as "a sincere group of people who are trying to improve the community in which we live." In addition to that, the Quakers also offered to give Kenyatta money to maintain the building, or as they put it, "to offer as much support as they can to provide maximum opportunity for success of their venture."

One day after the Quakers capitulated to Kenyatta's demands, Kenyatta announced that the seizure of the Chester settlement house was the "first step in taking over all of Chester."

"This is a model for our intent to eventually seize all of Chester and set up a new law and order," Kenyatta announced at the building which used to belong to the Quakers but now functioned as his headquarters.

"The important thing is that yesterday in the eyes of the majority we were outlaws who had seized a piece of property and encamped on it," Kenyatta said. "Today we are legal residents. This marks an important step, not just for Chester but for the state and the country."

Kenyatta then renewed his vow to take over the city of Chester "by any means necessary." He also added that while he was opposed to violence, he could not rule it out.

Throughout the summer of 1969, Kenyatta would show up at the services of various churches in the Philadelphia area and renew his demands for reparations payments. On July 13, he arrived at Abington Presbyterian Church, after obtaining permission in advance from church pastor Rev. William J. Evans. In the course of his hour-long harangue, Kenyatta told the congregation that if it failed to respond to his demands, it would face the prospect of demonstrations. Twenty people walked out in the course of Kenyatta's speech. On the same day in New York city, James Foreman tried the same thing at New York's Washington Square Church in Greenwich village and was presented with a check for $15,000 for his pains. In the meantime, and perhaps encouraged by his initial successes, Forman raised the reparation demands to a cool $3 billion. In addition to that, the Congress of Racial Equality or CORE jumped on the bandwagon by demanding $6 billion in reparations from the nation's banks. Pretty soon, as the saying goes, the civil rights movement was talking real money.

On February 1, 1970, Mrs. Jane Cosby, Bill Cosby's aunt and a member of the BEDC, demanded $500,000 from the Quakers at their Philadelphia Yearly meeting.

"We wanted you to see us," Mrs. Cosby told the Friends, "we are real; we are human; we are in a great deal of pain, and we are very black by God's creation."

At around the same time as Mrs. Cosby shared her pain with the Quakers, the Philadelphia branch of the Unitarian Universalists announced they were increasing the $250,000 they were already paying in reparations payments to a nice round $5 million.

"The program," a spokesman for the Unitarians announced at a press conference, "represents a major new direction for churches struggling to be relevantly involved in repairing the long-damaged black community."

The incongruity of the whole campaign was never more apparent than when Kenyatta (with the advance permission of the pastor, of course) marched into St. Anthony's Roman Catholic Church in Chester on May 19 and made the same demands.

"Racist" churches, the "silent and attentive" congregation was told, must help build schools and colleges and help finance black businesses. The irony of his statement was apparently lost on Mr. Kenyatta. The Catholics had been involved in building schools and colleges throughout their existence in the United States. "Separate but equal" was something they aspired to but never achieved in the realm of funding, as *Lemon v. Kurtzman* would show two years later. In the realm of ideas, the blacks and the Catholic liberals had the same problem. They kept trying to apply the lessons of the segregated south to the ethnic parishes and neighborhoods of the north and never noticed the incongruity of what they were proposing.

In this regard, the article reporting the incident in the *Philadelphia Inquirer* is instructive. St. Anthony's is described as an "all-white church," which was in a sense true. It would have been probably more accurate to describe St. Anthony's as an "all-Italian church," since that is what it was by intention. The parish was founded in an Italian neighborhood in 1911 by Italians for Italians. All of the 500 member families of the parish, according to its pastor, were of Italian origin. Not only did the parish exclude Black baptists and Black Muslims, it also excluded Irish, Polish and German Catholics and for that matter any group other than Italian Catholics. That was in effect the definition of the ethnic parish that had been the mainstay of church life in the Philadelphia archdiocese since the time of Bishop Neumann. To see this as segregation required a leap of faith that only the civil rights movement and its increasingly bizarre spin off organizations could provide.

Equally tenuous was the connection between this Church and slavery. "The great cathedrals," Kenyatta informed the Italians at St. Anthony's, "have been built on the blood and free labor of black men." One can only wonder which cathedrals he had in mind. One can also wonder what was going through the mind of this Italian congregation during Kenyatta's diatribe, especially when he added that "the Catholic Church alone controls an 'empire' larger than America's greatest corporations." It was just one more instance of the old nativism and the new liberalism finding themselves in the same bed again.

Within a matter of months Stanley Branch, Kenyatta's erstwhile collaborator, had had enough. On January 13, 1970, the Chester civil rights leader condemned Kenyatta's actions a little over a week after he threw communion bread and wine on the floor of the Swarthmore Presbyterian Church in the middle of one of his diatribes. According to a report in the *Bulletin*, ("Branch Raps Kenyatta," John F. Morrison, the *Evening Bulletin*, 1/13/70), Branch claimed that the local civil rights movement had "taken a giant step backwards with the latest in misguided leadership of one Donald Jackson, who likes to call himself Muhammad Kenyatta." Branch called the demand for $500 million in reparations "stupid." He was also critical of other black leaders who stood by in silence as Kenyatta spun out of control.

Most of Branch's anger, however, was reserved for the liberal Protestant leadership in Philadelphia which caved in to

Kenyatta's demands. The main villain in the matter, according to Branch was Bishop Robert L. DeWitt, head of the Episcopal Diocese of Pennsylvania, who "coddled, fostered and perpetuated Mr. Jackson."

According to Branch, the "shameful act of attacking the churches has to stop, and the so-called white liberals and the supposed black leaders who condone such vicious acts, must be brought to task by the public."

Bishop DeWitt, it should be remembered, was the main proponent in the state of Pennsylvania for the government-funded distribution of contraceptives. He and the other mainline Protestant groups had made up in fervor for the civil rights movement what they lacked in defending the sixth commandment, and now they were being devoured piecemeal by the monster they created. DeWitt's handling of the racial situation created divisions in the Episcopal Church in Philadelphia which never healed. By the time the passions had died down the Episcopal Church was dying as well, as was the city of Philadelphia. All were victims of the liberal religious leaders who Branch excoriated in 1970. "In the white community," the *Bulletin* opined in August of 1969, "Kenyatta's only read source of encouragement has been Episcopal Bishop Robert L. DeWitt."

Kenyatta, however, was not completely successful in his march through the Churches. The Catholic Church entertained his proposition and then turned him down. As early as 1969, Kenyatta knew that the message that was getting across to the Episcopalians was not resonating with the Catholics. "We are very serious about this money," Kenyatta told the *Bulletin*, and no one could say he wasn't being perfectly serious. As a result, Kenyatta was watching the Archdiocese of Philadelphia "closely."

"We will move on them," Kenyatta promised, "but that man," he continued referring to John Cardinal Krol, "is tough."

In the early '70s, Cardinal Krol had more pressing things on his mind than writing reparation checks payable to Muhammad Kenyatta. As Father Meehan had indicated, the cultural revolution was causing a crisis of faith, especially among priests and Religious. Because the priests were incapable of functioning in what they considered an effective manner, they began to have doubts about whether they should have become ordained in the first place. That coupled with the loosening of sexual mores was causing a hemorrhage of Religious out of the body of the Church.

Beginning in 1970 Tony Massamini, also anointed a cultural hero in the '67 *Philadelphia Magazine* article, was having severe doubts about his own vocation. Rather than discuss them with a spiritual advisor, Tony went to a psychiatrist with predictable results.

In the late fall '70, Massamini went to the authorities at the seminary, where he was back teaching theology, and announced his intention to leave the priesthood. Massamini was convinced that he was not a good priest. When asked why, he responded, "because I was a misfit."

"My reasoning was I'm not a good priest, because to be a good priest I can't be a hundred per cent free to be who I am, and this is holding me back. It's restricting my soul. So there has gotta be something wrong. So therefore I can't give myself a hundred per cent to being a priest as I see being a priest, because I can't put a hundred percent of my soul into it, therefore I'm not a good priest. Because I believe there's a lot of good to being a priest."

By the end of 1970 Massamini's rapport with the students at the seminary had deteriorated as well. It might have been the result of his crisis of faith, or it might have been the cause of it.

"I wasn't preparing my classes," Massamini continued, "because I had this sense that I want to teach you guys theology, but you're not going to use theology. And what I should be teaching you is how to be a good priest, but then again I wasn't a real good priest because my heart was not in it. I was trying to put my heart in it, but the soul's not in it."

Because of that the '70-'71 academic year at St. Charles was "pretty bad." Massamini continued seeing the same psychiatrist until during one session, a light went on when he made up his mind to leave the priesthood. When the psychiatrist asked for a reason, Massamini replied, "My soul told me, not my mind." And the psychiatrist responded, "Okay, I understand."

At this point Massamini decided that he had to talk to Cardinal Krol. When they finally met in Krol's offices, just before Christmas of 1970, Krol's first statement was "I understand that you're one of the people that's been misled by the Second Vatican Council."

Massamini had always felt that there were two John Krols, and he was in no mood to argue with the official one now. All he said in response was "I really feel it is the right thing to do. I gotta leave."

In an age dominated by the infallibility of personal feeling, it was an irrefutable argument.

"I can't be preaching to anybody if I'm empty inside," Massamini continued. "How can I preach life to people if I'm dying? I can't do that."

Krol, however, refused to accept this as a explanation. Instead he handed Massamini a holy card with a picture of St. John Neumann on it and said, "Say this prayer and put yourself in God's hands."

"Your Eminence," Massamini responded, "I'm 43 years old. I have no job. And I have no money. If I'm not in God's hands, I don't know where I am."

"That was my last statement to him," Massamini recounted 20 years later.

"He looked up to me with utter pain," Massamini said of Krol, "because he wasn't getting through to me, and because we had nothing else left to say to each other. And so the last, official thing that happened between us was this pain on his face and me just sitting there and saying, 'are we finished? I want out of here; I don't want to argue with you. You don't understand what I'm saying. And I'm not sure I understand what I'm saying, except I need to lead my own life in a much more expansive way than I was doing right now. And I can see that you don't understand; its hurting you, its hurting me. We shouldn't be doing this. Let's finish it.'"

Massamini later learned from a priest who was a mutual friend that Krol took his defection personally.

"It hurt him," Massamini continued, "because there was an attachment, this priestly attachment, this love," which was more important than the need to hang on officially and canonically to his priest. He was doing the official stuff, but it wasn't just that. There was something very deeply moving going on there. Very deeply moving. Because he wasn't rejecting me coldly and all that stuff. Even though I was the cause, no question, of a lot of pain, and this was the worse thing I could be saying to him. Krol, the Churchman just couldn't tolerate what I was saying to him or the fact that I was walking away from the priesthood. But there was a lot more to it. John the person was extremely forgiving about this whole thing, even though he was in great anguish."

During the 1970 Christmas break, Tony Massamini moved out of the seminary and into makeshift quarters at the Newman Center of the University of Pennsylvania, where he lived, sleeping on a couch and getting washed in the men's room, for the next six months. Eventually campus security caught up with him and he had to move out of that arrangement as well.

"The authorities finally caught up with me. 'Do you have any money?" they asked, and I said no. 'You mean nothing?' I said, 'No.'

In June of 1971, right around the same time the Supreme Court handed down *Lemon*, Tony Massamini went to see Krol for the last time. There was nothing much to talk about. Massamini was determined to leave, and there was nothing Cardinal Krol could say to dissuade him.

"So he finished with me," Massamini continued. "He was behind his desk, and I was sitting in front of his desk with this holy card in my hand. And then he switched. All of a sudden there was a switch in his whole personality. When I got up he said: 'Let me show you what I just got from Poland.' And we walked over to a table. And he picked up a book, a picture book with drawings, pictures on Polish culture and costume—you know the old traditional Polish thing—and he said: 'Look, this is where my parents came from.' He said, 'Look. This is how they dressed. And we went through this like the two friends that we were. When that was finished, I took a few steps toward the door, and I turned around, and said: 'May I have your blessing?' And I got that of course. He gave he a blessing. I kissed his hand and his ring. And I walked out."

"The Church is like the moon," Cardinal Krol said on the 25th anniversary of his arrival in Philadelphia, "It waxes and it wanes."

"There was a bit of turbulence following the Council," the cardinal continued, "but change is a rule of life. Unlike some of our ecumenical friends in the various denominations who tend to split and separate, the Catholic church has the capacity of self renewal. And every time you have change there's a bit of dust, a bit of turbulence, a bit of turmoil."

On November 17, 1971, Cardinal Krol was elected president of the NCCB. In a speech following his election, Krol announced that, "without minimizing the crisis in the Church," the Church's main objective was "getting back to the simplicity of the Gospel command of Christ to unite man with God and man with each other." The crisis was still in full swing and would in many ways get worse, but the man God had chosen to lead from the meat department at Kroger's to the head of the Archdiocese of Philadelphia had long since decided the Church never finished with its battles. Like the moon, the Church's maximal effulgence is only a prelude to its apparent disappearance. Like the moon, the Church never really declines, but it does seem that way sometimes.

A Note on Sources

Because of the scope of this book, the bulk of its research material was taken from the Krol Papers of the archives of the Archdiocese of Philadelphia. I am grateful to the Archdiocese of Philadelphia and Cardinal Krol for making these papers available to me. I would also like to thank the Rockefeller Archives for granting me access to their files on Father Theodore Hesburgh and the conference on contraception funded by the Population Council at Notre Dame in 1963. The Urban Archives at Temple University proved to be a valuable source of information on the 1964 riots in North Philadelphia as well as the source for the two photos which comprise the cover of this book. What follows are the principal nonarchival sources cited in this book.

Alpert, Hollis. *Fellini: A Life* . New York: Atheneum, 1986.

Anderson, Floyd, ed. *The Council Day Book*. Washington, DC: National Catholic Welfare Conference, 1965.

Associated Press. "Sen Clark Urges Intensified Drive for Birth Control,"1/24/64

Barzini, Luigi. *The Italians*. Atheneum: New York, 1964.

Baum, Gregory, ed. *Journeys: The Impact of Personal Experi ence on Religious Thought.*. New York: Paulist Press, 1975.

Berard, Aram, S.J., trans. *Preparatory Reports of the Second Vatican Council* . Philadelphia: The Westminster Press, 1965.

Berelson, Bernard and Morris Janowitz, eds. *Public Opinion and Communication*. Glencoe, Illinois: The Free Press, 1950.

Berson, Lenora E. *Case Study of a Riot: The Philadelphia Story*. New York: Insitute of Huamn Relations Press, the American Jewish Committee, 1966.

Blumberg, Leonard. *Migration as a Program Area for Urban Social   Work: A Pilot Study of Recent Negro Migrants into*

Philadelphia. Philadelphia: Urban League of Philadelphia, 1958.

Bonnot, Rev. Bernard R. *Pope John XXIII: An Astute, Pastoral Leader*. New York: Alba House, 1979.

Bork, Robert H. *The Tempting of America..* New York: The Free Press, 1990.

Brown v. Board of Education of Topeka et al, 347 US 483

Brunette, Peter. *Roberto Rossellini*. New York: Oxford University Press, 1987.

Collier, Peter and David Horowitz. *Destructive Generation: Second Thoughts About the Sixties. New York: Summit Books*, 1989.

Collier, Peter and David Horowitz. *The Rockefellers*. New York: Holt, Rinehart and Winston, 1976.

Connelly, Msgr. James. *St. Charles Seminary, Philadelphia: A History of the Theological Seminary of Saint Charles Borromeo, Overbrook, Philadelphia, Pennsylvania, 1832-1979,* Philadelphia: Published by St. Charles Seminary, 1979.

Crump, David *et al. Cases and Materials on Constitutional Law.*   New York: Mathew Bender, 1989.

Curran, Charles E. *Faithful Dissent*. Kansas City, MO: Sheed & Ward, 1986.

de Pauw, Gommer, *Sounds of Truth and Tradition: Catholic Traditionalist Movement, #4,* 1979.

Douglas, William O. *Points of Rebellion*. New York: Random House,1969.

Ershkowitz, Miriam and Joseph Zikmund II, eds. *Black Politics in Philadelphia*. New York: Basic Books, Inc., 1973.

Fellini, Federico. *Federico Fellini's La Dolce Vita. New York: Ballentine Books, 1961.*

Fink, Joseph Richard. *Reform in Philadelphia: 1946-51* Rutgers U. Ph.D. 1971. Ann Arbor: University Microfilms, 72-819.

Fisher, Paul A. *Behind the Lodge Door: Church, State and Freemasonry in America* . Bowie: Shield Publishing, Inc., 1988.

Fonzi, Gaeton. "The Pill," *Greater Philadelphia Magazine.*, July 1966.

Gard, Connie Schultz. "Anna Quindlen," *The Plain Dealer*, January 24, 1993.

Glancy, Dorothy J. "Douglas's Right of Privacy: A Response to His Critics." *"He Shall Not Pass This Way Again" The Legacy of Justice William O. Douglas*. Edited by Stephen L Wasby. Pittsburgh: University of Pittsburgh Press for the William O. Douglas Institute, 1990.

Griswold v. State of Connecticut, 381 US 479

Harr, John Ensor and Peter J. Johnson, *The Rockefeller Century: Three Generations of America's Greatest Family*. New York: Charles Scribner's Sons, 1988.

Harr, John Ensor and Peter J. Johnson, *The Rockefeller Conscience: An American Family in Public and Private*. New York: Charles Scribner's Sons, 1991.

Hitchcock, James. *Years of Crisis: Collected Essays, 1970-1983*. San Francisco:Ignatius, 1985.

Ickinger, Therese. *"Religion" Texts: An Indictment*. Philadelphia: POPE, May 30, 1970.

Johnson, Paul. *Pope John XXIII*. Boston: Little, Brown and Company, 1974.

Joseph Burstyn, Inc v Wilson, Commissioner of Education of NewYork, et al. 343 US 495

Kelly, Msgr. George A. *The Battle for the American Church*. Garden City: Image Books, 1981.

Kerouac, Jack. *On the Road*. New York: Viking, 1957.

Kerouac, Jack.*The Subterraneans*. New York: Grove Press, 1958.

Lader, Lawrence. "Hidden Threat to Education," *Liberty Magazine* (a publication of the Religious Liberty Association of America and the Seventh Day Adventist Church), Nov/Dec 1970.

Lemann, Nicholas. *Promised Land: The Great Black Migration and How it Changed America.* New York: A. A. Knopf, 1991.

Leff, Laurel. "Reich's Return: What a Long, Strange Trip It's Been." *Legal Times. 20 April 1992.*

Leff, Leonard J. and Jerold L. Simmons. *The Dame in the Kimono: Hollywood, Censorship, and the Production Code from the 1920's to the 1960's.* New York: Grove Weidenfeld,1990.

McCormick, Bernard. "The Troubled See: The Church is being renewed. Here, as elsewhere, it is a time of pain ful uncertainty." *Philadelphia Magazine,* 1967, p.52 ff.

McNally, Dennis. *Desolate Angel,* New York: Random House, 1979

Madden, Thomas J. "White Gang is Resentful of 'Takeover' in Area," *The Philadelphia Inquirer,* May 16, 1971.

Mailer, Norman. *Advertisements for Myself.* New York: G.P. Putnam's Sons, 1959.

Mankowski, Paul V., S. J. "There are no conservative Catho lics" talk prepared for the Conference Springing Eternal in December at the Jacques Maritain Center of the Uni versity of Notre Dame, December 12-14, 1992.

Meehan, Joseph J. "Changing Priest and Changing Parish: The Land of Jacob's Ladder."*Dimensions,* 1975.

Miranda Prorsus. Pius XII. August, 1957.

Moran, Gabriel. *The New Community: Religious Life in an Era of Change.* New York: Herder and Herder, 1970.

Moran, Gabriel. "Catechetics RIP." *Catechetics.,* Dec 18, 1970, p. 299.

Morris, Joe Alex. *The Richardson Dilworth Story*. Philadel phia: Mercury Books, Inc., 1962.

Muggeridge, Anne Roche. *The Desolate City*. San Francisco: Harper& Row, Publishers, 1986.

Murphy, Paul I. *La Popessa*. New York: Warner Books, 1983.

Novak,Michael "Abandoned in a Toxic Culture: How we failed the New Generation," *Crisis*, December 1992, pp. 15-19.

—— *A New Generation: American and Catholic*. New York: Herderand Herder , 1964.

——*Naked I Leave: A Novel*. New York: The Macmillan Co., 1970.

—— *The Open Church: Vatican II, Act II*. New York: The Macmillan Company, 1964.

Panzarella, Brother Andrew, F.S.C. *Growth in Christ*. New York: W. H. Sadlier, Inc., 1968.

Pfeffer, Leo. "The 'Catholic' Catholic Problem." *Comonweal1* August 1975, pp 302-305.

—— God, Caesar, and the Constitution.. Boston: Beacon Press, 1975.

—— "Issues that Divide: The Triumph of Secular Human ism." *Journal of Church and State* , vol 19, Spring 1977, pp. 203-216.

Phillips, B.J. "Catholic schools go back to basics,"*The Phila delphia Inquirer*, 4/6/93, B1

Quindlen, Anna. *Object Lessons*. New York: Random House, 1991.

——"Perhaps it's time for us to adopt our old neighbor hoods," May   19, 1992, NYT News Service.

Reich, Charles A. *The Greening of America*. New York: Ran dom   House, 1970.

——*The Sorcerer of Bolinas Reef*. New York: Random House, 1976.

Roszak, Theodore. *The Making of a Counter Culture*. New York: Doubleday, 1969.

Rynne, Xavier. *Vatican Council II.* New York: Farrar, Strauss, and Giroux, 1968.

Simon, James E. *Independent Journey: The Life of William O. Douglas.* New York: Harper & Row, 1980.

Sjoeman, Vilgot. *I am Curious (Yellow): a film by Vilgot Sjoeman*, translated from the Swedish by Martin Minow and Jenny Bohman. New York: Grove Press,1968.

Spike, Paul. *Photographs of my Father*. New York, Alfred A Knopf, 1973.

Spike, Robert W. *The Freedom Revolution and the Churches.* New York: Association Press,1965.

Tillich, Hannah. *From Time to Time*. New York: Stein and Day, 1973.

Vagnozzi, Egidio "Thoughts on the Catholic Intellectual," address delivered June 3, 1961 at baccalaureate services at Marquette University, Milwaukee WI, in the *American Eccesiastical Review,* vol. 145 (1961) p. 73-79.

Van Alstyne, William W. *First Amendment: Cases and Materi als*. University Casebook Series. Westbury: The Founda tion Press,   Inc., 1991.

Walker, Alexander. *Sex in the Movies: The Celluloid Sacrifice.* Baltimore Maryland: Penguin Books, 1966.

Witt, Michael J., FSC. I. *Phil*. Winona: Saint Mary's Press, 1987.

Woodward, Bob & Scott Armstrong. *The Brethren: Inside the Supreme Court*. New York: Simon and Schuster, 1979.

Wormser, René A. *Foundations: Their Power and Influence.* New York: The Devin-Adair Company, 1958.

Wrenn, Msgr. Michael J. *Catechisms and Controversies*. San Francisco: Ignatius Press, 1991.

Index